Real-Time Animation Toolkit in C++

REX E. BRADFORD

JOHN WILEY & SONS, INC.

NEW YORK • CHICHESTER • BRISBANE • TORONTO • SINGAPORE

Publisher: Katherine Schowalter
Senior Editor: Diane D. Cerra
Managing Editor: Micheline Frederick
Text Design & Composition: North Market Street Graphics

Library of Congress Cataloging-in-Publication Data:

ISBN: 0471-12147-9

Printed in the United States of America

10 9 8 7 6 5 4 3 2 1

This book is dedicated to my father,
who taught me how to think.
Thanks, Chuck.

ABOUT THE AUTHOR

Rex Bradford was introduced to computers in a psychology research lab in the late 1970s, where his first job was to type the contents of a hard disk back into the computer from paper listings. He quickly gravitated to programming and began a career developing computer games in 1981. He worked first for Parker Brothers, creating "The Empire Strikes Back" cartridge for the Atari Video Computer System. After a brief interlude at Activision during the Great Videogame Shakeout, he formed Microsmiths in 1984. In 1986 he wrote "Mean 18," the first of the modern 3D golf simulators. He and Microsmiths developed many other original games, educational programs, and "ports" to and from many game platforms, including Commodore-64, Apple-II, Atari ST, Amiga, Nintendo, SEGA, Macintosh, and, of course, the PC. Most recently, he teamed up with LookingGlass Technologies on "Terra Nova," a sprawling CD-ROM-based science fiction simulation. Bradford is known as "Dr. Documentation" by many of his colleagues; this is his first book. He lives in Massachusetts with his sweet wife and zany critters.

C O N T E N T S

vi Contents

Part 2: Animation and Composition   283

285   Chapter 8: Frame Animation

318   Chapter 9: Animation Files

363   Chapter 10: Scene Composition

412   Chapter 11: Animated Actors and Scrolling Backgrounds

Part 3: Palettes and Color Effects   493

Contents

Preface
and Acknowledgments

The personal computer revolution is just warming up. The success of Microsoft Windows™, by freeing video board makers from rigid adherence to the basic VGA hardware standard, has fueled an explosion in graphics chip technology. This graphics revolution will rapidly culminate in high-resolution, true-color displays, with hardware-assisted 2D and 3D rendering and full-screen digital video.

At the same time, the CD-ROM has arrived as a standard delivery medium for graphics, animation, video, sound, music, and text, in an inexpensive and attractive package. The convergence of these technologies has powerful implications for education and entertainment, and is just beginning to be explored. Accompanying this book is an interactive CD-ROM disk which you can use to enhance your understanding of the material and code presented in these pages.

In the book, I have essentially done a "brain dump" of the techniques developed over a dozen or so years of commercial computer game programming. The basics of video modes and graphics file formats are recapped quickly, so that more time may be devoted to the meatier and more exciting realms of real-time digital picturemaking. These topics include animation, composition of overlapping screen elements, realistic color shading techniques and special effects, digital video, and 3D transformations and texture mapping. The book is not about game programming per se, but about the graphics techniques which underlie real-time screen animation on today's PCs.

The code presented in both the book and CD (easily installable to your hard disk) is more than a hodgepodge of techniques. It is organized as a full-featured C++ graphics class library, with accompanying tools and sample programs. Feel free to use it and build upon it in your own projects. This animation toolkit is especially relevant to the realms of animated presentations, education and training software, scientific visualization, image processing, and, of course, computer gaming. Also present on the CD is interactive documentation for the toolkit, to aid you in exploring the world of animation programming. I hope you find both the book and the CD enlightening, entertaining, and useful.

There are many people I'd like to thank for their help along the way. Thanks to George Karalias, Joanne Murphy, and Gail Robertson for the artwork used in sample programs and some of the figures. Thanks to Frank Davis for many very helpful comments on the text of the book as it was developed. Other individuals who aided me in various ways include Joe Huffman at Flashtek, Kevin Gilette of the VESA VBE Committee, and helpful people at Autodesk, Criterion, Symantec, and Adobe Systems, among others. I'd also like to thank many folks at LookingGlass Technologies for their creativity, enthusiasm, and talent, including Sean Barrett, Doug Church, Dr. Eric Twietmeyer, Carol Angell, Andrea Carnevali, and the rest of the gang, plus Paul Neurath and Ned Lerner for building the environment for us to play in. Thanks to my editor, Diane Cerra, for ongoing support and a very nice dinner indeed. Special thanks to Mark Lesser for longstanding encouragement and confidence in "Mr. Bitmap."

I thought I wouldn't have to include the obligatory "thanks to my wife for putting up with me" in this preface. The last couple of months proved me wrong. Work is heck, as somebody must have said, and writing is much play but also much work. Today is Wednesday; it must be Chapter 17. Have I told my family about my plans for Figure 17.3 yet? Hey, where are you going?

Thanks very much, Liz.

Introduction

What This Book Is About

I want to take you on a journey in this book. This statement may be a cliche, or even pretentious in the face of bookshelves full of books on computer graphics, but I mean it nonetheless. This book is not an academic textbook, nor a reference work, nor a catalog of APIs. It is one person's answer to the question "How do I get cool-looking stuff onto my computer screen at high speed?"

This book is a journey into the realm of real-time animation, a topic that's been part of my work on a daily basis for the past fourteen years. There is an abundance of tricks and techniques that are regularly employed by those of us in the game development community, most of which are applicable to animation in general, and this book is an attempt to share some of these ideas with a wider audience.

This book is a "journey" in another aspect. In most books, computer code is used merely as a "proof" of the ideas expressed in the text—the code is not useful on its own merits. The code in this book is different. The book builds, from the ground up, a full-featured C++ class library, composed of over sixty classes. Accompanied by useful tools as well as sample programs written using the class library, the body of code contained herein is eminently usable in your own projects. This book lets you peer behind the scenes into the process by which professional graphics code is structured and put together, and then take away the results of the effort.

On yet another level, this book is a journey into the real world of C++ class library design. My hope is that the class library built in these pages will serve as a useful model in other realms of programming. You don't have to be a C++ expert to understand the code here—in fact I have purposely avoided advanced C++ idioms in order to make the library readable. My hope is that the design decisions made in the book will stimulate your thinking. We programmers spend far too little time reading one another's code. The code in this book is broken down into digestible pieces and well-documented; it is meant to be read. For that reason, I have intermingled it with the text, rather than collecting it into large listings.

Another aspect of this project is a journey for me, into the world of interactive authoring. Accompanying this book is a **CD-ROM**. This CD serves as a repository for all the source code and related artwork files, but it is more than that. Contained on the CD is the "manual" for the C++ library and programs, delivered in a hypertext format with plenty of cross referencing, popups, and graphics.

What's in the Book?

The number and variety of computer graphics books available now is staggering. There are classic texts which elucidate fundamental principles, books which unlock the secrets of various image file formats, and books which display staggering details about the VGA and SuperVGA devices (Ferraro's *Programmer's Guide to the EGA, VGA, and SuperVGA Cards* weighs in at 1,600 pages!). There are specialty books about morphing, fractals, raytracing, radiosity, digital video, virtual reality, and more. Although there were none when I started writing this book, there are now at least a dozen books about game programming, not to mention several about animation in general. What's left to write about?

Plenty. Desktop computer graphics is on the move, more so than it has been at any time in its history. The success of Microsoft Windows has freed hardware developers from slavish imitation of IBM's VGA hardware standard, since the standard now is adherence to Windows, which is accomplished through a software driver. Even low-end boards now feature hardware-accelerated true-color graphics. Real-time hardware-assisted digital video playback is becoming a commodity item, and 3D hardware acceleration is just around the corner. Coupled with fast 486s and Pentiums to drive these boards, graphics performance is skyrocketing. This is not your father's PC.

What was the question again? Oh yes, what is this book about. It's about high-resolution graphics running under both DOS and Windows. It's about animation files and animation playback. It's about seamlessly composing a multitude of moving and animating objects against a scrolling background, with no visible glitching. It's about scaling bitmaps to any size in real time. It's about real-time color effects, including darkening and lightening, hazing, and translucency. It's about palette fading and color cycling. It's about 256-color graphics, the current standard in high-speed animation, and tomorrow's standard, which is 15-bit and 24-bit true-color graphics. It's about digital video playback. It's about texture-mapped 3D objects. It's about what you see happening on your PC every day.

This is not rocket science, by the way, and you don't need a PhD or Hacker of the Year credentials to learn this stuff. Not that there aren't brilliant game programmers. But real-time animation, which is fundamental to the graphics side of game development, consists mostly of clever adaptations of ideas which have been around for a while in computer science. It helps that the "real" academic graphics community blazes the theoretical trail on high-speed graphics workstations. We computer game programmers follow behind, read the papers and books, and then figure out when and how to make already-known ideas practical on a **PC**. High-quality, high-speed graphics on a **PC** is a combination of hard science and folklore, with a little sleight-of-hand thrown in for good measure. This book is an introduction to the combination of techniques that makes computer games look as good as they do. These techniques are also eminently suitable to the fields of presentation graphics, educational software, multimedia authoring, and scientific visualization, and anywhere else computer graphics are used.

What Is ARTT?

The chapters of this book build, from the ground up, a C++ class library and an associated set of tool programs, collectively called ARTT—Animation in Real-Time Toolkit. ARTT's class library encompasses VGA, SuperVGA, 15-bit *hi-color*, and 24-bit *true-color* displays, and runs under both **DOS** and **Windows**. The classes that make up ARTT provide a fairly full-featured "lab" in which to do high-speed graphics work. Rendering capabilities include simple geometric primitives such as lines, rectangles, and polygons. But sophisticated bitmap rendering is the heart of real-time animation, and ARTT provides a great deal of support for rendering bitmaps in various formats and with various effects. Support for extracting images and animations from popular file formats is provided.

That's just the foundation for the real stuff, however. The heart of ARTT is animation. Code to read animations from standard "FLIC" files is developed, along with animation playback code. Fundamental to ARTT is a sophisticated "scene and actor" system, which seamlessly composes multiple animating and moving graphics objects. Several actor classes are developed, including graphical user interface elements, and the system is easily extended. Advanced features include real-time shading and lighting effects, special effects such as translucency, palette fading, and color cycling, and 3D texture-mapping.

Besides the C++ classes, ARTT includes a set of useful adjunct "tool" programs and sample applications which use it, all including full source code. Many of these programs are listed in this book; some are included only on the accompanying CD.

As a purchaser of this book, you have the right to use ARTT in your own projects, including commercial ones. Since full source code is provided, you may also modify ARTT to your liking. You are free to distribute your own programs built using the ARTT toolkit. However, you may not redistribute the library source, tools, or sample programs which make up the ARTT toolkit. The license agreement packaged with the enclosed CD-ROM provides additional information.

Who Can Use This Book

The content of the book is directed at practicing programmers, both professional and hobbyist. It is not a beginner's book, but it is meant to be meaningful and useful to novice and intermediate programmers. Even the experts may find a few tricks they have missed. All the code in ARTT was developed specifically for this book, with instruction as well as utility in mind—this is not a "heap of old code" shoehorned into C++ with some vague text sprinked around it. Those currently practicing or considering involvement in programming graphics for presentations, education, scientific visualization, graphic user interfaces, or entertainment should find a wealth of useful information here.

No previous graphics programming is assumed, although the book does not dally overlong on the basics. All code is written in C++; at minimum a working knowledge of C and at least some exposure to C++ is assumed. The code makes heavy use of the basic C++ features such as classes, encapsulation, data hiding, inheritance, and virtual functions. However, the more obscure features of the language are not used, and C programmers who have seen C++ code before shouldn't have trouble understanding most of the code developed herein. Programmers who have dabbled in graphics, perhaps using one of the C toolkits available, can use this book to expand their understanding of the field, and get an extensible toolkit included in the bargain.

Organization of the Book

The book is divided into 4 parts: Part 1 lays the foundation for the rest of the book. Chapter 1 covers the fundamentals of bitmapped graphics and introduces ARTT's bitmap formats. Chapter 2 describes ARTT's rendering strategy, using bitmap-based "drawing surfaces" called *canvases,* and shows how to render such simple primitives such as pixels, rectangles, and bitmaps. Chapter 3 explores graphics file formats, and shows how to extract bitmaps from PCX and BMP files. Chapter 4 introduces *clipping,* which keeps graphics routines from overwriting other windows, or worse, your program itself, and then discusses fixed-point arithmetic and line-drawing. Chapter 5 investigates SuperVGA display modes, which are based on *bank-switching* to access the huge amounts of screen real estate they encompass, and provides SVGA support in ARTT through the VESA BIOS Extensions. Chapter 6 covers run-length compression of bitmaps, and real-time bitmap scaling. Chapter 7 builds support for Microsoft Windows into ARTT, using Microsoft's WinG library, which provides a speedy conduit between a program and its display window.

Part 2 is all about bitmapped animation. Chapter 8 introduces frame-based animation, describes various techniques for animating displays, and shows how to use the PC timer under DOS and Windows. Chapter 9 presents code to read animations from the popular FLIC format developed by Autodesk. Chapter 10 discusses the seamless composition of overlapping screen elements, and introduces the important *scene* and *actor* classes which are used to drive screen animation and composition. Chapter 11 looks at character animation, and features sample programs which highlight use of the scene and actor system. Chapter 12 covers user interaction, and develops keyboard and mouse drivers under DOS and Windows, as well as actor classes which provide a range of graphical user interface elements.

Part 3 presents a toolbox full of techniques for dealing with color palettes, color tables, and a variety of color effects, for use with 15-bit and 24-bit *direct-color* displays as well as the 8-bit ones used in the first two parts. Chapter 13 presents some basic color theory, and then shows how to render images stored in 15-bit and 24-bit form onto 8-bit displays, including generation of *inverse tables* to speed the process. Chapter 14 provides detailed development of rendering code for 15-bit *hi-color* and 24-bit *true-color* displays. Chapter 15 explains the use of Color Look Up Tables (CLUTs) to achieve a variety of color effects, including shading and lighting, hazing and fog effects, filtering, palette translation, and translucency.

Part 4 provides information and code on some advanced topics. Chapter 16 covers the fast-moving topic of digital video, including discussion of JPEG, MPEG, Apple QuickTime, Microsoft Video for Windows, and a new hybrid system called WinToon. Chapter 17 begins a foray into the realm of 3D graphics, explaining the basic mathematics of 3D projection and rendering of polygons and polygon-based objects. Chapter 18 spruces up the polygons' look using *texture mapping*. Chapter 19 finishes off the 3D coverage with a wide-ranging discussion of 3D scene rendering. Chapter 20 ends the book with a discussion of a variety of ideas and directions for optimizing, porting, and extending and enhancing ARTT.

What's on the CD?

This book features a lot of code, but even so lists only a portion of ARTT. The entire toolkit, including makefiles for several popular compilers, is included on the CD. Full source of all classes, tools, and sample programs is provided on the CD, along with the artwork used in the sample programs.

Also on the CD is the "manual" for ARTT, in the form of a Windows help file. This hypermedia document serves as the official documentation of the ARTT toolkit. It features cross-referenced, graphically enhanced "pages" of information about all classes, tools, and sample programs. In addition, it provides information on building the toolkit under various compilers. All source code is available within the help file at the click of a button. In addition, screen shots, class hierarchy diagrams, and other graphics bring the information to life.

More About ARTT

ARTT is composed of two major components:

1. A C++ graphics class library
2. Tools and sample programs (built using the class library)

The C++ class library contains more than 60 classes, organized into the following general categories:

- Low-level classes, for performing math, manipulating rectangles, etc.
- Bitmap and *canvas* classes for performing rendering

- Screen access classes for VGA, Super VGA, and Windows
- Classes for reading and writing image and animation files
- *Scene, actor,* and other composition-related classes
- Input device classes
- Graphical user interface classes
- Color palette and color lookup table classes
- 3D-related classes

ARTT includes many command-line based tools to aid in animation work. Some are listed in this book; others are simply referenced in the text. See Appendix B for a complete listing of the tools provided, highlights of which are presented below:

- GFXSHOW, a tool for viewing graphics files of various types (three versions)
- GFX2GFX, a tool for converting graphics files between formats
- ANIMPLAY, a tool for playing back animation files
- ANM2ANM, a tool for converting animation files to ARTT'S ASA format
- MAKEITAB, a tool for making inverse tables for fast color conversions
- MAKECLUT, a tool for making color tables for shading, hazing, filtering, etc.
- PIXBLITZ, a display rendering speed benchmarker
- VESALIST, a tool for identifying VESA VBE modes supported by a given PC

In addition to these tools, several fun demonstration programs are developed which illustrate various concepts, and again both source and executables are included. Some of these tools have dual DOS/Windows versions; others are provided in only one version. See Appendix B for a complete listing of the sample programs, which include:

- BBALL, a bouncing-ball demo
- WEB, a Windows-based animated demo
- TEXCUBES, a 3D textured-cube demo
- AQUARIUM, a sample program with fish swimming in it
- AMUCK, a wacky laboratory instrument simulation
- HELIFIRE, a pseudo-3D shoot-'em-up featuring fast bitmap scaling and color effects
- ROMNRACE, a side-scrolling foot race set in Roman times

Compilers and Environments Supported

ARTT has been designed to be as portable as possible. All code has been compiled under the following compilers for use under both DOS and Windows 3.1:

- Borland C++ 4.5
- Symantec C++ 6.11 and 7.0
- Watcom C++ 10.0

ARTT has been designed primarily for 32-bit operation, although it can run in 16-bit environments with some restrictions. Under DOS, ARTT can be compiled for either 16-bit "regular" DOS or 32-bit *extended DOS*. Because ARTT does not make use of expanded memory or *huge* pointers, 16-bit ARTT buffers can't exceed 64K in size, limiting graphic images to areas of roughly 320×200 pixels or less. The same buffer size limitations exist in 16-bit Windows. In 32-bit extended DOS or 32-bit Windows using Win32s, no such restrictions exist.

Compile-time flags are used to handle some differences between 16-bit and 32-bit operation, and between various compilers, so the entire library should be recompiled under whatever environment you choose to run. Makefiles are provided to make this process easier, and the ARTT "manual" provides more information on the issues associated with each. See Appendix D for restrictions which apply to some compilers. Portability to other compilers, if necessary, should be reasonably straightforward, and Chapter 20 includes useful information for those interested in porting ARTT to other systems altogether, such as OS/2 or X-Windows.

Why Use ARTT? Doesn't Windows do Graphics?

Microsoft Windows, being a graphical operating environment, of course "does" graphics via its Graphics Device Interface (GDI). Windows also does a lot more, providing a full user interface built on top of GDI, memory and device management, and a host of extensions from Video for Windows to Object Linking and Embedding. But the GDI itself, which provides a device-independent toolset for rendering graphics to the screen, in some respects falls far short of the capabilities provided by a library such as ARTT. GDI provides basic rendering primitives, good text font support, and a reasonable set of bitmap operations, and pretty much leaves it at that. Want to load an image from a graphics file? Do it yourself. Want to animate the screen instead of just drawing a static picture? You're on your own. Want to provide shading, hazing, or translucency color effects? Start writing some code.

This is not to fault Windows—it provides a competent basic graphics engine, albeit one with a few performance problems which are primarily due to its general and device-independent nature. The kinds of features provided by ARTT are just not in its domain. Even Windows programmers who want to provide top-notch graphics must find some way of creating those graphics by non-Windows means, and then use GDI to get the resulting pixels to the screen. WinG is a major step forward in Windows' ability to let such programs create their own graphics and then move their pixels to the screen as fast as possible. ARTT uses WinG as its display engine when running under Windows.

Is C++ Fast Enough for Real-Time Graphics?

This book does not include a single line of assembler code. I made this decision consciously, and with the full expectation of some ridicule by those who think that fast graphics means assembly language. I made the no-assembler decision in order to create a library with maximum teaching value, readability, maintainability, and portability. But I wouldn't have taken this path if C++, in the hands of modern compilers, wasn't capable of moving pixels at very high speed. Furthermore, good algorithms and precalculated lookup tables beat poor algorithms optimized with assembler any day—less code or no code is the best optimization.

The question "Is C++ fast enough for real-time graphics?" is really two questions. Since C++ is a superset of C, the first question is "Is C fast enough for real-time graphics?" My answer is emphatically yes, and assembler is faster. Until advances in artificial intelligence, which remains as always poised for big breakthroughs in ten years, endows compilers with human brains, a clever human will be able to code a given function significantly better than a compiler. Compilers are smart enough already, however, that to beat them sometimes requires more than an understanding of the CPU register and instruction set and a book of "official" instruction timings. The best assembly programmers have intimate knowledge of prefetch queues, instruction scheduling and pipelining (which vary widely from 386 to 486 to Pentium, of course), and other issues which are not for the faint of heart. The Pentium CPU already executes multiple instructions simultaneously; when the next generation of CPUs takes such *superscalar* design to the next level, optimization via assembly programming may truly be dead by virtue of sheer complexity.

In the interim, for instance, right now when we all still have to get our programming done, assembler has its place, and is certainly used for critical portions of graphics code in commercial work, including my own. The final chapter of this book details several functions in ARTT which could be improved by conversion to good assembly code. Sometimes, though, the speedup due to such effort may be less than you might imagine. For example, in ARTT the inner loop of a standard pixel copying routine is based on memcpy(). Horrors! A function call in an inner loop of an important routine! Well, as it turns out, when you compile with optimization turned on, modern compilers "inline" the memcpy() code, and produce the exact same assembly code that a good programmer would write. As Socrates said, *know your compiler.*

By the way, I think that knowing assembly language is a very valuable skill for a graphics programmer, even if you never use it. If nothing else, it helps you read disassemblies of the code created by your compiler, so you can tell if it's doing a reasonable job in a given situation. Beyond that, it's extremely helpful when writing a piece of C or C++ code to have a good sense of what the compiler is likely to do with that code, and whether structuring it another way would likely give you better compiled code.

The second part of the question "Is C++ fast enough for real-time graphics?" is the question "Is C++ as fast as C?" By definition the answer is yes, if C++ is used just like C. But the attractiveness of C++ lies in its classes, inheritance, and other *object-oriented* features. Will using these features slow us down? The answer is, it depends on how they are used. Virtual functions, a powerful C++ mechanism for indirectly calling the right function for a particular object, are used heavily in ARTT—most rendering calls are virtual! However, any graphics system which supports more than one type of output device must provide for such runtime function dispatch; C++ virtual functions are equivalent to tables of function pointers in C or assembler, which is the typical technique used in those languages. In my experience, constructors and destructors, especially as objects are passed to functions via the stack, tend to be the worst unnecessary gobblers of execution time in C++ code. ARTT avoids most such overhead by passing such arguments by *reference* in most cases, equivalent to passing a pointer to the object in C. So my answer to this half of the question is, yes, if you know what your C++ compiler is doing.

C++ *Feature Usage*

ARTT is written from the ground up in C++. It makes heavy use of such basic C++ features as classes, inheritance, virtual functions, and data hiding (well, usually). For performance, ARTT makes liberal use of *inline* functions, which are like C macros but more powerful and type secure. The book assumes that C++ code is familiar to you, even if you may not already use it in your programming. Some readers may balk at some of the strange constructs, but I have attempted to explain, in context and in "C++ Note" boxes, any language feature or usage which might be unfamiliar. Experienced and enthusiastic C++ users may object to the lack of rigor in data hiding, lack of use of the const keyword, and other failures to toe the object-oriented line. In this section and in C++ Note boxes, I also attempt to explain and justify usage which is not considered "good C++." Most such "compromises" are made either to enhance readability for C++ novices, or for the sake of runtime efficiency.

Much thinking went into deciding which features of the evolving C++ language to use in ARTT, and which to avoid. ARTT is limited to a subset of C++ for the following reasons:

- Some features are unfamiliar to a majority of readers or are hard to read and understand. Operator overloading is modestly used in ARTT because its abuse can lead to unreadable code. It is mostly used in low-level computational classes and in classes which are arraylike.

- Some features are nonstandard or not yet available on all compilers, so that their usage would leave a large subset of readers unable to compile the code. Templates and exception handling are not used in ARTT for this reason.

- C standard i/o (printf, fread, etc.) is used instead of C++ streams. ARTT makes very little use of i/o anyway; it is restricted mostly to printing error messages and reading data from files. I thought that using streams would just "get in the way" of readability for enough readers that it didn't make sense to use it for such simple i/o needs. Not to mention the erratic and nonstandard ways in which streams seem to be implemented from compiler to compiler.

- ARTT does not include a single use of the *const* keyword. Const marks items as being read-only, and helps the compiler optimize code and check it for errors. The downside is that, once you start using const, you must essentially use it everywhere, to keep the compiler from complaining. And the function prototype for a member function taking const arguments and returning a const value, where also the function itself is const because it doesn't modify the object, can make James Joyce look like a Dick and Jane book. Sorry— books are meant to be read and understood.

To my mind, the point of C++ is to use classes and other language features to build a loosely connected set of components relevant to the task at hand, and easily extensible to future needs. I hope that the ARTT class library is useful as is, but even more I hope that you find it easy to understand and build upon. If you've developed a useful extension to ARTT, I'd love to have a look. Send me mail and/or your code on CompuServe at id 73040,2050.

Enjoy the journey.

Bitmaps
and Rendering

Bitmaps

The Basics: How a Computer Makes Pictures

How *does* a computer put pictures onto a display screen, really? Like many questions, technical and otherwise, this one can be answered at many different levels. An electrical circuit engineer might describe how an electrical waveform is used to drive the showering of electrons against the phosphor-coated surface of a display monitor's tube, which lights up to create a picture. That's useful information, but how is this electrical waveform generated? We might turn to the designer of the display card, which creates these electrical waveforms in the first place. He or she might answer our question in terms of commands and data bytes, and how these are sent from a computer and routed to the circuitry which creates the electrical signals to drive a display. After talking to both of these people, we would know how data bytes are converted into pictures on the display.

But if our goal is to create a realistic-looking three-dimensional scene on the display, these answers are hardly enough. It is time to talk to the software engineers. A system-level graphics programmer would tell us how the hardware architecture of a display card can be manipulated to create basic lines, rectangles, and other images. Now we're getting somewhere, but then again a complex scene doesn't look a whole lot like lines and rectangles. Our next stop is the creator of a full-fledged graphics program, such as a two-dimensional drawing package or a 3D raytracing program. Such a person can describe how to create sophisticated images using the system software as a base from which to build—our discussion turns to bitmaps, shaded polygons, depth-sorting of objects, and such. Now that we know how pictures are created from these higher levels of software, we might want to continue on and talk to users of such systems, such as graphic artists. Their answer to the question of how graphics are created might be given in terms of the colors, brushes, effects, and other tools presented by an application program.

In this book, we will focus primarily on two of these levels, those of the system-level programmer and the application creator. However, it never hurts to have understanding of any field at multiple levels. Knowledge of "lower" levels in computer graphics is especially useful when rendering speed matters—and it always does. Your users will thank you for your understanding of the problems they face using the "higher" levels of a graphics system.

The design of graphics hardware—displays, printers, scanners, plotters—is intimately related to the design of graphics software systems, and the two have evolved together over the last couple of decades. Fundamentally, however, hardware design operates under many more constraints than software, and sets the basic architecture around which software systems are developed. There are only so many ways to light up a screen or apply ink to paper, and the cost of various mechanical or electronic devices determines what designs will be commercially viable.

The Old: Vector Devices

For instance, in the 1960s the most common graphics devices were the pen plotter and its electronic corollary, the vector display terminal. Both devices displayed line segments and line segments only, one by moving a pen across paper, the other by controlling the spray of an electron gun against the surface of a display tube. By feeding the coordinates of line segments to either of these devices, a computer could draw certain kinds of pictures, such as scientific graphs or architectural drawings.

While most plotters were designed to accept vector drawing commands "on the fly" as they operated, with perhaps a small memory buffer to hold pending commands, vector terminals operated under a different hardware constraint which influenced their design. Rather than just drawing an image once, a terminal must *refresh* its screen by redrawing its image many times per second, in order to present an unflickering image. Without such refreshing, the image quickly fades away. For this reason, the vector terminal must hold the set of lines representing an image in memory inside the terminal, so that the attached computer is not required to send the same line coordinates over and over again. At typical slow serial connection speeds, this would be unfeasible anyway. The memory used to hold the line segment coordinates is usually referred to as a *display list*. Software to drive vector terminals, then, is designed around the setting and updating of the terminal's display list. Figure 1.1 diagrams the operation of a vector terminal.

The New: Bitmapped Devices

Pen plotters and vector terminals were limited compared to current laser printers and color monitors in a fundamental way. Representing pictures as line segments, even color line segments, is unsuitable for many types of images, for instance photographs. How much better if the graphics terminal could display such color images, like a television screen. Color televisions were already popular in the 1960s, so what kept them from being used for computer graphics? The answer to this question is derived from the way in which a television works. Like a vector terminal, the picture on a television screen must be

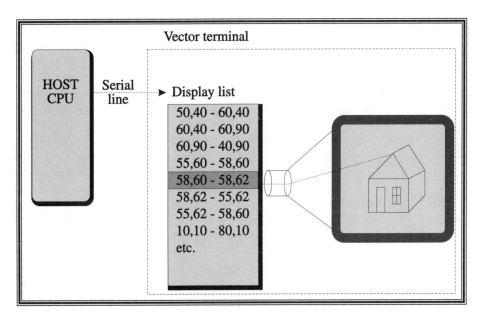

Figure 1.1 Operation of a vector terminal. Vector coordinates are stored in a display list which is used to refresh the display.

refreshed, at a rate of at least 30 times a second to avoid flicker. However, the type of storage needed to "hold the image" in this case is not just a display list of line segments, but is in fact the set of color values for every point on the screen. In television, each image is stored on videotape back at the transmitting TV station; each television just displays what is received over the air or cable. A computer must store its own images, and the cost of this storage kept such displays inaccessible to computers until the 1970s.

In such graphics devices, which are now in use on every desktop computer, the screen or page is represented by a grid array of tiny discrete elements called *pixels;* the term is derived from *pic*ture *ele*ment. Random-access memory chips inside the device hold the contents of the entire screen or page of such pixels. Because bits in these memory chips are "mapped" directly to screen or page pixels, these devices are often referred to as *bitmapped devices*, and the memory itself as a *bitmap*.

The way in which memory bits are physically used to drive screen pixels depends on the nature of the display hardware. The two most common types of displays in use today are *monitors*, based on cathode-ray tube technology, and LCD panels, based on liquid crystal physics. The two technologies are quite different in their physical operation, although the outcome is similar.

Cathode-Ray Tubes

The display monitors which sit atop the tens of millions of personal computers in use today are variations on the basic television set design in use since the 1930s. Inside every television and monitor, and filling up most of the space, is a vacuum tube (yes, there really is no air in it), referred to as a cathode-ray tube. Hence the designation CRT (cathode-ray tube) for computer displays. The term *cathode* refers to the negatively charged pole in an electrical system; the positive pole is the *anode*. The cathode in a cathode-ray tube is a source of electrons which it releases in great numbers across that vacuum toward its anode, which is the back of the screen itself. A large magnetic coil called the *yoke* is wrapped around the cathode, and manipulating the yoke's magnetic charge causes the flowing electrons to be pulled up, down, left, or right from the center of the screen.

By controlling this magnet in a systematic way, the electrons being ejected from the cathode can be caused to scan across the screen from top to bottom in a series of horizontal lines, and from left to right within each line. This scanning pattern is called a *raster*. Now, if the amount of electrons being fired at any given instant can be modulated during the raster scan, then different parts of the screen can be lit up with different levels of intensity. A television signal provides both the continually fluctuating intensity level and the "synchronization" pulses used to control the raster scanning process. In a computer monitor, these functions are carried on separate wires within the cable, but the principle is the same. Figure 1.2 illustrates the raster scanning pattern.

Color televisions and color display monitors are variants on the basic monochrome design. In a typical color monitor, the screen's *phosphor* (the material on the back of the screen which lights up when struck by electrons) is composed of a large array of triplets of dots. Each of the three types of dots gives off a different *primary* color when struck by the electrons. These three primary colors are red, green, and blue; a wide range of visible colors can be represented by a combination of different amounts of these three colors. For instance, violet is the combination of red and blue, with no green. In Chapter 13, the theory of color will be explored more fully.

In a color monitor, instead of one electron gun there are three, anchored relative to each other in such a way that electrons from each gun can strike only the proper member of each triplet of dots on the screen. The raster scanning operation operates on all three guns in unison, so that each screen dot is visited in a fixed pattern, but the intensity of each gun is independently controlled. As the three electron streams visit any triplet of phosphors, the amount of radiation striking each phosphor can be precisely controlled to produce the desired color at that location. For instance, as the electron stream passes by a particular pixel, the red and blue guns could be turned up to full intensity, and the green one turned off, to create a violet pixel.

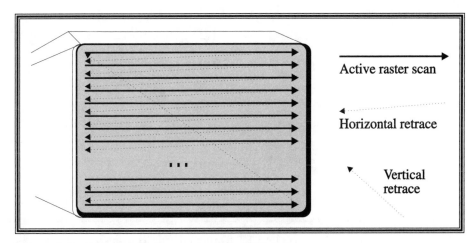

Figure 1.2 Raster scanning pattern of a CRT device.

Figure 1.3 shows how the three electron guns are used to light up triplets of phosphors.

By the way, the *dot pitch* referred to in monitor ratings is the distance between such RGB phosphor triplets. A typical dot pitch is .28 millimeters, which is about 3600 dot triplets per meter. A 15″ diagonal picture tube is 12″ across and 9″ down, and so would have roughly 1150 dots across by about 850 down. Note that the correspondence between these RGB (red-green-blue) triplets and screen pixels is not one-to-one (this could also be deduced by the fact that the same monitor can display different numbers of pixels across and down in different graphics *modes*). Screen *resolution* refers to the number of pixels across and down as delivered by the display card circuitry. 640 × 480, a common medium-level resolution, refers to a screen with 640 pixels across by 480 down. In the case of our hypothetical monitor, each such pixel would occupy roughly 2 × 2 phosphor dots—but not exactly! The same monitor driven by a 1024 × 768 pixel mode would barely use one phosphor dot per pixel. *Multisync* monitors, capable of adapting to the raster scanning patterns of different resolutions, are the norm today.

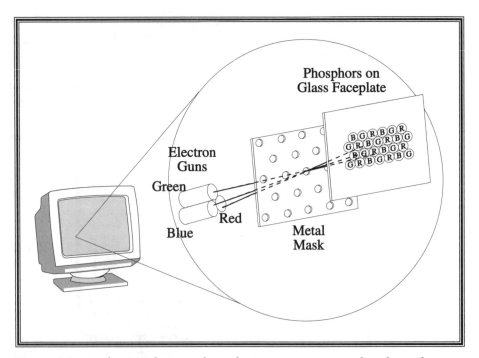

Figure 1.3   A color CRT features three electron guns, one per phosphor color.

Liquid Crystal Displays

Liquid crystal displays (LCDs), like the one on the notebook computer I am using to write this chapter, are similar in concept to television monitors, but are far different in how they physically create images. There is no electron gun in an LCD panel. Instead, electric current is used to change the state of a pixel grid of liquid crystal elements from transparent to opaque. When transparent, light reflected from the environment or *backlit* from behind makes the pixel appear bright; when opaque it appears dark. Passive-matrix LCDs are similar to CRTs in that the display is "scanned" in a refresh pattern which decays over time. Because of a typically slow refresh cycle, passive LCD displays have a sluggish feel, most easily seen by watching the mouse cursor blur as it is moved quickly. Active-matrix LCDs, on the other hand, devote a transistor to each screen pixel (3 per pixel for color screens), so each pixel maintains its state until changed, and no refresh scan is needed. Because of the large number of transistors required (on the order of a million for a 640×480 color screen, and a few bad transistors is all it takes to send a panel to the defective bin), these panels are more expensive to produce.

Display Control Circuitry

Now we've gotten at least a cursory answer, from the electrical engineer, to the question of how a computer displays pictures. In the case of CRTs and passive-matrix LCD displays, electrical waveforms containing color information for all the pixels in a screen image are fed to the screen. Combined with synchronization signals to control the raster scanning pattern which sweeps across and down the screen, these pixel values are used to vary the intensity of electron guns or liquid-crystal opacity. Active-matrix LCD screens are simpler in theory, because the image is "stored" directly in the LCD pixels themselves.

Now we turn to the next level in answering our original question, which is to ask how this electrical waveform is generated. To answer that, let's examine the video circuitry inside a typical PC. The waveform-generating circuitry is usually built into a *display card* which plugs into the PC bus, except in portable computers where it is built into the system's motherboard. Regardless of its location, the video circuitry has several jobs to do in transforming a bitmapped image inside the computer into the signals which drive the display monitor or LCD screen. These functions include bitmap storage, control and synchronization, and digital-to-analog conversion. Each is covered below:

- *Bitmap storage*—In almost all cases, the display card has on-board *video memory* to hold the screen bitmap, typically one megabyte or more. The memory is specially constructed and dedicated to the video circuitry. This is because it must be accessed continually to drive the display device, and grabbing pixels from normal system memory would put too much strain on the system bus. In fact, this memory is accessed at such a high rate to refresh the display that very often the CPU must wait to access the memory when changing the image. Instead of normal *dynamic ram* (DRAM) chips, high-performance designs employ more expensive "dual-ported" *video ram* (VRAM) which can be updated in parallel with screen refresh. One access port is devoted to screen refresh, and the other is always available for use by the CPU. The difference between DRAM and VRAM is transparent to the software, other than in speed of display update.

- *Controller*—The signals used to drive a monitor or LCD device include synchronization (sync) signals as well as the red, green, and blue intensity signals. These signals are usually analog, that is, they are continually varying electric waveforms, not digital transmissions. In the case of monitor devices, sync signals drive the raster scanning pattern, causing the yoke to pull the electron stream back to the left of the screen for another row, or back to the top for the next entire frame. In passive-matrix CRT devices, sync signals are used to refresh the liquid crystals from display memory. In either case, proper sync signals are based on the desired timings, which depend on screen resolution and refresh rate. In addition to providing synchronization, the controller also sweeps through video memory, grabbing the next pixel value, and running it through the digital-analog converter in order to transform it to the required analog values of red, green, and blue. These are fed to the next stage, the DAC.

- *DAC*—The "output stage" of the video circuitry is the DAC, which stands for *digital-analog converter*. This is a general term in electronics which has a specific meaning in the context of display circuits. It is the job of the DAC to take the discrete numeric values which are read from video memory, and convert them to the proper intensity (voltage) levels to be delivered to the display monitor or LCD. If the color pixel specifies each of the red, green, and blue components as separate values—usually 5 to 8 bits each to give a sufficient range of intensity—this is relatively straightforward. In typical low-cost graphic systems, however, each pixel value represents the color value indirectly, as we shall see when we discuss bitmap formats in more detail. A very common display format gives each pixel a single 8-bit byte, which is used as an index into a color table located in the DAC, where the full red, green, and blue values are located. These three values are then converted to analog form in the usual manner. This indirection allows a color screen to be specified using one-third as much video ram as would otherwise be required, with a tradeoff of less flexibility in assigning color values to screen elements. Much more on this later, as techniques for programming such 8-bit *indexed color* systems is a primary focus of this book.

In summary, then, the job of the video card is to continually read pixel values from video ram, transform to full RGB color values, convert these numeric values to analog signals, construct analog sync signals, and present both color and sync signals to a connector which can be hooked up to the display device. At the same time, the CPU must be granted access to write and read back values placed into the video memory. Figure 1.4 portrays a block diagram of a hypothetical basic display card.

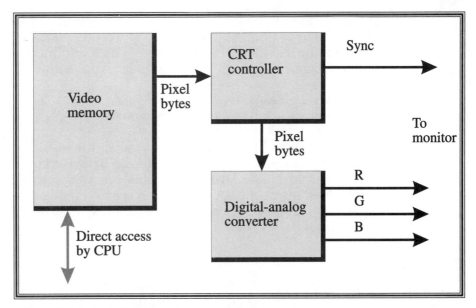

Figure 1.4   Block diagram of a typical display card.

Display Bitmaps

We have seen that memory bits can be used to drive the contents of a physical display device. But what exactly is the coding of these bits that represent pixels in video memory? The answer to this question (we are still talking to our hypothetical display card designer) will drive the development of the foundation layer of software for the graphics toolkit we will build in this book. And the answer is—there are several different codings, depending on which computer model and display card we are talking about! But don't panic—the varieties are sensible and fall into a few patterns. The different varieties are called *bitmap formats*.

The simplest bitmap formats are monochrome; color adds a layer of complexity. Monochrome formats are usually very straightforward. The original Macintosh computer and several of its descendent models displays only black and white pixels, and has a screen consisting of 512 pixels across by 342 high (512 × 342 resolution). These 171,104 pixels are each driven by a single memory bit—a 1 bit for black and 0 for white.[1] The 8 bits in each byte represent 8 horizontally adjacent pixels, and thus 64 bytes (512/8) across represent

---

[1] Of course, IBM monochrome systems use 1 for white and 0 for black, showing that, when it comes to computers, there is no issue so basic that there can't be disagreement on it.

each display row. The next 64 bytes represent the next row, going from top to bottom, and so on, as Figure 1.5 illustrates. Thus, given a *x,y* location, it is easy to calculate the byte and bit which drives that screen location. The magic formula is given below:

```
byte address = base address + (y * 64) + (x / 8)
bit number = x & 7 (low 3 bits of x-coordinate)
```

Most monochrome display bitmaps (for instance, monochrome VGA modes) are formatted similarly. The Hercules monochrome card, an older standard which lives on as accessible functionality embedded inside most VGA chips, has an oddball addressing scheme, in which successive rows of memory represent display rows which are not sequentially ordered.

Color Bitmaps

As we saw in the discussion of color display hardware, color is produced in these systems by combining various amounts of red, green, and blue. In a bitmapped color display, each pixel is assigned a certain amount of each of these three primary colors. Ideally, each pixel can take on any possible hue in the color spectrum. In such cases the term *direct-color* display is used, because each pixel's color is represented directly by its associated data bits in the bitmap. So-called

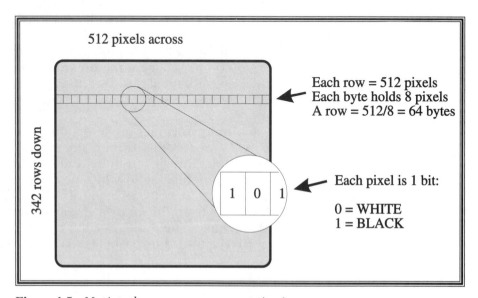

Figure 1.5   Macintosh screen memory organization.

true-color display systems give a full byte each to the red, green, and blue components of a pixel, giving them each 256 different intensity values. Colors which differ by only one increment of red, green, or blue are barely distinguishable by human vision. The following structure shows the memory layout of typical true-color pixels.

```
// Layout of typical true-color pixel (3 bytes)
   typedef struct {
       uchar blue;      // 8 bits of blue component
       uchar green;     // 8 bits of green component
       uchar red;       // 8 bits of blue component
} TrueColorPixel;
```

Note that true-color systems require three bytes per pixel—a 640 × 480-pixel true-color display requires nearly a megabyte of display memory. In the mid 1990s, this amount of memory is not exceptional, and because of this, true-color displays will rapidly take over the marketplace in the next few years. But in the early days of color displays, a megabyte was an unheard-of luxury. So how to provide the color everyone clearly wanted? The most commonly adopted solution to this problem was to provide a color lookup table in the DAC. Today's popular 8-bit VGA and *Super VGA* displays use such an approach, assigning only a single byte to each pixel.

How then does this single value generate color? It is used as an index into the DAC-based table of 256 RGB entries, each of which supplies the full red, green, and blue pixel component values. Thus 1 byte per pixel plus 768 bytes (256 entries × 3 bytes each) for the DAC color table can be used for an entire color display. Such displays are called *indexed-color* displays, as opposed to direct-color displays, because the data bits of a pixel are used as an index into a color table to determine the pixel's true color.

Indexed-color displays use far less display memory, but, of course, you don't get something for nothing. While any RGB color value can be put into the DAC color table, each pixel on the screen can't have a unique color—the entire display must share a single set of 256 RGB colors. No more than 256 unique colors can appear at once on the display, which may contain hundreds of thousands of pixels. Finding the best set of such colors to represent an image, or a set of images, is an interesting research topic in its own right.

There are other varieties of color bitmaps; 15-bit and 16-bit *hi-color* displays, which are direct-color but with less bits for each color component than true-color, are popular now and supported by a wide range of PC display cards. They provide better color than 8-bit lookup-based displays, but are much faster to program than 24-bit true-color displays (three-byte pixels are unwieldy to program;

two bytes is much simpler). For the near future they will be used widely, and they are particularly appropriate in digital video applications where their speed advantage over 24-bit displays is currently needed. In a matter of a few years, however, hardware acceleration will speed 24-bit cards up sufficiently to make the performance issue moot, and it seems likely that the superior picture quality of 24-bit will carry the day.

Other bitmap formats abound, but are no longer mainstream; 4-bit EGA and VGA displays capable of only 16 colors are thankfully disappearing. Home video-game machines, where cost of memory chips is paramount, typically do not even represent the screen in a fully bitmapped sense as we have been discussing it. Instead, the screen is divided into character cells, typically 8 or 16 pixels on a side. A limited number of character cells can be defined (each is its own minibitmap), then the screen is represented by a two-dimensional grid of character cell indexes. Figure 1.6 shows the display memory layout of a hypothetical video game machine. Ironically, this layout is essentially the same as that used by DOS in its "text modes." Each text character is represented by an index into a set of minibitmaps which describe the text font.

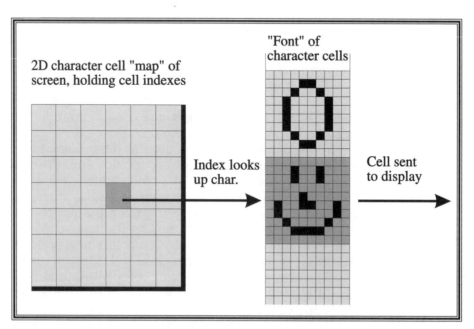

Figure 1.6 Hypothetical video game display memory layout.

Bitmaps Forever?

There is a large variety of bitmap formats across the spectrum of graphic devices, but this book is concerned only with modern PC displays. We will deal primarily with three types of color display formats—the currently preeminent 8-bit VGA and Super VGA displays, the also-popular 15-bit hi-color format, and the next coming standard—24-bit true-color displays. And what's after that? Do these 24-bit cards represent the end of the line in PC displays?

Hardly, young Grasshopper. The activity in graphics hardware development today is astounding. Virtually every PC display card sold now has added hardware acceleration to speed the rendering of pixels into video memory. Many of these cards are currently being outfitted with special hardware for decoding compressed digital video images in real time. And hardware support for 3D imaging is just beginning to find its way onto PC video cards. Fundamentally, though, there's still a bitmap on the card being shown on the display monitor, and these fancy features are aids to help us put pixel values into that bitmap.

Will displays of the future always have a bitmap as the fundamental underlying representation of the image? Who knows? Perhaps in 40 or 50 years, computer displays will be driven directly from fractal image representations, or each pixel will have a stochastic neural network computer driving it while chattering away with neighbor pixel drivers. More likely, the whole notion of a two-dimensional display will be an anachronism by then.

In the nearer term, say the next 10 or 20 years, it is pretty likely that the underlying image representation will remain a bitmap, with ever-more sophisticated hardware to manage its contents. In that time frame, the topics discussed in this book will be relevant to an increasingly smaller circle, mainly those developing graphics hardware and the accompanying built-in software, firmware, and microcode.

But the topics of this book are hardly obsolete today. Today's software must work on today's hardware. And today's hardware doesn't perform animation, it doesn't have sophisticated color effects, it doesn't draw 3D texture maps, and it doesn't compose multiple image sources together.[2] So, for the next several years, plotting pixels will still be a useful and rewarding activity.

---

[2]Actually, a $100 video game machine does provide for a large number of overlays, but the brightest minds in the business can't seem to figure out how to get this technology onto a PC! *Sigh.*

Back to the present. Our hypothetical display card engineer has given us a short overview of display circuitry. Armed with this knowledge, it's time to talk to the system-level graphics programmer about building the foundation level of our graphics software. Hey, that person is us! The answer to the question of how a computer generates pictures, at the system-software level, will be quite a bit lengthier. It is what this book is about.

C++ *Classes: A Quick Recap*

Soon, the C++ code will be flying by fast and furious. Now is a good time to take stock of some of the concepts and terminology that will be bandied about. Many of the C++ classes we'll be designing make heavy use of inheritance and virtual functions. This short section is meant as a refresher for those who may not be fully up to speed on these concepts. For a more detailed discussion, see any of the many available books on the C++ language.

A *class*, remember, is a way of defining both a structure of data and the set of functions which operate on that data. A class is an abstract concept; you create *instances* of a given class by declaration or via the *new* operator. These instances are often called *objects*, and the whole process goes by the overused buzzword *object-oriented programming*. A class is very much like a C struct with associated functions, called *methods*, declared alongside the *member variables* inside the curly braces. Each such function implicitly takes a pointer to an instance as an invisible argument, so it knows which particular instance of the structure is being referred to. When you see member variables being manipulated inside a method, these are actually the variables belonging to the instance referred to by the invisible pointer. C++ streamlines the coding process by letting you avoid using *p->member* everywhere inside these methods, like you would if you were using C in a similar fashion.

To give a short example of what's going on "under the hood," take a look at a very simple C++ class.

```
// C++ version of choo-choo train class
class Train {
   int numberOfCars;
   void BlowWhistle();
};


void Train::BlowWhistle()
{
   printf("Blowing whistle for %d cars\n", numberOfCars);
}
```

Now examine an "equivalent class" done in C. Note that, whereas Train::BlowWhistle() referred implicitly to a particular Train instance in C++, in C we must supply the instance pointer explicitly. Also, references to the 'numberOfCars' structure member must be referenced through an explicit pointer in C, whereas the pointer is implied in C++.

```
// C version of choo-choo train class
typedef struct {
    int numberOfCars;
} Train;

void BlowWhistle(Train *ptrain)
{
printf("Blowing whistle for %d cars\n", ptrain->numberOfCars);
}
```

Methods may be explicitly or implicitly declared *inline,* which advises the compiler to expand the body of the method *in place* when called instead of making an actual function call. This is a feature akin to C macros but better in many ways—inlines are easier to return values from than macros, and they don't have troublesome side effects. Also, inline methods enforce type-checking of their arguments, and other C++ features such as default arguments are available to them. Our toolkit uses inline methods heavily for performance reasons.

Member variables and methods may be declared *private, public,* or *protected.* Private members are accessible only to methods of the class itself and to specifically declared *friend* classes or functions. Public members are accessible to any code. Protected members are accessible to the class itself, to friends, and to methods in derived classes. Table 1.1 illustrates the protection levels.

Instances of an object can be created globally by declaration outside any function, locally by declaration inside a function, or on the memory heap via the new operator. These correspond to the ways

Table 1.1 C++ Protection Levels

Protection Level	*Accessibility*
Private	Class methods, friend functions, and methods of friend classes
Protected	All of above, plus methods in derived classes
Public	Any code

Table 1.2   C++ Object Storage Classes

Storage class	Location	Comments
Static	Global memory	Declared outside any function, or inside with static keyword. Statics are constructed before main(), destructed after exit().
Automatic	Stack	Declared inside function. Automatics are constructed at the start of function or enclosing block, and are destroyed at the end of the block or function.
Dynamic	On heap	Allocated and constructed via new(), destroyed via delete().

in which C storage can be allocated (globally, locally on the stack, or allocated on the heap). In all cases, a *constructor* is implicitly called to initialize the object. The constructor is a special method that you write to perform this task. When the object goes out of *scope*, the *destructor* is called. For global objects, this happens at the end of the program; for local objects, it's at the end of enclosing block or function. Objects allocated dynamically via new never go out of scope—they must be destroyed explicitly via the *delete* operator. Table 1.2 summarizes the storage classes for C++ objects.

Some classes stand alone, like the ABitmap class to be discussed later in this chapter. Others are *derived* classes; that is, they *inherit* some of their functionality from one or more *ancestor* classes. When you see the declaration of a derived class, the member variables and methods shown exist in addition to the member variables and methods of the ancestor classes. That is, an instance of a derived class has the member variables of both classes, and can be operated on by the methods of both as well. This is a powerful feature of the C++ language—it allows classes which are "just like some other class, only with these differences" to be easily created. A whole "tree" of classes related by a common ancestor class is often called a *class hierarchy*. We'll be creating several class hierarchies, and many standalone classes, unlike some libraries wherein all classes are derived from a single *root* class. Figure 1.7 shows a small class hierarchy, one whose classes will be discussed in Chapter 3.

Sometimes adding functionality to a class to make a new one isn't enough. Sometimes what is needed is to replace the functionality of some method with a new method. C++ provides *virtual functions* for this purpose. If a function is declared to be virtual, a

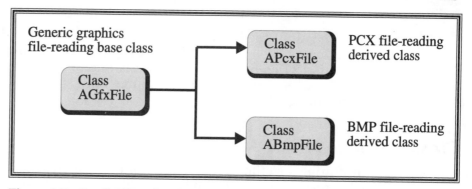

Figure 1.7   Small ARTT class hierarchy.

descendant class can *override* the definition of this method with a new one. Whenever the method is invoked on an object, the appropriate version of the virtual function is called, depending on which class the object is a member of. Virtual functions provide the method whereby the proper rendering routine for a given format of rendering surface is invoked, and they will be used heavily.

Whew! If some of this discussion of C++ is old news but some is unfamiliar, march on—we'll explain more as we go. If the entire thing sounded like Klingon, perhaps some review of an introductory C++ book would be helpful before proceeding.

The ARTT Toolkit

In this book, we will be developing a full-scale, high-performance graphics toolkit in C++, *from the ground up*. By that I mean that the software will interact directly with the graphics hardware and on-board firmware. Our toolkit will be called ARTT—*Animation in Real-Time Toolkit*. By the time we're done, we'll have a full system capable of:

- Running on VGA and Super VGA, on 8-bit, 15-bit, and 24-bit displays
- Running under Microsoft Windows using WinG
- Drawing geometric primitives such as lines, rectangles, and boxes
- Drawing color text in proportionally spaced fonts
- Reading images and animations from popular file formats
- Displaying and animating bitmapped images, at nominal size or scaled
- Composing several moving, overlapping images, and scrolling backgrounds
- Creating user interface elements such as icons, pushbuttons, and menus
- Producing a variety of color effects such as shading, hazing, and translucency

- Drawing 3D objects using texture mapping

The ARTT toolkit will be built from the ground up, by presenting each class or tool as it's needed. We'll get the ball rolling in this chapter with ARTT's bitmap class. This is one of the most fundamental ARTT classes, used as both the source and destination of most rendering operations.

Class ABitmap

In putting together a C++ class library, it is instructive to consider what the objects in the application domain might be. The classes of objects included in the design should be representations of the concepts used in thinking about the "problem"[3] domain. We've seen one such concept come up several times so far—the bitmap. That makes it a good candidate to be made into a class in our library.

What should our bitmap class look like, and what should it do? What data does it encapsulate, and what behavior does it need to support? Think for a second about what a bitmap needs to do. Bitmaps will be used to represent the display screen, of course, but we want them to do more than that. Professional graphics software needs to be able to access *off-screen* bitmaps, too. These are bitmaps which exist in some other memory besides the display screen's memory, often in regular *system ram* allocated with malloc() or new(). Using off-screen bitmaps is handy when composing a scene of multiple overlapping elements, when you don't want the poor user to have to watch the unsightly composing process. Instead, all the work goes on backstage in the off-screen buffer, which you finally copy, or *blit*, to the screen as the final step. This keeps the screen free from unprofessional-looking glitches.

Another use for bitmaps is for predrawn images to be rendered. Computer games and animated multimedia programs are full of animated characters, backgrounds, and other images, most of which are in bitmapped form. Hopping monsters, talking heads, solitaire cards, text characters, and even the cursor are all bitmapped images, defined by a 2D grid of pixels much like the screen itself. Thus our bitmaps will be used not only as destinations of drawing commands, but as sources for images as well.

An instance (object) of our bitmap class needs to include a pointer or some other kind of reference to the bits which make up the bitmap. It must also describe some attributes of these bits. Since not

---

[3]The word *problem* shows up often in object-oriented metholodogy literature. The people who write this stuff should switch to computer graphics—nobody writes about the problem of displaying graphics on a screen—it's kinda fun, in fact.

all bitmaps are screen-sized, it needs to describe the bitmap's width and height. Also, as we have seen, not all bitmaps are formatted identically, so format codes must be included. If the bitmap is in an indexed-color format, we need a pointer to the table of colors, or *palette,* that the indexes refer to. We will program this palette into the DAC color table, in order to view the image in the appropriate colors.

Below is the header file for class ABitmap. Since bitmaps are at the heart of ARTT, in the next sections we'll go over it in fine detail.

```
//    Abitmap.h   Bitmap class
//    Rex E. Bradford

#ifndef __ABITMAP_H
#define __ABITMAP_H

#include "atypes.h"
#include "apalette.h"
#include "aerror.h"

// Bitmap formats:

#define BMF_LIN8    0  // linear 8-bit (one byte per pixel)
#define BMF_LIN15   1  // linear 15-bit (two bytes: ORRRRRGGGGGBBBBB)
#define BMF_LIN24   2  // linear 24-bit (three bytes: BLUE, GREEN, RED)
#define BMF_BANK8   3  // 8-bit bank-switched bitmap (BMF_LIN8 w/64K banks)
#define BMF_BANK15  4  // 15-bit bank-switched bitmap (BMF_LIN15 w/banks)
#define BMF_BANK24  5  // 24-bit bank-switched bitmap (BMF_LIN24 w/banks)
#define BMF_RLE8    6  // run-length encoded 8-bit (token stream)

// Bitmap header structure:

class ABitmap {
    static uchar bmPixelSize[];   // size of 1 pixel for each mode
    static uchar bmCompatibleLinearFormat[]; // format lookup table

public:
    union {
        uchar *pbits;    // ptr to pixel bits, or
        ulong vaddr;     // if bank-switched, virtual address
        };
    uchar format;        // BMF_XXX
    uchar transparent;   // are 0 pixels drawn?
    short width;         // width in pixels
    short height;        // height in pixels
    short rowbytes;      // number of bytes per row
    long length;         // length of bits data
    APalette *ppalette;  // for 8-bit only, ptr to palette or NULL

// Constructors:
//    1. Default: for those who want to fill in by hand
```

```
//    2. Standard: sets fields, if pb == NULL, allocate's bitmap bits
//    3. Bank-switched: for BMF_BANKXX, sets vaddr = OL
//    4. Sub-bitmap: take subarea of existing bitmap

   ABitmap() {}
   ABitmap(uchar *pb, uchar form, bool transp, short w, short h,
      short row = 0);
   ABitmap(uchar form, short w, short h, short row = 0);
   ABitmap(ABitmap &bm, short x, short y, short w, short h);

// Allocate bitmap memory

   static uchar *Alloc(long length);
   uchar *AllocBits() {pbits = Alloc(length); return pbits;}

// Clone a bitmap

   AError Clone(ABitmap &bm);

// Compute byte-length of a given number of pixels

   int RowSize(int w) {return(w * bmPixelSize[format]);}

// Look up linear format compatible with supplied format

   static uchar CompatibleLinearFormat(uchar format) {
      return bmCompatibleLinearFormat[format];}
};

#endif
```

ABitmap Fields

Since the ABitmap class is so fundamental to the toolkit we are developing, let's look at each of its fields (member variables) in detail:

```
union {
      uchar *pbits; // ptr to pixel bits, or
      ulong vaddr;  // if bank-switched, virtual address
      };
```

The first field tells where to find the bits that this bitmap refers to. Usually the 'pbits' field will be a pointer to them. In some cases, namely Super VGA displays which have *bank-switched* memory not fully accessible through simple pointer manipulation, the 'vaddr' half of the union will be used instead of the pointer, to provide a *virtual address* to the bits which a simple pointer can't get to.

```
uchar format;          // BMF_XXX
```

The format field describes how the bits in the bitmap are formatted. ARTT recognizes seven bitmap formats. We will cover each of these formats in more detail shortly.

```
uchar transparent;        // are 0 pixels drawn?
```

This field determines whether or not the bitmap has *transparency*. In bitmaps with this flag set, any pixel with a color value of 0 is assumed to be transparent. When such a bitmap is used as the source image in a rendering operation, these pixels are not drawn. If the transparent flag is not set, all pixels are drawn, and 0 is not special.

```
short width;              // width in pixels
short height;             // height in pixels
```

Finally, some sensible fields! These two encode the width and height of the bitmap, in pixels.

```
short rowbytes;           // number of bytes per row
```

The 'rowbytes' field may seem strange at first, but it is absolutely essential. It contains the number of bytes in a single horizontal row of the bitmap. This number is handy to have when skipping rows or simply advancing from one row to the next during a rendering operation. Why not just calculate it? After all, in an 8-bit color bitmap the rowbytes field is equal to the width * 1, and in a 24-bit true-color bitmap it's equal to the width * 3.

Even if the above formulas were always true, for performance reasons it would be handy to have this value precalculated in the bitmap instead of having to compute it all the time. But, it turns out, the rowbytes field is not always calculable!

Suppose we have a full-screen bitmap, and we want to create a "window" as a subarea of that bitmap. For example, assume a 640 × 480-pixel 8-bit color screen, with a 320 × 240-pixel window centered in the middle of the screen. The width of the screen bitmap is 640 and so is its rowbytes. Now take the window's bitmap, whose bits, remember, are embedded in the overall screen memory. Its width is 320, and its rowbytes is—640! After all, it's embedded in the same screen memory with its 640-pixel-wide rows, and so we must skip 640 bytes to get from one row to the next, as Figure 1.8 illustrates. Because ARTT will depend a great deal on these *sub-bitmaps*, a rowbytes field is essential.

```
long length;              // length of bits data
```

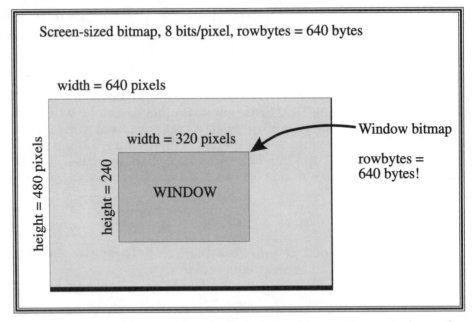

Figure 1.8 Screen bitmap with embedded window bitmap. Note equivalence of 'rowbytes' field.

This field holds the length of the bitmap's bits; that is, the distance between the first pixel and the next byte after the last pixel. The length is expressed in bytes. Like the rowbytes field but for a different reason, this field is usually calculable, but not always. For six of the seven bitmap formats, the bitmap's length is equal to its rowbytes times its height. However, one bitmap format, BMF_RLE8, represents a compressed bitmap whose rowbytes field is meaningless, since each row may be a different length due to variation in compression. For this format, the length field holds the length of the compressed bit data, and is the only way to get this information short of scanning through the entire compressed data stream. To make life easier for bitmap users, the length field is valid for all bitmap formats.

```
APalette *ppalette;          // for 8-bit only, ptr to palette or NULL
```

The 'ppalette' field is valid for 8-bit formats only (BMF_LIN8, BMF_BANK8, and BMF_RLE8), since they are the only indexed-color formats. The 'ppalette' field is a pointer to an instance of class APalette, which represents a color palette, that is, the table of color values which is indexed by the 8-bit pixel values. This palette is conceptually very similar to the DAC-based color table on the VGA card, but don't get the two confused. There is only one hardware-based DAC, whereas each bitmap can in theory have its own palette of colors. We need to load the palette for a given bitmap into the DAC to view it properly, of course, otherwise the color indexes in the bitmap will make no sense.

The definition of the APalette class will be deferred to Chapter 2, but essentially it encapsulates a set of 256 color triplets (red, green, and blue). If the 'ppalette' field is non-NULL, it points to an object of class APalette, which may be unique to this image or shared among several images. It may be NULL, in which case rendering code will use a default palette based on the current rendering destination or the current hardware DAC setting.

The member variables (fields) of class ABitmap are all public, which allows them to be modified at will by any code. This invites errors and is considered poor practice, and ARTT does a better job of data hiding in most other classes. Some low-level classes like ABitmap, however, require frequent read access to their fields by a wide variety of code, in this case, for rendering operations involving bitmaps. C++ inline functions can be used to provide read-only access to such fields, and the fields could then be made private. There's a practical hitch, though—many C++ compilers generate actual function calls for inlines when compiling with debugging flags turned on. The performance hit on a class like ABitmap would be astronomical in such a situation. Follow good programming practices as long as they don't hurt you.

ABitmap Formats

The 'format' field in the bitmap tells us how to interpret the data bits being referred to by the 'pbits' pointer or the 'vaddr' virtual address; that is, how to interpret the data bits as individual pixel values. While the ARTT toolkit we will be building is extensible to more bitmap formats, we can go a long way with the seven formats which are built in. Each of these formats is discussed below.

BMF_LIN8

Standing for "linear 8-bit format," BMF_LIN8 is our workhorse color format, applicable to a wide range of PC-based display systems and modes. For instance, the screen in "mode 13," the 320×200 resolution, 256-color video mode used by many PC computer games, is in

BMF_LIN8 format. Each pixel is represented by a single byte, laid out with adjacent bytes representing horizontally adjacent pixels from left to right. All 8-bit bitmaps, including BMF_LIN8, are indexed-color bitmaps—the exact RGB color value of each of the 256 different values a pixel can take on is determined by the palette (pointed to by the 'ppalette' field in the bitmap, or taken from a default palette). Figure 1.9 shows the layout of a BMF_LIN8 bitmap.

BMF_LIN15

The first of two direct-color linear formats, BMF_LIN15 packs 5 bits each of red, green, and blue into a two-byte word for each pixel. The high bit is unused, and is followed by red, green, and blue from high to low bits. Being a direct-color format, the 'ppalette' field is ignored. The overall linear layout of a BMF_LIN15 bitmap matches that of a BMF_LIN8 bitmap, except that each pixel occupies two bytes instead of one. Figure 1.10 illustrates the direct-color interpretation of a pixel in a BMF_LIN15 bitmap.

BMF_LIN24

The other direct-color linear format, BMF_LIN24, takes up three bytes for each pixel. Each pixel is given three successive bytes, in the

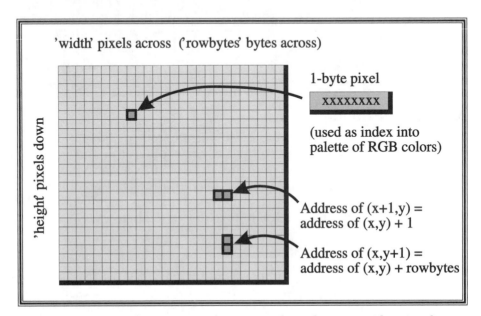

Figure 1.9 Layout of a BMF_LIN8 bitmap. Each pixel occupies 1 byte in a linear arrangement.

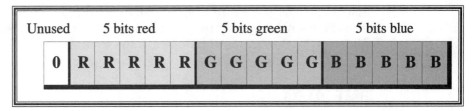

Figure 1.10 Bit-coding of a 15-bit direct-color pixel, taken from a BMF_LIN15 bitmap.

order of blue, green, and then red. Like BMF_LIN15, the color is expressed directly and therefore the 'ppalette' field is ignored. Figure 1.11 illustrates the format of a single pixel in a BMF_LIN24 bitmap.

BMF_BANK8, BMF_BANK15, BMF_BANK24

Super VGA displays contain more memory than can fit into the address space allocated to them under DOS. Therefore, the display memory must be accessed in chunks, known as *banks*. Such bitmaps are no longer "linear"; the entire bitmap cannot be accessed by simple pointer manipulation. Chapter 5 covers Super VGA and bank switching in detail. The BMF_BANK8 format is an 8-bit indexed-color format just like BMF_LIN8; the only difference is in the fact that bank switching must be done to access different portions of the bitmap. Similarly, BMF_BANK15 and BMF_BANK24 are analogous to BMF_LIN15 and BMF_LIN24.

The actual mechanics of bank switching is not contained within the bitmap itself, but is external to it. The format merely records that bank switching must take place; bank-switched bitmaps must be used in the context of an object which knows how to perform bank switching and convert a virtual address into addressable memory. In bank-switched formats such as BMF_BANK8, the 'vaddr' field is used

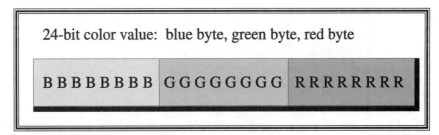

Figure 1.11 Bit-coding of a 24-bit direct-color pixel, taken from a BMF_LIN24 bitmap.

instead of the 'pbits' field—this virtual address specifies the offset into the overall bank-switched memory space, usually video memory. Figure 1.12 illustrates a block of bank-switched memory and a virtual address which points into it.

BMF_RLE8

The first six bitmap formats are all the same in one respect—every pixel in a given bitmap uses the same number of bits. In 8-bit bitmaps (BMF_LIN8 and BMF_BANK8), each pixel is one byte. BMF_LIN15 and BMF_BANK15 have two-byte pixels, and in BMF_LIN24 and BMF_BANK24 bitmaps pixels take three bytes.

Such bitmaps can consume memory voraciously. Even at one byte per pixel, a 640×480 bitmap takes up over 300,000 bytes! Maybe we can save some memory by applying data compression to the bitmap pixel bits. But what kind of compression? Can we come up with a compression format that can be used directly in real time during rendering operations, or should compression be relegated simply to disk-based images, which would then be decompressed when loaded into memory?

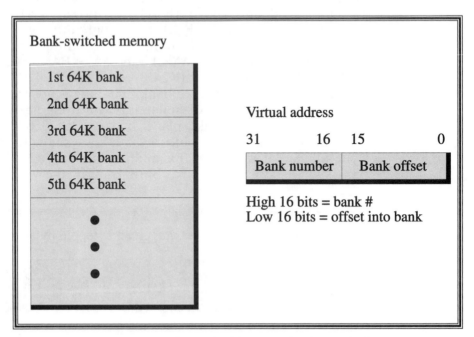

Figure 1.12 Interpretation of virtual address into bank-switched memory.

Run-length encoding is a classical image compression technique that can be used in real time. In run-length encoding, *runs* of adjacent same-valued pixels are encoded into a single "token." Not only can run-length encoding achieve a reasonable level of compression for many images, it can actually be faster to render in some situations than an uncompressed linear format. This is attributable to the compactness of the data (less memory needs to be accessed, thus taking less time) and to the fact that multiple pixels can be processed at once.

Format BMF_RLE8 is a run-length-encoded 8-bit indexed-color format. It is described fully in Chapter 6, along with code that renders directly from this format. For reasons discussed in that chapter, there are no corollary run-length formats for 15-bit and 24-bit bitmaps.

The astute reader may be wondering why different bitmap formats are all included in the same class and differentiated by a 'format' field. Why isn't there just a base bitmap class and several derived subclasses, one for each format? The answer to this is somewhat complex and lies in the lack of a "multi-method" of function dispatch in C++ (see section 13.8 of Bjarne Stroustrup's The Design and Evolution of C++, *Addison Wesley, for more information on multi-methods). In essence, the answer is this: Since bitmaps are both the source and destination of rendering operations, the virtual function mechanism by itself cannot be used to locate a function capable of rendering bitmap format A onto bitmap format B. A bitmap format field is necessary, unless we can afford the overhead of virtual function calls to read each source pixel, which we can't.*

ABitmap Constructors

Class ABitmap is a very low-level class, created for the purpose of encapsulating the information used to describe a bitmap. The rendering operations supported on bitmaps will be carried out by other classes, particularly the ACanvas class and its descendants presented in the next chapter. There are only a few methods included in the ABitmap class definition, including some constructors and miscellaneous methods.

Four constructors are provided, each of which is appropriate in different circumstances. In C++, you can write as many different constructors as you want, as long as they can be distinguished by the number and type of arguments. Two of these constructors are used for special purposes, and their implementation is discussed later in this book, as they are first used. The two remaining constructors include:

- A default "empty" constructor.
- A "standard" constructor.

The empty constructor doesn't do anything. It is used when declaring bitmaps whose fields will later be filled in by hand.

```
ABitmap() {}
```

The "standard" constructor initializes a bitmap from supplied arguments and some logic. The arguments include a data bits pointer, a bitmap format, a transparency flag, width and height in pixels, and an optional rowbytes field (defaults to 0 if not supplied).

The fields of the bitmap are filled in from these values, and some extra work is done. If the 'rowbytes' field is 0, it is calculated from the bitmap format and width—this is done as a convenience to the programmer. The length is then calculated by multiplying the rowbytes by the height. If the data bits pointer is NULL, the constructor allocates sufficient space for the bitmap from the heap using the AllocBits() method. Finally, the 'ppalette' field is set to NULL—this field must be subsequently set by hand if the bitmap uses a nondefault palette.

```
ABitmap::ABitmap(uchar *pb, uchar form, bool transp, short w, short h,
    short row)
{
// This is std constructor, fill in basic fields from arguments

    format = form;
    transparent = transp;
    width = w;
    height = h;

// Set rowbytes from arg unless 0, in which case use std calc
// Compute length as rowbytes × height

    if (row)
        rowbytes = row;
    else
        rowbytes = RowSize(width);
    length = long(rowbytes) * long(height);

// Set pbits field, if NULL then allocate

    pbits = pb;
    if (pbits == NULL)
```

```
    AllocBits();

// Set ppalette to NULL initially

    ppalette = NULL;
}
```

Other ABitmap Methods

The standard ABitmap constructor makes use of two other methods, RowSize() and AllocBits(). RowSize() is used to determine the number of bytes needed to represent a row of pixels of a given width (its 'rowbytes'). This is dependent on the bitmap format, and the actual calculation is done via a table of pixel sizes. The width is multiplied by 1, 2, or 3, according to bmPixelSize[format]. RowSize() should not be called for BMF_RLE8 bitmaps, for which the 'rowbytes' field is meaningless anyway.

```
int RowSize(int w) {return(w * bmPixelSize[format]);}

uchar ABitmap::bmPixelSize[] = {
        1,      // BMF_LIN8 (1 byte per pixel)
        2,      // BMF_LIN15 (2 bytes per pixel)
        3,      // BMF_LIN24 (3 bytes per pixel)
        1,      // BMF_BANK8 (1 byte per pixel)
        2,      // BMF_BANK15 (2 bytes per pixel)
        3,      // BMF_BANK24 (3 bytes per pixel)
        1,      // BMF_RLE8 (don't use to clip, though)
};
```

The bmPixelSize[] table is a static class member. This means it is shared across all instances of class ABitmap. Static class members are like global variables, but their access is restricted to class members and friends. If a static class member is public, other code still has to precede its name with Classname:: *to access it, so at least naming conflicts across modules are reduced.*

The AllocBits() method sets the 'pbits' field of the bitmap equal to the return value from the Alloc() method. Alloc() is just a wrapper around the standard heap allocator new(). Why not just use new() directly? Well, bitmaps can get very large—they are quite often larger than 64K. For compatibility with 16-bit code with its 64K limit on memory allocation, Alloc() checks for sizes which are too large, and returns NULL (without this check, new() will truncate the

size to something under 64K and allocate this amount, which is not very safe!).

```
uchar *AllocBits() {pbits = Alloc(length); return pbits;}

uchar *ABitmap::Alloc(long length)
{
// If 16-bit mode, we can't allocate over 64K

   if ((sizeof(size_t) == 2) && (length & 0xFFFF0000L))
      return NULL;

// If 16-bit and size under 64K, or 32-bit mode, call new()

   return new uchar[length];
}
```

Class ABitmap includes two other methods, namely Clone() and CompatibleLinearFormat(). These are discussed in context when they are first used in ARTT.

ARTT's Additional "Basic" Types

Some readers may be wondering about some of the oddball types used by the ABitmap class declaration, namely 'uchar' and 'ulong'. The first file I create when programming in a new environment is one which sets up these simple aliases for unsigned versions of built-in types char, short, int, and long. "Unsigned" is just too tedious to type—unsigned versions of the built-in types are provided in a header file named ATYPES.H, which is included explicitly or implicitly by every ARTT file. ATYPES.H also rounds up some of the other usual suspects, such as definitions or TRUE and FALSE and a boolean type.

```
//   ATypes.h   Basic types
//   Rex E. Bradford

#ifndef __ATYPES_H
#define __ATYPES_H

// Basic types

typedef unsigned char uchar;
typedef unsigned short ushort;
typedef unsigned long ulong;
typedef unsigned int uint;
typedef uchar bool;

// For disk-based structures
typedef uchar ABYTE;
```

```
typedef short AWORD16;
typedef long AWORD32;

// True, false, and null

#define TRUE 1
#define FALSE 0
#ifndef NULL
#define NULL OL
#endif
#endif
```

The header files listed in this chapter use ARTT's standard header-file wrapping. This encapsulates the entire file in an #ifdef which checks to see if a name derived from the filename is defined, and if not proceeds to define the name. This ensures that the contents of the header file are processed only once. It also allows both C++ files and header files which include other header files to speed compilation by incorporating their #include's inside #ifdef's, which can be derived by rote:

```
//      Some C++ file or header file
.....
#ifndef __OTHER_H
#include "other.h"
#endif
.....
```

Note that wrapping the #include statement is unnecessary and is only recommended where it is likely to speed compilation, for instance, in header files which include other header files.

Error Handling

The future of error handling in C++ lies in exception handling. However, at the time of this writing exception handling is not implemented by all compilers. Furthermore, it is unfamiliar to a great many programmers, and its use would serve only to distract by focusing attention on error handling and not on algorithms.

ARTT uses a C-like scheme for error handling. Routines capable of reporting an error condition do so by returning an argument of type AError, either as the return value or as an argument passed by reference. The error codes are all negative, and their meanings are listed in AERROR.H. A table of error strings is available to aid in reporting errors to the user. AERROR.H is listed below:

```
//   AError.h    Standard error codes
//   Rex E. Bradford

#ifndef __AERROR_H
#define __AERROR_H

#define AERR_OK          0       // no error
#define AERR_NOMEM       -1      // out of memory
#define AERR_FILEOPEN    -2      // can't open file
#define AERR_READ        -3      // read error
#define AERR_WRITE       -4      // write error
#define AERR_BADNAME     -5      // invalid filename or extension
#define AERR_BADFORMAT   -6      // file/data in bad format
#define AERR_NODRIVER    -7      // missing software driver
#define AERR_BADVERSION  -8      // wrong version of driver/file
#define AERR_BADMODE     -9      // invalid mode
#define AERR_DEVICE      -10     // can't access device
#define AERR_OVERFLOW    -11     // exceeded limit

typedef int AError;

class AErr {
    static char *errText[];      // array of error message strings

public:
    static char *Msg(AError err) {return errText[-err];}
};

#endif
```

AERROR.CPP holds the table of error strings.

```
//   AError.cpp   Standard error message strings
//   Rex E. Bradford

#include "aerror.h"

char *AErr::errText[] = {
    "NO ERROR",
    "Out of memory",
    "Can't open file",
    "Read error",
    "Write error",
    "Invalid filename or extension",
    "File/data format is bad",
    "Missing driver",
    "Driver/file is wrong version",
    "Invalid mode",
    "Can't access device",
    "Exceeded limit",
};
```

Memory Management and 16/32-Bit Programming

ARTT does not make use of special memory such as "expanded memory." It relies on the standard C library heap, accessed exclusively via new() and delete(). Because of this, and the fact that ARTT does not make use of the *huge* keyword, 16-bit programs are limited in the size of the bitmaps that may be allocated. Bitmaps larger than 64K cannot be used in 16-bit mode; this limits 16-bit DOS programs to the low-resolution VGA mode 13, and 16-bit Windows programs are limited to bitmaps of comparable size. A 320 × 200 8-bit bitmap, for comparison, takes up 64000 bytes (just under 63K). 32-bit DOS and Windows programs have no such restrictions.

The future and the present both lie in 32-bit programming, whether under DOS or Windows or some other environment. ARTT is designed primarily for 32-bit operation. However, ARTT can be compiled to run under 16-bit DOS and Windows, subject to the memory allocation restrictions noted above. Sixteen-bit ARTT programs must be compiled using the *large model*, since ARTT does not make use of the *far* keyword.

Allocation Protection

The ABitmap::Alloc() routine listed earlier traps 16-bit bitmap allocation requests and automatically returns NULL if the request exceeds 64K. Without this protection, serious problems can result. Both new() and malloc() take an argument of type size_t, which on 16-bit systems is defined as an unsigned short, which is a 16-bit value. A size argument greater than 64K is truncated, a buffer of a smaller size than desired is allocated, code later overwrites the too-small buffer and wipes out other data, and soon after that the user reaches for the Big Red Switch.

The new() operator returns NULL on memory allocation failure, and this result should always be checked (ARTT's routines do so, and usually pass an error code on up to calling routines). Programmers familiar with set_new_handler() may use it to trap memory allocation failures and perform some recovery operation.

Class AMem

Two other memory-management services are needed in order for 32-bit protected-mode DOS programs to work properly. One is the need to allocate memory which is guaranteed to lie below the 1 megabyte real-mode boundary, in order to communicate with real-mode code such as the VESA BIOS Extensions covered in Chapter 5. Class AMem provides the MallocLow() routine to allocate such a memory buffer for 32-bit programs, in such a way that 16-bit programs work fine too. AMem::MallocLow() returns the segment value of the allocated buffer. This can be converted to a pointer using GetPhysPtr(), discussed below.

The second memory-management service provides a pointer to memory which is not allocated on the heap or part of the program's data, but is instead specified by actual physical address. The video memory on VGA and Super VGA cards, for instance, lies at physical address 0xA0000L. In 16-bit mode, constructing a pointer to this address is trivial, using MK_FP(), but 32-bit mode requires the help of the extender environment to turn a physical address into a usable pointer. AMem::GetPhysPtr() provides this translation service, and works in both 16-bit and 32-bit modes.

The header file for class AMem is listed below.

```
//    AMem.h      Memory allocator
//    Rex E. Bradford

#ifndef __AMEM_H
#define __AMEM_H

#include "atypes.h"

class AMem {
public:

// Allocate memory below 1 Mb (special code for protected mode)
// Return segment.

   static ushort MallocLow(ushort size);

// Convert a physical address to a C pointer. In protected mode,
// this is not simply MK_FP().

   static void *GetPhysPtr(long addr);

   static void *GetPhysPtr(ushort seg, ushort off) {
      return GetPhysPtr(((long(seg)) << 4) + off);}
};

#endif
```

The AMem class is entirely composed of static methods. No instances of class AMem are ever created—the class serves merely as a "bundling" mechanism for the memory-management functions.

The implementation of AMem::MallocLow() is both word-size dependent and compiler-dependent. Here is the implementation for the Symantec compiler in 32-bit mode. The underlying DOS memory allocator is called using int86_real().

```
ushort AMem::MallocLow(ushort size)
{
   union REGS regs;

   regs.h.ah = 0x48;
   regs.x.bx = (size + 15) >> 4;
   int86_real(0x21, &regs, &regs);
   return(regs.x.ax); // segment in AX
}
```

AMem::GetPhysPtr() is listed next. It too, is word-size and compiler-dependent. The implementation for the Symantec compiler in 32-bit mode is listed. See the source on accompanying CD for other versions.

```
void *AMem::GetPhysPtr(long addr)
{
static uchar *pAllLowMem; // ptr to physical address 0

// 32-bit mode, physical memory must be accessed through extender
// One time only, map the entire low 1 Mb of physical memory

   if (pAllLowMem == NULL)
       pAllLowMem = _x386_map_physical_address(0, 0xFFFFF);

// Return ptr to 0 physical memory plus the address

   return (pAllLowMem + addr);
}
```

Other Coding Issues

My idiosyncracies in terms of tabbing distance, placement of curly braces, comment formatting, and the various "pretty printing" issues are, of course, idiosyncratic. As this is often a religious issue among programmers, other sects may prefer variants; feel free to run the code through an automatic heathen converter.

2

Basic VGA Graphics

In the last chapter we saw how modern computer screens are represented by a bitmap, which is an area of computer memory which maps data bits onto a two-dimensional color display. This chapter will do two things. First we'll introduce the VGA, which is the standard graphics mechanism used in virtually all IBM-compatible PCs. Then we'll begin building the C++ classes that perform *rendering*, the action of getting those screen pixels to light up the way we want. By the end of the chapter, we'll have a framework for putting images onto a PC screen, which will be shown off in a bouncing ball demo. This framework will be the foundation for all rendering done in this book; the smooth animation and dazzling effects of future chapters will be elaborations on the core structure set forth here.

The Video Graphics Array: VGA

Originally introduced by IBM when it unveiled the PS/2 computers in 1987, the VGA (Video Graphics Array) has become the standard in PC graphics. While many display adapter boards offer higher resolutions, more colors, faster performance, and extra features, virtually every PC computer graphics system has a VGA-compatible core. In desktop

PCs, the VGA is usually sold as a plug-in board bundled with the computer. In laptop and notebook computers, the VGA *chipset* is built right into the system board. Figure 2.1 shows a typical VGA card.

Originally an enhancement of the popular EGA device, the VGA achieved popularity because it offered decent resolution (640 pixels across × 480 pixels down) in a convenient-to-program square-pixel format. At this resolution, the original VGA could display only 16 col-

Figure 2.1 Photo of VGA card. Courtesy of Diamond Flower Instrument Co. Inc.

ors at a time, a limitation that has been swept away by enhanced Super VGA devices. Another mode in which the original VGA could be run offered 256 colors at once on screen, albeit in a lower resolution of 320 × 200 pixels. This mode took the computer gaming world by storm and remains the most common graphics mode used in games,[1] due to the richness of color available, the speed at which graphics can be rendered, and the simplicity of programming. It is this mode that we will use in our first explorations of the VGA.

VGA Graphics Modes

The VGA is a superset of the EGA, the Enhanced Graphics Adapter, which was a superset of the CGA, the original Color Graphics Adapter sold with the IBM PC when it was introduced in 1981. Each of these adapters maintained compatibility with its ancestors, while adding several new *video modes* in which the display could be run. A given program can select which mode is most appropriate, and program the adapter to switch to that mode. Not all of these modes are graphics modes. Some are text modes, in which the smallest graphics element which can be displayed is an entire character, not a pixel. We will not focus on text modes at all in this book—they're just not as fun as graphics!

Table 2.1 contains a complete list of the graphics modes supported by the basic VGA, including the pixel resolution of each and the number of colors which may simultaneously appear on a screen in that mode. Note that mode numbers are expressed in hexadecimal.

Setting VGA Modes—Class AVga

So how do we tell the VGA to switch to a particular mode? Through the BIOS, the *Basic Input Output System,* which is code in *Read-Only Memory* (ROM) in the PC. Every VGA card comes with a small ROM, which contains code to do various chores such as set the video mode, manipulate the available color set, and even do simple drawing of pixels and characters. When the computer boots up, initialization code sets up some information in system memory which makes this code available to us.

The drawing code in the ROM is pretty slow and unusable for "real" graphics, so we'll bypass it and program the VGA's display memory directly. But there's no better way to switch in and out of graphics modes than through the adapter's BIOS. The exact mechanism is through software interrupt 10H, which is reserved for video

---

[1]This is changing rapidly, however, as even real-time 3D simulations make the leap into Super VGA resolutions.

Table 2.1 Standard VGA Graphics Modes

Mode	Resolution	Colors	Comments
04H	320 × 200	4	First introduced in CGA
05H	320 × 200	4	First introduced in CGA
06H	640 × 200	2	First introduced in CGA
0DH	320 × 200	16	First introduced in EGA
0EH	640 × 200	16	First introduced in EGA
0FH	640 × 350	2	Monochrome, first introduced in EGA
10H	640 × 350	16	First introduced in EGA
11H	640 × 480	2	Square pixels, first introduced in VGA
12H	640 × 480	16	Square pixels, first introduced in VGA
13H	320 × 200	256	First introduced in VGA

services. In C or C++, setting a video mode is as simple as calling the int86() function with the right arguments.

The AVga class in ARTT provides an interface to basic features of the VGA such as mode setting and access to the DAC color table. The header file for the AVga class is given below:

```
//    AVga.h       VGA hardware access
//    Rex E. Bradford

#ifndef__AVGA_H
#define__AVGA_H

#include "atypes.h"

class AVga {

    static ushort prevMode;       // previous video mode

public:

    static void SetMode (ushort mode);  // set new mode
    static void SaveMode ();            // save old mode in 'prevMode'
    static void RestoreMode ();         // restore mode from 'prevMode'

    static void WaitForVerticalSync (); // wait till start of vsync

    static void SetDAC (uchar *prgb, int index = 0, int num = 256);
    static void GetDAC (uchar *prgb, int index = 0, int num = 256);
};

#endif
```

AVga::SetMode() uses the int86() call to set the VGA into the supplied mode number, as can be seen from its listing below:

```
void AVga::SetMode (ushort mode)
{
   union REGS regs;
   regs.x.ax = mode;             // AH = func 0 (setmode), AL = mode
   int86(0x10, &regs, &regs);    // call video BIOS to set mode
}
```

Voila! The PC screen is cleared to black and placed into the graphics mode as indicated. To return to text mode at the end of the program, you can call the same function with a mode number equal to one of the VGA text modes (not supplied in the above table—use 03H for 80 columns × 25 rows of text). Or, better yet, use a different BIOS call to read the current mode before going into graphics mode, and store this number away. Then, before exiting the program, use the saved mode number to return the PC back to the original mode. The whole process is as follows:

1. Read current video mode and store in a variable.

2. Set desired mode using code such as listed above.

3. Run program in this mode until time to exit.

4. Set original mode retrieved in step 1, again using code listed above.

AVga::SaveMode() and AVga::RestoreMode() have what we need:

```
ushort AVga::prevMode; // previous video mode

void AVga::SaveMode()
{
   union REGS regs;
   regs.x.ax = 0x0F00;           // AH = func 0F (getmode)
   int86(0x10, &regs, &regs);    // call video BIOS to get mode
   prevMode = regs.h.al;         // returns AL = mode, save away
}

void AVga::RestoreMode()
{
   SetMode (prevMode);           // just restore saved mode by setting
}
```

We'll put off the implementation of AVga::WaitForVerticalSync() until Chapter 13, when we have need for it. The last two methods, AVga::SetDAC() and AVga::ReadDAC(), are worth looking at now.

Programming the DAC Color Table

In mode 13H and other 8-bit indexed-color modes, each pixel represents color only indirectly. The VGA has a 256-entry "hardware palette" inside the DAC (digital-analog converter). The standard VGA DAC contains 256 18-bit values, where each value contains 6 bits of red, 6 bits of green, and 6 bits of blue. Thus the VGA is capable of displaying 2^{18} or 262,144 different colors in this mode, but only 256 at one time, which is the number of entries in the DAC. Figure 2.2 is a diagram of the VGA DAC color table.

Most representations of RGB colors, including those in the graphics files we'll explore in the next chapter, use 8 bits for each of the three color components, rather than the 6 bits available in the VGA hardware. When setting the DAC, we'll use the most significant 6 bits of each component, and lose some color fidelity encoded in the bottom 2 bits. Some new Super VGA cards have DACs with 8 bits of each component, but these must be programmed by special nonstandard means so that existing software using 6-bit components will still work.

The VGA DAC can be programmed in either of two ways. The first method is through the BIOS, using software interrupt 0×10, which is used for video-related functions. Function 0×10 is used for

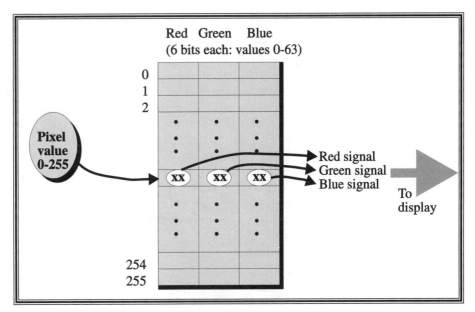

Figure 2.2   Diagram of VGA DAC color table.

DAC-related calls, and there are several. The most useful of these are subfunctions 0×10 and 0×12. Subfunction 0×10 sets a single DAC entry, and subfunction 0×12 sets a contiguous block of DAC entries (the entire set if desired).

The other method of programming the VGA DAC is the "direct" approach, using input-output (i/o) registers. A pair of such registers is used to program the DAC directly. Register 0×3C8 is written with the index of the DAC entry that is to be set (0 to 255). Then, three values are written to register 0×3C9, in the order of red, green, and blue. Each of these values should have the component value in the low 6 bits (value 0 to 63). If multiple successive entries are to be written, register 0×3C8 need only be written to once; it will autoincrement every time three values are written to 0×3C9.

This direct-to-hardware method is reliable and is faster than the BIOS calls. If that was the entire story, I would prefer the BIOS approach, since it is theoretically at least more "compatible" with variant hardware. But the problem with the BIOS call has to do with timing. Some VGA card BIOS implementations, when called with one of the DAC-setting functions, wait until the next vertical retrace period in the display's scanning cycle before actually changing the color table. This delay can be up to 16 milliseconds depending on the graphics mode and the happenstance timing of the call. They do this to avoid the possibility of the display "flashing" when the color table changes during a frame. Other VGA BIOS implementations don't insert a delay. Neither way is inherently right or wrong, as there is no specification to adhere to. But for real-time animation, the delay is bad enough, and the fact that a delay may or may not happen is intolerable. ARTT accesses the DAC directly through i/o ports because of this. Modern VGA cards exhibit far less flashing during color table update, but a call to AVga::WaitForVerticalSync() can be used in order to ensure update during the monitor's retrace.

AVga::SetDAC() sets one or more contiguous entries in the DAC. It is past the index of the lowest-numbered entry at which to begin setting (defaults to 0), and the number of RGB entries to set (defaults to 256). Note that this method expects the color triplets in the order blue, green, and red, but the VGA hardware takes them in the order red, green, and blue. The blue/green/red ordering is the standard ARTT RGB ordering, because it matches the layout of most true-color devices.

```
void AVga::SetDAC (uchar *prgb, int index, int num)
{
    outp(0×3C8, index);  // set index of first entry to write
    while (num-- > 0)    // loop num times
      {
```

```
      outp(0x3C9, *(prgb+2) >> 2);      // put 6-bit red component
      outp(0x3C9, *(prgb+1) >> 2);      // put 6-bit green component
      outp(0x3C9, *prgb >> 2);          // put 6-bit blue component
      prgb += 3;                        // advance to next rgb entry
      }
}
```

AVga::GetDAC() is the reverse of AVga::SetDAC(), reading DAC entries back into a memory buffer.

```
void AVga::GetDAC (uchar *prgb, int index, int num)
{
   outp(0x3C7, index);  // set index of first entry to read
   while (num-- > 0)    // loop num times
      {
      *(prgb+2) = inp(0x3C9) << 2;      // read 6-bits red, convert to 8
      *(prgb+1) = inp(0x3C9) << 2;      // then green
      *prgb = inp(0x3C9) << 2;          // then blue
      prgb += 3;                        // advance to next rgb entry
      }
}
```

Class APalette

Remember the ABitmap class from Chapter 1, which included a mysterious member variable called 'ppalette', which is a pointer to an instance of class APalette? This field is used to point to the color palette associated with a particular bitmap. When we load graphics files in the next chapter, we'll see that each graphics file carries around with it the palette appropriate to that image. When we read such images into bitmap format, we'll read in the image's palette as well, and set the 'ppalette' field to point to that palette. When we need to display the image, we can program the VGA DAC from this palette. In Part 3 of this book, we'll explore advanced uses of palettes, including finding ways of working with bitmaps which don't all share the same color palette.

Class APalette, then, contains a 256-entry color palette. The version we'll present here is actually a simplified version—the real class contains additional member variables and advanced methods such as color conversion routines. In Chapter 13 we will fill out the APalette definition when we explore color conversion, direct-color modes, and other related topics. The simplified APalette header file is presented below.

```
//   APalette.h    Palette class
//   Rex E. Bradford

#ifndef __APALETTE_H
#define __APALETTE_H
```

```
class APalette {
public:
   uchar rgb[768];        // 256 3-byte RGB entries (blue low, red high)

// Palette construction

   APalette() {}
   APalette(uchar *prgb) {Set(prgb);}

// Palette set (full or partial palette)

   void Set (uchar *prgb, int index = 0, int num = 256);
};

#endif
```

Two constructors are included—one simply declares an uninitialized APalette for later setting, and the other uses the Set() method to fill in an entire palette. APalette::Set() may be called at any time to set all or part of a palette. It copies the supplied RGB 3-byte triplets into the rgb[] array of the APalette instance, in the correct position. The simplified version of this method is supplied below; Chapter 13 shows the real version.

```
void APalette::Set(uchar *prgb, int index, int num)
{
   memcpy (rgb + (index * 3), prgb, num * 3); // set 24-bit entries
}
```

Rendering to the VGA Display

The VGA display memory is a bitmap. It exists in special memory associated with the VGA, on the VGA adapter card if there is one, or on the system board if the VGA is built-in. For all VGA graphics modes, the bitmap begins at address 0xA0000 in memory. This address corresponds to the pixel in the upper-left of the screen. Is this enough information for us to begin rendering to the VGA?

Not quite. As we observed in Chapter 1, not all bitmaps are *formatted* the same way. That is, the representation of a pixel in memory bits is not the same across all display devices. As it turns out, bitmap formatting is not at all the same across the various VGA graphics modes! For instance, 16-color modes require only 4 bits (half a byte, often called a *nibble*) to represent a single pixel in memory, and thus 2 pixel values can be stored in a byte. Four-color modes require only 2 bits per pixel, and thus can pack 4 pixels into a byte. Mode 13H, the 256-color mode, fits one pixel into a byte exactly. Figure 2.3 illustrates the various VGA pixel sizes.

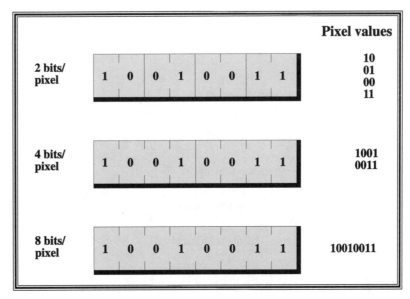

Figure 2.3   Sample byte in various pixel formats.

The differences don't end there. Most VGA modes don't even represent the screen bitmap in a single contiguous chunk of memory. In these modes, the bits which make up each pixel are often split across various *planes* of memory, and special programming of hardware registers is needed to access different planes.[2] Why this complication? The answer lies in the arcane history of the original IBM PC and the Intel 8088 processor inside. Most PC programmers soon run across the fact that the first 1 megabyte of memory in their PC is special, and that only this area of memory can be accessed by normal means when the CPU chip is in *real mode,* which is what DOS runs in. The first 640K of this megabyte is available for program code and data. When it introduced the PC, IBM reserved the remaining 384K for use by system components such as disk drives, video cards, and the computer's ROM BIOS. Only 64K was allocated to video memory at that time, but since the original CGA adapter needed only 16K, there was plenty of room for expansion, as the PC memory layout of Figure 2.4 shows.

Well, for plenty of room it ran out quickly. A VGA screen consisting of 640 × 480 pixels in 16 colors (2 pixels per byte) requires 640 × 480/2 = 153,600 bytes! If such a bitmap started at 0xA0000 in mem-

---

[2]Memory planes are not the same as memory banks. In planar modes, the bits of a single pixel are literally split across bytes in different memory registers. Bank-switched modes, covered in Chapter 5, aren't quite this evil.

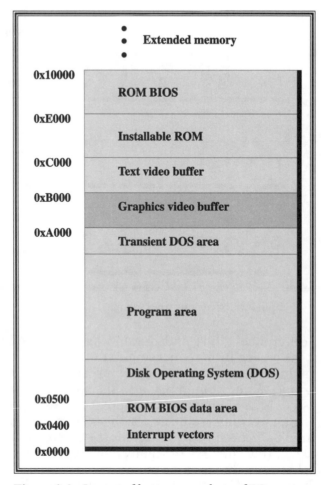

Figure 2.4   Layout of bottom megabyte of PC memory.

ory, it would end around address 0×C6000, which would overrun other important areas of memory, as Figure 2.4 indicates. Thus, the solution, first adopted in the EGA with its 64K-busting modes, was to add hardware which enabled the display card to carry more than 64K of memory, but to split it into multiple planes, each of which occupies the same memory from A0000 to B0000. Hardware registers are programmed to select which plane of memory is being read from or written to. Other special hardware registers are used to assist rendering, by supplying a mechanism to write bits to multiple planes at the same time.

If computers weren't so unnecessarily overcomplicated, programming wouldn't be such a challenging and rewarding profession!

The intricacies of writing graphics into this *planar* memory occupied many programmers, including myself, for several years. Since color displays featuring less than 256 simultaneous colors are quickly becoming an anachronism, however, only one of the basic VGA graphics modes is of interest to us, namely mode 13H. This mode is not planar, which happily makes it an ideal mode in which to begin our rendering explorations. When we expand our horizons to include Super VGA graphics modes in Chapter 5, we will encounter a different kind of memory space partitioning called *bank switching*.

Mode 13H Graphics

For the first few chapters in this book, we will use mode 13H exclusively. This is because it is the only basic VGA mode with good color, and it is very straightforward to program. This will enable us to focus on the architecture of the graphics toolkit we'll be building. We can ignore arcane details of VGA device programming and focus on the algorithms and content of the graphics techniques themselves.

Mode 13H couldn't be much simpler. The entire screen is a single *linear* bitmap of 8-bit pixels, where each pixel occupies a byte. The first 320 bytes represent the uppermost row of pixels on the screen, from left to right. The next 320 bytes represent the next row, and so on for 64000 pixels total (200 rows). The last 1536 bytes of the 64K video memory are unused. If the display card has more than 64K of display memory (these days, most have 512K or 1 Mb or more), these bytes are unavailable for use in mode 13H. If this linear pixel layout sounds familiar, it should. It is exactly the format of a BMF_LIN8 bitmap as described in Chapter 1.

The particular color that appears in a given pixel is a combination of the byte value that appears there, which can range from 0 to 255, and the RGB value stored in the VGA DAC at that index. In mode 13H, each pixel value is routed through the DAC on the way to the display monitor, transforming the 8-bit index into an 18-bit RGB value. Graphics modes like mode 13H are often called 256-color modes, or alternatively, 8-bit modes. Figure 2.5 shows the organization of display memory in mode 13H.

ARTT Coordinate System

Before we start building the classes necessary for rendering, the graphics coordinate system used in ARTT needs to be understood. Any bitmap, screen-based or otherwise, is divided into a rectangular grid of pixels. Note that the pixels need not be square; the ratio of the height of a pixel to its width is its *aspect ratio*, and not all graphics

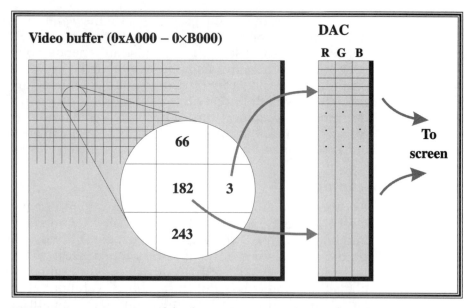

Figure 2.5 Organization of display memory in mode 13H. Each byte represents one pixel. Its value is used as an index into the DAC, where full RGB colors are stored.

modes provide a 1:1 aspect ratio. In fact, mode 13H pixels are 20 percent taller than they are wide, and have an aspect ratio of 1.2:1.

Each pixel has an *x,y* coordinate value. The upper-left pixel of a bitmap is at 0,0. *X*-coordinates increase from left to right, and *y*-coordinates increase from top to bottom. These directions correspond to increasing memory addresses of pixels in video memory, which makes for a more direct and therefore more efficient mapping between *x,y* coordinates and pixel addresses. Most, though not all, graphics systems share this coordinate space.

To be precise, ARTT places the coordinates on a grid, with the pixels hanging down and to the right off the coordinate grid, as Figure 2.6 illustrates. Looking at it this way helps in appreciating ARTT's method of defining rectangles, wherein the lower-right coordinates of the rectangle are not *inclusive* of the pixels at those coordinates. A rectangle with upper-left coordinates of 20,20 and lower-right of 21,21 is one pixel in size, not four.

ARTT Rendering Architecture

With a defined coordinate system and knowledge of the VGA and the BMF_LIN8 linear 8-bit bitmap format, we really know all we need to begin rendering onto a mode 13H screen. Now let's step back for a minute. Our goal is not just to render in mode 13H, but to build the bottommost levels of our graphics toolkit, the ARTT toolkit. We should set up classes that will allow us to add other graphics modes later, and to render into bitmaps which are not located on the screen but in system memory. Furthermore, we need to think about what mechanisms and protocols we will use to do rendering. Apart from the actual rendering functions we need (lines, rectangles, bitmaps, text, etc.), let's lay down a few basic requirements of our toolkit:

- It should be easily extensible to new graphics modes, and user code should not have to make different calls depending on the mode in use. In other words, it should have some sort of *display driver* which shields user code from the details of a particular mode. C++ virtual functions will help us here.

- It should support different screen resolutions (this is implied by supporting different modes). However, the toolkit should work in a pixel-based coordinate system—no automatic "scaling" of images should happen (though explicit scaling is allowed and important).

- It should support rendering onto 8-bit, 15-bit, and 24-bit displays. Support for 16-color, monochrome, or other display formats is not required.

- It should easily support screen windows (sub-areas of the screen). Our ABitmap class, with its 'rowbytes' field, is designed to make this easy.

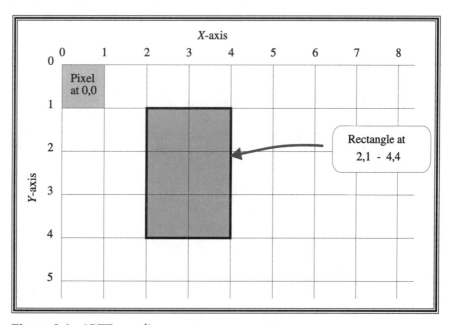

Figure 2.6 ARTT coordinate system.

- It should support rendering into off-screen bitmaps, so that complex rendering operations can be done behind the scenes and the final product moved to the screen seamlessly.

- It should provide some minimal "graphics state," particularly a "current color." Then each rendering call need not include such values as arguments.

The ABitmap class designed in Chapter 1 provides enough flexibility to handle the first five requirements. The last falls outside its scope. Rather than rendering into bitmaps per se, then, we should invent a new class, which combines a bitmap with a set of current drawing attributes. We will call such a combination a *canvas*, the name used for such a construct in *Computer Graphics Principles* by Foley and Van Dam. The term canvas invokes images of an artist's canvas with a palette of tools and colors.

Some graphics systems provide a large graphics state, also known as "drawing attributes." In ARTT, we'll be more minimalist. In fact, only two state variables will be defined:

- Current color, for lines, rectangles, boxes, and so on
- Current clipping rectangle, which defines the area where drawing is allowed

The uses of these drawing attributes will become more clear in the next few chapters as we begin to put them to work. Other drawing attributes, such as the font to be used when drawing text, or the color lookup table to be used when translating color values, are supplied as arguments to the rendering functions which use them.

Canvas Classes

The ACanvas class, our base canvas class, serves to glue together a bitmap and a set of drawing attributes, for the purpose of rendering onto that bitmap. The functions that we will use in ARTT to do the actual rendering will be methods in the ACanvas class—in fact, all rendering will be done to some canvas, whether on-screen or off-screen. But, as we've already seen, there are a host of bitmap formats to render into. Will the methods in ACanvas include all the code to do all the possible rendering combinations (for instance, drawing a BMF_RLE8 source bitmap onto a BMF_LIN8 canvas, or a BMF_LIN24 source bitmap onto a BMF_BANK8 canvas)? There are a lot of possible combinations here, and we don't want the drawing methods in ACanvas to be giant switching stations!

First of all, we will restrict our canvases to six of the seven bitmap formats. No canvas will be built from a BMF_RLE8 bitmap—such bitmaps will be used only as rendering sources, not destinations. This decision comes from practical necessity—rendering lines and bitmaps into already-compressed images is perhaps an interesting research topic, but not on our plate. Still, we have six possible bitmap types in our canvas, and a large number of varied drawing operations which need special code for each case. How do we organize this for sanity and efficiency?

Derived classes and virtual functions to the rescue! Class ACanvas will serve as the base class for a set of derived canvas classes. For each bitmap format we want to render into, we'll create a canvas class derived from ACanvas. By making the rendering methods virtual, a call to a rendering method will automatically invoke the version of the method specific to the right type of canvas. This version will "know" how to perform the rendering operation on the bitmap format it supports.

Canvas Class Hierarchy

The *canvas class hierarchy* is, in fact, ARTT's largest class hierarchy, both in breadth and depth. First, we need the base ACanvas class, which will serve at least as the place where all the virtual rendering methods are declared. By having a base canvas class, we can pass around a pointer to any canvas class, and code which makes rendering calls can use the pointer *without even knowing what type of canvas it really points to,* just that it's some descendent of ACanvas. This is very important. It's too much to ask that user code know or care which type of canvas is being rendered onto—the whole point of virtual functions is to avoid needing such knowledge. User code says, "Hey, you're a canvas. No, I don't know what type of wood your easel is made of. Draw this line already, willya?"

The base ACanvas class does a lot more than just serve as a declaration point for the virtual functions, as we will see later. It will also serve as the base class of a hierarchy of canvas classes, as depicted in Figure 2.7. Canvas classes derived from ACanvas handle the particulars of 8-bit, 15-bit, and 24-bit bitmaps, and canvas classes derived from them provide fast rendering routines specialized for the six renderable bitmap formats we'll encounter. And, of course, the hierarchy is extensible to new bitmap formats and devices which require special programming.

Class ACanvas Overview

The base class ACanvas is useful for a number of reasons. First off, it defines the basic structure of a canvas; it includes as members a bitmap and a set of drawing attributes. That means that all canvases have these members. The bitmap is used as the rendering surface,

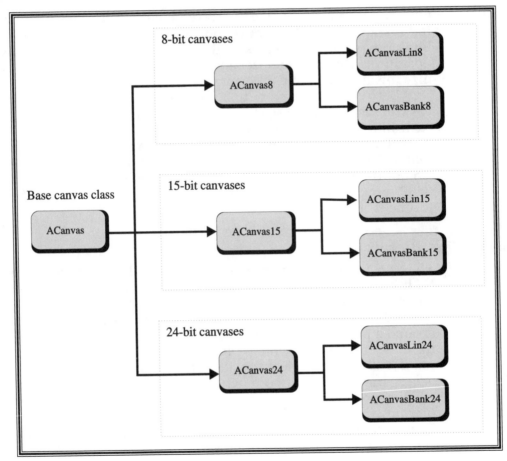

Figure 2.7   ARTT canvas class hierarchy.

and the drawing attributes supply additional "context" information for rendering routines.

By declaring most rendering operations as virtual functions in class ACanvas, user code which makes rendering calls does not need to know which type of canvas it is drawing to. Any such code can just use a generic canvas pointer (ACanvas*) as the rendering destination—all canvases will support the methods defined in the base canvas class, and virtual functions will ensure that the proper method for the type of canvas is invoked. Class ACanvas doesn't even implement the simplest rendering routine—the one that sets a single pixel to the current color. Why? Because it doesn't know how. As far as ACanvas knows, the bitmap could be any of the six renderable formats.

So does this make the ACanvas class just a shell—a template which has no real functionality of its own? Hardly. ACanvas doesn't know how to draw a pixel, maybe, but it can draw a line. How? A line can be drawn as a successive set of calls to draw a pixel, once for each position along the line. The operation of deciding which pixels make up a given line is a generic one—ACanvas doesn't need to know anything about bitmap formats to do this. So, the line-drawing routine can be written to do all the figuring and then call a separate pixel-drawing routine for each pixel on the line. Even though the line-draw routine resides in ACanvas, the correct pixel-drawer for the canvas will be invoked, by the magic of virtual functions, as Figure 2.8 illustrates.

In general, ACanvas can implement code for "high-level" rendering operations which can be broken down into other "lower-level" operations. Another example is a box, which can be drawn by making four line-rendering calls (for speed, it is actually implemented as two calls to a specialized horizontal-line drawer and two calls to a specialized vertical-line drawer). Since the operation of deciding which lines make up a box is generic and not dependent on canvas type, we can put this routine into ACanvas too.

Now suppose the box-drawing method is invoked on a canvas of some descendent class. The base ACanvas box drawer is invoked, and

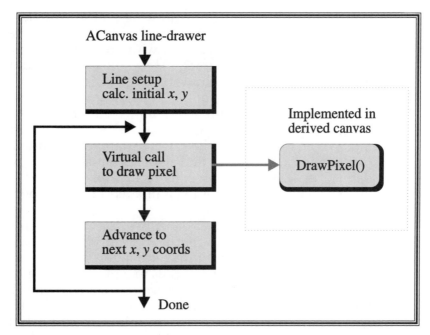

Figure 2.8   Line-drawing using virtual function to draw each pixel.

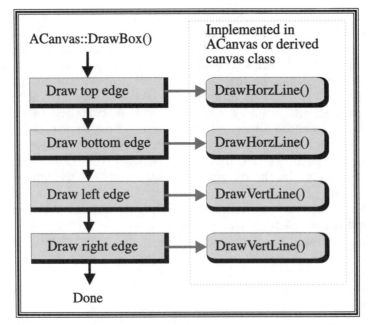

Figure 2.9   Box-drawing using virtual functions to draw lines.

it makes two horizontal-line-drawing and two vertical-line-drawing calls. These horizontal- and vertical-line-drawers, remember, are implemented in class ACanvas, with code which makes a series of pixel-drawing calls. Figure 2.9 shows how the box drawer is implemented in terms of line-drawers.

Efficiency afficionados may rightly worry that using virtual functions and performing drawing operations in terms of other lower-level drawing operations may be too slow. Certainly this can be taken to an extreme. In the extreme case, each canvas would implement only pixel drawing, and all other rendering operations could be defined in ACanvas using calls to this pixel drawer. This approach would be much too slow for animated business logos, never mind first-person asteroid fields.

However, look back at our box-drawing case. Now suppose that we wrote a line-drawing routine optimized for a particular canvas, one that took advantage of the bitmap format to set pixels directly in the line without making any calls to a pixel-drawing routine. Now, if we call the line drawer for a canvas of this type, the virtual function mechanism ensures that this sped-up version is called. But wait, it gets better. Let's call the box drawer. This is still defined in the base class ACanvas—we haven't written a special version for it. But it makes four calls to the line drawer, which *is* sped up. Drawing a box in terms of four lines, where each line is rendered using an optimal routine, makes for a pretty fast box drawer, without having to write one. About as close to a free lunch as it gets in programming.

This will be our approach. The base class, ACanvas, will contain implementations of nearly all graphic operations. Conspicuously left missing from ACanvas will be definitions of routines to set and get a single pixel. The base class cannot implement these routines, because it is independent of any particular bitmap format and therefore does not know how to set the bits to draw a pixel. Notwithstanding its inability to draw a simple pixel, the base canvas class will implement nearly all other drawing operations, and will implement each in terms of the pixel-drawing routine or other higher-level drawing routines. Thus, to make a fully functional derived canvas class, we need only write methods to get and set a single pixel. In practice, we'll enhance each derived class significantly to give it good performance.

C++ allows methods, such as ACanvas's pixel-drawers, to be declared but left unimplemented. Such pure virtual functions *are denoted by putting =0 at the end of the declaration. The presence of any pure virtual functions makes the class an* abstract base class. *Declaring instances of an abstract class is not allowed in C++, as the class is incomplete. If a derived class implements these functions, that class is not abstract and may be used. No instances of ACanvas can be declared in ARTT.*

By carefully choosing how we build higher-level operations out of lower-level operations, and by carefully choosing which ones we optimize in the derived classes, we can get very good performance by optimizing only a small fraction of the drawing methods. Let's dive in and see how this works.

ACanvas Class Declaration

Here is a subset of the declaration of class ACanvas. The full header file includes declarations of methods for a wide variety of drawing operations that won't make sense yet, so they're left out till later. Only a few very basic drawing routines, the ones that we'll use in this chapter, are included. Building up this base canvas class will be part of what we do throughout this book.

```
//   ACanvas.h    Canvas class
//   Rex E. Bradford

#ifndef __ACANVAS_H
#define __ACANVAS_H
```

```
        ... various include files ...

    class ACanvas {
    public:
        ABitmap bm;          // embedded bitmap
        ARect clipRect;      // clipping rectangle

    // Constructor: build us a nice fresh canvas

        ACanvas(ABitmap *pbm);

    // Destructor: nothing to do here, derived classes may need teardown

        virtual ~ACanvas() {};

    // Set current color, in various flavors

        virtual void SetColor8(uchar c8) = 0;
        virtual void SetColorNative (long c) = 0;

    // Retrieve current color, in various flavors

        virtual uchar GetColor8() = 0;
        virtual long GetColorNative () = 0;

    // Set and retrieve clipping rectangle

        void SetClipRect(ARect &rect) { clipRect = rect; }
        void SetClipRect (int 1, int t, int r, int b) { clipRect.left = 1;
            clipRect.top = t; clipRect.right = r; clipRect.bott= b; }
        void GetClipRect(int &left, int &top, int &right, int &bott) {
            left = clipRect.left; top = clipRect.right;
            right = clipRect.right; bott = clipRect.bott;}
        void GetClipRect(ARect &rect) { rect = clipRect; }

    // Set palette of the canvas' bitmap

        void SetPal(uchar *prgb, int index = 0, int num = 256);

    // Draw pixels

        virtual void DrawPixelU(int x, int y) = 0;
        virtual void DrawPixel8U(int x, int y, uchar c8) = 0;
        virtual void DrawPixelNativeU(int x, int y, long c) = 0;

    // Get pixel color

        virtual uchar GetPixel8U(int x, int y) = 0;
        virtual long GetPixelNativeU(int x, int y) = 0;

    // Basic geometric primitives: pixel, horz & vert line, box, filled rect

        virtual void DrawHorzLineU(int y, int xleft, int xright);
        virtual void DrawVertLineU(int x, int ytop, int ybott);
```

```
    virtual void DrawRectU(ARect rect);
    virtual void DrawBoxU(ARect rect);

    void DrawRectU(int left, int top, int right, int bott) {
        ARect rect(left,top,right,bott); DrawRectU(rect);}
    void DrawBoxU(int left, int top, int right, int bott) {
        ARect rect(left,top,right,bott); DrawBoxU(rect);}

// Bitmap drawing

    virtual void DrawBitmapLin8U(ABitmap &bm, int x, int y);
};


#endif
```

Like ABitmap, ACanvas is so fundamental that it's worth looking in detail at the member variables and methods listed so far. Remember, the actual ACanvas declaration is much bigger than this—we'll be adding more methods throughout this book.

```
ABitmap bm;              // embedded bitmap
ARect clipRect;          // clipping rectangle
```

The above represents the member variables of ACanvas. Every canvas has a bitmap, whose elements describe the bitmap's format, width and height, and so on as described in Chapter 1. The drawing attributes in ACanvas consist solely of a "clip rectangle," which is used to restrict rendering to an area of the canvas.

Where's the current color, the other drawing attribute that we need? It's not defined in ACanvas, and the reason has to do with color representation. For maximum drawing speed, the current color should be represented in the "native" format of the canvas, that is, an 8-bit indexed color value for 8-bit canvases, a 15-bit direct color value for 15-bit canvases, and a 24-bit direct color value for 24-bit canvases. So we won't even put the current color here in ACanvas, but will instead put a current color of the appropriate type as a member variable in derived classes.

Just because we don't have a current color member, that doesn't mean we can't include an interface for setting and retrieving the current color. We just can't provide the implementation. The following methods are used to set and retrieve the current color.

```
virtual void SetColor8(uchar c8) = 0;
virtual void SetColorNative(long c) = 0;
virtual uchar GetColor8() = 0;
virtual long GetColorNative() = 0;
```

SetColor8() is used to set the current color to the 8-bit indexed color supplied. In a hypothetical 8-bit derived canvas class, this will be easy—we'll just copy it. In 15-bit and 24-bit canvases, *color conversion* will have to occur. Chapter 13 discusses conversions between *color spaces*. GetColor8() retrieves the current color as an 8-bit indexed color, and again is easy for 8-bit canvases and requires conversion otherwise. SetColorNative() and GetColorNative() are used in places where a current color needs to be passed around, but the code involved doesn't know or care about its format. The native color format is whatever the canvas wants it to be, and users of this routine don't make any assumptions other than that it will fit into a long.

The current color can be set using colors in a format other than 8 bit, also. Methods SetColor15(), GetColor15(), SetColor24(), and GetColor24(), deferred to Chapter 13, are used to set and retrieve the current color in the other standard formats used by ARTT.

The clipping rectangle is set and retrieved using the inline methods listed below. Clipping is covered in chapter 4—don't worry about how this member variable is used yet.

```
void SetClipRect(ARect &rect) { clipRect = rect; }
void SetClipRect(int 1, int t, int r, int b) { clipRect.left = 1;
   clipRect.top = t; clipRect.right = r; clipRect.bott= b; }
void GetClipRect(int &left, int &top, int &right, int &bott) {
   left = clipRect.left; top = clipRect.right;
   right = clipRect.right; bott = clipRect.bott;}
void GetClipRect(ARect &rect) { rect = clipRect; }
```

The constructor for class ACanvas, the implementation of which is listed below, is used to initialize an instance of ACanvas. More precisely, it is used to initialize the ACanvas portion of a derived canvas, since an object of class ACanvas itself can't be created (it is an abstract base class with unimplemented virtual functions). The constructor takes a pointer to a bitmap as its sole argument. The canvas's internal bitmap is initialized by copying the supplied one, and the clipping rectangle is initialized with the bounds of the canvas's bitmap.

```
ACanvas::ACanvas(ABitmap *pbm) : bm(*pbm),
   clipRect (0,0,pbm->width,pbm->height)
{
   // Nothing to do but set up bitmap and clip rectangle!
}
```

The ACanvas destructor does nothing special, apart from the default implicit behavior of destroying its member variables. The destructor is declared virtual, which allows derived canvas classes to have their specific destructor called.

The 'bm' and 'clipRect' members in the constructor are initialized via their own constructors, rather than by assignment in the body of the function. Member variables with constructors should generally be initialized in this way to avoid double initialization, once by a default constructor and once by the assignment in the body of the function. Note that the bitmap 'bm' is initialized by a constructor which takes an ABitmap argument, and no such constructor exists in the ABitmap class definition! The default copy constructor, which initializes by copying each member of the object, is invoked automatically by the C++ compiler.

```
virtual ~ACanvas() {};
```

The DrawPixelXX() family of methods are used to draw a pixel onto the screen at the supplied *x,y* coordinate. The first draws the pixel in the canvas's current color. The next supplies the color to be drawn as an 8-bit indexed color—again, this is easy for 8-bit canvases and requires color conversion for 15-bit and 24-bit ones. The last pixel drawer supplies a color in native format. DrawPixel15U() and DrawPixel24U() are not shown. Note that all of these are pure virtual functions, with no implementation.

```
virtual void DrawPixelU(int x, int y) = 0;
virtual void DrawPixel8U(int x, int y, uchar c8) = 0;
virtual void DrawPixelNativeU(int x, int y, long c) = 0;
```

The GetPixelXX() family of methods retrieves the color of the pixel at the supplied *x,y* coordinate. The first retrieves in 8-bit format, and the second in native format. Color conversion may take place. GetPixel15U() and GetPixel24U() are not shown. Again, ACanvas does not implement these methods, relying on derived classes to do so.

By the way, the U at the end of these method names stands for Unclipped. The real header file for ACanvas also includes "clipped" versions of each of these, named without the trailing U.

```
virtual uchar GetPixel8U(int x, int y) = 0;
virtual long GetPixelNativeU(int x, int y) = 0;
```

The remainder of the class declaration lists methods which provide rendering of entities more complicated than a single pixel. The next section shows how the ACanvas class can implement them, even without being able to draw a pixel (note that the DrawPixelXX() routines were all pure virtual functions).

Setting the Canvas's Palette

SetPal() is used to put color values into the palette of the canvas's bitmap. If the canvas's bitmap doesn't currently have an associated palette, one is automatically allocated. Then, the specified range of the palette is set from the supplied RGB values. Note that this sets only the palette associated with the canvas—the real screen DAC is not updated. To do that, we must call AVga::SetDAC(). Why bother setting a canvas's palette at all, then? For simple programs, we don't need to. But ARTT allows sophisticated programs to maintain several palettes, and convert colors from one to another. Each window in a multiwindow program could have its own palette, maintained in the canvas associated with each window. Then, the VGA DAC could be set to match whichever window is active at any given time.

```
void ACanvas::SetPal(uchar *prgb, int index, int num)
{
    if (bm.ppalette == NULL)
        bm.ppalette = new APalette();
    if (bm.ppalette)
        bm.ppalette->Set(prgb, index, num);
}
```

Basic Drawing Operations: ACanvas::DrawHorzLineU()

The drawing operations shown in this section include four basic geometric operations and a single bitmap renderer. First, we will look at the *geometric primitives*.

Method DrawHorzLineU() draws a horizontal line in the current color, which for class ACanvas is just an unimplemented abstraction. However, since there is a pixel-drawer routine declared which draws a pixel in the current color, we don't have to worry about it here. Here's the implementation of DrawHorzLineU().

```
void ACanvas::DrawHorzLineU(int y, int left, int right)
{
    for (int x = left; x < right; x++)
        DrawPixelU(x, y);
}
```

Our horizontal line drawer takes three arguments. The first is the *y*-coordinate, which is the row at which to draw the line. As previously discussed, *y*-coordinates start at 0 and increase from top to bottom; *x*-coordinates start at 0 and increase from left to right. The other two arguments are left and right *x*-coordinates. As in all the drawing operations we implement in the ARTT toolkit (except the exceptions, of course), we will draw up to but not including the second of a pair of coordinates. As we'll see later, this makes rectangles and clipping operations more straightforward to think about and implement.

The base class horizontal-line drawer is very simple. It traverses in *x*-coordinates from left to right, calling the DrawPixelU() method to draw each pixel. Note that DrawPixelU() is a pure virtual function and is not implemented in the ACanvas class. However, derived classes will implement it, and then our DrawHorzU() routine will work like a charm (well, perhaps a little slowly).

As noted previously, the U at the end of each name stands for Unclipped. If we provide invalid coordinates, for instance negative numbers, or numbers outside the range of the canvas bitmap's size, or if we provide a right coordinate which is smaller than the left coordinate, this routine will fail to operate properly, to the point where it could easily crash the program entirely. In Chapter 4, we will introduce the notion of clipping, and provide clipping versions of all drawing operations. These will provide safety at the cost of a little performance. Most programs will use clipped versions of the routines in most cases, but having unclipped versions of everything is very handy too. For instance, a higher-level drawing routine may "know" that its coordinates are okay (having been checked out already, for instance), and so would call unclipped versions of lower-level drawing methods.

ACanvas::DrawVertLine()

DrawVertLineU() is a vertical-line renderer similar to DrawHorz-LineU(), and works in basically the same way. It takes a single *x*-coordinate (column) and top and bottom *y*-coordinates, and draws a vertical line in the current color.

```
void ACanvas::DrawVertLineU(int x, int top, int bott)
{
    for (int y = top; y < bott; y++)
        DrawPixelU(x, y);
}
```

ACanvas::DrawRectU()

DrawRectU() draws a filled rectangular area in the canvas's bitmap, in the current color. It takes a rectangle argument as input. The care and feeding of rectangles will not be covered until Chapter 4; for now it suffices to know that a rectangle is composed of the following fields:

```
short left;     // x-coordinate of left edge
short top;      // y-coordinate of top edge
short right;    // x-coordinate of right edge
short bott;     // y-coordinate of bottom edge
```

Note again that drawing proceeds up to but not including the lower-right coordinates. For instance, a rectangle given by coordinates 0,0 1,1 contains only one pixel, the one at 0,0. Only that pixel would be drawn.

```
void ACanvas::DrawRectU(ARect rect)
{
   for (int y = rect.top; y < rect.bott; y++)
      DrawHorzLineU(y, rect.left, rect.right);
}
```

DrawRectU() loops from top to bottom, calling DrawHorz-LineU() for each row. As it stands now, DrawHorzLineU() is implemented by successive calls to DrawPixelU(), and so DrawRect() would end up calling DrawPixelU() for each pixel in the rectangle. However, a derived class can (and will, or our users will not like us!) write a more optimal version of DrawHorzLineU(), one which takes advantage of its knowledge of the particular bitmap format for that canvas. By virtue of speeding up DrawHorzLineU(), rectangle drawing will be sped up for that canvas, even without that canvas redefining DrawRectU()!

ACanvas::DrawBoxU()

DrawBoxU() takes the same arguments as DrawRectU(), but instead of filling the rectangle it draws a one-pixel-thick box. It does so by making calls to DrawHorzU() for top and bottom, and to DrawVertU() for left and right sides. Again, DrawBoxU() can be magically sped up for a given canvas class by improving the operation of DrawHorzU() and DrawVertU().

```
void ACanvas::DrawBoxU(ARect rect)
{
   DrawHorzLineU(rect.top, rect.left, rect.right);
   DrawHorzLineU(rect.bott - 1, rect.left, rect.right);
   DrawVertLineU(rect.left, rect.top + 1, rect.bott - 1);
   DrawVertLineU(rect.right - 1, rect.top + 1, rect.bott - 1);
}
```

Basic Bitmap Rendering: ACanvas::DrawBitmapLin8U()

The last method in our minimal version of the ACanvas class is DrawBitmapLin8U(). This routine draws a source bitmap into our (destination) canvas's bitmap. What exactly is this bitmap that we're going to draw? It could be almost anything. Icons are made from bitmaps, for instance. The bugeyed critters and creatures inhabiting most computer games are predrawn bitmaps, made with programs such as Windows Paintbrush, Electronic Arts' DeluxePaint, Adobe Photoshop, or any of a host of *paint programs,* which allow the user to create a bitmapped image and save it in a file. The next chapter will show how bitmapped images can be extracted from the files produced by such programs. For now, we'll just assume that somehow we have some image in the form of a bitmap.

Now, what is the format of the bitmap we want to render? Well, it could be almost any format, and the code to draw such a bitmap will be different depending on the bitmap format, because it has to extract the bitmap's pixels in order to render them. Theoretically, we could extract the pixels one at a time from *any* type of bitmap, and use a C++ virtual function to do so, in order to generalize the drawing of a bitmap. But that would be *really* slow. Instead, we're just going to write several bitmap rendering methods, one for each format we want to render (actually, eventually we'll write more than one per format because of the various options and color effects we'll want to achieve during rendering). Later, for convenience, we'll also create functions which can be supplied any type of bitmap, and which will dispatch to the appropriate routine based on the format of bitmap to be drawn.

For now, we're going to present just one bitmap renderer, one that can render bitmaps which are formatted in the BMF_LIN8 format. That is, the bitmap consists of one byte per pixel, in a linear ordering. DrawBitmapLin8U() uses its knowledge of this format to get the pixels, and uses the generic DrawPixelU() function to draw them. Notice that the routine checks the 'transparent' flag of the source bitmap format, to see whether or not to draw pixels with the value 0. Using 'transparent' frees bitmaps from having to have an apparently rectangular shape, which otherwise is implied by having a width and height define the bitmap shape. A transparent bitmap must reside in a rectangular area, but may include or exclude any of the pixels within the rectangle. The little guy in Figure 2.10, for instance, is a bitmap with transparency. Most such creatures and critters are transparent bitmaps, unless perhaps they are the Rectangle-Shaped Warriors from Cubeworld.

The other nonintuitive thing the DrawBitmapLin8U() method does is its treatment of the data ptr "p". See how the pointer is updated every row to take into account the source bitmap's "rowbytes" field, which may not be the same as its width.

DrawBitmapLin8U(), like all bitmap rendering operations, takes a *reference* to the source bitmap as its first argument. The other arguments are the *x,y* position of the upper-left coordinate at which to draw the bitmap.

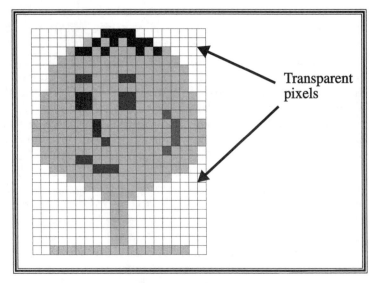

Figure 2.10   Bitmapped critter with transparency.

```
void ACanvas::DrawBitmapLin8U(ABitmap &bms, int x, int y)
{
// Copy pointer to source bitmap into local ptr 'p'
   uchar *p = bms.pbits;

// Loop through rows of source bitmap
   for (int iy = y; iy < (y + bms.height); iy++)
       {
// Loop through columns of source bitmap, incrementing bits ptr
       for (int ix = x; ix < (x + bms.width); ix++, p++)
           {
// If pixel is non-zero, or if bitmap is not transparent, draw pixel
           if (*p || !bms.transparent)
               DrawPixel8U(ix, iy, *p);
           }
// Since already advanced ptr by width, just add remainder of rowbytes
       p += bms.rowbytes - bms.width;
       }
}
```

References are very useful. They are typically imple-mented using pointers, but allow a more natural syntax to be used for the object referred to (i.e., bm.member *with references in place of* pbm->member *with pointers). For inline functions, references are especially useful—since the compiler is aware of the exact object being manipu-lated, it need not "turn the reference into a pointer," but can instead operate directly on the object. This is a big win.*

Class ACanvas8: 8-Bit Canvas Class

If we're going to render pixels onto an actual screen, we're going to have to derive a new canvas class from ACanvas, and define the methods which set and get pixels to and from the canvas. Our goal is to put pixels onto a VGA mode 13H screen before this chapter is out. But we're actually a couple of steps away from this, as can be seen by the canvas class hierarchy previously shown in Figure 2.7. This section discusses ACanvas8, the derived canvas which "specializes" the canvas for 8-bit bitmaps.

There are two renderable 8-bit bitmap formats, BMF_LIN8 and BMF_BANK8. These require different code to render onto, so class ACanvas8 will, like ACanvas, be unable to render even a single pixel. What's the point?

Remember, ACanvas doesn't know how to store the current color drawing attribute, because it doesn't know what format the color should be in. But 8-bit canvases clearly want the current color to be an 8-bit index color. The ACanvas8 class includes an 8-bit color member, thus specializing for 8-bit bitmaps.

A subset of the header file for the ACanvas8 class is listed below. It's a pretty simple class—it exists solely for the purpose of storing an 8-bit current color, and providing methods to convert colors to and from 8-bit format. SetColor8(), GetColor8(), SetColorNative(), and GetColorNative() all read and write the 8-bit color member. DrawPixelNativeU() and GetPixelNativeU(), to draw a pixel and retrieve its color, can now be implemented—by calling DrawPixel8U() and Get-Pixel8U()—which don't exist yet!

```
//   ACanvas8.h   Base 8-bit canvas class
//   Rex E. Bradford

#ifndef__ACANVAS8_H
#define__ACANVAS8_H

#include "acanvas.h"

class ACanvas8 : public ACanvas {
public:

    uchar color8;    // current color is 8-bit

// Constructor: nothing to see here

    ACanvas8(ABitmap *pbm) : ACanvas(pbm) {color8 = 0;}

// Set current color in various formats
```

```
    void SetColor8(uchar c8) {color8 = c8;}
    void SetColorNative(long c) {color8 = c;}

// Get current color in various formats

    uchar GetColor8() {return color8;}
    long GetColorNative() {return color8;}

// Draw pixel, convert to 8-bit form, which is not implemented

    void DrawPixelNativeU(int x, int y, long c) {DrawPixel8U(x, y, c);}

// Get pixel, convert from 8-bit form, which is not implemented
    long GetPixelNativeU(int x, int y) {return GetPixel8U(x, y);}
};

#endif
```

The version supplied above is actually a simplification. The other important job of the ACanvas8 class is to be the repository of color conversion to and from 8-bit color. Methods to set, get, and draw pixels using 15-bit and 24-bit color values require color conversion. They are implemented in this class but not covered until the topic of color conversion is addressed in Chapter 13.

Class ACanvasLin8: 8-Bit Linear Canvas Class

Our goal is to put some pixels on that screen before the chapter is out, using VGA mode 13H, the 320 × 200 8-bit (256-color) mode. But we're not quite there yet. The mode 13H screen is laid out linearly in memory, and in fact can be represented by a bitmap in format BMF_LIN8. Clearly, we need a canvas class which can do some real work, namely putting pixels into a bitmap of this format.

Class ACanvasLin8 will be a workhorse canvas class. It requires that the bitmap used to initialize it have format BMF_LIN8. Besides finally being able to read and write pixels from the canvas, it will contain faster versions of many of the rendering methods of class ACanvas. These will be faster because they won't use DrawPixelU() in their body; rather, the routine will have pixel-setting code expressed directly in C++ statements, as we'll shortly discover.

The relevant portion of the header file for class ACanvasLin8 is given below:

```
//   ACvLin8.h   8-bit linear canvas class
//   Rex E. Bradford

#ifndef__ACVLIN8_H
#define__ACVLIN8_H
```

```
#include "acanvas8.h"

class ACanvasLin8 : public ACanvas8 {

// Compute pointer from x,y

    uchar *Ptr(int x, int y) {return(bm.pbits +
        (long(y) * long(bm.rowbytes)) + x);}

public:
// Constructor: once again, pass the buck (bitmap) down the line

    ACanvasLin8(ABitmap *pbm) : ACanvas8(pbm) {}

// Draw pixel in 8-bit form (15/24-bit converted in class ACanvas8)

    void DrawPixelU(int x, int y);
    void DrawPixel8U(int x, int y, uchar c8);

// Retrieve color of pixel in 8-bit form (15/24-bit converted in ACanvas8)

    uchar GetPixel8U(int x, int y);

// Some drawing primitives, replacing slow ones in ACanvas

    void DrawHorzLineU(int y, int xleft, int xright);
    void DrawVertLineU(int x, int ytop, int ybott);
    void DrawRectU(ARect rect);

// Bitmap rendering routines

    void DrawBitmapLin8U(ABitmap &bm, int x, int y);
};

#endif
```

The ACanvasLin8 constructor takes a bitmap pointer as input, and has nothing to do other than the default behavior of calling base class constructors. The ACanvas constructor initializes the bitmap and clip rectangle, and the ACanvas8 constructor initializes the current color. Nothing more needs to be done. Make sure you pass in a pointer to a valid bitmap, with format BMF_LIN8.

The Ptr() method is private, and is used by many drawing routines to compute the address of a pixel within the bitmap. This pointer is calculated as follows: Start with the base bitmap data bits pointer (which points to 0,0), add the *y*-coordinate times the 'rowbytes' to get to the beginning of the desired row, and finally add the *x*-coordinate to get to the desired pixel within the row. Figure 2.11 shows how the calculations work.

```
uchar *Ptr(int x, int y) {return(bm.pbits +
    (long(y) * long(bm.rowbytes)) + x);}
```

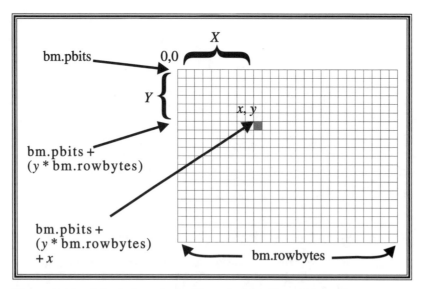

Figure 2.11   Calculating pixel address in 8-bit linear bitmap.

Class ACanvasLin8: Drawing and Retrieving Pixels

Below is the implementation of the ACanvasLin8 methods for setting and getting pixels. Note that, unlike the ACanvas routines, they take advantage of their knowledge of the pixel format of a BMF_LIN8 bitmap. Since the ACanvasLin8 class deals with a known bitmap type, namely BMF_LIN8, it has enough knowledge to implement the routines to get and set pixels.

```
void ACanvasLin8::DrawPixelU(int x, int y)
{
    *Ptr(x,y) = color8;  // draw pixel in current color
}

void ACanvasLin8::DrawPixel8U(int x, int y, uchar c8)
{
    *Ptr(x,y) = c8;      // draw pixel in supplied color
}

uchar ACanvasLin8::GetPixel8U(int x, int y)
{
    return *Ptr(x,y);    // retrieve color of pixel at x,y
}
```

Class ACanvasLin8: Higher-Level Drawing Methods

DrawHorzLineU() is easy with a linear 8-bit bitmap. Since a linear 8-bit bitmap has all the pixels in a row adjacent to each other, a horizontal line can be drawn using the C memset() function, which in most optimizing compilers is implemented using superfast embedded inline assembly language.

```
void ACanvasLin8::DrawHorzLineU(int y, int xleft, int xright)
{
   memset (Ptr(xleft, y), color8, xright - xleft);
}
```

A vertical line can't be drawn quite so quickly, since its pixels are not contiguous in memory. But at least we can calculate the address of each successive pixel by incremental addition, instead of calculating it from scratch each time.

```
void ACanvasLin8::DrawVertLineU(int x, int ytop, int ybott)
{
   uchar *p = Ptr(x, ytop);
   for (int y = ytop; y < ybott; y++, p += bm.rowbytes)
      *p = color8;
}
```

Since we now have pretty fast versions of the horizontal-line and vertical-line drawers, the default rectangle and box drawers defined way back in ACanvas now are fast too. Since filled rectangles are so important, however, we'll write a custom version of this routine too. DrawBoxU() is not so important and works well enough to leave alone.

```
void ACanvasLin8::DrawRectU(ARect rect)
{
   uchar *p = Ptr(rect.left, rect.top);
   for (int y = rect.top; y < rect.bott; y++, p += bm.rowbytes)
     memset(p, color8, rect.right - rect.left);
}
```

The last method we'll develop for the ACanvas8 class in this chapter draws a linear 8-bit bitmap onto the canvas, which itself is in 8-bit linear format. The major complication will be handling transparency, since this routine will be called for source bitmaps which are transparent (0-valued pixels not to be drawn) and nontransparent (draw all pixels). In the case of nontransparent bitmaps, we can use the C function memcpy() to quickly copy all the pixel values in a particular row.

```
void ACanvasLin8::DrawBitmapLin8U(ABitmap &bms, int x, int y)
{
// Set up source and destination pointers, and get # rows to draw
```

```
    uchar *ps = bms.pbits;       // get ptr to start of bitmap bits
    uchar *pd = Ptr(x, y);       // calc ptr into canvas
    int h = bms.height;          // get height for row countdown

// Loop through rows

    while (h-- > 0)
        {
// If source bitmap is transparent, check each pixel for value 0
// to decide whether or not to draw into canvas

        if (bms.transparent)
            {
            int w = bms.width;       // grab width for countdown
            while (w-- > 0)          // for each pixel in row:
                {
                if (*ps) *pd = *ps; // if source pixel !0, write to dest
                ++ps;                // increment source ptr
                ++pd;                // increment dest ptr
                }
            ps += bms.rowbytes - bms.width;  // advance source to next row
            pd += bm.rowbytes - bms.width;   // advance dest to next row
            }

// If source bitmap is not transparent, just copy row of pixels and
// update source and destination pointers.

        else
            {
            memcpy(pd, ps, bms.width);    // copy entire row from src->dest
            ps += bms.rowbytes;           // advance source to next row
            pd += bm.rowbytes;            // advance dest to next row
            }
        }
}
```

Class AMode13: Initializing and Terminating Mode 13H

Finally, we have all the canvases and rendering methods we need to use mode 13H, the basic 320×200 VGA graphics mode. To make life easy for us, let's define a very simple "interface" class to get us in and out of mode 13 graphics. Here's the header file for class AMode13:

```
//   AMode13.h    Mode 13 screen class
//   Rex E. Bradford

#ifndef__AMODE13_H
#define__AMODE13_H

#include "acanvas.h"
```

```
extern ACanvas *gCanvasScreen;    // ptr to screen canvas

class AMode13 {

public:

   static ACanvas *Launch (); // launch mode 13 (save old mode), make cv
   static void Term();        // exit mode 13, restore old mode, del cv
};

#endif
```

AMode13::Launch() does a few things for us. First, it retrieves and stores the current VGA mode (so we can restore it before we exit the program), and then it sets the VGA to mode 13H. Both these tasks are implemented using methods in the AVga class defined earlier in this chapter. Then, Launch() creates a canvas of class ACanvasLin8, passing in a bitmap constructed using the base physical address, format, and width and height of the mode 13H video buffer. The bitmap's 'pbits' pointer must point to physical address 0xA0000L, the start of VGA video memory. Because pointers to physical memory are constructed differently under 16-bit DOS in real mode versus 32-bit extended DOS in protected mode, AMem::GetPhysPtr() is used to create the 'pbits' pointer value.

This canvas covers the entire mode 13H screen. A pointer to it is passed back by Launch(), and is also put into a global variable called 'gCanvasScreen', so that any code can directly use this special canvas. In order to do any rendering onto the screen, programs will need to use this canvas pointer.

```
ACanvas *gCanvasScreen;     // ptr to screen canvas

ACanvas *AMode13::Launch()
{
// Save old mode, set mode 13

   AVga::SaveMode();      // save old (text) mode
   AVga::SetMode(0x13);   // set mode 13

// Create linear canvas to cover mode 13 screen

   ABitmap bmTemp((uchar *) AMem::GetPhysPtr(0xA0000L),
      BMF_LIN8, FALSE, 320, 200);
   gCanvasScreen = new ACanvasLin8(&bmTemp);

   return gCanvasScreen; // return ptr to canvas

}
```

AMode13::Term() should be called before exiting a program which has called AMode13::Launch(). It destroys the screen canvas and returns to the original video mode.

```
void AMode13::Term()
{
   delete gCanvasScreen; // delete screen canvas
   AVga::RestoreMode();   // restore old (text) mode
}
```

BBALL: The Bouncing Ball

This chapter ends with a little demonstration program to show off what we've accomplished. This program displays a ball bouncing around the screen, careening off each wall as it reaches it. It may not be impressive, but we've laid the foundation for a lot of flashier graphics to come. And maybe even the humble bouncing ball could be the start of a screen saver that you write!

```
//    Bball.cpp     Bouncing ball demo
//    Rex E. Bradford

#include <conio.h>
#include <string.h>
#include <dos.h>

#include "amode13.h"
#include "avga.h"

static uchar bmBallBits[] = {    // the ball's graphic shape is a bitmap
    0,0,0,0,0,0,0,0,0,0,0,0,0,0,  // whose pixel values are encoded here
    0,0,0,0,0,0,1,1,0,0,0,0,0,0,
    0,0,0,0,1,2,2,2,2,1,0,0,0,0,
    0,0,0,1,2,3,3,3,3,2,1,0,0,0,
    0,0,0,2,3,4,4,4,4,3,2,0,0,0,
    0,0,1,2,4,5,5,5,5,4,2,1,0,0,
    0,0,1,2,4,5,5,5,5,4,2,1,0,0,
    0,0,0,2,3,4,4,4,4,3,2,0,0,0,
    0,0,0,1,2,3,3,3,3,2,1,0,0,0,
    0,0,0,0,1,2,2,2,2,1,0,0,0,0,
    0,0,0,0,0,0,1,1,0,0,0,0,0,0,
    0,0,0,0,0,0,0,0,0,0,0,0,0,0,
};
static ABitmap bmBall (bmBallBits, BMF_LIN8, FALSE, 14, 12);

static uchar ballPal[] = {       // ball's palette of colors
    0x80,0x80,0x80,   // 0: GRAY
    0xFF,0x00,0x00,   // 1: BLUE
    0xC0,0x00,0x40,   // 2: BLUE-BLUE-RED
    0x80,0x00,0x80,   // 3: BLUE-RED
```

```
    0x40,0x00,0xC0,    // 4: BLUE-RED-RED
    0x00,0x00,0xFF,    // 5: RED
};

void MoveBall (ABitmap &bm, int &x, int &y, int &xvel, int &yvel);

// -----------------------------------------------------------
//    MAIN DRIVER PROGRAM
// -----------------------------------------------------------

void main()
{
// Fire up graphics mode 13

    AMode13::Launch();

// Set VGA DAC directly

    AVga::SetDAC(ballPal, 0, 6);

// Set ball's initial location and velocity. Velocity is expressed
// in terms of pixels per pass through the drawing loop - the ball's
// actual speed is determined by the computer's speed.

    int x = 176;       // start near screen center but offset a little
    int y = 110;
    int xvel = +2;     // move 2 pixels horizontal for every 1 vertical
    int yvel = +1;
    int pass = 0;      // counter for drawing passes per movement

// Move that ball until the cows come home (or user presses key)

    while (TRUE)
      {
      if (kbhit())       // if key pressed
        {
        getch();         // swallow key
        break;           // and exit loop
        }
      if (++pass == 30) // only move ball once per 30 drawings
        {
        MoveBall(bmBall, x, y, xvel, yvel);    // move the ball
        pass = 0;
        }
      gCanvasScreen->DrawBitmapLin8U(bmBall, x, y);    // redraw it
      }

// Return to text mode

    AMode13::Term();
}
// -----------------------------------------------------------
//
```

```
// MoveBall() moves the ball by adding its current velocity to its
// current location, and bouncing off the walls by inverting the
// velocity when it hits the wall. Note the use of gCanvasScreen
// to get the screen's width and height.

void MoveBall(ABitmap &bm, int &x, int &y, int &xvel, int &yvel)
{
// Add x-velocity to x-position, bounce off left & right edges

  x += xvel;
  if (x <= 0)
     { x = 0; xvel = -xvel; }
  else if ((x + bm.width) > gCanvasScreen->bm.width)
     { x = gCanvasScreen->bm.width - bm.width; xvel = -xvel; }

// Add y-velocity to y-position, bounce off top & bottom edges

  y += yvel;
  if (y <= 0)
     { y = 0; yvel = -yvel; }
  else if ((y + bm.height) > gCanvasScreen->bm.height)
     { y = gCanvasScreen->bm.height - bm.height; yvel = -yvel; }
}
```

Figure 2.12 shows a screen shot from BBALL. The static shot doesn't convey the frenetic bouncing of the ball off the edges of the screen—you'll have to run it yourself to see.

The bouncing ball demo program cheats. If the ball weren't defined with a blank space around it as part of its shape definition, it would leave copies of itself behind as it moved. And it must currently

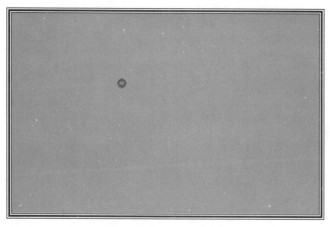

Figure 2.12   Screen shot from BBALL, the Bouncing Ball demo program.

careen around on top of a blank background, otherwise it would wipe out the background as it moved across it. In Part 2 of this book, powerful techniques for *composing* moving and overlapping graphics will be developed, and these limitations will be removed. In Part 2 we'll also use the PC timer to control the speed of moving objects—the ball free-runs in this simple program, making its speed dependent on the speed of the computer it's run on.

Finally, note that the ball's bitmap had to be defined in C code in the program. It would be much better if we could extract the ball's shape from a graphics file. Then we could use a paint program to make the ball look like whatever we wanted. Next on our agenda, in Chapter 3, is information and code to unlock the secrets of these graphics files, and to enable us to extract images from them.

Graphics File Formats

The graphic shape and color of the bouncing ball in the last chapter's demo was defined in an array of 'uchars'. This is less than ideal. Imagine creating the definition of a person's face in this manner— "Let's see, do I want a 0x5D here for the nose earring, or a 0x5E?" Clearly what is called for is to be able to import the images from graphic files of the kind created by programs such as Microsoft Paintbrush, Adobe Photoshop, and Electronic Arts' DeluxePaint, among many others. This chapter discusses the formats of such graphics files, and develops code to extract images from two of the most popular formats.

A Plethora of Standards

It has been said, "Standards are good—that's why we have so many to choose from." Nowhere is this more true than in the world of file formats for graphic images. A whole industry has sprung up to supply software to convert images from one format to another! The reason for this graphical Tower of Babel is mostly historical. In the early days of so-called "paint programs," each manufacturer developed a custom file format for saving images in, mostly because there were no standards. More recently, advances in image technology and image compression have created a need for more sophisticated standards, and some new file formats have been created by committees. Fortunately for users, most image creation programs will read and write files in several formats.

Table 3.1 lists the names of the popular formats most likely to be encountered by PC users. The format of a file can be identified uniquely by the file's three-letter extension. Where the common acronym for the format differs from the extension, it is noted.

Early PC Graphic File Formats

The first five of the formats listed in Table 3.1 (PCX, BMP/DIB, GIF, IFF/LBM, and TARGA), were created by software manufacturers to serve specific products. Each was created for a similar purpose, and there are some valid reasons why these different formats were created. ZSoft invented PCX when it developed PC Paintbrush, a paint program which came out not long after the IBM PC was introduced in 1981. The PCX format was created in a vacuum—there was no standard file format at the time for representing images. The IFF format was created by Electronic Arts as a general file format for use on the Amiga computer. IFF files can hold digital sounds and other data in addition to images. When the DeluxePaint program was ported from the Amiga to the PC, the IFF format came with it.

Table 3.1	Popular Graphics File Formats
Format	*Description*
PCX	Created by ZSoft for *PC Paintbrush*, common format
BMP,DIB	Microsoft Windows standard bitmap files (one format, two extensions)
GIF	Created by CompuServe for image downloading
IFF,LBM	Created by Electronic Arts for *DeluxePaint*
TARGA	Created by AT&T/Truevision, extension TGA
TIFF	Tagged Image File Format, extension TIF
JFIF	JPEG File-Interchange Format, extension JPG
WMF	Microsoft Windows metafile format
EPS	Encapsulated Postscript

The other manufacturers created new formats for various reasons. AT&T's high-end (at the time) TARGA board and associated software, later spun off into the Truevision company, handled more colors than then-current hardware or software. None of the existing file formats could handle its "true-color" needs, so the TGA format was born. CompuServe's primary concern was the time it takes to download a graphic image, and so it used an advanced compression scheme to reduce file sizes in its GIF format. Microsoft, of course, is Microsoft, and so we have the BMP/DIB format.

More Recent Formats

Each of the original PC-based graphic file formats met the needs of the hardware and software it was developed for, and each has gone through revisions as PC graphics boards have supported more colorful displays in higher resolutions. However, none of these formats is very sophisticated, which made them inadequate for the burgeoning desktop publishing industry in the mid 1980s. The Tagged Image File Format (TIFF) was developed jointly by Microsoft and Aldus, the company that created the *PageMaker* desktop publishing program. This format is far more sophisticated than the earlier formats. Beyond storing the image per se, it includes a great deal of optional descriptive information about the image, including *gamma correction* tables, which can be used to ensure accurate color reproduction on any output device. TIFF files can hold monochrome images, including faxes, as well as grayscale images and color images. The format itself is somewhat complex and has nonstandard variations, which has kept it from replacing more primitive file formats outside the realm of desktop publishing.

The JFIF format was created as a way of storing images compressed using the JPEG algorithm. JPEG stands for Joint Photographic Experts Group, a committee of the International Standards Organization (ISO). The JPEG compression algorithm, which is discussed briefly in Chapter 16, is a highly mathematical approach suitable for grayscale and full-color images such as photographs and captured images. Unlike other file formats, it is *lossy*, meaning that the compressed image does not match the original image pixel for pixel. However, JPEG can achieve remarkable compression ratios (such as 20 to 1 and higher) with very little noticeable picture degradation. The JFIF format is a standard format for putting JPEG-compressed images into files.

The other two formats listed, WMF and EPS, are arguably not image file formats at all. They are both "metafile" formats. Rather than encoding pixel values per se, they describe images in terms of graphic operations and primitives such as lines, rectangles, curves, and polygons. The EPS format contains an image described as a set of Postscript commands, Postscript being the image description language built into many printers and popularized by the Apple Macintosh. EPS is used fairly heavily in desktop publishing. WMF, the Windows Metafile Format, is specific to Microsoft Windows and is not generally used outside this domain.

What's in a Graphics File?

Most image-storage file formats are pretty simple. They typically contain a single image and some descriptive information about it. The image may be monochrome, grayscale, or color, and is represented using some number of bits per pixel (common color formats are 4, 8, and 24 bits per pixel). In the case of color images represented by 4 or 8 bits per pixel, the color palette which contains the red/green/blue values for each color index is also stored in the file. The image data may be a simple two-dimensional array of pixel values, or it may be subjected to some data compression algorithm. Descriptive information about the image typically includes its width and height in pixels, color depth (number of bits per pixel), data compression technique, and sometimes the original image size in inches or meters. Often the file will indicate which version of the file format is in use.

The simpler image formats basically consist of a fixed-size header followed by the image data, which is of variable length depending on image width and height, color depth, and data compression technique applied to the image. Figure 3.1 shows the structure of a typical fixed-header image file.

More complex formats such as IFF and TIFF consist of a series of variable-length *chunks*, each of which is tagged with a type field and some data. Different chunk types include image description chunks, color palette chunks, annotation chunks for author information, and actual image data chunks. The advantage of this scheme is that later versions of the file format can include new chunk types not originally envisioned, and old software will still work if it simply skips over chunks whose type it does not recognize. Figure 3.2 shows a typical chunk-based graphics file.

Reading Images from Graphics Files

What does it mean to use an image from a graphics file? We want to do more than just display the image on the screen directly from the file; we may want to keep it around in memory so we can render it at any time. What we really want to do is to extract the image into a

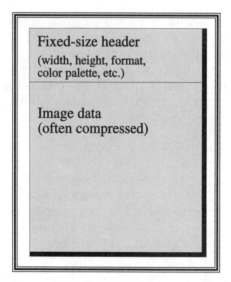

Figure 3.1   General structure of a fixed-header image file.

bitmap, into an object of class ABitmap in our case. The code in this chapter will allow us to do just that. In Chapter 8, we will develop code to extract multiple small images from a single graphics file, where each subimage is marked by enclosing it with a specially colored border. This technique is commonly used in computer game

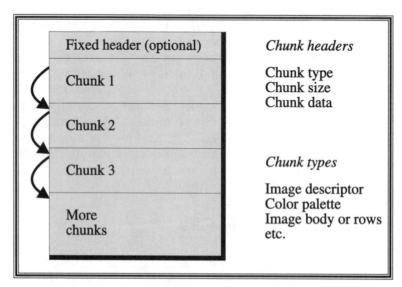

Figure 3.2   General structure of a chunk-based image file.

development to keep related images together, saving directory space and artists' time. We will also learn to apply our own run-length compression to an image.

Class AGfxFile: Reading and Writing Graphics Files

There are several formats of graphics files, but in each case we have the same goal—to extract the full image of the file into a bitmap, along with an associated palette if there is one. The extraction of bordered subimages in Chapter 8 will be done from the full bitmap once it is in memory. Since the goal is to support image extraction from multiple file formats, the appropriate place to start is to define a base class for all image file formats. This class will define the *interface* by which we "talk to" image files. The classes we will develop will also support writing of image files.

Here is the header file for the AGfxFile class, which implements the interface for accessing graphics files:

```
//    AGfxFile.h   Base Graphics File
//    Rex E. Bradford

#ifndef __AGFXFILE_H
#define __AGFXFILE_H

#include <stdio.h>
#include "abitmap.h"
#include "aerror.h"

class AGfxFile {

protected:
   FILE *fp;

   AGfxFile(FILE *fp_, bool read = TRUE) {fp = fp_;}
   virtual ~AGfxFile() {if (fp) fclose(fp);}

public:
   static AError Read(char *filename, ABitmap &bm);
   static AError Write(char *filename, ABitmap &bm);
};

#endif
```

The interface is pretty simple. In fact, there are only two public methods, one to read an image from a file into a bitmap, and another to write a bitmap into an image file. Talk about keeping the details under the hood! The static Read() method does everything needed to determine the type of graphics file from the filename's extension, open the file, allocate a bitmap in memory, and read the image into the bitmap. Read() also loads a palette if there is one, and even closes the file before returning. If all goes well, the empty bitmap passed in by reference will be "filled in" and become a usable bitmap, which can then be used for rendering or other purposes. If anything goes wrong (unknown file extension, can't open file, bad data in file, memory allocation problem, etc.), an error code is returned and the bitmap should not be used.

As we'll see shortly, the Read() method does some of the work, and relies upon classes derived from AGfxFile to do the hard work of interpreting the data inside a particular format of file. There will be one derived class for each type of file we wish to be able to load from. Read() knows which derived class to use by virtue of the extension of the filename, which it looks up in an internal table of graphics file formats. Write() works in the reverse direction, taking a filename and a bitmap, and creating an image file of the appropriate type.

Here is some sample user code to read from a graphics file:

```
char *filename = "somefile.pcx";
ABitmap bm;
AError err = AGfxFile::Read(filename, &bm);
if (err)
    {
    // error condition: don't use bitmap
    printf("Problem with file %s (%s)\n", filename, AErr:Msg(err));
    }
else
    {
    // use graphics file (for instance, call DrawBitmapLin8U(&bm,...) etc.
    }
```

Below is the implementation of AGfxFile::Read().

```
AError AGfxFile::Read(char *filename, ABitmap &bm)
{
    AError err;
    AGfxFile *pGfxFile = NULL;

// Open file, if can't then return error

    FILE *fp = fopen(filename, "rb");
    if (fp == NULL)
        return AERR_FILEOPEN;

// Opened file. Let's create a new instance of the proper type,
// based on file extension. If the file extension is improper,
// set error code
```

```
    bm.pbits = NULL; // so if never set, won't free
    bm.ppalette = NULL;

    switch (GrabExt (filename))
        {
        case MAKE_EXT('P','C','X'):
            pGfxFile = new APcxFile(fp, bm, err);
            break;
        case MAKE_EXT('B','M','P'):
        case MAKE_EXT('D','I','B'):
        case MAKE_EXT('R','L','E'):
            pGfxFile = new ABmpFile(fp, bm, err);
            break;
        default:
            return AERR_BADNAME;
        }

// If there's an error, free up bitmap bits and palette

    if (err)
        {
        if (bm.pbits) { delete bm.pbits; bm.pbits = NULL; }
        if (bm.ppalette) { delete bm.ppalette; bm.ppalette = NULL; }
        }

// We don't need the gfxfile obj anymore, since the bitmap has everything

    if (pGfxFile)
        delete pGfxFile;
    return err;
}
```

AGfxFile::Read() does the following:

1. Open the file, using fopen().

2. Clear pointer fields in the bitmap in case of error (so won't free garbage pointers).

3. Grab the file's extension, and switch based on it.

4. Construct an instance of the appropriate subclass; this loads bitmap from file.

5. Delete subclass instance and return.

All along the way, error conditions are checked for and handled, and the relevant error code is returned. If there are no errors, the bitmap is filled in with the contents of the image. Memory is allocated for the pixel data bits and they are read into this memory from the file, and the bitmap's width, height, and other fields are set appropriately as well. Sounds easy so far.

Looking up File Types by Extension

In AGfxFile::Read(), a function named GrabExt() is used to grab the three-letter file extension from the pathname passed in. This is a generally useful function, not specific to graphics files. GrabExt() will be used later when we read from animation files. The extension is put into a longword for easy comparison via a switch statement. The three characters of the extension are put into the low 3 bytes of the longword, whose typedef is AExt. The high byte is set to 0.

The header file which provides the declaration of AExt and the prototype for GrabExt() is listed below. It also includes MAKE_EXT(), a macro for building an AExt from three characters.

```
//    AExt.h      Routine to look up file type based on extension
//    Rex E. Bradford

#ifndef __AEXT_H
#define __AEXT_H

#include "atypes.h"

// An extension fits into a long, and is built with MAKE_EXT()

typedef ulong AExt;

#define MAKE_EXT(c1,c2,c3) (ulong(c1) | (ulong(c2) << 8) | \
    (ulong(c3) << 16))

// GrabExt() returns the extension portion of a filename in an AExt

AExt GrabExt(char *fname);

#endif
```

GrabExt() itself is pretty simple and is the sole function in file AEXT.CPP.

```
//    AExt.cpp    Routine to grab file extension
//    Rex E. Bradford

#include <string.h>
#include <ctype.h>
#include "aext.h"

// GrabExt () grabs the extension portion of a filename, and returns
// it in the form of an AExt.

AExt GrabExt(char *filename)
{
// Look for last period, if none then no extension
```

```
    char *p = strrchr(filename, '.');
    if (p == NULL)
        return 0;

// Found period, if it's succeeded by \ or /, it's part of path

    ++p;
    if ((*p == '/') || (*p == '\\'))
        return 0;

// Grab characters into 3-byte array

    uchar ext[3] = {0,0,0};
    int iext = 0;
    while (*p && (iext < 3))
        {
        ext[iext++] = toupper(*p);
        ++p;
        }

// Make extension from character array

    return MAKE_EXT(ext[0], ext[1], ext[2]);
}
```

Writing Image Files

AGfxFile::Write() works similarly to Read(), but in reverse. If the bitmap has no associated palette (the 'bm.ppalette' field is NULL), it uses the contents of the system palette when writing the file. Under DOS, the system palette is the VGA DAC. Under Windows, it is obtained from the Windows environment. AGfxFile::Write() is not listed here—see the accompanying CD for the full listing.

ARTT File Formats Supported

This chapter will present subclasses of AGfxFile for handling two of the most popular file formats. These are PCX, which may be the most widely used of all the PC graphics formats, and BMP/DIB, which is the standard format used in Microsoft Windows. Most graphics tools can export files in one or both of these formats, so it usually isn't a problem to convert files to one of these. Both formats support 8-bit and 24-bit images, as well as other color depths. Both formats feature very simple image compression algorithms, which makes them easy to work with. The downside of this, of course, is that they don't compress images very well, and thus graphics files in these formats tend to be fairly large.

The PCX File Format

Created by ZSoft for use by the PC Paintbrush series of paint pro-grams, the PCX format has gone through several revisions, almost literally tracking the development of PC-based graphics hardware. The original version of the format supported only monochrome and 4-color images; this capability matched that of the original IBM Monochrome Display Adapter (MDA) and Color Graphics Adapter (CGA). Version 2 added support for 16-color images, a capability of IBM's Enhanced Graphics Adapter (EGA). Version 5, the most recent revision, supports both 8-bit and 24-bit color images.

PCX files are pretty simple to decode. The file begins with a 128-byte header, which contains all descriptive information about the image, including the image's color palette if the image is a 4-color or 16-color image. This header is immediately followed by the image data itself, which is usually compressed according to a simple run-length compression algorithm. The header is described by the fol-lowing structure:

```
typedef struct {
    ABYTE manufacturer;      // must be 10
    ABYTE version;           // 0, 2, 3, or 5 (what happned to 1 and 4?)
    ABYTE encoding;          // 1 = run-length image compression, 0 = uncomp.
    ABYTE bitsPerPixel;      // number of bits per pixel per plane
    AWORD16 xmin;            // left edge
    AWORD16 ymin;            // top edge
    AWORD16 xmax;            // right edge
    AWORD16 ymax;            // bottom edge
    AWORD16 hres;           // horizontal resolution in dpi
    AWORD16 vres;           // vertical resolution in dpi
    ABYTE colorMap16[48];    // palette for 16-color images
    ABYTE reserved;          // 0
    ABYTE nplanes;           // number of planes per pixel
    AWORD16 rowbytes;        // number of bytes per line (even)
    AWORD16 paletteInfo;     // 1 = color/bw 2 = grayscale
    AWORD16 screenWidth;     // in pixels
    AWORD16 screenHeight;    // in pixels
    ABYTE pad[54];           // 0
} PcxHeader;
```

If this 128-byte header is followed directly by a variable-length compressed image, which it is, where, then, does the palette for 8-bit images go (remember, 24-bit images are direct RGB representations and thus have no palette)? This dilemma was faced by ZSoft when revising the format to handle 8-bit images, and highlights the prob-lems inherent in revising graphics file formats. In previous versions of the format, before the advent of 8-bit images, the 16-entry palette built into the header was sufficient.

The typedefs ABYTE and AWORD16 are used in this and other structures which refer to disk-based information. These types are used instead of the obvious 'uchar' and 'short', because the latter types are not guaranteed by the compiler to be any particular size on a given machine. On a 64-bit processor, for instance, a 'short' might be 32 bits in length. The header file ATYPES.H allows the types ABYTE, AWORD16, and AWORD32 to be modified to match the appropriate types for such a compiler. The definitions currently supplied in this file work on all 16-bit and 32-bit compiler implementations. It's also important to make sure your compiler is aligning structure members properly on byte boundaries. The compiler flags specified in ARTT's makefiles specify byte-alignment.

If the PCX format was a chunk-based format like IFF or TIFF, a new chunk could have been defined to hold the palette, and everything would have been fine. But the PCX header has space defined in it for only 16 color palette entries, and there is not enough room to fit a 256-entry palette. So where *does* it go? At the end of the file, after the image data, of course! Where else *could* it go? The palette is found by seeking to the end of the file, backing up 769 bytes (a 256-

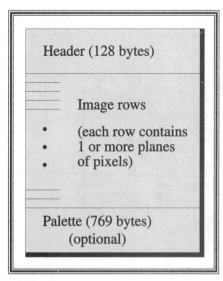

Figure 3.3 Structure of a PCX graphics file.

entry palette is 3 * 256 = 768 bytes), and checking for the special "palette marker" byte with the value 12, which verifies the existence of the palette. Why this marker byte is necessary, and what prevents some random PCX file from having a pixel byte with this value in this position by happenstance, is a mystery (to me at least). Figure 3.3 shows the overall structure of a PCX file.

Eight-bit images have a 'bitsPerPixel' setting of 8 and an 'nplanes' of 1. Twenty-four-bit images also have a 'bitsPerPixel' of 8, but have an 'nplanes' of 3. The idea here is that 24-bit images have 8 bits of each of the red, green, and blue components, and there are three such components.

The image data in a PCX file may be compressed or uncompressed, although I have never yet encountered one that wasn't compressed. Regardless of compression, the image data consists of a series of rows, starting from the top of the picture and working to the bottom. In the case of 8-bit uncompressed images, each row of the image is simply an array of 8-bit pixel values. If the 8-bit image is compressed, each row is compressed separately, according to an algorithm to be described shortly. In the case of 24-bit images, each of the three color components is stored separately, one component's row after another—a full row of pixels in a 24-bit PCX image consists of three independent subrows, one per component. Figure 3.4 shows the ordering of image data in a 24-bit PCX file.

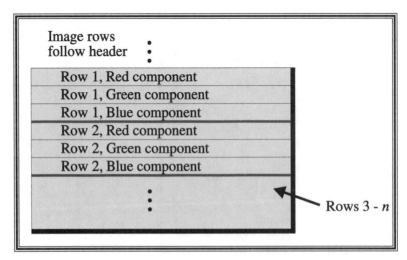

Figure 3.4 Ordering of image data in a 24-bit PCX file.

PCX Run-Length Compression

The method used to compress a row of pixels in a PCX file is very simple. It is a form of *run-length* compression, in which a "run" of adjacent and identical pixel values is encoded into a single two-byte token. Run-length compression in general offers good compression of images which feature large areas of solid color, and is generally poor on complex images, particularly natural or photographic ones, where there is very little in the way of runs of identical pixels. The form of run-length compression used in PCX files is poorer than most run-length schemes—the RLE8 bitmap format used in ARTT offers better compression and faster decoding too, without being any more complex.

When reading from a compressed PCX row, each byte must be examined to see if the high 2 bits are set. If they are, the value represents a run of identical pixels. In this case, the number of pixels in the run is encoded in the low 6 bits of this byte, and the pixel value to be replicated is in the next byte. On the other hand, if the first 2 bits of the byte are not both set, then the byte itself is the pixel value, with a run count of 1. Figure 3.5 shows a flowchart for decoding a PCX row.

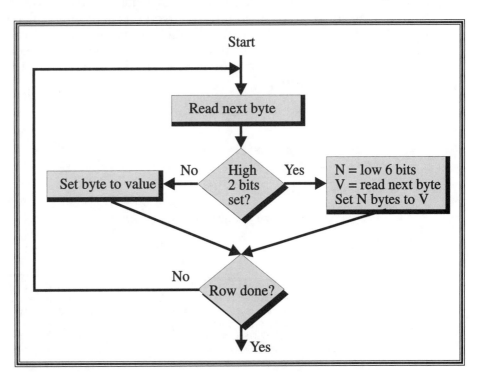

Figure 3.5 Flowchart for decoding a row of compressed pixels from a PCX file.

Note that pixel values from 0xC0 to 0xFF (high 2 bits set) must be represented in runs, because storing a single pixel in this range would cause the decoder to misinterpret the byte as a run count. Thus a single pixel value in this range takes 2 bytes to represent— not much compression there! I have seen several real compressed PCX files which are greater in length than they would be if the image data was uncompressed. The PCX standard has survived more because of its roots and its simplicity than because it offers good compression.

Class APcxFile: Reading and Writing PCX Files

Because of the wide variety of color depths the PCX format supports and its various versions, providing a full implementation of a PCX reader requires a fair amount of effort. Since version 5 has been around since 1991, the ARTT reader implementation ignores other versions. Also, this reader only supports 8-bit and 24-bit images. Monochrome, 2-bit, and 4-bit PCX images are rare nowadays and can always be converted to 8-bit before use with ARTT if need be.

The header file for class APcxFile is listed below. Note that only the constructor is public, and even it is generally called only by AGfx-File::Read() or AGfxFile::Write(), not by user code directly. The 'compressed' member variable and the other methods are private, and are used by the constructor in loading the image from the file into the supplied bitmap.

```
//   APcxFile.h    Graphics File for PCX files
//   Rex E. Bradford

#ifndef __APCXFILE_H
#define __APCXFILE_H

#include "agfxfile.h"

class APcxFile : public AGfxFile {

    bool compressed; // is PCX data run-length compressed?

// Private methods
    AError ReadFile(ABitmap &bm);                    // read entire bitmap
    AError ReadPalFromFile(ABitmap &bm);             // read palette
    AError ReadBitsFromFile(ABitmap &bm);            // read bitmap bits
    AError ReadBits8(ABitmap &bm);                   // read 8-bit bits
    AError ReadBits24(ABitmap &bm);                  // read 24-bit bits
    AError ReadRow(ABitmap &bm, uchar *p);           // read a single row
    void ReadPcxToken(uchar &c, short &count);       // read a single token
```

```
    AError WriteFile(ABitmap &bm);              // write entire bitmap
    void WriteRow(uchar *p, int len);           // write a single row
    void WriteToken(int &currVal, int &count);  // write a single token

public:
    APcxFile(FILE *fp, ABitmap &bm, int &err, bool read = TRUE);
};


#endif
```

The APcxFile constructor checks the state of the 'read' argument, and calls APcxFile::ReadFile() or APcxFile::WriteFile().

```
APcxFile::APcxFile(FILE *fp, ABitmap &bm, AError &err, bool read) :
    AGfxFile(fp)
{
    if (read)
        err = ReadFile(bm);
    else
        err = WriteFile(bm);
}
```

APcxFile::ReadFile() is responsible for reading in the image and palette into the supplied bitmap, while verifying that the image data is valid. It first reads the header and verifies that the file is a valid PCX file, of version 5, in 8-bit or 24-bit format. If all is well, it constructs the bitmap, using the ABitmap constructor which allocates memory for the bitmap's data bits (field 'pbits') when passed a NULL pointer argument. It then calls ReadBitsFromFile() to read the image data into the bitmap. If there are no errors yet, it calls ReadPalFromFile() for 8-bit images only, to read the bitmap's color palette.

```
AError APcxFile::ReadFile(ABitmap &bm)
{
// Read image header

    PcxHeader hdr;
    fread(&hdr, sizeof(hdr), 1, fp); // read in 128-byte header

// Verify manufacturer, version, bitsPerPixel, and numPlanes

    if (hdr.manufacturer != 10) return AERR_BADFORMAT;
    if (hdr.version != 5) return AERR_BADFORMAT;
    if (hdr.bitsPerPixel != 8) return AERR_BADFORMAT;
    if ((hdr.nplanes != 1) && (hdr.nplanes != 3)) return AERR_BADFORMAT;

// Allocate and init bitmap
```

```
    bm = ABitmap(NULL,
        (hdr.nplanes == 1) ? BMF_LIN8 : BMF_LIN24,
        FALSE,
        (hdr.xmax - hdr.xmin) + 1,
        (hdr.ymax - hdr.ymin + 1));
    if (bm.pbits == NULL)
        return AERR_NOMEM;

// Set compression flag, read image and optionally palette

    compressed = hdr.encoding;
    AError err = ReadBitsFromFile(bm);
    if (!err && (bm.format == BMF_LIN8))
        err = ReadPalFromFile(bm);
    return err;
}
```

The routine to read the palette, which is called only for 8-bit images, is listed below. It seeks to the location 769 bytes before the end of the file and looks for the magic value 12 there. If this test is passed, the next 768 bytes are read and a palette is constructed from them. Before the palette is constructed, the RGB triplets are run through a "swapper," because ARTT stores them in the order blue, green, red (to match typical 24-bit video cards), whereas PCX files store them in the order red, green, blue. Life was easier when we all just bought IBM (there was no green or red then, only blue).

```
AError APcxFile::ReadPalFromFile(ABitmap &bm)
{
    fseek(fp, -769L, SEEK_END);    // go to end of file, back up 769
    uchar palFlag = fgetc(fp);     // check for magic value 12
    if (palFlag == 12)
        {
        uchar rgb[256 * 3];
        fread(rgb, 256 * 3, 1, fp);        // read in palette
        uchar *prgb = rgb;
        for (int i = 0; i < 256; i++, prgb += 3)
            {
            uchar temp = *prgb;
            *prgb = *(prgb+2);
            *(prgb+2) = temp;
            }
        bm.ppalette = new APalette(rgb); // construct palette
        if (!bm.ppalette)
            return AERR_NOMEM;                // if can't alloc, return err
        }
    return AERR_OK;
}
```

Reading the image data is done in APcxFile::ReadBitsFrom-File() and other routines which it calls. ReadBitsFromFile() simply hands off to one of two other methods, based on whether the image is an 8-bit image or a 24-bit one.

```
AError APcxFile::ReadBitsFromFile(ABitmap &bm)
{
   fseek(fp, sizeof(PcxHeader), SEEK_SET);    // seek to data past header

   if (bm.format == BMF_LIN8)
      return(ReadBits8(bm));            // call 8-bit read routine
   else
      return(ReadBits24(bm));          // or 24-bit read routine
}
```

APcxFile::ReadBits8() reads an 8-bit image, using successive calls to ReadRow() for each row in the image.

```
AError APcxFile::ReadBits8(ABitmap &bm)
{
   uchar *p = bm.pbits;

   for (int y = 0; y < bm.height; y++, p += bm.rowbytes)
      {
      AError err = ReadRow(bm, p);    // for each row, read it
      if (err) return(err);           // if error, return it
      }
   return AERR_OK;
}
```

APcxFile::ReadBits24() loads 24-bit images. For each row of the bitmap, one call to ReadRow() is made, to read the red, green, and blue components into a temporary buffer. Then an interleaving pass is made through this buffer, transferring the color bytes into the destination bitmap's row in ARTT BMF_LIN24 format. Here, each pixel is composed of blue, green, and red bytes stored together.

```
AError APcxFile::ReadBits24(ABitmap &bm)
{
   uchar *p = bm.pbits;
   uchar *prgb = new uchar[bm.rowbytes];         // allocate 1 row buff
   int numRgb = bm.rowbytes / 3;

   AError err = AERR_OK;
   for (int y = 0; y < bm.height; y++)           // loop thru rows
      {
      err = ReadRow(bm, prgb);                   // read all 3 planes
      if (err)
         break;
      uchar *pred = prgb;
      uchar *pgreen = pred + numRgb;
      uchar *pblue = pgreen + numRgb;
      for (int x = 0; x < numRgb; x++)           // interleave data
```

```
            {
            *p++ = *pblue++;
            *p++ = *pgreen++;
            *p++ = *pred++;
            }
        }

    delete prgb; // free row buffer
    return err;
}
```

APcxFile::ReadRow() is called to read a single row, for one or three planes. In the rare case where the row is uncompressed, a simple fread() does the trick. Compressed rows are handled using the algorithm flowcharted in Figure 3.5 on page 91.

```
AError APcxFile::ReadRow(ABitmap &bm, uchar *p)
{
    if (!compressed)
        {
        fread(p, bm.rowbytes, 1, fp);      // uncompressed, just read row
        return AERR_OK;
        }
    else
        {
        uchar *pend = p + bm.rowbytes;     // else if compressed, set row end
        while (p < pend)                   // loop until reach end
            {
            uchar c;
            short count;
            ReadPcxToken(c, count);        // get pixel value and run count
            if ((p + count) > pend)        // check for overrun error
                return AERR_BADFORMAT;
            memset(p, c, count);           // else copy run into buffer
            p += count;                    // and update buffer ptr
            }
        return AERR_OK;
        }
}
```

Finally, APcxFile::ReadPcxToken() is used by ReadRow() to read a single token from the PCX file, returning the color value and count. If the high 2 bits of the current byte are both set to 1, this represents a compressed token—the low 6 bits are the pixel count, and the next byte supplies the value. If the high 2 bits are not both set to 1, the byte is the value, and the count is 1.

```
void APcxFile::ReadPcxToken(uchar &c, short &count)
{
    c = fgetc(fp);                     // get next byte value
    if (0xC0 == (0xC0 & c))            // if both high bits set
        {
        count = c & 0x3F;             // then count in low 6 bits
```

```
      c = fgetc(fp);                // and pixel value in next byte
      }
   else
      count = 1;                    // else byte is value, with count 1
}
```

That's all there is to reading PCX files, at least those which have 8-bit or 24-bit images in them. The bitmap returned by the APcxFile constructor, assuming no errors, is ready for rendering.

Writing PCX files is similar. The code for APcxFile::WriteFile() and associated methods is not included here—see the CD.

The BMP File Format

The BMP format was invented by Microsoft for its Windows environment, and a variant of the format is used in OS/2. BMP files are used by Windows itself for its logo screen and desktop wallpaper files (just search your \WINDOWS directory for *.bmp files). Icons are *not* typically stored in BMP files; there is a separate ICO format which allows for multiple versions of the icon for different screen resolutions and color depths (Windows can decide "on the fly" which of several variants will look best on the display).

Windows programmers hear a lot about *device-independent bitmaps,* and such DIBs are often stored in files ending in the extension DIB. There is absolutely no difference between a BMP file and a DIB file other than the extension. A third extension, RLE, is also sometimes used for these files.

The BMP file format is somewhat similar to the PCX format in overall structure, although the BMP image compression format is a little more complex. The file begins with a header, which is optionally followed by a color palette. Following the palette, if any, is the image data, which may or may not be compressed. Figure 3.6 shows a block diagram of a BMP file.

The BMP File Header

Every BMP file begins with a 14-byte file header, which can be used to verify that this is indeed a BMP file, and furthermore gives the offset of the image bits in the file. The structure of this header is given below:

```
typedef struct {
   AWORD16 bfType;      // 'BM'
   AWORD32 bfSize;      // size of file (for error-check)
   AWORD16 bfReserved1; // 0
   AWORD16 bfReserved2; // 0
   AWORD32 bfOffbits;   // byte offset in file to bits
} BmpFileHeader;
```

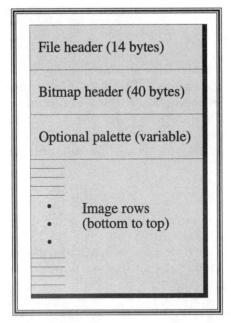

Figure 3.6 Structure of a BMP graphics file.

This file header is immediately followed by a second header, which contains information about the image contained in the file. This information includes the image's width, height, color depth, and compression format, among other things. To allow for future growth of the format, the first longword in the information header gives its own length. This should be used to compute the location in the file of the color palette, by adding it to the size of the fixed-size file header. This way, if a new version of the BMP file format has a larger information structure, the palette can still be reliably found.

The bitmap information structure is given below:

```
typedef struct {
    AWORD32 biSize;            // size of this struct (usually 40)
    AWORD32 biWidth;           // in pixels
    AWORD32 biHeight;          // in pixels
    AWORD16 biPlanes;          // always 1
    AWORD16 biBitCount;        // num bits per pixel (1, 4, 8, 16, 24, 32)
    AWORD32 biCompression;     // BI_RGB, BI_RLE8, BI_RLE4
    AWORD32 biSizeImage;       // image size in bytes
    AWORD32 biXPelsPerMeter;   // horizontal resolution
    AWORD32 biYPelsPerMeter;   // vertical resolution
    AWORD32 biClrUsed;         // number of colors, or 0 for max
    AWORD32 biClrImportant;    // number of important colors
} BmpInfoHeader;
```

The last two fields are a bit odd. They are hints to Microsoft Windows as to the number of colors in the palette actually used in the image, and how important they are to maintain image fidelity. Windows can take this information into account when trying to achieve the best color palette across a set of windows, each of which want a different palette.

Note that OS/2 BMP files use a variant of the bitmap info header. The ABmpFile class cannot read or write these files.

Images may consist of 1, 4, 8, 16, 24, or 32 bits per pixel. The 4-bit images, which contain up to 16 unique colors, are still fairly common, and the ARTT reader we're about to see supports them by converting them to 8-bit format. The 16-bit images are in the same 5-5-5 RGB format used in ARTT's BMF_LIN15 format; the high bit of each word is unused and set to 0. Two true-color formats are available, 24-bit and 32-bit. The 32-bit form, as well as the 16-bit form, are recent additions to the standard which match bitmap formats supported by newer graphics cards. The ARTT reader doesn't support the 32-bit form, which is quite rare anyway. Another recent addition to the standard allows the specification of "bitfields" which allow the red, green, and blue components of an arbitrary format to be specified in terms of bit masks. This format is very new and little used, and is similarly unsupported here.

Unless the image is a 24-bit or 32-bit true-color image, a color palette follows the information header. Even 1-bit images are not necessarily monochrome; they have a 2-entry palette. Four-bit images have a 16-entry palette, and 8-bit images have a 256-entry palette. The 'biClrUsed' field of the information header specifies how many colors actually appear in the image, not how many entries exist in the palette.

If there is a palette, it is composed of an array of 4-byte entries. A byte each of red, green, and blue is present, followed by an unused pad byte. The structure of such an 'RgbQuad' entry is given below:

```
typedef struct {
    uchar b;          // blue
    uchar g;          // green
    uchar r;          // red
    uchar pad;        // so 4 bytes long
} RgbQuad;
```

BMP Image Data

The image data in a BMP file consists of a series of rows, which may be compressed or uncompressed. Unlike typical image file formats, in most BMP files the image data starts at the *bottom* row of the image and works up. This format seems upside down, and is in fact upside down in relation to the memory layout of all PC-based video hardware. What gives? The bottom-up layout has its roots in OS/2 Presentation Manager, which was originally a joint venture between Microsoft and IBM. Presentation Manager coordinates place 0,0 at the bottom-left corner of the screen, and *y* increases up the screen. The BMP layout matches this. Some programmers and mathematicians feel that this is a more "correct" coordinate system.[1]

Uncompressed BMP image rows are very like uncompressed PCX image rows, and there isn't a whole lot to say about them. One important point is that, for memory access efficiency reasons, all uncompressed rows are aligned on 4-byte boundaries. Rows are padded to the right to observe this requirement. For instance, an 8-bit bitmap with a width of 62 pixels will have 2 pad bytes at the end of each row, because 64 is the closest multiple of 4. In 4-bit BMP images, by the way, the leftmost pixel is stored in the high nibble of a byte, and the rightmost pixel in the low nibble.

BMP Compression Formats

The compression format is specified in the 'biCompression' field of the bitmap info header. It may take on one of the following values, although values for new compression schemes may be added in the future.

```
#define BI_RGB 0        // no compression (always used for 15/24 bit)
#define BI_RLE8 1       // 8-bit RLE compression
#define BI_RLE4 2       // 4-bit RLE compression
#define BI_BITFIELDS 3  // customized bitfields (NOT SUPPORTED BY ARTT)
```

The BI_RGB format identifies the image data as uncompressed, and is currently required for 1-bit, 16-bit, 24-bit, and 32-bit bitmaps. This can make for some very large files. For instance, a 640×480 24-bit image file will be almost a megabyte in length.

Four-bit and 8-bit images may be compressed or uncompressed. In either the BI_RLE8 (8-bit) or BI_RLE4 (4-bit) cases, a compressed image row is comprised of a series of "tokens." Each token begins with a 2-byte sequence which gives the token type and some auxiliary information. Some tokens consist only of the 2-byte sequence; others make use of successive bytes. There are five token types in the format, as listed in Table 3.2.

---

[1]Much of IBM's Presentation Manager development was done in England, where they drive on the wrong side of the road, after all.

Table 3.2   Tokens in BMP Compressed Image Encoding

Token	Meaning
00 00	End of row—begin next row.
00 01	End of image—stop decompressing.
00 02 dx dy	Delta vector—advance to different row/column of image.
00 nn [...]	Copy pixels—copy *nn* successive pixels into image.
nn vv	Run of pixels—copy *nn* pixels of value *vv* to image.

These tokens are described in more detail below:

00 00 - End of row

When this token is encountered, the decoding of the current row is complete. The next token in the file will be at the start of the next row.

00 01 - End of image

When this token is encountered, the decoding of the entire image is complete.

00 02 dx dy - Delta vector

Delta vectors are used to encode a "jump" to another location in the image. Delta encoding is very useful in animation, where one of a succession of *frames* of an image may change only slightly from the previous frame. Delta encoding can then quickly skip over unchanged pixels and go directly to the part of the image that is changing. Delta vectors could also be used to implement transparency, skipping over pixels which shouldn't be drawn. However, I have never encountered a BMP file which has a delta vector in it. Since the image data in a BMP file is essentially the same as a device-independent bitmap (DIB) in memory, it may be that delta vectors are meant for use with in-memory DIBs and not really with BMP files. In any case, the two bytes after the token are used to hold the relative number of rows and columns of pixels to advance by.

00 nn [...] - Copy pixels

If the first byte is 0 and the second is 3 or higher, the token is a "copy" token. The number of pixels to copy is given in the second byte. Therefore at least 3 pixels must be copied. The number of bytes in the data following the token must be even, so there may be an unused byte after the pixels are copied that must be skipped over. For instance, the following sequence in an 8-bit image specifies that the 3 bytes 66, 67, and 68 must be copied, and the next byte (00) skipped over, so that the total number of bytes in the sequence is even:

```
00 03 66 67 68 00
```

In the case of 4-bit copy tokens, each byte contains two pixels, the leftmost in the high nibble and the rightmost in the low nibble. Since the data must be an even number of *bytes*, as many as 3 nibblesized pixels may be unused. For instance, the following token copies the 5 pixel values 8, 5, and 2, 1, and 6:

```
00 03 85 21 60 00
```

```
nn vv - Run of pixels
```

A first byte which is nonzero signifies a run of pixels. The first byte holds the number of pixels to be written, and the second byte holds the pixel value(s). In the case of 8-bit images, the second byte is just the pixel value. In the case of 4-bit images, the second byte holds two pixel values, one in each nibble, and the two values are not necessarily the same. The two nibble pixel values are alternately written. For instance, in a 4-bit run the sequence 05 71 causes the following pixels to be written: 7 1 7 1 7.

Bottom-Up versus Top-Down

While most BMP files are bottom-up, meaning that the bottommost row of the bitmap appears first in the file, the format has been modified to allow specification of top-down bitmaps as well. A good BMP reader should be able to handle both varieties, even though most BMP files are still bottom-up. Since the top-down format matches the hardware of all display cards more directly, the quest for rendering speed under Windows has pushed the adoption of top-down DIBs, at least for memory-based bitmaps.

How are top-down bitmaps differentiated from bottom-up ones? The 'biHeight' field of the bitmap info header is set to a negative number if the bitmap data is top-down. The real height, then, is the absolute value of 'biHeight'. The BMP reader we will build shortly will support both bottom-up and top-down files, converting both into one of ARTT's bitmap formats, which are all top-down.

Class ABmpFile: Reading and Writing BMP Files

The implementation of the BMP access class in ARTT does not handle 1-bit or 32-bit images, but does handle the other color depths. Since ARTT itself does not support 4-bit bitmaps, 4-bit images are expanded to 8-bit bitmaps during the read process. Support for 4-bit BMP files is important because so many of the BMP files in existence are 4-bit (16-color) files.

The header file for class ABmpFile is listed below. Like the APcx-File class, only the constructor is public; the other methods are used by the constructor to assist it in reading and writing images.

```
//    ABmpFile.h    Graphics File for BMP files
//    Rex E. Bradford

#ifndef __ABMPFILE_H
#define __ABMPFILE_H

#include "agfxfile.h"

class ABmpFile : public AGfxFile {
    ulong bitsOffset;    // file offset to image bits
    ulong palOffset;     // file offset to palette dat
    ulong compression;   // compression format
    ushort bitsPerPixel; // 4, 8, 15, or 24
    long height;         // true height of bitmap
    int direction;       // +1 = top-down, -1 = bottom-up

    AError ReadFile(ABitmap &bm);                     // read entire file
    AError ReadPalFromFile(ABitmap &bm);              // read palette
    AError ReadBitsFromFile(ABitmap &bm);             // read bitmap image
    AError ReadBitmapNotCompressed(ABitmap &bm);// read uncompressed
    AError ReadBitmapCompressed(ABitmap &bm);    // read compressed

    AError WriteFile(ABitmap &bm);                    // write entire file

public:
    ABmpFile(FILE *fp, ABitmap &bm, int &err, bool read = TRUE);
};

#endif
```

Note that several member variables are used by the file-reading code. These are read or calculated from the file's header, and put into these variables to make them accessible to the various methods which read image data from the file.

The ABmpFile constructor checks the 'read' argument and calls ReadFile() or WriteFile().

```
ABmpFile::ABmpFile(FILE *fp, ABitmap &bm, AError &err, bool read) :
    AGfxFile(fp)
```

```
{
   if (read)
      err = ReadFile(bm);
   else
      err = WriteFile(bm);
}
```

ABmpFile::ReadFile() is responsible for verifying the file, and reading in the image (and palette for 8-bit images). Its overall flow closely parallels that of APcxFile::ReadFile().

```
AError ABmpFile::ReadFile(ABitmap &bm)
{
   BmpFileHeader hdr;
   BmpInfoHeader info;

// Read both parts of header

   fread(&hdr, sizeof(hdr), 1, fp);
   fread(&info, sizeof(info), 1, fp);

// Verify 'BM' marker, file length, other info

   if (hdr.bfType != 0x4D42) return AERR_BADFORMAT;
#ifdef CHECK_FILE_LENGTH
   fseek(fp, 0L, SEEK_END);
   if (ftell(fp) != hdr.bfSize) return AERR_BADFORMAT;
#endif
   if (info.biSize != sizeof(info)) return AERR_BADFORMAT;
   if (info.biPlanes != 1) return AERR_BADFORMAT;
   if (info.biBitCount == 1) return AERR_BADFORMAT;

// See if bottom-up or top-down, set direction and positive height

   direction = -1;              // assume bottom-up
   height = info.biHeight;      // width positive height
   if (height < 0)
      {
      direction = +1;           // nope, top-down
      height = -height;         // negative, height, make positive
      }

// Allocate and init bitmap

   switch (info.biBitCount)
      {
      case 4:        // 4-bit images are aligned on long (8-pixel) bounds
         bm = ABitmap((uchar *) NULL, BMF_LIN8, FALSE, info.biWidth,
            height, (info.biWidth + 7) & 0xFFF8);
         break;
```

```
      case 8:        // 8-bit images are aligned on long (4-pixel) bounds
         bm = ABitmap((uchar *) NULL, BMF_LIN8, FALSE, info.biWidth,
            height, (info.biWidth + 3) & 0xFFFC);
         break;

      case 16:        // 16-bit images are aligned on long (2-pixel) bounds
         bm = ABitmap((uchar *) NULL, BMF_LIN15, FALSE, info.biWidth,
            height, ((info.biWidth * 2) + 3) & 0xFFFC);
         break;

      case 24:        // 24-bit images are aligned on long bounds
         bm = ABitmap((uchar *) NULL, BMF_LIN24, FALSE, info.biWidth,
            height, ((info.biWidth * 3) + 3) & 0xFFFC);
         break;

      default:
         bm.pbits = NULL;
         return AERR_BADFORMAT;
      }

// Check for bitmap allocation error

   if (bm.pbits == NULL)
      return AERR_NOMEM;

// Set some variables needed by image reader

   bitsOffset = hdr.bfOffbits;
   palOffset = sizeof(hdr) + info.biSize;
   compression = info.biCompression;
   bitsPerPixel = info.biBitCount;

// Read image and palette

   AError err = ReadBitsFromFile(bm);
   if (!err && bm.format == BMF_LIN8)
      err = ReadPalFromFile(bm);
   return err;
}
```

The routine to read the palette, which is called for 4-bit and 8-bit images, is listed below. It must convert from the file's RgbQuad format into ARTT's palette format, and also cope with the fact that the palette in the file may have less than 256 colors.

```
AError ABmpFile::ReadPalFromFile(ABitmap &bm)
{
// Palette to read into is on stack, zero it in case partial-pal

   uchar rgb[256 * 3];
   memset(rgb, 0, sizeof(rgb));
```

```
// Seek to palette, determine number of entries

    fseek(fp, palOffset, SEEK_SET);
    int numPalette = 1 << bitsPerPixel;

// Read palette entries from file, convert from 4-byte to 3-byte format

    uchar *pp = rgb;
    for (int i = 0; i < numPalette; i++)
        {
        RgbQuad rgbq;
        fread(&rgbq, sizeof(RgbQuad), 1, fp);
        *pp++ = rgbq.b;
        *pp++ = rgbq.g;
        *pp++ = rgbq.r;
        }

// Construct palette, err if can't, else groovy

    bm.ppalette = new APalette(rgb);
    if (!bm.ppalette)
        return AERR_NOMEM;
    else
        return AERR_OK;
}
```

Reading the image data is done in ABmpFile::ReadBitsFrom-File() and other routines which it calls. ReadBitsFromFile() hands off to one of two methods, depending on whether the image data is compressed or not.

```
AError ABmpFile::ReadBitsFromFile(ABitmap &bm)
{
// Seek to start of image, call compressed or uncompressed decoder

    fseek(fp, bitsOffset, SEEK_SET);
    if (compression)
        return(ReadBitmapCompressed(bm));
    else
        return(ReadBitmapNotCompressed(bm));
}
```

ABmpFile::ReadBitmapNotCompressed() handles uncompressed images. Besides some logic for setting up top-down versus bottom-up reading, the only complication is expanding 4-bit images into 8-bit form. For 8-bit, 16-bit, and 24-bit images, the data is in precisely the format we want, so a simple fread() is used to load each row.

```
AError ABmpFile::ReadBitmapNotCompressed(ABitmap &bm)
{
// Assume top-down bitmap
```

```
        uchar *pd = bm.pbits;              // assume top-down
        long rowAdjust = bm.rowbytes;      // and moving downwards
        int ystart = 0;                    // from 0 to height
        int yend = height;

// If bottom-up, adjust parameters

        if (direction < 0)
            {
            pd += (long(height - 1) * long(bm.rowbytes));
            rowAdjust = -rowAdjust;
            ystart = height;
            yend = 0;
            }

// Traverse rows, either top-down or bottom-up

        for (int y = ystart; y != yend; y += direction, pd += rowAdjust)
            {

// If 4-bit image, expand to 8-bit bitmap

            if (bitsPerPixel == 4)
                {
                uchar *pd1 = pd;
                for (int x = 0; x < bm.rowbytes; x += 2)
                    {
                    uchar c = fgetc(fp);
                    *pd1++ = c >> 4;
                    *pd1++ = c & 0x0F;
                    }
                }

// Else 8-bit, 15-bit, or 24-bit image, just read row straight in

            else
                fread(pd, bm.rowbytes, 1, fp);
            }
        return AERR_OK;
}
```

ABmpFile::ReadBitmapCompressed() is fairly complex, particularly because it is capable of handling both the 4-bit and the 8-bit varieties. The method starts by setting up for top-down or bottom-up processing, and then enters a loop for each row. Within a row, it decodes the compression tokens until it encounters an end-of-bitmap or end-of-line token. Support for the delta vector token is included, even though I couldn't find a single image which included one to test on!

```
AError ABmpFile::ReadBitmapCompressed(ABitmap &bm)
{
// Assume top-down bitmap

    uchar *pdbase = bm.pbits;          // assume top-down
    long rowAdjust = bm.rowbytes;      // and moving downwards
    int ystart = 0;                    // from 0 to height
    int yend = height;

// If bottom-up, adjust parameters

    if (direction < 0)
        {
        pdbase += (long(height - 1) * long(bm.rowbytes));
        rowAdjust = -rowAdjust;
        ystart = height;
        yend = 0;
        }

// Traverse rows, either top-down or bottom-up

    for (int y = ystart; y != yend; y += direction, pdbase += rowAdjust)
        {
        uchar *pd = pdbase;

// Loop thru two-byte compression tokens until hit 0,0 code

        while (TRUE)
            {
            uchar c = fgetc(fp);
            uchar c2 = fgetc(fp);

// If 1st byte of token is nonzero, this is a run

            if (c)
                {
// Run of 8-bit pixels: run count in first byte, pixel value in 2nd byte

                if (bitsPerPixel == 8)
                    {
                    memset(pd, c2, c);
                    pd += c2;
                    }

// Run of 4-bit pixels: run count in 1st byte, pixel pair in 2nd byte

                else
                    {
                    for (int i = 0; i < c; i++)
                        {
                        if (i & 1)
                            *pd++ = c2 & 0x0F;
                        else
```

```
                            *pd++ = c2 >> 4;
                        }
                }
            }

// Else if 1st byte of token is a zero, it's a special token

            else
                {
                switch (c2)
                    {
                    uchar dx,dy,dummy;
                    int nbytes;

// 0,0 token: end of line, break out of loop

                    case 0:
                        break;

// 0,1 token: end of bitmap

                    case 1:
                        return AERR_OK;

// 0,2 token: delta token, read dx,dy from next bytes and advance
// Adjust y and pdbase by (dy - 1) because loop does 1 for us

                    case 2:
                        dx = fgetc(fp);
                        dy = fgetc(fp);
                        pd += dx;
                        y += (dy - 1) * direction;
                        pdbase += (dy - 1) * rowAdjust;
                        break;

// 0,n token (n >= 3): copy n pixels from file

                    default:

// Copy 8-bit pixels: read from file, keep file word-aligned

                        if (bitsPerPixel == 8)
                            {
                            fread(pd, c2, 1, fp);
                            pd += c2;
                            if (c2 & 1)
                                dummy = fgetc(fp);
                            }

// Copy 4-bit pixels: read from file, keep file word-aligned

                        else
                            {
                            nbytes = ((int) c2) >> 1;
```

```
                    while (nbytes--)
                        {
                        c = fgetc(fp);
                        *pd++ = c >> 4;
                        *pd++ = c & 0x0F;
                        }
                    if (c2 & 1)
                        *pd++ = fgetc(fp) >> 4;
                    if (((c2 & 3) == 1) || ((c2 & 3) == 2))
                        dummy = fgetc(fp);
                    }
                break;
                }
            if (c2 == 0) // make 0,0 case break out of while(TRUE)
                break;
            }

// Processed token: check for overrun

        if ((pd - pdbase) > bm.rowbytes)
            return AERR_BADFORMAT;
        }
    }

// I can't believe we made it without crashing...

    return AERR_OK;
}
```

Adding Support for Additional Graphics File Formats

Adding support for a new format is pretty straightforward. Besides the hard part of writing a new AGfxFile-derived class along the lines of APcxFile and ABmpFile, the AGfxFile::Read() and Write() methods must be modified to include a new case in the extension-based switch statement. That's it—with a recompile and relink, any program which handled PCX and BMP files will now handle the new types as well!

GFXSHOW1: Image Viewer, Version 1

Armed with the ability to read in bitmapped images and their palettes, program the VGA palette registers, and display bitmaps (we learned how to do that in Chapter 2), we are ready to enjoy the fruits of our labor. GFXSHOW1 is a program which takes the name of a PCX or BMP/DIB file on the command line, reads in the image, and displays it onscreen with the proper palette. Any keypress exits the program. We may not be writing DOOM yet, but the pieces are beginning to fall into place.

This version of GFXSHOW does not work with 15-bit or 24-bit images. It does handle both 8-bit images and the 4-bit images encountered in BMP files. Also, the program uses mode 13H, which has a screen resolution of 320×200. If the picture is greater than 320 pixels wide or 200 lines high, GFXSHOW1 will fail to display it, since it's not Chapter 4 yet and we haven't learned how to clip the image to the confines of the screen. In Chapter 5 we'll dive into Super VGA 8-bit modes, and a coming GFXSHOW2 will be able to display high-resolution, clipped images (but still not 15- or 24-bit; GFXSHOW3 comes later still).

If the file cannot be opened, or the data in the file is bad, or any other error is detected, GFXSHOW1 displays an appropriate error message. Here's the code:

```
//    Gfxshow1.cpp    Show graphics file (320 x 200, 256-color only)
//    Rex E. Bradford

#include <stdio.h>
#include <stdlib.h>
#include <conio.h>

#include "amode13.h"
#include "agfxfile.h"
#include "avga.h"

void main(int argc, char **argv)
{
// Make sure filename is specified

    if (argc <= 1)
        {
        printf("usage: gfxshow1 filename.ext\n");
        exit(1);
        }

// Read bitmap from file, check for error

    ABitmap bm;
    AError err = AGfxFile::Read(argv[1], bm);
    if (err)
        {
        printf("Problem with file: %s (%s)\n", argv[1], AErr::Msg(err));
        exit(1);
        }

// Make sure bitmap format is BMF_LIN8

    if (bm.format != BMF_LIN8)
        {
        printf("Can't handle format of gfx file (format: $%x)\n", bm.format);
```

```
        exit(1);
        }

// Make sure bitmap doesn't overflow screen

    if ((bm.width > 320) || (bm.height > 200))
        {
        printf("Image too large for mode 13 screen: %d x %d\n",
            bm.width, bm.height);
        exit(1);
        }

// Ok: construct mode 13 canvas, set DAC from bitmap, draw bitmap,
// wait for keystroke, and return to text mode

    AMode13::Launch();
    AVga::SetDAC(bm.ppalette->rgb);
    gCanvasScreen->DrawBitmapLin8U(bm, 0, 0);
    getch();
    AMode13::Term();
}
```

Figure 3.7 shows a sample screen shot from GFXSHOW1.

Figure 3.7 Screen shot from GFXSHOW1, the first version of a graphics file viewer.

GFX2GFX: A Graphics File Converter

One way of conquering the graphics file Tower of Babel is to have tools which can convert images between formats. With the ability to read and write graphics files, it's easy to "roll our own" solution! GFX2GFX is almost too easy—39 lines counting comments and blanks—the bulk of the code is spent parsing arguments and checking for errors. See the CD for the source listing.

While only PCX and BMP files can be converted currently, any new image file formats you write classes to support will automatically be handled by GFX2GFX, with only a relink. GFX2GFX is run from the command line, like so:

```
GFX2GFX infile outfile
```

Clipping, Rectangles, Lines, and Fixed-Point Numbers

So far, we've developed a basic rendering methodology centered around bitmaps and canvases, which are renderable bitmaps with associated "drawing attributes." We can place the PC display into a low-resolution graphics mode, and return to text mode before returning to DOS. We can pull bitmapped images out of graphics files in the PCX and BMP formats, and if they are 8-bit indexed color images we can render them onto the screen. We can also render such simple shapes as points, horizontal lines, vertical lines, boxes, and filled rectangles. Not bad for three chapters. This chapter and the next few will round out our knowledge of rendering "static" graphics onto 8-bit displays. Then, in Part 2, we'll add dazzling animation capabilities to our feast of graphics!

But first, we must eat our broccoli.

Clipping Basics

Depending on your personality type, you will find the topic of *clipping* to be: (a) a fascinating look at how perfect orderliness can be maintained in a computer graphics system, or (b) a pedantic bore that can't be over too soon. What is clipping? It refers to the business of confining a rendering operation to a portion of the drawing surface that the rendering operation would otherwise cover. Clipping is necessary for at least one very practical reason—to avoid crashing your computer. Figure 4.1 shows a bitmap whose bottom extends below the bottom of the canvas it is being rendered into. What happens if our rendering code just ignores the canvas bottom and keeps going—as our DrawBitmapLin8U() or similar routines would definitely do?

The results vary depending on circumstance, but none of them are pretty. Let's assume that the canvas being drawn to is the screen canvas, and we are in mode 13H. The memory address of the screen starts at physical address 0xA0000, and extends nearly to 0xB0000. If our bitmap extends below the screen bottom far enough, we will keep writing to memory all the way to 0xB0000 and beyond. What happens then? If there is a monochrome card in your system attached to a secondary monochrome display, random characters will start appearing on this display, because these memory addresses are used by the monochrome card. And if our mad rendering code keeps going all the way to address 0xC0000, where the VGA card's ROM "firmware" usually resides, and you have a memory manager like QEMM or 386MAX installed, which shadows ROM into RAM, it's reboot time.

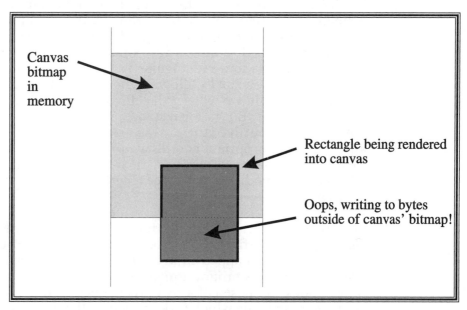

Figure 4.1   Drawing operation extending past bottom of canvas.

Less harmful but visually annoying is the case where the bitmap extends off the right edge of the canvas. Since the rightmost pixel of a row is followed in memory by the leftmost pixel of the next row, the image will "wrap around" one row down. Kind of unsightly.

And what if the canvas being rendered into is an off-screen canvas, whose bitmap memory has been allocated with new()? Draw past the bottom of this canvas, and you will be writing values into other memory in the heap. If you're running in a protected-mode environment, you may only get a "page fault" and termination of the program. Under plain vanilla DOS, it's probably reboot time again.

Clipping has other uses besides protecting your software from crashes, although this is certainly a noble goal in itself. Efficiency (read "speed") is another. If only a part of an image has changed since the last time it was rendered, it is not necessary to rerender the entire image, only the portion that has changed. In Part 2, we will develop a *screen composition* methodology that makes use of clipping to avoid excessive redraw of unchanged areas. This is one of the keys to snappy animation.

Clipping Regions

What does it mean to restrict rendering to a portion of a drawing surface? What is the shape of such a portion? In the case of canvases, the canvas is based on a bitmap, which by our definition has a rectangular shape to it (it has a width and height, and contains all the pixels defined inside that bounding rectangle). Thus, clipping rendering operations to a *clipping rectangle* is clearly what is called for to keep rendering confined to the canvas boundary. Since we know we need to be able to clip to a rectangular region for canvas safety, we can generalize this concept by allowing the clip rectangle to take on other values. By default, we will set the clipping rectangle to exactly cover the entire canvas. But if, for instance, we want to restrict drawing to the upper-one-fourth of the canvas, we can just set the clipping rectangle to the appropriate coordinates. The ACanvas class defined in Chapter 2 contains a 'clipRect' field to hold a clipping rectangle which can be modified as needed. Figure 4.2 shows an example clip rectangle.

A rectangle is not the only shape that an image or geometric primitive can be clipped to. Certainly one can imagine clipping to a *clipping region* defined by circle, a triangle, a set of rectangles, or even another bitmapped image, often called a clipping *mask*. The Windows graphics programming toolbox, called GDI, supports clipping regions composed of a set of rectangles—a drawing operation is confined to the area which is described by the *union* of all these rect-

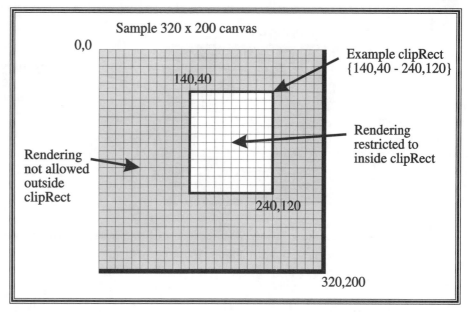

Figure 4.2 Sample canvas with clipping rectangle.

angles. The Macintosh's Quickdraw toolbox goes one step further, allowing a clipping region to be built from essentially arbitrary drawing calls. Internally, the region is represented by a nonpublic and more complicated data structure.

Clipping Masks

The problem with clipping regions defined by arbitrary shapes is that rendering methods must be written which confine themselves to these shapes, and coding such algorithms is a pain in the butt. The algorithms required to clip a given drawing operation to a circle, for instance, can be both difficult to program and time-consuming to execute. Of all the possibilities, clipping to a rectangle is by far the easiest to code and fastest to execute. More complex clipping regions are best represented by an image mask, which is a monochrome bitmap in which 1-valued pixels represent areas within the region and 0-valued pixels represent areas outside the region. The mask itself, being a bitmap, specifies only the region inside a rectangular area; clipping to a mask implies preclipping to the rectangle boundaries of the mask. Figure 4.3 depicts a sample clipping mask.

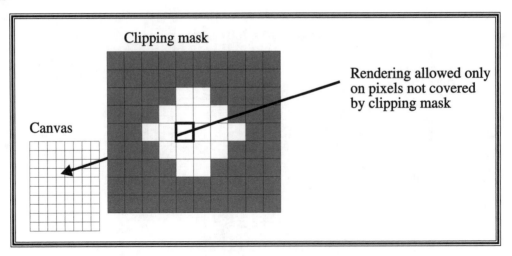

Figure 4.3   Rendering through a clipping mask.

Clipping Span Lists

Another way to represent a clipping mask is via a set of spans, where each span is given by a y-coordinate and left and right x-coordinates, similar to the horizontal line segments drawn by DrawHorzLineU(). More than one span can appear on the same line. This representation has the advantage that it can be more compact and faster to clip to than a bitmask, because each pixel need not be checked independently. The disadvantage of span clipping is that the span list itself can be difficult to build and maintain. If the clipping region is allowed to be built from rendering operations into the clip region itself, then these operations are themselves complex, involving splitting of spans and other modifications to the span list. A hypothetical structure for such a clipping spanlist might be:

```
typedef struct {
    ClipSpan *next; // ptr to next span in this row, or NULL if last
    ClipSpan *prev; // ptr to previous span in this row, or NULL if first
    short xleft;    // left edge of a given span
    short xright;   // right edge of a given span
} ClipSpan;

ClipSpan *spanList[MAX_HEIGHT];  // ptr to 1st span in each row
```

As can be imagined from this data structure, managing clipping spans is no fun.

ARTT Clipping Methodology

For real-time work, nothing beats rectangles for clipping speed. Furthermore, clipping rectangles accomplish most of what clipping is needed for, namely protection of memory outside the canvas and restriction of rendering for purposes of efficiency. It would be silly to use clipping regions to speed up rendering only to find that the clipping itself is eating up all the time that is supposedly being saved! In ARTT, clipping regions will be defined by a single rectangle, period. That rectangle is defined by the 'clipRect' field of the canvas, which may be set to a new rectangle value at any time.

Each rendering primitive will be available in clipped and unclipped versions. In Chapter 2, we developed unclipped versions of rendering routines for points, horizontal lines, vertical lines, boxes, rectangles, and 8-bit linear bitmaps. Now, we will develop the clipped versions of each of these operations. The advantage of having both clipped and unclipped routines available is that there are times when code doing the rendering "knows" that the operation to be performed lies within the boundaries of the clip rectangle. In this case, it can avoid the overhead of clipping calculations and go straight to the unclipped version of the operation. Also, some rendering operations are broken down into lower-level operations, and if the higher-level routine provides full clipping it is wasteful for it to call rendering functions which provide their own redundant clipping.

Rectangles

Before we start clipping to rectangles, we should know a little more about them. We all know what they look like, but how are they really defined, and what operations should we allow on them? As for definition, a rectangle is fully defined by the coordinates of its upper-left and lower-right corners, that is, two *x,y* coordinate pairs. The right and bottom coordinates in ARTT will be *exclusive;* that is, a rectangle does not include the pixels with those coordinates. Think of the rectangle coordinates as lying on a grid at the upper-left corner of each pixel, as Figure 4.4 illustrates.

This definition has many important benefits over the *inclusive* approach. The width of a rectangle can be calculated by subtracting the left from the right coordinate; with an inclusive rectangle we would have to add one afterwards. An "empty" rectangle, one which contains no pixels, is one in which the left coordinate equals the right or the top equals the bottom. With inclusive rectangles, the right coordinate would have to be less than the left coordinate to denote an

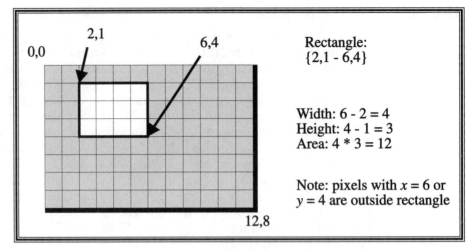

Figure 4.4 Sample rectangle. Note that right and bottom coordinates are outside rectangle.

empty rectangle. Exclusive rectangles make life easier; trust me on this one.

The operations we would like to perform on rectangles include the following:

- Initialization of coordinates, via constructors
- Width and height calculations
- Area computation and "emptiness" test
- Equality test (is this same as another rectangle?)
- Test for enclosure of a point within the rectangle
- Test for enclosure of another rectangle within the rectangle
- Intersection test and calculation of intersection area (with another rectangle)
- Calculation of smallest rectangle enclosing two other rectangles
- Calculation of area inside one rectangle but not in another (disjoint area)

Other operations are possible too, of course, but these are the basics that we need. Most of these are very simple and can be done with inline methods, and that's just what we'll do in the ARect class.

Class ARect: ARTT Rectangles

Rectangles in ARTT are instances of class ARect, whose header file is listed below.

```
//   ARect.h      Rectangle class
//   Rex E. Bradford
```

```
#ifndef __ARECT_H
#define __ARECT_H

#include "atypes.h"

class ARect {
public:
   short left;  // x-coord of upper-left pixel
   short top;   // y-coord of upper-left pixel
   short right; // x-coord to right of rect's last pixel
   short bott;  // y-coord below rect's last pixel

// Constructors

   ARect::ARect(short l, short t, short r, short b) {
      left=l; top=t ; right=r; bott=b;}
   ARect::ARect() {}

// Various simple computations

   short Width() {return(right - left);}
   short Height() {return(bott - top);}
   bool IsEmpty() {return((left >= right) || (top >= bott));}
   long Area() {return(long(right - left) * long(bott - top));}

// Tests with points and other rectangles

   bool Equal(ARect &rect) {return((left == rect.left) &&
      (right == rect.right) && (top == rect.top) && (bott == rect.bott));}
   bool TestSect(ARect &rect) {return((left < rect.right) &&
      (right > rect.left) && (top < rect.bott) && (bott > rect.top));}
   bool Encloses(int x, int y) {return((x >= left) && (x < right) &&
      (y >= top) && (y < bott));}
   bool Encloses(ARect &rect) {return((rect.left >= left) &&
      (rect.right <= right) && (rect.top >= top) && (rect.bott <= bott));}
   bool EnclosedBy(ARect &rect) {return((left >= rect.left) &&
      (right <= rect.right) && (top >= rect.top) && (bott <= rect.bott));}

// Compute more complex interactions with other rectangles

   ARect Intersect(ARect &rect);
   ARect SmallestEnclosing(ARect &rect);
   int Disjoint(ARect &rect, ARect *pResultArray);
};

#endif
```

Basic ARect Methods

Many of these methods are pretty self-explanatory and don't need much discussion.

- Width() returns the width of the rectangle, by subtracting the left coordinate from the right.
- Height() returns the height of the rectangle, by subtracting the top coordinate from the bottom.
- IsEmpty() tests whether the rectangle encompasses any pixels. A rectangle with coordinates 0,0,0,0 is empty, but is not the only possible empty rectangle.
- Area() multiplies the width by the height to compute the area inside the rectangle.

The various "test" methods are a little more complex, but all basically involve checking coordinates for less than or greater than.

- Equal(ARect &rect) tests whether the rectangle has exactly the same coordinates as another rectangle.
- TestSect(ARect &rect) quickly determines whether the rectangle has any intersection, or overlap, with another rectangle (but does not compute the area of intersection).
- Encloses(int x, int y) tests whether the rectangle encloses a point.
- Encloses(ARect &rect) tests whether the rectangle fully encloses another rectangle.
- EnclosedBy(ARect &rect) tests whether the rectangle is fully enclosed by another one.

Encloses() is an example of overloading. *Two methods with the same name are defined, with different implementations. They are distinguishable by the compiler by virtue of the number and type of arguments they take. Using overloaded names can be dangerous, but sometimes is useful when the two are variations which perform very similar operations, and coming up with two different names seems silly. ARTT uses overloading heavily when giving a class multiple constructors, where it is not possible to provide different names, since all constructors must be named with the class name.*

Rectangle Intersection and Enclosure

The intersection of two rectangles is defined by the rectangle which represents the area of overlap of two rectangles, which may be empty. Figure 4.5 shows a few cases of rectangle intersection.

The TestSect() inline method shown in the header file does a quick overlap test. For a full computation of the area of intersection, use Intersect(), listed below.

```
ARect ARect::Intersect(ARect &rect)
{
```

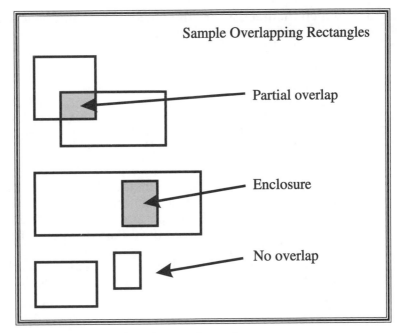

Figure 4.5 Examples of rectangle overlap.

```
return(ARect(
    left > rect.left ? left : rect.left,      // rightmost left
    top > rect.top ? top : rect.top,          // bottommost top
    right < rect.right ? right : rect.right,  // leftmost right
    bott < rect.bott ? bott : rect.bott));    // topmost bottom
}
```

The Intersect() method returns a rectangle (not a pointer or reference to one). Using the constructor and returning the rectangle made by it directly is more efficient than declaring a temporary rectangle, filling in its fields, and returning it. The method used here involves less copying.

Intersection testing will be very important in Part 2, where we use it to quickly determine which of a set of sprite objects overlaps a screen area scheduled for updating, so that we can restrict rendering to only those objects that matter. The inline TestSect() is about as fast as it gets for doing this test.

The smallest rectangle which encompasses two rectangles is also a handy computation to be able to make. If an object moves a short distance, for instance, we might decide to redraw the screen area which includes where the object is now and where it previously was. SmallestEnclosing() does this.

```
ARect ARect::SmallestEnclosing(ARect &rect)
{
   return(ARect (
      left < rect.left ? left : rect.left,     // leftmost left
      top < rect.top ? top : rect.top,         // topmost top
      right > rect.right ? right : rect.right, // rightmost right
      bott > rect.bott ? bott : rect.bott));   // bottommost bottom
}
```

The computation of the area included in one rectangle but not in another, calculated by the Disjoint() method, can require up to four rectangles to represent. This operation is somewhat complex, and discussion of it will be deferred until Part 2, when screen recomposing code which uses this operation is discussed.

That's it for rectangles—they're pretty easy to work with, which is why real-time graphics uses them for clipping. Now, let's put them to work for us.

Clipping to Rectangles

Now that we have a rectangle class and a set of rectangle operations, we can start using rectangles for clipping regions. Let's turn back to class ACanvas, which uses an ARect object to represent a canvas' clipping region. We'll define a set of clipping routines in the ACanvas class which can clip a variety of graphic objects to the clipping rectangle, so that we won't draw outside of it. Since all canvas classes are derived from ACanvas, they will inherit this functionality.

Setting and Retrieving the Clipping Rectangle

The inline methods in class ACanvas for setting and retrieving the clip rectangle are repeated below. The base ACanvas constructor also takes care of initializing the clip rectangle to the full area of the canvas' bitmap.

```
void SetClipRect(ARect &rect) { clipRect = rect; }
void SetClipRect(int l, int t, int r, int b) { clipRect.left = l;
   clipRect.top = t; clipRect.right = r; clipRect.bott= b; }
void GetClipRect(int &left, int &top, int &right, int &bott) {
   left = clipRect.left; top = clipRect.right;
   right = clipRect.right; bott = clipRect.bott;}
void GetClipRect(ARect &rect) { rect = clipRect; }
```

Clipping Pixels

Even a single pixel drawn outside a canvas can crash your PC. Clipping pixels is important, and it's definitely not very hard, so we'll start there. The ClipPixel() routine returns TRUE if the pixel at the supplied coordinates lies inside the clip rectangle. This and other clipping routines will reside in the ACanvas class, where the clipped versions of the rendering routines can get at them easily.

The pixel-clipping calculation is actually performed by a call to an inline function in the ARect class. ARect::Encloses() takes the *x* and *y* coordinates of a point, and returns TRUE if the point is inside the rectangle (see the ARect header file previously listed for its definition). ACanvas::ClipPixel() is just a "wrapper" around this function.

```
bool ACanvas::ClipPixel(int x, int y) {return(clipRect.Encloses(x, y));}
```

Mirroring the unclipped versions seen in Chapter 2, there are various clipped DrawPixel() methods, one of which uses the current color, and the others of which use supplied color values. These all just call ClipPixel(), and then call the appropriate unclipped pixel drawer if it returns TRUE. If ClipPixel() returns FALSE, indicating that the pixel is outside the clip rectangle, no drawing is done.

```
void ACanvas::DrawPixel(int x, int y)
{
    if (ClipPixel(x, y)) DrawPixelU(x, y);
}

void ACanvas::DrawPixel8(int x, int y, uchar c8)
{
    if (ClipPixel(x, y)) DrawPixel8U(x, y, c8);
}

void ACanvas::DrawPixelNative(int x, int y, long c)
{
    if (ClipPixel(x, y)) DrawPixelNativeU(x, y, c);
}
```

Clipping Horizontal and Vertical Lines

Clipping lines or indeed anything other than points involves more than just deciding whether to draw or not to draw. A line or bitmap or other shape may lie partially inside and partially outside the clip rectangle. It is the job of the clipping version of the drawing routine to determine what portion of the shape is inside the clip rectangle, and then draw only that portion. Figure 4.6 illustrates a horizontal line being clipped.

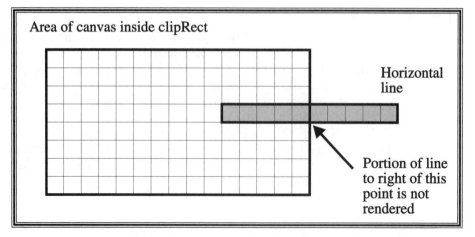

Figure 4.6   Horizontal line clipped to canvas' clipping rectangle.

For most shapes, a clipping routine can return a "modified" version of the primitive or image, which can then be passed to the unclipped version of the drawing routine. Take a horizontal line, for instance. The portion of a horizontal line inside the clip rectangle, if it exists, is guaranteed by definition to be another horizontal line, albeit one which may have different endpoint coordinates. The clip routine, then, is responsible both for determining whether a portion of the line lies inside the clip rectangle, and for returning the coordinates of such a line if it does.

The routine ClipHorzLine() in class ACanvas returns TRUE if any portion of the line lies inside the clip rectangle, and if so it also modifies the left and right endpoint coordinates of the line. Note that these arguments are passed by reference (instead of by value), so that ClipHorzLine() can modify the values in the calling routine. In C, these would be pointers to the endpoint coordinates; C++ provides references in part to reduce the need for pointer syntax.

```
bool ACanvas::ClipHorzLine(int y, int &left, int &right)
{
   if ((y < clipRect.top) || (y >= clipRect.bott))
     return FALSE;
   if (left < clipRect.left) left = clipRect.left;
   if (right > clipRect.right) right = clipRect.right;
   return(left < right);
}
```

DrawHorzLine() draws a clipped horizontal line. It calls Clip-HorzLine(), and if the result is TRUE, calls DrawHorzLineU() with the potentially modified endpoints.

Arguments passed by reference, and access to them inside a function, is typically internally implemented using pointers. The difference between using references and pointers is often one of syntax. However, references are important and necessary, particularly in operator overloading, as a way of referring to an object without specifying whether value or pointer is to be used in the implementation. In an inline function, for instance, an argument passed by reference may be accessed directly and not by pointer at all, because at the time of "expansion" during compilation, the object being referred to by the reference is known. See the C++ Reference Manual (Addison Wesley) by Stroustaup and Euris for more information.

```
void ACanvas::DrawHorzLine(int y, int left, int right)
{
    if (ClipHorzLine(y, left, right))
        DrawHorzLineU(y, left, right);
}
```

Clipping vertical lines is a similar process. ClipVertLine() and DrawVertLine() are listed below:

```
bool ACanvas::ClipVertLine(int x, int &top, int &bott)
{
    if ((x < clipRect.left) || (x >= clipRect.right))
        return FALSE;
    if (top < clipRect.top) top = clipRect.top;
    if (bott > clipRect.bott) bott = clipRect.bott;
    return(top < bott);
}

void ACanvas::DrawVertLine(int x, int top, int bott)
{
    if (ClipVertLine(x, top, bott))
        DrawVertLineU(x, top, bott);
}
```

Clipping Rectangles and Boxes

Clipping filled rectangles is easy. We already have a function in the ARect class which computes the intersection of two rectangles, and an inline to test whether a rectangle is empty. Since the clipping area is a rectangle, we can use ARect::Intersect() to determine the area of overlap between the rectangle we want to draw and the canvas' clipping rectangle. This area of overlap is what we want to draw, and we can use ARect::IsEmpty() to see if this area of intersection has anything in it. The ClipRect() routine is short enough to code as an inline directly in the ACanvas class declaration:

```
bool ClipRect(ARect &rect) {
    rect = rect.Intersect(clipRect); return(!rect.IsEmpty());}
```

The method DrawRect() then draws a clipped rectangle by calling ClipRect(), which returns whether or not there is an overlap and modifies the rectangle to equal the intersection if there is. This can be passed to DrawRectU(), the unclipped rectangle drawer. Here's DrawRect():

```
void ACanvas::DrawRect(ARect rect)
{
    if (ClipRect(rect)) DrawRectU(rect);
}
```

The portion of a hollow box which lies inside a rectangle cannot be expressed by a rectangle. Often, one or more of the sides of the box will lie fully or partially inside the clipping rectangle, and one or more sides will lie fully outside it. Because of this, it is not possible for DrawBox(), which takes a rectangle describing the box as its sole argument, to compute a new rectangle and pass it to DrawBoxU(). DrawBox() must clip and draw the box using horizontal and vertical line primitives. The most straightforward way to do this is to just draw each of the four bounding lines of the box, calling the clipped version for each and letting the underlying drawing routines take care of clipping altogether.

```
void ACanvas::DrawBox(ARect rect)
{
    DrawHorzLine(rect.top, rect.left, rect.right);
    DrawHorzLine(rect.bott - 1, rect.left, rect.right);
    DrawVertLine(rect.left, rect.top + 1, rect.bott - 1);
    DrawVertLine(rect.right - 1, rect.top + 1, rect.bott - 1);
}
```

Clipping Bitmaps to Rectangles

Since a bitmap is defined by its width and height, it is in effect enclosed in a rectangle. The intersection of such a rectangle with the clip rectangle is by definition another rectangle, therefore it should be possible to define the portion of the bitmap inside the cliprect as another bitmap. This new bitmap can be thought of as a "sub-bitmap," because it is "inside" the original bitmap. Figure 4.7 illustrates.

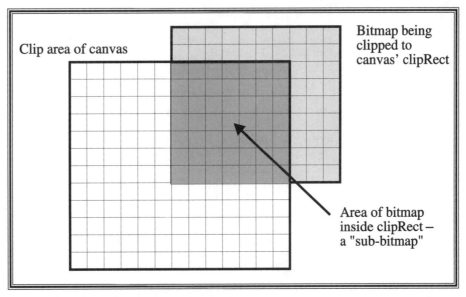

Clip area of canvas

Bitmap being
clipped to
canvas' clipRect

Area of bitmap
inside clipRect –
a "sub-bitmap"

Figure 4.7 Area of bitmap inside canvas' clipping rectangle - a "sub-bitmap."

How do we represent this sub-bitmap? We certainly don't want to have to copy the actual data bits to another area of memory—that would be too time-consuming. The trick is to make a new bitmap which points to the relevant sub-area of the original bitmap. The width and height of the sub-bitmap will obviously change from those in the original bitmap. In the case where the upper-left pixels of a bitmap have been clipped off, the 'pbits' field must be changed to point to the new "start point" of the bitmap. Since the sub-bitmap references the same data bits, the 'rowbytes' field does not change. In fact, the major reason for having a 'rowbytes' field at all is to allow such sub-bitmaps to be represented easily, by decoupling the width of the resulting bitmap from the width of the data bits it is derived from.

The ClipBitmap() method

The ClipBitmap() method listed below examines the bitmap and the clip rectangle, and modifies the bitmap to "include" only the area within the clip rectangle. It modifies the *x,y* coordinates passed in as well if they lie outside the clip rectangle. The resulting sub-bitmap can then be drawn at the new *x,y* coordinates using an unclipped renderer.

```
bool ACanvas::ClipBitmap(ABitmap &bms, int &x, int &y)
{
// If top of bitmap cut off, advance pbits, reduce height, new y
```

```
    if (y < clipRect.top)
        {
        bms.pbits += long(clipRect.top - y) * long(bms.rowbytes);
        bms.height -= (clipRect.top - y);
        y = clipRect.top;
        }

// If bottom of bitmap cut off, reduce height

    if ((y + bms.height) > clipRect.bott)
        bms.height = clipRect.bott - y;

// If left of bitmap cut off, advance pbits, reduce width, new x

    if (x < clipRect.left)
        {
        bms.pbits += bms.RowSize(clipRect.left - x);
        bms.width -= (clipRect.left - x);
        x = clipRect.left;
        }

// If right of bitmap cut off, reduce width

    if ((x + bms.width) > clipRect.right)
        bms.width = clipRect.right - x;

// Return TRUE if width and height both greater than zero

    return((bms.width > 0) && (bms.height > 0));
    }
```

Drawing Clipped Bitmaps

ACanvas::DrawBitmapLin8() is used to draw a BMF_LIN8 bitmap with clipping enabled. It calls ClipBitmap() first to clip the bitmap. If ClipBitmap() returns TRUE, the appropriate unclipped drawing routine is called with the sub-bitmap returned by ClipBitmap(), at the modified *x,y* coordinates. Note that the clipping is done on a local copy of the source bitmap—otherwise ClipBitmap() would end up modifying the original bitmap passed in by reference!

```
void ACanvas::DrawBitmapLin8(ABitmap &bm, int x, int y)
{
    ABitmap bmlocal = bm;
    if (ClipBitmap(bmlocal, x, y))
        DrawBitmapLin8U(bmlocal, x, y);
}
```

A Lifetime of Clipping

Whether you found clipping to be an exciting adventure in precision graphics or as fun as raking leaves, we're done with it for the moment. As further graphics operations are presented in this chapter and throughout the book, clipping will be an integral part of "doing them right." Another important vegetable to eat before we can have our animation turkey is the topic of fixed-point number representation. Open wide.

Floating-Point and Fixed-Point Numbers

In this chapter, we're going to learn how to do line-drawing. These lines will feature arbitrary endpoints, and so can't be drawn with the simple horizontal and vertical line-drawers introduced so far. But first, we're going to take a detour into the land of numeric representation. Why? Because there are many quantities that can't be expressed adequately using just integers. In later chapters, we'll want to talk about the frame rate of an animation in frames per second, or the speed of a sprite in pixels per second. These quantities will not always be whole numbers, but may include a fractional part.

The obvious solution is to use floating-point for those quantities which can't be expressed by integers. But most floating-point calculations are slower than integer calculations, even on a Pentium, never mind a 486SX which has no floating-point hardware.

Floating-Point Quick Recap

To see why floating-point math is slower than integer math, let's quickly look at how floating-point numbers are stored and manipulated. C defines two floating-point types, float and double, which differ in the range of numbers they can represent and their resolution. Resolution is measured in the number of "significant digits" that such a number can represent.

The bits of a floating-point number are divided into two fixed-size portions, the *exponent* and the *mantissa*, and a sign bit which determines whether the number is positive or negative. The mantissa can be thought of as holding the "significant digits," while the exponent determines the scale of the number. If the computer inherently worked in base 10, for instance, 4.562 and 4562 would have the same mantissa, but the exponent of the second would be greater by 3, because the decimal point is three digits further to the left. Floating-point numbers work just like that, except that they use base 2, so that the exponent increases by one each time the value doubles, instead of each time it is multiplied by 10.

Figure 4.8 illustrates the layout of floating-point numbers, and shows the sizes of exponent and mantissa on Intel 86-series processors. Floats are 32 bits wide, and doubles are 64 bits wide. The "extended" format, which matches the floating-point processor registers on Intel processors, is an 80-bit format.

The exponent field itself can be thought of as signed. If it is greater than 0, the number is larger than one, and the mantissa holds significant digits to the left (and possibly also the right) of the decimal point. If the exponent is less than 0, the mantissa is wholly fractional, and the number is less than 1.

The mantissa/exponent layout is very flexible. It allows for very tiny fractions and very huge numbers, because the exponent "slides the scale" at which the number is represented. The mantissa, which holds the significant digits of the value, doesn't care whether these digits are far to the left or right of the decimal point. The decimal point "floats," which, of course, is how floating-point got its name.

Floating-Point Calculations

The nature of the floating-point representation immediately highlights why it is inherently slower to work with than integer math. As it turns out, multiplication and division are simpler than addition and subtraction. To multiply two floating-point numbers, essentially what happens is the exponents are added, and the mantissas are mul-

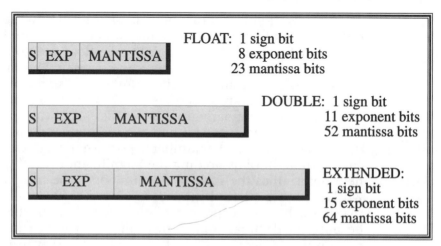

Figure 4.8   Bit layouts of three formats of floating-point numbers on Intel processors.

tiplied. Adding two large exponents yields an even larger one, which is what happens when two large numbers are multiplied. Adding a positive and negative exponent tend to wholly or partially cancel out and produce an intermediate exponent, which is what happens when a large number and a fractional number are multiplied. Adding two negative exponents yields an even more negative exponent; thus multiplying two small fractions yields an even smaller one. In the real world, the algorithm for floating-point multiplication is complicated by the need to check for overflow of various kinds and deal with other subtleties.

Floating-point division is similar to multiplication, except that the exponents are subtracted rather than added, and the mantissas are divided instead of multiplied. Floating-point addition and subtraction, on the other hand, is even messier. To add two floating-point numbers, for instance, the exponents need to be aligned, so that the mantissas can be added in the same frame of reference.

Floating-Point Speed

Table 4.1 shows the speeds at which various processors execute floating-point versus integer calculations, in terms of machine cycles (on a 50 Mhz machine, there are 50 million cycles per second). Each number of cycles is presented as a range—the exact timing of any given operation depends on the values involved, memory cache hits or misses, and other factors. See Michael Abrash's *Zen of Code Optimization* for the detailed story on why instruction timing is a black art these days.

Table 4.1   Times of Various Operations (in machine cycles)

Operation	486SX (no built-in FP)	486DX (built-in FP)	Pentium (built-in FP)
Integer add	1	1	<= 1
Integer sub	1	1	<= 1
Integer mpy	13–42	13–42	10–11
Integer div	19–44	19–44	22–46
Floating add	software	8–20	1–3
Floating sub	software	8–20	1–3
Floating mpy	software	11–17	1–3
Floating div	software	73	39

With a Pentium floating-point hardware unit, floating-point multiplication and division actually take less time than their integer counterparts, although this doesn't count the extra cycles it takes to move values in and out of the CPU's floating-point registers, or convert to and from integer format. Addition and subtraction, on the other hand, are much faster with integers, which can execute in less than one cycle on a Pentium due to its multiple integer processing units. The 486's floating-point hardware is much slower than the Pentium's, however. And take away the floating-point hardware, as Intel did with the 486SX processor, and floating-point performance drops through the floor into the sub-basement.

Fixed-Point Number Representation

While floating-point is getting more practical as Pentium-class chips take over, even then it still suffers from a minor performance penalty compared to integer math when the time to load and unload the floating-point registers and other overhead is factored in. But we need those fractions that floating-point offers! Well, Virginia, there is a solution. The speed problem inherent in floating-point addition and subtraction is almost entirely due to the need to align the mantissas of numbers which have different exponents. That is, the two "floating" decimal points have to be lined up before "normal" math can be applied to them. What if we kept them permanently lined up?

What we'd have is "fixed-point" representation, where a number can have a fraction, but the decimal point is always in the same place. Such fixed-point numbers have much less range than floating-point ones—in essence we're chopping up the bits of an integer into a whole number part and a fractional part, and no exponent. Figure 4.9 shows the layout of a sample fixed-point value. In this 32-bit fixed-point format, 16 bits are devoted to a signed whole number, and 8 bits are devoted to a fractional part. This isn't much fractional resolution, but it's sufficient for many purposes. The remaining 8 bits are devoted to an "overflow" area for temporary use during calculations.

Fixed-Point Math

Adding two fixed-point numbers is easy—just add them like integers! Since the decimal point is aligned by definition, the whole number parts add together, as do the fraction parts, and the fractions even overflow properly into the whole number part. Figure 4.10 illustrates fixed-point addition. Subtraction works the same way.

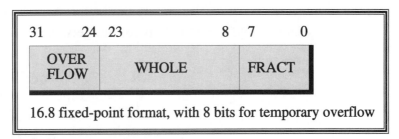

Figure 4.9 Fixed-point number representation used by ARTT.

Multiplication and division are a little trickier. The floating-point method of adding/subtracting exponents and multiplying/dividing mantissas works the same in fixed-point. We can speed up the process, though, by avoiding splitting the exponent and mantissa halves. For instance, multiplication can be achieved by using integer multiplication on the two fixed-point numbers, which produces a number with 16 bits of integer result and 16 bits of fraction. Then, we shift the number 8 bits to the right, in order to return it to the 16.8 format. This method shows the need for the 8 bits of overflow area. Figure 4.11 illustrates fixed-point multiplication.

Division works similarly. The dividend is first shifted up by 8 bits, and then divided by the divisor. Again, the overflow area is needed. Note that the whole number range of this 16.8 fixed-point representation is −32768 to +32767, the same as a 16-bit integer. Care must be taken to avoid trying to use this format to hold larger numbers.

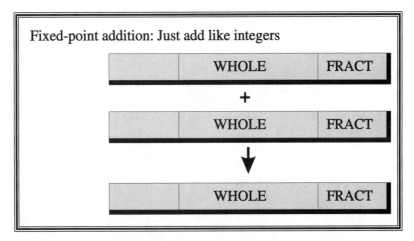

Figure 4.10 Fixed-point addition.

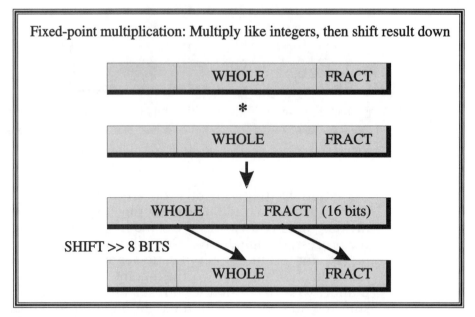

Figure 4.11   Fixed-point multiplication.

Class AFix: Fixed-Point Numbers

One of the finest features of C++ is the ability to create new types, which can then be used almost as if they were built into the language. With operator overloading, we can design a fixed-point class, and then use it like this:

```
// Sample code using fixed-point numbers
AFix a(4.5);         // declare a fixed-point number, initialized from float
AFix b(10);          // declare another, initialized from an integer
AFix c = a + (b * 1.25); // do some math using C operators
```

Using inline methods and a good optimizing compiler, we can create a fixed-point class which has speed as well. This is too good to resist. Let's design class AFix, a class for representing fixed-point numbers.

AFix Representation

In ARTT, we'll use the 16.8 fixed-point representation illustrated in the previous discussion. Only 8 bits of fraction is a bit skimpy, so our fixed-point class definitely shouldn't be used for calculating moon trajectories. But for animation playback rates, flying missile speeds, and fractional-pixel calculations, it'll do nicely. If we were able to get at the CPU's internal 64-bit register pairs used in multiplication and division, we could go with a 16.16 fixed-point format, and have a more robust fractional precision. But C++, like C, is not always as powerful as assembly language, and there's no way of getting at these 64-bit quantities without using assembler. Without them, we need to leave 8 bits of overflow space, as Figure 4.11 illustrates.

Rather than print the full listing of the AFix header file, we're going to view it piecemeal, to show how the design of such a class is built up. The first snippet shows the internal representation of an AFix, which is simply a longword.

```
class AFix {
   long v; // 8 bits overflow, 16 bits signed whole, 8 bits fraction

... methods ...

};
```

AFix Constructors

We need to be able to declare fixed-point numbers and put valid values into them, so we need one or more constructors. Several flavors of constructors make sense. One takes no arguments and does no initialization—it can be used to declare AFix variables for later setting. Another constructs an AFix from an integer, simply by shifting that value into the high 24 bits and leaving the 8 bits of fraction set to 0. The final two constructors initialize an AFix by converting from floating-point to fixed-point representation.

```
AFix() {}
AFix(int val) {v = long(val) << 8;}
AFix(float f) {v = long(f * 256.0);}
AFix(double f) {v = long(f * 256.0);}
```

Here is some sample code which uses the various constructors:

```
// SAMPLE CODE SHOWING USE OF AFIX CONSTRUCTORS
AFix a;           // value undefined, set later (using a = expression)
AFix b(22);       // sets to 22.0 (22 whole part, 0 fractional part)
AFix c(1.55);     // sets to 1.55 (1 whole part, .55 fractional part)
short value = 13;
AFix e(value);    // short value promoted to int, sets to 13.0
```

AFix Type-Conversion Operators

Now we can convert from integer or floating-point representations to AFix; it's helpful to go the other way as well. Type-conversion operators allow us to explicitly and implicitly convert AFix values to other types. Here are the conversion operators built into class AFix:

```
operator int() {return(v >> 8);}
operator float() {return (float(v) / 256.0);}
operator double() {return (double(v) / 256.0);}
```

Conversion to floating-point is done by converting the internal longword to a float, and then dividing by 256. The 256 comes from the fact that the internal longword is shifted up by 8 bits, which is equivalent to multiplication by 256.

Here are some examples of explicit and implicit conversions:

```
// SAMPLE CODE SHOWING USE OF AFIX CONVERSION OPERATORS
AFix a(10.5);           // declare an AFix
int b = int(a);         // explicit conversion to int
int c = a;              // implicit conversion to int
double d = double(a);   // explicit conversion to double
```

AFix Assignment Operators

The next stop for design in a basic numeric class such as AFix is to write assignment operators. Because we have defined type-conversion operators for the basic integer and floating-point types, simple assignment of integer and floating-point expressions to an AFix just works. Yea!—less coding is fine by me! But there are other assignment operators, such as += and *=, that we do need to write. They are listed below, and show off the implementation of the four basic math operations. The implementation of *= and /= shows why we needed the extra 8 bits of room in AFix for temporary usage.

```
AFix &operator+=(AFix a) {v += a.v; return *this;}
AFix &operator-=(AFix a) {v -= a.v; return *this;}
AFix &operator*=(AFix a) {v = (v * a.v) >> 8; return *this;}
AFix &operator/=(AFix a) {v = (v << 8) / a.v; return *this;}
```

We could stop there, but suppose we wanted to multiply an AFix by an integer, say 2. The above *= method would work, by autoconstructing a temporary AFix with the value 2, and multiplying the original AFix by it. But see what that means. The constructor makes an AFix out of 2 by shifting up 8 bits. Then a multiply happens, and then the result is shifted down 8 bits. It's more direct to avoid such upshifting and downshifting, by writing special operators which take an integer argument.

```
AFix &operator*=(int a) {v *= a; return *this;}
AFix &operator/=(int a) {v /= a; return *this;}
```

There's no point in writing such special versions for adding or subtracting integers, because in those cases there's still going to be one shift-by-8, whether it's in the operator or the constructor called to convert an integer to an AFix.

We could stop there with assignment operators, and I did the first time through, until I discovered a nasty bug. Take a look at the following sample code:

```
// SAMPLE CODE TO DEMONSTRATE NASTINESS OF AUTO-CONVERSION
AFix a(10.0); // construct 'a' with value 10.0
a *= 2.5;     // multiply by 2.5, or is it 2?
```

With just the AFix class we've designed so far, 'a' gets multiplied by 2, not 2.5! Why? Since there's no *= operator defined which takes a floating-point argument, C++ decides to convert 2.5 to the something that will work with *=. We would like it to pick AFix, and construct a temporary AFix using 2.5. But C++ prefers its built-in types, and it knows how to convert a float to an integer, which it notices can be used as an argument to *=. So, it constructs a temporary integer, assigns 2.5 to it in all its truncated glory, and the resulting 2 gets passed to the integer version of *=.

We fix this problem by forcing the compiler's hand, supplying it with versions of operator*=() and operator/=() that use doubles:

```
AFix &operator*=(double a) {return(*this *= AFix(a));}
AFix &operator/=(double a) {return(*this /= AFix(a));}
```

Two other assignment operators are handy. C and C++ programmers used to worrying about efficiency know that multiplying and dividing integers by numbers which are powers of 2 can be done with shifting. This trick works for fixed-point numbers too.

```
AFix &operator>>=(int nbits) {v >>= nbits; return *this;}
AFix &operator<<=(int nbits) {v <<= nbits; return *this;}
```

Below are some examples which use the assignment operators.

```
// SAMPLE CODE USING AFIX ASSIGNMENT OPERATORS
AFix a(.125);      // declare AFix with value .125
AFix b(4);         // declare AFix with value 4.0
a *= b;            // multiply a by b, a now is .5
b /= b;            // divide b by itself, b is now 1.0
a += .01;          // add AFix(.01) to a, a is now roughly .51
a *= 3;            // multiply a by integer 3, a is now roughly 1.53
a >>= 2;           // shift a 2 bits (divide by 4), a is now about .38
```

AFix Relational Operators

Comparing fixed-point numbers can be done by simply comparing their longword representations, so the relational operators are easy. Watch out for the fact that the fractional part of a number is very imprecise. Roundoff error can accumulate in a series of calculations, so the value of a fixed-point number may not be exactly what you think it should be.

```
int operator==(AFix a) {return(v == a.v);}
int operator!=(AFix a) {return(v != a.v);}
int operator>(AFix a) {return(v > a.v);}
int operator>=(AFix a) {return(v >= a.v);}
int operator<(AFix a) {return(v < a.v);}
int operator<=(AFix a) {return(v <= a.v);}
```

Below is some example code which shows the potential rounding problems:

```
// SAMPLE CODE USING AFIX RELATIONAL OPERATORS
AFix a = 1.0;          // initialize a using implicit conversion to 1.0
a /= 3;                // divide by 3, a about .333
a *= 3;                // multiply by 3, a about .996
if (a != 1.0)          // compare a to AFix(1.0)
   printf("oops!\n");  // you will get this "oops"
```

AFix Math Operators

We've developed the assignment operators for math, namely +=, −=, *=, and /=, but what about the basic binary math operators themselves? These we define as friend functions, taking two AFix arguments and returning a third, in case we want to string operations together such as $a + b + c$. We also want to be able to multiply and divide by integers. The binary math operators are defined below:

```
inline AFix operator+(AFix a, AFix b) {return(AFix(a.v + b.v, 0));}
inline AFix operator-(AFix a, AFix b) {return(AFix(a.v - b.v, 0));}
inline AFix operator*(AFix a, AFix b) {return(AFix((a.v * b.v) >> 8, 0));}
inline AFix operator/(AFix a, AFix b) {return(AFix((a.v << 8) / b.v, 0));}

inline AFix operator*(AFix a, int b) {return(AFix(a.v * b, 0));}
inline AFix operator/(AFix a, int b) {return(AFix(a.v / b, 0));}
```

If you look closely, something odd is going on. For instance, operator+, which is called by the C++ compiler when you perform $a + b$ on two AFix's, is implemented using a constructor we haven't seen. Furthermore, this constructor takes two arguments, one of which is the result of the calculation, and the other of which is the value 0! What's going on here?

At the risk of looking like an idiot when someone points out a better way of doing this, I'll explain. What's going on is that the set of constructors in AFix precludes our doing what we really want to do. What we'd like is to calculate the internal longword value in the appropriate way, and then stuff this value into the longword of the AFix that we are returning. But if we just say: return AFix(calculated_value), the calculated value, which is a longword, will get shifted up by 8 bits by the constructor! We need a constructor into which we can stuff the result value without modification, and that's what our special two-value constructor does. The second argument is a dummy value and is not used.

Here is the private two-argument "stuff and go" constructor, with the original comments left for all to see.

```
// This horrible ugly hack constructor is used in order to "stuff"
// a long value which is already in the correct form (shifted up by 8)
// into the new AFix. Since a long can be used in a "normal" constructor,
// a second dummy argument is used to distinguish the two constructors.
// This argument, an int for no apparent reason, is not used. Any
// compiler worth its salt will just optimize it away, leaving the
// constructor we want but can't seem to get any other way. I'm sure
// some C++ expert is going to cringe - I wish s/he was here now.

    AFix(long val, int captainDunsel) {v = val;}
```

Here are some examples using the math operators:

```
// SAMPLE CODE USING MATH OPERATORS
AFix a(10);              // construct a with value 10.0
AFix b = a * a * a;      // set b to 10 * 10 * 10 = 1000.0
b += (b + (a / 2));      // add 1000 + 5 to b, b now 2005.0
AFix c = b / 2;          // divide b by integer 2, c is 1002.5
```

AFix Shift Operators

The binary shift operators use the same ugly hack constructor to do their work:

```
inline AFix operator<<(AFix a, int nbits) {return(AFix(a.v << nbits, 0));}
inline AFix operator>>(AFix a, int nbits) {return(AFix(a.v >> nbits, 0));}
```

Some examples:

```
// SAMPLE CODE TO SHOW USE OF AFIX SHIFT OPERATORS
AFix a = 128;        // initialize a to 128.0
a >>= 4;             // shift a down by 4 (divide by 16), now 8.0
AFix b(1);           // construct b to 1.0
b <<= 3;             // shift b up by 3 (multiply by 8), now 8.0
if (a == b)          // we're lucky this time, since fractions were 0
   printf("no oops this time\n"); // whole numbers always exact in AFix's
```

Miscellaneous AFix Methods

A couple of miscellaneous methods are defined in class AFix to aid their use. These are the unary minus operator, and friend functions abs(), sign(), and round(). AFix::abs() returns the absolute value of an AFix, sign() returns its sign as +1 or –1, and round() converts to integer by rounding up or down (conversion using the int() operator just truncates).

```
AFix &operator-() {v = -v; return *this;}

inline AFix abs(AFix a) {return(AFix(labs(a.v), 0));}
inline int sign(AFix a) {return (a.v >= 0 ? +1 : -1);}
inline int round(AFix a) {return int(a + AFix::onehalf);}
```

And some examples:

```
// SAMPLE CODE TO SHOW USE OF AFIX ABS() AND SIGN() METHODS
AFix a = -20;              // initialize a to -20.0
AFix b = abs(a);           // b is abs(-20.0), so b is 20.0
int s = sign(a);           // s is sign(-20.0), so s is -1
int r = round(AFix(1.7));  // r is round(1.7) = 2
```

AFix Special Values

The AFix::round() method makes use of a special value named AFix::onehalf. This is one of several static precalculated values provided by the class as a convenience. The following variables are available for use in computation—please don't modify them just because I left off the const keyword.

```
// These special values are available for use. They have major
// inaccuracies with 8 bits of fraction - caveat emptor.

AFix AFix::onehalf = AFix(1)/2;        // 1/2, or .5
AFix AFix::e(2.718282);                // e, about 2.718
AFix AFix::pi(3.14159);                // pi, about 3.142
AFix AFix::epsilon(1L, 0);             // smallest AFix, ~.004
AFix AFix::max((32768L << 8) - 1, 0);  // largest, ~32767.996
```

Here is an example:

```
// SAMPLE CODE SHOWING USE OF AFIX SPECIAL VALUE
AFix veryCloseToEdge = AFix(rect.right) - AFix::epsilon;
```

Uses for Fixed-Point Numbers

In ARTT, we'll use fixed-point numbers of type AFix in most places where we might be otherwise tempted to use floating-point. The 3D classes presented in Part 4 will use floating-point, because they need the accuracy, but we'll use AFix everywhere else. Uses for fixed-point will include:

- Timekeeping, including animation rates and duration of a frame in fractions of a second
- Speed of moving objects, in pixels per second
- Exact position of moving objects, for smoothness
- Incremental calculations in bitmap scaling, line-drawing, and polygon-drawing

Our first use of fixed-point math follows next.

Rendering Lines

After all the effort to create a fixed-point number class, we'd better put it to good use. Line-drawing is actually one place where it turns out to be handy. In Chapter 2, we learned how to draw horizontal and vertical lines, but that's hardly the end to line-drawing. The ability to draw straight lines at any angle is fundamental to computer graphics, including real-time animated graphics. High-end graphics systems oriented toward scientific graphics, for instance, provide a great deal of support for line-drawing, because there are many ways to embellish a simple line. Some of the options include:

- Line color or pattern
- Line thickness
- Line style (dashed, dotted, etc.)
- Line beveling (shape of endpoints and connections to other lines)
- Anti-aliasing (smoothing edges of lines)

In computer games, multimedia presentation software, education and edutainment software, and related areas, line-drawing is not used nearly so heavily as in such fields as scientific visualization. Also, it is pretty time-consuming to render complex lines featuring adjustable thickness, internal color pattern-filling, dash-styling, and bevelled endpoints. Real-time work always has its tradeoffs. In ARTT, our line-drawer will be restricted to a single thickness, and no styling or bevelling. The line will be drawn in the current canvas color, so at least we'll have our choice of color. Note that a dashed line can be simulated by breaking up the line "by hand" into segments and calling the line-drawer for each segment.

How a Line Is Drawn

In the days of vector terminals, line-drawing was easy. The terminal did it in hardware, by directing the electron gun to sweep between

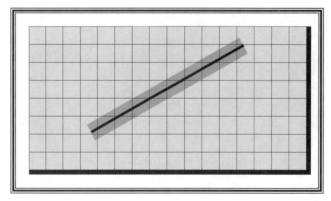

Figure 4.12   Line embedded in imaginary 1-pixel-thick border.

the endpoints. In the days of bitmapped graphics, though, things are a little tougher. We have to somehow turn a line, traditionally defined by two *endpoints* (each endpoint consists of an *x* and *y* coordinate), into a set of pixel locations to be colored. This is the central issue—how to decide which pixels fall on the line and are to be colored, and which fall outside the line.

Ideally, our lines will all look like they are one pixel thick, regardless of the angle at which they lie. Our horizontal and vertical line-drawers meet this requirement, and the general line-drawer we'll develop here should approximate this ideal as closely as possible. To do so, it is helpful to think of an infinitely thin line connecting the endpoints, and a one-pixel-wide boundary surrounding it, as Figure 4.12 shows.

One approach to rendering the line is to color all pixels which are 50 percent or more contained within the boundary around the line. Another approach is to color all pixels whose midpoint lies within the boundary around the line. These approaches will give similar, but not identical, results. High-end computer graphics spends much time worrying about such issues, including the bevelling of line endpoints to give them a pleasing look. For a very good discussion of the issues involved in high-end line-drawing, including Bresenham's classic technique (from 1965!), see *Computer Graphics: Principles and Practice* by Foley and van Dam, or any of the many other good sources on the subject.

We're not so fussy, as long as we can draw a reasonably good-looking line that matches the endpoints, and in a hurry, thank you. We'll create a variant of the standard line-drawing techniques, using fixed-point math. The overarching principle in all fast line-rendering algorithms is to plot pixels *incrementally*. This means starting at one of the endpoints and advancing along the line, stepping diagonally some times and horizontally or vertically other times, drawing each pixel "visited" along the way, until the endpoint is reached. The Bresenham technique and others like it use purely integer math accompanied by an "error term" that bounces negative and positive, telling the algorithm when to step diagonally and when to step horizontally or vertically.

Switching from integer to fixed-point math simplifies line-drawing conceptually; we just step along the line by a fractional amount in x or y, drawing a pixel along the way each time.

The ARTT Line Drawer

The DrawLineU() method presented here, implemented in base class A Canvas, uses fixed-point increments in x and y to step from pixel to pixel along the line. Note that even the endpoint coordinates passed in are fixed-point numbers! This can be useful, especially in 3D scenes—even though only whole pixels can be plotted. Lines drawn between endpoints which differ only by a fraction may start and end on the same whole pixel, but draw different pixels along the line.

In cases where we just want to use integer endpoints, our AFix constructors will automagically promote integer coordinates passed to DrawLineU() to their fixed-point equivalents. The code for Draw-LineU() is remarkably simple—once some setup is done, it's just a matter of stepping fractionally down the line, drawing a pixel at each step.

```
void ACanvas::DrawLineU(AFix x1, AFix y1, AFix x2, AFix y2)
{
// Set up line-drawer stepping factors


    AFix dx, dy;
    int count = SetupLine(x1, y1, x2, y2, dx, dy);


// Iterate, drawing a point along each step


    while (count-- > 0)            // loop through pixels
      {
      DrawPixelU(x1, y1);          // plot this pixel (implicit int(x1,y1))
      x1 += dx;                    // move in x
      y1 += dy;                    // move in y


      }
}
```

The DrawLineU() method makes use of SetupLine() to calculate the '*dx*' and '*dy*' stepping values, and to determine the number of pixels (steps) total to be drawn. SetupLine() determines which of the two axes, horizontal or vertical, is longer. The step value for this major axis is set to 1.0 or −1.0, or one pixel. This ensures that we don't waste valuable time drawing over the same pixel multiple times, and don't skip any pixels either. The minor axis is computed to be a fraction whose absolute value is less than 1.0.

```
int ACanvas::SetupLine(AFix x1, AFix y1, AFix x2, AFix y2,
   AFix &dx, AFix &dy)
{
// Calculate x,y difference and absolute values too

   AFix xdiff = x2 - x1;     // xdiff = distance from x1 to x2
   AFix ydiff = y2 - y1;     // ydiff = distance from y1 to y2

   AFix xdabs = abs(xdiff); // xdabs = absolute value of xdiff
   AFix ydabs = abs(ydiff); // ydabs = absolute value of ydiff

// Try to avoid dividing by 0, if it's not too much trouble

   if ((xdabs == AFix(0)) && (ydabs == AFix(0)))
      return 0;

// Find longer of two distances in absolute value, make that axis
// step by 1 pixel, and the other by a fraction of 1.

   if (xdabs > ydabs)             // if x-distance larger in absolute terms
      {
      if (xdiff < AFix(0))        // then x steps by 1.0 in pos or neg
         dx = AFix(-1);
      else
         dx = AFix(1);
      dy = ydiff / xdabs;         // and y steps by fraction
      return(((int) xdabs) + 1); // return total steps
      }
   else if (ydabs > AFix(0))      // else if y-distance larger in absolute
      {
      dx = xdiff / ydabs;         // then x steps by fraction
      if (ydiff < AFix(0))
         dy = AFix(-1);           // and y steps by 1.0 in pos or neg.
      else
         dy = AFix(1);
      return(((int) ydabs) + 1); // return total steps
      }
   else
      return(0);                  // if x,y distance both 0, no line!
}
```

Note that, unlike ARTT's horizontal and vertical line-drawing routines, and every other drawing routine so far encountered, the line-drawer draws up to and *including* the second endpoint (the point is not exclusive). All other primitives encountered so far had a source object in rectangular form (a horizontal or vertical line can be thought of as a 1-pixel-thick rectangle), and our rule is that rectangles are defined by integer coordinates, where the right and bottom edges are outside the rectangle. The two endpoints of a line, however, may be in arbitrary fractional locations, and the line's shape is not rectangular. For this reason and for ease in specifying endpoints, lines *include* their endpoints.

Line Clipping

As we know after reading the first half of this chapter, we are very keen not to plot pixels at any old x,y location, lest we overstep the canvas and write over some other data or even the program code itself! That means it's time for line clipping, wherein we ensure that no pixels are drawn outside the clip rectangle of the canvas being rendered into. Clipping a line to a rectangle is first a matter of figuring out which sides of the rectangle, if any, are intersected by the line. If any such intersection occurs, the relevant endpoint must be replaced by the point of intersection with the clipping rectangle. Figure 4.13 shows a line clipped to a rectangle.

Cohen-Sutherland Line Clipping

Several algorithms to perform this clipping have been developed. One of the best-known and most widely used is the Cohen-Sutherland algorithm. This algorithm provides very quick "trivial

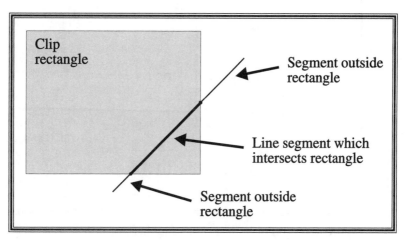

Figure 4.13 Line clipped to a rectangle.

reject" and "trivial accept" clipping. That is, a line which lies wholly inside or wholly outside the clip rectangle will be processed very quickly, and only when an intersection occurs is significant time spent performing clipping calculations.

The algorithm relies on computing special "clip codes" for both endpoints. These clip codes contain 4 bits each, and each bit denotes the relation of the endpoint to each of the 4 sides of the clip rectangle. Figure 4.14 shows the clip codes and their meaning.

The ClipCode() method in class ACanvas calculates the clip code of an endpoint.

```
//   ClipCode() calculates 4-bit clipcode for point vs. rect.
//
// 000x: set to 1 if x < clipRect.left
// 00x0: set to 1 if x >= clipRect.right
// 0x00: set to 1 if y < clipRect.top
// x000: set to 1 if y >= clipRect.right

uchar ACanvas::ClipCode(int x, int y)
{
    uchar flag = 0;                         // assume no intersections
    if (x < clipRect.left)  flag = 1;       // crosses left edge
    if (x >= clipRect.right) flag |= 2;     // crosses right edge
    if (y < clipRect.top)   flag |= 4;      // crosses top edge
    if (y >= clipRect.bott) flag |= 8;      // crosses bottom edge
    return(flag);
}
```

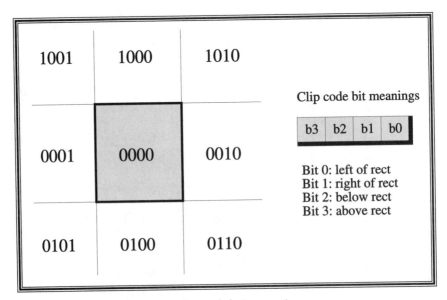

Figure 4.14 Line clipping codes and their meaning.

The Cohen-Sutherland clipping algorithm proceeds as follows. The clip codes of the two endpoints are calculated. If both are zero, then the endpoints both lie within the rectangle, and the clipping routine is exited. If the two clip codes contain any bits in common, that means that both points lie on the outside of one of the rectangle's sides, and therefore the line does not intersect the rectangle at all. Figure 4.15 illustrates various clipping cases.

If both clipcodes are nonzero, and they share no bits in common, then the line may intersect one of the sides of the rectangle, and must be clipped. In this case, we pick the endpoint with the nonzero clipcode (if both are nonzero, we can choose either one), and compute its intersection with the side it lies outside, replacing the endpoint with the new intersection coordinates. This process is then repeated until both endpoints lie inside the clipping rectangle. An endpoint may lie outside two sides; for example, it may be off the top and right of the cliprect. In this case, it will be clipped to these two sides one at a time, in successive passes through the loop. In the worst case, four passes through the clipping loop will be required, two for each endpoint. It is possible that after one or more iterations, a line will turn out to be fully outside the clipping rectangle, and will be rejected.

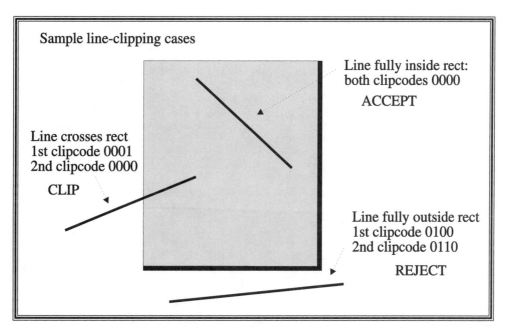

Figure 4.15 Sample lines and their clipping codes.

The ClipLine() method in base class ACanvas, an implementation of the Cohen-Sutherland algorithm customized for fixed-point coordinates, is listed below:

```
bool ACanvas::ClipLine(AFix &x1, AFix &y1, AFix &x2, AFix &y2)
{
// Compute 4-bit clipcodes for both endpoints

    uchar flag1 = ClipCode(x1, y1);
    uchar flag2 = ClipCode(x2, y2);

// Repeat until no more clipping can be done

    while (TRUE)
        {

// Check for acceptance of both endpoints or rejection of both

        if ((flag1 | flag2) == 0) // if both points within rect,
            return TRUE;          // we've finished clipping
        if (flag1 & flag2)        // if flags contain any common bits,
            return FALSE;         // then entirely outside cliprect

// Pick endpoint to clip. To simplify clip code, we always clip the
// 2nd endpoint. If 2nd endpoint is already inside cliprect, we swap
// the two endpoints so that we're really clipping endpoint 1

        if (flag2 == 0)           // if 2nd endpoint is within cliprect:
            {
            AFix txy = x1; x1 = x2; x2 = txy; // swap x coords
            txy = y1; y1 = y2; y2 = txy;      // swap y coords
            uchar flag = flag1; flag1 = flag2; flag2 = flag; // swap codes
            }

// If either of two low bits of clipcode set, we'll clip against
// left or right this time. Compute intersection with the appropriate
// side and set new endpoint x,y.

        if (flag2 & 3)            // clip against left or right edge?
            {
            AFix xedge;                       // will hold edge x coord
            if (flag2 & 1)                    // if crosses left, clip left edge
                xedge = AFix(clipRect.left);
            else                              // else right, clip right edge
                xedge = AFix(clipRect.right) - AFix::epsilon;
            AFix slope = (y2 - y1) / (x2 - x1);   // compute slope of line
            y2 = y1 + (slope * (xedge - x1));     // calc y-crossing & set y2
            x2 = xedge;                           // set x2 to crossing
            }

// Else clip against top or bottom. Compute intersection with the
// appropriate side and set new endpoint x,y
```

```
    else                        // else clip against top or bottom edge
      {
      AFix yedge;               // will hold y edge coord
      if (flag2 & 4)            // if crosses top, clip top edge
         yedge = AFix(clipRect.top);
      else                      // else bott, clip bott edge
         yedge = AFix(clipRect.bott) - AFix::epsilon;
      AFix slope = (x2 - x1) / (y2 - y1);   // compute slope of line
      x2 = x1 + (slope * (yedge - y1));     // calc x-crossing & set x2
      y2 = yedge;               // set y2 to crossing
      }

// Recompute clipcode of endpoint 2 for next time through loop

    flag2 = ClipCode(x2, y2);
    }
}
```

Once we can clip a line's endpoints to the cliprect, the clipped version of the line drawer is easy:

```
void ACanvas::DrawLine(AFix x1, AFix y1, AFix x2, AFix y2)
{
   if (ClipLine(x1, y1, x2, y2;))
      DrawLineU(x1, y1, x2, y2);
}
```

PIXBLITZ: A Rendering Speed Tester

On the accompanying CD is a program, including source, that tests the speed of the various rendering primitives developed over the past few chapters. PIXBLITZ flashes the screen annoyingly for about a minute and a half, and then prints out to the screen a report which gives the speed of each operation in terms of pixels per second. Redirecting the output to a file creates a permanent record of the results. For instance, type:

```
PIXBLITZ >pixblitz.out
```

The speeds reported vary from machine to machine, and are a function of:

- The speed of your CPU, determined by CPU type (386/486/Pentium), clock speed, cache design, and other factors
- The speed of your VGA card's bus and display memory
- The compiler used to compile PIXBLITZ, and the optimization flags used

The results for a Gateway 90 Mhz Pentium with a PCI-bus ATI Mach64 VGA, using code compiled using Symantec C++ 6.11 with optimization fully on, are listed in Table 4.2. Your mileage may vary.

The numbers are approximate due to the calling overhead built into PIXBLITZ—the actual speed of the rendering methods themselves is somewhat higher than reported here. Horizontal lines reported a rate of over 13 million pixels per second. That's over 190 screenfulls per second at 320 × 200 resolution! Not bad for mere C++ code. Speaking of screenfulls, it's time to move beyond the chunky pixels of mode 13H, and switch into high-resolution modes. High resolution means Super VGA, the subject of the next chapter.

Table 4.2 Results from PIXBLITZ, Run on Gateway P5-90 with ATI Mach 64

Primitive	*Speed (in Pixels/Second, Unclipped)*
Pixel	2303136
HorzLine	13138272
VertLine	5587960
Box	7511205
Rect	12425600
Line	1691584
Lin8 bitmap (transp)	5355420
Lin8 bitmap (not tr)	6564936

C H A P T E R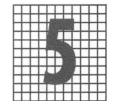

Super VGA Graphics

Up to this point, all our rendering has been done under the VGA's mode 13H, which offers 320 × 200 resolution in 8-bit color. This mode has been the standard for PC games since soon after the VGA was introduced with IBM's PS/2 series in 1987, but it's getting a little tired. Higher-resolution Super VGA graphics cards are the norm now, and they are finally getting zippy enough for real-time animation. Commercial games such as *Sim City* and *Syndicate* run in Super VGA, and a broad transition among developers is in the works. This chapter introduces the Super VGA (SVGA) and the *VESA* standard for accessing it. We'll develop a display driver for ARTT which works with a variety of 8-bit SVGA modes. Later on, in Chapter 14, we'll explore SVGA modes which feature more than 8 bits of color depth. High resolution lives!

The Super VGA

In 1987, IBM introduced the PS/2 series of computers, and with them the new Video Graphics Array (VGA) standard. VGA is a superset of EGA, the Enhanced Graphics Adapter introduced a few years earlier in 1985. The VGA came standard with 256K of display memory, and

153

featured several modes unavailable on the EGA. One of these, mode 13H, was the first mode to support 256 simultaneous onscreen colors, albeit in a low 320 × 200 resolution. Other modes supported 640 × 480 in up to 16 simultaneous colors (4-bit per pixel color).

Why didn't IBM supply a standard mode capable of 256 colors in higher resolutions? The answer, as far as I can tell, is a combination of math and marketing. A 640 × 480 mode in 256 colors was out of the question, for the simple reason that 640 × 480 = 307,200 bytes of display memory, more than that available on the VGA. However, 640 × 400, double the 320 × 200 in each dimension, does fit in 256K of display memory, with a few kilobytes to spare. Why not provide this mode? I don't know, but my best guess lies in the fact that some PS/2 computers were shipped with the Multi-Colored Graphics Array (MCGA), a subset of the VGA with only 64K of display memory. The MCGA was capable of 320 × 200 in 256 colors, but just barely. A 640 × 400 mode would not have run on a PS/2 with MCGA. So one might think that IBM abandoned higher-resolution modes in order to keep mode support common between VGA and MCGA, but in fact there are other modes not common to both adapters. Perhaps nobody thought that a 640 × 400 256-color mode would be useful! And 64K is all the memory a computer will ever need, if I remember correctly.

Third-party graphics board manufacturers had cut their teeth making clones of the EGA, and cloning the VGA was a logical next step. Within a year, VGA chip and board makers such as ATI, Tseng, Western Digital, Cirrus Logic, and others were shipping products. They quickly began competing on more than price, offering enhancements in the form of new text and graphics modes featuring higher resolutions. In the last few years an explosion of other sorts of enhancements has occurred, including increased color depths, hardware-assisted pixel drawing, hardware cursor overlays, digital video playback support, enhanced DAC color table resolution, and more. And with precious little standardization across manufacturers, as we shall see.

Super VGA Basics: Planar and Packed-Pixel Modes

A Super VGA card is very much like a VGA card, and indeed must be a strict superset of the VGA, supporting all its modes and features. Beyond VGA compatibility, the central identifying factor of a Super VGA card is its support for text and graphics modes not supported by the VGA. The first SVGA cards supported 800 × 600 resolution in 16 simultaneous colors, up from the 640 × 480 maximum of the VGA in mode 12H. Because of the way 16-color (4-bit color) modes are implemented on the VGA, it turns out that higher-resolution 16-

color modes can be programmed using exactly the same code and techniques, except, of course, that the number of pixels across and down is higher, and the new mode must be given a mode number and activated somehow. But the video memory organization and hardware registers used to access that memory need not be changed. VGA and SVGA 16-color modes organize display memory in a *planar* fashion, wherein each pixel is composed of 4 bits, divided into one bit per pixel across 4 planes at the same memory address. Figure 5.1 illustrates.

Splitting a 4-bit pixel across 4 planes, and writing a bit into each plane, would be tedious enough to program, but the fact that the 4 bits in a pixel all exist at the same memory location (but in different memory planes, selected via i/o ports) makes access tedious and slow. On the EGA and VGA, the way 16-color pixels are typically accessed involves special hardware. A 4-bit color value is first written to a "current color" hardware register, and then writing to a single plane of memory causes the color bits to be split and written "across the planes" appropriately. Another hardware register, a "mask" register, can be used to determine which of the 8 pixels in a byte (per plane) is to be updated—up to 8 pixels can be written across all 4 planes in a single memory write!

The 16-color modes are essentially obsolete, so we won't dwell further on the zany intricacies of their programming, of which the

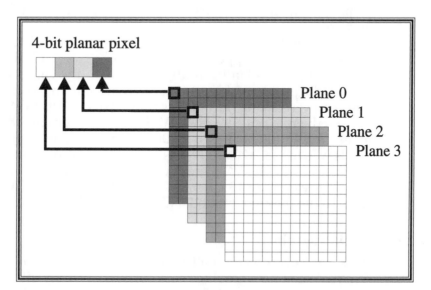

Figure 5.1 Planar memory organization. In this case, 4 planes each contribute a bit to the pixel.

above description is just a small taste. The point here is that, because the display memory is split across 4 planes which all seem to exist at the same memory location, these modes only take up one-fourth the video "address space" they otherwise would. So, a 640 × 480 16-color mode, which requires 640 × 480 / 2 = 153,600 bytes of memory, uses only 153,600 / 4 = 38,400 of address space, starting at 0xA0000 and extending to 0xA9600. Thus, the original SVGA higher-resolution mode, 800 × 600 × 16 colors, can use more memory without spilling over the 64K area allocated to the VGA graphics-mode video memory. It extends from 0xA0000 to 0xAEA60, well below the limit at 0xB0000.

But what about higher-resolution 16-color modes, or indeed 256-color modes beyond 320 × 200? How are they kept from spilling past 0xB000? First of all, it's interesting to note that IBM abandoned the planar architecture for its first 8-bit mode, mode 13H. The various hardware registers associated with planar memory access are 8-bit registers, and the upper four bits of each were reserved for expansion, so it would have been easy enough for IBM to claim the reserved bits and extend planar programming to 8 bits. Why they didn't do this is unclear, but it's a blessing to us poor graphics programmers, because planar programming is slow for certain operations and is just plain tedious and complex. By contrast, the *packed-pixel* mode chosen by IBM for mode 13H, wherein each pixel sits in a byte by itself, is simplicity itself. In Chapter 2, we saw how straightforward it was to access such pixels in a linear format bitmap.

The good news about the packed pixel approach, which is that memory planes disappear, is also the bad news. With the video memory no longer hidden in multiple planes at the same address, we're back to the problem of how to address more than 64K bytes of pixels, without overflowing the address range assigned to VGA devices. This may be the real reason why IBM didn't introduce any 8-bit modes at higher resolution than 320 × 200. Once the decision to used packed pixels was made, 320 × 200 was the highest resolution available that didn't overflow the VGA graphics memory space. At 320 × 200 × 1 = 64000 bytes, mode 13 extends from 0xA0000 to 0xAFA00, perilously close to the 0xB0000 boundary. There's nowhere to go!

Super VGA Bank-Switching

IBM's approach to the fact that the VGA's limits had been reached was to design new graphics cards around entirely different architectures. The Professional Graphics Adapter came and went, followed by the 8514/A and the XGA. While these later two have had some modest success, they have not become mainstream graphics technology. Instead, the clonemakers struck out on their own and captured the marketplace for advanced graphics. How did they get past the video memory limit?

Bank-switching is a time-honored way of sneaking past memory address roadblocks. It was used to get around the 64K memory limit on the Apple-II series and Commodore 128, and is the basis for *expanded memory* on the PC. In bank-switching, a large set of memory is divided into banks, only one or a small number of which can be accessed at a time. Hardware registers are used to select which bank or banks are "active," and such banks then appear at standard memory locations. In the case of the SVGA, a large amount of video memory can be broken into 64K banks, only one of which occupies the space from 0xA0000 to 0xB0000 at a time. See Figure 5.2. This "memory aperture" through which a portion of video memory is "seen" goes by the name *window,* not to be confused with a graphical window.

Using bank-switching, video cards were developed with 512K of memory, then with 1 Mb, and now cards routinely ship with 2 or even 4 Mb of video memory. But, at any given moment, only 64K of this memory is accessible by the CPU.

There is one catch, of course. The VGA has no assigned registers to perform this bank-switching. There is no way to perform the operation which informs the SVGA card which bank or banks of memory to activate. So, in the face of this hurdle, SVGA makers made up their own registers, and assigned them i/o port addresses out of thin air. Or

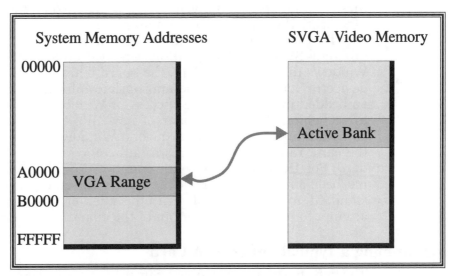

Figure 5.2 Access to a bank of SVGA video memory via addresses 0xA0000 to 0xB0000.

out of a hat, if you will, and each manufacturer picked a different number out of the hat.

Another Tower of Babel

If you thought the lack of standardization in graphics file formats was bad, you're in for a real treat now. Not ones to share ideas with their competitors, each SVGA manufacturer assigned the bank-switch selection registers to different i/o port addresses. In their zeal to avoid incompatibility with the VGA, some found unused bits in existing registers, and used them so as to avoid allocating a new i/o port address which might conflict with some other equipment, such as a network card. Some manufacturers created a "master switch" bit, so that the SVGA card would run in a "total compatibility" mode until that bit was flipped on, and would otherwise ignore access to the new registers. The number of ways in which a few bank selection bits could be strewn randomly across the PC's hardware addressing mechanism is staggering. Find a hard-core SVGA graphics programmer and mention this topic if you have a few hours to kill and want to see some *real* animation.

Besides the assignment of i/o ports for bank registers and other registers, such as compatibility switches, the other major incompatibility arose in the selection of mode numbers. Remember, to put a VGA card into a particular graphics mode requires calling a BIOS software interrupt routine (INT 0x 10, function 0) with the appropriate number of the desired mode. What are the mode numbers for these new modes being invented and reinvented by each SVGA manufacturer? Ha ha. More random numbers.

This would all be funnier if there weren't literally hundreds of different SVGA implementations and variations. Under Microsoft Windows this isn't a problem; the board maker supplies a Windows device driver which has the appropriate information for that card embedded in it. In fact, the success of Windows has been a driving force behind the development of new SVGA capabilities, because compatibility is defined in terms of a Windows driver supplied with the card, rather than in terms of adherence to some abstract standard. For DOS-based programming, however, the lack of standards has been a real stumbling block. Luckily, the emergence of the VESA standard, to be discussed later in this chapter, is a largely successful attempt to bring some order out of the chaos.

Programming a Typical Super VGA Card

The first step to programming a Super VGA card, of course, is to detect whether you have one at all. Since the IBM VGA standard does not include Super VGA, this step itself is by definition nonstandard. Each manufacturer recommends procedures for verifying the presence of its particular board or boards, usually by searching the board's ROM for special strings and/or poking at various registers. Besides the headache of keeping track of the various detection schemes, this approach has inherent problems. One experienced SVGA graphics library developer told me that some detection schemes work fine on the board for which they were intended, and when run on other hardware cause the system to hang. Apparently, the moral is to attempt to detect hardware only if you already know it's there.

Assuming you know you have a particular SVGA card, either by detection or by virtue of a user query (or maybe you bought the card yourself), you can go about putting it into the desired mode. For a given resolution and color depth (say, 640×480 with 8-bit color), the card can be put in that mode by issuing the regular BIOS video mode-set call with the appropriate mode number, *appropriate* meaning whatever the card manufacturer decided. You can return to text mode at the end of the program by the normal means as well. So far so good.

As far as displaying graphics on the screen, happily most SVGA cards are programmed by similar means. In 8-bit packed-pixel SVGA modes, each pixel resides in a single byte, just like good old mode 13H. The only difference is that the graphics memory doesn't all fit between 0xA0000 and 0xB0000, and so bank-switching must be used to access various portions of the screen. Figure 5.3 shows the bank layout for a typical SVGA mode.

The location of bank-switch registers and the exact means by which they are programmed vary from card to card; if you know which card you are running on, you can implement the appropriate i/o instructions. Figure 5.4 shows how an *x,y* coordinate can be converted into a "virtual address" in the SVGA memory, which can then be divided into a bank number and an offset within the bank.

The calculations shown in Figure 5.4 assume a few things. First, the 'rowbytes' of the display is assumed to be the same as its width in pixels. This is generally true, but not always in all modes. If it is, the linear offset into the display memory can be calculated by multiplying the *y*-coordinate by the width, and adding the *x*-coordinate. If not, a separate 'rowbytes' field must be supplied. This is very similar to pixel address calculations used for mode 13H and indeed all linear 8-bit canvases.

Another assumption is that banks are 64K in size, the same size as the video memory address space allocated to the VGA. Again, this is usually true but not always, and is also often under program control, via more nonstandard i/o registers. If the bank size is 64K, then

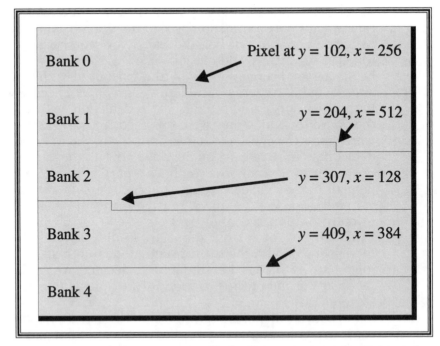

Figure 5.3   Areas of screen occupied by banks in 640 × 480, 8-bit SVGA modes.

the bank number for a given offset is computed by dividing the offset by 64K, which is the same as shifting 16 bits. This example further assumes that there is a single bank switch register into which this bank number can be written, which is often *not* true. Sometimes different bits of the value must be written to different registers.

Once the appropriate bank is selected, the low 16 bits of the memory offset can be added to 0xA0000 to get the true physical address of the pixel, which is then written with the color value. The following sample pseudocode shows how a pixel might be plotted on a hypothetical SVGA card. Note that this pseudocode computes an address and uses it directly, which does not generally work in 32-bit protected-mode environments—ARTT uses AMem::GetPhysPtr() to retrieve a pointer to a physical address.

```
// SAMPLE CODE TO PLOT A PIXEL ON AN SVGA CARD
void PlotPixelSvga8(int x, int y, uchar color)
{
long virtualAddr = (y * display_width) + x;  // calc offset into display
*BANK_SWITCH_REG = virtualAddr >> 16;         // set bank from high 16 bits
*((uchar *) 0xA0000 + (virtualAddr & 0xFFFF)) = color; // set byte
}
```

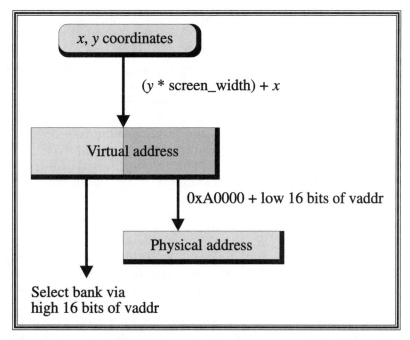

Figure 5.4 Converting an *x,y* coordinate into a virtual address, then bank and pointer.

Bank-Switched Bitmaps in ARTT

Take a look at the ARTT bitmap formats listed in Chapter 1. There are three with the word "bank" in them, namely BMF_BANK8, BMF_BANK15, and BMF_BANK24. These bitmap formats are bank-switched variants of the 8-bit, 15-bit, and 24-bit linear bitmaps named BMF_LIN8, BMF_LIN15, and BMF_LIN24. In ARTT, bank-switched bitmaps are essentially linear, except that they are divided into banks at 64K intervals. Fixing the bank size at 64K allows bank address calculation to be hardcoded and speedy, and even SVGA cards which feature bank sizes other than 64K can be programmed to use 64K bank sizes.

In an 8-bit SVGA mode, then, the screen will be one big bitmap of format BMF_BANK8. Because it is divided into banks, our ACanvasLin8 class, upon which the mode 13H driver is based, cannot be used. A new class, ACanvasBank8, will be the canvas upon which 8-bit SVGA modes will be built. This class will contain the code used to access pixels in a BMF_BANK8 bitmap. Why can't we use ACanvasLin8? Because the bitmap does not fit into one continuous set of addresses—instead, it consists of a set of addresses repeated several times in the bitmap, each with a different hardware bank setting.

In bank-switched bitmaps, the notion of a pointer to a given position in the bitmap is a little strange. After all, by switching banks various portions of the bitmap can be windowed into the same memory address range. For this reason, the 'pbits' field in ABitmap is unioned with 'vaddr', which stands for *virtual address*. The virtual address is the offset into the overall display memory, regardless of which portion is currently selected by the bank setting. Given the virtual address of a pixel, the bank in which it resides and the offset from that bank's beginning can be calculated. In fact, with 64K banks, the bank number is in the high word and the offset in the low word. BMF_BANK8 bitmaps use the 'vaddr' member of the union instead of the 'pbits' member.

Handling Bank Transitions

Take, for instance, a simple example, that of drawing a horizontal line. With a linear bitmap, we just compute a pointer to the first pixel on the line, and then set each pixel at successive memory addresses. However, in a bank-switched bitmap, the line may straddle a bank transition. Note that bank boundaries are not required to fall at the end of display rows—in fact, they are just about guaranteed not to! In a 640-wide 8-bit canvas, the first 64K pixels, bank 0, take up 65536 / 640 = 102 rows + 256 bytes left over. That means the transition from bank 0 to bank 1 occurs after the 256th pixel in the row 102. The switch to bank 2 occurs after the 512th pixel in row 204. Table 5.1 lists the location of bank transitions in a few popular SVGA modes.

Let's think about how to draw a horizontal line in a bank-switched bitmap. Since we'll be drawing from left to right, we first must calculate the virtual address of the leftmost pixel in the line, and make sure the bank that pixel lies in is currently selected. If it is, we needn't bother re-selecting the same bank. If it isn't, we must

Table 5.1 Location of Bank Transitions in Popular 8-bit SVGA Modes	
Mode	*Transitions (y,x)*
640 × 480	102,256 204,512 307,128 409,384
800 × 600	81,736 163,672 244,608 325,544 406,480 487,416 568,352
1024 × 768	64,0 128,0 192,0 256,0 320,0 384,0 448,0 512,0 576,0 640,0 704,0

appropriately reprogram the bank-switch hardware. Then, we determine whether the rightmost pixel lies in the same bank. If it does, then we can just compute a pointer to the first pixel and use a single memset() to write all the pixels. If the line crosses a bank boundary, however, then the line must be drawn in two halves, one memset() for the left half, followed by a bank switch and pointer recalculation, followed by a memset() for the right half. More concretely:

1. Calculate virtual address of leftmost pixel (vaddrL = (y * rowbytes) + xleft).
2. If bank portion of virtual address (high 16 bits) != current bank setting, switch banks.
3. Calculate virtual address of rightmost pixel (vaddrR = (y * rowbytes) + xright).
4. Calculate physical pointer to leftmost pixel (ptr = 0xA0000 + (vaddrL & 0xFFFF)).
5. If bank portion of rightmost virtual address == current bank setting, memset() pixels.
6. Else, memset() to end of current bank, increment bank, recalc pointer, and memset() remaining pixels.

Class ABankMgr: A Bank Manager

In order to aid in the computation of banks and pointers from virtual addresses, we're going to invent a "bank manager" which handles all this for us. Then, when we go to write a canvas class for a new bank-switched bitmap format, we don't have to reinvent the bank-handling logic each time. This bank manager won't actually know how to change the physical bank register settings—this will be done in an unimplemented virtual function and left to a derived class to implement. However, it will provide everything else needed to manage bank-switched memory.

The situation is slightly complicated by the fact that some SVGA devices use a single bank register to control the set of pixels accessed for both reading and writing, whereas other devices have separate bank registers for reading versus writing pixels. Class ABankMgr keeps track of separate "current" bank settings for read versus write, and knows (by being told in its constructor) whether these are really tied to the same physical hardware setting.

Class ABankMgr, our bank manager, provides the following services:

- Constructor: Initializes bank manager instance with base address of "memory window"
- CalcBank(): Calculates bank given a virtual address (high 16 bits)
- Ptr(): Computes pointer from virtual address (adds low 16 bits to base address)

- CrossesBank(): Determines whether virtual address range crosses bank boundary
- BytesLeftInBank(): If range crosses bank, returns number of bytes on "left" side of crossing
- GetWriteBank(): Retrieves current setting of "write" bank
- GetReadBank(): Retrieves current setting of "read" bank
- SetWriteBank(): Sets new "write" bank via SwitchWriteBank(), updates current setting
- SetReadBank(): Sets new "read" bank via SwitchReadBank(), updates current setting
- EnsureWriteBankAtAddr(): Checks if current write bank ok, else calls SetWriteBank()
- EnsureReadBankAtAddr(): Checks if current read bank ok, else calls SetReadBank()

Declared in ABankMgr, but implemented only in derived classes, are the methods which actually do the reprogramming of the bank-switch registers:

- SwitchWriteBank(): Reprograms bank-switch write bank register
- SwitchReadBank(): Reprograms bank-switch read bank register

ABankMgr provides an efficient bank-switching mechanism by keeping track of the current hardware setting(s), and accessing the hardware only when necessary. As another concession to efficiency, ABankMgr works only with banks which are exactly 64K in size. This allows it to provide super-fast inline methods for conversion of virtual addresses to bank numbers and pointers. Most SVGA modes on most devices provide 64K-sized banks. ABankMgr doesn't hardcode 0xA0000 as the base address of the "memory window"—this base address is taken from an argument in the constructor. This is necessary to make the class work in protected-mode environments, where physical pointers must be obtained from the operating system.

The header file for class ABankMgr is listed below. No associated C++ file is necessary—the entire class is defined via inline methods. Note in particular the implementation of CalcBank() and Ptr(). CalcBank() returns the bank associated with a virtual address, by simply shifting the virtual address down 16 bits, equivalent to dividing by 64K. Ptr() converts a virtual address to a physical pointer, assuming the bank is set correctly for that virtual address, by simply masking off the high 16 bits and adding to the base address.

```
//   ABankMgr.h    Bank-switched manager class
//   Rex E. Bradford


#ifndef __ABANKMGR_H
#define __ABANKMGR_H
```

```cpp
#include "atypes.h"

class ABankMgr {

    int writeBankCurr;      // current write bank
    int readBankCurr;       // current read bank
    bool readWriteTied;     // same bank reg for read/write
    uchar *pBankBaseAddr;   // ptr to physical base addr of bank

// Perform actual bank-switching operation

    virtual void SwitchWriteBank(int bank) = 0;
    virtual void SwitchReadBank(int bank) = 0;

public:

// Constructor: set basic bank info

    ABankMgr(uchar *baseAddr, bool rwTied) {
       writeBankCurr = readBankCurr = 0;
       pBankBaseAddr = baseAddr; readWriteTied = rwTied;}

// Calculate bank and pointer at a virtual address

    static int CalcBank(long vaddr) {return (vaddr >> 16);}
    void *Ptr(long vaddr) {return(pBankBaseAddr + (vaddr & 0xFFFF));}

// Check if segment crosses bank boundary, also find amt before split

    static bool CrossesBank(long vaddr, int len) {
       return((vaddr ^ (vaddr + len)) >> 16);}
    static int BytesLeftInBank(long vaddr) {
       return(0x10000L - (vaddr & 0xFFFFL));}

// Get current read and write banks

    int GetWriteBank() {return writeBankCurr;}
    int GetReadBank() {return readBankCurr;}

// Set read & write banks

    void SetWriteBank(int bank) {SwitchWriteBank(bank);
       writeBankCurr = bank; if (readWriteTied) readBankCurr = bank;}

    void SetReadBank(int bank) {SwitchReadBank(bank);
       readBankCurr = bank; if (readWriteTied) writeBankCurr = bank;}

// Calculate bank, ensure correct bank given virtual address

    void EnsureWriteBankAtAddr(long vaddr) {
       if ((vaddr >> 16) != writeBankCurr) SetWriteBank(vaddr >> 16);}
    void EnsureReadBankAtAddr(long vaddr) {
```

```
            if ((vaddr >> 16) != readBankCurr) SetReadBank(vaddr >> 16);}
    };


    #endif
```

Class ACanvasBank8: 8-Bit Bank-Switched Canvases

Now that we have a bank manager, we can develop a generic canvas class for handling 8-bit bank-switched bitmaps. ACanvasBank8 will be derived from ACanvas8, because it is an 8-bit canvas. It will hold a pointer to the particular bank manager used to handle bank-switching, so that it can work with different bank-switching methods. This frees us to derive bank-switching implementations for different SVGA devices—in fact, it frees us to derive bank-switching implementations which are not tied to SVGA at all! One could imaging writing a class to perform rendering into files larger than can exist in memory, and using bank-switching as a paging mechanism to bring the desired section of the file into a single 64K memory window. This is, in fact, possible by creating an appropriate bank manager derived from ABankMgr and hooking it up to a bank-switched canvas. See the discussion in Chapter 20.

We're getting ahead of ourselves. Let's get back to ACanvas-Bank8, which is a generic canvas class for handling all 8-bit bank-switched bitmaps. ACanvasBank8 handles all rendering into such bitmaps, either itself or by inheriting from ACanvas and ACanvas8. For instance, the DrawLine() method in ACanvas will work automatically, as long as we implement DrawPixelU() here in ACanvasBank8.

Here is the header file for class ACanvasBank8, simplified to leave out rendering methods we haven't even seen yet in ACanvas or ACanvasLin8.

```
//   ACvBank8.h     8-bit bank-switched canvas class
//   Rex E. Bradford

#ifndef __ACVBANK8_H
#define __ACVBANK8_H

#include "acanvas8.h"
#include "abankmgr.h"

class ACanvasBank8 : public ACanvas8 {

    ABankMgr *pBankMgr; // ptr to bank manager object

// Compute virtual address from x,y
```

```
   long Vaddr(int x, int y) {return(bm.vaddr +
     (long(y) * long(bm.rowbytes)) + x);}

// Hand off to bank manager for easy coding in rendering methods

   uchar *Ptr(long vaddr) {return(uchar*) (pBankMgr->Ptr(vaddr));}
   void EnsureWriteBankAtAddr(long vaddr) {
     pBankMgr->EnsureWriteBankAtAddr(vaddr);}
   void EnsureReadBankAtAddr(long vaddr) {
     pBankMgr->EnsureReadBankAtAddr(vaddr); }
   static bool CrossesBank(long vaddr, int len) {
     return(ABankMgr::CrossesBank(vaddr, len));}
   static int BytesLeftInBank(long vaddr) {
     return(ABankMgr::BytesLeftInBank(vaddr));}

public:

// Constructor: initializes underlying 8-bit canvas

   ACanvasBank8(ABitmap *pbm, ABankMgr *pBankMgr_) : ACanvas8(pbm)
     {pBankMgr = pBankMgr_;}

// Draw pixel

   void DrawPixelU(int x, int y);
   void DrawPixel8U(int x, int y, uchar color);

// Get pixel

   uchar GetPixel8U(int x, int y);

// Geometric drawing routines

   void DrawHorzLineU(int y, int xleft, int xright);

// Bitmap drawing

   void DrawBitmapLin8U(ABitmap &bm, int x, int y);
};

#endif
```

ACanvasBank8 Constructor

The constructor for class ACanvasBank8 takes a pointer to a bitmap and a pointer to a bank manager instance. The bank manager pointer should point to an initialized bank manager—later in this chapter, we'll create a derived bank manager class to handle SVGA devices, and put it to work. The bitmap pointer argument should be pointing

> *In the above class definition, the methods Ptr(), Ensure WriteBankAtAddr(), EnsureReadBankAtAddr(), Crosses-Bank(), and BytesLeftInBank() might seem curious. They simply "hand off" to methods of the same name in class ABankMgr. They are simply present as a syntactic convenience to rendering methods in class ACanvas-Bank8, so that such code can access these bank manager routines without preceding them by pBankMgr-> or ABankMgr::.*

to a bitmap which is already appropriately constructed. Such a bitmap should have a 'format' field set to BMF_BANK8, signifying that it is an 8-bit bank-switched bitmap. Its 'vaddr' field, the base offset into the bank-switched memory, is 0 for a full-screen SVGA canvas. There is a special "convenience" constructor in class ABitmap for initializing bank-switched bitmaps. We skipped over the definition of this constructor in Chapter 1. Here it is now.

```
ABitmap::ABitmap(uchar form, short w, short h, short row)
{
// This constructor is for bank-switched bitmaps, vaddr starts at 0

    vaddr = 0;

// Fill in fields from args, assume not transparent

    format = form;
    transparent = FALSE;
    width = w;
    height = h;

// Set rowbytes from arg unless 0, in which case use std calc
// Compute length as rowbytes × height

    if (row)
        rowbytes = row;
    else
        rowbytes = RowSize(width);
    length = long(rowbytes) * long(height);

// Set ppalette to NULL; must set by hand if desired

    ppalette = NULL;
}
```

Computing Virtual Addresses

The first thing any bank-switched rendering routine needs to do is convert *x,y* coordinates into virtual addresses, which can then be used to compute banks and pointers. The inline method Vaddr() computes a virtual address from an *x,y* coordinate. Note that this computation is basically identical to the way a linear canvas computes a pointer, except that the type of the return value is long instead of uchar*. This similarity is not surprising, because the virtual address space is linear, even if the bank-switched device memory is not.

```
long Vaddr(int x, int y) {return(bm.vaddr +
        (long(y) * long(bm.rowbytes)) + x);}
```

ACanvasBank8 Pixel Setting and Getting

Drawing a pixel in a bank-switched canvas is a little more involved than in a linear canvas, but it's still pretty simple. DrawPixelU() draws a pixel in the current color at the specified *x,y* location. First, it uses Vaddr() to calculate the virtual address at that pixel. The next step is to make sure the correct bank is selected for that virtual address, using the inline EnsureWriteBankAtAddr() method (which hands off to ABankMgr::EnsureWriteBankAtAddr()—see the header file and accompanying C++ note). Finally, the color pixel can be written to the pointer calculated from the virtual address by Ptr(). Don't be alarmed by the function calls—all are inlined. An actual function call occurs only when a bank register needs to be changed to a new value.

```
void ACanvasBank8::DrawPixelU(int x, int y)
{
    long vaddr = Vaddr(x, y);      // calc virtual addr
    EnsureWriteBankAtAddr(vaddr);  // make sure right bank is set
    *Ptr(vaddr) = color8;          // calc video ptr, set pixel there
}
```

DrawPixel8U() is the same, except that the color value is passed in.

```
void ACanvasBank8::DrawPixel8U(int x, int y, uchar c8)
{
    long vaddr = Vaddr(x, y);      // calc virtual addr
    EnsureWriteBankAtAddr(vaddr);  // make sure right bank is set
    *Ptr(vaddr) = c8;              // calc video ptr, set pixel there
}
```

Retrieving the current color of a pixel is similar. Note that Ensure-ReadBankAtAddr() is used instead of EnsureWriteBankAtAddr(). In the case where there is only one shared bank register, the bank manager ensures that the current read and write bank values stay in sync.

```
uchar ACanvasBank8::GetPixel8U(int x, int y)
{
    long vaddr = Vaddr(x, y);      // calc virtual addr
```

```
EnsureReadBankAtAddr(vaddr);     // make sure right bank is set
return(*Ptr(vaddr));             // calc video ptr, get pixel there
```

ACanvasBank8 Horizontal Line-Drawer

The routines to draw and retrieve pixel values are sufficient to make the bank-switched driver work. All higher-level operations have implementations in the base ACanvas class which use these pixel primitives to get the job done. However, relying on pixel-by-pixel operations makes for a pretty slow display driver. We can achieve dramatic improvement in performance by writing bank-switch-specific versions of the horizontal line-drawer (on which boxes and rectangles are based) and bitmap renderer.

As we saw previously, care must be taken to detect and handle horizontal lines which cross a bank boundary. We could do this by simply calling EnsureWriteBankAtAddr() for every pixel, but that wouldn't be very efficient. Instead, we'll use the CrossesBank() method to detect whether a bank-crossing occurs. If it doesn't, we'll just use memset() to draw the entire line. If a crossing does occur somewhere in the line, we'll use two memsets(), one for each half. It's not nearly as simple as ACanvasLin8::DrawHorzLineU(), but that's bank-switching for you.

```
void ACanvasBank8::DrawHorzLineU(int y, int xleft, int xright)
{
// Compute virtual address of 1st pixel, make sure we're in right bank

    long vaddr = Vaddr(xleft, y);
    EnsureWriteBankAtAddr(vaddr);

// See if horz line lies across a bank boundary, if so split

    if (CrossesBank(vaddr, xright - xleft))
        {
        int numLeft = BytesLeftInBank(vaddr);
        memset(Ptr(vaddr), color8, numLeft);
        EnsureWriteBankAtAddr(vaddr + numLeft);
        memset(Ptr(0), color8, (xright - xleft) - numLeft);
        }
    else
        memset(Ptr(vaddr), color8, xright - xleft);
}
```

ACanvasBank8 Bitmap Drawing

Bitmap drawing is more complex still, because of the additional burden of transparency handling. For each row of the bitmap, a test to see whether the row spans a bank boundary must be made. The case where a bank boundary occurs is handled with special code, and the normal case is written to go as fast as possible. In each of these two cases, separate code is used for transparent bitmaps versus non-transparent bitmaps, so essentially there are four different pieces of code to handle a given row. This routine is long because of this, but it's an important one that should be as efficient as possible. Overall, this routine is just about as fast as its counterpart in ACanvasLin8, which renders the same bitmap into a linear 8-bit canvas.

```
void ACanvasBank8::DrawBitmapLin8U(ABitmap &bms, int x, int y)
{
// Setup: get source ptr and compute virtual address

    uchar *ps = bms.pbits;
    long vaddr = Vaddr(x, y);

// Loop through rows

    int h = bms.height;                 // local copy of height
    while (h-- > 0)
        {
// Make sure we're at the right bank for the start of this row

        EnsureWriteBankAtAddr(vaddr);   // make sure the bank is right
        uchar *pv = Ptr(vaddr);         // compute ptr to leftmost pixel


// Does this row lie across a bank boundary?

        if (CrossesBank(vaddr, bms.width))
            {

// Yes and transparent, punt efficiency and go pixel by pixel

            if (bms.transparent)
                {
                long vaddrTransp = vaddr;  // local copy of virtual address
                int w = bms.width;         // and local copy of width
                while (w-- > 0)
                    {
                    if (*ps) *pv = *ps;    // write non-zero pixel
                    ++ps;                  // increment source ptr
                    ++pv;                  // increment dest ptr
                    if ((++vaddrTransp & 0xFFFFL) == 0)
                        {
                        EnsureWriteBankAtAddr(vaddrTransp); // bank cross!
                        pv = Ptr(vaddrTransp);       // get new dest ptr
                        }
                    }
                }
```

```
// Yes, across bank, but not transparent, split into two memcpy's

        else
            {
            int numLeft = BytesLeftInBank(vaddr);     // # pixels on left
            memcpy(pv, ps, numLeft);                  // copy them
            EnsureWriteBankAtAddr(vaddr + numLeft);   // bank switch
            memcpy(Ptr(vaddr + numLeft),              // copy right pixels
                ps + numLeft, bms.width - numLeft);
            ps += bms.rowbytes;                       // advance src ptr
            }
        }


// No, row does not lie across bank boundary (like a LIN8 row!)

        else
            }
// Not split but transparent: go pixel by pixel

        if (bms.transparent)
            {
            int w = bms.width;            // local copy of width
            while (w--> 0)
                {
                if (*ps) *pv = *ps;       // write non-zero pixel
                ++ps;                     // increment source ptr
                ++pv;                     // increment dest ptr
                }
            ps += bms.rowbytes - bms.width; // advance src to next row
            }

// Not split, not transparent, just memcpy()

        else
            {
            memcpy(pv, ps, bms.width); // just copy bytes, how easy!
            ps += bms.rowbytes;        // and advance src ptr to next row
            }
        }


// Update virtual address for next row

        vaddr += bm.rowbytes;
        }
    }
```

Clipping in ACanvasBank8

What about clipping? It's all handled in the base ACanvas class—the clipped versions of these routines located there do clipping calculations and then call the unclipped versions listed here via virtual function calls.

Bank-Switched Super VGA Canvases

Class ACanvasBank8 works, and we needn't derive from it any further. However, we can't use it yet, because we have no way of instantiating a bank manager for it to use. Class ABankMgr is an abstract base class, with methods SwitchWriteBank() and SwitchReadBank() left unimplemented. So what we need to do is write a class, derived from ABankMgr, which can handle the bank-switching for SVGA devices. With this new class, we could use ACanvasBank8 with Super VGA screen modes.

The problem, of course, is that each Super VGA device has special quirks, including nonstandard mode numbers, different register and bit assignments for bank-switching, special "master" switches for accessing extended functionality, and other oddities. The issue of detecting which card is in a given machine is no small matter either. Nevertheless, we could pick the several most popular cards and supply bank manager implementations for them at least. But given that nowadays each manufacturer seems to come out with a new graphics card every six months, this approach will require constant maintenance to stay current. One's thoughts begin to turn to methods of torture, applied slowly, perhaps one water drop for each line of code required to support a given card.

Fortunately, there's a better way.

The VESA BIOS Extensions

By the late 1980s it was clear that the Super VGA "Tower of Babel" was quickly getting out of control, and some standardized way of accessing these cards was needed. The Video Electronics Standards Association (VESA), a consortium of chip and board manufacturers, took up the task of defining a common interface to SVGA, a set of BIOS extensions that eventually became known as the VBE (VESA Bios Extension). The VESA committee did a good job of focusing on the heart of the problem, that of developing standard mechanisms for accessing SVGA modes and performing bank switching. To its credit, the committee did not overreach and attempt to create an entire graphics programming interface. Such an effort would surely fail, especially given the need to implement any new standard within the confines of the limited video card BIOS space and RAM for device drivers.

The original VBE spec was published in 1989. Version 1.2, issued in October 1991, has been the common standard supported by most manufacturers. At the time of this writing in mid-1995, version 2.0 has recently been finalized. The version of the VBE described in this chapter is 1.2, but discussion of relevant 2.0 features will be included.

The VBE includes a standard list of resolutions and the mode numbers assigned to these modes. It also includes an application programming interface (API) with the following functionality, accessible by software interrupts:

- Detect presence of VBE support.
- Query supported VBE modes and capabilities.
- Set and restore SVGA modes.
- Save and restore SVGA state information.
- Control bank-switch hardware.
- Access advanced features, such as enhanced DACs and logical line length (rowbytes).

Initially, VBE support was implemented by a TSR (terminate and stay-resident) module that could be loaded at boot time, and some cards still require a TSR to provide VESA support. The TSR "maps" the VESA mode numbers and requests onto card-specific functionality. In general, a TSR is specific to a given SVGA card, although "universal" VBE drivers are available which can provide VBE support for a wide variety of SVGA hardware. In particular, SciTech has a product called UniVBE which is widely used.

In the last few years, many hardware manufacturers have built VBE support right into the ROM BIOS along with the basic VGA support software. No TSR is necessary. This has the advantage of not using any precious RAM or requiring the end user to install the TSR via AUTOEXEC.BAT.

VESA VBE Modes

Table 5.2 lists standard mode numbers defined in the 1.2 specification. SVGA cards are not required to support all modes—a query facility is provided to determine what modes and features are implemented by a given card. In version 2.0, no new mode numbers have been added, and, in fact, mode numbers are being phased out in favor of generic queries based on resolution and color depth.

VESA modes start at 100h (they have bit 8 set, which defines them as VESA mode numbers). For historical reasons, the VESA spec also defines an "alias" mode number for mode 102h, that alias being 0x6Ah.

VBE Application Programming Interface

All calls to the VBE implementation are done through the standard video software interrupt, int 10h. VESA defined a new BIOS function number for the extended calls, namely 4Fh, and several subfunctions. In assembly language, the function number is passed to the int

Table 5.2 VBE Standard Modes

Mode number	Resolution	Colors
100h	640 × 400	256 (8-bit indexed color)
101h	640 × 480	256
102h/6Ah	800 × 600	16 (4-bit planar memory)
103h	800 × 600	256
104h	1024 × 768	16
105h	1024 × 768	256
106h	1280 × 1024	16
107h	1280 × 1024	256
10Dh	320 × 200	32K (5:5:5—5 red, 5 green, 5 blue, direct-color)
10Eh	320 × 200	64K (5:6:5—5 red, 6 green, 5 blue, direct-color)
10Fh	320 × 200	16.8M (8:8:8—8 red, 8 green, 8 blue, direct-color)
110h	640 × 480	32K
111h	640 × 480	64K
112h	640 × 480	16.8M
113h	800 × 600	32K
114h	800 × 600	64K
115h	800 × 600	16.8M
116h	1024 × 768	32K
117h	1024 × 768	64K
118h	1024 × 768	16.8M
119h	1280 × 1024	32K
11Ah	1280 × 1024	64K
11Bh	1280 × 1024	16.8M

10h handler in register AH and the subfunction in register AL; ARTT uses the int86() library function and passes in arguments through the REGS pseudoregister structure used by int86(). The new int 10h functions handled by the VBE through function 4Fh are listed in Table 5.3.

Each of these functions returns status information as to whether the function is supported, and whether the function was successful in performing the desired operation. These status codes are returned in registers AL and AH, and are coded as follows:

Table 5.3   VBE 1.2 Functions (subfunctions of int 10, function 4Fh)

Func.	Purpose	Comments
0	Return Super VGA information	Detect if VBE present & return info
1	Return Super VGA mode information	Check for mode, return info on it
2	Set Super VGA video mode	Launch this mode
3	Return current VGA video mode	Get mode so can restore before exit
4	Save/Restore Super VGA video state	Allows entire "context" switch
5	CPU video memory window control	Performs bank-switch
6	Set/Get logical scan line length	Manipulate screen "rowbytes"
7	Set/Get display start	Perform hardware scrolling
8	Set/Get DAC palette control	Enable 8-bit DAC color table

AL == 4Fh: Function is supported
AL != 4Fh: Function is not supported
AH == 00h: Function call successful
AH == 01h: Function call failed

Like all BIOS calls, the VBE functions must be executed in "real mode." Programs executing in protected mode under a DOS extender must take care when calling such functions. In particular, data buffers must reside in "real memory" below 1 Mb, and all addresses passed must be translated between the segment:offset format of real mode and the protected mode format of the particular extended environment.

Besides handling the business of translating mode numbers and providing an interface for applications to query the various modes supported by the hardware, VESA supplies a mechanism to get at the bank-switch hardware. While we have so far assumed that banks must be aligned on 64K boundaries, in fact many SVGA cards allow finer control over the placement of the 64K memory window. The *granularity* at which banks may be positioned is often 4K or even less; it is always a power of 2 to simplify conversion from virtual address to bank number. Bank granularities of less than 64K can provide a modest rendering boost in some cases where an image crosses a 64K bank boundary. For instance, if an image lies across the division between the first and second 64K of video memory on an implementation with a bank granularity of 4K, the hardware can be pro-

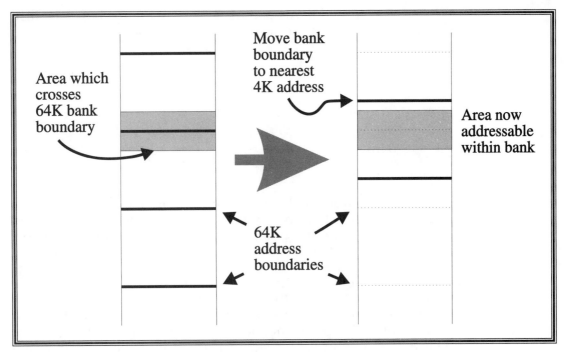

Figure 5.5 Using fine granularity of bank window to avoid bank-crossing.

grammed to set the bank to the nearest 4K boundary prior to the image, and voilà, the image no longer crosses a bank boundary. See Figure 5.5.

The performance improvement gained by using such a technique is very minor, and can even be outweighed by the performance gained by "hardcoding" the 64K bank alignment into rendering code. ARTT banks are hardcoded to 64K alignment, and so ARTT does not need to make use of bank granularity.

The information about VBE function calls given in the following sections is somewhat brief, and focuses on what we need to know in order to program Super VGAs under ARTT. For more in-depth information, including how to order the latest VBE specification, see Appendix E.

VBE Function 0: Return Super VGA Information

This call serves to detect whether VBE support is available at all, and to obtain general information if so. The AH and AL registers should be set to 4Fh and 0, respectively, and the address of a 256-byte buffer is passed to this function in the register pair ES:DI. The return status,

as always, is returned in AH and AL. If successful, the buffer is filled in with useful information, according to the following structure:

```
typedef struct {
    ABYTE signature[4];          // 'VESA'
    AWORD16 version;             // major version in high byte, minor in low
    AWORD16 oemStringOff;        // real-mode offset of oem string
    AWORD16 oemStringSeg;        // real-mode segment of oem string
    AWORD32 capabilities;        // capabilities flags
    AWORD16 videoModeOff;        // real-mode offset of supported mode list
    AWORD16 videoModeSeg;        // real-mode segment of supported mode list
    AWORD16 memory;              // number of 64K memory segments on card
} AVesaInfo;
```

If the 'signature' field does not contain the four characters "VESA," something has gone wrong and further VESA calls should not be made. The VESA version number is returned in the 'version' field. A pointer to a manufacturer-supplied string, usually identifying board or chipset, is pointed to by 'oemStringOff' and 'oemStringSeg'. This is informational only and is not needed in order to program the SVGA. Version 1.2 of the VBE defines only the lowest bit of the 'capabilities' field. If set, it denotes that this card has a DAC which can be switched into 8-bit per component operation. A pointer to a list of supported mode numbers is supplied in 'videoModeOff' and 'videoModeSeg'. These mode numbers are word-sized and terminated by a mode number of 0xFFFF(–1). Finally, the 'memory' field identifies the amount of video memory on the card, in terms of 64K-sized chunks.

VBE Function 1: Return Super VGA Mode Information

Once VBE support has been established, an application can obtain information about a particular mode number using function 1. The AH and AL registers are set to 4Fh and 1, respectively, the mode number about which information is desired is placed in CX, and the address of a 256-byte buffer is passed in ES:DI. This function then fills in the buffer with information about the mode, and returns status in AH and AL.

The mode number to be queried might be a standard mode number taken from the standard list in Table 5.2, or it might be obtained by iterating over the list supplied by function 0. In any case, function 1 returns a wealth of information about the mode, in particular information about its "window" (bank) support.

The information returned by function 1 is described by the structure given below.

```
typedef struct {
    AWORD16 modeAttributes;      // mode attributes, VESA_MODEATTR_XXX
    ABYTE winAAttributes;        // flags whether window A absent/read/write
```

```
    ABYTE winBAttributes;       // flags whether window B absent/read/write
    AWORD16 winGranularity;     // granularity of window placement in K
    AWORD16 winSize;            // size of window in K
    AWORD16 winASegment;        // location of window A memory
    AWORD16 winBSegment;        // location of window B memory
    AWORD16 winFuncOff;         // offset of real-mode bank switch function
    AWORD16 winFuncSeg;         // segment of real-mode bank switch function
    AWORD16 bytesPerScanLine;   // rowbytes of display
// The following information was optional before VESA 1.2, required now
    AWORD16 xResolution;        // width of screen in pixels
    AWORD16 yResolution;        // height of screen in pixels
    ABYTE xCharSize;            // width of character cell in pixels
    ABYTE yCharSize;            // height of character cell in pixels
    ABYTE numberOfPlanes;       // number of bitplanes
    ABYTE bitsPerPixel;         // number of bits in each pixel
    ABYTE numberOfBanks;        // number of groupings for nonlinear modes
    ABYTE memoryModel;          // display memory layout, VESA_MEMMODEL_XXX
    ABYTE bankSize;             // size of groupings for nonlinear modes
    ABYTE numImagePages;        // number of image pages
    ABYTE reserved;             // set to 1
// The following are used in direct-color modes
    ABYTE redMaskSize;          // size of direct color red mask in bits
    ABYTE redFieldPos;          // bit position of lsb of red mask
    ABYTE greenMaskSize;        // size of direct color green mask in bits
    ABYTE greenFieldPos;        // bit position of lsb of green mask
    ABYTE blueMaskSize;         // size of direct color blue mask in bits
    ABYTE blueFieldPos;         // bit position of lsb of blue mask
    ABYTE rsvdMaskSize;         // size of direct color reserved mask in bits
    ABYTE rsvdFieldPos;         // bit position of lsb of reserved mask
    ABYTE directColorModeInfo;  // direct-color mode attributes
} AVesaModeInfo;

#define VESA_MODEATTR_DISPSUPP   0x01  // does display supports this mode?
#define VESA_MODEATTR_OPTINFO    0x02  // is optional info present?
#define VESA_MODEATTR_BIOSTEXT   0x04  // are BIOS text output funcs avail?
#define VESA_MODEATTR_COLOR      0x08  // is mode color? (else monochrome)
#define VESA_MODEATTR_GRAPHICS   0x10  // is mode graphics? (else text)

#define VESA_MEMMODEL_TEXT    0     // text mode
#define VESA_MEMMODEL_CGA     1     // 2 bit/pixel CGA mode
#define VESA_MEMMODEL_HERC    2     // Hercules monochrome mode
#define VESA_MEMMODEL_4PLANE  3     // 16-color planar mode
#define VESA_MEMMODEL_PACKED  4     // Byte-wide packed mode
#define VESA_MEMMODEL_NOCHAIN 5     // Mode X style
#define VESA_MEMMODEL_DIRECT  6     // Direct-color mode
#define VESA_MEMMODEL_YUV     7     // YUV-encoded mode
```

The first element, 'modeAttributes', has bit flags which indicate some information about the mode. The constants named beginning with VESA_MODEATTR_ describe the use of each bit. The next fields provide a variety of information about the A and B windows (one for reading and one for writing, if both are present). For each, this includes the "window" segment, which is nearly always 0xA000 for the primary A window, and the window granularity, which specifies the granularity of window placement in 'K' (1K is the minimum allowed granularity). ARTT thinks in terms of 64K banks, whereas VBE bank numbers are in terms of units of the granularity. The granularity value is needed in order to convert ARTT 64K bank numbers into those expected by the VBE, which are expressed in units of the supplied granularity.

The mode information structure contains much more mode-specific information—see the comments next to each field.

VBE Function 2: Set Super VGA Video Mode

Once we have determined that a mode number is valid, and have obtained the relevant information about that mode, we can set the SVGA into that mode. VBE function 2 does just that, and is essentially a VBE version of the standard VGA BIOS mode set routine at int 10h, function 0. The AH and AL registers are set to 4Fh and 2, respectively, and the mode to be set is placed into BX. This function then sets the mode if it is a valid one, and returns status in AH and AL.

For SVGA modes, this function should be used instead of the standard BIOS mode set routine.

VBE Function 3: Return Current VGA Video Mode

VBE function 3 is used to determine the current VGA or Super VGA video mode, in order that later we may return the card to that mode. The AH and AL registers are set to 4Fh and 3, respectively. The function returns the current mode number in BX, and status in AH and AL. Since the current mode may be a Super VGA mode, this function is preferable to the standard VGA BIOS mode-retriever (int 10, function 0Fh) when VESA is present.

VBE Function 4: Save/Restore Super VGA Video State

VBE function 4 is used to save or restore the Super VGA "video state." It is used by software which must perform a full "context" switch and be able to restore it later. This function is akin to the standard video BIOS calls to save or restore VGA state (int 10, function 1Ch). The video state consists of the video hardware state, the BIOS data area state, the DAC color table state, and the Super VGA register state. Any or all of these four components may be saved or restored with this call. ARTT does not require or support such context switches.

VBE Function 5: CPU Video Memory Window Control

VBE function 5 is used to perform bank-switching, or "windowing" in VBE parlance. It can be used, depending on arguments, to either set or retrieve the state of the bank register. It can do so for either window A or window B. ARTT uses the mode information returned by function 1 to determine which window is the "write" window and which is the "read" window, or whether, in fact, both reading and writing are tied to a single window (usually A if this is the case).

To set a given window to a desired bank number setting, AH and AL are set to 4Fh and 5, respectively, BH is set to 0, BL is set to 0 for window A or 1 for window B, and DX is set to the bank number to be set (in window granularity units). Status, as always, is returned in AH and AL.

To retrieve the current bank register setting, AH and AL are again set to 4Fh and 5, BH is set to 1, and BL is set to 0 for window A or 1 for window B. On return, DX is set to the current bank setting in window granularity units, and AH and AL hold the status. ARTT does not bother to read current bank settings, instead opting to remember them. This saves an enormous amount of overhead.

The VBE provides an alternate and somewhat faster method for setting the bank. The information block supplied by function 0, Return Super VGA information, includes a pointer to a function for performing the bank switch. This function may be called directly to set or retrieve the bank, instead of going through software interrupt 10h. The function is a real-mode function, however, and so is not directly accessible from a protected-mode program. ARTT uses VBE function 5 instead of a direct call.

Other VBE Functions

The remaining functions defined in version 1.2 of the VBE are used to control advanced aspects of the SVGA hardware. Function 6 provides control over the "logical scan-line length" of the screen, which is what we have called 'rowbytes'. Exact control is not guaranteed— the SVGA card may ignore a request or select a 'rowbytes' which is greater than that asked for. Function 7 is used to program the "start address" of the display, which can be used to perform limited hardware panning. The screen becomes in essence a window into the full display memory. Function 8 is used to enable 8-bit DAC color table support; remember, normal VGA DACs use only 6 bits each for red, green, and blue. Not all SVGA cards include these enhanced DACs.

VBE Version 2.0

Version 2.0 of the VBE specification, published in early 1995, adds many enhancements to version 1.2, including:

- Facilities for direct access to VBE functions from 32-bit protected mode
- Support for linear frame buffers in extended memory (access SVGA without bank-switching)

- Access to gamma correction tables in direct-color modes
- Enhanced Super VGA information block
- More detailed error return coding

Some of these additions are built into existing VBE functions, using previously reserved fields. Two new functions have been added:

Function 9 Set/Get palette data (for DAC programming
        through VBE)
Function 10   Return VBE protected mode interface

Class AVesa: An Interface to the VESA BIOS Extensions

The AVesa class is used to present to the rest of ARTT a view of the VBE that is easy to work with. The class is an "interface" class with only static members; that is, no instances of class AVesa are ever created. The header file for class AVesa is listed below.

```
//    AVesa.h      VESA Interface
//    Rex E. Bradford

#ifndef __AVESA_H
#define __AVESA_H

#include "aerror.h"
#include "acanvas.h"

extern ACanvas *gCanvasScreen; // ptr to screen canvas

    ..... AVesaInfo and AVesaModeInfo structs previously listed .....

// ARTT helper structure: overall VESA information

typedef struct {
// overall:
    void *pLowMemBlock; // ptr to VESA low memory interface block
    ushort lowMemSeg;   // real-mode segment of VESA interface block
    AVesaInfo info;     // info returned from VESA function 0
    short numModes;     // number of VESA modes supported by card
    ushort *pModeList;  // ptr to list of VESA modes
// active mode:
    void *pBaseAddr;    // ptr to base video address
    int granShift;      // # bits to shift bank by to get window gran
} AVesaStats;

// ARTT helper structure: useful mode information

typedef struct {
    ushort mode;        // mode number
    ushort width;       // screen width in pixels
    ushort height;      // screen height in pixels
```

```
    ushort depth;          // color depth (8, 15, 24)
    uchar writeWin;        // window to use for writing (0 = A, 1 = B)
    uchar readWin;         // window to use for reading (0 = A, 1 = B)
} AVesaMode;

class AVesa {
    static ushort prevMode;       // previous mode

    static bool CallVesa(int func, ushort bx, ushort cx, ushort dx);

public:
    static AVesaStats stats;      // overall vesa statistics

// Check for presence of VESA and initialize

    static AError Init();

// Get number of modes, index through list of modes

    static int NumModes() {return stats.numModes;}
    static ushort GetModeNum(int i) {return stats.pModeList[i];}

// Get detailed mode info given mode number

    static AVesaModeInfo *GetModeInfo(ushort mode);

// Verify that ARTT can handle this mode

    static bool ArttApprovedMode(AVesaModeInfo *pvmi);

// Get summary mode info based on number or width/height/depth

    static bool GetModeSummary(ushort mode, AVesaMode &vesaMode);
    static bool GetModeSummary(int w, int h, int depth,
        AVesaMode &vesaMode);

// Launch a mode given width/height/depth, mode, or mode summary info

    static ACanvas *Launch(int width, int height, int depth);
    static ACanvas *Launch(ushort mode);
    static ACanvas *Launch(AVesaMode &vesaMode);

// Exit VESA mode

    static void Term();

// THE FOLLOWING ARE NOT TYPICALLY CALLED BY APPLICATIONS

// Save and restore mode

    static void SaveMode();
    static void RestoreMode();
```

```
// Set mode and return filled in bitmap

  static AError SetMode(AVesaMode &vesaMode, ABitmap &bm);

// Program hardware bank-switch

  static void SetBank(int bank, uchar window);
};
```

```
#endif
```

A "simple" application uses the AVesa class in the following manner:

1. Call one of the first two flavors of AVesa::Launch(), specifying a mode number or a desired resolution and color depth. Launch() returns a screen canvas or NULL if the mode could not be launched. Checking this return value is important, unlike in mode 13H, which was guaranteed to work.

2. Use AVesa::SetBank() to perform bank-switching. This is done transparently through class ABankMgrVesa, a bank-switch manager customized for VESA that will be covered later in this chapter.

3. Before exiting the program, call AVesa::Term() to exit the SVGA mode. AVesa::Term() restores the previous mode, automatically saved before launch.

A more advanced application, one interested in finding the best mode for its needs, might use the AVesa interface like this:

1. Call AVesa::Init() to verify presence of VBE support. In the "simple" application, AVesa::Launch() calls AVesa::Init() internally as a convenience. Here, we'll use other functions which don't check for VBE presence first, so we must.

2. Call AVesa::NumModes() to retrieve the number of modes available on this card.

3. Iterate over available modes using AVesa::GetModeNum(), supplying an index from 0 to AVesa::NumModes() – 1.

4. Optionally, for any given mode in the list, call AVesa::GetModeInfo() to get detailed information about this mode.

5. Call AVesa::GetModeSummary() to get summary information about a mode, and automatically determine if it is compatible with ARTT's requirements (ARTT doesn't support 16-color modes, for instance). An alternate version of GetModeSummary() provides information on any mode which meets specified resolution and color-depth requirements, and can be used directly after step 1 in applications that know what resolutions and color depths they want to try for.

6. Call one of the three versions of AVesa::Launch(). One takes a mode number, another takes resolution and color depth, and the third takes a mode summary structure (returned by AVesa::GetModeSummary). Proceed as in the "simple" method from here.

As a convenience, AVesa::Launch() recognizes mode number 13H, and uses AMode13::Launch() in that case. The version of

Launch() which takes resolution and color-depth arguments also traps 320 × 200 8-bit as a special case and invokes mode 13H. Thus, programs which can run in multiple resolutions can include mode 13H support without having to code special calls to the AMode13 class.

Class AVesa: Implementation

The implementation of class AVesa is listed below, split up for discussion purposes. It starts with declarations of a few static variables.

```
AVesaStats AVesa::stats;            // stats, created by init routine
ushort AVesa::prevMode;             // previous mode
bool isMode13;                      // are we in mode 13?
ABankMgrVesa *pVesaBankMgr;         // ptr to bank manager
```

AVesa::CallVesa() : Accessing the VBE

AVesa::CallVesa() is used to actually communicate with the VESA BIOS Extensions. This is done through software interrupt 0 x 10, the normal video BIOS software interrupt. However, accessing this interrupt from 32-bit protected mode is implementation-dependent. Under the Symantec compiler, int86x_real() can be used to gain access to this "real mode" interrupt. Under Watcom, the DOS Protected Mode Interface manager must be called to "simulate" the real mode interrupt on the application's behalf. The Symantec implementation is listed below - see the CD for other versions.

Besides the VBE function number, three arguments are passed in, and these are assigned to the BX, CX, and DX registers when the software interrupt is invoked. Additionally, some VBE calls require a pointer to a buffer to be passed in ES:DI. A single low-memory buffer whose segment is stored in 'stats.lowMemSeg' is supplied. This buffer is allocated in AVesa::Init() using AMem::MallocLow().

```
bool AVesa::CallVesa(int func, ushort bx, ushort cx, ushort dx)
{
   union REGS regs;
   struct SREGS sregs;

// Set up registers for real-mode interrupt

   regs.x.ax = 0x4F00 | func;
   regs.x.bx = bx;
   regs.x.cx = cx;
   regs.x.dx = dx;
   sregs.es = stats.lowMemSeg;
   regs.x.di = 0;

// Invoke the real-mode software interrupt
```

```
#if __INTSIZE == 4
   int86x_real(0x10, &regs, &regs, &sregs);
#else
   int86x(0x10, &regs, &regs, &sregs);
#endif

// Function 3 (retrieve mode) has a return value, which is copied
// into 'prevMode'.

   if (func == 3)
      prevMode = regs.x.bx;

// Return error as boolean

   return (regs.x.ax == 0x4F);
}
```

AVesa::Init(): Detect VBE and Obtain General Information

AVesa::Init() allocates a low-memory buffer used to communicate with the VBE, and then calls VBE function 0 to detect its presence and obtain general information. The list of modes supported by the implementation is copied to another buffer. If anything goes wrong, an appropriate error code is returned.

```
AError AVesa::Init()
{
static bool init = FALSE;

// Only go thru here once, even if multiple mode launches

   if (init)
      return AERR_OK;

// Allocate low memory block for VESA information return

   stats.lowMemSeg = AMem::MallocLow(256);
   if (stats.lowMemSeg == 0)
      return AERR_NOMEM;
   stats.pLowMemBlock = AMem::GetPhysPtr(stats.lowMemSeg, 0);

// Call VESA BIOS FUNC 0: Return SVGA information

   if (!CallVesa(0, 0, 0, 0))
      return AERR_NODRIVER;

// Copy VESA info out of low memory, check special VESA signature

   memcpy(&stats.info, stats.pLowMemBlock, sizeof(stats.info));
   if (memcmp(stats.info.signature, "VESA", 4))
      return AERR_NODRIVER;
```

```
// Check for at least VESA 1.2
// #define REQUIRE_VERSION_1.2
#ifdef REQUIRE_VERSION_1.2
   if (stats.info.version < 0x0102)
      return AERR_BADVERSION;
#endif

// Count modes in stats.numModes

   ushort *pmodes = AMem::GetPhysPtr(stats.info.videoModeSeg,
      stats.info.videoModeOff);
   for (stats.numModes = 0; ; stats.numModes++)
      if (pmodes[stats.numModes] == 0xFFFF) break; // -1 marks end of list

// Allocate array to hold modes, copy out of VESA low-memory buffer

   stats.pModeList = new ushort[stats.numModes];
   if (stats.pModeList == NULL)
      return AERR_NOMEM;
   memcpy(stats.pModeList, pmodes, sizeof(ushort) * stats.numModes);

// All good things come to an end

   init = TRUE;
   return AERR_OK;
}
```

Obtaining Information About a Mode

Detailed information can be obtained about a numbered mode through VBE function 1. AVesa::GetModeInfo() makes this call and returns a pointer to a structure of type AVesaModeInfo. As this structure resides in the low-memory communications block, it is valid only until the next VBE call is made.

```
AVesaModeInfo *AVesa::GetModeInfo(ushort mode)
{
   if (!CallVesa(1, 0, mode, 0))
      return NULL;
   return((AVesaModeInfo *) stats.pLowMemBlock); // ret ptr to info
}
```

In order for a given mode to be usable with ARTT, several conditions must be met. These are delineated in the comment preceding AVesa::ArttApprovedMode(), which returns TRUE if a mode passes all the tests.

```
// ArttApprovedMode() checks to see if a given mode lives up
// to ARTT's high standards for it. These include:
//
// 1. Must be graphics mode
```

```
// 2. Display must support this mode
// 3. Window size must be 64K
// 4. Number of planes must be 1 (non-planar mode)
// 5. Must have at least 8 bits per pixel
// 6. Must be "packed" or "direct" memory model

bool AVesa::ArttApprovedMode(AVesaModeInfo *pvmi)
{
    if (!(pvmi->modeAttributes & VESA_MODEATTR_GRAPHICS)) return FALSE;
    if (!(pvmi->modeAttributes & VESA_MODEATTR_DISPSUPP)) return FALSE;
    if (pvmi->winSize != 64) return FALSE;
    if (pvmi->numberOfPlanes != 1) return FALSE;
    if (pvmi->bitsPerPixel < 8) return FALSE;
    if ((pvmi->memoryModel != VESA_MEMMODEL_PACKED) &&
        (pvmi->memoryModel != VESA_MEMMODEL_DIRECT))
            return FALSE;
    return TRUE;
}
```

There are two AVesa::GetModeSummary() routines, each taking different arguments. C++ allows such *overloading* of function names, which can be preferable to having to come up with two names for functions that do essentially the same thing with different arguments.

The first version of GetModeSummary() takes a mode number as input, and returns TRUE if the mode is capable of being launched, and FALSE otherwise. Before returning TRUE, it also fills in a mode summary structure passed in by reference. This structure is of type AVesaMode, and includes the mode number, resolution, color depth, and window characteristics. The application can examine this structure to determine if it wishes to launch the mode using AVesa::Launch(). GetModeSummary() calls ArttApprovedMode() and returns TRUE only if this test is passed, so an application need not do this itself.

```
bool AVesa::GetModeSummary(ushort mode, AVesaMode &vesaMode)
{
// First look in VESA info mode list

    for (int i = 0; i < stats.numModes; i++)
        {
        if (stats.pModeList[i] == mode)
            {
// Found mode in list, make sure it's ARTT-approved

            AVesaModeInfo *pvmi;
            if ((pvmi = GetModeInfo(stats.pModeList[i])) != NULL)
                {
                if (ArttApprovedMode(pvmi))
                    {
// Copy mode information to caller and return TRUE
```

```
                    vesaMode.mode = mode;
                    vesaMode.width = pvmi->xResolution;
                    vesaMode.height = pvmi->yResolution;
                    vesaMode.depth = pvmi->bitsPerPixel;
                    vesaMode.writeWin = (pvmi->winAAttributes & 4) ? 0 : 1;
                    vesaMode.readWin = (pvmi->winAAttributes & 2) ? 0 : 1;
                    return TRUE;
                    }
                }
            break;
            }
        }

// Couldn't find mode or verify info about it, no go

    return FALSE;
}
```

The second variant of GetModeSummary() is used when you don't care about mode numbers. It takes a width, height, and color depth (8, 15, or 24) as input. Of course, you had better be pretty careful to pick a resolution that VBE is likely to find acceptable. See Table 5.2 on page 175 for the commonly supported values.

```
bool AVesa::GetModeSummary(int width, int height, int depth,
    AVesaMode &vesaMode)
{
// Search VESA info mode list, getting info on each, looking for match

    for (int i = 0; i < stats.numModes; i++)
        {
        AVesaModeInfo *pvmi;
        if ((pvmi = GetModeInfo(stats.pModeList[i])) != NULL)
            {
// Found match, make sure it meets ARTT's requirements

            if (ArttApprovedMode(pvmi))
                {
// Check that width/height/depth all match

                if ((pvmi->xResolution == width) &&
                    (pvmi->yResolution == height) &&
                    (pvmi->bitsPerPixel == depth))
                    {
                    vesaMode.mode = stats.pModeList[i];
                    vesaMode.width = width;
                    vesaMode.height = height;
                    vesaMode.depth = depth;
                    vesaMode.writeWin = (pvmi->winAAttributes & 4) ? 0 : 1;
                    vesaMode.readWin = (pvmi->winAAttributes & 2) ? 0 : 1;
                    return TRUE;
                    }
                }
```

```
        }
      }

// No match

    return FALSE;
}
```

AVesa::Launch(): Launching a Mode

Three versions of AVesa::Launch() are available, providing maximum convenience. The first takes width, height, and depth arguments, and attempts to find a matching mode and launch it. If successful, it returns a constructed canvas which can be used for rendering onto the screen. The canvas is of type ACanvasBank8 (or ACanvas-Bank15/24 for color depths beyond 8, but don't worry about that just yet). This canvas is attached to a bank manager capable of doing VBE bank-switching—we'll look at this bank manager class when we're finished with AVesa.

Note that AVesa::Launch() ends with a call to Launch()! No, this is not recursion. It's just calling one of the other versions of this over-loaded method.

```
ACanvas *AVesa::Launch(int width, int height, int depth)
{
    AVesaMode vesaMode;

// If 320×200×8, that's mode 13H!

    if ((width == 320) && (height == 200) && (depth == 8))
        {
        isMode13 = TRUE;
        return AMode13::Launch();
        }

// Else make sure VESA is initialized

    if (AVesa::Init())
        return NULL;

// Try to get mode summary, return NULL if mode not found

    if (!AVesa::GetModeSummary(width, height, depth, vesaMode))
        return NULL;

// Else try to launch it!

    return(Launch(vesaMode));
}
```

The second version of AVesa::Launch() takes a mode number as input, but otherwise works the same.

```
ACanvas *AVesa::Launch(ushort mode)
{
   AVesaMode vesaMode;

// If mode 0×13, that's mode 13H!

   if (mode == 0×13)
      {
      isMode13 = TRUE;
      return AMode13::Launch();
      }

// Else make sure VESA is initialized

   if (AVesa::Init())
      return NULL;

// Try to get mode summary, return NULL if mode not found

   if (!AVesa::GetModeSummary(mode, vesaMode))
      return NULL;

// Else try to launch it!

   return(Launch(vesaMode));
}
```

The final version of AVesa::Launch() takes a mode summary block as input. It's the "real" version of Launch() that the previous two make use of, and it may be called directly by an application too. It saves the current mode before launching the mode specified in the mode summary. The SetMode() call fills in a bitmap which describes the screen, and Launch() uses that bitmap to construct a canvas for the screen. The canvas constructor also requires a bank manager, and one of class ABankMgrVesa (covered shortly) is created and supplied to it. When Launch() returns, the global screen canvas is ready for rendering.

```
ACanvas *AVesa::Launch(AVesaMode &vesaMode)
{
   ABitmap bmVesa;

// Make sure VESA is initialized

   if (AVesa::Init())
      return NULL;
```

```
// Save current mode and try to set the mode using SetMode().
// If successful, SetMode() fills in the bmVesa bitmap

   AVesa::SaveMode();
   if (AVesa::SetMode(vesaMode, bmVesa))
      return NULL;

// Build canvas using bitmap filled in by SetMode(), and new bankmgr

   pVesaBankMgr = new ABankMgrVesa(vesaMode.writeWin, vesaMode.readWin,
      (vesaMode.writeWin == vesaMode.readWin) ? TRUE : FALSE);
   switch (vesaMode.depth)
      {
      case 8:
         gCanvasScreen = new ACanvasBank8(&bmVesa, pVesaBankMgr);
         break;
      case 15:
         gCanvasScreen = new ACanvasBank15(&bmVesa, pVesaBankMgr);
         break;
      case 24:
         gCanvasScreen = new ACanvasBank24(&bmVesa, pVesaBankMgr);
         break;
      default:
         gCanvasScreen = NULL; break;
      }

// Return canvas ptr

   return gCanvasScreen;
}
```

AVesa::Term(): Exiting Graphics Mode

Before exiting a program which has used AVesa::Launch(), AVesa::Term() must be used to terminate graphics mode and return to the previously saved mode, which is usually a text mode. Term() also works properly if Launch() actually launched mode 13H instead of a VESA mode.

```
void AVesa::Term()
{
   if (isMode13)
      {
      AMode13::Term();          // if mode 13, terminate specially
      isMode13 = FALSE;         // and mark as no longer in mode
      }
   else
      {
      delete gCanvasScreen;     // delete screen canvas
      delete pVesaBankMgr;      // delete VESA bank manager
      AVesa::RestoreMode();     // restore old (text) mode
      }
}
```

Internal AVesa Methods

The following methods of AVesa are not normally accessed by applications, though they are public in case some application wishes to use them.

AVesa::SaveMode() uses VBE function 3 to retrieve the current mode. The CallVesa() function automatically stores this in the static variable 'prevMode'.

```
void AVesa::SaveMode()
{
    CallVesa(3, 0, 0, 0); // puts prev mode into 'prevMode'
}
```

AVesa::RestoreMode() uses VBE function 2 to set the mode previously saved.

```
void AVesa::RestoreMode()
{
    CallVesa(2, prevMode, 0, 0);
}
```

AVesa::SetMode() does an actual mode set using VBE function 2. It does some additional work as well. This includes computing the number of bits by which a bank number in 64K units must be shifted to specify it in "window granularity" units—the bank-switch routine uses this value. Its other job is to construct a bitmap which describes the entire SVGA screen. Launch() uses this to build a canvas for the screen.

```
AError AVesa::SetMode(AVesaMode &vesaMode, ABitmap &bm)
{
// Get mode info

    AVesaModeInfo *pvmi;
    if ((pvmi = GetModeInfo(vesaMode.mode)) == NULL)
        return AERR_BADMODE;

// Compute granShift factor for this mode
// Granularity must be 1K,2K,4K,8K,16K,32K,64K
// stats.granShift becomes number of bits, 0 to 6, needed to
// shift this granularity to make it equal 64K

    for (int i = 0; i <= 6; i++)
        {
        if (pvmi->winGranularity == (1 << i))
            {
            stats.granShift = 6 - i;
            break;
            }
```

```
        }
    if (i == 7)
       return AERR_BADMODE;

// Get base physical addres

    stats.pBaseAddr = AMem::GetPhysPtr((long) pvmi->winASegment << 4);

// Launch the mode!

    if (!CallVesa(2, vesaMode.mode, 0, 0))
       return AERR_BADMODE;

// Figure out the bitmap format for this mode

    uchar format;
    if (pvmi->bitsPerPixel == 8)
       format = BMF_BANK8;
    else if (pvmi->bitsPerPixel == 15)
       format = BMF_BANK15;
    else if (pvmi->bitsPerPixel == 24)
       format = BMF_BANK24;
    else
       return AERR_BADMODE;

// Construct the bitmap for this mode

    bm = ABitmap(format, vesaMode.width, vesaMode.height,
       pvmi->bytesPerScanLine);
    return AERR_OK;
}
```

SetBank() does the bank switch operation, using VBE function 5. This method is not typically called directly. The VBE-aware bank manager class, coming up, does that.

```
void AVesa::SetBank(int bank, uchar window)
{
    CallVesa(5, window, 0, bank << stats.granShift);
}
```

VESALIST: A Program to List VESA-Supported Modes

Included on the enclosed CD is a program called VESALIST, which uses the AVesa methods to print out a lot of useful information about the VESA implementation on the machine on which it is run. This includes a dump of the Super VGA information returned by sub-function 0, as well as the mode information for every mode contained in the mode list obtained thereby. VESALIST.CPP, the source code for this program, is included on the CD as well.

Class ABankMgrVesa: A Bank Manager for VESA

The final piece in our SVGA puzzle is a bank manager class, derived from ABankMgr, which can perform bank-switching through the VBE. The SVGA screen canvas built by AVesa::Launch() uses a bank manager of class ABankMgrVesa, which is what we'll look at now.

This class is very simple, and the header file listed below defines the class completely. Two private methods, SwitchWriteBank() and SwitchReadBank(), call AVesa::SetBank() to perform the bank-switching. SwitchWriteBank() and SwitchReadBank(), remember, are virtual functions left unimplemented in class ABankMgr. They are called whenever the bank manager determines that a new bank is being accessed.

The third and final method is the constructor, which takes three arguments. The first two are the numbers of the write window and read window (0 for A, 1 for B)—these are supplied in the mode summary information which class AVesa gathers. The third argument is the "rwTied" argument, which is passed along to construct the base ABankMgr. This tells the underlying ABankMgr whether the read and write banks are tied to the same physical window.

```
//    ABnkMgrV.h     VESA-based bank manager class
//    Rex E. Bradford

#ifndef __ABNKMGRV_H
#define __ABNKMGRV_H

#include "abankmgr.h"
#include "amem.h"

class ABankMgrVesa : public ABankMgr {

   uchar writeWindow;   // window to use for writing
   uchar readWindow;    // window to use for reading

// Perform actual bank-switching operation: thru VESA!

   void SwitchWriteBank(int bank) {
      AVesa::SetBank(bank, writeWindow);}

   void SwitchReadBank(int bank) {
      AVesa::SetBank(bank, readWindow);}
```

```
public:

// Constructor: set up VESA bank manager, mark write/read windows

    ABankMgrVesa(uchar writeW, uchar readW, bool rwTied) :
        ABankMgr((uchar *) AMem::GetPhysPtr(0xA0000L), rwTied)
            {writeWindow = writeW; readWindow = readW;}
};


#endif
```

That's the entire story for SVGA, VBE, and 8-bit bank-switched canvases. We'll write more advanced rendering methods for both linear and bank-switched canvases, but the code in this chapter is sufficient to use Super VGA modes with the same ease as the mode 13H screen. Let the Super VGA rendering begin!

GFXSHOW2: Super VGA Version of GFXSHOW1

GFXSHOW2 is an updated version of GFXSHOW1, the graphics file viewer introduced in Chapter 3. This version checks the width and height of the graphics file brought in. If the image is wider than 320 pixels or taller than 200 pixels, GFXSHOW2 invokes a 640×480 8-bit VESA mode; otherwise, it asks for a 320×200 one, which will give us mode 13H. Compare the code to the GFXSHOW1 program to see how easy it is to add high-resolution Super VGA to your programs. Note that this version also calls the clipping method DrawBitmapIn8(), so that images larger than 640×480 will not cause bad side effects other than not being fully visible.

```
//   Gfxshow2.cpp    Show graphics file (8-bit, any resolution)
//   Rex E. Bradford

#include <stdio.h>
#include <conio.h>

#include "agfxfile.h"
#include "avesa.h"
#include "avga.h"

void main(int argc, char **argv)
{
// Check for filename and read graphics file

    if (argc <= 1)
        {
        printf("usage: gfxshow2 filename.ext\n");
```

```
        exit(1);
        }

    ABitmap bm;
    AError err = AGfxFile::Read(argv[1], bm);
    if (err)
        {
        printf("Problem with file: %s (%s)\n", argv[1], AErr::Msg(err));
        exit(1);
        }

// Launch graphics mode (320x200 or 640x480, depending on image)
// and render bitmap
    switch (bm.format)
        {
        case BMF_LIN8:
            if ((bm.width > 320) || (bm.height > 200))
                AVesa::Launch(640, 480, 8);
            else
                AVesa::Launch(320, 200, 8);
            if (gCanvasScreen == NULL)
                {
                printf("Unable to launch VESA mode\n");
                exit(1);
                }
            if (bm.ppalette)
                AVga::SetDAC(bm.ppalette->rgb);
            gCanvasScreen->DrawBitmapLin8(bm, 0, 0);
            break;

        default:
            printf("can't handle format of gfx file (format: $%x)\n",
                bm.format);
            exit(1);
        }

// Wait for key, restore text mode, exit

    getch();
    AVesa::Term();
    exit(0);
}
```

Figure 5.6 shows a sample picture being viewed at 640 × 480 resolution with GFXSHOW2.

Figure 5.6   Screen shot from GFXSHOW2, the SVGA version of the graphics file viewer.

C   H   A   P   T   E   R

6

Bitmap Compression and Bitmap Scaling

In this chapter, we return to bitmaps with a vengeance. Two major topics are included here. The first is bitmap compression, which is the encoding of bitmap data to reduce its space requirements. Run-length encoding is used in ARTT for compression of 8-bit images in a format from which they can be rendered directly, without a separate decompression step. The other major topic of this chapter is scaled rendering of bitmaps, that is, the rendering of bitmaps into an area of a canvas whose width and height differ from that of the source bitmap being rendered. These topics will form a firm foundation for bitmap rendering that the animation system in Part 2 will build on.

Bitmap Compression

In Part 2 of this book, we're going to put together classes to handle sophisticated bitmapped animation. Bitmapped animation means lots of bitmaps, one for each animation frame. Let's do some math. A single frame of animation, say 320 pixels wide by 200 pixels high, at 8 bits per pixel, requires 64,000 bytes to represent in the BMF_LIN8 format. Animated at 16 frames per second, that adds up to 1,024,000 bytes per second. Thirty seconds of such animation is 30,720,000 bytes, or about 30 megabytes. *Hmmm.*

This is a problem. First of all, hard disks don't grow on trees. At 1995's price of 50 cents per megabyte of hard disk space, our thirty-second animation just cost us $15 of hard disk space. The delivery medium for our animation could be CD-ROM, of course, which is a far less expensive storage medium. Speaking of CD-ROM, a double-speed drive has a maximum transfer rate of 300K per second from the disk to memory, which means it's not fast enough by a factor of three to deliver the animation frames to us. Even many hard disks have trouble supplying a megabyte per second of sustained data transfer.

Data compression is the obvious answer. Programmers often use utilities such as PKZIP by PKWARE to compress files to a fraction of their original size. Can't we do the same thing with our animation frames? Sure, and we can do one better. We can compress them with a method which can be decompressed in real time. In fact, we can render the compressed image directly to a screen or canvas, without having to decompress it first.

Image Compression Techniques

The variety and complexity of compression techniques could fill several books, and it has. Even *image compression*, compression specifically designed for bitmapped images, is a large topic. The arrival of digital video as a new medium has focused enormous attention on the design of data formats and fast algorithms appropriate to images. In Chapter 16, we'll have a look at some of the most popular techniques for compressing digital video images, such as the JPEG and MPEG standards. Some of these algorithms can run in real time in software on current personal computers. Others, including MPEG, require hardware assistance, usually in the form of a specially programmed *digital signal processing* (DSP) chip. Most of the compression techniques used in digital video are inherently *lossy*, which means that the image which goes in to the compressor isn't exactly the same as the one that comes out. When the compressor is allowed to change a pixel's value to one which "isn't too far off," it can greatly reduce the amount of data needed to represent the compressed image.

Run-Length Encoding of Bitmaps: The BMF_RLE8 Format

For 8-bit images, which are still the best choice for high-speed animation, another class of techniques works quite well. These *run-length* compression methods have the advantage of being *lossless*—what comes out is exactly what goes in. They also have the advantage of being very fast to decompress. In fact, it is often *faster* to render a run-length compressed image than it is to render the uncompressed version, as we will see. What's the downside? The *compression ratio*, which is the ratio between the size of the uncompressed image and the compressed one, isn't very high. The run-length compressed frames, while smaller than the uncompressed ones, aren't as reduced as can be achieved by other techniques. Still, for 8-bit images run-length is the way to go when speed is important, and the data reduction gained can be pretty substantial.

How does run-length compression work? As the name implies, run-length compression gathers together *runs* of a particular color, and represents the entire run in a few bytes regardless of its length. For instance, a sequence of 10 consecutive pixels of value 7 could be represented by a two-byte sequence containing the run's length (10) and its value (7), as shown in Figure 6.1. That's a 5:1 compression ratio for these pixels.

Obviously, run-length compression performs best when there are lots of areas of solid color in an image, and fares more poorly with busy images filled with changing shades and detailed patterns. Video images don't compress well with run-length techniques. Because true-color images rarely have consecutive pixels with *exactly* the same shade of a given color, these images don't compress well either. However, many 8-bit images have solid runs of color precisely because there are few color values available, so many adjacent pixels use the same value. Also, images which have transparency benefit greatly from run-length compression. Transparent pixels, remember, are represented by the color value 0. This is just another color value which can show up in runs, and in fact transparent pixels usually clump together naturally in images.

The BMF_RLE8 Format

ARTT has one bitmap format which is different from all the others, because it represents compressed images. This is the BMF_RLE8 format, which is used for 8-bit images which are run-length compressed. There are many possible ways to run-length compress a bitmap; the

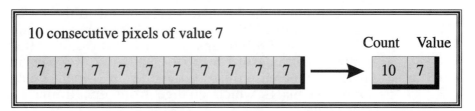

Figure 6.1 Encoding a run of identical pixels in a two-byte token.

PCX and BMP graphics file formats support different variants of the technique. What exact format should be used in ARTT's BMF_RLE8 format?

We would like a format which is simple enough that rendering routines can use it directly without first decompressing the image into a linear format. To aid clipping, each row should be compressed independently—this makes it easier to skip over clipped rows. Compressing each row separately will lose us a little bit of compression, since runs that wrap from one row to the next will have to be broken into two halves (and runs of transparency often *would* wrap).

The simplest format we could invent would be to represent the bitmap by a series of *tokens,* each of which has a count and a color value. The problem with this approach is that if each pixel is a different color from its neighbor, every pixel will require two bytes: one for the count (always 1), and one for the value. Thus, our compressed image could be twice as big as the uncompressed one!

To avoid this serious problem, the BMF_RLE8 technique has two types of tokens. A *run token* represents a run of pixels of the same color, just like the method described above. A *dump token* represents a series of values which don't consist of runs, and should just be treated like a set of linear, uncompressed pixels. In essence, a BMF_RLE8 bitmap is like a linear bitmap with run tokens interspersed where they make sense.

A BMF_RLE8 bitmap, then, consists of a series of tokens. Each token begins with a single byte which identifies the type of token and the number of pixels represented by the token. The type (run or dump) is indicated in the high bit; the count is in the low 7 bits. A run token is followed by a single byte color value, so run tokens are always two bytes long. A dump token is followed by a set of bytes whose length is indicated in the count. A special *end token,* of value 0, is added to the end of the *token stream.* Figure 6.2 shows the format of the tokens.

Since a token's count field is 7 bits wide, it is limited to representing runs or dumps of 1 to 127 pixels. If a run or dump is longer than 127 pixels in length, it must be broken up into multiple tokens. Note that the special end token value of 0 does not conflict with the other tokens, since count fields must be at least 1. Figure 6.3 shows a small bitmap in linear format along with the set of tokens which describes it in BMF_RLE8 format. For sprite figures, icons, and the like, BMF_RLE8 bitmaps offer a compression ratio which is typically in the range of 1.5:1 to 4:1. In Part 2, we'll see how we can dramatically increase this ratio further by using *delta encoding,* where only the pixels which change from one frame to the next are encoded.

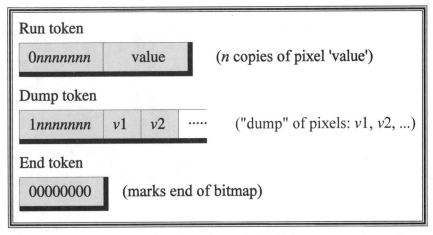

Figure 6.2 Encoding of run, dump, and end tokens in BMF_RLE8 format.

Transparency in BMF_RLE8 Bitmaps

One of the annoying things about drawing bitmaps with transparency in them is the need to check every single pixel to see if it has the value 0. This constant checking can slow down rendering considerably. With run-length-encoded bitmaps, we have an opportunity to ameliorate this somewhat. If we require that all transparent pixels appear in runs (even if they appear by themselves, with a run of 1), then the dump tokens don't need to be checked for transparency pixel by pixel. This means that the dump tokens can be written with memset() or other similar fast techniques previously reserved for nontransparent bitmaps. And since run tokens have one value to check regardless of the number of pixels in the count, transparency-checking overhead is greatly reduced here too. This is a big win and is one of the reasons why it is often faster to render BMF_RLE8 bitmaps than their BMF_LIN8 counterparts.

BMF_RLE8 Data Bits Layout

A BMF_RLE8 bitmap, like a BMF_LIN8 bitmap, consists of a set of rows of pixel data, as specified in the 'height' field of the ABitmap. In the case of a BMF_RLE8 bitmap, however, the row data consists of a series of tokens, some of them run tokens and some of them dump tokens. The number of pixels accounted for by these tokens (in their count fields) will exactly match the width of the bitmap in pixels, as specified by its 'width' field. In fact, checking the number of pixels processed in a row is the only way to detect when a row is done, since

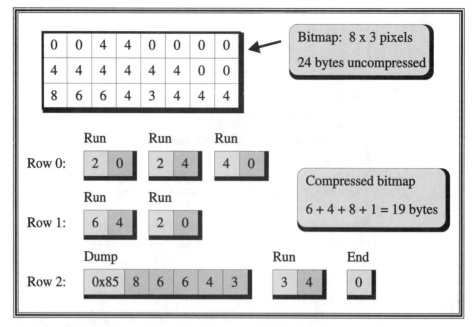

Figure 6.3   Small linear bitmap, and its run-length encoding.

there is no "end of row" token. After the data for all rows, there is a single "end" token, represented by a single byte of the value 0. Strictly speaking, this token is unnecessary, but it can be handy for code which is scanning through the data without keeping track of the number of rows processed.

Each row of a BMF_RLE8 bitmap is encoded as a set of tokens. Each token is one of the following three types:

00000000	End of bitmap
0nnnnnnn vvvvvvvv	Run - n copies of pixel value v
1nnnnnnn [. . . data . . .]	Copy - n bytes follow, copy them unmodified

The header file ARLE8.H summarizes the encoding of a BMF_ RLE8 bitmap.

```
//   ARle8.h    RLE-8 bitmap formatting
//   Rex E. Bradford


#ifndef __ARLE8_H
#define __ARLE8_H


// BMF_RLE8 streams consist of the following token formats:
//
```

```
//      00000000                end of stream
//      0nnnnnnn vvvvvvvv        1-127 copies of pixel value
//      1nnnnnnn [...]           dump of next 1-127 pixels

#define ARLE8_DUMP 0×80         // test mask for token type (else run)
#define ARLE8_COUNT 0×7F        // mask to get count field

#endif
```

What About BMF_RLE15 and BMF_RLE24?

You may have noticed that BMF_RLE8 is the only compressed bitmap format defined in ARTT. The reason is that run-length encoding does not work particularly well with direct-color images, whether 15-bit or 24-bit. While there is nothing to prevent images in these formats from having large stretches of the exact same color, they rarely do in practice. If such images are composed of solid swaths of a few colors, they should be converted to 8-bit format and then run-length encoded.

Other compression techniques, especially the "frequency-based" algorithms such as JPEG, do work well with direct-color images. However, decoding images encoded in these formats is hardly a real-time affair, at least without hardware support. For real-time work, the fastest approach is to use 8-bit images, even if the display screen is 15-bit or 24-bit. In Part 3, we'll develop code to quickly render 8-bit images onto 15-bit and 24-bit screens.

Class ARle8Reader: Decoding BMF_RLE8 Bitmaps

The logical next step would be to discuss how an image is encoded (compressed) into the BMF_RLE8 format. However, it's helpful first to see how such an image is decoded (decompressed)—decoding is easier and will give us a feel for the format of the tokens that make up a BMF_RLE8 image.

When it comes to working with run-length-encoded bitmaps, it makes sense to provide some "helper" routines, rather than force each rendering method to repeat all the token decoding logic. Since this is C++, let's make a small class. Class ARle8Reader provides a standard interface for retrieving data from BMF_RLE8 bitmap data. When a routine needs to read from a BMF_RLE8 bitmap, it constructs an object of class ARle8Reader, and then uses this object to pull the data tokens from the bitmap. This approach reduces errors and redundant coding.

The ARle8Reader object encapsulates the "state" of the reader, which includes the current pointer into the token stream, the width of each row, and whether zeroes should be skipped or written. This last option is important when such a bitmap is decoded straight into

the destination canvas—transparent pixels are not written when this option is set.

ARle8Reader Methods

The ARle8Reader class has two constructors, which differ in how they set up the reader to handle transparency. The first takes a bitmap as its sole argument, and initializes the reader object to point to the beginning of the bitmap, with the proper row width, and with the 'skipZero' flag set according to the transparency of the bitmap. The other constructor allows the 'skipZero' flag to be set explicitly regardless of the bitmap's transparency; this is sometimes handy, as we'll see.

Once an ARle8Reader object has been constructed, uncompressed bitmap data can be extracted from it, using the four methods provided:

More()	Determines whether the compressed data has been exhausted
SkipRow()	Skips over one or more rows of data (handy for clipping)
UnpackRow()	Unpacks (decodes) an entire row of data into a buffer
UnpackAll()	Unpacks the entire bitmap into a buffer

```
//   ARle8Rd.h     RLE-8 bitmap reader class
//   Rex E. Bradford

#ifndef __ARLE8READER_H
#define __ARLE8READER_H

#include "abitmap.h"
#include "arle8.h"

class ARle8Reader {

    uchar *prle;        // ptr to current spot in rle buffer
    short widthRow;     // width of row in pixels
    bool skipZero;      // if TRUE, don't write runs of zero

public:

// Constructor: sets up rle8 reader to read from bitmap, Skip
// over zeroes when unpacking if bitmap is transparent.

    ARle8Reader(ABitmap &bm) {prle = bm.pbits; widthRow = bm.width;
        skipZero = bm.transparent;}

// Constructor: sets up rle8 reader to read from bitmap. Skip
// over zeroes according to 'transp' argument.
```

```
    ARle8Reader(ABitmap &bm, bool transp)
        {prle = bm.pbits; widthRow = bm.width; skipZero = transp;}

// Unpacking methods

    bool More() {return(*prle);}          // is there more to read?
    void SkipRow(int numRows = 1);        // skip 1 or more rows
    uchar *UnpackRow(uchar *buff);        // unpack row into buffer
    void UnpackAll(uchar *buff);          // unpack all rle data
};


#endif
```

Skipping Rows With ARle8Reader

Skipping a row of uncompressed bitmap data is easy—just add the 'rowbytes' field to the current pointer. With a compressed BMF_RLE8 bitmap, which has a variable number of tokens representing each row, the 'rowbytes' field is meaningless and can't be used. There is no silver bullet when it comes to skipping a row of compressed data—it must be scanned through until the correct number of pixels have been skipped.

```
void ARle8Reader::SkipRow(int numRows)
{
   while (More() && (numRows-- > 0))
      {
      int width = widthRow;                // get copy of width to count down
      while (width > 0)
         {
         int count = *prle & ARLE8_COUNT;  // get count of pixels
         if (*prle++ & ARLE8_DUMP)         // if hibit set, it's a dump
            prle += count;                 // advance to next token
         else
            ++prle;                        // skip past run value
         width -= count;                   // count down width
         }
      }
}
```

Decoding Rows With ARle8Reader

Decoding a row of run-length data is similar to skipping over it, except that the tokens need to be expanded into a pixel buffer as they are processed. A dump token is processed by using memcpy() to copy the token's pixels into the destination buffer. A run token is processed by using memset() to set destination-buffer pixels with the token pixel value, unless the pixel value is 0 and the 'skipZero' flag is set, in which case the destination bytes are skipped over unwritten. If the destination buffer happens to be part of a canvas into which the bitmap is being directly unpacked, this achieves transparency! Remember that our definition of BMF_RLE8 tokens guarantees that we don't need to check pixel values in a dump for 0.

On exit, ARle8Reader::UnpackRow() returns a pointer to the next byte in the destination buffer.

```
uchar *ARle8Reader::UnpackRow(uchar *buff)
{
    if (!More()) return buff;

    int width = widthRow;                // get copy of width to count down
    while (width > 0)
        {
        int count = *prle & ARLE8_COUNT; // count is in low 7 bits
        if (*prle++ & ARLE8_DUMP)        // if hibit set, it's a dump
            {
            memcpy(buff, prle, count);   // copy into dest buffer
            buff += count;               // update dest buffer ptr
            prle += count;               // advance to next token
            }
        else
            {
            if (*prle || !skipZero)       // skip if 0 and in skip0 mode
                memset(buff, *prle, count);
            ++prle;                      // skip past run value
            buff += count;               // update dest buffer ptr
            }
        width -= count;                  // count down width
        }
    return buff;                         // return ptr to end of buffer
}
```

Full Bitmap Decoding With ARle8Reader

As a convenience, the ARle8Reader::UnpackAll() method is provided. It simply unpacks the entire bitmap into a buffer. Note how the return value of UnpackRow() is used to advance the destination buffer pointer along.

```
void ARle8Reader::UnpackAll(uchar *buff)
{
    while (More())
        buff = UnpackRow(buff);
}
```

Soon, we'll use the ARle8Reader class to render BMF_RLE8 bitmaps. But first, let's see how we can compress bitmaps into this format.

Class ARle8Writer: Encoding BMF_RLE8 Bitmaps

Decoding BMF_RLE8 bitmaps is pretty easy, because the tokens tell us what to do. Encoding is not quite as simple, because here a mass of undifferentiated pixels must be shaped into the appropriate set of tokens, and hopefully into the *optimal* set of tokens so our compression will be as good as possible. We could just turn each pixel into a run or dump of length 1, but that wouldn't help the cause much!

The ARle8Writer class is used to perform the encoding, and it can be used to encode a row at a time or a whole bitmap in one shot. The header file for class ARle8Writer is given below.

```
//   ARle8Wr.h     RLE-8 bitmap writer class
//   Rex E. Bradford

#ifndef __ARLE8WRITER_H
#define __ARLE8WRITER_H

#include "abitmap.h"
#include "arle8.h"

class ARle8Writer {
    uchar *pbeg;          // ptr to start of dest buffer
    uchar *pend;          // ptr to end of dest buffer
    uchar *pdest;         // ptr to current spot in dest buffer
    short widthRow;       // width of a row in pixels
    bool zeroInRuns;      // should 0 pixels always go in runs?
    bool overflow;        // did we attempt to overflow dest buffer?

#define RLE8WR_END 0      // end of rle8 stream
#define RLE8WR_RUN 1      // run on n copies of pixel
#define RLE8WR_DUMP 2     // dump of n pixels

    typedef struct {      // ARle8Token: helper structure for encoding
        uchar type;       // RLE8WR_XXX
        uchar count;      // for run or dump
        union {
            uchar pixel;  // if RLE8WR_RUN
            uchar *ptr;   // if RLE8WR_DUMP
            };
    } ARle8Token;

    bool WriteToken(ARle8Token &tok);     // write a token to output

public:

// Constructor: set up buffer to begin compressing into

    ARle8Writer(uchar *buff, long buffSize, int width, bool transp);
```

```
// Encode an entire lin8 bitmap, return length or 0 if overflowed

    long EncodeLin8Bitmap(ABitmap &bm);

// Encode a single row of length "width", return FALSE if overflowed

    bool EncodeRow(uchar *psrc);

// Write END token to rle buffer

    void WriteEnd() {if (!overflow) *pdest++ = 0;}

// Info routines

    long Length() {return(pdest - pbeg);} // length of rle data
    bool Overflow() {return overflow;}     // overflowed?
};

#endif
```

ARle8Writer Buffer Management

Since the size of a BMF_RLE8 bitmap is not known until after it is
encoded, the issue of how much memory to allocate before encoding
begins is a tricky one. The ARle8Writer object is given a buffer and its
size when constructed. ARle8Writer then ensures that data is never
written past the end of this buffer, even if that means abandoning the
compression. The encoding routines return status codes which convey
this information. Typically, a BMF_RLE8 bitmap is encoded from a
source bitmap of format BMF_LIN8, and the buffer is allocated at the
size of the uncompressed source bitmap. If overflow occurs, there is
no point in representing the bitmap by a compressed version which is
larger than the original anyway, and so the caller abandons the compression attempt. The following example code shows a typical usage:

```
// Example code, assume bm is a BMF_LIN8 bitmap
uchar *buff = new uchar[bm.length];         // allocate buffer to orig bm size
ARle8Writer rle8wr(buff, bm.length, bm.width, bm.transparent); // init
long len = rle8wr.EncodeLin8Bitmap(bm);   // attempt to encode it
if (len)                                   // if successful, make BMF_RLE8 bm
    {                                      // with the buffer as its data bits
    ABitmap bmrle8(buff, BMF_RLE8, bm.transparent, bm.width, bm.height);
    ... use 'bmrle8' ...
    }
else                                       // else abandon compression
    {
    delete buff;                           //clean up buff
    ... abandon compression, just use 'bm' ...
    }
```

Encoding a Bitmap With ARle8Writer

Encoding a bitmap is begun by constructing an "rle8 writer" object of class ARle8Writer, giving it information on the buffer to be used for encoding, the width of each row, and whether the bitmap has transparency. This is followed by a call to ARle8Writer::EncodeBitmap() to attempt to encode the entire bitmap. The ARle8Writer constructor is listed below:

```
ARle8Writer::ARle8Writer(uchar *buff, long buffSize, int width,
   bool transp)
{
   pdest = pbeg = buff;       // set beg and current ptr to buffer
   pend = buff + buffSize;    // set ptr to end of buffer
   widthRow = width;          // set row width
   zeroInRuns = transp;       // decide whether 0 must go only in runs
   overflow = FALSE;          // we haven't filled the inn yet!
}
```

ARle8Writer::EncodeBitmap() encodes the bitmap a row at a time, making successive calls to ARle8Writer::EncodeRow(). It checks the return of EncodeRow() for buffer overflow, and abandons the compression attempt if this occurs. EncodeBitmap() returns the length of the compressed data, including the end token, or 0 if compression is abandoned.

```
long ARle8Writer::EncodeLin8Bitmap(ABitmap &bm)
{
   uchar *psrc = bm.pbits;    // begin at the beginning, they do say
   for (int y = 0; y < bm.height; y++) // loop thru each row
      {
      if (!EncodeRow(psrc))    // encode row
         return(0);            // if overflowed, return 0 length
      psrc += bm.rowbytes;     // advance source ptr to next row
      }
   WriteEnd();               // write end token to end of stream
   return(Length());         // return length of stream
}
```

Encoding a Bitmap Row

The basic algorithm used to encode a particular row is somewhat complex. It is implemented in terms of a "state machine," where the current state is defined in terms of a "current token." The current token may be a run token or a dump token. If it is a run token, the new pixel must match the color value of the current run; otherwise the run token is written out and a new run begun. If the current token is a dump token, on the other hand, the new pixel is added to the dump. It's actually more complex than this. For instance, a run

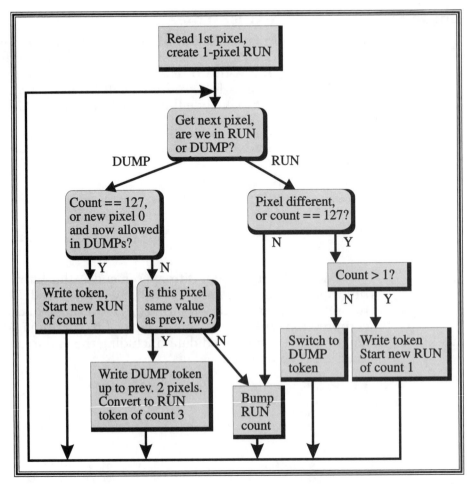

Figure 6.4 Flowchart of run-length bitmap row encoding (ARle8Writer::Encode-Row()).

token of length 1, added to a different-valued pixel, is transformed into a 2-pixel dump token. Similarly, a dump token may have three identical pixels added to it. When this happens, it is split into a dump portion and a 3-pixel run portion. Figure 6.4 is a flowchart of the full algorithm, which finds the optimal encoding for a given row.

The ARle8Writer::EncodeRow() method implements this algorithm. It is fairly heavily commented, so you can follow how the array of pixel values is turned into a stream of tokens.

```
bool ARle8Writer::EncodeRow(uchar *psrc)
{
// Start off in a run of length 1
```

```
        ARle8Token currTok;
        currTok.type = RLE8WR_RUN;
        currTok.count = 1;
        currTok.pixel = *psrc++;

// Read thru pixels till done

        int numPixels = widthRow = 1; // we already grabbed 1st pixel
        while (numPixels > 0)
            {
            if (currTok.type == RLE8WR_RUN)
                {
// If currently in run, check for different pixel value or maximum
// length run.

                if ((currTok.pixel != *psrc) || (currTok.count == 127))
                    {
// We must end the current run. If it's long enough, we'll write it
// out as a run, and start a new run of length 1. But if it's too
// short, we'll just convert the current run to a dump and add this.

                    if (currTok.count > 1)
                        {
                        if (!WriteToken(currTok))
                            return FALSE;
                        currTok.pixel = *psrc;
                        currTok.count = 1;
                        }
                    else
                        {
                        currTok.type = RLE8WR_DUMP;
                        currTok.ptr = psrc - currTok.count;
                        ++currTok.count;
                        }
                    }

// If we're in a run and the current pixel is the same color, great!
// Bump the token count.

                else
                    ++currTok.count;
                }
            else
                {
// We're currently in a dump token. If we've hit our limit of 127
// pixels, or the new pixel is a 0 and can't go in a dump, write out
// current token and switch to a run of length 1.

                if ((currTok.count == 127) ||
                    ((*psrc == 0) && zeroInRuns))
                    {
                    if (!WriteToken(currTok))
                        return FALSE;
                    currTok.type = RLE8WR_RUN;
```

```
                    currTok.pixel = *psrc;
                    currTok.count = 1;
                    }
                else if ((currTok.count > 2) && (*psrc == *(psrc - 1)) &&
                    (*psrc == *(psrc - 2)))
                    {
// Well, we're in this dump, see. But it turns out that this pixel
// matches the previous two pixels. So, we want to write out the
// dump, MINUS THE PREVIOUS TWO PIXELS, and then convert into a
// 3-pixel run (the previous two plus this one).

                    currTok.count -= 2;
                    if (!WriteToken(currTok))
                        return FALSE;
                    currTok.type = RLE8WR_RUN;
                    currTok.pixel = *psrc;
                    currTok.count = 3;
                    }

// If there's nothing special going on, just bump the dump count.

                else
                    ++currTok.count;
                }

// In either run or dump case, bump source ptr and count down pixels

            ++psrc;
            --numPixels;
            }

// Successfully ran through all source pixels, write out last token.

        return(WriteToken(currTok));
    }
```

Writing Tokens

EncodeRow() uses the private method WriteToken() to write a token
to the output stream.

```
bool ARle8Writer::WriteToken(ARle8Token &tok)
{
// Compute size of token + END, make sure enough room for both
// If not, write out an END token and set the overflow flag.

    int len = (tok.type == RLE8WR_RUN) ? 3 : 2 + tok.count;
    if ((pdest + len) >= pend)
        {
        overflow = TRUE;
        *pdest++ = 0;
```

```
        return FALSE;
        }

// Write RUN or DUMP token

    if (tok.type == RLE8WR_RUN)
        {
        *pdest++ = tok.count;
        *pdest++ = tok.pixel;
        }
    else
        {
        *pdest++ = ARLE8_DUMP | tok.count;
        memcpy(pdest, tok.ptr, tok.count);
        pdest += tok.count;
        }
    return TRUE;
}
```

Rendering BMF_RLE8 Bitmaps

Encoding and decoding run-length bitmaps is all well and good, but we're not writing an archiving package. What we really want to do is draw these critters on the screen, and fast. That means we don't want to unpack the BMF_RLE8 into some huge buffer and then draw it as a BMF_LIN8 bitmap. At the very least, we should unpack a row at a time, to avoid having to allocate a whole bunch of memory. As we'll soon see, in certain situations we can go one step better, and decode the run-length bitmap *directly into the destination canvas.*

Rendering a BMF_RLE8 Bitmap into Any Canvas

As always, we want to put a method to render a BMF_RLE8 bitmap into class ACanvas, so that we can render such a bitmap onto any canvas. By virtue of being generic, such a method will not run at optimum speed, but at least it works. How should such a method be written? We could unpack the entire bitmap into a big buffer and then draw it as a BMF_LIN8 bitmap, since we already have a method to do that. But there are better solutions. We could unpack the bitmap a row at a time and call the generic DrawPixel8U() routine to draw each pixel, but this approach is likely to be maddeningly slow. An intermediate approach is to unpack each row, and draw the row as a 1-row-high BMF_LIN8 bitmap. This is the method we'll use.

ACanvas::DrawBitmapRle8U() draws an unclipped BMF_RLE8 bitmap into a canvas. First, it creates a 1-row-high bitmap. This bitmap uses a temporary memory buffer, ACanvas::tempBuff, as the place where its bits are stored. ACanvas::tempBuff is an 8K buffer declared in class ACanvas for purposes such as these, as an alternative to using new(). If we have a bitmap wider than 8192 pixels, we'll have to increase the size of this buffer, but this is pretty unlikely.[1]

Notice how an object of class ARle8Reader is initialized in such a way that 0-valued pixels are not skipped over. This is because we want the UnpackRow() routine to always set every pixel in the temporary buffer. After all, there could be garbage pixels lying around in the buffer. DrawBitmapLin8U(), which we'll call to render the row, will take care of skipping over 0 pixels if the bitmap is transparent.

```
void ACanvas::DrawBitmapRle8U(ABitmap &bms, int x, int y)
{
// Set up 1-row bitmap in temporary buffer

    ABitmap bmrow(tempBuff, BMF_LIN8, bms.transparent, bms.width, 1);

// Initialize a rle8 reader, tell it not to skip over 0's.

    ARle8Reader rle8rd(bms, FALSE);

// Unpack each row into 1-row-high bitmap, then draw using lin8
// bitmap renderer.

    int yend = y + bms.height;          // pre-calc row to end at
    while (y < yend)                    // loop from top to bottom
        {
        rle8rd.UnpackRow(tempBuff);     // unpack row into temp buffer
        DrawBitmapLin8U(bmrow, x, y);   // draw 1-pixel tall BMF_LIN8 bm
        ++y;                            // advance to next row
        }
}
```

By using the DrawBitmapLin8U() method to draw each row, the above routine is actually pretty fast in any canvas. This is because DrawBitmapLin8U() is a virtual function, and we have already written good versions of this routine for both linear and bank-switched canvases. So the only penalties we pay are for row unpacking and the overhead of calling a virtual function for each row.

Rendering a BMF_RLE8 Bitmap into an 8-Bit Linear Canvas

The beauty of a linear canvas is that it's, well, linear. If we just use the generic ACanvas::DrawBitmapRle8U() method for an 8-bit linear can-

---

[1]My 87-inch monitor isn't due to arrive for another few years.

vas, we're paying the price of unpacking each row into a 1-row-high linear bitmap, and then copying this row to another linear bitmap. Let's cut out the middleman! ACanvasLin8::DrawBitmapRle8U() does just that, unpacking each row directly into the destination canvas. In this case, it sets up the rle8 reader to skip over 0 pixels if the bitmap is transparent, so that transparency is handled directly in the unpacking process! For this reason, this method can often draw run-length bitmaps faster than the equivalent linear bitmap could be drawn.

```
void ACanvasLin8::DrawBitmapRle8U(ABitmap &bms, int x, int y)
{
// Setup: init rle8 reader which will skip over 0's if this
// bitmap is transparent. Then compute ptr to 1st pixel to be drawn.

   ARle8Reader rle8rd(bms); // set up for reading rle8 data
   uchar *pd = Ptr(x, y);   // get ptr into canvas at x,y

// Unpack each row directly into the canvas bitmap!!
// Advance dest ptr by rowbytes for each row.

   int yend = y + bms.height;
   for ( ; y < yend; y++, pd += bm.rowbytes)
      rle8rd.UnpackRow(pd);
}
```

Rendering a BMF_RLE8 Bitmap into an 8-Bit Bank-Switched Canvas

The basic version of DrawBitmapRle8U() in ACanvas doesn't do a bad job for almost any derived canvas, because it calls DrawBitmap-Lin8U() to draw each unpacked row of the BMF_RLE8 bitmap. Since ACanvasBank8, for instance, already has a good version of DrawBitmapLin8U(), this means that DrawBitmapRle8U() will work pretty quickly. We certainly could write a custom version of DrawBitmapRle8U() for class ACanvasBank8, one which unpacked rows directly into the canvas when no bank-crossing occurred and did something else to handle bank-crossing rows.

However, since the animation system we'll be building in Part 2 renders run-length-encoded images to off-screen linear canvases, and then copies the (linear) results to the screen, rendering BMF_RLE8 bitmaps directly to a bank-switched canvas is less important than it might seem. For this reason, a more optimal ACanvasBank8::Draw-BitmapRle8U() is left as an exercise for the energetic reader.

Clipped Rendering of BMF_RLE8 Bitmaps

The process of rendering BMF_RLE8 bitmaps is complex, but worth it. And we're done, right? We haven't forgotten anything,

218

have we? Oh no, we almost forgot about clipping. We mustn't over-write the canvas and crash the poor computer, must we Precious? *Hissssssshhh.* . . .

Clipping run-length-encoded bitmaps is a nuisance. We can't take advantage of our old trick of creating a "sub-bitmap" which is the clipped area of the original bitmap. We might have a single token which is half in the clip area and half outside, for instance! Unfortunately, the clipping has to be done as an integral part of the rendering.

Clipping BMF_RLE8 Bitmaps

In order to help the various methods which might want to render BMF_RLE8 bitmaps, let's define a special clipping routine that does as much of the work as possible. ACanvas::ClipRle8Bitmap() takes a reference to a bitmap and an *x,y* position, like our regular bitmap clipper, but it takes two additional arguments: a reference to an ARle8Reader object, which it needs in order to skip over rows clipped from the top of the image, and a reference to a clip structure of type Rle8Clip, which it uses to convey other clipping information back to the caller.

Below is the Rle8Clip structure, taken from the ACanvas class declaration. It is used to report back which pixels should be drawn in a given row in 'xbeg' and 'xend'. These are expressed in terms of indexes into the unpacked row buffer. The third item, 'yend', is in canvas coordinates, and represents the row to end drawing at.

```
typedef struct {
    short xbeg;    // index into row at which to begin drawing
    short xend;    // index into row at which to end drawing
    short yend;    // y row at which to end drawing
} Rle8Clip;
```

ACanvas::ClipRle8Bitmap() compares the bitmap's extents against the canvas clip rectangle. For rows at the top of the bitmap which lie outside the clip rectangle, these rows must be skipped. Unlike uncompressed bitmaps, this can't be done by incrementing the 'pbits' pointer by some multiple of the 'rowbytes' field. Instead, ARle8Reader::SkipRow() must be called to scan through the tokens that make up these rows.

ClipRle8Bitmap() checks left, right, and bottom edges against the clip rectangle, setting the three fields in the Rle8Clip structure appropriately. It returns TRUE if any part of the bitmap lies within the clip rectangle, and FALSE if no part does. The caller uses this to determine whether to proceed with any drawing at all.

```
bool ACanvas::ClipRle8Bitmap(ABitmap &bms, int &x, int &y,
    ARle8Reader &rle8rd, Rle8Clip &rclip)
```

```
{
// Clamp relative xend to clip rectangle

   rclip.xend = bms.width;
   if ((x + bms.width) > clipRect.right)
      rclip.xend = clipRect.right - x;

// Set rclip.xbeg to # pixels to skip at start of each row
// If clip, modify x to point to real drawing start

   rclip.xbeg = 0;
   if (x < clipRect.left)
      {
      rclip.xbeg = clipRect.left - x;
      x = clipRect.left;
      }

// If no unclipped columns, bail out of rendering

   if (rclip.xbeg >= rclip.xend)
      return FALSE;

// Clip bottom

   rclip.yend = y + bms.height;
   if (rclip.yend > clipRect.bott)
      rclip.yend = clipRect.bott;

// Clip top, skip rows when clip

   if (y < clipRect.top)
      {
      rle8rd.SkipRow(clipRect.top - y);
      y = clipRect.top;
      }

// Return whether or not anything left

   return(y < rclip.yend);
}
```

Rendering Clipped BMF_RLE8 Bitmaps

ACanvas::DrawBitmapRle8() is used to draw a clipped BMF_RLE8 bitmap. Because the unclipped version can be significantly faster, it first checks to see if the entire bitmap lies within the clip rectangle, and if so just calls DrawBitmapRle8U() and returns. Assuming we're not that lucky, it sets up an ARle8Reader for the bitmap and calls ClipRle8Bitmap() to compute the clipping information and skip over any rows at the top of the bitmap which are clipped off.

Next, DrawBitmapRle8() constructs a 1-pixel-high linear bitmap to hold a single row, again using the temporary memory buffer for the bits area. After some fancy footwork to adjust the bitmap based on the clipping information, it goes into a loop, unpacking each row and rendering it with DrawBitmapLin8U(). The fancy footwork is needed so that, while the entire row must be unpacked, only the unclipped portion is drawn.

```
void ACanvas::DrawBitmapRle8(ABitmap &bms, int x, int y)
{
// If bitmap fully within clip rectangle, use unclipped version

    if ((y >= clipRect.top) && ((y + bms.height) <= clipRect.bott) &&
        (x >= clipRect.left) && ((x + bms.width) <= clipRect.right))
            {
            DrawBitmapRle8U(bms, x, y);
            return;
            }

// Initialize rle8 reader, tell it not to skip 0's
// "Clip" rle8 bitmap, return if fully clipped

    ARle8Reader rle8rd(bms, FALSE);
    Rle8Clip rclip;
    if (!ClipRle8Bitmap(bms, x, y, rle8rd, rclip))
        return;

// Set up 1-row bitmap in temporary memory

    ABitmap bmrow(tempBuff, BMF_LIN8, bms.transparent, bms.width, 1);

// Adjust bitmap to draw just what we want

    bmrow.pbits += rclip.xbeg;          // clip off left side
    bmrow.width = rclip.xend - rclip.xbeg; // adjust width

// Unpack each row & draw as 1-pixel-high bitmap

    while (y < rclip.yend)              // loop from top to bottom
        {
        rle8rd.UnpackRow(tempBuff);    // unpack row into temp buffer
        DrawBitmapLin8U(bmrow, x, y);  // draw 1-pixel tall BMF_LIN8 bm
        ++y;                           // advance to next row
        }
}
```

What about a clipped version for ACanvasLin8 canvases? It turns out that our trick of unpacking directly into the canvas won't work in the clipped version, because part of the row may need to be clipped off. Because of this, the generic version in ACanvas works almost as well as we could do anyway. For ACanvasBank8 as well, the complications are significant and the gains are not worth the effort.

That's all there is to working with run-length bitmaps. The effort is worth it, as the savings in bitmap size, and sometimes even rendering speed, can be significant. Cartoon-style graphics compress particularly well, and can be rendered quite quickly. For instance, imagine a bitmap of a sky backdrop which washes from a deep blue at the top to a sunset red at the bottom, where each row is a different solid color. This bitmap can be represented in a few tokens per row (depending on its width, because of the 127-pixel token limit), so the compression ratio is on the order of 64:1. And when rendered into an 8-bit linear canvas, ARle8Reader::UnpackRow() does the actual rendering, using memset() to draw each set of 127 pixel runs. Very compact, and very speedy.

Scaling Bitmaps

Thus far when rendering bitmaps, we have maintained a one-to-one correspondence between pixels in a source bitmap and pixels on the destination canvas. A bitmap 10 pixels high and 10 pixels wide renders onto the same pixel area on the canvas. But that's not always what we might want. In 3D games such as *Doom* and *Dark Forces*, bitmapped objects appear large when an object is close, and smaller when it is further away. Theoretically, this could be done by storing a huge number of versions of each bitmap, each at a different size, but the enormous memory costs of this approach make it impractical. We need to *scale* the bitmap, converting its representation to a roughly equivalent one with a different width and height. Ideally, we should scale on the fly during a rendering method, rather than having to scale as a separate step before rendering.

Bitmap Scaling Basics

What does it mean, actually, to scale a bitmap? We can't change the size of the pixels themselves. Instead, we need to think in terms of a destination bitmap, each of whose pixels are taken from an appropriate position in the source bitmap. Each pixel in the destination bitmap should be colored according to the pixel or pixels in the same relative area of the source bitmap.

Let's look at an example. Suppose we have a 6 × 4-pixel bitmap, which we want to render into a 3 × 2-pixel destination area. In this case, we are scaling down by a factor of 2 in both width and height. Taking the view from the destination bitmap, each pixel should be related to a 2 × 2 group of pixels in the source bitmap, as Figure 6.5 illustrates.

How exactly do we color each destination pixel? There are a number of ways, which we can choose from depending on how good we want the result to look, and how fast we want to render. The fast way is to just take any pixel out of the 2 × 2 group, for instance the upper-left one, and copy it to the destination pixel. To get a better look, we would "average" the color of the four pixels in the 2 × 2 group, and color the destination pixel with the average. How do we compute such an average? After all, in the 8-bit indexed color modes that we are using, we can't just average the color indexes, which are arbitrary numbers. We need to average in RGB color space, and somehow turn this back into a color index. In Part 3, we'll see how to quickly perform such color calculations.

Suppose we are scaling to a larger size instead of a smaller size? Figure 6.6 shows a 3 × 3 bitmap being scaled up to cover a 6 × 6 area. Here, each pixel in the source bitmap is being turned into a 2 × 2-pixel block in the destination canvas. Another way to look at it is that each destination pixel is taken from a ½-pixel block in the source bitmap. The dotted lines in the left-hand bitmap of Figure 6.6 show these "half-pixels." A fractional pixel? Sure, with the help of fixed-point numbers, of course!

When scaling a bitmap upward in size, we can opt for the fast route of setting each destination pixel to the closest whole pixel in the source, or we can compute an average based on which actual pixels the fractional pixel is near. In the fast case, we'll get a "blocky" look to the bitmap, which can look crude when scaling up by a factor of two or more. Using pixel averaging, however, is far slower, and requires some color-calculation tools we haven't yet developed.

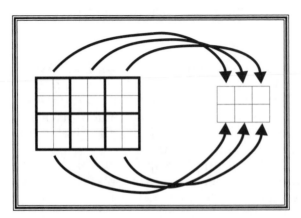

Figure 6.5   Scaling a 6 × 4 bitmap into a 3 × 2 area.

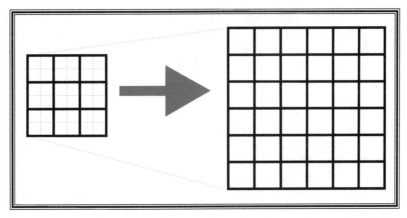

Figure 6.6 Scaling a 3 × 3 bitmap into a 6 × 6 area. Dotted lines highlight "fractional" pixels.

Fast Bitmap Scaling in ARTT

In ARTT, we'll develop bitmap scaling routines using the fast non-averaging approach. We will, however, allow arbitrary scaling factors, not just powers of two as in our examples. The scaling factor in the horizontal direction need not equal the vertical scaling factor, and we can produce some mighty strange effects by exploiting that. Furthermore, we will eventually be able to scale bitmaps in a variety of formats, including run-length-encoded bitmaps!

The bitmap scaling routines will take as arguments a bitmap reference and a rectangular area of the destination canvas onto which the bitmap should be projected. The scaling routine will take care of figuring out the scaling factor from the bitmap's width and height and the area supplied. The following sample code shows how we will use the bitmap scaler.

```
// SAMPLE CODE WHICH RENDERS A SCALED BITMAP
// assume 'bms' is a valid BMF_LIN8 bitmap
ARect area(20, 20, 200, 60);                  // area in canvas coords
gCanvasScreen->DrawScaledBitmapLin8(bms, area); // scale bms into that area
```

How should we structure and write the internals of such a bitmap scaling routine? The general approach will be to take the point of view of the destination canvas. For each pixel in the area to be scaled into, we compute the corresponding fractional pixel location in the source bitmap, round to the nearest whole pixel, and render the pixel that we find there. We won't actually calculate the source pixel location from scratch each time; instead we'll step incrementally through the source bitmap by a fractional amount, as we step through the destination a pixel at a time.

The x and y source pixel increments will be fixed-point numbers. If we are scaling down by a factor of 2, they would be set to 2, because we want to step over 2 source pixels for every pixel in the destination. If we are scaling up by a factor of 2, the source increments would be .5, so that we visit each source pixel twice for each destination pixel. If we are scaling up by 25 percent, the source increments would be .8, so that by the time 5 destination pixels are rendered, 4 pixels in the source bitmap have been stepped through.

Note that the fractional increment in the x-direction need not be the same as the y-increment. Figure 6.7 shows a bitmap being scaled up by 200 percent in the horizontal direction while being scaled down to 50 percent of its height in the vertical direction. The distortion shown in this case is fairly severe, but is pretty much a worst-case scenario. Larger, more detailed bitmaps fare much better, especially when scaled by a factor of two or less in either direction.

Row-Based Scaling

Like all bitmap rendering routines, the scalers will work a row at a time, copying pixels from source to destination using the fractional stepping. At the end of each row, stepping in the y-direction will occur, and the process repeats for the next row. The overall steps are listed below:

1. Compute fractional x-increment from bitmap width and area width.
2. Compute fractional y-increment from bitmap height and area height.
3. For each row in destination, copy pixels from source with fractional stepping, when row is done step source y by fractional y-increment.

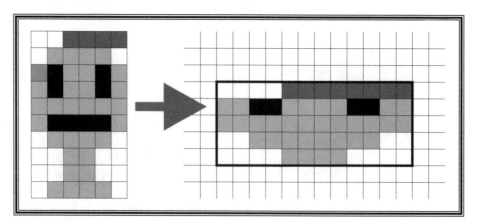

Figure 6.7   Scaling a 6×10 bitmap into a 12×5 area—200% horizontal scale, 50% vertical.

Variations on the Scaling Theme

Before we jump into writing methods to scale bitmaps, let's think about where we're headed. We currently have two different bitmap types we'd like to render scaled versions of, namely BMF_LIN8 and BMF_RLE8. We have transparent and nontransparent versions of these as well. Plus, we have several destination canvas classes that we want to render onto.

One approach would be to just write the two appropriate bitmap scaling routines (for BMF_LIN8 and BMF_RLE8 bitmaps), put them in class ACanvas, and be done with it. The problem with this approach is that the routines in class ACanvas have to use a virtual function to draw every pixel, because ACanvas is generic and doesn't know how to. This makes for slower scaling than we'd like.

At the other extreme is to write a full-fledged version of each routine for each canvas type. Instead of two routines, we'd have six, because we'd have to duplicate the two methods in ACanvasLin8 and ACanvasBank8, as well as class ACanvas. This still might be workable, though tedious. However, in Part 3 we are going to open up a Pandora's Box of new bitmap formats, new canvas classes, and color transformations. The number of bitmap rendering combinations, assuming every combination is allowed, is mind-boggling. Want to render a BMF_LIN15 bitmap scaled onto a 24-bit bank-switched canvas, with translucency? Sure, pal, let me put some fuel in my automatic code generator, and we'll throw in the shaded version for free!

Let's not panic yet—in Part 3, we'll bring order out of the exploding chaos with a combination of slow generic ACanvas methods for the cases that we don't care about, and lots of coding for the ones we do.

Rendering Scaled BMF_LIN8 Bitmaps

Even though we only need to write a few bitmap scaling routines now, let's take advantage of the row-based nature of the fast scaling method we intend to implement. If we can write a fast row-scaler for each combination of bitmap format and canvas type we need, we can put a single version of the "outer loop" of the routine in ACanvas and leave it there. We'll get a minor performance penalty for calling a virtual function to render each row, but we can live with the overhead of one virtual function call per row. That means that all the setup for the scaling, and calculating the fractional stepping factors and so forth, can be done in just one place too. Figure 6.8 shows the overall architecture we're adopting.

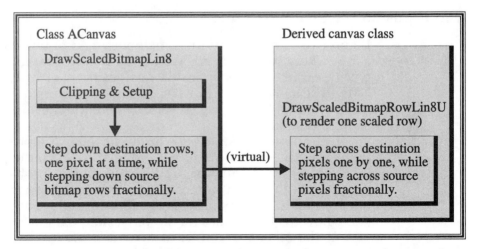

Figure 6.8 Architecture of bitmap scaling method, using virtual row-renderer function.

AScaledRowInfo: Horizontal Row Scaling Information

Let's look at the methods we need from the inside out, beginning with the routine that draws a single scaled row. This routine needs to have some information supplied to it, such as the *y* coordinate of the destination row being written in the canvas and its left and right *x*-coordinates. It also needs to know where to find the bits for the relevant row of the source bitmap, its starting *x*-coordinate (which may not be 0 due to clipping), and the all-important fractional step factor. The following structure holds all this information and then some—the last four members are for use by the overall routine that is controlling the row-by-row rendering process.

```
typedef struct {
// this info used in a row-renderer
    AFix srcFx;            // starting source x-coord, fractional
    AFix srcFxStep;        // source x-coord step, fractional
    uchar *srcPbits;       // ptr to source bits for entire row
    APalette *palette;     // palette of source image
    short transparent;     // is source transparent?
    short destY;           // destination y pixel row
    short destXleft;       // left destination pixel
    short destXright;      // right destination pixel (exclusive, no draw)
// this info used in overall renderer, not in row-renderer
    short destYtop;        // top coord of dest
    short destYbott;       // bottom coord of dest (exclusive)
    AFix srcFy;            // fixed-point source y coord
    AFix srcFyStep;        // fixed-point source y step
} AScaledRowInfo;
```

DrawScaledBitmapRowLin8U(): Scaling a BMF_LIN8 Row

The AScaledRowInfo structure holds all the information necessary to scale a row. A generic row scaler in ACanvas shows how this information is used to render a row of a bitmap of type BMF_LIN8. This routine is called DrawScaledBitmapRowLin8U(), and am I glad today's linkers allow function names of more than the 6-character limit I started out on!

```
void ACanvas::DrawScaledBitmapRowLin8U(AScaledRowInfo &sri)
{
// Start at initial source fixed-point x-coord

   AFix fx = sri.srcFx;

// Traverse from left to right in destination pixel row

   for (int x = sri.destXleft; x < sri.destXright; x++)
      {
      uchar c8 = *(sri.srcPbits + int(fx));  // grab source pixel
      if (c8 || !sri.transparent)            // if non-zero, or not transp
         DrawPixel8U(x, sri.destY, c8);      // draw it at dest
      fx += sri.srcFxStep;                   // step in src w/fraction
      }
}
```

The inner loop of the above routine does the nitty-gritty scaling work. First, the source pixel is extracted from the row by using the integer portion of the current fractional *x*-coordinate as an offset from the base of the row. This pixel is then drawn to the current destination pixel (unless it is 0 and the bitmap is transparent), in this case using the virtual function DrawPixel8U(). Finally, the source *x*-coordinate is incremented by a fractional amount, before moving on to the next destination pixel. Certainly it's more work than the normal nonscaling case, but not by much.

DrawScaledBitmapLin8(): Rendering a Scaled BMF_LIN8 Bitmap

With a scaling row-renderer in place in class ACanvas, we can write the outer shell, the routine that we call from our programs. Because there is a fair amount of setup involved before rendering a scaled bitmap, we're going to abandon our traditional approach of supplying both clipped and unclipped versions of each routine. The sole version will be a clipping version. Because of the nature of the row-rendering process, we can also get away with needing only an *unclipped* version of the row-rendering routine. This is a win–win— we pay a tiny setup overhead for clipping, but then the actual rendering code uses unclipped row-scaling routines throughout.

ACanvas::DrawScaledBitmapLin8() calls ClipAndSetupScaled-Bitmap() to fill in the AScaledRowInfo structure, which includes both information used by the row-renderer and other information used to control stepping from row to row. Then it enters a loop which it executes once per row in the destination, calling the row-renderer and then stepping fractionally in *y*. The *y*-stepping code computes the difference in the whole portion of the old and new *y*-coordinate, and uses this to determine how many bytes to advance in the source bitmap (multiplying the difference by the source bitmap's rowbytes). DrawScaledBitmapLin8() is listed below.

```
void ACanvas::DrawScaledBitmapLin8(ABitmap &bms, ARect &area)
{
    AScaledRowInfo sri;

// Clip and setup bitmap

    if (!ClipAndSetupScaledBitmap(bms, area, sri))
        return;

// Loop thru rows, drawing each (preclipped) strip

    int ysrc = int(sri.srcFy);
    for (sri.destY = sri.destYtop; sri.destY < sri.destYbott; sri.destY++)
        {
        DrawScaledBitmapRowLin8U(sri);    // render row!
        sri.srcFy += sri.srcFyStep;       // advance y fract
        sri.srcPbits += (int(sri.srcFy) - ysrc) * long(bms.rowbytes);
        ysrc = int(sri.srcFy);            // and src pbits
        }
}
```

ClipAndSetupScaledBitmap(): Scaling Setup

The last piece in our puzzle is ACanvas::ClipAndSetupScaledBitmap(), which takes the bitmap and destination area as input, and returns as output a filled AScaledRowInfo structure. Like all our clipping routines, it also returns TRUE if any portion of the bitmap is to be drawn, and FALSE otherwise. This routine is moderately complex because it handles clipping as an integral part of the setup. Basically, it does the following:

1. If the area to be rendered into is an empty rectangle, it returns FALSE.

2. Calculate the source *y*-stepping value as the ratio of the bitmap's height to the area's height.

3. Set the initial source *y*-coordinate to half the *y*-stepping value. This centers the destination area in our source bitmap.

4. Check the bottom and top coordinates against the clip rectangle, and adjust the source *y*-coordinate and the drawing area appropriately.

5. Calculate the source *x*-stepping value as the ratio of the bitmap's width to the area's width.

6. Check the left and right coordinates against the clip rectangle, and adjust the source *x*-coordinate and the drawing area appropriately.

7. Set the source bits pointer based on the source *x*- and *y*-coordinates.

8. Set the palette and transparent flag from the source bitmap. Ignore the BitmapOrDefaultPal() call here—Chapter 13 explains this routine and its use in 15-bit and 24-bit canvases.

9. Return FALSE if clipped area empty, TRUE if anything to draw.

```
bool ACanvas::ClipAndSetupScaledBitmap(ABitmap &bms, ARect &area,
    AScaledRowInfo &sri)
{
// If destination area is empty, don't draw anything

    if (area.IsEmpty())
        return FALSE;

// Source ystep is source height divided by dest height,
// and start y source at half a step

    sri.srcFyStep = AFix(bms.height) / area.Height();
    sri.srcFy = sri.srcFyStep / 2;

// Clip to top edge of clip rect, recalc bits ptr

    sri.destYtop = area.top;
    if (sri.destYtop < clipRect.top)
        {
        sri.srcFy += sri.srcFyStep * (clipRect.top - sri.destYtop);
        sri.destYtop = clipRect.top;
        }

// Clip to bottom edge of clip rect

    sri.destYbott = area.bott;
    if (sri.destYbott > clipRect.bott)
        sri.destYbott = clipRect.bott;

// Xstep and start x are calculated similarly

    sri.srcFxStep = AFix(bms.width) / area.Width();
    sri.srcFx = sri.srcFxStep / 2;

// Clip to left edge of clip rect
```

```
    sri.destXleft = area.left;
    if (sri.destXleft < clipRect.left)
        {
        sri.srcFx += sri.srcFxStep * (clipRect.left - sri.destXleft);
        sri.destXleft = clipRect.left;
        }

// Clip to right edge of clip rect

    sri.destXright = area.right;
    if (sri.destXright > clipRect.right)
        sri.destXright = clipRect.right;

// Set src ptr

    sri.srcPbits = bms.pbits + (int(sri.srcFy) * long(bms.rowbytes));

// Pick a palette, set transp flag

    sri.palette = BitmapOrDefaultPal(bms);
    sri.transparent = bms.transparent;

// Return whether anything to draw

    return((sri.destYtop < sri.destYbott) &&
        (sri.destXleft < sri.destXright));
}
```

Scaled Row-Rendering into an ACanvasLin8 Canvas

Well. That handles the case of a BMF_LIN8 bitmap being scaled onto any canvas. Not bad, but before we move on, let's speed up the code for 8-bit linear canvases, such as the mode 13H screen. The nice thing about the design approach we've taken is that we're not starting from scratch. We've got our outer loop routine and the setup routine that it uses. All we need to do is write the routine to render a scaled row onto the 8-bit linear canvas, in class ACanvasLin8.

ACanvasLin8::DrawScaledBitmapRowLin8U() can scale a row pretty quickly. After some setup which includes calculating the pointer to the first pixel we're going to render into the destination canvas, one of two short inner loops is used to render each pixel. One loop is for transparent bitmaps; the other for nontransparent. Note how this version avoids the overhead of a function call for each pixel. In fact, the nontransparent case is a pretty tight loop.

```
void ACanvasLin8::DrawScaledBitmapRowLin8U(AScaledRowInfo &sri)
{
// Initialize source x-coord, calc ptr into bitmap row, set width

    AFix fx = sri.srcFx;
    uchar *pd = Ptr(sri.destXleft, sri.destY);
```

```
        int w = sri.destXright - sri.destXleft;

// If transparent, check each pixel for 0 before write

    if (sri.transparent)
        {
        while (w--)
            {
            uchar c8 = *(sri.srcPbits + int(fx)); // grab pixel from source
            if (c8)
                *pd = c8;                          // only write if non-zero
            ++pd;                                  // bump canvas dest ptr
            fx += sri.srcFxStep;                   // advance fractional x
            }
        }

// Else non-transparent, grab pixels & write, step fractionally

    else
        {
        while (w-- > 0)
            {
            *pd++ = *(sri.srcPbits + int(fx));     // grab pixel and write
            fx += sri.srcFxStep;                   // advance fractional x
            }
        }
    }
```

Voilà! Instant faster version of DrawBitmapScaledLin8() for ACanvasLin8, and all we had to do was write a routine to render a single row.

Scaled Row-Rendering into an ACanvasBank8 Canvas

While we're on a roll, let's finish off the row-scalers by adding a row-scaler to class ACanvasBank8. ACanvasBank8::DrawScaledBitmap-RowLin8U() is complicated by the fact that a given row might cross a bank boundary, so it can't just be written to dash off pixels one after another. Like other rendering routines in ACanvasBank8, it needs to determine if there is a bank crossing, and if so split the rendering into "before" and "after" portions, inserting a bank-switch call between them. Other than that, it's the same game here—maybe we should dust off that code generator after all.

```
void ACanvasBank8::DrawScaledBitmapRowLin8U(AScaledRowInfo &sri)
{
// Setup for row, make sure correct bank is selected

    AFix fx = sri.srcFx;
    long vaddr = Vaddr(sri.destXleft, sri.destY);
    EnsureWriteBankAtAddr(vaddr);
```

```
// Set up ptr into canvas, set width of row

    uchar *pd = Ptr(vaddr);
    int w = sri.destXright - sri.destXleft;

// Check for bank crossing, if so do left half and set up for right

    if (CrossesBank(vaddr, w))
        {
// Split across bank: do left half

        int numLeft = BytesLeftInBank(vaddr); // # pixels on left
        int numRight = w - numLeft;         // the rest on right
        w = numLeft;                        // w = width on left half
        while (w-- > 0)                     // count down left half pixels
            {
            uchar c8 = *(sri.srcPbits + int(fx)); // grab source pixel
            if (c8 || !sri.transparent)
                *pd = c8;                   // if non-zero, write
            ++pd;                           // bump dest ptr
            fx += sri.srcFxStep;            // advance x by fractional amt
            }
        vaddr += numLeft;                   // at end of left, bump virtual addr
        EnsureWriteBankAtAddr(vaddr);       // make sure we're at right bank
        pd = Ptr(vaddr);                    // and recalc dest ptr
        w = numRight;                       // set up width for right half
        }

// Do entire row, or right half in split case

    while (w-- > 0)                         // loop thru pixels
        {
        uchar c8 = *(sri.srcPbits + int(fx)); // grab source pixel
        if (c8 || !sri.transparent)
            *pd = c8;                       // write if non-zero
        ++pd;                               // bump dest ptr
        fx += sri.srcFxStep;                // advance x by fractional amt
        }
    }
```

Rendering Scaled BMF_RLE8 Bitmaps

Scaling directly from a bitmap which is encoded in run-length format is a somewhat daunting prospect. While it is possible to step fractionally through pixels which are stored inside run and dump tokens, the coding of such an algorithm is not for the faint of heart. Take that as a challenge! In ARTT, we're going to do something a little less aggressive. The approach will be to unpack each row as it is needed into a temporary buffer, and then call the same row-scalers we used to scale BMF_LIN8 bitmaps. After all, an unpacked row is stored as one pixel

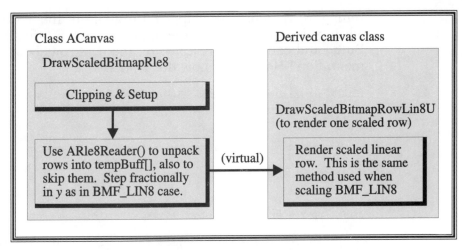

Figure 6.9 Architecture of BMF_RLE8 bitmap scaling.

per byte, just like a row in a BMF_LIN8 bitmap. This will save us an enormous amount of effort, and the results will be reasonably speedy too. Figure 6.9 gives an overview of the approach.

Because we can rely upon the row-scaling routines in the various canvas classes to do their job well, the main outer loop routine need only be written once, in class ACanvas. ACanvas::DrawScaled-BitmapRle8(), listed below, draws a scaled BMF_RLE8 bitmap onto any canvas.

After calling the same ClipAndSetupScaledBitmap() setup routine used for linear bitmaps, it sets up a "reader" for the run-length bitmap to be scaled. One row is unpacked at a time into tempBuff[], the temporary buffer that class ACanvas makes available for temporary memory usage. If any rows were clipped off in ClipAndSetup-ScaledBitmap, ARle8Reader::SkipRow() is called to skip through these rows in the BMF_RLE8 bitmap. Then, the first row is unpacked before entering the main loop of the routine.

The main loop then runs once per row of the destination area. Since an unpacked row of a BMF_RLE8 bitmap is just a linear row like one in a BMF_LIN8 bitmap, the same row-rendering routines we just wrote can be used here. The row-scaler is called to render the row, and then the destination is stepped using fractional stepping as in the linear bitmap case. The only extra complication is that, when the source bitmap is stepped in the vertical direction, this means unpacking another row instead of just updating a 'pbits' pointer. Further, if the source bitmap is stepped by more than one row, the intervening rows must be skipped through. If the *y*-stepper doesn't advance by an entire row, the unpacked row is still sitting in temp-Buff[] and can just be rescaled on the next row. Look at the implementation below to see how this works.

```
void ACanvas::DrawScaledBitmapRle8(ABitmap &bms, ARect &area)
{
    AScaledRowInfo sri;

// Clip and setup scaled bitmap with local copy of area

    if (ClipAndSetupScaledBitmap(bms, area, sri))
        {

// Set up reader for run-length bitmap

        ARle8Reader rle8rd(bms, FALSE);   // FALSE: don't skip over transp

// Set up initial integer src y-offset, skip rows if need to

        int ysrc = int(sri.srcFy);        // get whole part of init yfract
        if (ysrc)                         // check to see if rows to skip
            rle8rd.SkipRow(ysrc);         // skip them if so

// Unpack first row, then loop through each row of destination

        rle8rd.UnpackRow(tempBuff);       // use tempBuff[] for row
        sri.srcPbits = tempBuff;
        for (sri.destY = sri.destYtop; sri.destY < sri.destYbott;
            sri.destY++)
            {
            DrawScaledBitmapRowLin8U(sri);    // draw row
            sri.srcFy += sri.srcFyStep;       // advance y by fraction
            int ny = int(sri.srcFy) - ysrc;   // get # rows to advance
            if (ny)                           // did we advance?
                {
                if (ny - 1)                   // yes, check for skipped rows
                    rle8rd.SkipRow(ny - 1);   // if so, skip them
                rle8rd.UnpackRow(tempBuff);   // unpack row
                }
            ysrc = int(sri.srcFy);            // get whole y for next compare
            }
        }
}
```

Generic Bitmap-Rendering Interface

Now that we've got two different bitmap formats, we have two sets of methods for rendering using them. When calling a rendering routine, we've had to call the "right" one based on the format of the bitmap we're rendering, BMF_LIN8 or BMF_RLE8. If some piece of code must be able to handle either, it has to look something like this:

```
// SAMPLE CODE TO RENDER A BITMAP OF EITHER BMF_LIN8 OR BMF_RLE8
if (bm.format == BMF_LIN8)
    pCanvas->DrawBitmapLin8(bm, x, y);
else if (bm.format == BMF_RLE8)
    pCanvas->DrawBitmapRle8(bm, x, y);
```

This is kind of silly, and will get worse when we add more bitmap formats. Let's nip it in the bud. We'll write a single Draw-Bitmap() which can handle any bitmap format, including those we haven't seen yet. While we're at it, let's also make a generic Draw-ScaledBitmap().

How do we write such generic routines? One way would be to use a switch statement:

```
// HYPOTHETICAL DRAWBITMAP()
void ACanvas::DrawBitmap(ABitmap &bm, int x, int y)
{
    switch (bm.format)
        {
        case BMF_LIN8:
            DrawBitmapLin8(bm, x, y); break;
        case BMF_RLE8:
            DrawBitmapRle8(bm, x, y); break;
        // ... other cases
        }
}
```

Generic Interface Using Pointers to Member Functions

There's a better way, though, using pointers to member functions. This is an advanced C++ idiom which allows us to create a pointer, or better yet a table of pointers, to class methods. We can make a table of such pointers with one entry per bitmap format, and enter into the table the "pointers" to the appropriate method for a bitmap of that format.

ACanvas::DrawBitmapU(), which draws an unclipped bitmap of any format, is listed below, along with its associated member function pointer table.

```
void (ACanvas::*pfDrawBitmapU[])(ABitmap &bm, int x, int y) = {
    &ACanvas::DrawBitmapLin8U,
    &ACanvas::DrawBitmapLin15U,
    &ACanvas::DrawBitmapLin24U,
    &ACanvas::DrawBitmapBadFormat,
```

```
        &ACanvas::DrawBitmapBadFormat,
        &ACanvas::DrawBitmapBadFormat,
        &ACanvas::DrawBitmapRle8U,
};


void ACanvas::DrawBitmapU(ABitmap &bms, int x, int y)
{
    (this->*pfDrawBitmapU[bms.format])(bms, x, y);
}
```

Inside DrawBitmapU(), the appropriate member function pointer is looked up in the table and invoked. This may be DrawBitmapLin8U, DrawBitmapRle8U, or another bitmap-rendering method for a format we haven't encountered yet.

But something more dramatic than it looks is going on here. If the entries in the table were actually just function pointers, like you might imagine in C, they would all be pointing at the implementations of these methods in class ACanvas. But here's the amazing thing—when this very ACanvas::DrawBitmapU() is invoked on a derived canvas class, say ACanvasLin8, that canvas's implementations of these methods are called, not the ones in class ACanvas! This single table, defined once, gets us to the proper virtual function for whatever canvas class is being rendered onto. If this doesn't make sense to you, it surprised me too—but it works!

Pointers to member functions are obviously not implemented as simple pointers. They are usually, in fact, stored as offsets into the table of virtual functions associated with each class. Then, the invocation of such a "function pointer" looks up the address of a virtual function at that offset, and dispatches to it. Since each class has its own virtual function table, and each object carries a pointer to that table, the single member function pointer table can be used to access an unbounded variety of actual functions.

Two other generic bitmap renderers are implemented in the same manner as DrawBitmapU(). These are ACanvas::DrawBitmap(), which draws a generic bitmap with clipping, and ACanvas::DrawScaledBitmap(), which draws a generic bitmap scaled to an area.

Figure 6.10   Various screen shots taken during a run of SCALSHOW.

Figure 6.10   *(Continued)*

SCALSHOW: A Sample Scaling Program

SCALSHOW is a simple demo program which shows off bitmap scaling. It takes the name of a graphics file as input, and scales the image up and down in size as fast as it can go. Press any key to exit. Run via:

```
SCALSHOW filename.ext
```

For the source to SCALSHOW, see the accompanying CD. Figure 6.10 shows three snapshots of the program in action.

C H A P T E R

Microsoft Windows and WinG

Up to this point, we have been programming VGA and Super VGA devices directly, using programs written under DOS and 32-bit extended DOS. The bare-bones quality of DOS has allowed us to focus on the mechanisms of bitmap manipulation and display, without the added complexity of working within a graphical environment with its own rules. But DOS is dead, as they've been saying for a while now. Microsoft Windows is the new king of the desktop, and most new applications are written to run under its graphical environment. In this chapter, we'll rework ARTT to work with Windows.

Does this mean a complete overhaul? Hardly. Windows has device-independent bitmaps (DIBs), which, as we'll see, look remarkably like linear canvases. A new Windows API, called WinG, allows fast copying of offscreen DIBs to windows on the screen. We're going to write two new classes in this chapter, and ARTT will be brought into the world of Windows. Our programs will run under Windows 3.1 and Windows 95 systems equipped with WinG (included on the CD). The rest of this book will then build upon the dual DOS/Windows foundation set up in this chapter.

But we're getting ahead of ourselves. First, let's review what Windows is and how it's programmed, before leaping into efforts to fit ARTT into it.

Windows Overview

Microsoft Windows is a Graphical Operating Environment. Version 1.0 was released in November 1985, and largely met with a collective yawn from the industry. PC compatibles at the time were barely capable of supporting such a graphics-based system. The Macintosh, which Windows was clearly modeled after, was also underpowered in its early versions, but the Mac had the advantage of a better processor, a monochrome-only display, far less hardware add-ons to contend with, and a truly brilliant team of designers behind it. Windows had to contend right off the bat with a wide variety of (color) displays, a huge variety of printers and add-on cards, a wimpy processor (the 8088), and the limitations of a clunky DOS operating system under it.

Like the feudal lord in Monty Python's *The Holy Grail*, who kept building castles even though each one sank in the swamp, Microsoft persevered, and in November 1987 released version 2.0, followed shortly by Windows/386 for the new 80386-based machines. The first version which "stayed up" in a big way was version 3.0, introduced in May 1990. Version 3.0 was the first to make use of the protected-mode features of the 286 and 386 chips, and allowed access to up to 16 Mb of RAM. Version 3.1, released in April 1992, added TrueType fonts, multimedia features, and more, and built upon the success of 3.0.

Windows is dominant now. Nearly all major applications are written for it, and Windows 95 is likely to cement Windows' dominance on the PC desktop. Windows 95 sports a much-improved user interface and greater support for 32-bit operation. Microsoft's declaration that DOS has been banished from the Windows kingdom is apparently a little overstated, but Windows 95 does move further in the direction of relegating DOS to a compatibility mode of Windows, from its current role as underlying operating system and shaky foundation.

Windows Look and Feel

While each version of Windows has enhanced the visual appeal and user interface of the environment, all versions have contained the basic interface elements of resizable windows, icons, pushbuttons, pull-down menus, dialog boxes, and the other now-familiar elements which make up its "look and feel." Figure 7.1 is a screenshot from a sample Windows 3.1 screen.

The screen in Figure 7.1 shows some of the interface elements available to Windows application developers. Table 7.1 lists the most common elements found in modern Windows programs.

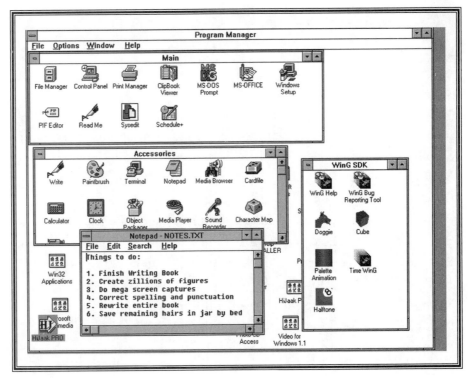

Figure 7.1 Screen shot of typical Windows 3.1 screen, showing user-interface elements.

Windows Applications

Application programs need not be modified to "simply work" under Windows. The ARTT programs developed so far can be launched from within Windows. Upon doing a video mode set, the Windows screen disappears, replaced by the same full-screen VGA or Super VGA screen that would be seen when running from DOS. When the program exits, the Windows screen magically reappears.

A true Windows program is not so rude, however. First of all, it runs on the same screen with the Windows desktop and other Windows programs. It runs inside one or more windows on that screen, and these windows can make use of a huge host of services made available by the Windows environment. These services include creation of the user-interface components such as those listed in Table 7.1, a large set of rendering routines (GDI, the Graphics Device Interface), sound and video services, network connections, and more advanced services such as Object Linking and Embedding (OLE). Literally over a thousand functions are available, and the "dynamic

Table 7.1   Common Windows Interface Elements

Name	Use
Window	Screen area holding view of information, optionally with border area
Menu	List of selectable commands
Icon	Visual glyph, representing file, program, or operation
Scroll bar	Control element used to scroll window contents
Button	Control element which can be "pushed" to send command
Check box	Control used to toggle state of an option
Radio button	Control used to select one of a set of choices
Slider	Control used to set the value of a continuously varying option
Edit field	Control into which text can be typed
Toolbar	Array of icons
Status bar	Screen area devoted to status message display
Dialog box	Special window holding related controls
Property sheet	One page of a set of sheets, each similar to a dialog box

linking" capabilities allow new API sets, such as WinG, to be added at any time.

Programming Windows

For programmers used to text-mode or even graphics programming under DOS, stepping into the world of Windows programming is a disorienting experience. Besides the sheer volume of new functions and structures to learn about, the basic control flow mechanisms are turned on their heads. Many simple DOS programs flow from top to bottom, following a mostly linear path. Windows programs, on the other hand, are inherently "event driven." After initialization, they enter a loop, where *messages* are pulled from a queue and processed, until one message finally informs the program that it is to terminate. Additionally, Windows sends other messages directly to procedures associated with the windows that the program has created.

Whoa! Messages? Window procedures? Let's back up a second, lay out a few terms, and then try again. Table 7.2 lists some of the terms and concepts Windows programmers must be familiar with.

In the next section, we'll see how these concepts are used in the creation of a basic Windows program. This discussion will move quickly, and cover only a tiny portion of the overall Windows paradigm and API tonnage. If you're already familiar with Windows programming, great. This will be a recap and some new information specific to WinG. If you're not familiar with Windows programming, get ready for a crash course on just what we need to know to make ARTT work under Windows. For further information, take a look at one of the many books which are devoted to this topic. The best known of these, and for good reason, is Charles Petzold's *Programming Windows 3.1*, published by Microsoft Press (see Appendix E).

WinMain: The Entry Point to a Windows Program

Right off the bat, Windows programs are different. Rather than start with a main() function, a Windows program uses WinMain() as its entry point. WinMain() takes four arguments:

HANDLE hInstance	Handle of this instance of the application
HANDLE hPrevInstance	Handle to previous instance, or NULL if no other instances
LPSTR lpszCmdParam	Pointer to command line
int nCmdShow	Recommended initial state for main window

Table 7.2 Some Windows Programming Terms

Name	*Definition*
Message	Numeric command code, with 2 associated arguments (wParam and lParam)
Handle	Id associated with a window or other system "object"
Window procedure	Function which handles messages for a window
Window class	Set of windows sharing a window procedure and other attributes
Device context	Drawing surface and drawing attributes
Resource	Data object contained in EXE file or external resource file

What are these new types, such as HANDLE and LPSTR? In WIN-DOWS.H, which every Windows program includes, a huge number of new types are defined. The definitions of all these types are beyond the scope of this book, but a few comments are in order. HANDLEs are integer quantities used to hold "magic cookie" identifiers for windows, palettes, device contexts, drawing objects, and many other "objects" in Windows. LPSTR is a string pointer. Part of the reason for Windows' convoluted type system is its roots in 16-bit segment-based programming, in which only pointers declared "far" can access more than a limited region of memory. With 16-bit "large model" and 32-bit programming (the only two modes supported by ARTT), the use of the FAR keyword is unnecessary. That's fortunate, because we don't want to have to go back and modify all the classes developed so far!

WinMain Contents

A typical WinMain() takes the following actions:

1. Copy the instance handle into a global variable, for later use by the program.
2. Register one or more window classes.
3. Create and show the main application window.
4. Enter a loop of getting and dispatching messages.
5. On exit from the loop, return an exit code to Windows.

Let's look at a typical (minimal) WinMain(), and see each of the five actions.

WinMain: Copying the Instance Handle

Below is listed the header of a minimal Windows program, and the first few lines of the WinMain() function.

```
#include <windows.h>


HANDLE hInst;    // global copy of instance handle
HWND hWndApp;    // global copy of handle to main application window
char *szAppName = "Sample App Name"; // application name

int PASCAL WinMain(HANDLE hInstance, HANDLE hPrevInstance, LPSTR lpszCmdLine,
    int nCmdShow)
{
    MSG msg;                 // message structure (for event loop)

    hInst = hInstance;   // save the instance handle
```

WinMain: Registering the Window Class

A window class supplies information to Windows about a class of windows, and registering one or more classes is necessary before creating any custom application windows. The WNDCLASS structure used for registration holds several fields, and a full discussion of them is beyond the scope of this book. The 'style' field gives information to Windows such as what kinds of messages should be sent to windows of this class, whether each window gets its own device context, and under what conditions the window needs redrawing by the application. The next field, 'lpfnWndProc', identifies the user-supplied function which will process messages directed to windows of this class. Fields 'cbClsExtra' and 'cbWndExtra' identify how many "extra" bytes should be allocated with the class and with each window, in which can be stored class- or window-specific data. The next four fields hold handles to various window-related entities. Field 'lpszMenuName' holds the name of the menu resource which supplies the menu for windows of this class. Finally, 'lpszClassName' holds the name of the window class we are registering.

```
if (!hPrevInstance)
   {
   WNDCLASS wndclass;      // window class structure (for registration)
   wndclass.style = CS_BYTEALIGNCLIENT | CS_VREDRAW |
      CS_HREDRAW | CS_DBLCLKS;
   wndclass.lpfnWndProc = WndProc;
   wndclass.cbClsExtra = 0;
   wndclass.cbWndExtra = 0;
   wndclass.hInstance = hInstance;
   wndclass.hIcon = LoadIcon(hInstance, "REX");
   wndclass.hCursor = LoadCursor(NULL, IDC_ARROW);
   wndclass.hbrBackground = GetStockObject(WHITE_BRUSH);
   wndclass.lpszMenuName = NULL;
   wndclass.lpszClassName = szAppName;
   if (!RegisterClass(&wndclass))
      return FALSE;
}
```

WinMain: Creating and Showing the Main Application Window

The CreateWindow() function takes several arguments, and returns the handle to a newly created window. The first argument is the window class name previously used to register the class. This is followed by the window caption title. The next argument specifies the "window style," including whether the window has a title, a thick frame for user resizing, a system menu, minimize and maximize icons, and other features. The style argument is followed by two pairs of coordinates. The first pair specifies the window's upper-left screen location; in this case we are letting Windows decide. The second pair is the initial size of the window. This size includes the window title and frame—to control the size of the *client area* of the window (its inside), the AdjustWindowRect() function can be used. A later example will highlight this. Following the size coordinates are three handles and an optional "creation data" pointer.

If all goes well, an invisible window has been created. To show it on the screen, the ShowWindow() call must be used. Making this a separate step allows a program to perform operations on the window to prepare it for visibility after it has been created, for example, to create the data structures needed for rendering it. ShowWindow() takes two arguments. The first is the window handle returned by CreateWindow(). The second specifies how the window will be shown—minimized, maximized, or normal. Typically, programs let Windows decide, passing along the 'nCmdShow' argument supplied to WinMain().

```
hWndApp = CreateWindow(
    szAppName,                    // window class name
    "Sample Window Caption",      // window caption text
    WS_OVERLAPPED | WS_CAPTION | WS_SYSMENU |
        WS_MINIMIZEBOX | WS_MAXIMIZEBOX | WS_THICKFRAME; // window style
    CW_USEDEFAULT, CW_USEDEFAULT, // initial window upper-left location
    400,400,       // initial window size
    NULL,          // parent window handle
    NULL,          // window menu handle
    hInstance,     // application instance handle
    NULL);         // pointer to optional creation data

ShowWindow(hWndApp, nCmdShow);    // show window
```

WinMain: The Event Loop

After initialization, a Windows program enters a loop. In this loop, it receives messages from Windows which are directed at one of its windows, dispatches them to the appropriate window, and loops to receive another message. The process is often so simple that some people wonder why it's located in the application at all—an alternative would be to just call some hypothetical WinTellMeWhenItsOver(). Putting the event loop in the application is important, however, because it does give the application some flexibility over how it handles messages, and it gives the application the ability to perform other recurrent processing which is not prompted by user events or by Windows.

The simplest event loop looks like the one listed below. Later, we'll create a slightly more complicated one to serve our animation needs.

```
while (GetMessage(&msg, NULL, 0, 0)) // wait for next message
    {
```

```
        TranslateMessage(&msg);        // support accelerator keys
        DispatchMessage(&msg);         // dispatch to appropriate window procedure
    }
```

WinMain: On Exit From Event Loop, Clean Up and Return

GetMessage() returns FALSE on receipt of a particular message, one which tells the application that it has been shut down by the user or some other event. The application should clean up and return to Windows with the supplied return code. In our example, there's not much to do.

```
        UnregisterClass(szAppName, hInstance); // unregister window class
        return msg.wParam;                     // return exit code to Windows
    }
```

The Window Procedure

Is our sample program done? Not quite. Remember that we supplied the name of a function when registering the window class. This function is a "window procedure," which is a very special function which handles the messages which Windows, and indirectly the user, supply to our window. This function takes as arguments the window handle, a message code, and two message-specific arguments.

Window message codes are typically named in the form WM_XXXX, and there are a large number of them. Some are merely informative—the application is notified whenever the window is moved or resized, or the system palette changes. Others demand attention by most applications. Such messages include keystrokes or mouse clicks, menu selections, scrolling commands, and the important WM_PAINT message, which tells the application to redraw the window. Since a window may be overlapped and later uncovered, or minimized and later restored, an application must remain ready at any time to redraw the full contents of the window on receipt of the WM_PAINT message. Applications can force WM_PAINT messages to be sent to themselves, using the InvalidateRect() call, which notifies Windows that the program has determined that some or all of a window needs to be redrawn. The program may do this because it is animating the display, or a mouse click or other user action has caused a change in state which should be reflected in the window.

A minimal window procedure, minus the actual code to draw into the window, is presented below. Note that unhandled messages are passed on to a function called DefWindowProc(). This "default window procedure" is supplied by Windows. It responds sensibly to a great many messages on the application's behalf, and all unhandled messages should be passed on to it.

```
LRESULT CALLBACK WndProc(HWND hwnd, UINT message,
    WPARAM wParam, LPARAM 1Param)
{
    PAINTSTRUCT ps;        // structure used when repainting window

    switch (message)
        {
        case WM_PAINT:
            hdc = BeginPaint(hwnd, &ps);
            ... draw contents of window ...
            EndPaint(hwnd, &ps);
            return(0);

        case WM_DESTROY:
            PostQuitMessage(0);        // window destroyed, let's shut down app
            return(0);
        }

    return DefWindowProc(hwnd, message, wParam, 1Param); // use default proc
}
```

What Else Goes in a Windows Program?

The example code given above is not exactly the next killer app, but it will work, displaying a blank white window which can be resized, minimized and maximized, dragged around the screen, and closed. Most programs will add an "about box" and a menu bar, if not more advanced interface elements such as a toolbar of icons. Also, we obviously need to put something inside our blank white window. To do so, Windows developers usually dive into the depths of GDI, the Graphics Device Interface. GDI supplies a host of drawing functionality, from lines and rectangles and polygons to bitmaps and outline fonts.

We're going to take a different route in this chapter, however. Shortly we'll explore WinG, a new API which allows us to render into windows blindingly quickly, directly from off-screen buffers which we manage with our own rendering code. What rendering code is that? Why, ARTT canvas rendering code, of course. We'll tie an off-screen canvas to a WinG-managed window, and in one fell swoop all the rendering code we've developed so far (and all the animation and special effects to come) will be usable inside our windows. It's also possible to mix GDI calls in as well, so we can write text using True-Type fonts, for instance.

WinG is based on device-independent bitmaps, known as DIBs. That's our next stop on this fast-moving train to high-performance Windows graphics.

DIBs: Device-Independent Bitmaps

In Windows' early days, most users ran Windows on a 16-color VGA display, usually at a resolution of 640 × 480 pixels (or 640 × 350 for

EGA users). This 16-color mode is a *planar* mode, meaning that the four bits which make up each pixel are not stored together, but are distributed across four *planes* of memory. (Refer back to Figure 5.1 for an illustration of planar modes.)

Writing rendering code for such a display format is nontrivial, and thankfully those days are behind us now. But the impact on the design of Windows lingers on. Until recently, Windows assumed that most displays ran in such planar modes, and programs were required to go through contortions to work with the *device-dependent bitmaps* compatible with such displays. The simple act of rendering a bitmap read from a file involved a surprising number of function calls to create "compatible device contexts," select them into the display context, and so on. But these days are numbered.

The DIB

Beginning with Windows 3.0, Microsoft introduced the DIB—the device-independent bitmap. The DIB format is a "chunky pixel" format in which each pixel's bits are contained together in memory. The DIB format encompasses pixels with 1, 4, 8, 16, and 24 bits per pixel. The invention of the DIB is a recognition of the fact that the vast bulk of current Windows users are running 256-color Super VGA displays, and those that are not are mostly those who have moved on to hi-color and true-color displays. These displays all work in chunky pixel format, although they usually add the complication of bank-switching to access all that display memory.

The future of Windows bitmap manipulation lies with the DIB. WinG, the fast-blitting API we will cover shortly, works exclusively with DIBs. In Windows 95, the whole notion of what a display driver has to do changes in light of the DIB takeover. Display device drivers written for Windows 3.1 and previous versions are huge, bloated monstrosities of rendering code, much of it the same from driver to driver. In Windows 95, a "DIB engine" is available to perform most rendering operations, and display driver functions often just call this engine to do the work (unless they can take advantage of on-board hardware to do the job faster). This DIB engine is hand-crafted, highly optimized, 32-bit assembler code, and it exists in one place, available for all drivers to use. Figure 7.2 is somewhat simplified, but contrasts the overall rendering architecture used in Windows 3.1 and Windows 95.

The Format of a DIB

So then, what is the format of a DIB? At this point, I could begin listing the structures that lay out the contents of a DIB, discussing the meaning of each field. But we've already done that! Remember Chap-

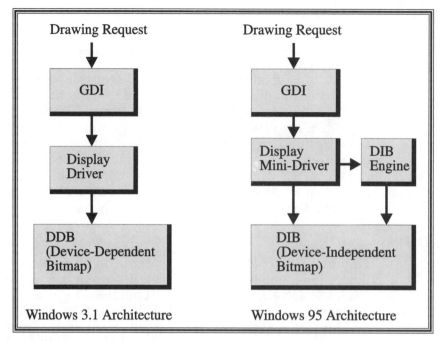

Figure 7.2 Simplified comparison of Windows 3.1 and Windows 95 rendering architectures.

ter 3, when we discussed the format of a BMP file, which incidently could use the extension DIB instead of BMP? That's a DIB. Take a look now to refresh your memory. Table 7.3 recaps the overall structure of a DIB file.

In order to render into a DIB, or to render a DIB into a window, we need to have it in memory, not just sitting there in a file. That's easy. An in-memory DIB is just the same as a file-based DIB, minus the initial 14-byte file header. The bitmap info header, color table, and bitmap bits are all present in the exact format in which they appear in the file. End of format discussion.

What Do We Do With a DIB?

Since we already have code to read DIBs from a file into our own ABitmap format, we're not going to bother writing new code to read a DIB. What we are going to do is create off-screen buffers in the form of a DIB, and then create a canvas which can be used to render into that DIB. We'll also explore how to copy that rendered DIB onto the screen (in our window, of course). Creating and deleting a DIB, managing its palette, and copying it to a window—that's the functionality we need, because ARTT can do the rest. This brings us to WinG.

Table 7.3 Structure of a DIB File

Component	Size (in bytes)	Contents
File Header	14	'BM' signature, file size, offset to data bits
Bitmap Header	40	width, height, depth, compression type, other info
Palette	variable	up to 256 RGBQUAD entries
Data bits	variable	data bits, usually uncompressed

WinG: G For Games?

Microsoft must have been frustrated to see entertainment programs stay DOS-based for so long after the rest of the developer community had moved to Windows. Word processors, spreadsheets, databases, image editing programs, utilities, and every other application software category is firmly Windows-based by now. Games, educational software, and other entertainment titles have remained in the DOS fold even despite the huge success of Windows 3.0 and 3.1. Why?

Performance, performance, performance. The lure of a dazzling array of graphic interface elements and a host of other APIs was enough of an attraction for most other developers to hang up their DOS hats. If a little graphics performance was lost in the bargain, so be it—that loss of performance also brought the delightful prospect of not having to write drivers for a hundred different display adapters. But game developers want to put that pedal to the metal. In a 3D simulation, nobody cares much about pretty dialog boxes. The name of the game is fast screen update, to create the illusion that you really are traveling through some other world.

It's not that the creators of Windows drivers are stupid or sloppy. For one thing, Windows has to be a general graphics system serving applications with widely varying needs, and so cannot hope to compete with hard-wired graphics routines. And that's not the only problem. Ironically, Windows' high-resolution screen also made it unsuitable for gaming until quite recently. A screen at 640×480 resolution has about five times as many pixels as one at 320×200. That translates into roughly one-fifth the speed of update. This is also one reason why high-speed games had been largely unavailable on the Macintosh until the advent of Power Macs, which have enough horsepower to handle such a detailed display in real time.

Three things have come together to cure Windows' inability to handle high-speed screen updating of the kind that entertainment software requires. One is the advent of the DIB, which allows developers to use their own customized code to render into off-screen buffers. The second is the emergence of widely available display cards which are able to perform hardware scaling, wherein a smaller-than-full-screen bitmap can be blown up to full screen *in hardware*. The third is WinG, which creates the interface whereby DIBs can be moved to the screen at blazing speeds, by optimized code or by hardware if available.

The WinG API

When I explain what WinG is to some of my colleagues, often I get a curious puzzled reaction. They keep asking for more information, uncertain as to what the big deal is. They thought that Windows must have done these things all along. As we'll see, the WinG API is pretty small, and does contain functions, particularly the one which "blits" a DIB to a window, that many people are surprised didn't exist before. Anyway, WinG is here now, available for Windows as a free add-on, (WinG is actually taken from code developed by the Windows 95 team). Table 7.4 lists the ten API calls which make up WinG.

Before we go into the API in more detail, have a look at Figure 7.3, which shows in flowchart form how WinG is typically used.

Table 7.4 WinG API Set

Function name	Purpose
WinGCreateDC	Create a WinG device context
WinGCreateBitmap	Create a new off-screen WinG bitmap (DIB)
WinGGetDIBPtr	Return pointer to bitmap bits inside WinG bitmap
WinGRecommendDIBFormat	Recommend optimal DIB format for blitting to screen
WinGGetDIBColorTable	Return the DIB color table of a WinG bitmap
WinGSetDIBColorTable	Set the DIB color table of a WinG bitmap
WinGBitBlt	Copy all or part of a WinG device context to another device context
WinGStretchBlt	Like WinGBitBlt, with scaling
WinGCreateHalftoneBrush	Create dithered pattern brush based on WinG halftone palette
WinGCreateHalftonePalette	Create a copy of the WinG halftone palette

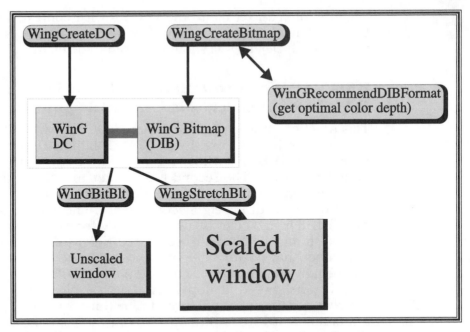

Figure 7.3 Basic usage of WinG functions in a simple application.

WinG Device Contexts and Bitmaps

The first six of the ten WinG functions have to do with manipulating WinG device contexts and WinG bitmaps, which are DIBs. Let's examine each of them. For more information about WinG and the API, a help file accompanies the WinG developer files on the Microsoft Developer CD. The Developer CD, available by subscription from Microsoft, is a treasure trove of information about Windows programming, and should be subscribed to by serious Windows programmers. The help file, WING.HLP, is included on the CD accompanying this book as well.

HDC WinGCreateDC()

This function creates a WinG device context. A Windows device context is similar in concept to an ARTT canvas. It has a drawing surface, accompanied by a set of drawing attributes. In Windows, the drawing attributes are far more extensive than ARTT's color and clip rectangle—Windows attributes include current color, font, pen, brush, palette, and more. When a WinG DC is created, it is equipped with a default monochrome bitmap surface of size 1 × 1 pixels. WinGCreateBitmap() should be used to create a larger color bitmap, which is then *selected* into the WinG device context. When a WinG DC is no longer needed, usually after the window it is associated with is destroyed, DeleteDC() should be used to delete it.

HBITMAP WinGCreateBitmap(HDC hWinGDC, BITMAP-INFO FAR *pHeader, void FAR* FAR* ppBits)

This function creates a WinG bitmap. In Windows, a bitmap is a special object referred to by its HBITMAP handle. Internally, a WinG bitmap is a DIB. The first argument is the WinG DC returned by WinGCreateDC(). The second is a pointer to a BITMAPINFO structure (see Chapter 3's BmpInfoHeader), which should be filled in with the bitmap's width, height, color depth, and so on. WinGRecommendDIBFormat() can be used to query for an optimal format, but the width and height still need to be filled in. Speaking of which, remember that positive height values are used for bottom-up DIBs, and negative heights are used for top-down DIBs. In ARTT, we'll use negative heights and top-down DIBs exclusively, because that matches our linear canvas format. The third argument is a pointer to a pointer. WinGCreateBitmap() fills in the referenced pointer with the address of the first pixel in the bitmap, and we'll use this to construct a bitmap for our canvas.

By the way, in this and all WinG functions, the use of the FAR keyword is unnecessary for our purposes. As long as we're using the large model in 16-bit Windows programming, or compiling in 32-bit mode for use under Win32s or Windows 95, the FAR keyword is redundant and need not be used.

void FAR *WinGGetDIBPtr(HBITMAP hWinGBitmap, BITMAPINFO FAR *pHeader)

This function returns the address of the first pixel in a WinG bitmap. This is the same value returned in the third argument to WinGCreateBitmap(). Typically, an application will save that value in a variable, and never have to call WinGGetDIBPtr().

BOOL WinGRecommendDIBFormat(BITMAPINFO FAR *pHeader)

This function fills in the supplied bitmap header with "recommended" values for a WinG bitmap. Using WinGRecommendDIB-Format() is easier than filling in all the fields in a BITMAPINFO structure by hand, and it fills in values that match the display device for best performance. WinGRecommendDIBFormat() returns a nonzero value if it is successful in filling in the structure, and zero if

Bill Gates' net worth drops below $5 billion before it has finished filling in all the fields.

The most critical information to be determined in this way is the bitmap orientation (top-down or bottom-up) and the number of bits per pixel. The recommended orientation is set in the returned bitmap height field ('biHeight'), which will be +1 for bottom-up and −1 for top-down. We can multiply this by the actual height we need before calling WinGCreateBitmap(). However, in order to support a recommended orientation, we'd need code able to render both "rightside up" and "upside down" images. ARTT only handles top-down bitmaps with its linear canvas formats, and so in this book we're going to ignore the recommended orientation, and always supply a negative height.

The recommended pixel depth in the current version of WinG always returns 8. In fact, the current version of WinG *requires* that the WinG DIB's color depth be 8. WinG can work with display devices of greater color depths, supplying color depth translation on the fly during blitting. But to support off-screen WinG buffers of depth 16 or 24, apparently Win95 and its new CreateDIBSection() call must be used. WinG is something of a stopgap measure until we all fork over for the upgrade to Win95.

UINT WinGGetDIBColorTable(HDC hWinGDC, UINT StartIndex, UINT NumberOfEntries, RGBQUAD FAR *pColors)

This function returns some or all of the color table entries associated with the specified WinG device context. We'll dive more into Windows color tables later in this chapter; in essence, this returns the palette of the bitmap associated with the device context. The starting index and number of entries specify which part of the color table to extract into the memory area pointed to by the last argument. These color tables are in the RGBQUAD format seen in Chapter 3 in the BMP file-reading code. WinGGetDIBColorTable() returns the number of entries copied.

UINT WinGSetDIBColorTable(HDC hWinGDC, UINT StartIndex, UINT NumberOfEntries, RGBQUAD FAR *pColors)

This function modifies the color table, or palette, associated with the specified WinG device context. Again, 'StartIndex' and 'NumberOf-Entries' specify the range of the color table to be set, and the color table entries are copied from the memory pointed to by the last argument. Like WinGGetDIBColorTable(), WinGSetColorTable() returns the number of entries copied.

WinG Blitting

The six functions previously discussed allow us to create a WinG device context and a DIB-based bitmap to go with it. We can then render onto this DIB surface with Windows GDI calls, and, just as importantly, with our own rendering code. Remember, however, that this WinG bitmap is off screen, in system memory. Whatever we render into it will remain forever unseen, unless we perform additional work. The next step, then, is to copy the bitmap's contents to a window on the screen. This window will be a normal window created with the CreateWindow() call. To move pixels from our off-screen DIB to the window, two WinG calls are available. We use one to copy the pixels unchanged, and the second if we want to scale the bitmap to fit a window which is larger or smaller than the off-screen bitmap.

BOOL WinGBitBlt(HDC hdcDest, int nXOriginDest, int nYOriginDest, int nWidthDest, int nHeightDest, HDC hdcSrc, int nXOriginSrc, int nYOriginSrc)

This function copies all or part of an off-screen WinG DC to another DC, which is often a DC associated with a window. It need not be—WinGBitBlt() can be used to copy pixels to a printer device context or another off-screen DC. Usually, however, our destination will be a window.

The destination of the blit is defined by a handle to a DC (again, usually a window's DC), the upper-left coordinate at which to place the bitmap, and the width and height of the area to copy. Note that this is a sort of a rectangle, which means that we can use WinGBitBlt() to copy any rectangular sub-area of the bitmap to the window. We needn't always blit the entire thing. The source for blitting is specified by a handle to a DC (in this case, the WinG DC returned by WinGCreateDC()), and the upper-left corner coordinate of the off-screen bitmap at which to begin copying. This is 0,0 in the case of a full blit. WinGBitBlt() returns nonzero if successful. Figure 7.4 illustrates the blit process.

BOOL WinGStretchBlt(HDC hdcDest, int nXOriginDest, nYOriginDest, int nWidthDest, int nHeightDest, HDC hdcSrc, int nXOriginSrc, int nYOriginSrc, int nWidthSrc, int nHeightSrc)

This function is used when the bitmap to be blitted should be scaled. Often, a smaller off-screen bitmap will be blown up to a full-screen window, with each source pixel appearing multiple times on the des-

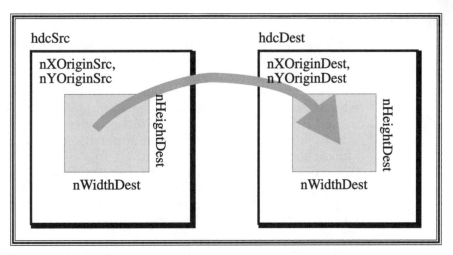

Figure 7.4 Operation of WinGBitBlt(). Pixels are copied in a one-to-one manner.

tination display. WinGStretchBlt() takes all the same arguments as WinGBitBlt(), plus two more. These are 'nWidthSrc' and 'nHeight-Src', which with the source upper-left coordinates specify a rectangular area of the source bitmap to be copied. WinGStretchBlit(), then, is supplied with essentially a source and destination rectangle, and performs scaling of pixels if those rectangles are not the same size. Figure 7.5 illustrates the stretch-blit process.

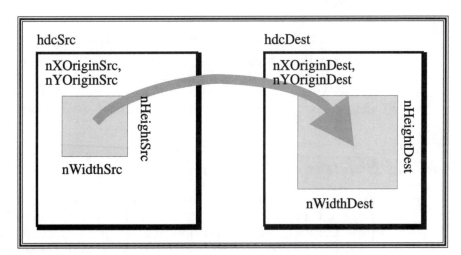

Figure 7.5 Operation of WinGStretchBlt(). Pixels are scaled up or down during copy.

WinG Halftoning

The final two WinG API calls are used to aid in simulating true-color operation on 8-bit display devices. WinG contains an internal definition of a special palette known as a "halftone palette." This palette features a mixture of colors which is intended to provide a good distribution across the color spectrum. Coupled with WinG's ability to create "brushes" which contain a dithering of colors from this palette to approximate a 24-bit color, an application can create reasonably realistic graphics. The halftone brush, like all Windows brushes, is a GDI object which can only be used with GDI rendering calls. Since we'll be rendering into our WinG DIB using ARTT and not GDI, we won't focus on the details of halftoning. For completeness, though, here are descriptions of the remaining two calls.

HBRUSH WinGCreateHalftoneBrush(HDC hdc, COLORREF color, enum WING_DITHER_TYPE DitherType)

This function creates a halftone brush and returns a handle to it. The first argument is the DC with which the brush will be compatible (the WinG DC). The second argument is a COLORREF holding the 24-bit color to be simulated, and the third argument specifies the type of dithering to be performed in creating the brush, from the following possibilities:

```
WING_DISPERSED_4×4
WING_DISPERSED_8×8
WING_CLUSTERED_4×4
```

HPALETTE WinGCreateHalftonePalette()

This function creates a palette containing the WinG halftone colors, and returns a handle to it. Such a palette is like one built using the CreatePalette() call, which builds a palette from an application-defined array of colors. In the next section, we'll discussion Windows palettes in more detail.

Windows Palettes and the Palette Manager

One topic remains before we can dive in and create the code which ties WinG and ARTT together, and that subject is palettes. In our DOS programming, we've seen how we can program the VGA or Super VGA card's DAC with the 256 RGB color values we want, and then render 8-bit images using that palette. In Windows, life is more complicated. Primarily, the complication arises from the fact that we are sharing the screen with other applications, each of which may want to set the palette according to its own needs. On top of that, the window borders and menus and minimized icons and so forth all need to be drawn in some colors. If some ill-behaved program set the hardware palette to 256 shades of blue, our pull-down menus couldn't have black text or a yellow background, and the nearby word processor document wouldn't have white pages any more!

So, on an 8-bit display device anyway, our application must share the palette with other applications and with the system. This sharing is mediated by the Windows Palette Manager. We can no longer attempt to talk to the VGA DAC hardware directly—attempting to do so will cause a protection violation and will fail. We must submit our palette-changing requests to the Palette Manager, and cope with the fact that these requests may fail or only partially succeed. We must mutter magic incantations (in code) to "select" and "realize" palettes when we draw into our windows, and we must process a couple of palette-related messages in our main window procedure.

The following information is only an overview of the mysteries of the Palette Manager. For more detail, I recommend two good sources of information. One is the relevant chapters (2, 3, and 4) of the book *Animation Techniques in Win32*, written by Nigel Thompson and published by Microsoft Press (see Appendix E). The other is the article *Palette Manager: How and Why* by Ron Geary, which is located on the Microsoft Developer CD. This article is the ultimate information resource on the Palette Manager. I've read it three times, and I think after the fourth I'll have it all figured out.

Palette Manager Policies

First off, the Palette Manager sets a few policies which applications must observe:

1. The first 10 and last 10 colors in the overall Windows palette are set by the system for use in borders, menus, icons, and other interface elements. These are called the *static* colors. They may be used, but they should not be changed, although there are complex and scary methods for doing so if the need is great. Applications should try mightily to use only the middle 236 *nonstatic* colors for their needs.

2. The foreground application has priority over the Windows palette, and other applications get their color needs fulfilled only if there is room left in the hardware DAC for them. Because of this policy, the DAC is continually adjusted as windows are moved to the foreground as a result of user actions. The messages WM_QUERYNEWPALETTE and WM_PALETTECHANGED are usually processed by palette-using applications in order to support this policy. If a background window doesn't get many of its palette needs met, well, it looks a little funny. The idea is that you're looking at your foreground window anyway, so you won't feel so bad.

Palette Objects and CreatePalette()

In order to juggle palette needs across applications, the Palette Manager requires that applications create "logical palettes." This is done using the CreatePalette() function, or now also via WinGCreate-HalftonePalette(). The CreatePalette() routine is prototyped below:

```
HPALETTE CreatePalette(LOGPALETTE *pLogPal);
```

The LOGPALETTE structure, a pointer to which is the sole argument to CreatePalette(), is defined below:

```
typedef struct {
    WORD palVersion;            // should be 0x0300 (version 3.0)
    WORD palNumEntries;         // number of entries in palPalEntry[]
    PALETTEENTRY palPalEntry[1]; // palette color entries
} LOGPALETTE;
```

Note that the structure is defined with one entry, but that in reality from 1 to 256 entries may be present. The LOGPALETTE structure definition is fine for reading such a structure, since C and C++ will happily index past the first entry. For defining logical palettes, however, either malloc() should be used with a computed size large enough to fit all required entries, or a compatible structure with the desired number of entries should be defined and used.

The LOGPALETTE structure contains entries of type PALETTEENTRY. This structure is defined below:

```
typedef struct {
    BYTE peRed;          // red component value, 0 - 255
    BYTE peGreen;        // green component value, 0 - 255
    BYTE peBlue;         // blue component value, 0 - 255
    BYTE peFlags;        // 0 or special value PC_XXXX
} PALETTEENTRY;
```

The three RGB values in a PALETTEENTRY should be no surprise. What's the 'peFlags' field all about, though? Herein lies the pathway toward the complexity of the Palette Manager. Besides simply managing application palette requests in foreground-to-background order, the Palette Manager tries to give the application a way to supply hints so it can do its job better. Table 7.5 lists the possible values for the 'peFlags' field.

Table 7.5 Possible Values for 'peFlags' Field of PALETTEENTRY Structure

Name	Value	Meaning
PC_RESERVED	0×01	This entry may be used for palette animation (it may be modified during the program). Therefore, don't let other entries with similar colors be "mapped" onto this entry.
PC_EXPLICIT	0×02	This entry is not a color at all, but an explicit reference to a palette index. Used when actual DAC entries must be shown.
PC_NOCOLLAPSE	0×04	Give this entry its own slot in the system palette, even if the color matches an existing one. Useful when creating an "identity palette."

How the Palette Manager Works, Sort Of

We're now armed with enough knowledge to get a sense of how the Palette Manager works. In general, each application creates one or more logical palettes using CreatePalette(), and saves the handle(s) returned by this routine. Then, whenever an application moves to the foreground, Windows sends it a WM_QUERYNEWPALETTE. In response to this message, the application usually calls SelectPalette() and RealizePalette(), using the desired palette handle. These are magic functions which set up the palette and associated color translation tables for that application's window. This new palette activity then causes a WM_PALETTECHANGED message to be broadcast to all applications, in front-to-back order. In response to this message, each does its own SelectPalette() and RealizePalette(). The ordering of the "realization" of the various palettes causes an overall "physical" palette to be accumulated, and programmed into the VGA DAC by Windows.

Take a look at Figure 7.6. It shows two logical palettes, each containing 200 colors, being mapped into Windows' single physical palette. Note how the first window, the foreground window, takes up most of the available slots. The second window's logical palette has more entries than can fit in the remaining slots, so the remaining entries are simply mapped to existing slots in the physical palette,

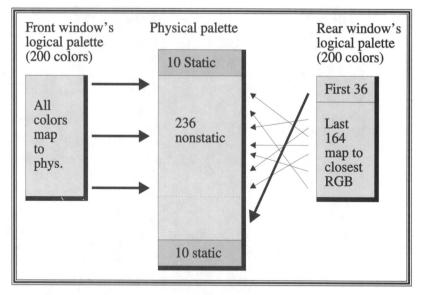

Figure 7.6   Two logical palettes mapping into a single physical palette.

based on closest color match. This diagram is a simplification of what really goes on, which is dependent on the flags associated with each logical palette entry.

Identity Palettes

In the above example, notice how the second logical palette's entries got mapped all over the place in the physical palette. What happens, then, when drawing is done in that window? How are the colors specified in source bitmaps mapped into the actual color slots in the DAC, which is programmed from the physical palette? It's done internally in the Windows GDI through color lookup tables, a subject we'll learn a lot more about in later chapters. The color index translation is all done on your behalf, so you don't really need to know it's happening, except, of course, if you want top-notch performance. If you do, you'll try to ensure an *identity palette* in your application.

An identity palette is simply one in which the color indexes used in a logical palette map exactly to the same indexed slots in the physical palette. In the interface between WinG and ARTT we'll be building in the next section, we'll develop code which attempts to ensure this mapping. This involves use of the PC_NOCOLLAPSE flag in our logical palette, and careful treatment of the 20 static color entries.

I Hate Palettes

If the above discussion was pretty confusing, don't despair. The code we'll be developing gets basic palette manipulation right, and you can just use it and forget about how it works. If you need to do more advanced palette work or just want to understand things better, take a look at one of the references mentioned earlier. Someday soon we'll all have true-color displays, and all this nonsense will be history to tell our grandchildren about. Until then, issues like palette management help keep our profession exciting and well-paid.

Class AWingWindow: ARTT Meets WinG

The actual code we need to write to make ARTT work under Windows is surprisingly modest. We're only going to develop two classes, and then we'll have the WinG beast tamed. One class, AWingPal, will represent a logical palette. The other class, AWingWindow, will tie a window, a WinG DC, and an off-screen buffer together. Furthermore, it will supply a canvas which operates on that WinG buffer. Don't we need new canvas classes too, then? No, WinG buffers, which are DIBs, are just linear canvases! Figure 7.7 shows the relationship between

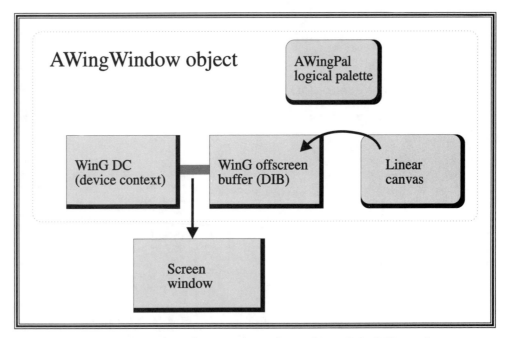

Figure 7.7   An AWingWindow object, and its relationship to DCs, DIBs, and canvases.

the window, the off-screen WinG DIB, the AWingWindow object, and the linear canvas, which is an object of class ACanvasLin8.

WinG only supports 8-bit DIBs, unfortunately. For higher color depths, the Windows 95 call CreateDIBSection() needs to be used, and such a program won't run under Windows 3.1. At least our 8-bit WinG program can run on screens of any color depth, because WinG provides built-in color depth translation during blitting.

The classes we will develop are "straight Windows," not built using the Microsoft Foundation Classes or some other *application framework*. This makes them useful to the widest audience of programmers. If you're really into MFC, OWL, or some other C++/Windows paradigm, feel free to develop classes which provide a wrapper around the ones included in ARTT.

Without further ado, let's see the header for class AWingWindow.

```
//    AWingWin.h    WinG Window class
//    Rex E. Bradford

#ifndef __AWINGWIN_H
#define __AWINGWIN_H

#include <windows.h>
#include "awingpal.h"
#include "acanvas.h"

class AScene;

typedef struct {
    BITMAPINFOHEADER bmhdr;      // bitmap header
    RGBQUAD colors[256];         // color palette
} WingOffBuffer;

class AWingWindow {
public:
    AScene *pscene;              // ptr to attached scene, or NULL
    ACanvas *pcv;                // ptr to off-screen linear canvas
    HWND hwnd;                   // window handle
    HDC hdcWin;                  // handle to window device context
    HBITMAP hbmWin;              // offscreen bitmap
    HBITMAP hbmOld;              // original selected bitmap
    short widthScreen;           // width of window on screen
    short heightScreen;          // height of window on screen
    AWingPal *ppal;              // ptr to palette
    WingOffBuffer offBuff;       // offscreen buffer

    static AWingWindow *mainWin; // 1st window created

// Constructor and destructor, attach scene
```

```
    AWingWindow(AError &err, int width, int height, APalette *ppalette,
        char *lpszClassName, char *lpszWindowName, DWORD windowStyle,
        int xWindow, int yWindow, int widthWindow, int heightWindow,
        HWND hwndParent, HMENU hmenu, HINSTANCE hinst, void *lpvParam);
    ~AWingWindow();
    void AttachScene(AScene *pscene_) {pscene = pscene_;}

// Palette handling

    void CopyPalIntoOffbuff();
    void SetPal (uchar *prgb, int index, int numcols) {
        ppal->SetPal (prgb, index, numcols);
        CopyPalIntoOffbuff();}
    void GetPal (uchar *prgb, int index, int numcols) {
        ppal->GetPal (prgb, index, numcols);}

// Other methods

    void SetScreenArea();
    void Blit (HDC hdc, ARect *parea = NULL);
    LRESULT StdHandler(HWND hwnd, UINT message, WPARAM wParam,
        LPARAM lParam);
};

#endif
```

AWingWindow Constructor

The AWingWindow constructor has to do many things:

1. Create a WinG device context (DC) which can be used for rendering, using WinGCreateDC().

2. Create an object of class AWingPal, initialized from the APalette pointer passed in. This object will create a Windows logical palette for use with the window.

3. Create an off-screen WinG buffer, used to hold the off-screen contents of the window, using WinGCreateBitmap().

4. Create an ARTT canvas which points into the off-screen WinG buffer, of class ACanvasLin8.

5. Create a window, using CreateWindow().

The constructor first calls WinG to create a device context (DC) and an off-screen bitmap (DIB). The 'width' and 'height' arguments determine the size of the off-screen bitmap, which need not match the window size specified in 'widthWindow' and 'heightWindow'. If they do match, better performance results because WinGBitBlt() is used for blitting instead of WinGStretchBlt(). The 'widthWindow' and 'heightWindow' arguments refer to the *client area* of the window to be created—the constructor uses AdjustWindowRect() to tell CreateWindow() what size overall window to create to make this so.

Before creating the off-screen buffer, an object of class AWingPal is created. Then, AWingWindow::CopyPalIntoOffbuff() is used to copy the RGB values into the structure used to create the off-screen bitmap. Each window gets its own logical palette.

A canvas of class ACanvasLin8 is constructed, using the off-screen bitmap returned by WinGCreateBitmap(). Care is taken to ensure that the rowbytes for the bitmap are set to a multiple of four, as Windows requires.

Finally, CreateWindow() is called with a huge number of arguments, most of them passed in unchanged from the constructor arguments. AdjustWindowRect() is used to find the desired window size, including borders, menu, and title, which matches the desired client area size.

Assuming all goes well, the constructor returns an invisible window ready for use. When the constructor returns, everything is set for rendering into the window's canvas to occur, followed by a call to ShowWindow() to make it visible. If anything goes wrong, the 'err' argument is set appropriately.

```
WingOffBuffer stdHdr;                // info from WinGRecommmendDIBFormat()
AWingWindow *AWingWindow::mainWin; // main (1st) window

AWingWindow::AWingWindow(AError &err, int width, int height,
   APalette *ppalette,
   char *lpszClassName, char *lpszWindowName, DWORD windowStyle,
   int xWindow, int yWindow, int widthWindow, int heightWindow,
   HWND hwndParent, HMENU hmenu, HINSTANCE hinst, void *lpvParam)
{
   void *pBuffer;   // will hold pointer to bits in offscreen bitmap

// Clear things in case fail out of here

   hbmWin = NULL;
   pscene = NULL;
   pcv = NULL;
   ppal = NULL;
   err = AERR_DEVICE; // assume the worst, what a pessimist

// Create device context, or return AERR_DEVICE

   hdcWin = WinGCreateDC();
   if (hdcWin == 0)
      return;

// 1st time through, get recommended dib format, even though
// we're basically going to ignore everything it says.

   if (stdHdr.bmhdr.biSize == 0)
      {
      if (WinGRecommendDIBFormat((BITMAPINFO *) &stdHdr) == 0)
         return;
```

```
      }
    offBuff.bmhdr = stdHdr.bmhdr;
    offBuff.bmhdr.biBitCount = 8;

// Create wing palette, and copy its colors into the offBuff member,
// which we'll then use when creating the offscreen bitmap.

    ppal = new AWingPal (ppalette);
    CopyPalIntoOffbuff();

// Create offscreen bitmap (always top-down). The pointer to the
// bits is returned in pBuffer.

    offBuff.bmhdr.biWidth = width;
    offBuff.bmhdr.biHeight = -height;
    offBuff.bmhdr.biClrUsed = 256;
    hbmWin = WinGCreateBitmap(hdcWin, (BITMAPINFO *) &offBuff,
        &pBuffer);
    if (hbmWin == 0)
        return;

// Select new bitmap into the DC, get old and save away

    hbmOld = (HBITMAP) SelectObject(hdcWin, hbmWin);

// Create linear canvas into offscreen bitmap

    ABitmap bm((uchar *) pBuffer, BMF_LIN8, FALSE, width, height);
    bm.rowbytes = (bm.rowbytes + 3) & 0xFFFC;
    pcv = ACanvas::NewCompatibleCanvas(bm, FALSE);
    if (pcv == NULL)
        {
        err = AERR_NOMEM;
        return;
        }

// Set width,height of screen area of window

    widthScreen = widthWindow;
    heightScreen = heightWindow;

// Compute the size of the real window from the desired client area
// width and height.

    RECT rect;
    rect.left = 0;
    rect.top = 0;
    rect.right = widthWindow;
    rect.bottom = heightWindow;
    AdjustWindowRect(&rect, windowStyle, FALSE);

// Create the window, we hope anyway
```

```
hwnd = CreateWindow (lpszClassName, lpszWindowName,
    windowStyle, xWindow, yWindow,
    rect.right - rect.left, rect.bottom - rect.top,
    hwndParent, hmenu, hinst, lpvParam);
if (hwnd == NULL)
    return;

// OK! Success is ours. If this is the first window, set mainWin
// as a convenience to the app writer. Return OK.

if (mainWin == NULL)
    mainWin = this;
err = AERR_OK;
}
```

AWingWindow Destructor

The destructor cleans up, deleting the off-screen buffer, the device context, the AWingPal palette object, and the canvas created by the constructor. It does not delete the window itself, as it is typically called in response to a message that the window has already been destroyed.

```
AWingWindow::~AWingWindow()
{
    if (hdcWin)
        {
        SelectObject(hdcWin, hbmOld);       // select out curr. bitmap
        if (hbmWin)
            DeleteObject(hbmWin);            // and then delete it
        DeleteDC(hdcWin);                    // delete device context
        }
    if (ppal)
        delete ppal;                         // delete wing palette
    if (pcv)
        delete pcv;                          // delete canvas
}
```

AWingWindow Blitting

Usually, a program will want to copy the off-screen buffer to the screen under one of at least two conditions. One such condition is in response to a WM_PAINT message, which is sent by Windows whenever it determines that the window needs repainting. This may happen because another window which previously obscured this one has moved or been deleted. Another reason may be that the application has called InvalidateRect(), after a palette change or change in the application state requires redrawing of the window. The second condition is when the application has just plain changed the contents of the off-screen buffer. This is an animation book, after all, and we'll be changing the window all the time.

AWingWindow::Blit() takes two arguments. The first is a handle to a device context, which is returned by BeginPaint() in response to the WM_PAINT message, or simply obtained by calling GetDC(). Note that this device context handle is *not* the one obtained by WinGCreateDC(), which is the DC for the off-screen buffer and not the window.

The second argument is a pointer to the rectangular area in the off-screen buffer to be copied to the window. This argument defaults to NULL, and is ignored in the case where scaling through WinGStretch-Blt() is required. If set, though, it can be very useful in controlling what areas of the window are repainted. In Chapter 10, we'll see how *dirty-rectangle animation* can be used to speed up our screen updates.

AWingWindow::Blit() first mutters the magic SelectPalette() and RealizePalette() incantations, followed by a call to WinGBitBlt() or WinGStretchBlt(), depending on whether the off-screen buffer size matches the window size.

```
void AWingWindow::Blit(HDC hdc, ARect *parea)
{
// Select and realize palette

    if (ppal->hPal)
        SelectPalette(hdc, ppal->hPal, FALSE);
    RealizePalette(hdc);


// If buffer matches screen, just bitblit, else stretchblit

    if ((pcv->bm.width == widthScreen) &&
        (pcv->bm.height == heightScreen))
        {
        ARect area;
        if (parea == NULL)
            {
            parea = &area;
            area.left = 0;
            area.top = 0;
            area.right = pcv->bm.width;
            area.bott = pcv->bm.height;
            }
        WinGBitBlt(hdc,
            parea->left, parea->top, parea->Width(), parea->Height(),
            hdcWin, parea->left, parea->top);
        }
    else
        {
        WinGStretchBlt(hdc, 0, 0, widthScreen, heightScreen,
            hdcWin, 0, 0, pcv->bm.width, pcv->bm.height);
        }
}
```

Miscellaneous AWingWindow Methods

When the window changes size, the AWingWindow object needs to be kept up to date. The AWingWindow::StdHandler() method, to be covered shortly, does this automatically, by processing the WM_SIZE message sent to a window when it is resized. AWingWindow:: ScreenArea() is called to recompute the 'widthScreen' and 'height-Screen' members.

```
void AWingWindow::SetScreenArea()
{
    RECT wrect;

    GetClientRect (hwnd, &wrect);      // get client area 0,0 - width,height
    widthScreen = wrect.right;          // set width and height from rect
    heightScreen = wrect.bottom;
}
```

AWingWindow::SetPal(), an inline method, is used to change the logical palette associated with a window. This method should be used instead of directly accessing the AWingPal object's methods. The reason is that the AWingWindow object needs to be aware of any changes to the logical palette maintained by AWingPal, and copy its changed contents into the RGBQUAD color table embedded in the off-screen DIB. This is done via AWingWindow::CopyPalIntoOff-buff(), which is called by SetPal() and also in the constructor. Copy-PalIntoOffbuff() keeps the off-screen buffer DIB's color table in sync with the logical palette in the associated AWingPal.

```
void AWingWindow::CopyPalIntoOffbuff()
{
    RGBQUAD *pc = &offBuff.colors[0];
    PALETTEENTRY *pe = &ppal->logPal.entries[0];
    for (int i = 0; i < 256; i++, pc++, pe++)
        {
        pc->rgbRed = pe->peRed;
        pc->rgbGreen = pe->peGreen;
        pc->rgbBlue = pe->peBlue;
        pc->rgbReserved = 0;
        }
}
```

AWingWindow Standard Message Handler

One of the annoying aesthetics about many Windows programs, particularly sample programs, is how the message-handling window procedures become humongous switch statements brokering giant swaths of code. The entire application seems to be inside a giant case statement. Some C++ *application frameworks*, such as Microsoft's

MFC, attempt to bring some structure to this mess by redirecting each message case into its own C++ virtual function. We're not going to use such techniques here, but we will help reduce the clutter in ARTT-based Windows programs by providing a "standard handler" for certain messages. The main window procedure in the application can then hand off relevant messages to this routine for processing.

The version of AWingWindow::StdHandler() given below is a portion of the full routine. When we cover keyboard and mouse input in Chapter 12, we'll add relevant message cases to this routine. For now, the job of the standard handler is to handle the following messages:

WM_PAINT	Blit the off-screen buffer to the screen
WM_SIZE	Call SetScreenArea() to keep 'widthScreen' and 'heightScreen' fields up to date
WM_PALETTECHANGED	Select and realize palette, invalidate window
WM_QUERYNEWPALETTE	Essentially the same as WM_PALETTECHANGED

Unhandled messages are passed on to DefWindowProc(). Thus, an application's window procedure can handle whatever it wants and then pass all other messages on to this standard handler, knowing that DefWindowProc() will be called in the end. In the sample program at the end of this chapter, we'll see how little an application window procedure really needs to do.

In the handler of the WM_SIZE message, a check is made to see if the 'pscene' member is non-NULL, and if so a ChangeScreenArea() method is invoked for it. In Chapter 10 we'll introduce ARTT's "scene and actor" system, which is used to handle full-screen animation of multiple overlapping objects. The scene object needs to know whenever the window it is managing changes, and that's why WM_SIZE checks for a scene which is "attached" to this window. Other than this connection, the window doesn't need to worry about the scene playing into it (the scene worries more about the window, of course).

```
LRESULT AWingWindow::StdHandler(HWND hwnd, UINT message,
   WPARAM wParam, LPARAM lParam)
{
   HDC hdc;
   BOOL f;
   PAINTSTRUCT ps;

// Dispatch based on message type
```

```
        switch (message)
            {
// WM_PAINT: blit contents of offscreen buffer
        case WM_PAINT:
            hdc = BeginPaint(hwnd, &ps);
            Blit(hdc);
            EndPaint(hwnd, &ps);
            return(0);

// WM_SIZE: recompute client area rectangle
// If attached scene, let it know too
        case WM_SIZE:
            SetScreenArea();
            if (pscene)
                {
                ARect area(0, 0, widthScreen, heightScreen);
                pscene->ChangeScreenArea(area, AScene::UPDATE_UNCHANGED,
                    FALSE);
                }
            break;

// WM_PALETTECHANGED: if it's us, just ignore
        case WM_PALETTECHANGED:
            if ((HWND) wParam == hwnd)
                break;
// Else fall through to WM_QUERYNEWPALETTE
// WM_QUERYNEWPALETTE: select & realize pal, invalidate area
        case WM_QUERYNEWPALETTE:
            hdc = GetDC(hwnd);
            if (ppal->hPal)
                SelectPalette(hdc, ppal->hPal, FALSE);
            f = RealizePalette(hdc);
            ReleaseDC (hwnd,hdc);
            if (f)
                InvalidateRect (hwnd, 0, FALSE);
            return f;
        }

// Otherwise, call default window proc

    return DefWindowProc(hwnd, message, wParam, lParam);
    }
```

Class AWingPal: The Window's Palette

Each AWingWindow creates its own AWingPal object, and uses it to manage the window's logical palette. The contents of the logical palette are initially taken from an ARTT APalette, but may be subsequently changed. The AWingPal keeps track of the HANDLE to the internal Windows logical palette, which is created using the Windows call CreatePalette(). Below is listed the header for class AWingPal.

```
//   AWingPal.h     WinG Palette class
//   Rex E. Bradford

#ifndef __AWINGPAL_H
#define __AWINGPAL_H

#include <windows.h>
#include "apalette.h"

// Logical palette structure (Windows-defined)
typedef struct {
   WORD version;                  // palette version
   WORD numEntries;               // number of entries
   PALETTEENTRY entries[256];     // palette entries
} AWinLogPal;

// WinG palette class

class AWingPal {
public:
   HPALETTE hPal;                 // handle to logical palette
   AWinLogPal logPal;             // logical palette structure

   AWingPal (APalette *ppal);     // constructor
   ~AWingPal();                   // destructor

// Set/get entries in logical palette
   void SetPal (uchar *prgb, int index, int numcols);
   void GetPal (uchar *prgb, int index = 0, int numcols = 256);

// Clear system palette before any palette use
   static void ClearSystemPal();
};

#endif
```

AWingPal Constructor and Destructor

The AWingPal constructor creates a full 256-color logical palette, grabbing the first and last ten colors from the system palette. Doing this allows us to create an identity palette, which will speed up WinG's blitting. Class AWingPal has no facilities for palettes with less than 256 entries. Plus, the first and last ten entries in the supplied APalette are totally ignored! Artwork for use with Windows generally needs special preparation, and in this case that means restricting color usage to entries 10 through 245.

```
AWingPal::AWingPal(APalette *ppalette)
{
// Set up version 3.0, 256-entry palette
```

```
    logPal.version = 0x300;
    logPal.numEntries = 256;
    memset (logPal.entries, 0, sizeof(logPal.entries));

// Create an identity palette from thin air:
// get the 20 system colors as PALETTEENTRIES

    HDC ScreenDC = GetDC (NULL);
    GetSystemPaletteEntries(ScreenDC, 0, 10, logPal.entries);
    GetSystemPaletteEntries (ScreenDC, 246, 10,
        logPal.entries + 246);
    ReleaseDC (NULL, ScreenDC);

// Copy middle 236 from the supplied palette

    SetPal (ppalette->rgb + (10 * 3), 10, 236);

// Create palette

    hPal = CreatePalette ((LOGPALETTE *) &logPal);
}
```

The destructor deletes the palette created with CreatePalette().

```
AWingPal::~AWingPal()
{
    DeleteObject (hPal);
}
```

AWingPal Palette Access

AWingPal::SetPal() is called inside the constructor, and may be called at any time to modify the logical palette. It converts the standard RGB triplets into logical palette entries. This method should generally not be called directly—use AWingWindow::SetPal(), which calls AWingPal::SetPal() and then updates the window's DIB too.

```
void AWingPal::SetPal (uchar *prgb, int index, int numcols)
{
// If trying to set 1st 10 or last 10, don't allow it

    if (index < 10)
        {
        numcols -= (10 - index);
        prgb += (3 * (10 - index));
        index = 10;
        }
    if ((index + numcols) > 246)
        numcols = 246 - index;
    if (numcols <= 0)
        return;
```

```
// Copy entries from rgb array into logical palette

   PALETTEENTRY *pe = &logPal.entries[index];
   for (int i = index; i < numcols; i++, pe++)
      {
      pe->peBlue = *prgb++;
      pe->peGreen = *prgb++;
      pe->peRed = *prgb++;
      pe->peFlags = PC_NOCOLLAPSE;
      }
}
```

AWingPal::GetPal() retrieves a portion of the logical palette. Unlike SetPal(), it gives access to the first and last ten "static" colors. They are read-only, in essence.

```
void AWingPal::GetPal (uchar *prgb, int index, int numcols)
{
   PALETTEENTRY *pe = &logPal.entries[index];
   for (int i = index; i < numcols; i++, pe++)
      {
      *prgb++ = pe->peBlue;
      *prgb++ = pe->peGreen;
      *prgb++ = pe->peRed;
      }
}
```

AWingPal::ClearSystemPalette(): The Final Magic Incantation

Before any windows or palettes are created in an ARTT-based Windows program, a single call to the static method AWingPal::ClearSystemPal() should be made. ClearSystemPal() creates a 256-entry palette with all PC_NOCOLLAPSE entries, in order to flush out other applications' use of the system palette. This should be followed immediately by a window creation, which creates a logical palette.

```
void AWingPal::ClearSystemPal (void)
{
// Dummy palette, 256 entries

static AWinLogPal Palette = {0x300,256};

// Reset everything in the system palette to black

   memset(Palette.entries, 0, sizeof(Palette.entries));
   int i;
   PALETTEENTRY *pe;
   for (i = 0, pe = Palette.entries; i < 256; i++, pe++)
      pe->peFlags = PC_NOCOLLAPSE;

// Create, select, realize, deselect, and delete the palette
```

```
HDC ScreenDC = GetDC(NULL);
HPALETTE ScreenPalette = CreatePalette((LOGPALETTE *)
    &Palette);
if (ScreenPalette)
    {
    ScreenPalette = SelectPalette(ScreenDC,
        ScreenPalette, FALSE);
    RealizePalette(ScreenDC);
    ScreenPalette = SelectPalette(ScreenDC,
        ScreenPalette, FALSE);
    DeleteObject(ScreenPalette);
    }

ReleaseDC(NULL, ScreenDC);
}
```

WEB: A Sample WinG Program

The code for a simple WinG-based program is listed below. WEB displays a web of points connected by lines. Each point moves independently around the window, bouncing off of the edges. The overall effect is that of a single shape continually morphing. The window is resizable and can be minimized. When minimized, the program continues to run with scaled-down graphics! When scaled up to full-screen, the web looks blocky. This is because the AWingWindow class uses WinGStretchBlt() to scale the off-screen buffer, whose size is fixed, up to full-screen size. The implementation of WinGStretchBlt() uses fast scaling which is very similar to what we developed in the last chapter, with the same artifacts.

A few other points are worth noting:

1. The canvas pointer contained in the AWingWindow object is public. Rendering into this canvas is done simply via: pSomeWin->pcv->SomeRenderingRoutine(. . .).

2. PeekMessage() is used instead of GetMessage() in the main loop. Programs which animate the screen do not want to go to sleep waiting for the next message, as would happen with a call to GetMessage(). Using PeekMessage allows an application to be well-behaved and yield control to other programs, while at the same time performing periodic application activities, such as animating the screen.

3. The application's window procedure handles only WM_DESTROY, which is called when a window is destroyed. In this one-window example, this is a signal to shut down the program, so PostQuitMessage() is called to do so. All other messages are passed on to AWingWindow::StdHandler(), and in most cases implicitly on to DefWindowProc().

```
//   WEB.cpp   WEB-drawing Windows sample program
//   Rex E. Bradford
```

```
#include <windows.h>
#include <stdio.h>
#include <stdlib.h>
#include <string.h>

#include "wing.h"
#include "awingwin.h"
#include "afix.h"

// Application info

static char *szAppName = "WEB"; // app name (window class name)

#define WIN_WIDTH 400   // offscreen buffer width
#define WIN_HEIGHT 400  // offscreen buffer height

// Web structure and associated data

typedef struct {
    AFix x;            // x-coord of web point
    AFix y;            // y-coord of web point
    AFix xspeed;       // signed x-speed in pixels/iteration
    AFix yspeed;       // signed y-speed
} WebPoint;

#define NUM_WEB_POINTS 8            // # points in web
WebPoint ptWeb[NUM_WEB_POINTS];     // the points themselves
#define WEB_MAX_SPEED 1.0           // max speed in pixels/iteration

#define COLOR_BKG 10   // index of background color
#define COLOR_WEB 11   // index of foreground (web) color

uchar rgbWeb[] = {     // web palette (back & fore colors)
    0xFF,0xFF,0xFF,    // white background
    0xC0,0x00,0x40,    // violet lines
};

AWingWindow *pMainWin; // ptr to window obj

// Prototypes

int PASCAL WinMain(HANDLE, HANDLE, LPSTR, int);
LRESULT CALLBACK WndProc(HWND, UINT, WPARAM, LPARAM);

void DrawWeb(ACanvas *pcv);
void MoveWeb();
AFix FixRand (AFix low, AFix high);

// --------------------------------------------------------------
//
// WinMain() is the program's entry point.
```

```
int PASCAL WinMain(HANDLE hInstance, HANDLE hPrevInstance,
    LPSTR lpszCmdLine, int nCmdShow)
{
// Register window class

    if (!hPrevInstance)
        {
        WNDClass wndclass;
        wndclass.style = CS_BYTEALIGNCLIENT | CS_VREDRAW |
            CS_HREDRAW | CS_DBLCLKS;
        wndclass.lpfnWndProc = WndProc;
        wndclass.cbClsExtra = 0;
        wndclass.cbWndExtra = 0;
        wndclass.hInstance = hInstance;
        wndclass.hIcon = NULL;
        wndclass.hCursor = LoadCursor(NULL, IDC_ARROW);
        wndclass.hbrBackground = (HBRUSH) NULL;
        wndclass.lpszMenuName = NULL;
        wndclass.lpszClassName = szAppName;
        if (!RegisterClass(&wndclass))
            {
            MessageBox(NULL, "Can't register class\n", NULL, MB_OK);
            return FALSE;
            }
        }

// Clear system palette and create web palette

    AWingPal::ClearSystemPal();
    APalette *gPalette = new APalette();
    gPalette->Set(rgbWeb, 10, 2);

// Create window

    DWORD windowStyle = WS_OVERLAPPED | WS_CAPTION | WS_SYSMENU |
        WS_MINIMIZEBOX | WS_MAXIMIZEBOX | WS_THICKFRAME;
    AError err;
    pMainWin = new AWingWindow(err, WIN_WIDTH, WIN_HEIGHT,
        gPalette,
        szAppName,
        "The Web",
        windowStyle,
        CW_USEDEFAULT, CW_USEDEFAULT,
        WIN_WIDTH, WIN_HEIGHT,
        NULL,
        NULL,
        hInstance,
        NULL);
    HWND hWndApp = pMainWin->hwnd;

// If can't create, bail out

    if (err)
        {
```

```
            delete pMainWin;
            UnregisterClass (szAppName, hInstance);
            MessageBox(NULL, "Can't create window\n", NULL, MB_OK);
            return 1;
            }

// Initialize web points: location and speed

    for (int i = 0; i < NUM_WEB_POINTS; i++)
        {
        ptWeb[i].x = FixRand(0, WIN_WIDTH);
        ptWeb[i].y = FixRand(0, WIN_HEIGHT);
        ptWeb[i].xspeed = FixRand(-WEB_MAX_SPEED, +WEB_MAX_SPEED);
        ptWeb[i].yspeed = FixRand(-WEB_MAX_SPEED, +WEB_MAX_SPEED);
        }

// Draw web into offscreen buffer, then show window

    DrawWeb(pMainWin->pcv);
    ShowWindow(hWndApp, nCmdShow);

// Poll messages from event queue, update web

    MSG msg;
    while (TRUE)
        {
        if (PeekMessage(&msg, 0, 0, 0, PM_REMOVE))
            {
            if (msg.message == WM_QUIT)
                break;
            TranslateMessage(&msg);
            DispatchMessage(&msg);
            }
        else
            {
            MoveWeb();                      // move web points
            DrawWeb(pMainWin->pcv);         // redraw offscreen buffer
            HDC hdc = GetDC (hWndApp);      // get DC of window
            pMainWin->Blit (hdc);           // blit to it
            ReleaseDC(hWndApp, hdc);        // release window DC
            }
        }

// Delete window, unregister class, and exit

    delete pMainWin;
    UnregisterClass(szAppName, hInstance);
    return msg.wParam;
}


// ----------------------------------------------------------------
//
// WndProc() is the window message handler.
```

```
LRESULT CALLBACK WndProc (HWND hwnd, UINT message,
   WPARAM wParam, LPARAM lParam)
{
// Handle messages not handled by StdHandler() or DefWindowProc().

   switch (message)
      {
      case WM_DESTROY:
         PostQuitMessage(0); // when window destroyed, close up shop
         return(0);
      }

// Pass the rest on to StdHandler(), some go on to DefWindowProc

   return pMainWin->StdHandler(hwnd, message, wParam, lParam);
}


// ----------------------------------------------------------------
//
// DrawWeb() draws the web into the offscreen buffer canvas.

void DrawWeb(ACanvas *pcv)
{
// Cover canvas with background color

   pcv->SetColor8(COLOR_BKG);
   pcv->DrawRect(0, 0, WIN_WIDTH, WIN_HEIGHT);

// Draw connected web points

   pcv->SetColor8(COLOR_WEB);
   for (int i = 0; i < NUM_WEB_POINTS; i++)
      for (int j = i + 1; j < NUM_WEB_POINTS; j++)
         pcv->DrawLine(ptWeb[i].x, ptWeb[i].y, ptWeb[j].x, ptWeb[j].y);
}


//----------------------------------------------------------------
//
// MoveWeb() moves the web, and bounces each point off walls.

void MoveWeb()
{
   for (WebPoint *pw = &ptWeb[0]; pw < &ptWeb[NUM_WEB_POINTS]; pw++)
      for (int i = 0; i < NUM_WEB_POINTS; i++)
         {
         pw->x += pw->xspeed;
         if ((pw->x <= AFix(0)) || (pw->x >= AFix(WIN_WIDTH)))
            pw->xspeed = -pw->xspeed;
         pw->y += pw->yspeed;
         if ((pw->y <= AFix(0)) || (pw->y >= AFix(WIN_HEIGHT)))
            pw->yspeed = -pw->yspeed;
```

```
        }
}


// ------------------------------------------------------------
//
// FixRand() computes a fixed-point random number between low,high.

AFix FixRand(AFix low, AFix high)
{
   float r = float(rand());
   float scale = (float(high) - float(low)) / 32768L;
   r = (r * scale) + float(low);
   return AFix(r);
}
```

Figure 7.8 shows a screen shot from the WEB program.

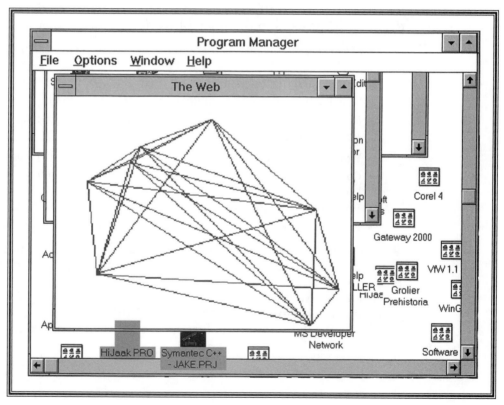

Figure 7.8   Screen shot from WEB, a WinG-based sample program.

Onward to Animation

This chapter covered a *lot* of ground. If you're an experienced Windows programmer, then probably only the WinG API and the ARTT code was new. If you're unused to Windows, this chapter was probably a little bewildering. Don't worry—it turns out that you don't need to know very much about Windows in order to use ARTT in that environment, if all you want to do is run ARTT-based animation inside a window. If you want to build full-fledged Windows programs, then there's no substitute for diving in to the books and manuals and tools and sample programs that come with today's Windows programming environments. ARTT by no means attempts to replace the huge set of APIs and functionality built into Windows. ARTT is a (partial) replacement for GDI for high-speed rendering into windows. For menus, dialogs, OLE, and all the rest, other toolkits and the Windows API itself are where you should turn.

Together, these first seven chapters have laid a solid foundation for the really fun stuff to come in the rest of the book. The capabilities we now possess in the form of working classes includes:

- Setting screen to 320 × 200 VGA or higher Super VGA resolutions in 8-bit color
- Reading and writing graphic images in PCX and BMP files
- Drawing basic geometric primitives, including lines, rectangles, and pixels
- Drawing 8-bit color bitmaps, including those with transparency
- Clipping all drawing operations to within rectangular areas
- Working with fixed-point numbers for high-speed fractional math
- Compressing bitmaps using run-length encoding, and rendering directly from that format
- Drawing scaled bitmaps, both linear and run-length, with clipping
- Rendering into WinG-based canvases, and then blitting them to the screen

With this foundation, we are now ready to tackle the business of moving and animating images on the screen at high speed, without flicker, just like the pros. We'll do this in high-resolution, under DOS or Windows. We have a solid base upon which to build animation file reading, timed animation playback, composition of moving and overlapping sprites, and much more. Stay tuned for Part 2.

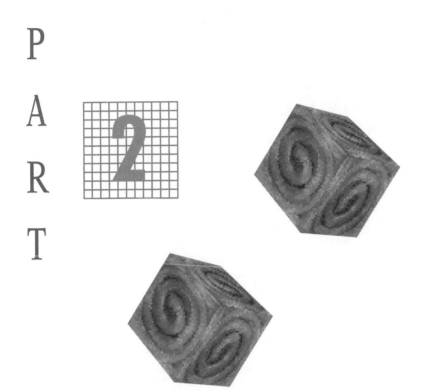

Animation
and Composition

Frame Animation

Part 1 laid a solid foundation of "static" graphics rendering. The ARTT library developed so far includes bitmaps and renderable canvases, images grabbed from graphics files, geometric shapes such as rectangles and lines, VGA and Super VGA display modes, run-length bitmap encoding, and scaled rendering of bitmaps. Part 2 builds on this foundation, adding animation, composition of multiple moving sprites, scrolling and tiled backgrounds, cartoon animation, input devices and user interaction, and much more.

In this chapter, we'll cover some animation basics and introduce *sprites*, which are a fundamental unit of animation, and develop code to grab an array of sprites from a single graphics file. We'll see how the PC hardware timer is used to control the rate of animation of these sprites. Finally, we'll look at GFXPLAY, a utility for playing back an animation consisting of a series of sprites grabbed from a graphics file.

Animation Creation

Everyone has seen computer animation, whether on a computer screen or in a movie such as *Jurassic Park*, in which computer-created dinosaurs terrorized children and stalked their parents' extra spending money. Computer animation has gotten very sophisticated in the last several years—movies such as *Jurassic Park* employ teams of animators working for months or years to create a few minutes of visual fantasy. These animators use complex *modeling* programs to create three-dimensional creatures and scenes, which are then *rendered* as two-dimensional images over long hours by fast workstations. The software used is very expensive, but software packages affording some of the same features are now available on the PC for reasonable cost, meaning several hundred to a few thousand dollars. Autodesk's "3D Studio" is very popular among commercial PC game developers. Alias Research, maker of some of the best high-end software used in TV commercials and movies, is now offering low-end versions of its wares on the PC platform. Other newcomers, such as "TrueSpace" by Caligari, are offering good-quality animation software at ever-lower prices.

How is such software used to create animated images? Color plate 1 shows a few screen shots depicting this process. A three-dimension wireframe model is laboriously constructed using a mouse, tablet, or 3D input device. Then, color and texture is applied to the surface of the model. Multiple models can be placed into a scene, and given motion and animation commands. Simulated light sources are placed into the scene, the "OK" button is selected, and boring hours go by while the software laboriously generates a series of images depicting the scene in motion, carefully calculating the color value of each pixel in each image based on the positions of the models, light sources, and shadowing.

Real-Time Animation

What does the above discussion have to do with a book about *real-time* animation? We want monsters racing down corridors at speeds greater than one pixel per hour, after all. In commercial game and educational software development, the animation software described above is used to generate a *series of bitmapped images,* which can then be drawn at high speed using the bitmap-rendering code we already know how to write. Color plate 4 shows a series of such rendered snapshots, in bitmap form.

Each item in an animation series is called an animation *frame,* and real-time animation is at its heart the process of presenting successive frames to the viewer at high speed. The rate at which new images are presented is called the *frame rate.* With a sufficiently high frame rate, the different frames fuse in the viewer's mind into a single changing image. Since the refresh rate of the display device is typically 60 or 70 times per second, it is not possible to present a series of animation frames at a rate higher than this. Remember, images are written to the video system's display memory, which is "scanned out" to the monitor at a fixed rate. If a second image is written to the display memory too quickly after the first, the second image will overwrite the first before it has even been displayed on the monitor.

Displaying animated scenes too quickly for the display hardware is seldom a problem, however, and would be a welcome one. Usually, the problem is one of not being able to process and render frames at a high enough rate. The frame rate necessary for good fusion depends on several things, including the contrast and other characteristics of the scene or object, how much the image changes from frame to frame, and the individual viewer's perception. Typically, frame rates in the range of 15 to 30 frames per second are quite adequate. Below about 10 frames per second, a noticeable "jumpiness" in the image occurs. If the object is moving across the screen, a higher frame rate may be needed to give the illusion of fluid motion. Otherwise, the gaps between successive locations of the object become noticeable.

Table 8.1 shows the frame rates of various display systems.

Animation Frames: Sprites and Class ASprite

For real-time animation, then, we've come back to bitmaps. Whether the images are scanned in from drawings, "hand-drawn" using a paint program, or rendered using sophisticated 3D modeling programs, the form of each frame of animation will often be a bitmap.

Table 8.1 Frame Rates of Various Display Systems	
Display	***Frame Rate***
Film	24 frames per second
Television	NTSC system (US, Japan, elsewhere): 30 frames per second, each in 2 interlaced fields
	PAL system (Europe, elsewhere): 25 frames per second, each in 2 interlaced fields
	SECAM system (France, elsewhere): 25 frames per second, each in 2 interlaced fields
Video game	Uses television, image updated typically at 30 frames per second but may be less
PC game	Variable, typically 10 to 40 frames per second depending on software/hardware combo

That means that we can use the rendering code from Part 1 as the base for our animation system. All we need to add is a method for getting access to a series of bitmapped images and a timing mechanism, and we'll be well on the way to animating the PC screen.

Reference Points (Hotspots)

As it turns out, we're going to make a subclass of the ABitmap class for use in animation. Most of the animation we'll be doing involves graphic objects which are smaller than the screen in size, for instance human figures, cartoon characters, vehicles, natural objects, and even the mouse cursor. These objects share in common the fact that each frame has a natural "reference point" which is not necessarily the upper-left corner of the image. Bitmaps, remember, are drawn at an *x,y* coordinate, and that coordinate specifies where the upper-leftmost pixel will be drawn. For most animating images (and many that don't animate), however, the upper-left corner of the bitmap is not what we usually mean when we refer to the "position" of the image. Figure 8.1 shows a couple of sample images and their refer-

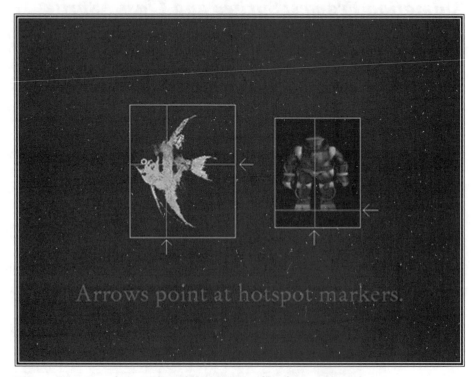

Figure 8.1   Sample images and their "natural" reference points.

ence points. In the case of the fish, the "center of gravity" around which the fish swims is chosen. In the case of the mechanized warrior, the bottom of his feet are chosen (centered between the feet). Using these locations to mark the true "position" of an object helps anchor successive animation frames sensibly, especially when they change width or height.

The "reference point" of an image is sometimes called its *hotspot*. This term is often used with mouse cursors, because it denotes the point on the cursor which is "hot"; that is, which is used when deciding what the cursor is selecting.

Class ASprite: A Bitmap With a Hotspot

As a basic component in our animation system, then, we're going to define a subclass of ABitmap called ASprite. The term *sprite* is video-game and computer-game terminology to describe an object on the screen which may be animating and/or moving. ASprite adds a hotspot to the data which makes up a bitmap, specified as an 'xoff' and a 'yoff' coordinate. The pair xoff,yoff specifies the pixel offset into the image where its hotspot, or reference point, is located. Since an ASprite is also an ABitmap, it can be drawn using the same bitmap rendering routines developed in Part 1 of this book. Such rendering code must offset the x,y drawing location by the hotspot, as shown in Figure 8.2.

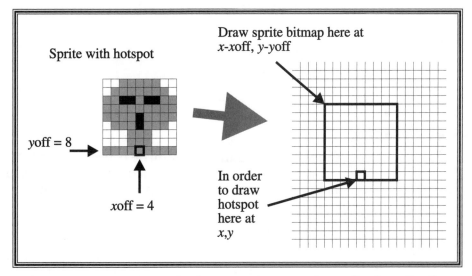

Figure 8.2 Drawing a sprite by drawing its bitmap with x,y offset by xoff,yoff.

The header file for the ASprite class is listed below. There are two constructors. One merely lets an ASprite be declared and initialized later. The other takes a reference to a bitmap as an argument, along with *x* and *y* hotspot coordinates. This constructor creates a sprite whose underlying bitmap is taken from the supplied bitmap, combined with the hotspot. The hotspot coordinate arguments have default values of 0, so that a sprite initialized with simply an ABitmap as a sole argument will get a hotspot of 0,0. Such a sprite would render in precisely the same location as the bitmap from which it was initialized.

```
//   ASprite.h      Sprite class (bitmap with hotspot)
//   Rex E. Bradford

#ifndef __ASPRITE_H
#define __ASPRITE_H

#include "abitmap.h"
#include "aerror.h"

class ASprite : public ABitmap {
public:
    short xoff;  // x-offset of anchor point (hotspot)
    short yoff;  // y-offset of anchor point

// Empty constructor and one which constructs from bitmap
    ASprite() {}
    ASprite(ABitmap &bm, short x = 0, short y = 0)
        {*(ABitmap *)this = bm; xoff = x; yoff = y;}

// Clone existing sprite

    AError Clone(ASprite &sp);
};

#endif
```

Sprite Cloning

The Clone() method in class ASprite is used to make the sprite into a copy of an existing sprite. This includes making a separate copy of the data bits that make up the sprite's image, not just a copy of the bitmap structure.

```
AError ASprite::Clone(ASprite &sp)
{
    AError err = ABitmap::Clone(sp);    // clone bitmap portion of sprite
    if (err) return err;                // if can't allocate, bail out
```

```
    xoff = sp.xoff;                          // copy hotspot
    yoff = sp.yoff;
    return AERR_OK;
}
```

ASprite::Clone() uses ABitmap::Clone() to do most of the work. We skipped over this routine when introducing the ABitmap class in Chapter 1; it is presented below. Note that ABitmap::Clone() doesn't blindly copy the entire bitmap set of data bits in the bitmap that is being cloned. If the source bitmap's width doesn't match its 'row-bytes,' which can happen if the source bitmap is a sub-bitmap embedded in a larger one, Clone() allocates the minimum memory necessary to fit a new copy of the bitmap, and copies only the portion of the source bitmap's rows that are "inside" the bitmap.

```
AError ABitmap::Clone (ABitmap &bm)
{
// Copy all fields, except pbits

    format = bm.format;
    transparent = bm.transparent;
    width = bm.width;
    height = bm.height;
    rowbytes = bm.rowbytes;
    length = bm.length;
    ppalette = bm.ppalette;

// If embedded bitmap, set new (minimal) rowbytes and length

    if ((format != BMF_RLE8) && (rowbytes != RowSize(width)))
        {
        rowbytes = RowSize(bm.width);
        length = long(rowbytes) * long(height);
        }

// Allocate bits, return error code if can't

    if (AllocBits() == NULL)
        return AERR_NOMEM;

// Copy bitmap bits, either in one fell swoop or row-at-a-time

    if (rowbytes == bm.rowbytes)
        memcpy(pbits, bm.pbits, length); // if rowbytes match, just copy
    else
        {
        uchar *ps = bm.pbits;                 // else set up for row-by-row
        uchar *pd = pbits;
        for (int y = 0; y < height; y++) // loop thru all bitmap rows
            {
```

```
            memcpy(pd, ps, rowbytes);      // copy row
            pd += rowbytes;                // advance dest ptr
            ps += bm.rowbytes;             // advance src ptr
            }
        }
    return AERR_OK;
}
```

That's it. The ASprite class is a simple extension of the ABitmap class. It exists solely to supply the hotspot needed by animated screen objects but not needed by all bitmaps. For animation, however, we need more than just single sprites. We need a set of sprites to describe an animation. We need an array of sprites.

Class ASpriteArray: An Array of ASprites

Class ASpriteArray is designed to allow us to create "containers" for ASprites, and to access elements in these containers by array index. Unlike built-in arrays of ints or other basic types, sprite arrays can grow dynamically as sprites are added.

Each element in a sprite array is a pointer to an object of class ASprite. This array of sprite pointers is reallocated as needed to grow the array. The implementation does this in blocks of 16 pointers to avoid making a memory allocation request for every sprite added to the array. Figure 8.3 presents a conceptual diagram of an ASpriteArray object.

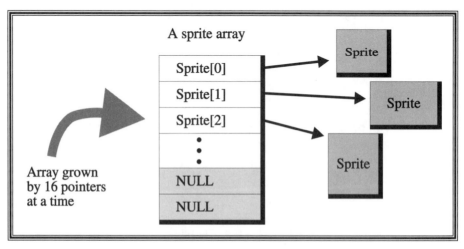

Figure 8.3   Conceptual diagram of a sprite array (class ASpriteArray).

ASpriteArray Memory Management

One of the issues which comes up in all class design, but array class design in particular, is memory management. When a sprite is added to the array, should a copy of it be made? If the sprite array doesn't make copies of the sprites added to it, but just points to existing ones, who takes responsibility for deleting the sprites when they are no longer needed? Since sprites are so small (24 bytes, if you must know), the solution chosen here is for ASpriteArray to always copy sprites which are added to it. The application can do what it will with the sprite it "added" to the array, and the array takes responsibility for deleting the copy it contains.

Copying the bitmap bits pointed to by the 'pbits' field of the sprite is another matter. This bitmap data is potentially very large, and indiscriminant copying can take a lot of time and memory. In order to simplify data management without excessive overhead, ASpriteArray implements the following policy:

1. The application decides for each sprite whether its data bits are "cloned" when the sprite is added to the array.

2. If the data bits are cloned, the application retains responsibility for the original sprite bits, and the sprite array takes responsibility for the cloned sprite bits.

3. If the data bits are not cloned, the sprite array takes over responsibility for data pointed to by the original sprite, and the application must not attempt to delete its data bits.

This policy is simple since the sprite array doesn't need to keep track of which sprites it owns and which it doesn't. It owns them all, and deletes their data bits when the sprite is deleted from the array.

ASpriteArray Implementation

The header file for class ASpriteArray is listed below.

```
//   ASpriteA.h     Sprite array class
//   Rex E. Bradford

#ifndef __ASPRITEA_H
#define __ASPRITEA_H

#include "asprite.h"

class ASpriteArray {

    ASprite **ppSprites;        // ptr to array of sprite ptrs
    short numAlloc;             // number of sprite ptrs allocated
```

```
    AError Grow(int index);        // grow array to include supplied index

#define DEFAULT_SPARRAY_NUMALLOC 16     // default # ptrs allocated
#define SPARRAY_GROW_AMT 16             // # ptrs to grow array by

public:

// Constructor and destructor

    ASpriteArray(int numAlloc = DEFAULT_SPARRAY_NUMALLOC);
    ~ASpriteArray();

// Access element of sprite array

    ASprite *operator[](int index)
        {return (index < numAlloc) ? ppSprites[index] : NULL;}

// Set sprite into array at specified index

    AError SetSprite(ASprite &sp, bool clone, int index);

// Remove sprite from array

    void DelSprite(int index);
};

#endif
```

Note the use of overloading of the [] operator to access a member of the array. ARTT uses operator overloading primarily for numeric classes like AFix and the AVector and AMatrix classes in Part 4. Array indexing seems like another natural use for operating overloading, so ARTT uses it in ASpriteArray and other arraylike classes. In this case, the implementation of the overload operator protects against going past the end of the array:

```
ASprite *operator[] (int index)
        {return (index < numAlloc) ? ppSprites[index] : NULL;}
```

The code below gives a short example of how sprite arrays are used.

```
// Sample code showing use of a sprite array
ASpriteArray sa;                        // create empty sprite array
sa.SetSprite(someSprite, FALSE, 0);  // sprite entry 0, without cloning
ASprite *psp = sa[0];                 // get ptr to sprite 0
gCanvasScreen->DrawBitmapLin8(*psp, x - psp->xoff, y - psp->yoff); // draw it
```

The ASpriteArray constructor creates an empty sprite array. While there are no sprites in a newly constructed array, an array of pointers is allocated for future use. The amount of space allocated for the internal array of sprite pointers may be set using the sole constructor argument; it defaults to 16 pointers. Regardless of whether the pointer array size is specified, it still automatically grows as sprites are added.

```
ASpriteArray::ASpriteArray(int numAlloc_)
{
// Allocate sprite ptr array, clear ptrs to 0

    ppSprites = (ASprite **) new char[sizeof(ASprite *) * numAlloc_];
    if (ppSprites == NULL)
        numAlloc = 0;                 // if alloc fails, protect ptrs
    else
        {
        memset(ppSprites, 0, sizeof(ASprite *) * numAlloc_);
        numAlloc = numAlloc_;
        }
}
```

The destructor deletes all the sprites currently in the array, including the bitmap data pointed at by them.

```
ASpriteArray::~ASpriteArray()
{
    if (ppSprites)
        {
        for (int i = 0; i < numAlloc; i++)      // delete all sprites
            DelSprite(i);
        delete (char *) ppSprites;              // then delete ptr array
        }
}
```

ASpriteArray::DelSprite() method is used by the destructor to delete a sprite from the array and set its pointer to NULL. DelSprite() may also be called by user code when an array element is no longer needed.

```
void ASpriteArray::DelSprite(int index)
{
    ASprite *psp = ppSprites[index];  // get ptr to sprite at this index
    if (psp)
        {
        delete psp->pbits;               // delete its data bits
        delete psp;                      // delete sprite
        ppSprites[index] = NULL;         // set sprite ptr to NULL
        }
}
```

Adding Sprites to Sprite Arrays

ASpriteArray::SetSprite() is used to place a sprite into the array. It takes three arguments: a reference to the sprite to be added, a 'clone' flag which determines whether the bitmap bits should be copied, and the array index at which to add the sprite. The array is grown if needed, and if the array element is already in use that sprite is deleted and replaced.

```
AError ASpriteArray::SetSprite(ASprite &sp, bool clone, int index)
{
// If index past array, grow it

    if (index >= numAlloc)
        {
        AError err = Grow(index);
        if (err)
            return err;
        }

// Delete sprite at current index, if any

    DelSprite(index);

// Make new sprite at this index

    ASprite *pSp = new ASprite;
    if (pSp == NULL)
        return AERR_NOMEM;
    ppSprites[index] = pSp;

// Clone sprite or copy it in

    if (clone)
        return(pSp->Clone(sp));
    else
        {
        *pSp = sp;
        return AERR_OK;
        }
}
```

Since the ASprite class has a constructor which takes an ABitmap reference as an argument, a bitmap can be added to a sprite array (with a default hotspot of 0,0). This can be done as follows:

```
ASpriteArray sa;                        // empty sprite array
ABitmap bm(....);                       // invent a bitmap
sa.SetSprite(ASprite(bm), TRUE, i);     // set bm in array as
                                        //      sprite
```

The SetSprite() method grows the array of sprite pointers if needed, using the private method Grow(). Grow() extends the array by 16 pointers at a time to reduce memory allocation overhead, and sets the new pointers to NULL.

```
AError ASpriteArray::Grow(int index)
{
// Start with current # alloc'ed, bump in steps past supplied index

    int numWant = numAlloc;
    while (numWant <= index)
        numWant += SPARRAY_GROW_AMT;

// If this number is greater than current allocation, realloc array

    if (numWant > numAlloc)
        {
// Allocate new sprite array, fail if out of memory

        ASprite **ppSp = (ASprite **) new char[sizeof(ASprite *) * numWant];
        if (ppSp == NULL)
            return AERR_NOMEM;

// Copy current array into new one, and clear new entries

        memcpy(ppSp, ppSprites, sizeof(ASprite *) * numAlloc);
        memset(ppSp + numAlloc, 0,
            sizeof(ASprite *) * (numWant - numAlloc));

// Delete old array, set new array as the real one, mark # alloc'ed

        delete (char *) ppSprites;
        ppSprites = ppSp;
        numAlloc = numWant;
        }
    return AERR_OK;
}
```

Filling Sprite Arrays

Now we have a mechanism for storing arrays of sprites, and accessing them by index. This is a good step toward a frame animation system. The problem is, we don't have a very good way of getting source bitmap data into the sprite arrays. Sure, we can read full-screen images from graphics files, but most of the animation we want to do involves images which are smaller than that. Reading a dozen graphics files to get a dozen frames of animation is cumbersome and uses up a lot more memory than we'd like.

In the next chapter, we'll tackle animation file formats, which allow multiple animation frames to be stored as successive bit-mapped images in one file. That will definitely do the trick. But there's an alternative that is also a very useful technique, used all the time in the computer game industry. Why not draw several images all "on the same page" of one graphics file, and then extract them each as a separate bitmap? The graphics file can be a PCX or BMP file, which we already know how to read. In order to allow the computer to easily locate these images, a rectangular border is drawn around each one, in a special color that isn't otherwise used. Figure 8.4 shows a sample graphics file done in this way, and the next section will show how we can extract the images from it.

Extracting Multiple Images from a Graphics File

Extracting partial images directly from a graphics file can be a messy business. Since the bitmap data is usually compressed, skipping over

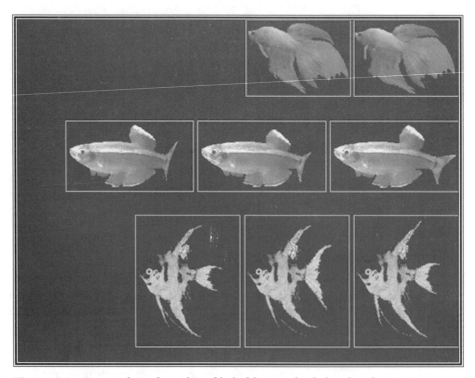

Figure 8.4   Screen shot of graphics file holding multiple bordered sprite images.

the unwanted pixels is not as simple as it might seem. Fortunately, there's no need to extract them directly from the file itself. We already know how to read a graphics file into memory in the form of a bitmap. If we take this step first, then all we really need to do is extract images from a bitmap! That simplifies the problem considerably, and means that we can extract such images from any bitmap, not just those read in from a graphics file.

Image Extraction Methodology

The image extraction technique we will use will work on any linear format bitmap, whether it has 8, 15, or 24 bits per pixel. More precisely, it will work with bitmaps of format BMF_LIN8, BMF_LIN15, and BMF_LIN24. Since the graphics file readers of classes derived from AGfxFile produce only bitmaps of these classes, any bitmap read from a graphics file will be available for extraction.

The technique relies on the use of a special color value which is not otherwise used in the bitmap. This color is used for drawing rectangular borders around each image to be extracted. For 8-bit images, a common convention is to use color index 255, the highest possible color index. In 8-bit indexed-color images, this value can be set to any desired color shade to make the border stand out, for instance, a bright pink or bright green. For 15-bit and 24-bit images, some 15-bit or 24-bit color must be found which is not used elsewhere in the image. The color value chosen is specified to the extraction code, and thus may vary among a set of graphics files.

Class ABitmapFind: A Class for Finding and Extracting Images

A special class, ABitmapFind, is used to facilitate the image extraction process. After AGfxFile::Read() is used to read a graphics image into a bitmap, an object of class ABitmapFind is created. When constructed, this object is passed in a reference to the bitmap and the value of the special border color to be used in locating images. Once initialized, any of three methods can be used to extract images from the bitmap. Images are found by looking for a border's upper-left corner as defined by three pixels in the arrangement shown in Figure 8.5. This figure also shows the order in which a sample set of images would be extracted.

The methods used to extract images in class ABitmapFind are:

NextBitmap()—extract next image as a bitmap

NextSprite()—extract next image as a sprite

CaptureSprites()—extract an entire set of sprites into an existing sprite array

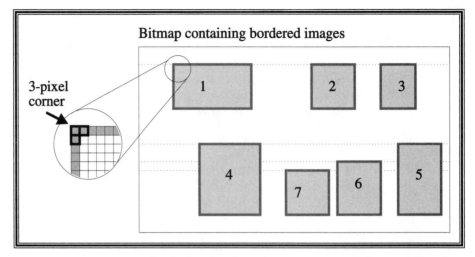

Figure 8.5   Scanning order for bordered image extraction, and closeup of border corner.

NextBitmap() and NextSprite() fill in objects of class ABitmap and ASprite, respectively, with the contents of the next bordered image. These routines do not copy the actual bitmap data bits; the bitmap or sprite they return is specified as a sub-bitmap of the bitmap in which they are found. This bitmap or sprite can be cloned using ABitmap::Clone() or ASprite::Clone() to get a copy with its own data bits. CaptureSprites() automatically clones the bitmap data bits, in accordance with the policy of sprite arrays that the array must assume ownership of these bits. (If the sprite array tried to delete a sprite whose bits were embedded in another bitmap, you wouldn't be happy with the outcome.)

The header for class ABitmapFind is listed below:

```
//    AbmFind.h   Bitmap finder, generic
//    Rex E. Bradford

#ifndef __ABMFIND_H
#define __ABMFIND_H

#include "acanvas.h"
#include "aspritea.h"

class ABitmapFind {
    short x;            // current x-loc in search
    short y;            // current y-loc in search
    long color;         // border color, in "native" format
    ACanvas *pcv;       // ptr to canvas used to peek into bitmap
```

```
// Private methods, used internally

    bool IsStart();              // are we at a border corner?
    void Grab(ABitmap &bm);      // grab
    void GetHotspot(ABitmap &bm, short &xoff, short &yoff);

public:

// Constructor: specify bitmap to begin searching

    ABitmapFind(ABitmap &bm, long color);

// Destructor: free up canvas used in search

    ~ABitmapFind() {if (pcv) delete pcv;}

// Get next bordered bitmap or sprite

    bool NextBitmap(ABitmap &bm, bool transp);
    bool NextSprite(ASprite &sp, bool transp);

// Capture a set of sprites into a sprite array

    int CaptureSprites(ASpriteArray &sa, bool transp, int num = 32767);
};

#endif
```

ABmFind Constructor

The constructor for ABitmapFind gets ready for subsequent border-searching. It initializes the current search point to just before the upper-leftmost pixel in the bitmap and sets the color to be used for the border. Note that this color is not specified as an 8-bit, 15-bit, or 24-bit color. It is in fact a "native" color, specified in the bit depth appropriate to the format of the bitmap being used as the extraction source. Here is where the native color methods of class ACanvas begin to shine. By using native color throughout, the ABitmapFind implementation remains untied to bitmap formats, and can be used equally well for 8-bit, 15-bit, and 24-bit bitmaps without fancy color conversion.

```
ABitmapFind::ABitmapFind(ABitmap &bm, long color_)
{
    x = 32766;              // when we advance, we'll start at 0,0
    y = -1;
    color = color_;         // set native format border color
```

```
// Create canvas compatible with this bitmap

    pcv = ACanvas::NewCompatibleCanvas(bm, FALSE);
}
```

The last thing the constructor does is to construct a canvas, using the supplied bitmap as the bitmap for the canvas. This is done using the method ACanvas::NewCompatibleCanvas(), not previously discussed. The idea here is to create a canvas which can then be subjected to graphics routines to search for colored borders and extract images. What class of canvas is to be created? It needs to match the format of the supplied bitmap. NewCompatibleCanvas() exists for the purpose of constructing a canvas compatible with the supplied bitmap, and is shown below. We're calling it with a second argument of FALSE, telling it not to allocate a copy of the bitmap data bits. We just want a canvas which points to the existing bitmap data bits.

Don't worry about the fact that NewCompatibleCanvas() references classes ACanvasLin15 and ACanvasLin24, which we haven't seen yet. These classes will be covered in Chapter 14, and I'll bet you can guess that they are canvas classes for 15-bit and 24-bit linear bitmaps.

```
ACanvas *ACanvas::NewCompatibleCanvas(ABitmap &bm, bool allocBits)
{
// Copy bitmap, then if 'allocBits' set, allocate bits for new canvas

    ABitmap bmnew = bm;
    if (allocBits)
        {
        bmnew.rowbytes = bmnew.RowSize(bmnew.width);
        bmnew.pbits = ABitmap::Alloc(long(bmnew.height) *
            long(bmnew.rowbytes));
        if (bmnew.pbits == NULL)
            return NULL;
        }

// Construct new canvas using bitmap created above

    switch (bm.format)
        {
        case BMF_LIN8:
            return(new ACanvasLin8(&bmnew));
        case BMF_LIN15:
            return(new ACanvasLin15(&bmnew));
        case BMF_LIN24:
            return(new ACanvasLin24(&bmnew));
        default:
            return NULL;
        }
}
```

ABitmapFind Extraction Methods

ABitmapFind::NextBitmap() method extracts the next bitmap found with the special colored border. Again, remember that it does not actually make a copy of the bitmap data bits, but rather returns a sub-bitmap which points into the overall bitmap. The 'transp' flag is passed in to set whether the returned bitmap should have its 'transparent' flag set. NextBitmap() returns TRUE if it was able to find another bordered image, and FALSE if no more could be found in the bitmap.

```
bool ABitmapFind::NextBitmap(ABitmap &bm, bool transp)
{
    if (pcv == NULL) return FALSE;        // if no canvas, no grabby

    while (TRUE)
        {
// Advance x-coord, if hit edge of bitmap wrap to next row

        if (++x >= (pcv->bm.width - 1))
            {
            x = 0;
            if (++y >= (pcv->bm.height - 1))// check for end of canvas
                return FALSE;
            }

// Check for 3-pixel corner of border, if so grab bitmap and return it

        if (IsStart())
            {
            Grab(bm);
            bm.transparent = transp;
            return TRUE;
            }
        }
}
```

ABitmapFind::NextSprite() returns the next sprite in the bitmap. There is no distinction between bitmap and sprite images inside the bitmap being scanned, and NextBitmap() and NextSprite() will each return the same result in the same circumstances. The difference is that NextSprite() returns the extracted image as an ASprite instead of an ABitmap. Furthermore, NextSprite() scans the right and bottom edges of the border for special "hotspot markers," which are pixels in the border which are of any color other than the border color. If they are found, they are taken to mark the x,y hotspot of the sprite. To find the reference point visually, draw a horizontal line from the hotspot pixel on the right edge, draw a vertical line from the hotspot pixel on the bottom edge, and see where these lines meet—this is the reference point. See Figure 8.6 for an example.

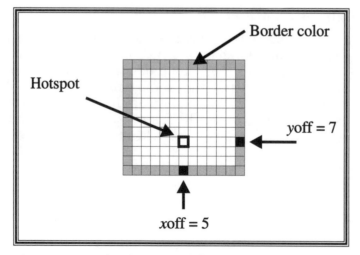

Figure 8.6   Bordered image with hotspot markers embedded in right and bottom borders.

If no hotspot pixels are marked on the border, the hotspot is assumed to be at 0,0. The NextSprite() method is listed below.

```
bool ABitmapFind::NextSprite(ASprite &sp, bool transp)
{
   if (!NextBitmap(sp, transp))          // try for bitmap
      return FALSE;                      // nope, no sprite then
   GetHotspot(sp, sp.xoff, sp.yoff);     // yep, look for hotspot
   return TRUE;
}
```

CaptureSprites() is the last of the three extraction routines. This method takes as arguments a reference to a sprite array, a 'transp' transparency flag, and the number of sprites to search for, which defaults to 32767, meaning "as many as you can find." It extracts the sprites it finds up to the specified limit, and copies them into the sprite array using ASpriteArray::SetSprite(), starting at index 0. The sprites are cloned; that is, copies of the bitmap data bits are made so that the sprite array can take over their management. Capture-Sprites() returns the number of sprites added.

```
int ABitmapFind::CaptureSprites(ASpriteArray &sa, bool transp, int num)
{
   int isp;
   for (isp = 0; isp < num; isp++)       // loop for up to 'num' sprites
      {
      ASprite sp;
      if (!NextSprite(sp, transp))       // get next sprite
         break;                          // if no more, break out
```

```
      if (sa.SetSprite(sp, TRUE, isp))   // set clone of sprite in array
         break;                          // if can't add, break out
      }
   return(isp);                          // return num of sprites added
}
```

ABitmapFind Internal Methods

A few private methods are used to aid the extraction routines. IsStart() checks to see if the current *x,y* location being examined is the start of a bordered image. More precisely, is the pixel at *x,y* of the border color, and are the pixels immediately to the right and below also of the border color? This is as smart as ABitmapFind gets at finding borders, so make sure the border color isn't used anywhere in such a way that this simple "border corner" detection scheme would misfire. Note the use of ACanvas::GetPixelNativeU(), which doesn't know or care what the color format in use is.

```
bool ABitmapFind::IsStart()
{
   if ((pcv->GetPixelNativeU(x,y) == color) &&
      (pcv->GetPixelNativeU(x+1,y) == color) &&
      (pcv->GetPixelNativeU(x,y+1) == color))
         return TRUE;
   return FALSE;
}
```

Once a border corner has been found, Grab() is used to extract a bitmap. Grab() finds the size of the bordered image by scanning down the top and left borders to find their ends, looking for the first pixel which doesn't match the border color. It then constructs a bitmap using the size information it has gathered.

```
void ABitmapFind::Grab(ABitmap &bm)
{
// Scan top border for right edge (non-border color pixel)

   for (int xend = x + 2; xend < pcv->bm.width; xend++)
      if (pcv->GetPixelNativeU(xend, y) != color)
         break;

// Scan left border for bottom edge (non-border color pixel)

   for (int yend = y + 2; yend < pcv->bm.height; yend++)
      if (pcv->GetPixelNativeU(x, yend) != color)
         break;

// Grab (sub-)bitmap

   bm = ABitmap(pcv->bm, x + 1, y + 1, xend - (x + 2), yend - (y + 2));
}
```

Note that Grab() makes use of a special ABitmap constructor, one which we skipped over in Chapter 1. This is a sub-bitmap constructor, which takes an existing bitmap and a rectangular area (specified as *x,y,* width, height), and constructs a new bitmap which represents just that area. No bitmap data bits are copied—the new bitmap just "points into" the bitmap from which it is constructed. Note that this would not be possible without the 'rowbytes' field, which decouples the bitmap's width from the width of the image inside which it may reside.

The 'pbits' field of the new bitmap is set to its "parent's" bitmap plus the appropriate offset to reach the upper-left corner of the sub-area. This constructor, by the way, works for bank-switched as well as linear bitmaps. The 'vaddr' field occupies the same place as the 'pbits' field (they are unioned), and so it is offset by the appropriate amount. This constructor should *not* be called on BMF_RLE8 bitmaps, since the compressed data format makes it impossible to specify a sub-area inside it.

Here's the sub-bitmap constructor for class ABitmap:

```
ABitmap::ABitmap(ABitmap &bm, short x, short y, short w, short h)
{
// This constructor used for sub-bitmaps, fill in format

    format = bm.format;

// Adjust pbits for sub-bitmap (if bank-switched, it's really vaddr)

    pbits = bm.pbits + (long(y) * long(bm.rowbytes)) +
        (x * bmPixelSize[format]);

// Fill in some fields from args, copy others from parent bm

    transparent = bm.transparent;
    width = w;
    height = h;
    rowbytes = bm.rowbytes;

// Compute length as rowbytes × height
// Copy palette from parent

    length = long(rowbytes) * long(height);
    ppalette = bm.ppalette;
}
```

When a sprite is being extracted, ABitmapFind::GetHotspot() is called to see if there are hotspot markers on the right or bottom edges. This method initially sets the hotspot to default values of 0,0 in case no hotspot markers are found.

```
void ABitmapFind::GetHotspot(ABitmap &bm, short &xoff, short &yoff)
{
   xoff = yoff = 0;      // set default hotspot

   int x1 = x + 1;             // since x is at corner, advance into image
   int y1 = y + 1;             // same for y

// Scan bottom edge for non-border color, if so set hotspot

   for (int ix = 0; ix < bm.width; ix++)
      {
      if (pcv->GetPixelNativeU(x1 + ix, y1 + bm.height) != color)
         { xoff = ix; break; }
      }

// Scan right edge for non-border color, if so set hotspot

   for (int iy = 0; iy < bm.height; iy++)
      {
      if (pcv->GetPixelNativeU(x1 + bm.width, y1 + iy) != color)
         { yoff = iy; break; }
      }
}
```

That's all there is to bitmap extraction. The following sample code shows how easy it is to fill up a sprite array with images from a graphics file.

```
// SAMPLE CODE TO READ BORDERED IMAGES INTO SPRITE ARRAY
ABitmap bmGfx;                         // declare bitmap for entire file's image
if (AGfxFile::Read("somefile.pcx", bmGfx))  // read file image into bmGfx
   { ... handle error condition ... }
ASpriteArray sa;                       // declare sprite array
ABitmapFind bmfind(bmGfx, 255);  // construct bitmap finder, bordcol = 255
int numFrames = bmfind.CaptureSprites(sa, FALSE);  // extract all images
```

Timing and the PC

Sprite arrays are very useful, if only as an organizer for libraries of images. But they can be more than just undifferentiated arrays of images. A sprite array can hold, in order, the successive frames of an animation sequence. Then, rendering that sequence is simply a matter of indexing through the sprite array, drawing each frame. This brings us back to frame rate, a concept discussed earlier in this chapter. How fast do we want to play back the sequence? And even if we know how fast, how do we make that happen? Animating frames at a particular rate presupposes that we have a method for keeping track of time. Since we haven't developed one for ARTT so far, apparently it is time to do so now, so that our animation doesn't free-run as fast as we can display it.[1] This should be easy, right? A machine as powerful as a personal computer ought to have timekeeping down pat.

PC Timing Hardware

Never underestimate the power of short-sightedness. The PC, after all, is a business computer, and adding fifty cents' worth of sophisticated timing hardware to time a word processor would just be a waste of money. Therefore, the standard for timekeeping laid down in the dawn of the PC era is not as straightforward or accurate as we might like. Here's the deal: There is a clock generator chip (originally an Intel 8253 chip; nowadays usually a small part of an integrated chip) which generates an interrupt at a programmable rate. This rate, by default, is roughly 18.2 times per second. The interrupt is handled by a routine in the ROM BIOS, which increments a count of ticks in a special longword variable kept in low memory at location 0040:006Ch (linear address 046Ch). This variable holds the number of ticks elapsed since midnight. DOS makes use of this variable in conjunction with the date supplied by a separate battery-backed chip to compute the exact date and time. Figure 8.7 shows the relationship between the various hardware and software timekeeping components.

What's wrong with this picture? For one, a tick frequency of 18.2 times per second (more precisely, 18.2065 times per second) is not ideal. It's an oddball number, and doesn't provide as much resolution as we'd like. More to the point for animation, it's unrelated to the refresh of the display screen, so that it's not possible to synchronize our animation frame rate to the real frame rate of the screen. The VGA standard doesn't support *vertical retrace interrupts* in a usable way, so we can't use the VGA card itself for our timing, which is really unfortunate.

Reprogramming the PC Timer Hardware

What to do? The two main choices are: (a) live with 18.2-ticks-per-second accuracy, and (b) take over the timer hardware and speed up the tick rate. This second option is used in many commercial games. The method relies on the fact that 18.2 ticks per second is the *default*

---

[1] Amazing as it may seem now, most early PC games did not synchronize to any timer. Instead, the game ran "flat out," displaying new frames as fast as the machine could handle. The modest variations in speed between XT and AT-class PCs made this annoying enough, but nowadays such an approach would be simply unacceptable. For a laugh, trying playing Origin's original "Wing Commander I" on a Pentium, and see if you can catch a glimpse of the Kilrathi warships as they jet by at warp 9.

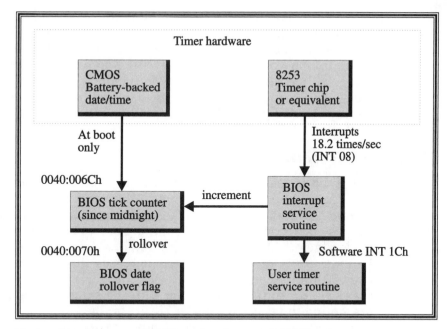

Figure 8.7 Diagram of PC timer hardware and BIOS software.

interrupt rate. Internally, the timer chip uses a countdown timer which runs at 1.19318 million counts per second, and generates the interrupt pulse every time this count reaches 0. The default interrupt rate occurs when the countdown timer is initialized at a count of 65,536, which is its maximum value. Reprogramming the timer chip to count down from 32,768, for instance, doubles the interrupt rate to 36.4 per second. Many games bump the rate up to 200 interrupts per second or more to get smoother animation plus good timer resolution for other purposes.

Reprogramming the timer hardware involves more than just jamming a different countdown value into the chip. If you did simply this, the DOS clock would start running wildly ahead, because the BIOS interrupt service routine would still think the interrupts were coming in at 18.2 per second, and increment the timer value at 0040:006CH every interrupt. Instead, you must *redirect* the interrupt to your own service routine, which increments your own private timer tick counter, and then *chains to* (calls) the real BIOS service routine only 18.2 times per second. (If you speed up the timer by a factor of 8, for instance, chain to the BIOS routine every eighth time through.) On interrupts where you don't chain to the BIOS routine, you must include the proper code to reset the timer hardware for the next countdown.

All this is not quite as complicated as it sounds, and nowadays can often be done totally in C, until protected-mode 32-bit programming is introduced. Here, the issues become magnified, because the interrupt may come in when the CPU is in real mode or when it is in protected mode, and so *dual-mode* handlers are needed. These handlers usually must be written in assembly language, depending on the capabilities of the compiler.

ARTT Timer System

The DOS-based timer code included with ARTT punts the timer speedup method in favor of portability, and relies on the 18.2-per-second tick counter. Since the screen refresh rate is typically 60 or 70 frames per second, and synchronizing to it is difficult, there is always a "slop factor" in PC-based animation of at least 15 or 16 milliseconds. Using the unmodified PC timer increases this slop factor to a little over 50 milliseconds, which is not ideal but works well enough in many circumstances. For those with the skills and interest in reprogramming the timer for better accuracy, the ARTT timer code is very small and easy to modify to take advantage of alternative methods.

Under Microsoft Windows, other methods for reading the time are available, some with better resolution than the DOS method. Windows has a function call, GetTickCount(), which returns time in milliseconds. This seeming millisecond-accuracy should not be taken too seriously—Windows uses the same old 18.2-tick-per-second unmodified timer, and so the values returned by GetTickCount() jump by about 55 milliseconds. A more accurate timer can be accessed via the TOOLHELP DLL. A function called TimerCount() uses the same low-resolution timer hardware, but peeks into the timer chip to see how far into its current countdown it is, and uses this information to supply a more accurate version of the current time. This function can be used for Windows-based ARTT programs. Yet another Windows-based timing mechanism is provided by the timeGetTime() function in the Multimedia extensions API.

We'll provide one timer mechanism for DOS and one for Windows, but we'll give them an identical interface. That way, our programs just need to link with the version of the timer class appropriate for the environment they want to run under (DOS or Windows), and don't even need recompiling for this purpose, much less code changes.

Class ATime: The Interface

There's no need for us to invent a fancy interface. Class ATime will offer a single static method named Read(), which returns the elapsed time since the first time it was called. We only care about "relative time" anyway when doing animation. ATime::Read() returns this time as a fixed-point number of seconds. Since fixed-point numbers have 8 bits of fraction, this gives us a resolution of 1/256 of a second, or about 4 milliseconds. That's more resolution than we're really getting under DOS anyway, and plenty for our animation purposes.

The header file for class ATime, which is the same regardless of how many implementations we invent for different environments beyond DOS and Windows, is listed below.

```
//   ATime.h      Timekeeping
//   Rex E. Bradford

#ifndef __ATIME_H
#define __ATIME_H

#include "afix.h"
class ATime {
public:

    static AFix Read();  // read current timer value
};

#endif
```

Class ATime: DOS Version

The DOS implementation of ATime::Read() is pretty simple. The first time through, it does some setup, including obtaining a physical pointer to the low-memory BIOS tick counter location and reading its initial value. It then returns a time of 0. Subsequent calls to Read() read the current value of the tick counter and convert the difference between it and the original value into fixed-point seconds. For efficiency, if Read() is called multiple times in quick succession, a check is made to see if the tick counter is the same as the last time read. If so, a repeat of the conversion to seconds is skipped (the last value returned is simply returned again).

If the tick counter *has* changed since the last Read(), the conversion to seconds is done by subtracting the current tick count from the original reading, and multiplying this difference by the length of a tick (about 55 milliseconds, the reciprocal of 18.2 ticks per second). The only complication is accounting for rollover of the tick count at midnight, when it resets to 0. If the current tick count is less than the original one read on startup, the routine compensates by adding the number of ticks in a day. Note that this scheme works only if the program has been running for less than 24 hours. Beyond 24 hours of

continuous operation, the timer reports incorrect values. This could
be fixed by checking the date, but then again maybe such users
should be encouraged to get out of the basement, walk the dog, and
so on. Just a suggestion.

```cpp
//    ATimeDos.cpp      DOS-based timer
//    Rex E. Bradford

#include <dos.h>
#include "atime.h"
#include "amem.h"


static ulong *pBiosTime;        // ptr to low-memory BIOS time counter
static ulong tBiosStart;        // time value at start of program
static ulong tBiosPrev;         // last time value read
static AFix tCurr;              // current time in seconds

#define TIMER_ROLLOVER 0x1800B0       // # BIOS ticks in 24 hours
#define TIMER_TICKDUR .05492549323    // duration of one tick


//-------------------------------------------------------------
//
// Read() initializes the timer if that has not been done already.
// It then checks the BIOS time value. If the BIOS ticks counter
// has changed since the last time read, the current time is
// recalculated. The midnight rollover is checked for, although
// only one such rollover is allowed, so a single run of a program
// cannot cross two midnights and get the right time.

AFix ATime::Read()
{

// First time through, do setup and return time 0

    if (pBiosTime == NULL)
        {
        pBiosTime = AMem::GetPhysPtr(0x46cL);    // get pointer to 0040:006C
        tBiosStart = tBiosPrev = *pBiosTime;     // grab current value
        tCurr = 0;                               // reset time to 0
        return tCurr;                            // return 0
        }

// Grab BIOS time and compare to previously-read time

    ulong t = *pBiosTime;       // grab BIOS time
    if (t != tBiosPrev)         // check for diff from last read
        {

// If different, get # ticks diff from start & convert to seconds

        ulong tdiff;
        if (t >= tBiosStart)    // calculate diff in ticks
```

```
          tdiff = t - tBiosStart;  // accounting for midnight rollover
      else
          tdiff = (t + TIMER_ROLLOVER) - tBiosStart;
      tCurr = AFix(double(tdiff) * TIMER_TICKDUR); // compute secs
      tBiosPrev = t;               // set for next time
      }

// Return the current time since first read in fixed-point seconds

   return tCurr;                   // return time in seconds
}
```

Class ATime: Windows Version

The Windows implementation of ATime::Read() has a compile-time flag which determines whether it uses the high-resolution TOOL-HELP routine TimerCount(), or the low-resolution Windows API routine GetTickCount(). Both of these return time in milliseconds since application startup, so we don't even need to compare to some previously read value.

```
//    ATimeWin.cpp   Windows-based timer
//    Rex E. Bradford

#include <windows.h>
#include "atypes.h"
#include "atime.h"

// Uncomment this and link with lib made from toolhelp.dll
//#define USE_ACCURATE_TOOLHELP_TIMER
#ifdef USE_ACCURATE_TOOLHELP_TIMER

typedef struct tagTIMERINFO    // copied from toolhelp.h
{
   DWORD dwSize;
   DWORD dwmsSinceStart;
   DWORD dwmsThisVM;
} TIMERINFO;

BOOL WINAPI TimerCount(TIMERINFO FAR* lpTimer);

#endif

//-----------------------------------------------------------
//
// Read() attempts to get an accurate millisecond count using the
// TimerCount() function in toolhelp.dll. If this fails, the
// 18.2 msec-accurate GetTickCount() is used.

AFIX ATime::Read()
{
```

```
    static ulong tStart = OL; // tick counter on 1st pass
       ulong ticks;


// Get ticks since Windows started

#ifdef USE_ACCURATE_TOOLHELP_TIMER
    TIMERINFO timerInfo;

    if (TimerCount (&timerInfo))         // use accurate TimerCount()
       ticks = timerInfo.dwmsSinceStart;
    else
#endif
       ticks = GetTickCount();           // or plain old GetTickCount()

// First time through, save ticks and return 0

    if (tStart == OL)
       {
       tStart = ticks;
       return AFix(0);
       }

// Else return diff in fixed-point

    return(AFix(double(ticks)/1000));    // convert to secs
}
```

GFXPLAY: *Playing an Extracted Animation*

The GFXPLAY program uses the code we've put together in this chapter to actually put an animation up on the screen. Supply GFX-PLAY with a graphics file consisting of multiple images surrounded by borders, the border color, and a frame rate. Then watch as these frames are displayed, one after the other, centered on your screen! The hotspots, if present in the border, are even used to make the frames align the way they should. Run the program like this:

GFXPLAY *filename borderColor frameRate*

That is:

GFXPLAY golfer.pcx 255 12.5

The code for GFXPLAY is listed below.

```
//   GfxPlay.cpp   Play extracted images as an animation
//   Rex E. Bradford
```

```
#include <stdio.h>
#include <stdlib.h>
#include <conio.h>

#include "agfxfile.h"
#include "abmfind.h"
#include "avesa.h"
#include "avga.h"
#include "atime.h"

void main(int argc, char **argv)
{
// Check args

    if (argc < 4)
        {
        printf("usage: gfxplay filename bordcol framerate\n");
        exit(1);
        }

// Open input file

    ABitmap bmGfx;
    AError err = AGfxFile::Read(argv[1], bmGfx);
    if (err)
        {
        printf("Problem with gfx file: %s (%s)\n", argv[1],
            AErr::Msg(err));
        exit(1);
        }

// Grab other arguments, compute frame duration

    long borderColor = atoi(argv[2]);
    AFix frameRate = atof(argv[3]);
    if (frameRate <= 0)
        {
        printf("Frame rate must be > 0!\n");
        exit(1);
        }
    AFix frameDur(1.0 / double(frameRate));

// Grab into sprite array

    ASpriteArray sa;
    ABitmapFind bmfind(bmGfx, borderColor);
    int numFrames = bmfind.CaptureSprites(sa, FALSE);

// Fire up screen

    if (bmGfx.format == BMF_LIN8)
        {
```

```
          if ((bmGfx.width > 320) || (bmGfx.height > 200))
             AVesa::Launch(640, 480, 8);
          else
             AVesa::Launch(320, 200, 8);
          if (gCanvasScreen == NULL)
             {
             printf("can't launch graphics mode\n");
             exit(1);
             }
          if (bmGfx.ppalette)
             AVga::SetDAC(bmGfx.ppalette->rgb);
          }
       else
          {
          printf("can't handle format of gfx file (format: $%x)\n",
             bmGfx.format);
          exit(1);
          }


// Set up for clearing last frame each time

    ARect lastRect(0,0,0,0);
    gCanvasScreen->SetColorNative(0);


// Loop through frames

LOOP:

    AFix tNext = ATime::Read();

    for (int i = 0; i < numFrames; i++)
        {
// Clear last frame

        gCanvasScreen->DrawRect(lastRect);


// Get next frame, compute rectangle, and display it

        ASprite *psp = sa[i];
        lastRect.left = (gCanvasScreen->bm.width / 2) - psp->xoff;
        lastRect.top = (gCanvasScreen->bm.height / 2) - psp->yoff;
        lastRect.right = lastRect.left + psp->width;
        lastRect.bott = lastRect.top + psp->height;
        if (psp->format == BMF_LIN8)
           gCanvasScreen->DrawBitmapLin8(*psp, lastRect.left, lastRect.top);


// Wait for time of next frame, checking keyboard to break out

        tNext += frameDur;
        while (TRUE)
            {
            AFix t = ATime::Read();
            if ((t >= tNext) || kbhit())
```

```
                    break;
            }

// If key hit, break out of frame playing

        if (kbhit())
            break;
        }

// Wait for keystroke, if not ESCAPE then loop

    int c = getch();
    if (c != 0x1B)
        goto LOOP;

// Return to text mode

    AVesa::Term();
}
```

Cramped Animations?

Grabbing image frames from PCX and BMP files is very useful, but doesn't work well for large images or long animation sequences. For these, we need to get our images from some kind of animation file. What kind? Stay tuned for Chapter 9.

9

Animation Files

You might think that the graphics file formats such as **PCX**, **BMP**, **GIF**, and the others are perfect candidates for extending into animation file formats. Just modify the format slightly to include multiple images, each one a frame in the animation sequence. If this were the case, we could make easy extensions to our graphics-reading code to handle these files. Well, forget it.

Animation File Formats: Tower of Babel, Part 37

For whatever reason, graphics file formats are stuck to representing a single image, and a new slew of formats have been developed for animation. Table 9.1 lists the most common ones likely to be encountered in the PC environment.

What's in an Animation File?

The animation file formats listed in Table 9.1 differ in capability as well as in format. AVI and MOV are *digital movie* formats, and as such include a digital sound track as well as image information. These will be discussed in more depth in Chapter 16. Authoring packages such as Macromind Director and Paul Mace Software's GRASP

Table 9.1 Common PC Animation File Formats

Extension	*Description*
FLC,FLI,CEL	FLIC format, invented by Autodesk for its Animator software
AVI	Microsoft Video for Windows digital video movie
MOV	Apple QuickTime for Windows digital video movie
DIR	Macromind Director movie (interactive)
SHW	CorelShow "slide show," part of CorelDraw package

(GRAphics System for Professionals) create complex files which include some form of script or code in them. When these files are run using a special player, they create interactive presentations in which the user can use the mouse or keyboard to branch to different parts of the movie by clicking on hotspots on the screen. The presentation packages, such as CorelShow, create simpler files which are usually just a set of images to be displayed one after another.

Of these simpler formats, the FLIC format has emerged as the closest thing there is to a standard animation file format. The FLIC format is the native file format of Autodesk's Animator and Animator Pro series. Animator Pro is the most popular of the two-dimensional animation packages, and offers a wide range of drawing and image processing tools. Other Autodesk products, notably 3D Studio, widely used for 3D scene modeling, can output FLIC files. Macromind Director and most other authoring software packages have the ability to import FLIC files.

Because of its dominance, the FLIC format will be the one that we'll develop code for in this chapter. This code will not only be able to "play" FLIC files onto the screen, but also to extract these images into bitmaps for any purpose. Before we begin, we need to learn about delta encoding, which is used in FLIC files.

Delta Encoding

In many full-screen animated sequences, much of the picture is constant from frame to frame. A spaceship zooms across a fixed starfield, or butterflies flitter over a field of daisies (actually, I haven't seen this second scene in a computer game lately). If the "camera" isn't moving, much of the background of the picture is unchanging. Even with a moving camera, you'd be surprised at the number of pixels which don't change value from one frame to another, especially in 8-bit animations with their limited palettes. When a camera sweeps across a starfield, most pixels are black on one frame and still black on the next. There must be a way to take advantage of this redundancy to increase our compression ratio and speed up our rendering.

Delta encoding is the way. In delta encoding, we don't compress the frame itself; what we compress is the difference, or *delta*, between this frame and the previous frame. How do we represent the difference between two frames? One possibility is to subtract the value of each previous frame's pixel from the current frame's pixel. If a pixel on frame n has a value of 11, and on frame $n + 1$ it has a value of 18, we encode the difference as $18 - 11 = 7$. If both pixels are 38, the difference is 0. Since presumably we'll get a lot of 0s this way as pixels remain constant from frame to frame, run-length compressing the delta frames should give us good compression. To reconstruct the image for a frame, we could just add the delta value to the previous frame's pixel, and voilà, new pixel. Figure 9.1 shows delta encoding via pixel subtraction.

However, pixel subtraction in 8-bit images has a few problems. The RGB colors associated with particular 8-bit indexes are essentially arbitrary. Color 11 might be bright green, and color 12 dark purple. So color difference values other than 0, when the pixel remains unchanged, are somewhat arbitrary. The 0s will definitely compress well, but the rest will be a mess. Generally, we'll do well to represent an unchanged pixel with a 0, and represent a changed pixel simply by the new pixel value itself. This helps speed our decoding, because for pixels which *do* change we don't need to read back the previous pixel's value to know what to draw. Figure 9.2 shows this form of delta encoding.

A marvelous side-effect of this coding scheme is that we can use our transparent bitmap rendering methods to play back these ani-

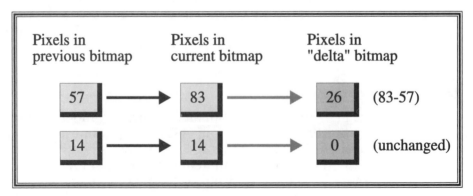

Figure 9.1   Computation of delta pixels via pixel subtraction.

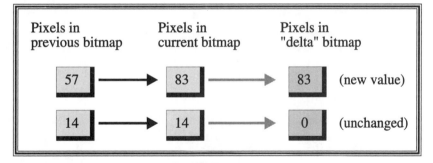

Figure 9.2 Computation of delta pixels via new/unchanged coding.

mations. Imagine frame 1 is already on the display, and we want to draw frame 2, which is delta encoded. All pixels in frame 2 which are 0 are skipped (they're considered transparent), and all (changed) pixels which are nonzero are drawn on top of frame 1. By the time we're done drawing frame 2 in this way, a perfect copy of the original *unencoded* frame 2 is sitting on the display.

There's one hitch, of course. The pixel value 0 is ambiguous. Does 0 mean that the pixel is unchanged, or that it has changed to a new value of 0? This is a similar problem to the one we faced using transparent bitmaps in ARTT, and in that case we just declared by fiat that no transparent bitmaps may use color 0, and it is reserved for transparency.

Animation files don't necessarily need to forbid the use of color 0. The FLIC format encodes each delta frame in a run-length format, wherein runs of unchanged pixels are stored in a token different from the tokens used to store new pixel values. Thus, it allows use of pixel value 0 and indeed all 256 colors.

The FLIC File Format

The FLIC file format has two variants and comes with three different filename extensions. An extension of FLI signifies an original Autodesk Animator file, which is hard-coded for 320 × 200 resolution images. An updated version of the format is signified by the FLC or CEL extension, which allow for different resolutions. FLC and CEL files are identical in format, but the extensions are typically used for different types of files. The FLC extension is generally used for full-screen animation, whereas the CEL extension is usually applied to smaller animated figures, objects, or textures.

The FLIC format is a chunk-based format. The file begins with a fixed-size header, after which comes a set of variable-length "frame chunks," each of which holds one frame of an animation. Within each frame chunk, nested chunks hold the image data and optionally other associated data, such as color palette information. Figure 9.3 gives the overall structure of a FLIC file.

FLIC File Header

FLI file headers are different from FLC/CEL headers, but both varieties start with the same base portion, and then have different extended parts. The following structure describes either header, using a union to include the two varieties. In FLI files, the 'magic' field is set to 0xAF11, and in FLC and CEL files it is set to 0xAF12. The header is pretty simple, and includes such basics as the width and height of the frames. In a FLIC, all frames must have the same width and height. Note that even though FLI files have a width and height, they are always set to 320,200. The color depth is always 8 in any FLIC file—frames are always 8-bit images.

```
typedef struct {
    ulong fileSize;       // size of entire file, including hdr
    ushort magic;         // 0xAF12 or 0xAF11
```

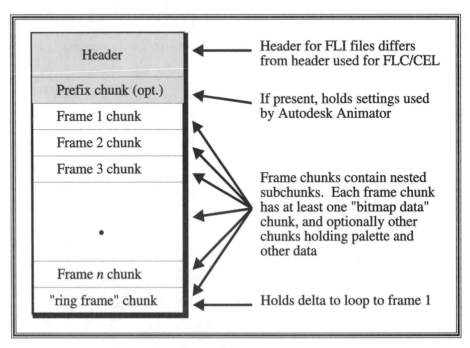

Figure 9.3   Overall structure of a FLIC file.

```
    ushort frames;         // number of frames, not including ring frame
    ushort width;          // width in pixels
    ushort height;         // height in pixels
    ushort depth;          // pixel depth (always 8)
    ushort flags;          // always 0x0003
    union {
        FliInfo fliInfo;   // if FLI file, use this info
        FlcInfo flcInfo;   // if FLC/CEL file, use this info
        };
} FlicHeader;
```

In a FLI file, the FliInfo header extension is very simple, and is shown below. It includes the animation frame rate, expressed in "jiffies," which tells the duration of each frame in units of 1/70 second. The remainder of the header, padded out to a length of 128 bytes total, is set to 0.

```
typedef struct {
    ushort jiffies;        // number of 1/70 second delays per frame
    uchar reserved[110];   // set to 0
} FliInfo;
```

FLI and CEL files have a different header extension, listed below. Besides representing frame duration in milliseconds instead of "jiffies," this header includes the aspect ratio of the display used when creating the frames and some auxiliary authoring information such as the date and time when the file was first created and first updated, along with the serial number of the program which did so (Animator Pro sets this; other programs may just use 0). The header also includes the file offset of the first two frames. The first frame offset is necessary because the first frame may not start right after the header, but may be preceded by an optional "prefix" chunk. The second frame offset is also useful, as we shall see later.

```
typedef struct {
    ulong speed;           // number of milliseconds between frames
    ushort reserved1;      // set to 0
    ulong created;         // MS-DOS creation time
    ulong creator;         // serial number of program which created file
    ulong updated;         // MS-DOS time of last update
    ulong updater;         // serial number of program which updated file
    ushort aspectx;        // x-portion of aspect ratio
    ushort aspecty;        // y-portion of aspect ratio
    uchar reserved2[38];   // set to 0
    ulong oframe1;         // offset of frame 1 (first frame)
    ulong oframe2;         // offset of frame 2 (second frame)
    uchar reserved3[40];   // set to 0
} FlcInfo;
```

FLIC File Frame Chunks

The header is followed by an optional "prefix chunk" (FLC/CEL files only), and then by a set of "frame chunks." Frame chunks and prefix chunks have chunk headers, which are 16-byte structures laid out according to the structure given below.

```
typedef struct {
   ulong size;          // size of frame chunk, including this header
   ushort type;         // 0xF1FA
   ushort numChunks;    // number of subordinate chunks
   uchar reserved[8];   // set to 0
} FlicFrameChunk;
```

Because the frame or prefix chunk header gives the chunk's size, any chunk can be skipped over without reading its contents by using fseek() to skip over the number of bytes given (minus the size of the frame chunk structure itself). The prefix chunk contains chunks which control Autodesk program settings for this animation. These settings are undocumented and unnecessary for decoding of the animation file, and for these reasons the prefix chunk should be skipped over.

Frame chunks include one or more subchunks within them. Each frame includes at least an image data chunk. Some frames, particularly the first, include additional chunks as well as the image data. Two varieties of such chunks are currently defined—one to set or modify the color palette, and another to provide a "postage stamp" iconic version of the animation, so that programs which provide browsing of animation files can easily obtain a small version of the animation's first frame for display to the user.

The number of frame chunks present in a FLIC file is one greater than the number of frames given in the animation header, because of a final "ring frame." The purpose of the ring frame has to do with the fact that the animation frames are delta-encoded, with each frame encoding just the difference between it and the previous frame. Because the first frame can't be delta encoded (there's no previous frame to compare to), it is usually substantially larger and slower to draw than subsequent frames. The final ring frame encodes the difference between the last frame and the first. This allows programs to display the animation in a continuous "looping" fashion without reloading the first frame. The ring frame, when applied to the last frame, achieves the same effect. See Figure 9.4.

The presence of the ring frame explains why the header includes the file offsets of the first two frames. On the second and subsequent passes of a looping animation, the ring frame should be followed by the second frame of the sequence, since the ring frame effectively gets us back to the first frame itself.

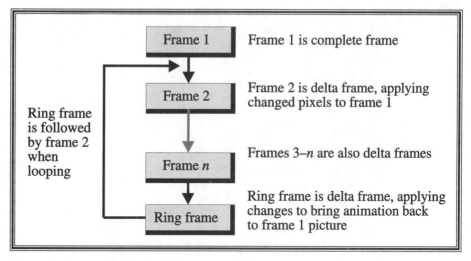

Figure 9.4   Use of delta ring frame to return animation to frame 1.

FLIC Chunks

Each frame chunk is made up of one or more subchunks, each of which begins with the 6-byte header given below. Like frame chunks, a chunk within a frame can be skipped over by virtue of the fact that its size is placed in its header. Besides the size, the other field in these chunks is a type field. This identifies a chunk as an image data chunk or some other type. The beauty of chunk-based schemes like this is that they can be extended to include new types of chunks, and old programs still work, as long as they just skip over chunks whose type is unknown to them.

```
typedef struct {
    ulong size;  // size of chunk, including this header
    ushort type; // chunk type, FLI_XXX
} FlicChunk;
```

Table 9.2 lists the types of chunks currently defined.

Color Palette Chunks

The first frame chunk in a FLIC file always includes a color palette chunk, which holds the color palette used in the animation. Subsequent frames may include color palette chunks as well, if the flic employs *palette animation*, wherein the palette itself is updated during playback. Most flics do not change the palette after the first frame, although some do.

Table 9.2 Chunk Types in FLIC Files

Type	Name	Description
4	FLI_COLOR256	Palette data, 256-level colors
7	FLI_SS2	Image data, word oriented, delta encoded
11	FLI_COLOR	Palette data, 64-level colors
12	FLI_LC	Image data, byte oriented, delta encoded
13	FLI_BLACK	Image data, entire frame is color index 0
15	FLI_BRUN	Image data, byte oriented, run-length encoded
16	FLI_COPY	Image data, uncompressed
18	FLI_PSTAMP	Postage stamp data, various encodings

Palette chunks come in two flavors: FLI_COLOR256 and FLI_COLOR. They differ by whether the red, green, and blue values in the palette data are represented by 8-bit or 6-bit values. Remember, the VGA's DAC uses 6-bit color registers, so the 6-bit format is more direct. However, in anticipation of display adapters with more color resolution, some flics store the color values as 8-bit values, and these must be scaled down to 6 bits when programmed into the VGA.

Other than the choice of 8-bit or 6-bit color values, the FLI_COLOR256 and FLI_COLOR chunks have an identical format. Palette chunks need not set the entire color palette; for this reason the palette data is arranged into *packets*, each of which contains data for a subset of the palette. The first frame usually has a palette chunk with one packet representing the entire palette from indexes 0 through 255. Subsequent palette animation chunks, if present, have one or more packets representing the entries to be changed. The format of a palette chunk is shown in Figure 9.5.

Postage Stamp Chunks

The first frame chunk in a FLIC often includes a postage stamp chunk, which features a miniature icon of the image for use by flic browsers. The postage stamp has no bearing on decoding the animation itself or any frame in it. The format of this icon is not covered in this book.

Image Data Chunks

Every frame chunk has an image data chunk which contains the pixel data for the frame. What format is this pixel data encoded in?

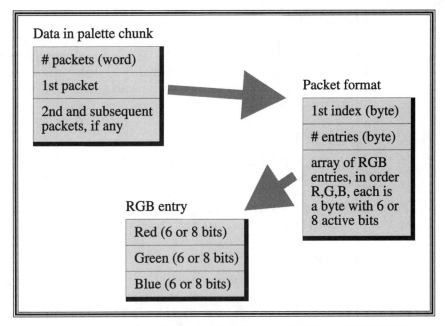

Figure 9.5   Format of a palette chunk (FLI_COLOR256 or FLI_COLOR).

Any of five different formats, and a flic reader must be capable of decoding an image chunk in any of these formats.

Why so many different formats? The answer is compression. Frames other than the first are usually delta encoded—the pixel data contained in them contains only those pixels which have changed from the previous frame. Chunk type FLI_SS2 signifies a particular form of delta encoding and is typically used, but FLI files use the older FLI_LC format, another form of delta encoding. The first frame in the animation has no previous frame to compare to, so delta encoding doesn't make much sense. First frames are usually encoded in FLI_BRUN format, a run-length format similar to ARTT's BMF_RLE8 format. Some frames are so busy that compression just doesn't work on them and can actually increase the amount of data needed to represent a frame—for these, FLI_COPY is used to signify an image that is in uncompressed format, which is identical to BMF_LIN8. Finally, a frame which consists of nothing but pixel 0 can be represented by the FLI_BLACK chunk type.

Note that a given frame may use any of the five image chunk types, so a reader must not make any assumptions. The chunk type field determines the type of image encoding used, and the data associated with the chunk must be interpreted in the appropriate manner.

Now we'll discuss each of the five image chunk types.

FLI_BLACK

This chunk type is somewhat misnamed, since it really says that the entire frame has pixel value 0, which need not be black in color. There is no data associated with this chunk—the header says it all. When encountering a chunk of type FLI_BLACK, we should set the entire image to 0.

FLI_COPY

Another simple image chunk type is FLI_COPY, which signifies that the pixel data that follows is an uncompressed array of 8-bit pixels. This data is laid out in a linear format identical to the BMF_LIN8 format ARTT uses. If we are reading into a bitmap in that format, a single fread() can be used to pull the data from the file into the bitmap.

FLI_BRUN

The first frame in an animation is typically encoded in FLI_BRUN (Byte RUN) format, which is a run-length format very similar to BMF_RLE8, though not identical. The data following the chunk header consists of a series of rows, one per row in the image. Each such row starts with a bytewide "packet count," which has been declared obsolete and should be ignored (probably because it's just not big enough to hold more than 255, and high-resolution images might have more than 255 packets).

The remainder of the row is a series of packets not unlike the tokens in BMF_RLE8 format. Each starts with a one-byte count field, in which the high bit specifies whether the packet is a "dump" packet or a "run" packet. If the high bit is 0, it's a run packet. In this case, the length of the run is encoded in the low 7 bits of the header, and the next byte contains the pixel value to be replicated that many times. If the high bit is 1, it's a dump packet. In this case, the count byte must be *negated* in order to obtain the proper count, which signifies how many successive bytes should be copied from the file to the bitmap. (This differs from ARTT's BMF_RLE8 format, where the high bit is stripped to get the count.) Figure 9.6 illustrates the layout of an FLI_BRUN image chunk.

Note that there is no packet to mark the end of a row or the end of a bitmap. The pixels must be counted during decoding, and the width and height of the frame used to determine when to stop.

FLI_LC

FLI_LC is one of two delta-encoded image chunk types, and it's the rarer of the two, having been bypassed by the more effective

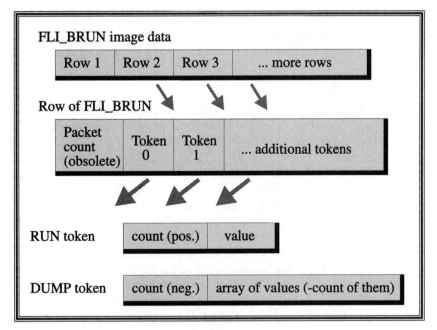

Figure 9.6 Format of an FLI_BRUN image chunk.

FLI_SS2. Still, many flics have FLI_LC frames in them, so we need to know how to decode them.

The data following the chunk header begins with two special word-sized values. The first is the number of rows, starting from the top of the image, to skip entirely. Remember, this is a delta-encoded frame, so this first value is nonzero if some lines at the top of the image don't change at all. This is followed by a row count, which specifies how many rows of data are encoded in the chunk. Any rows left over at the bottom of the image are unchanged. Following the two special words are a set of rows, the number of which has been specified in the row count. Each row consists of a series of packets. A packet begins with a bytewide column skip count, which tells how many pixels to skip over. This is followed by a series of run/dump tokens, whose format is maddeningly different from FLI_BRUN tokens. Here, the first byte is again a type/count field, but a high bit of 1 signifies a run and a high bit of 0 signifies a dump! Other than this sign bit change, such a packet is decoded in the same way as a FLI_BRUN packet—run packets are followed by a single value to be replicated, and dump packets are followed by an array of pixels. A negative count field (this time run tokens have them) must be negated before being used.

As always, there is no end-of-row marker—we must count pixels until the width of the frame has been reached in order to know when to stop. Figure 9.7 illustrates the layout of an FLI_LC image chunk.

FLI_SS2

FLI_SS2 image chunks are also delta-encoded, using a more complex scheme than FLI_LC chunks. This complexity pays off in better compression, and FLI_SS2 is used exclusively for delta compression in newer versions of Autodesk products. This format achieves better compression in two ways.

First, it allows for "line skipping" anywhere in an image. Suppose a frame has pixels changing at the top of the frame and the bottom, but nowhere else. In FLI_LC format, all the unchanging lines in between would have to be encoded. Since the column skip count field can handle only 255 skipped pixels, the remaining pixels in each row would have to be repeated. FLI_SS2 fixes this problem by allowing lines to be skipped over at any place in the image.

The other improvement in FLI_SS2 is to use 16-bit pixel pairs, instead of single pixels, as the fundamental unit of compression. This makes for better compression and faster playback.

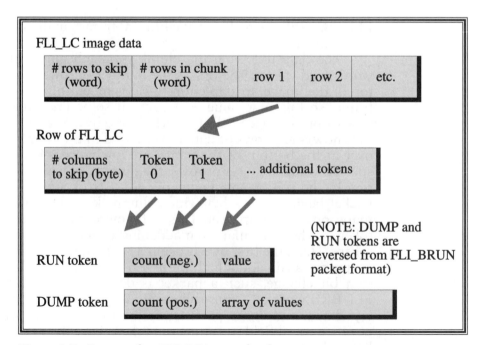

Figure 9.7   Format of an FLI_LC image chunk.

The data for a FLI_SS2 chunk starts with a word which determines how many "row chunks" are in the data. Each such row chunk contains both a row of data and, optionally, a count of the number of rows to skip before it. Thus rows can be skipped anywhere in the image.

Each row chunk begins with one or more word-sized packet headers, which are used to signify different things depending on the settings of the high two bits. Table 9.3 lists the meanings of each combination.

Packets used to signify line skipping or "last-byte" setting are immediately followed by another packet, unless all rows in the image have been processed. The last-byte packet is used to set the value of the last pixel in a row of odd width, since the format works with pairs of pixels and cannot otherwise get to a single pixel. This packet need not be present even on odd-width rows if the last pixel is unchanged from the previous frame.

After the optional "skip lines" and last-byte packets, a packet count is encountered. This is immediately followed by a set of packets, the number of which is denoted by the packet count. Each such packet begins with a bytewide column skip count. The skip count is followed by a bytewide run/dump marker similar to that used in FLI_LC—a marker with a high bit of 1 signifies a run and must be negated to get the count, and a high bit of 0 signifies a dump, with the count in the low 7 bits. The only difference is that the count refers to *words*, not bytes, to follow. Each word contains two pixels, the leftmost in the low byte and the rightmost in the high byte (the correct format for storing the word into any linear 8-bit bitmap). Figure 9.8 illustrates the layout of an FLI_SS2 image chunk.

Using FLIC Files in ARTT

FLIC files get pretty good compression with animations using a combination of the above compression schemes, particularly FLI_SS2 word-sized delta compression. Scenes with largely static backgrounds

---

Table 9.3 FLI_SS2 Row Packet Header

Packet Header	Description
11xxxxxx xxxxxxxx	Skip lines (negate word and skip this many lines)
10xxxxxx vvvvvvvv	Last byte in row should be set to vvvvvvvv
0nnnnnnn nnnnnnnn	Packet count, *n* packets follow

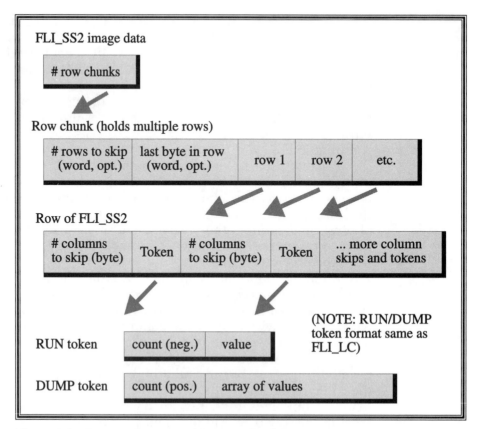

Figure 9.8   Format of an FLI_SS2 image chunk.

and a few moving foreground objects achieve dramatic compression compared with simply storing each frame uncompressed, often over 20:1. The cost of this is complexity. While FLI_SS2-encoded images are not too complicated to decode straight to screen or to an image buffer, try clipping them or applying the scaling or color effects we'll be applying to bitmaps later in this book. The format is a bit too complex for much other than straight rendering.

While ARTT's BMF_RLE8 run-length encoding does not provide compression as good as FLI_SS2, it can be used for delta encoding. Remember, in ARTT we have reserved color 0 for transparency. There's no law that says we can't use color 0 in delta-encoded bitmaps to mean "unchanged from previous frame." That's just what we're going to do. Therefore, the big savings of delta encoding will be ours, without having to invent a new complex format. Our compression ratio will be weaker than FLI_SS2 by 20 percent to 30 percent for typical animations, but we're still way ahead of the game.

Our next step, therefore, will be to write some code to extract images from FLIC files and be able to put them in BMF_LIN8 and BMF_RLE8 format.

Class AAnmFile: A Generic Animation File Class

In the spirit of the graphics file classes of Chapter 3, let's develop a generic class for reading and writing animation files, and derive any format-specific classes from it. Then, if we decide it's really important to read CorelShow animations or some other format, we won't have to build a framework from scratch.

What should a basic animation file reader provide? Let's lay down a few requirements for the capabilities our reader should provide:

- Structure for reading and writing animation files
- Derived class may be read-only, or may supply read/write capability
- Variable frame resolution and bit depth (8, 15, and 24 bit images, anyway)
- For 8-bit animations, color palette access (on-the-fly changes not required)
- Variable frame rate (fixed within a given animation) and number of frames

Given the above, what do we want to be able to do with an animation file? Here are a few ideas:

- Open file for reading, and read frames, palette, and descriptive information from it.
- Open file for writing, and write frames, palette, and descriptive information into it.
- Read entire animation file into a sprite array, or write a sprite array into an animation file.

These last two allow us to treat an animation file as a sort of on-disk sprite array. This won't be our normal mode—full-screen animations are usually very large, and must be read a frame at a time due to memory constraints. However, animation files are a convenient storage mechanism for arrays of small sprites, and it's nice to be able to read and write such arrays with a single call.

Class AAnmFile is the base class we'll develop for handling animation files. The header for this class is listed below.

```
//   AAnmFile.h    Base Animation File Reader
//   Rex E. Bradford

#ifndef __AANMFILE_H
#define __AANMFILE_H

#include <stdio.h>
#include "aspritea.h"
```

```c
#include "afix.h"
#include "aerror.h"

// Animation descriptor

typedef struct {
    short width;            // width of frames in pixels
    short height;           // height of frames in pixels
    short depth;            // pixel depth (8, 15, 24)
    short numFrames;        // number of frames
    AFix frameDur;          // duration of frames in seconds
    long maxFrameLen;       // length in bytes of biggest frame's bits
} AnimDesc;

// Animation file class

class AAnmFile {
protected:
    FILE *fp;               // file ptr
    AnimDesc desc;          // animation descriptor
    APalette *palette;      // ptr to palette for 8-bit anims
    short currFrame;        // index of current frame
    bool reading;           // TRUE if reading, FALSE if writing
    bool bmAlloced;         // was current bitmap allocated internally?

// Constructor and destructor (protected)

    AAnmFile(FILE *fp, bool read);       // called by OpenXXXX()
    virtual ~AAnmFile();                 // called by Close()

public:

// Read/write a sprite array from/to an animation file

    static ASpriteArray *ReadSpriteArray(char *filename, AError &err);
    static AError WriteSpriteArray(char *filename, ASpriteArray &sa,
        AFix frameDur);

// Open an animation file to read/write frames "by hand"

    static AAnmFile *OpenRead(char *filename, AError &err);
    static AAnmFile *OpenWrite(char *filename,AError &err);
    static AAnmFile *Open(char *filename, bool read, AError &err);

// Close anim file (same as delete)

    static void Close(AAnmFile *pAnmFile) {delete pAnmFile;}

// Read/write sprite array from open anim file

    AError ReadSpriteArray(ASpriteArray &sa);
    AError WriteSpriteArray(ASpriteArray &sa);

// Read animation frames
```

```
bool More() {return(currFrame < desc.numFrames);}
virtual AError ReadNextFrame(ABitmap &bm, uchar *buff = NULL) = 0;
virtual AError ReadNextSprite(ASprite &sp, uchar *buff = NULL) = 0;
void FreeFrame(ABitmap &bm) {if (bmAlloced) delete bm.pbits;}
virtual void Reset() {currFrame = 0;}

// Write animation frames

virtual AError WriteNextFrame(ABitmap &bm, bool compress = TRUE) = 0;
virtual AError WriteNextSprite(ASprite &sp, bool compress = TRUE) = 0;

// Set/Get info about animation

AnimDesc *GetAnimDesc() {return &desc;}
int CurrFrame() {return currFrame;}
void SetFrameDur(AFix frameDur) {desc.frameDur = frameDur;}

// Set/get info about palette

bool HasPalette() {return (palette != NULL);}
APalette *GetPalettePtr() {return palette;}
void SetPal(APalette *pal);
};

#endif
```

Reading and Writing Entire Sprite Arrays

For the ultimate in convenience, two methods are available which treat animation files just like on-disk sprite arrays. AAnmFile::ReadSpriteArray() constructs a new sprite array, and fills it with the frames of the specified animation file. AAnmFile::WriteSpriteArray() operates in reverse, writing the sprites in the specified sprite array into the animation file. ReadSpriteArray() is listed below; see the CD for a listing of WriteSpriteArray().

```
ASpriteArray *AAnmFile::ReadSpriteArray(char *filename, AError &err)
{
// Open anim file for reading, get ptr to AAnmFile object

    AnimDesc ad;
    AAnmFile *paf = OpenRead(filename, err);
    if (err)
        return NULL;

// Create new sprite array, bail out if can't

    AnimDesc *pad = paf->GetAnimDesc();
    ASpriteArray *psa = new ASpriteArray(pad->numFrames);
    if (psa == NULL)
        {
        Close(paf);
```

```
        err = AERR_NOMEM;
        return NULL;
        }

// Read sprite array from file

    err = paf->ReadSpriteArray(*psa);
    Close(paf);
    if (err)
        {
        delete psa;
        psa = NULL;
        }

// Return ptr to sprite array

    return psa;
}
```

Opening and Reading from AAnmFiles

For large animation files, using ReadSpriteArray() is impractical due to memory limitations. An alternate interface is available for reading individual frames from a file, and for writing individual frames into a file. AAnmFile::OpenRead() opens a file for reading, and AAnm-File::OpenWrite() opens one for writing. OpenRead() takes a filename as input, and returns a pointer to an instance of class AAnmFile. This pointer can be later used with other methods to read frames from the file in succession. Other methods can then be used to extract general information about the animation file.

AAnmFile::OpenRead() and AAnmFile::Open(), which Open-Read() calls internally, are listed below. Like AGfxFile::Read(), AAnm-File::Open() uses the extension of the filename to determine which derived class to use when creating a handler object. Two such classes will be developed later in this chapter, one of which will handle FLIC files and the other of which will handle a custom format.

```
AAnmFile *AAnmFile::OpenRead(char *filename, AError &err)
{
    return(AAnmFile::Open(filename, TRUE, err));
}


AAnmFile *AAnmFile::Open(char *filename, bool read, AError &err)
{
// Open file, if can't just return NULL

    char *openMode = read ? "rb" : "wb";
    FILE *fp = fopen(filename, openMode);
    if (fp == NULL)
        {
```

```
        err = AERR_FILEOPEN;
        return NULL;
        }

// File opened. Let's create a new instance of the proper type.
// The constructor will examine the file's header and set 'err'
// appropriately.

    AAnmFile *pAnmFile = NULL;

    switch (GrabExt(filename))
        {
        case MAKE_EXT('A','S','A'):
            pAnmFile = new AsaFile(filename, fp, read, err);
            break;
        case MAKE_EXT('F','L','C'):
        case MAKE_EXT('F','L','I'):
        case MAKE_EXT('C','E','L'):
            pAnmFile = new AFlcFile(fp, read, err);
            break;
// Insert your Microsoft AVI reader here!
        default:
            err = AERR_BADNAME;
            break;
        }

// If error, delete anim file and return error

    if (err)
        {
        Close(pAnmFile);
        return NULL;
        }

// If we got here, we're home free

    return(pAnmFile);
}
```

AAnmFile::Close() is called by the application to close an animation file when all frames have been read from or written to it. Close() simply deletes the animation file object; using delete directly achieves the same outcome.

```
static void Close(AAnmFile *pAnmFile) {delete pAnmFile;}
```

As an additional convenience, sprite arrays may be read from or written to an open animation file. An overloaded version of AAnm-File::ReadSpriteArray() fills a sprite array with the frames from an open animation file. WriteSpriteArray() is overloaded in a similar manner. ReadSpriteArray() is listed below.

```
AError AAnmFile::ReadSpriteArray(ASpriteArray &sa)
{
// Make sure we start at frame 0

   Reset();

// Go through all frames, loading sprites

   for (int i = 0; i < desc.numFrames; i++)
      {
      ASprite sp;
      AError err = ReadNextSprite(sp);  // alloc & read sprite
      if (err) return err;              // return error if problem
      err = sa.SetSprite(sp, FALSE, i); // set sprite, no clone
      if (err) return err;              // return error if problem
      }

   return AERR_OK; // all aboard!
}
```

AAnmFile Constructor and Destructor

When AAnmFile::Open() constructs an instance of some animation
file class derived from AAnmFile, the base AAnmFile constructor is
called implicitly during construction of the derived instance. This
base constructor does initialization common to all animation handlers. It makes a copy of the file pointer to be subsequently used when
reading and writing the file, marks whether reading or writing has
been selected, sets the palette pointer to NULL (this will later get set
for 8-bit animations with palettes), and resets the current frame to 0.

```
AAnmFile::AAnmFile(FILE *fp_, bool read)
{
   fp = fp_;              // set internal file ptr
   reading = read;        // reading/writing
   palette = NULL;        // no palette (yet)
   currFrame = 0;         // start at frame 0
}
```

The destructor, which should be called explicitly or implicitly
via AAnmFile::Close() (but not both!), cleans up memory allocated
for the palette and closes the file. This method is declared virtual, so
derived classes may perform additional format-specific cleanup in
their destructors.

```
AAnmFile::~AAnmFile()
{
   if (palette)
      delete palette;    // delete palette
   fclose(fp);           // close file
}
```

Reading Frames from Open AAnmFiles

Methods are provided to read frames into both bitmaps and sprites (a sprite is just a bitmap with a hotspot, remember). AAnmFile:: ReadNextFrame() and AAnmFile::ReadNextSprite() are both unimplemented virtual functions—these must be handled by the derived class. Besides a bitmap or sprite reference as the first argument, both take a second pointer argument which defaults to NULL. This is the buffer into which the data bits of the frame should be read. If NULL, the routine will allocate memory for that frame and use it. If non-NULL, the routine will load the frame's data into the supplied memory buffer. The application can find out how big such a buffer needs to be by accessing the "animation descriptor" structure of the animation (see the next section).

Three other related methods are defined:

More()	Returns TRUE if there are more frames, FALSE if last frame already read
FreeFrame()	Frees data bits for last frame, if and only if they were auto-allocated
Reset()	Resets reader to first frame, for looping

AAnmFile::Reset() merely sets the current frame number back to 0. Note, however, that Reset() is declared virtual, so that actual file readers can implement more code to do the actual reset, for instance, fseek()'ing the file pointer back to the first frame.

A derived class of AAnmFile really wants to set the current frame count to 0 as well as *doing additional class-specific work to reset the animation. With C++ virtual functions, the derived class' implementation of Reset() will be called* instead of *the AAnmFile implementation of Reset(). In order to do both jobs, the derived class' Reset() implementation should include a call to AAnm-File::Reset() as part of its code.*

Getting Information About Open AAnmFiles

The following methods are available to obtain more detailed information about an open animation file:

CurrFrame()	Returns number of next frame to be read, counting from 0
HasPalette()	Returns TRUE if animation has palette, FALSE otherwise

GetPalettePtr()	Returns pointer to animation's palette, or NULL if none
GetAnimDesc()	Returns pointer to animation's "descriptor," defined below:

```
typedef struct {
    short width;          // width of frames in pixels
    short height;         // height of frames in pixels
    short depth;          // pixel depth (8, 15, 24)
    short numFrames;      // number of frames
    AFix frameDur;        // duration of frames in seconds
    long maxFrameLen;     // length in bytes of biggest frame's bits
} AnimDesc;
```

An assumption is made that the width, height, and color depth of all frames is the same. This is certainly true of FLIC files and most other animation files. In the case of general sprite arrays, it is not necessarily true. In the ASA format to be defined later in this chapter, these three values describe the first sprite only.

The 'frameDur' field can be used by playback code to time the animation, leaving each frame displayed for this duration in seconds (fractional). The 'maxFrameLen' field denotes the largest frame in the file, and may be used by applications wishing to supply a buffer to ReadNextFrame() or ReadNextSprite().

Writing to Animation Files

The following methods apply to animation files opened for writing. They are not listed in this book—see the CD that accompanies this text.

OpenWrite()	Open animation file for writing
WriteSpriteArray()	Write sprite array to file
WriteNextFrame()	Write bitmap to next frame of file
WriteNextSprite()	Write sprite to next frame of file
SetFrameDur()	Set frame duration for animation
SetPal()	Set animation's palette

Class AFlcFile: A Derived Class for Reading FLIC Files

Now that we have a base class in place to provide the framework, the structure of a class for reading FLIC files falls into place. If all we are interested in doing is reading from FLIC files, then the only public methods we need to implement are a constructor, ReadNextFrame(), ReadNextSprite(), and Reset(). Other data and methods can be private to the implementation.

```
//    AFlcFile.h      Animation reader for Autodesk FLIC files
//    Rex E. Bradford

#ifndef __AFLCFILE_H
#define __AFLCFILE_H

#include "aanmfile.h"

class AFlcFile : public AAnmFile {

    friend class AAnmFile;        // so it can call our constructor

    long offsetFrame0;            // offset to frame 0
    uchar zeroSubst;             // color to substitute for 0

// Constructor: private - for use by AAnmFile::Open() only

    AFlcFile(FILE *fp, bool read, AError &err);

// Internal routines to access data in file

    AError ReadHeader();
    void ProcessChunk(int chunkType, ABitmap &bm);
    void ReadPalette(int shift);
    void ReadRow(int chunkType, uchar *buff, int &skipLines, int width);
    void ReadBrunRow(uchar *buff, int width);
    void ReadByteDeltaRow(uchar *buff, int &skipLines, int width);
    void ReadWordDeltaRow(uchar *buff, int &skipLines, int width);
    void FindZeroSubst();
    void SubstZero(uchar *buff, ushort len);

public:

// Read next frame as bitmap or sprite, reset to start
    AError ReadNextFrame(ABitmap &bm, uchar *buff = NULL);
    AError ReadNextSprite(ASprite &sp, uchar *buff = NULL);
    void Reset();

// Write next frame

    AError WriteNextFrame(ABitmap &bm, bool compress = TRUE)
        {return AERR_WRITE;}
    AError WriteNextSprite(ASprite &sp, bool compress = TRUE)
        {return AERR_WRITE;}
};

#endif
```

AFlcFile Constructor

The AFlcFile constructor, called from AAnmFile::Open(), is passed an open file pointer, so it doesn't need to worry about checking extensions or opening files. It is however, called during file opening for purposes of reading and writing. We're only going to handle reading, so the constructor should return an error code if the 'read' argument is FALSE.

```
AFlcFile::AFlcFile(FILE *fp, bool read, AError &err) :
   AAnmFile(fp, read)
{
   if (read)
      err = ReadHeader();
   else
      err = AERR_WRITE;
}
```

The constructor calls AFlcFile::ReadHeader(), a private method, to do the real work of reading in the file's header and verifying it. Read-Header() fills in the animation descriptor record in the base class, and also seeks to the first frame in anticipation of frame reading.

```
AError AFlcFile::ReadHeader()
{
   FlicHeader hdr;
   bool isFli;

// Read header & check it out

   fread(&hdr, sizeof(hdr), 1, fp);
   if (hdr.magic == 0xAF12) isFli = FALSE;
   else if (hdr.magic == 0xAF11) isFli = TRUE;
   else return AERR_BADFORMAT;

   if (hdr.depth != 8) return AERR_BADFORMAT;
   if (isFli && (hdr.flags != 0)) return AERR_BADFORMAT;
   if (!isFli && (hdr.flags != 3)) return AERR_BADFORMAT;

// Set up anim descriptor

   desc.width = hdr.width;
   desc.height = hdr.height;
   desc.depth = 8;
   desc.numFrames = hdr.frames - 1; // skip ring frame
   desc.maxFrameLen = long(desc.width) * long(desc.height);

// If .FLI, frame duration is in 1/70th seconds, and frame 0 follows

   if (isFli)
      {
      desc.frameDur = AFix(int(hdr.fliInfo.jiffies)) / 70;
      offsetFrame0 = ftell(fp);
      }
```

```
// Else if .FLC/.CEL, frame duration is in milliseconds, and offset
// of frame 0 is in header

    else
        {
        desc.frameDur = AFix(int(hdr.flcInfo.speed)) / 1000;
        offsetFrame0 = hdr.flcInfo.oframe1;
        fseek(fp, offsetFrame0, SEEK_SET);
        }

    return AERR_OK;        // Off to the movies!
}
```

Reading Frames from FLIC Files

AFlcFile::ReadNextFrame() processes all the chunks in the next frame chunk, which includes one image data chunk and possibly palette chunks. The first frame invariably contains a palette chunk, and this is used to determine the animation's palette. In our implementation, all subsequent palette chunks are ignored—ARTT's FLIC reader does not handle palette animation. ReadNextFrame() calls the private method ProcessChunk() to actually process each chunk; we will look at this routine in detail shortly. Note that ReadNextFrame() sets 'bmAlloced' to TRUE or FALSE, depending on whether or not a buffer to hold the image had to be allocated. AAnmFile::FreeFrame() later uses this flag to determine whether to delete the bits—this allows FreeFrame() to work properly whether or not a buffer was allocated.

```
AError AFlcFile::ReadNextFrame(ABitmap &bm, uchar *buff)
{
    FlicFrameChunk frameChunk;

// If read all frames, don't keep going

    if (currFrame >= desc.numFrames)
        return AERR_OVERFLOW;

// Set up bitmap for this frame, mark whether it is being allocated
// or not.

    bmAlloced = (buff == NULL) ? TRUE : FALSE;
    bm = ABitmap(buff, BMF_LIN8, TRUE, desc.width, desc.height);
    if (bm.pbits == NULL)
        {
        bmAlloced = FALSE;
        return AERR_NOMEM;
        }
```

```
// Read frame chunk header, if bad header bail out

    fread(&frameChunk, sizeof(frameChunk), 1, fp);
    if (frameChunk.type != 0xF1FA)
        return AERR_BADFORMAT;

// Compute file offset of next frame chunk

    long nextFrameOffset = ftell(fp) + frameChunk.size -
        sizeof(frameChunk);

// If no chunks in frame, create a blank frame

    if (frameChunk.numChunks == 0)
        ProcessChunk (FLI_BLACK, bm);

// Else process all chunks, one of them will fill in bitmap

    else
        {
        for (int i = 0; i < frameChunk.numChunks; i++)
            {
            FlicChunk chunk;
            fread(&chunk, sizeof(chunk), 1, fp);
            long nextChunkOffset = ftell(fp) + chunk.size - sizeof(chunk);
            ProcessChunk(chunk.type, bm);
            fseek(fp, nextChunkOffset, SEEK_SET);
            }
        }

// Seek to offset of next frame chunk

    fseek(fp, nextFrameOffset, SEEK_SET);

// Bump frame counter and return

    ++currFrame;
    return AERR_OK;
}
```

ReadNextSprite(), the alternate method for frame loading, is a no-brainer. Since FLIC files contain no hotspot information, it simply sets the hotspot to 0,0 and calls ReadNextFrame().

```
AError AFlcFile::ReadNextSprite(ASprite &sp, uchar *buff)
{
    sp.xoff = sp.yoff = 0;
    return(ReadNextFrame(sp, buff));
}
```

Reset(), used when looping back to the first frame of an animation, seeks the file pointer back to the frame 0 offset, which was saved off by the constructor.

```
void AFlcFile::Reset ()
{
    AAnmFile::Reset();                     // reset currFrame to 0
    fseek(fp, offsetFrame0, SEEK_SET);  // seek back to frame 0
}
```

Processing FLIC Chunks

The private method ProcessChunk() is used to process image data and palette chunks. Inside ProcessChunk(), image data chunks are handled by calling ReadRow() successively to retrieve each row of the image, and building up the BMF_LIN8 bitmap (passed in by reference) one row at a time. The ReadRow() method is passed in a current line skip count to aid those chunk types which do line-skipping. Certain chunk decoders update this counter whenever they encounter line-skipping tokens. At the beginning of the entire image, the counter is initialized to the special value −1 to indicate that this is the first row of the image. Some chunk types, such as FLI_SS2, have special header information at the beginning of the image; their readers need to know when they are being called for the first time.

```
#define SKIPLINES_FIRST   -1   // special indicator

void AFlcFile::ProcessChunk(int chunkType, ABitmap &bm)
{
    switch (chunkType)
        {
// Palette chunks:

        case FLI_COLOR256:
            ReadPalette(0);      // read palette with 8-bit colors
            break;

        case FLI_COLOR:
            ReadPalette(2);      // read palette, shifting 6-bit colors
            break;               // up by 2 bits into 8-bit form

// Frame bitmap chunks:

        case FLI_BLACK:
        case FLI_COPY:
        case FLI_BRUN:
        case FLI_LC:
        case FLI_SS2:
```

```
// Set up ptr to 1st row, signify that we aren't skipping any lines
// currently, and then loop through rows, reading them into bitmap.

        {
        uchar *pRow = bm.pbits;
        int skipLines = SKIPLINES_FIRST;
        for (int y = 0; y < bm.height; y++, pRow += bm.rowbytes)
            ReadRow(chunkType, pRow, skipLines, bm.width);
        }


// Ignore all other chunks

        default:
          break;
        }
}
```

Reading Palette Chunks

ReadPalette() reads a palette chunk. Remember FLI_COLOR256 chunks contain palette data with 8-bit color values and FLI_COLOR chunks contain 6-bit colors. Since we always want 8-bit RGB color values, ReadPalette() includes a shift value which is set to 0 in the case of 8-bit chunks and 2 for 6-bit chunks (shift them up 2 bits).

```
void AFlcFile::ReadPalette(int shift)
{
   ushort numPackets;
   uchar rgb[256 * 3];

// If we've already read a palette chunk, ignore subsequent
// updates. Our format can't handle palette changes during
// an animation.

   if (palette != NULL) return;

// Clear local rgb[] array to 0 so unused entries are black.

   memset(rgb, 0, sizeof(rgb));

// Read number of palette packets, and assume we're at index 0

   fread(&numPackets, sizeof(ushort), 1, fp);
   int palIndex = 0;

// For each packet, read index increment and rgb count.
// If count is 0, that means 256. Then read in colors into
// the proper slots in the rgb[] array, shifting into 8-bit form.

   for (int i = 0; i < numPackets; i++)
     {
     palIndex += fgetc(fp);              // bump pal index
```

```
    int count = fgetc(fp);               // get rgb count
    if (count == 0) count = 256;         // 0 means 256 entries
    uchar *prgb = rgb + (palIndex * 3);  // calc ptr into rgb[]
    for (int color = 0; color < count; color++, prgb += 3)
        {
        *(prgb+2) = fgetc(fp) << shift;   // read red first
        *(prgb+1) = fgetc(fp) << shift;   // then green
        *prgb = fgetc(fp) << shift;       // then blue
        }
    }

// Allocate a new palette with these rgb[] values

    palette = new APalette(rgb);

// Since we can't allow color 0 to be used (because it means 'skip'),
// find the closest color to the one at index 0, and assign
// its index to be substituted for 0 whenever it appears.

    FindZeroSubst();
}
```

ReadPalette() only bothers to read the palette on the first time through, which happens on frame 0. Subsequent calls to this routine are ignored, so palette animation won't happen. ReadPalette() also has another funny bit of behavior—it calls FindZeroSubst() after reading the palette in. What's this all about?

Remember that FLIC files can include color index 0 as well as transparency, whereas ARTT bitmaps reserve color 0 for transparency. So how can we read these animations into ARTT bitmaps and not get color 0 screwed up? We can by substituting another color index whenever we see 0. Which color index should we pick? The one whose color is closest to the color at index 0. FindZeroSubst() finds the closest color, by comparing the RGB values of each color in the palette to the one at color 0, and selecting the closest match. The theory behind such color math will be covered in Chapter 13—for now, you can just assume that it works. FindZeroSubst() stores the result in the member variable 'zeroSubst', where our image-reading routines can get at it.

```
void AFlcFile::FindZeroSubst()
{
    uchar cz[3];

// Get rgb color at index 0

    cz[0] = *palette->rgb;
    cz[1] = *(palette->rgb + 1);
    cz[2] = *(palette->rgb + 2);
```

```
// Start at index 1, and set our current best match to really really awful

   long diffBest = 999999;
   uchar *p = palette->rgb + 3;

// Loop thru colors 1 to 255, computing the squared distance in rgb
// space from color 0. If better than the best so far, mark in
// 'diffBest' and 'zeroSubst'.

   for (int i = 1; i < 256; i++)
      {
      long diff = 0;
      for (int comp = 0; comp < 3; comp++, p++)
         {
         if (*p < cz[comp])
            diff += (ushort) (cz[comp] - *p) * (ushort) (cz[comp] - *p);
         else
            diff += (ushort) (*p - cz[comp]) * (ushort) (*p - cz[comp]);
         }
      if (diff < diffBest)
         {
         diffBest = diff;
         zeroSubst = i;
         }
      }
}
```

Reading Image Data Chunks

ReadRow() reads the next row of the image data chunk into the supplied buffer, which ProcessChunk() sets to point to the appropriate row of the bitmap being loaded. ReadRow() must perform different actions depending on the chunk type, which tells how the image data is encoded in the file. Simple chunk types such as FLI_BLACK and FLI_COPY are handled directly, setting the row to a solid color or reading directly from a file. For the three compressed chunk types, an appropriate routine is called in each case to decode the row.

```
void AFlcFile::ReadRow(int chunkType, uchar *buff, int &skipLines,
   int width)
{
   switch (chunkType)
      {

// FLI_BLACK: just set the entire row to color index 0. Since this
// may mean a transparent frame, don't substitute for 0!!
      case FLI_BLACK:
         memset(buff, 0, width);
         break;

// FLI_COPY: read row directly from file, substitute all 0's.
```

```
            case FLI_COPY:
                fread(buff, width, 1, fp);
                SubstZero(buff, width);
                break;

    // FLI_BRUN: decompress byte-wide run-length row

            case FLI_BRUN:
                ReadBrunRow(buff, width);
                break;

    // FLI_LC: decompress byte-wide delta-encoded row

            case FLI_LC:
                ReadByteDeltaRow(buff, skipLines, width);
                break;

    // FLI_SS2: decompress word-wide delta-encoded row

            case FLI_SS2:
                ReadWordDeltaRow(buff, skipLines, width);
                break;
            }
    }
```

Decoding FLI_BRUN, FLI_LC, and FLI_SS2 Rows

ReadBrunRow() reads a row from a FLI_BRUN run-length-encoded
frame. See the discussion earlier in this chapter for more information on the exact form of this chunk. Note how 'zeroSubst' is substi-
tuted for 0 in a run packet, and SubstZero() is called to do the same
for an entire array of pixels in a dump packet.

```
void AFlcFile::ReadBrunRow(uchar *buff, int width)
{
    fgetc(fp);                   // first byte is unused packet count
    int numPixels = width;       // count down width

    while (numPixels > 0)                        // loop till row complete
        {
        signed char typeCount = fgetc(fp);       // grab packet header
        if (typeCount & 0x80)                    // check hibit for dump/run
            {
            typeCount = -typeCount;              // dump: negate hdr for count
            fread(buff, typeCount, 1, fp);       // read 'count' bytes from file
            SubstZero(buff, typeCount);          // substitute 0s
            }
        else
            {
            int c = fgetc(fp);                   // run: next byte is value
            if (c == 0) c = zeroSubst;           // if 0, substitute it
            memset(buff, c, typeCount);          // and set that many bytes
```

```
      }
    buff += typeCount;                    // bump row buffer ptr
    numPixels -= typeCount;               // and decrement width count
    }
}
```

ReadByteDeltaRow() is used to decode a row of an FLI_LC chunk. This and the FLI_SS2 chunks contain line skipping, and care is taken to preserve a current line skip count across the successive calls to this routine, one per row.

```
void AFlcFile::ReadByteDeltaRow(uchar *buff, int &skipLines, int width)
{
static ushort numChunkRows;         // used to count down active rows

// If 1st row in frame, read row skip count and number of active rows

    if (skipLines == SKIPLINES_FIRST)
        {
        ushort skip;
        fread(&skip, sizeof(ushort), 1, fp);
        skipLines = skip;
        fread(&numChunkRows, sizeof(ushort), 1, fp);
        }

// If we're currently skipping rows at the top of the frame, or
// have run through all active frames, set this row to fully
// transparent. If we're skipping at the top, count down skip.

    if (skipLines || (numChunkRows == 0))
        {
        memset(buff, 0, width);
        if (skipLines)
            --skipLines;
        return;
        }

// Read packet count, and calculate ptr to end of row

    uchar numPackets = fgetc(fp);
    uchar *buffEnd = buff + width;

// Process all packets

    while (numPackets--> 0)
        {
        uchar columnSkip = fgetc(fp);       // get column skip count
        if (columnSkip)
            {
            memset(buff, 0, columnSkip);    // if non-zero count,
            buff += columnSkip;             // set pixels to 0
            }
```

```
        signed char typeCount = fgetc(fp);   // get packet type/count
        if (typeCount & 0x80)                 // check for dump or run packet
            {
            typeCount = -typeCount;           // run: invert for count
            uchar c = fgetc(fp);              // get pixel value
            if (c == 0) c = zeroSubst;        // if 0, substitute
            memset(buff, c, typeCount);       // and set pixels in row
            }
        else
            {
            fread(buff, typeCount, 1, fp);    // dump: read directly into row
            SubstZero(buff, typeCount);       // substitute 0s
            }
        buff += typeCount;                    // bump buffer ptr
        }

    if (buff < buffEnd)                       // if row not fully written
        memset(buff, 0, buffEnd - buff);      // append 0s to fill it out
    numChunkRows--;                           // decrement active row count
}
```

ReadWordDeltaRow() reads a row from an FLI_SS2 chunk. Like ReadByteDeltaRow(), it maintains a line-skip count across invocations.

```
void AFlcFile::ReadWordDeltaRow(uchar *buff, int &skipLines, int width)
{
static ushort numChunkRows;   // used to count down active row chunks

// If 1st row in frame, read number of active chunk rows

    if (skipLines == SKIPLINES_FIRST)
        {
        fread(&numChunkRows, sizeof(ushort), 1, fp);
        skipLines = 0;
        }

// If we're currently skipping lines anywhere in the frame, or if
// we've run out of active rows, set the entire row to transparent.
// If we're skipping rows, count down skip.

    if (skipLines || (numChunkRows == 0))
        {
        memset(buff, 0, width);
        if (skipLines)
            --skipLines;
        return;
        }

// Read packet count field

    short packetCount;
    fread(&packetCount, sizeof(short), 1, fp);
```

```
// If 11xxxxxx xxxxxxxx, negate to get line skip count

   if ((packetCount & 0xC000) == 0xC000)
      {
      skipLines = -packetCount;  // get line skip count
      memset(buff, 0, width);    // set this row to transparent
      --skipLines;               // we just skipped this row
      return;                    // and we're done with this row
      }

// Else check for 10xxxxxx vvvvvvvv, if so grab value of last
// byte in row. If no such packet, mark 'lastByte' as -1.

   short lastByte = -1;
   if ((packetCount & 0xC000) == 0x8000)
      {
      lastByte = packetCount & 0xFF;
      fread(&packetCount, sizeof(short), 1, fp);
      }

// Process packets in a loop

   uchar *buffEnd = buff + width; // set buffEnd to end of row
   while (packetCount-- > 0)
      {
// Get # pixels to skip over, and skip them

      uchar columnSkip = fgetc(fp);
      if (columnSkip)
         {
         memset(buff, 0, columnSkip);
         buff += columnSkip;
         }

// Get type/count field, check for dump or run packet

      signed char typeCount = fgetc(fp);
      if (typeCount & 0x80)
         {
// Run packet, read word pixel pair, do tricky stuff to check
// both pixels for 0 and substitute. Then set that many pixel
// pairs in the row.

         ushort word;
         fread(&word, sizeof(ushort), 1, fp);
         if ((word & 0xFF00) == 0)
            word = (word & 0xFF) | (ushort(zeroSubst) << 8);
         if ((word & 0xFF) == 0)
            word = (word & 0xFF00) | zeroSubst;
         typeCount = -typeCount;
         for (int i = 0; i < typeCount; i++)
            {
            *(ushort *)buff = word;
            buff += sizeof(ushort);
```

```
                    }
                }
            else
                {
// Dump packet: read pixel pairs directly into buffer, then do a
// pass over them to substitute 0s.

                fread(buff, typeCount * sizeof(ushort), 1, fp);
                SubstZero(buff, typeCount * sizeof(ushort));
                buff += typeCount * sizeof(ushort);
                }
            }


// After all packets processed, fill remainder of row with 0.

        if (buff < buffEnd)
            {
            memset(buff, 0, buffEnd - buff);
            buff = buffEnd;
            }


// If got a last byte value, jam it at end of row

        if (lastByte >= 0)
            *(buff - 1) = lastByte;

// Count down number of active chunk rows

        numChunkRows--;
    }
```

The routines listed above use the SubstZero() method to replace all 0s in an array of pixels with the closest color match. SubstZero() is listed below.

```
void AFlcFile::SubstZero(uchar *p, ushort len)
{
    while (len--)
        {
        if (*p == 0)
            *p = zeroSubst;
        ++p;
        }
}
```

ANIMPLAY: An Animation File Player

We've developed a lot of code for reading animation files without much context. How do we use these classes to put animated images onto the screen? The AAnmFile interface allows for multiple methods. One way is to Open() the file, read each frame with Read-NextFrame() and display it, use FreeFrame() to free up each frame's data if it was allocated, and Reset() to loop or stop the animation at the last frame. The **ANIMPLAY** tool uses this method to play back an animation onto the screen.

ANIMPLAY is simple to use, just type:

```
ANIMPLAY filename        // (e.g., ANIMPLAY someflic.flc)
```

The code for this tool is listed below. Most of it is setup; the actual animation-handling code is pretty small.

```cpp
//    AnimPlay.cpp    FLIC file player
//    Rex E. Bradford

#include <stdio.h>
#include <stdlib.h>
#include <conio.h>

#include "aanmfile.h"
#include "amodel3.h"
#include "avesa.h"
#include "avga.h"
#include "atime.h"

#define USEBUFF

void main(int argc, char **argv)
{
// Check args

    if (argc < 2)
        {
        printf("usage: animplay filename\n");
        exit(1);
        }

// Open animation file

    AError err;
    AAnmFile *pAnmFile = AAnmFile::OpenRead(argv[1], err);
    if (err)
        {
        printf("Problem with anim file: %s (%s)\n", argv[1],
            AErr::Msg(err));
        exit(1);
        }
    AnimDesc *pAnimDesc = pAnmFile->GetAnimDesc();

// Allocate frame buffer
```

```
#ifdef USEBUFF
   uchar *frameBuff = ABitmap::Alloc(pAnimDesc->maxFrameLen);
   if (frameBuff == NULL)
      {
      printf("Unable to allocate buffer of size: $%x\n",
         pAnimDesc->maxFrameLen);
      exit(1);
      }
#endif

// Set screen mode

   bool hiRez = FALSE;
   if ((pAnimDesc->width > 320) || (pAnimDesc->height > 200))
      {
      if (!AVesa::Launch(640, 480, 8))
         {
         printf("Unable to launch 640×480,8 VESA mode\n",
            AErr::Msg(err));
         exit(1);
         }
      hiRez = TRUE;
      }
   else
      AModel3::Launch();

// Replay animation.

REPLAY:

// Read time, start 1st frame now

   AFix tNext = ATime::Read();
   int c = 0;

// Loop thru all frames

   while (pAnmFile->More())
      {
// Load next frame

      ABitmap bm;
      AError err;
#ifdef USEBUFF
      err = pAnmFile->ReadNextFrame(bm, frameBuff);
#else
      err = pAnmFile->ReadNextFrame(bm);
#endif
      if (err)
         {
         if (hiRez)
            AVesa::Term();
```

```
            else
                AMode13::Term();
            printf("Problem with animation (%s)\n", AErr::Msg(err));
            exit(1);
            }

// Wait for time to display frame

        if (pAnimDesc->frameDur != AFix(0))
            {
            while (ATime::Read() < tNext)
                {}
            tNext += pAnimDesc->frameDur;
            }

// Display frame, including palette on frame 1

        if ((pAnmFile->CurrFrame() == 1) && pAnmFile->HasPalette())
            AVga::SetDAC(pAnmFile->GetPalettePtr()->rgb);
        gCanvasScreen->DrawBitmap(bm, 0, 0);

// Free frame

        pAnmFile->FreeFrame(bm);

// If key, repeat or bail out

        if (kbhit())
            {
            c = getch();
            break;
            }
        }

// Bailed out or finished anim, get keystroke, ESC exits, else loop

    if (c != 0x1B)
        {
        pAnmFile->Reset();
        goto REPLAY;
        }

// Exiting, return to text mode

    if (hiRez)
        AVesa::Term();
    else
        AMode13::Term();
    }
```

The ASA Animation File Format

We've spent a lot of time talking about the Tower of Babel of file formats for graphic images and animations. We're going to revisit this topic again now. But this time, instead of whining, we're going to join the party! Let's invent a new animation file format, right now!

Are we insane? (Why am I always talking in the plural, anyway?) *Uh-oh*, 300 pages at the word processor and the twig has finally snapped. No, actually there are good reasons for inventing your own file formats—if I don't create a new one every month I feel I'm missing something. In this case, the reasoning has to do with the time it takes to decode FLIC file chunks into bitmaps and sprites. Since ARTT can only work with BMF_LIN8 and BMF_RLE8 8-bit bitmapped images, every time we load a frame from a FLIC file we have to convert it. This takes valuable time and can get quite annoying if we want to load and use a large number of animations. Further, converting directly from encoded FLIC image chunks to BMF_RLE8 bitmaps is complex and not included in our current AFlcFile implementation, so if we want BMF_RLE8 bitmaps we have to decode from FLIC chunk to BMF_LIN8 bitmap, then encode to BMF_RLE8. This is twice as much work.

Wouldn't it be nice if we could just read BMF_LIN8 and BMF_RLE8 frames directly from an animation file? Then the promise of a "sprite array on a disk" would really be met. But since no commercial programs make use of this format that we're about to invent, how do we get animations in this format? We write a conversion program, of course, and convert FLIC files into the new format. Since this conversion is done in an off-line tool and not in our "real" application, the conversion time is free.

The new format will be very simple: a very small header with overall descriptive information, followed by a color palette for 8-bit animations, followed by a series of sprites. Since this file really is basically a disk-based sprite array, we'll choose the extension ASA: ARTT Sprite Array.

Layout of an ASA Animation File

Figure 9.9 summarizes the layout of an ASA file. It consists of only very basic information, including number of frames and their width and height, color depth (so we can put 15-bit and 24-bit images into these files eventually), frame duration, and maximum frame length, to aid programs in allocating their buffers. This information is an AnimDesc, which we defined as an information structure when creating the AAnmFile file reader class. The ASA file header is merely an

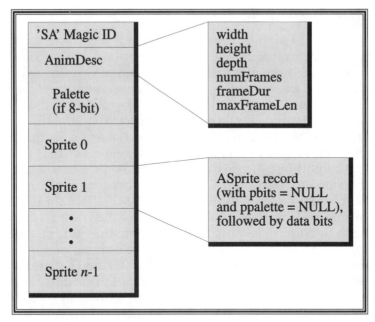

Figure 9.9   Layout of an ASA file.

AnimDesc, preceded by a two-byte identifier consisting of the letters 'SA', for Sprite Array.

If the 'depth' setting of the AnimDesc header is set to 8, and only then, a 256-entry color palette immediately follows the header. For 15-bit and 24-bit images, if we ever have any, a palette is not necessary. Note that we are assuming that all images in the file have the same number of bits per pixel, which we will make a requirement. Since we may want to use the ASA format for storage of large numbers of sprites which are not part of an animation per se, we won't require that all frames have the same width and height. The width and height fields in the header are merely advisory, and are not to be used in lieu of an actual frame sprite's width and height.

Immediately following the header and optional palette is a contiguous set of sprites, the number of which is noted in the header (there is no termination marker in the file). Sprites need not all be the same size, both because the width and height may vary, and because BMF_RLE8 sprites are subject to a variable amount of compression. The ASprite data fields, which are delineated in the ASprite and ancestor ABitmap classes, are stored "as is" in the file, except that the 'pbits' and 'ppalette' pointer fields are set to 0 in the file, and reconstructed on loading. Immediately following the ASprite data fields in each case are the data bits representing the image itself, in whatever format is signified by the ASprite 'format' member. Figure 9.10 shows the layout of a sprite in the ASA file.

Class AsaFile: A Class for Reading and Writing ASA Files

Class AsaFile, unlike AFlcFile, supports both reading and writing. The public interface to AsaFile is identical to that of AFlcFile. The header file for this class is listed below.

```
//   AsaFile.h    Animation reader for ARTT .asa files
//   Rex E. Bradford

#ifndef __ASAFILE_H
#define __ASAFILE_H

#include "aanmfile.h"

class AsaFile : public AAnmFile {

    friend class AAnmFile;  // so it can call our constructor

    char *fname;     // ptr to filename

// Constructor and destructor: private - used by AAnmFile

    AsaFile(char *filename, FILE *fp, bool read, AError &err);
    ~AsaFile();
```

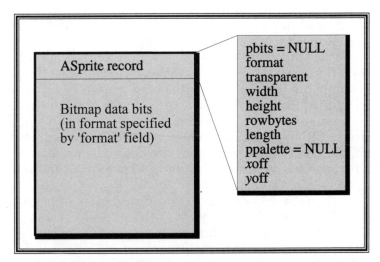

Figure 9.10 Format of a sprite in an ASA file.

```
// Internal methods to read/write file header

   AError ReadHeader();     // read in ASA header
   AError WriteHeader();    // write out ASA header

public:

// Read next frame as bitmap or sprite, reset to start

   AError ReadNextFrame(ABitmap &bm, uchar *buff = NULL);
   AError ReadNextSprite(ASprite &sp, uchar *buff = NULL);
   void Reset();

// Write next frame

   AError WriteNextFrame(ABitmap &bm, bool compress = TRUE);
   AError WriteNextSprite(ASprite &sp, bool compress = TRUE);
};

#endif
```

The implementation of this class is not listed—see the CD for full source. The implementation is pretty straightforward, since there is such a one-to-one mapping between sprites in memory and on disk in ASA files. WriteNextFrame() and WriteNextSprite() will, if the 'compress' argument is TRUE, compress BMF_LIN8 bitmaps into BMF_RLE8 format as they are written to disk.

ANM2ANM: Converting Animations Between Formats

Now that we can read FLIC files and write ASA files, we can write our handy tool to convert FLICs to ASA format. ANM2ANM reads from one animation file and writes to another.

One important caveat bears mentioning. The FLIC file format, by definition, stores each frame as the *delta* from the previous frame. When using bitmaps or sprites read from a FLIC format, they must be applied to a buffer which contains the previous frame, and cannot be used standalone. This applies to ASA files created by conversion from FLIC using ANM2ANM, which will also contain delta frames. If standalone animation frames are desired, create a PCX or BMP file with each frame inside a border, and use GFX2ANM (described next) to create an ASA file.

The source code is not reproduced here, but can be found in the file ANM2ANM.CPP on the CD-ROM. ANM2ANM is invoked from the command line as follows:

```
ANM2ANM infile outfile // e.g., ANM2ANM myflic.flc myflic.asa
```

GFX2ANM: Extracting Graphic Images into Animation Format

As stated earlier, the ASA format is ideal for storing sprite arrays. In the last chapter, we saw how multiple bordered images in a single graphics file could be used for sprite storage. Let's put the two together via another tool. GFX2ANM reads all the bordered images in a graphics file, and writes them out into an animation file as a sprite array (an ASA file now, or eventually any other derived animation file class). Reading sprites from an ASA file is more direct than reading a graphics file and extracting them using class ABitmapFind. GFX2ANM moves this "bitmap searching" into an off-line tool, so your program can read its sprites directly from convenient ASA files.

The source code for this tool can be found on the CD-ROM in file GFX2ANM.CPP. I would love to include the source for all these tools here in the book, but my editor is standing out on the ledge and claiming she *will* jump.

GFX2ANM is invoked as follows:

```
GFX2ANM infile outfile bordcol  // i.e., GFX2ANM imgset.pcx imgset.asa 255
```

ASALIST: Peering Inside an ASA File

An ASA file is a black box, unusable by programs outside the ARTT toolkit. To help in debugging problems which may arise when using ASA files, the ASALIST program is included. ASALIST prints out the file's header, and then prints information on each sprite, including its width, height, bitmap format, and so on. The output may be redirected to a file for viewing with a text editor.

ASALIST is invoked from the command line as follows:

```
ASALIST asafile [>outfile]     // i.e., ASALIST myanim.asa >myanim.out
```

ANIMVIEW: A Visual Look Inside an Animation File

Another tool, ANIMVIEW, allows a visual peek inside an ASA file or FLIC file. ANIMVIEW renders each frame of the animation, and waits for a key before proceeding to the next. Use the ESCAPE key to exit. ANIMVIEW is handy for viewing each sprite in an ASA file. It also provides an interesting "look under the hood" for FLIC files, showing each delta frame by itself. You can get a good idea of how much change exists in each frame of a FLIC file using this tool.

ANIMVIEW is run as shown below:

```
ANIMVIEW animfile      // i.e., ANIMVIEW someflic.flc
```

With these tools, we are now unleashed to scarf up animations and put them in a convenient-to-use format. It's getting to be time to do something with them! The next chapter will get the screen action happening in a big way, as we get into the composition of multiple moving, animating sprites against a scrolling background.

C H A P T E R

Scene Composition

In this chapter, the rubber hits the road. Part 1 laid the foundation by developing a system for loading and rendering static graphics, and the previous two chapters added bitmapped animation to our toolbox. Now, we're going to begin building the next level, the composition of fully animated *scenes*. By *composition* I mean the seamless display of multiple moving and animating elements, rendered with correct overlap. These *actors* can move across the scene, animate, and scale in size. The scene itself can *scroll* in *x* and *y* directions, and can itself be scaled when *blitted* to the screen. This chapter marks our entry into the big leagues of screen manipulation.

Screen Composition Methodologies

What's composition all about? Haven't we been doing fine so far drawing bitmaps and sprites and animations? The problem with our current techniques is that they fail to work properly if we try to draw an object which moves across the screen. Remember the bouncing ball from Chapter 2, which needed a black border around it to avoid leaving trails? Figure 10.1 is a screen shot showing what would hap-

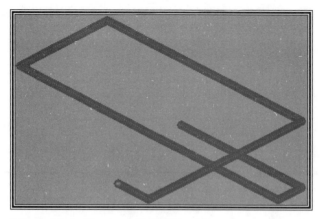

Figure 10.1   Version of BBALL without border to erase previous images.

pen without such a crutch, if we tried to draw a transparent ball in new positions without figuring out a way to *erase* the previous image.

The problem is not limited to moving objects. In an animated sprite which has transparency, what happens when we naively draw one frame of an animation on top of another? As Figure 10.2 shows, the "holes" in the new frame show pieces of the old frame. Since these holes are supposed to be transparent, they just aren't drawn, and the old frame is never erased.

It gets worse. How about two moving objects? They do badly enough by themselves, leaving trails behind them, but when they overlap the result depends on the order in which they get drawn. If object A is supposed to always be in front of object B, how do we ensure this when it comes time to draw object B, which may be occupying the same screen position as object A? Figure 10.3 illustrates the problem.

Composition Solutions Through the Ages

All is not lost. There are several ways of making sure our objects get erased and redrawn properly when they move and animate. The major screen update techniques used over the short history of computer graphics include:

- Exclusive-or rendering
- Hardware overlays
- Saveunders
- Hardware double-buffering ("page flipping")
- Software double-buffering

Let's look at each of these methods.

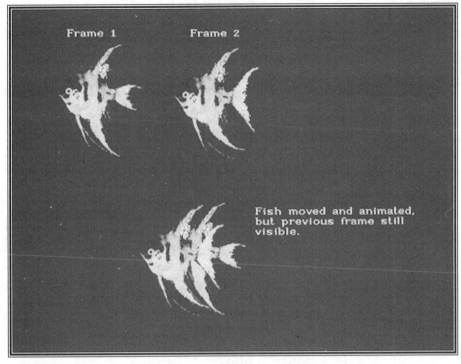

Figure 10.2 This is what happens if a transparent image is animated without erasing previous frame.

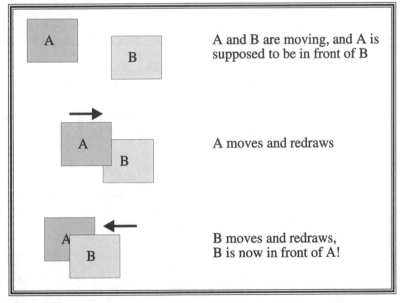

Figure 10.3 Moving object problem—if B moves and overlaps A, priority is incorrect.

Exclusive-Or Rendering

I only bring up this technique in an attempt to ridicule it so thoroughly that no computer graphics writer ever mentions it again. It is amazing that in the 1990s, with graphics systems powerful enough to render realistic full-screen 3D scenes in real time, writers still sometimes refer to this laughable hack as a realistic way of erasing old images and drawing new ones, as if anybody doing real graphics work has actually used it in the past two decades. What are these guys on?

There. I've done my bit for future generations. Now, what is exclusive-or rendering, you might ask out of baffled curiosity at this point? C and C++ programmers should be aware of the exclusive-or mathematical operator, denoted by the '^' symbol, as it is very handy for bit manipulation, along with its cousins 'and' ('&') and 'or' ('|'). The exclusive-or operator takes two arguments, and performs a bitwise (bit at a time) combination. The resulting value has a 1 in each bit position where the two input values have different values, and a 0 where they are the same. The "truth table" for each bit in the operation is given in Table 10.1.

For example, the value 0x07 exclusive-or'ed with 0x11 would be 0x16, because in binary:

```
00000111 ^ 00010001 = 00010110 // result has 1 where bits differ
```

What does this have to do with computer graphics? Well, an interesting property of the exclusive-or operator is that it can be applied a second time to recover the original value. For instance:

```
0x07 ^ 0x11 = 0x16      // 0000111 ^ 0010001 = 00010110
0x16 ^ 0x11 = 0x07!!    // 00010110 ^ 00010001 = 00000111
```

In monochrome graphics systems, where exclusive-or rendering was invented, drawing an image on a blank background by copying

Table 10.1 Truth Table for Exclusive-Or

Operand 1	Operand 2	Result	
0	0	0	// bits are the same, result is 0
0	1	1	// bits differ, result is 1
1	0	1	// bits differ, result is 1
1	1	0	// bits are the same, result is 0

is identical to doing so by exclusive-oring each image pixel with its destination pixel. Since the (blank) screen pixel starts out at 0, a 0 image pixel will get drawn as 0 (0 ^ 0 = 0), and a 1 image pixel will get drawn as 1 (0 ^ 1 = 1). The interesting part is that the image can be erased by drawing it a second time, if exclusive-or is used to "set" each pixel. The 1 pixel set the first time around, when exclusive-or'ed with 1, returns a 0 to the display.

Thus, a monochrome image can be moved about a blank background trivially. Just erase it by "drawing" it a second time, using exclusive-or, then draw it at the new position. What about backdrops that aren't black to begin with, and what about multiple overlapping objects? Here, the exclusive-or hack doesn't quite work. A pixel where two images overlap and each draws 1 pixel cancel to form a 0! The good news, I guess, is that when both images are erased, at least the screen pixel returns to its original value. The original use of exclusive-or rendering was for drawing wireframe models (like all new technologies, the bitmapped display was first used to recreate its predecessor, in this case the vector display), and it is a clever hack that isn't correct but worked well enough for that use.

What about color bitmapped images? Ha ha. Let's try it. Take a purple pixel in an 8-bit indexed color image. What's the color index of purple? I don't know—it could be anything—it depends on the palette. Suppose in our palette it happens to be color value 0x33. Now suppose we are drawing this pixel onto a blue background, which happens to be color 0x02 in this case. What gets drawn? Let's see, 0x33 ^ 0x02 = 0x31. What color is at 0x31? Who knows, let's say it happens to be yellow. That's just great. We go to draw purple on blue, and get yellow. At least when we draw it again, we get back to blue. I'm just *so* excited about using exclusive-or rendering for my next game.

Let's move on.

Hardware Overlays

"Graphics programmers do it as fast as they can, but still wish the hardware just did it by itself" is a bumper sticker I keep looking for. It's a valid point, though—why can't the graphics hardware handle the overlaying of images? We've been assuming that the screen is represented by a single bitmap, since that's the framework laid down since the start of this book and describes all current PC graphics hardware pretty well. Is this the only way to design a graphics system?

Of course not. The $100 video game systems from Nintendo or SEGA provide hardware which solves the bulk of the problem we've been grappling with. Instead of just one screen bitmap, they include a whole bunch of them, stacked one on top of the other. To conserve expensive memory, the bitmaps don't have to all be full-screen in size, other than the screen backdrop. These *hardware sprites* each have their own little bitmap representing a single object's image. The display hardware overlays the full set of images on the fly as it scans them out to the monitor. There is never a single bitmap which collects the full state of the display—it is continually pieced together on the fly by the hardware overlay circuitry. Figure 10.4 illustrates this design.

With such hardware overlays, the hard stuff of composition becomes easy. To move an object, just change the hardware x,y position of the sprite. Presto, it's in a new location, and no erasing need be done. To change the shape of an object, redraw into its private bitmap. Here you do have to take care to erase the old image, but at least you don't have to worry about overlap with other objects or the background. To delete an object permanently, just "turn off" the hardware sprite. Graphics programmers could be out of work if this stuff caught on! Wow, is this fantastic capability part of the new SuperVGA accelerator cards?

Luckily for those of us who need to make a living pushing pixels the hard way, real graphics system architects don't take their design ideas from cheapo $100 toy machines. Actually, lately SVGA cards have been coming with one hardware overlay, namely for the mouse cursor, which is the only sprite officially sanctioned in the business world, I suppose. Your teenager has about a hundred hardware

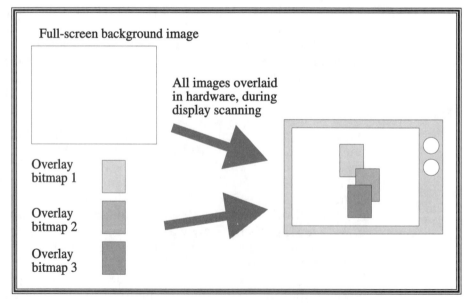

Figure 10.4   Graphics system featuring hardware "sprite" overlays.

sprites at his command, you've finally got your first. If you show you can take care of it responsibly, maybe they'll give you a second.

Saveunders

One way to erase an image is to save what's underneath before drawing it into a memory buffer (a bitmap, in fact). Then, erasing an image is as simple as drawing the "saveunder" bitmap back to the screen. To replace an image with a new transparent frame, simply draw the saveunder back before drawing the new frame. To move an object, follow these three steps: (1) Draw the saveunder back to the screen, (2) capture a new saveunder at the new location, and (3) draw the object. Moving an animated object works with this method as well. Figure 10.5 illustrates this very simple technique.

If there are multiple images on the screen, each can have its own saveunder buffer. Multiple images is this method's Achilles heel, though. What if two images overlap? Some of the problems are illustrated in Figure 10.6. First, there is the problem that when we move an image, we draw it on top of other images, even if it should be behind them. But that's just the beginning of the trouble. When we go to move image A to an area overlapping image B, A's new saveunder includes part of image B! Now, if we move B, its saveunder wipes out

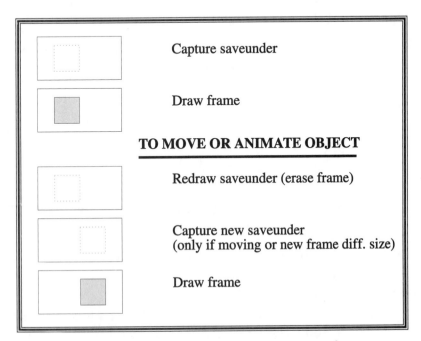

Figure 10.5 Moving and animating objects using saveunders.

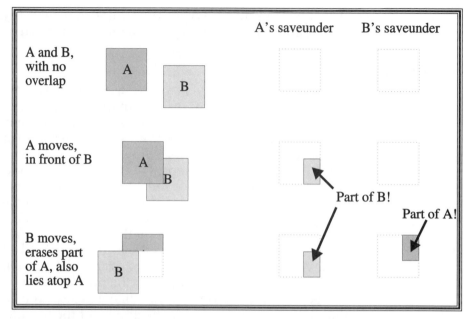

A's saveunder   B's saveunder

A and B,
with no
overlap

A moves,
in front of B

Part of B!

Part of A!

B moves,
erases part
of A, also
lies atop A

Figure 10.6   Some of the problems associated with simple saveunder buffering.

part of A. As A and B move apart, we are likely to leave part of one behind (because it will have been grabbed in the other's saveunder buffer).

These overlap problems can be solved. One solution is to erase all objects at once, writing back saveunder buffers in the reverse order from which they were grabbed, move all objects, get new saveunders for all objects, and then draw all of them. A more complex solution is to do the above for only "necessary" objects, which are those whose saveunders overlap the area being updated (or which overlap saveunders which overlap the area of interest!).

There's another problem with saveunders. All this erasing and redrawing causes unsightly glitches on the screen, where for a small fraction of a second an image disappears entirely. When lots of images are moving and animating, the flashing can be incredibly annoying. What's needed is a way to do this erasing and redrawing off the screen somehow, and present the finished result to the screen. The next two techniques provide this seamless update.

Hardware Double-Buffering

Graphics cards nowadays hold 1, 2, and even 4 megabytes of memory. If a 800 × 600 8-bit-per-pixel screen takes only half a megabyte to represent, is the rest of that video memory wasted? Not necessarily. It is possible to use this memory as an "off-screen" screen. The video memory can be written to just like the screen memory, only it's not visible. Clearly we can use this to prepare an off-screen picture of what we want the screen to look like, and we can also use bitmap copying operations to move these pixels to the "real" screen memory.

We can do even better. Graphics cards have a *start address* which tells them the address of the upper-left pixel to begin screen display at. In other words, the portion of video memory being viewed can be changed. So it's possible to have two "screens" in video memory, A and B. We can take advantage of this capability. While screen A is being displayed, software is busily updating B, erasing and redrawing and doing all sorts of unsightly pixel operations invisibly. Then, when the job is done, the VGA is reprogrammed to display portion B, and updating of A begins. This technique is called *hardware double-buffering*, and is also known as *page flipping*. Figure 10.7 illustrates the technique.

The software techniques used to update the "screen" which is not being viewed vary. The simplest technique is to redraw the entire contents of the screen from scratch, from back to front. It's simple and can't miss, but has the disadvantage of requiring a lot of rendering, which takes time. Still, a lot of commercial programs do just

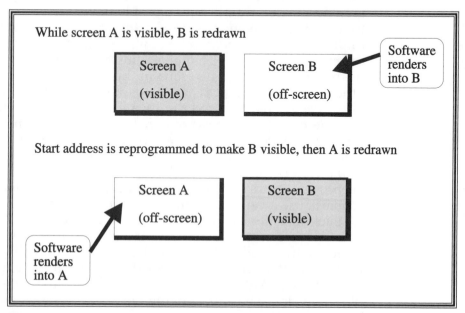

Figure 10.7   Hardware double-buffering (page flipping) in operation.

that. As an alternative, the saveunder technique previously discussed can be applied to hardware double-buffering. In this case, each of the two screens needs its own set of saveunders.

One problem with hardware double-buffering is that not all video modes and display cards can handle it. Dumb old mode 13H, which requires only 64K of video memory, is set up in hardware in such a way that the start address can't be reprogrammed to point to a second screen, no matter how much video memory there is. Other high-resolution video modes may easily use more than half the video memory of the card, which rules out a second screen. For this reason, hardware double-buffering can't be relied upon exclusively.

Software Double-Buffering

We've spent a fair portion of this book showing how a screen is just a bitmap. We have a class, ACanvasLin8, which can be used to render into any portion of linear memory, not just the screen. This memory can be located in system memory, for instance, allocated with new(). If we don't have enough video memory for a second screen, or the video hardware won't let us page flip the display between two hardware screens, maybe we can put the second screen in system memory.

Assuming we have the system memory for a full second screen (and this can run from 64K to over a megabyte depending on the graphics mode), we still have a problem. We can't force the hardware to display our "memory screen." However, we *can* copy those pixels to the real screen, and with luck we can do it quickly enough to fool the eye into thinking it happened instantaneously. In software double-buffering, we have two screens, but one is always visible, and the other is always "under repair," creating the next image. Figure 10.8 illustrates simple full-screen software double-buffering.

We pay the overhead of copying the entire frame from system memory to video memory every time we want an update, unless we can figure out how to copy *only the portions of the screen that have changed since the last frame.* There are several ways to represent and keep track of this information, and good software double-buffering schemes use a variety of schemes to copy as few pixels as they need to. Such schemes can do more than limit the amount of pixels copied from off-screen to screen—they can also limit redrawing of the off-screen buffer itself. Instead of redrawing the entire off-screen system memory buffer every frame, only those portions which are changing are redrawn. Within these areas, a full back-to-front redraw of all objects is done, but unchanging parts of the screen are unaffected. When rectangular areas are used to mark these "areas of update,"

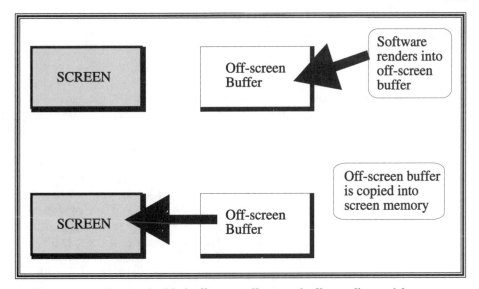

Figure 10.8   Software double-buffering. Off-screen buffer is allocated from system memory.

this optimization is often called *dirty rectangle* animation. The name is a little odd—the screen areas are not dirty, just in need of update—and probably has its genesis in the use of the term "dirty bit" in operating systems, to mark areas of a file which have changed and need to be rewritten to disk.

   ARTT uses software double-buffering exclusively. It keeps track of a list of dirty rectangular areas which need to be updated, and does a full back-to-front redraw of all objects into each of these areas. The theory and coding of this process is covered in further sections of this chapter.

ARTT Composition: Scenes and Actors

Because of its flexibility and universality, we're going to develop a software double-buffering scheme for ARTT and use it exclusively for screen composition. Before we jump in and do further design, let's step back and think about what we want such a system to accomplish. A screen composition methodology is intimately related to the overall screen architecture. For instance, do we want to support overlapping "windows" on the screen? Do we need windows at all, or should we just treat the screen as one big window? Does there need to be a one-to-one correspondence between pixels in our off-screen buffer and screen pixels, or do we want to support scaling windows?

What kinds of objects will inhabit a given window, and what capabilities will they have?

Scenes

Microsoft Windows manages multiple windows for us, so it's a nobrainer to build multiwindow support in this environment. Under DOS, we would have to do this work ourselves. Basically, it is trivial to support multiple windows, as long as they don't overlap. If we can have one instance of a window, we can have several. Window overlap is less trivial, as it means that the transfer of pixels from off-screen memory to the screen needs to take into account whether part of the window is obscured by another one. This problem is certainly not insurmountable, but it's no picnic either. Although it's a close call, we're going to punt window overlap under DOS, and require that DOS "windows" occupy distinct screen areas.

We will call such a window a *scene,* to avoid confusing it with the windows of Microsoft Windows or other graphical operating environments. A scene occupies a distinct rectangular area on the screen, and has a system-memory buffer backing it up (the double buffer). If the screen area does not match the double buffer in pixel width and height, the buffer is scaled when rendered to the screen.

A scene can be thought of as a view into some world of objects, and has its own "world coordinate system" in which those objects are located. The scene can scroll in x and y directions through this coordinate system, and object positions are scrolled accordingly. The scene has no inherent graphics other than an optional background color—all other graphics, including bitmapped backdrops, are provided by the objects, or *actors,* associated with the scene. See Figure 10.9.

Actors

The primary component of a scene is the list of actors which inhabit it. Each actor has a position in the scene's world coordinate system in x and y, as well as a z-coordinate which is used to control overlap ordering, and optional scaling of the object (which is distinct from scaling of the entire scene). Actors are members of some actor class—a base actor class implements such basics as inclusion in a scene, depth ordering, and motion. Derived classes provide specific rendering techniques and other behavior, such as response to mouse clicks on them. Derived actor classes included in ARTT provide the following kinds of scene objects, and more can be easily developed:

- Backdrops, including tiled and scrolling backdrops
- Sprites, including transparency and scaling based on z-coordinate

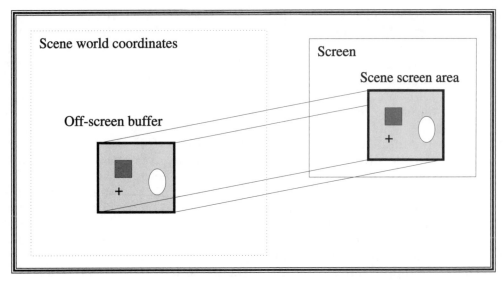

Figure 10.9   Scene window on screen, and off-screen buffer "located" in world coordinate system.

- Animated sprites
- Graphical user interface components such as buttons and icons

Actor classes are fairly simple to write, as the hard part of composition is done within the scene class.

Class AScene: A Window on a World

Class AScene will manage a scene, or window, on the display. In applications, we'll use derived scene classes depending on our graphic environment. Classes ASceneDos and ASceneWin will handle the two environments covered in this book. However, most of the "action" is in AScene—the others exist mainly to provide the "screen copying" mechanism.

The primary responsibility for the scene is to manage the list of actors inside it, as they will provide all of the graphic display inside the scene, with the exception of an optional background color that the scene can draw itself. Under DOS, such windows will be "raw" windows in the sense that they will not include a frame of any kind (no title bar or border). If we desire, we can create actors to provide this functionality. Under Windows, there will be a one-to-one correspondence between a scene and a window (using class AWingWindow from Chapter 7), and the scene fits into the client area of the window. The window may have whatever frame it wants surrounding the scene, courtesy of Windows.

Besides keeping a list of actors, another responsibility of the scene is managing the "update strategy," which defines how the screen is updated when changes in the scene and its actors occur. Class AScene provides a simple update strategy, in which the entire scene is redrawn each "update period," and it also provides two variants of the dirty-rectangle update approach. These make use of a list of rectangular areas; they differ by how that list is maintained during animation.

Each scene has its own world coordinate system, as previously mentioned, and can be scrolled through that world. When a scene is scrolled, its actors appear to move in the opposite direction. Think of the scene as a moving window onto the actors' world. Also, while the scene appears on the screen in a particular rectangular area defined for it at scene construction, that area can be changed—the scene can grow and shrink and move about the screen under program control. Furthermore, the software double buffer for it need not be the same width and height in pixels as the screen area. We'll be using our bitmap scaling code from Chapter 6 to scale this off-screen buffer, which is just a canvas by the way, when copying it to the screen.

Finally, the scene is responsible for taking mouse clicks and other mouse events and directing them to the appropriate actor, which is usually the one under the mouse cursor. The methods involved in this process will not be discussed until Chapter 12, when input devices and user interaction are covered.

Here is the header file for class AScene, which we'll go over in detail.

```
//   AScene.h     Scene class
//   Rex E. Bradford

#ifndef __ASCENE_H
#define __ASCENE_H

#include "acanvas.h"
#include "arectlst.h"
#include "afix.h"

class AActor;   // we need to declare ptrs to AActors

class AScene {

static AScene *pFirst; // ptr to first scene in list of scenes

public:

typedef enum {
    UPDATE_FULLAREA,     // recompose & reblit full scene each update
    UPDATE_SLOPPY,       // gather overlapping rects together
```

```
        UPDATE_EXACT,          // exact set of rectangles, no slop or overlap
        UPDATE_UNCHANGED,      // don't change from current setting
    } UpdateStrategy;

private:

    AScene *next;         // link to next scene
    AScene *prev;         // link to prev scene
    long color;           // background color, or 0 for none
    AFix xScale;          // scale factor for x, screen -> canvas
    AFix yScale;          // scale factor for y, screen -> canvas
    AFix xWorld;          // "world" x-coord
    AFix yWorld;          // "world" y-coord
    AActor *pFrontActor;  // ptr to frontmost actor in list (head)
    AActor *pRearActor;   // ptr to rearmost actor in list (tail)
    AFix tLastUpdate;     // time of last update

protected:

    ACanvas *pcv;                // ptr to offscreen canvas for composing
    ARect screenArea;            // area occupied on screen (or window)
    ARectList updateAreas;       // list of areas to update
    UpdateStrategy upStrategy;   // method of updating screen
    bool scaling;                // scaling (canvas w,h != screen w,h)

    void Redraw(ARect &area);             // recompose
    virtual void RedrawAndBlit() = 0;     // recompose and update screen
    virtual void Blit(ARect &area) = 0;   // update screen

public:

// Constructor and destructor, change size of scene window

    AScene(AFix xWorld, AFix yWorld, long color);
    virtual ~AScene();
    void ChangeScreenArea(ARect &screenArea,
        UpdateStrategy upStrategy = UPDATE_UNCHANGED,
        bool updateScreen = TRUE);

// Vital statistics

    ARect ScreenArea() {return screenArea;}
    short ScreenWidth() {return screenArea.Width();}
    short ScreenHeight() {return screenArea.Height();}
    short LogWidth() {return pcv->bm.width;}
    short LogHeight() {return pcv->bm.height;}
    AFix WorldX() {return xWorld;}
    AFix WorldY() {return yWorld;}

// Convert between world and canvas coords

    void ConvertWorld2Canvas(AFix &x, AFix &y) {
        x -= xWorld; y -= yWorld;}
```

```
        void ConvertCanvas2World(AFix &x, AFix &y) {
          x += xWorld; y += yWorld;}

// Convert between screen (scene-relative) and canvas coords

        void ConvertScreen2Canvas(short &x, short &y) {
          x = int(xScale * (x - screenArea.left));
          y = int(yScale * (y - screenArea.top));}
        void ConvertCanvas2Screen(short &x, short &y)
          {x = int(AFix(x) / xScale) + screenArea.left;
           y = int(AFix(y) / yScale) + screenArea.top;}

// Add and remove actors

        void AddActor(AActor *pActor);      // called by: new AActorXxx()
        void RemoveActor(AActor *pActor);   // called by: delete pActor
        bool ResortActor(AActor *pActor);   // resort in z

// Scroll scene

        void Scroll(AFix dx, AFix dy);      // scroll logical coords

// Update scene

        static void UpdateAll();            // update all scenes
        void Update();                      // update actors, compose, blit
        void Changed(ARect *parea = NULL);  // this area of scene has changed
};

#endif
```

Global Scene List

Class AScene keeps track of all scenes in existence in a linked list. This is useful when more than one scene is active in a program. For instance, events like mouse clicks can be checked against all possible scenes by the AScene system itself—because it has all the scenes in a list, it can iterate through them. A single UpdateAll() call can be made to update the display of all scenes, without the programmer having to specify them all.

The static variable 'pFirst' is a pointer to the first AScene object in a doubly linked list, or NULL if no scenes have been created yet. Being a static variable, it is global to the class, and not a member of each AScene. Inside each AScene, 'next' and 'prev' pointers are used to link together the list.

```
static AScene *pFirst;  // ptr to first scene in list of scenes
.....
AScene *next;           // link to next scene
AScene *prev;           // link to prev scene
```

Note that, since scenes may not overlap on the screen, there is no implied visual ordering based on position in the list. The constructor for a new scene simply puts the scene at the head of the list, and the destructor removes the scene from the list.

Scene Canvas Pointer

Each scene has associated with it an off-screen buffer, in the form of a canvas. The scene maintains a pointer to this canvas, and scene rendering is a matter of drawing into this canvas and then later *blitting* (copying) its contents to the screen window. It is the responsibility of the constructor in the derived scene class (ASceneDos or ASceneWin) to construct this canvas in some appropriate format. Of the formats we've seen so far, only the BMF_LIN8 bitmap format and its accompanying ACanvasLin8 canvas class fit the bill. In Part 3, we will develop code for 15-bit and 24-bit linear bitmaps (BMF_LIN15 and BMF_LIN24) and accompanying canvas classes, and then scenes may be created with these color depths.

Also supplied is a background color, expressed as a "native" long-word color. This color value, if nonzero, is the color in which the background behind any actors will be drawn. If zero, which is the default, no background is drawn behind the actors. The default should be used if the scene will include a "backdrop" actor which covers the entire scene—it's pointless to draw a background color behind something which occupies the entire scene. If used, this color should be specified in the color format of the chosen canvas format. For BMF_LIN8 canvases, the desired color index in the screen's palette should be supplied.

```
ACanvas *pcv;   // ptr to offscreen canvas for composing
long color;     // background color, or 0 for none
```

Scene World and Screen Coordinates

Besides a background color, the other arguments to the AScene constructor are its starting *x*- and *y*-location in world coordinates. The member variables 'xWorld' and 'yWorld', copied from these arguments, give the world coordinates of the upper-left pixel in the canvas, in fixed-point coordinates. This gives us a good bit of control over the position and motion of actors that we'll place into the scene, as fixed-point numbers let us specify fractional coordinates for positions and speeds. When a scene scrolls, the 'xWorld' and 'yWorld' coordinates are adjusted accordingly and the scene redrawn.

Other important coordinates include the 'screenArea' member, which marks the location and size of the scene on the screen. Under DOS, this is specified in screen coordinates, but in Windows the coordinates are window relative. (Under Windows, a given window is the "entire screen" as far as scene code is concerned.) The 'screenArea' rectangle is set by the ChangeScreenArea() method during construction and later times, such as after a window resize.

The scene computes three other variables, 'xScale', 'yScale', and 'scaling'. These are scaling factors which represent the ratio between the off-screen canvas size and the screen window size. For instance, a scene with an off-screen canvas width of 100 and a screen width of 200 has an 'xScale' factor of 100/200, or .5. The 'scaling' flag is set to TRUE if either 'xScale' or 'yScale' differs from 1.0.

```
AFix xScale;       // scale factor for x, screen -> canvas
AFix yScale;       // scale factor for y, screen -> canvas
AFix xWorld;       // "world" x-coord
AFix yWorld;       // "world" y-coord
.....
ARect screenArea;  // area occupied on screen
.....
bool scaling;      // scaling (canvas w,h != screen w,h)
```

Several inline methods are available to inspect the current screen area, world coordinates, and "logical" width and height, which is the width and height of the double-buffer canvas.

```
ARect ScreenArea() {return screenArea;}
short ScreenWidth() {return screenArea.Width();}
short ScreenHeight() {return screenArea.Height();}
short LogWidth() {return pcv->bm.width;}
short LogHeight() {return pcv->bm.height;}
AFix WorldX() {return xWorld;}
AFix WorldY() {return yWorld;}
```

Conversion routines are also available to convert between world coordinates and canvas-relative coordinates, and to convert between canvas coordinates and scene-relative screen coordinates (to account for scaling).

```
// Convert between world and canvas coords

    void ConvertWorld2Canvas(AFix &x, AFix &y) {
        x -= xWorld; y -= yWorld;}
    void ConvertCanvas2World(AFix &x, AFix &y) {
        x += xWorld; y += yWorld;}

// Convert between screen (scene-relative) and canvas coords

    void ConvertScreen2Canvas(short &x, short &y) {
        x = int(xScale * (x - screenArea.left));
        y = int(yScale * (y - screenArea.top));}
```

```
void ConvertCanvas2Screen(short &x, short &y)
  {x = int(AFix(x) / xScale) + screenArea.left;
  y = int(AFix(y) / yScale) + screenArea.top;}
```

Actor List

Each scene contains a linked list of the actors which are contained within it. Don't worry—someday we'll find out what the heck an actor is! The scene needs the list of actors in order to redraw the scene, which means redrawing the actors within it. It also needs the list so it can determine which actor is under the mouse cursor.

```
AActor *pFrontActor;     // ptr to frontmost actor in list (head)
AActor *pRearActor;      // ptr to rearmost actor in list (tail)
```

Scene Update Strategy

When it comes time to redraw a scene (because actors have moved or animated, for instance), class AScene offers three different update strategies. For 3D scenes or any time the whole scene is likely to change on every update, UPDATE_FULLAREA is an appropriate strategy. With UPDATE_FULLAREA set, the scene doesn't try to keep track of which areas of the scene are changing—it just redraws all the actors on every update.

For 2D scenes with small sprites moving around, or other scenes which are more static, redrawing the entire scene is wasteful. Why spend time copying the same pixels over and over again? Class AScene has two strategies for drawing only what needs to be drawn, both of which involve keeping a list of rectangular areas of the screen which need redrawing. UPDATE_SLOPPY and UPDATE_EXACT differ in the exact details of how this rectangle list is maintained as the actors move and animate across the scene, and each is appropriate in different circumstances. We'll examine these strategies in more detail later in this chapter.

Finally, a 'tLastUpdate' member variable is used to keep track of the last time the scene was updated. This is useful for controlling timed movement and animation of actors.

```
typedef enum {
   UPDATE_FULLAREA,       // recompose & reblit full scene each update
   UPDATE_SLOPPY,         // gather overlapping rects together
   UPDATE_EXACT,          // exact set of rectangles, no slop or overlap
   UPDATE_UNCHANGED,      // don't change from current setting
} UpdateStrategy;

   ARectList updateAreas; // list of areas to update
   UpdateStrategy upStrategy; // method of updating screen
   AFix tLastUpdate;      // time of last update
```

Scene Creation and Deletion

Class AScene has a single constructor which creates a new scene and links it into the list of existing scenes. This constructor may not be called directly—scenes must be created of type ASceneDos or AScene-Win. The AScene constructor exists to construct the base AScene portion of such derived scene objects.

The AScene constructor sets world coordinates and background color from supplied arguments. It also links this scene into the linked list of scenes (which have no implied ordering, since they can't overlap), initializes the actor list to empty, and reads the current time for use during the next update. Such a scene has no actors, and so if displayed it shows only a background color. To avoid this, the initial set of actors should be added before the first call to Update().

```
AScene::AScene(AFix xWorld_, AFix yWorld_, long color_)
{
// Init world coord current location

    xWorld = xWorld_;
    yWorld = yWorld_;

// Set us up at head of list

    if (pFirst)                     // set us up at head of scene list
       pFirst->prev = this;         // make current head point back to us
    next = pFirst;                  // and we point forward to it
    prev = NULL;                    // with no one behind us
    pFirst = this;                  // we are number one! (zero?)

// Misc init

    color = color_;                 // and backdrop color (or 0 for none)
    pFrontActor = NULL;             // init actor list to empty
    pRearActor = NULL;
    tLastUpdate = ATime::Read();    // set time of last update to now
}
```

The destructor deletes all the actors in the scene, and then unlinks the scene from the global scene list. Cleanup of the off-screen canvas is the responsibility of the derived class which created it.

```
AScene::~AScene()
{
// Delete all actors

    AActor *pActor = pFrontActor;           // start at head of actor's list
    while (pActor)
      {
```

```
            AActor *pnext = pActor->next; // delete() will screw up next field
            delete pActor;                  // delete the actor
            pActor = pnext;                 // advance to real next one
            }

// Unlink us from chain of scenes

    if (next)                   // if scene ahead of us, unlink us
        next->prev = prev;
    if (prev)                   // if scene behind us, unlink us
        prev->next = next;
    else
        pFirst = next;          // if no one behind, we were first
}
```

The scene's screen area and update strategy are set by AScene::ChangeScreenArea(), which must be called by the constructor of the derived scene class (ASceneDos and ASceneWin). It may also be called at any time to reflect a moving or resizing of the screen area. In addition to copying these arguments into the scene's member variables, the ChangeScreenArea() routine computes the scaling factors 'xScale', 'yScale', and 'scaling'. And because scaling of many individual update areas has performance problems and visual rounding errors, this routine forces UPDATE_FULLAREA if scaling is on. Finally, the Changed() routine is called, which marks the entire scene for redrawing during the next Update().

```
void AScene::ChangeScreenArea(ARect &screenArea_, UpdateStrategy
    upStrategy_, bool updateScreen)
{
// Copy screen area and update strategy

    screenArea = screenArea_;       // just copy screen area
    if (upStrategy_ != UPDATE_UNCHANGED)
        upStrategy = upStrategy_; // set update strategy

// Check if screen w,h same as canvas w,h, if so set scaling off

    if ((screenArea.Width() == pcv->bm.width) &&
        (screenArea.Height() == pcv->bm.height))
        {
        scaling = FALSE;
        xScale = AFix(1);       // scale factors are 1.0, just in
        yScale = AFix(1);       // case anybody looks at them
        }

// Else set scaling on and force FULLAREA update strategy

    else
        {
```

```
        scaling = TRUE;
        xScale = AFix(pcv->bm.width) / screenArea.Width();
        yScale = AFix(pcv->bm.height) / screenArea.Height();
        upStrategy = UPDATE_FULLAREA;
        }

// In any case, the entire scene has clearly changed

    if (updateScreen)
        Changed();
}
```

Adding Actors to a Scene

A scene isn't much without actors. In fact, at best it's a solid rectangular color. We need to add actors to the scene, and these actors are members of classes derived from AActor, the base actor class we'll explore later in this chapter. For now, it's necessary only to know that actors are graphic objects which can move and animate, and which take up a rectangular area in the scene. Because they can use transparency, actors need not *look* rectangular. The scene's update strategy makes use of the rectangular nature of actors to quickly decide who needs to be redrawn when overlapping occurs.

In order to decide visual priority when overlapping, each actor has a z-coordinate, which is a sort of distance back from the screen. The larger the z-position, the further back is the actor. For pseudo-3D scenes, we'll also use the z-coordinate to determine the scale of the actor sprite. Negative and zero z-coordinates are considered to be in front of the screen itself, and so actors with z-coordinates <=0 are not drawn, as Figure 10.10 illustrates.

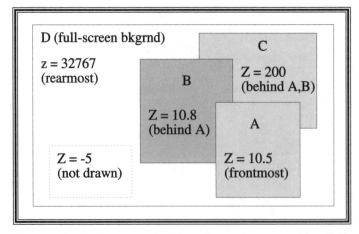

Figure 10.10 Sorting priorities of sample actors. Note full-screen background actor at Z = 32767.

The list of actors that a scene maintains is kept in a sorted order based on the *z*-coordinate of the actors. Overlap priorities can be changed on the fly by changing the *z*-coordinates of one or more actors, which the scene then dutifully resorts. Having an already-sorted list makes it *much* easier and quicker for the scene to redraw the actors when it needs to.

The constructor for the base class AActor, as we'll see later, automatically calls AScene::AddActor() to add the actor to the scene. This method does nothing more than add the actor to the list in the correct position based on its *z*-coordinate. As you can see from the size of the routine, this is not quite as simple as it sounds, mostly because of the need to handle the special cases of an empty list and actors which go at the front or rear of the list. Sounds like the linked list should be a class all its own!

```
void AScene::AddActor(AActor *pActor)
{
// Check for empty list, if so set sole entry

    if (pFrontActor == NULL)
        {
        pActor->next = pActor->prev = NULL; // no one ahead or behind
        pFrontActor = pRearActor = pActor;  // everyone points to us
        return;                             // and we're outta here
        }

// Else scan for 1st entry which is in behind new one (p)
// Keep track of the one behind too (pprev)

    AActor *pprev = NULL;        // currently, no 'prev'
    AActor *p = pFrontActor;     // start with frontmost actor
    while (p && (pActor->loc.z > p->loc.z)) // find one we're ahead of
        {
        pprev = p;               // while advancing, get new 'pprev'
        p = p->next;             // and 'p'
        }

// Now 'p' points to actor behind new one (or NULL), and 'prev'
// points to actor ahead of new one (or NULL). Insert new actor.

    pActor->next = p;            // new one's 'next' points to 'p'
    pActor->prev = pprev;        // and its 'prev' points to 'pprev'

// Patch up pprev and p pointers

    if (p)                       // if there's a 'p'
        p->prev = pActor;        // set its 'prev' to new one
    else
        pRearActor = pActor;     // else new one at rear
```

```
    if (pprev)                  // if there's a 'pprev'
        pprev->next = pActor;   // set its 'next' to new one
    else
        pFrontActor = pActor;   // else new one at front
}
```

Removing Actors

Old actors never die—they are deleted. When this happens, the base AActor class destructor calls AScene::RemoveActor() to pull them out of the actor list. The only complication here is handling actors at the front or rear of the list.

```
void AScene::RemoveActor(AActor *pActor)
{
// If actor behind this one, patch its 'next' field, else this one is
// frontmost and we need to redirect 'pFrontActor' to next in line

    if (pActor->prev)
        (pActor->prev)->next = pActor->next;
    else
        pFrontActor = pActor->next;

// If actor ahead of this one, patch its 'prev' field, else this one
// is behindmost and we need to redirect 'pRearActor' to prev in line

    if (pActor->next)
        (pActor->next)->prev = pActor->prev;
    else
        pRearActor = pActor->prev;
}
```

Resorting Actors

When an actor's z-coordinate changes, its position in the linked actor list may or may not change. AScene::ResortActor() is called whenever the z-coordinate changes, and decides whether or not resorting is necessary. If the actor still has a z-coordinate greater than the actor in front of it, and less than or equal to the actor behind it, no action is necessary. If one of these conditions fails, this lazy routine "resorts" the list by removing the actor from it and reinserting from scratch, using RemoveActor() and AddActor(). A more "stoked" version could update the links itself more quickly, but changing overlap priorities is a relatively rare event in the life of a graphics program, and AddActor() and RemoveActor() are pretty fast anyway.

```
bool AScene::ResortActor(AActor *pActor)
{
// If now in front of the actor which is currently in front of this
// one, resort by removing and adding back to list.
```

```
        if (pActor->prev && (pActor->loc.z <= pActor->prev->loc.z))
            {
            RemoveActor(pActor);    // remove from actor list
            AddActor(pActor);       // insert back in sorted order
            return TRUE;
            }

// Else if now behind actor which is currently behind this one, resort.

        else if (pActor->next && (pActor->loc.z > pActor->next->loc.z))
            {
            RemoveActor(pActor);    // remove from actor list
            AddActor(pActor);       // insert back in sorted order
            return TRUE;
            }

// Else we didn't need to do anything after all

        else
            return FALSE;
    }
```

Class ASceneDos: DOS-Based Scenes

A scene class derived from AScene really has three main responsibilities:

1. Provide a constructor which creates an off-screen canvas of an appropriate type.
2. Provide a destructor to clean up this canvas.
3. Provide a method for redrawing the buffer and blitting it to the screen.

Class ASceneDos does this for the DOS environment, and its header file is listed below.

```
//   AScenDos.h    DOS-based Scene class
//   Rex E. Bradford

#ifndef __ASCENEDOS_H
#define __ASCENEDOS_H

#include "ascene.h"

class ASceneDos : public AScene {

// RedrawAndBlit & Blit routines (private)

    void RedrawAndBlit();       // recompose and update screen
    void Blit(ARect &area);     // update screen
```

```
public:

// Constructor and destructor

    ASceneDos(ARect &screenArea, uchar bmFormat,
        int logWidth, int logHeight, AError &err,
        AFix xWorld = 0, AFix yWorld = 0,
        UpdateStrategy upStrategy = UPDATE_FULLAREA, long color = 0);
    ~ASceneDos();
};


#endif
```

The constructor for class ASceneDos takes a huge number of arguments. The first, 'screenArea', is used to set the screen area which the scene should take up. The next three, 'bmFormat', 'log-Width', and 'logHeight', are used to create the off-screen canvas where actor rendering will occur. Note that if 'logWidth' and 'logHeight' match the width and height of 'screenArea', a normal one-to-one pixel correspondence between the canvas and screen is maintained, and blitting can use the fast DrawBitmap(). Otherwise, blitting will be done using DrawScaledBitmap().

The 'err' argument is used to return an error code if the canvas cannot be created, for instance, because of insufficient memory. Arguments 'xWorld', 'yWorld', and 'color' are passed on to the base AScene constructor. Finally, 'upStrategy' is used to select a screen update strategy, defaulting to UPDATE_FULLAREA.

```
ASceneDos::ASceneDos(ARect &screenArea_, uchar bmFormat,
    int logWidth, int logHeight, AError &err,
    AFix xWorld_, AFix yWorld_, UpdateStrategy upStrategy_,
    long color_) : AScene(xWorld_, yWorld_, color_)
{
// Make a canvas out of a bitmap made from bmFormat and log w,h

    ABitmap bmTemp(NULL, bmFormat, FALSE, logWidth, logHeight);
    if (bmTemp.pbits == NULL)
        { err = AERR_NOMEM; return; } // can't allocate bitmap, oops!

    pcv = ACanvas::NewCompatibleCanvas(bmTemp, FALSE);
    if (pcv == NULL)
        { err = AERR_NOMEM; return; } // if can't allocate canvas, oops!

// Set screen area, update strategy, and scaling flag

    ChangeScreenArea(screenArea_, upStrategy_);

    err = AERR_OK;                     // no hits, no runs, no errors
}
```

The ASceneDos destructor deletes the canvas and its bitmap.

```
ASceneDos::~ASceneDos()
{
    delete pcv->bm.pbits;       // free canvas bits
    delete pcv;                 // free canvas itself
}
```

Discussion of DOS-based scene redraw and blitting will be deferred until later in this chapter.

Class ASceneWin: Windows-Based Scenes

Class ASceneWin manages scenes which are rendered into WinG-based windows. The header file for this class is listed below.

```
//    AScenWin.h    WinG-based Scene class
//    Rex E. Bradford

#ifndef __ASCENEWIN_H
#define __ASCENEWIN_H

#include "ascene.h"

class AWingWindow;

class ASceneWin : public AScene {

public:

    AWingWindow *pWin;    // ptr to Window

// Constructor (no destructor other than base)

    ASceneWin(AWingWindow *pwin, AFix xWorld = 0, AFix yWorld = 0,
        UpdateStrategy upStrategy = UPDATE_FULLAREA, long color = 0);

private:

// RedrawAndBlit & Blit routines

    void RedrawAndBlit();      // recompose and update screen
    void Blit (ARect &area);   // update screen
};

#endif
```

The ASceneWin constructor takes far fewer arguments than its DOS-based counterpart. This is due to the fact that it expects a window to already have been created, and the first argument is a pointer to the AWingWindow object which manages that window. This object contains information about such an already-created screen window, which already has a particular screen position and size, for instance. The ASceneWin constructor reacts to this information, as opposed to receiving it through arguments. Similarly, the AWingWindow object already has an off-screen canvas pointer, which references a WinG DIB. Rather than create yet another canvas, the scene canvas pointer is copied from this pointer.

```
ASceneWin::ASceneWin(AWingWindow *pwin, AFix xWorld_, AFix yWorld_,
    UpdateStrategy upStrategy_, long color_) :
        AScene(xWorld_, yWorld_, color_)
{
// Copy window ptr and canvas ptr from window, set screen area

    pWin = pwin;
    pcv = pwin->pcv;
    ARect area(0, 0, pwin->widthScreen, pwin->heightScreen);
    ChangeScreenArea(area, upStrategy_);
    pWin->AttachScene(this);
}
```

Because the WinG DIB canvas is managed by the AWingWindow object, class ASceneWin doesn't need to (and better not!) delete the canvas or its bitmap. Therefore, it has no destructor (the default AScene destructor is still invoked to do its own cleanup).

The remaining functionality in class ASceneWin relates to rendering and blitting the off-screen buffer. This is the subject of the next section.

Scene Updating, Composition, and Blitting

We've talked a lot about scene update, but what is it really and how does it work? Here's the deal: In a program using scenes, you should call AScene::UpdateAll() in your main loop, as often as possible:

```
while (TRUE)      // sample code for updating scenes
    {
    AScene::UpdateAll();
    ..... do anything else ....
    }
```

UpdateAll() uses code featuring no rocket science to update each of the scenes in the global scene list. It iterates through the global scene list, calling Update() for each scene.

```
void AScene::UpdateAll()
{
    AScene *pscene = pFirst;    // start at head of scene list
    while (pscene)
        {
        pscene->Update();       // update scene
        pscene = pscene->next;  // and advance to next
        }
}
```

So, we've passed the buck to AScene::Update(), which updates a particular scene. Update() reads the current time and computes the elapsed time since the last call to Update(). It then traverses the list of actors, calling each actor's Update() method with the elapsed time. (The AActor::Update() method has no C++ relation to AScene::Update().) This gives each actor the opportunity to move, animate, kill itself or other actors, or compute the value of pi to 155 digits while playing the National Anthem.

A second pass is made through the actor list to "sweep up" killed actors and actually delete them. This two-pass approach is important, as otherwise the traversal of the linked actor list could be thrown off by actors which were physically deleted and removed from the list during traversal. Getting the 'next' field from an actor which doesn't exist anymore, in order to move on to the next actor, which was perhaps also deleted, is a risky proposition at best. The Kill() now, delete later approach solves this problem.

Finally, after all actors have been updated and dead ones carried off, a call to RedrawAndBlit() is made to redraw all or part of the scene and *blit* it to the screen. The term "blit" is a shortened version of Bit-Block Image Transfer. The RedrawAndBlit() method is unimplemented in base class AScene, and is the responsibility of derived classes to implement. In the DOS version, ARTT routines will be used to do the final blit. Under Windows, the scene will pass the buck to AWingWindow::Blit(), which uses WinG calls to perform the actual transfer to the screen.

Let's look first at AScene::Update(), which drives the overall scene update and redrawing process.

```
void AScene::Update()
{
// Get current time and delta time

    AFix tCurr = ATime::Read();      // read current time
    AFix dt = tCurr - tLastUpdate;   // subtract last update t from it

// Update all actors, supplying delta time

    AActor *pActor = pFrontActor;    // start with front actor
    while (pActor)
```

```
      {
      if (!pActor->killed)      // if actor not killed:
         pActor->Update(dt);    // update the actor
      pActor = pActor->next;    // and advance to next
      }

// Set time of last update, for next time

   tLastUpdate = tCurr;

// Scan through actor list, remove killed ones

   pActor = pFrontActor;          // start with front actor
   while (pActor)
      {
      AActor *pActorNext = pActor->next;  // prefetch next actor ptr
      if (pActor->killed)
         delete pActor;          // if killed, do deletion now
      pActor = pActorNext;       // advance to next
      }

// Recompose changed areas of scene and blit them to screen

   RedrawAndBlit();
}
```

Scene Updating: Changed Areas

If a scene's update strategy is UPDATE_FULLAREA, the call to RedrawAndBlit() made by Update() is easy to implement. All the actors in the scene are redrawn into the canvas from back to front (after drawing the background color if one is set), and then the redrawn canvas is copied to the screen.

Other update strategies try to be a little more efficient by keeping track of a list of dirty rectangular areas in need of redrawing and blitting. How is this list created and maintained?

Each scene has a member of class ARectList, which maintains a list of rectangles. Whenever an actor is created, moved, modified in appearance, or deleted, the canvas area occupied by that actor must be redrawn. Note that no attempt is made to maintain saveunders to keep track of what used to be underneath the actor. Redrawing is still a matter of drawing all objects from back to front, but this time the drawing is confined to one or more rectangular areas, instead of the entire canvas. Clipping is used to confine the rendering operations, and furthermore, rectangle intersection tests can be done to quickly decide which actors don't even overlap the area being redrawn, so they can be skipped entirely. Figure 10.11 illustrates the process of redrawing a changed area.

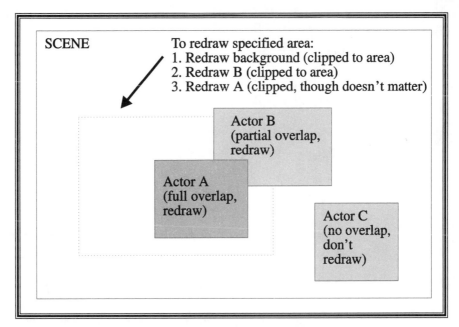

Figure 10.11 Redrawing a changed area by redrawing all actors which overlap it.

Note that if an actor moves or changes size, both the original area occupied by the actor and its new area must be redrawn. The two update strategies UPDATE_SLOPPY and UPDATE_EXACT differ in how they handle the cases where two or more update areas overlap, which is very common when actors move.

When actors notify the scene of an area to be redrawn, they do so using AScene::Changed(), passing in a pointer to a rectangular area, in canvas-relative coordinates. A NULL pointer signifies the entire scene. If the update strategy is UPDATE_FULLAREA, this call is ignored, since the whole scene is redrawn every Update(). Otherwise, the specified rectangle, clipped to the canvas area in case it lies partially off-canvas, is added to the rectangle list. This "adding" process is more than just tacking onto the end of the list—if this dumb strategy were used, we'd often wind up redrawing the same area many times. The update strategy determines which method of ARectList is used to *merge* the new area into the list, to keep multiple redraws down.

Take a look at Figure 10.12, which shows what happens when two moving sprites intersect. Four rectangle areas will have "changed," the old and new areas encompassed by each of the two sprites.

The last thing we want to do is redraw and blit these four areas, since so many of the pixels involved occur in more than one rectan-

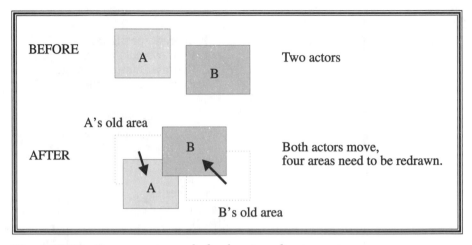

Figure 10.12   Four areas in need of redrawing after two actors move.

gle—we could end up redrawing and reblitting certain pixels up to four times! What we need is to collapse this set of rectangles into a set which has less redundancy in it. Two collapsing strategies are defined. Using UPDATE_EXACT, the resulting set will be an exact, and usually minimum, set of rectangles which covers the entire area with no pixel covered twice. The UPDATE_SLOPPY strategy, on the other hand, is looser, and instead collapses any rectangles which overlap into the smallest rectangle which encloses them. Figure 10.13 shows the resulting collapsed rectangle list using each of the two schemes, applied to a sample set of rectangles.

The "rectangle collapsing" is done on the fly as each rectangle is passed to ARectList::AddExact() or ARectList::AddSloppy(), which are called by AScene::Changed(). The ARectList class is not included here; see ARECTLST.H and ARECTLST.CPP, as well as ARECT.CPP for the ARect::Disjoint() method used by ARectList::AddExact().

Neither strategy is perfect. UPDATE_EXACT creates a rectangle list with the minimum number of pixels, but at the expense of a lot of rectangles and overhead in processing them. Remember, each rectangle is later submitted to a process whereby all actors are checked against it, and redrawn into it if there is overlap. Then, the rectangle is blitted, which has its own setup overhead. UPDATE_SLOPPY creates less rectangles and less overhead, but at the expense of drawing and blitting pixels which never really needed processing. Still, UPDATE_SLOPPY is generally preferable and should be used if you're not sure which is best in a given situation.

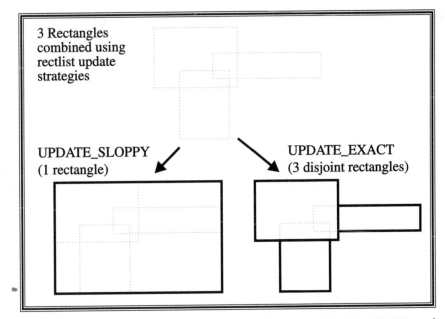

Figure 10.13 Collapsing 3 sample rectangles using UPDATE_EXACT and UPDATE_SLOPPY.

```
void AScene::Changed(ARect *parea)
{
// If update strategy is FULLAREA, we don't need to mark piddly areas

    if (upStrategy == UPDATE_FULLAREA)
        return;

// If NULL ptr passed in, use entire scene area, else intersect

    ARect area(0, 0, pcv->bm.width, pcv->bm.height);
    if (parea)
        area = area.Intersect(*parea);

// Calc intersection of area with scene, if non-empty then add
// this rectangle to the update rectlist

    if (!area.IsEmpty())
        {
        if (upStrategy == UPDATE_SLOPPY)
            updateAreas.AddSloppy(area);   // use sloppy rect adding
        else
            updateAreas.AddUnique(area);   // or exact method
        }
}
```

Scene Updating: Redrawing and Blitting the Scene

AScene::RedrawAndBlit() is called by AScene::Update() to redraw all or part of the scene and move the affected pixels from the off-screen canvas to the screen. If the strategy is UPDATE_FULLAREA, Redraw() is called with the entire canvas area to redraw all the actors into it, and then Blit() is called to copy the entire canvas to the screen. For the other update strategies, Redraw() is called for each rectangle in the current update list, if any. Then, these same areas are copied to the screen using Blit(). Finally, the update list is cleared to an empty state, in preparation for the next update.

The Windows version of RedrawAndBlit(), in class ASceneWin, turns out to be simpler than the DOS version, and is listed below. The DOS version is very similar, except for the added complication of composing the mouse cursor into the areas being blitted. See the CD for the gruesome details.

```
void ASceneWin::RedrawAndBlit()
{
// Compute entire area of canvas, we'll need it

    ARect entireArea(0, 0, pcv->bm.width, pcv->bm.height);

// Redraw (recompose): if FULLAREA, just redraw entire scene

    if (upStrategy == UPDATE_FULLAREA)
        Redraw(entireArea);

// Else scan through rectangles in update list, redraw each

    else
        {
        ARectEntry *pre = updateAreas.First();    // else scan rectlist
        while (pre)
            {
            Redraw(pre->rect);          // redraw this rect
            pre = pre->next;            // and advance to next rect
            }
        }

// Now see if should blit entire scene or just list of
// changed areas. Blit entire area if:
//      1. UPDATE_FULLAREA chosen, or
//      2. StretchBlt required

    if ((upStrategy == UPDATE_FULLAREA) ||
        (pcv->bm.width != pWin->widthScreen) ||
        (pcv->bm.height != pWin->heightScreen))
            Blit(entireArea);
    else
```

```
    {
    ARectEntry *pre = updateAreas.First();
    while (pre)
        {
        Blit(pre->rect);
        pre = pre->next;
        }
    }
  updateAreas.Clear();
}
```

AScene::Redraw(), which is generic to all scenes, redraws all or part of the scene, as specified by the canvas-relative coordinates passed in by AScene::RedrawAndBlit(). Redraw() sets the clip rectangle to the area of concern. While this isn't necessary for correctness (who cares if other portions of the canvas are redrawn?), it speeds up the process by rendering only that portion of each actor that overlaps the area. After setting the clip rectangle, all actors which overlap the area are drawn into it, from back to front (preceded by drawing a background rectangle if a background color has been set).

Not every actor is drawn. If the actor is "hidden" or has a z-coordinate less than or equal to 0, it is not drawn. Beyond that, a quick overlap test is made before drawing using ARect::TestSect(). Any actor which has no overlap with the area of interest is not drawn. Clipping would keep the object from drawing anyway, but TestSect() is an inline method which can check for overlap extremely quickly. For small rectangular areas, 90 percent of actors might have no overlap, so speeding up the handling of actors which don't need drawing can be quite significant.

```
void AScene::Redraw(ARect &area)
{
// Set clip rectangle to area

   pcv->SetClipRect(area);

// Draw background color, if any

   if (color)
      {
      pcv->SetColorNative(color);
      pcv->DrawRect(area);
      }

// Draw all actors which overlap area, back to front

   AActor *pActor = pRearActor;  // start with rearmost
   while (pActor)
      {
```

```
    if (!pActor->hidden &&      // check if hidden or z >= 0, no draw
        (pActor->loc.z > AFix(0)) &&
        area.TestSect(pActor->area))  // check for overlap with area
            pActor->Draw(pcv);   // draw with clipping
    pActor = pActor->prev;       // advance to next actor (in front)
    }
}
```

Finally, Blit() copies the area from canvas to screen. The Windows version in ASceneWin is trivial, passing the buck on to the AWingWindow::Blit() method shown in Chapter 7.

```
void ASceneWin::Blit(ARect &area)
{
    HDC hdc = GetDC(pWin->hwnd);  // get window device context
    pWin->Blit(hdc, &area);       // blit area to it
    ReleaseDC(pWin->hwnd, hdc);   // release window DC
}
```

The DOS version of Blit() in class ASceneDOS is also pretty simple. If no scaling is involved, a sub-bitmap which describes the portion of the double-buffer canvas bitmap is constructed, and the canvas's DrawBitmap() method is called. Scaling blits are done with DrawScaledBitmap().

```
void ASceneDos::Blit(ARect &area)
{
// If scaling, must be entire canvas by definition

    if (scaling)
        gCanvasScreen->DrawScaledBitmap(pcv->bm, screenArea);

// Else make bitmap of portion to blit, and render it

    else
        {
        ABitmap bmArea(pcv->bm, area.left, area.top,
            area.Width(), area.Height());
        gCanvasScreen->DrawBitmap(bmArea, screenArea.left + area.left,
            screenArea.top + area.top);
        }
}
```

Scene Miscellany

Scenes can be scrolled using AScene::Scroll(), which moves the "view" of the scene in the world coordinate system. Scrolling scenes and tiled, scrolling backgrounds are covered in the next chapter. Class AScene also provides methods to support handling of the mouse cursor and mouse events, and these are covered in Chapter 12.

Actors and AActor Classes

The scene provides all the smarts for composition and screen update, but scenes would be pretty empty without actors. ARTT defines a hierarchy of classes derived from the abstract class AActor, and it's easy to add your own too. An actor really only needs to be able to do a few things:

- Draw itself on command from the scene at any time.
- Compute the rectangular area it occupies in the scene (its "extent").
- Respond to Update() calls to perform animation or whatever.
- Move in x, y, z directions (handled by base AActor class).
- Optionally, respond to mouse events such as clicks.

The base class AActor provides much of the framework for actor classes, even though it's pretty small itself. Class AScene handles the tough stuff, such as manipulating the actor 'next' and 'prev' links, deleting Kill()'ed actors, and figuring out which actors must be redrawn.

Figure 10.14 shows the actor classes provided with ARTT, all based on class AActor.

Class AActor: The Base Actor Class

Class AActor provides the basic framework, which derived actor classes inherit from and extend. Objects of class AActor cannot be instantiated, because the important methods Draw() and Compute-Extent() are pure virtual functions which are not implemented. The base AActor class does not know how to draw an actor or compute its extent because it makes no assumptions about the actor's visual properties. The actor might be represented visually by a sprite, or it might be a full scrolling background. Or, it might be a complex 3D object rendered from a set of drawing calls.

Each actor is a member of a scene, and only one scene. The pointer to this scene is supplied in the AActor constructor, along with an x, y, z position in fixed-point coordinates. It's important to note that these are given in the scene's *world coordinates*. Sometimes, as when placing a menu overlay, it's desirable to position an actor using screen-relative or canvas-relative coordinates and not world coordinates. In these cases, AScene::ConvertScreen2Canvas() and AScene::Convert-Canvas2World() can be used to compute the world coordinates needed by the constructor.

Because of the way linked lists are managed, an actor should never be deleted by application code. AActor::Kill() should be used to mark the actor for later deletion by the scene. Note also that because

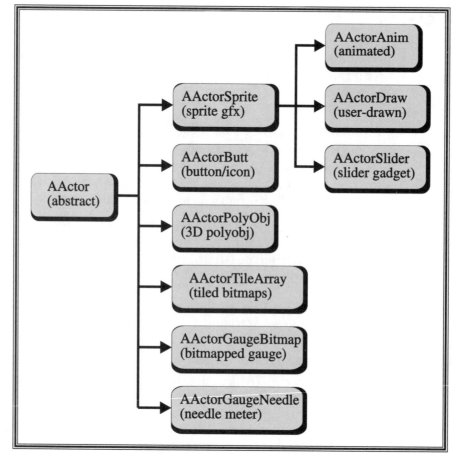

Figure 10.14 Actor class hierarchy.

the scene uses the C++ delete operator to delete the actor, actors should never be declared in static memory or on the stack—always use *new* to create an actor.

Various other flags and member variables are built into the base AActor class. Actors may be hidden and later reshown. They may be "sticky," which keeps them from scrolling when the scene scrolls (useful for such things as menu overlays, which you don't want sliding around when the background shifts). Timed movement is built into the AActor class—actors can be assigned a fixed-point speed (in pixels per second) in *x*, *y*, and even *z*, and they move automatically.

The header file for class AActor is listed below.

```
//   AActor.h   Base Actor class
//   Rex E. Bradford
```

```
#ifndef __AACTOR_H
#define __AACTOR_H

#include "ascene.h"
#include "afix.h"

class ACoord3 { // 2.5-D fixed-point coordinate class (z is depth)
public:
   AFix x;
   AFix y;
   AFix z;

   ACoord3() {}
   ACoord3(AFix x_, AFix y_, AFix z_) {x = x_; y = y_; z = z_;}
};

class AActor {
   friend class AScene; // scenes get special access

   AActor *prev;        // ptr to previous actor
   AActor *next;        // ptr to next actor

protected:

   AScene *pscene;      // ptr to scene actor is in
   ACoord3 loc;         // x,y,z location (scene-relative)
   ACoord3 speed;       // x,y,z speed in pixels per second
   ARect area;          // scene area encompassed by current frame

   ushort killed:1;     // killed this frame?
   ushort hidden:1;     // hidden from view?
   ushort sticky:1;     // sticky when scrolling?
   ushort moving:1;     // moving?
   ushort scalesInZ:1;  // scales when moves in Z

// Virtual function to compute extent into 'area'

   virtual void ComputeExtent() = 0;

// These are called by the scene

   virtual ~AActor();                        // delete actor (use Kill())
   virtual void Scroll(AFix dx, AFix dy);    // scroll actor
   virtual void Draw(Acanvas *pcv) = 0;      // draw actor onto canvas

public:

// Constructor: place actor into scene

   AActor(AScene *pscene, ACoord3 &loc);
```

```
    // Delete an actor with Kill(), don't use delete

        void Kill() {killed = TRUE;}

    // Return canvas-relative coords of actor

        int CanvasX() {return round(loc.x);}
        int CanvasY() {return round(loc.y);}

    // Return world coords

        AFix X() {return(loc.x + pscene->WorldX());}
        AFix Y() {return(loc.y + pscene->WorldY());}
        AFix Z() {return loc.z;}

    // Show and hide, redraw

        void Show() {hidden = FALSE; pscene->Changed(&area);}
        void Hide() {hidden = TRUE; pscene->Changed(&area);}
        void Redraw() {if (!hidden) pscene->Changed(&area);}
        void RedrawNewArea();

    // Update actor

        virtual void Update(AFix dt);

    // Motion control

        void SetSticky(bool onoff) {sticky = onoff;}
        void MoveBy(AFix dx, AFix dy, AFix dz = 0);
        void MoveTo(ACoord3 &newloc);
        void MoveToX(AFix x);
        void MoveToY(AFix y);
        void MoveToZ(AFix z);

        virtual void SetSpeed(AFix xspeed, AFix yspeed, AFix zspeed = 0);
        void SetSpeed(ACoord3 &speed) {SetSpeed(speed.x, speed.y, speed.z);}
        void SetXSpeed(AFix xspeed) {SetSpeed(xspeed, speed.y);}
        void SetYSpeed(AFix yspeed) {SetSpeed(speed.x, yspeed);}
        void SetZSpeed(AFix zspeed) {SetSpeed(speed.x, speed.y, zspeed);}

        virtual void StopMotion() {moving = FALSE;}
        virtual void ResumeMotion() {moving = TRUE;}

        bool IsMoving() {return moving;}
        AFix XSpeed() {return speed.x;}
        AFix YSpeed() {return speed.y;}
        AFix ZSpeed() {return speed.z;}
};

#endif
```

AActor Constructor and Destructor

The constructor for class AActor is passed a scene pointer and an *x, y, z* world-coordinate position expressed as an ACoord3, which is defined in the AActor header file. The base AActor constructor is called by other derived-class constructors to set the basic fields in the actor. The scene and position are initialized; the position is converted from world to canvas-relative coordinates internally because these are more efficient to work with. A bunch of flags are initialized to default states—the object starts out "not killed," "not hidden," "not moving," "not sticky," and "not scaling in Z." These states can be changed in the derived constructor or after the actor is created. Finally, the constructor adds the actor to the scene list using AScene::AddActor(), which, as we previously saw, inserts the actor into the scene's actor list in sorted order.

```
AActor::AActor(AScene *pscene_, ACoord3 &loc_) : loc(loc_), speed(0,0,0)
{
// Set scene pointer and and convert coords to canvas-relative

    pscene = pscene_;
    pscene->ConvertWorld2Canvas(loc.x, loc.y);


// Set defaults

    killed = FALSE;      // not dead yet (only resting!)
    hidden = FALSE;      // visible
    moving = FALSE;      // not moving
    sticky = FALSE;      // not sticky (if scene scrolls, actor scrolls)
    scalesInZ = FALSE;   // doesn't scale when moves in Z


// Add actor to scene in proper sort order

    pscene->AddActor(this);
}
```

The destructor is called when an actor is deleted, which, remember, should be done only by scenes—use Kill() instead. It calls Hide() in order to force a redraw of the area covered by the actor, so its ghost doesn't hang around for some indefinite time period. Then the actor is unlinked from the scene's list using AScene::RemoveActor();

```
AActor::~AActor()
{
    Hide();                      // hide actor (forces redraw under)
    pscene->RemoveActor(this);   // remove actor from scene
}
```

The approved way of deleting an actor, through Kill(), just sets the 'killed' flag for the scene to find later:

```
void Kill() {killed = TRUE;}
```

Actor Position

Often it's handy to get the position of an actor. Class AActor provides methods to get the world coordinates or canvas-relative coordinates of an actor at any time. Note that since coordinates are kept internally in canvas-relative form, returning world coordinates involves a computation, albeit a pretty simple one. The scene's world-coordinate (at its upper-left corner) must be added to the actor's canvas-relative coordinate, using fixed-point addition, to get the world coordinate.

```
// Return canvas-relative coords of actor

   int CanvasX() {return round(loc.x);}
   int CanvasY() {return round(loc.y);}

// Return world coords

   AFix X() {return(loc.x + pscene->WorldX());}
   AFix Y() {return(loc.y + pscene->WorldY());}
   AFix Z() {return loc.z;}
```

Showing and Hiding

Actors can be temporarily hidden with Hide(), and later reshown using Show(). These set the appropriate flag, and then call AScene:: Changed() to tell the scene to redraw the area covered by the actor. When the area is later redrawn, during the next scene update, the actor will be drawn or skipped based on the 'hidden' flag.

```
void Show() {hidden = FALSE; pscene->Changed(&area);}
void Hide() {hidden = TRUE; pscene->Changed(&area);}
```

Marking Actors for Redraw

When an actor decides it is time to be redrawn, for instance, because it has moved or animated, it calls either Redraw() or RedrawNew Area(). Neither call actually redraws the actor; both tell the scene to mark areas for later redrawing. Redraw() is used if the actor has not changed position or size, but merely has a new graphic appearance to be shown.

```
void Redraw() {if (!hidden) pscene->Changed(&area);}
```

If the actor has moved or changed shape, however, Redraw-NewArea() should be called to ensure that both the old and new areas covered by the actor are redrawn. Neither of these routines is typically called by client code—they are built into the actor classes themselves, called when the actor moves or animates.

```
void AActor::RedrawNewArea()
{
   Redraw();              // mark area encompassed by current extent
   ComputeExtent();       // recompute extent
   Redraw();              // mark new area
}
```

Moving Actors

An actor may be moved to a new location at any time using AActor::MoveTo(), which takes a new location in world coordinates and moves the actor there. If the actor needs to be moved in only one dimension, use MoveToX(), MoveToY(), or MoveToZ(). Motion by a relative amount is done using AActor::MoveBy(). MoveTo() and the other three methods all just call MoveBy() with the deltas between the desired coordinates and the current coordinates. Since coordinates are kept internally in canvas-relative form, the MoveTo() methods must convert the new coordinates to that form before calling MoveBy() with the deltas.

```
void AActor::MoveTo(ACoord3 &newloc)
{
   AFix xnew = newloc.x;                            // get new x,y loc
   AFix ynew = newloc.y;
   pscene->ConvertWorld2Canvas(xnew, ynew);  // convert to canvas coords
   MoveBy(xnew - loc.x, ynew - loc.y, newloc.z - loc.z); // move rel.
}

void AActor::MoveToX(AFix xnew)
{
   AFix ynew = 0;                            // dummy conversion
   pscene->ConvertWorld2Canvas(xnew, ynew);  // convert to canvas coords
   MoveBy(xnew - loc.x, 0, 0);               // move relative
}

void AActor::MoveToY(AFix ynew)
{
   AFix xnew = 0;                            // dummy conversion
   pscene->ConvertWorld2Canvas(xnew, ynew);  // convert to canvas coords
   MoveBy(0, ynew - loc.y, 0);               // move relative
}

void AActor::MoveToZ(AFix znew)
{
```

```
    MoveBy(0, 0, znew - loc.z);                    // move relative
}
```

MoveBy() is a little complicated, mostly because it tries to minimize unnecessary redraw. It first adds the *z*-coordinate delta and calls AScene::ResortActor() in case the actor has moved in front of or behind another actor as a result of the new *z*-position. ResortActor() returns TRUE if this took place, and MoveBy() remembers this result. It then adds the *x* and *y* deltas, after first saving the integer portion of the current coordinates. Finally, it calls RedrawNewArea() to draw the old and new areas encompassed by the actor, but only if one or more of the following is true:

1. The actor has been reordered in the actor list due to *Z* motion.
2. The actor scales based on *z*-position and has moved in *Z*, regardless of reordering.
3. The actor's *integer x,y* location has moved.

```
void AActor::MoveBy(AFix dx, AFix dy, AFix dz)
{
// If z-motion, move and resort

    bool z_redraw = FALSE;              // assume no redraw based on z
    if (dz != 0)                        // only worry if z-change != 0
        {
        loc.z += dz;                    // add dz to zpos
        if (pscene->ResortActor(this))  // resort actor in depth list
            z_redraw = TRUE;            // if moved in list, remember this
        if (scalesInZ)
            z_redraw = TRUE;            // if scales based on z, redraw
        }


// Move in x,y

    int oldx = int(loc.x);              // remember old integer x,y
    int oldy = int(loc.y);
    loc.x += dx;                        // move x,y by dx,dy
    loc.y += dy;

// If redrawing due to z motion, or if x,y moved in integer coords,
// redraw old and new areas.

    if (z_redraw || (oldx != int(loc.x)) || (oldy != int(loc.y)))
        RedrawNewArea();
}
```

Actors can also move automatically after being programmed with a speed. AActor::SetMotion() gives a speed to a sprite, where each of the *x,y,* and *z* components is expressed as a fixed-point number of pixels per second. AActor::StopMotion() turns the motion off, but without clearing the speed setting, and AActor::ResumeMotion() can be used to resume motion at the same speed.

```
void AActor::SetSpeed(AFix xspeed_, AFix yspeed_, AFix zspeed_)
{
    speed.x = xspeed_;    // copy speed coords
    speed.y = yspeed_;
    speed.z = zspeed_;
    moving = TRUE;        // and set moving flag
}


    void StopMotion() {moving = FALSE;}
    void ResumeMotion() {moving = TRUE;}
```

Other methods are available to retrieve the current speed of an actor, or to set a single component of the speed. See the header file for details.

Updating and Drawing Actors

Part of the operation of AScene::Update() is to call each actor's Update() routine. AActor::Update() is declared virtual, so that derived actor classes can do their own special update procedures. The base class's Update() has only one job, to move the actor if it is moving.

```
void AActor::Update(AFix dt)
{
    if (moving)
        Move(xspeed * dt, yspeed * dt, zspeed * dt);
}
```

Derived classes which override Update() should make sure they call AActor::Update() explicitly within their own Update() methods. Otherwise, objects of such classes will lose their ability to move.

Two of the most important methods in class AActor are not implemented, and must be defined in derived classes. ComputeExtent() computes the area encompassed by the actor, in canvas-relative coordinates, and places the result in the 'area' member. Draw() renders the actor at its current location, into the canvas supplied as an argument (this canvas will be the scene's off-screen canvas).

```
virtual void ComputeExtent() = 0;
virtual void Draw(ACanvas *pcv) = 0;
```

Class AActorSprite: A Working Actor Class

The base AActor class is all well and good, but you can't make an
actor out of it! We need to make a derived class that knows how to
draw something and can compute its rectangular extent. Then we
can actually create instances of this class in a scene, and start getting
some real screen composition happening.

A sprite is a pretty simple and useful graphic item, so it's a good
candidate. A bitmap is simpler still (a sprite is just a bitmap with a
positioning hotspot, remember), but a bitmap can always be turned
into a sprite through automatic type conversion, so let's use a sprite
and get bitmaps for free. The AActorSprite() class will be pretty simple—an AActorSprite will contain a pointer to a sprite, and thus can
draw that sprite and calculate its extent. We'll add one fancy feature,
which is the optional ability to scale in size based on the value of the
z-coordinate (depth into the scene). Being based on AActor, AActor-
Sprite will inherit all the functionality built into all actors, such as
motion.

The header file for class AActorSprite is listed below.

```
//    AActSp.h    Sprite Actor class
//    Rex E. Bradford

#ifndef _AACTSP_H
#define _AACTSP_H

#include "aactor.h"
#include "asprite.h"
#include "afix.h"

class AActorSprite : public AActor {
    ASprite *psp;               // ptr to sprite
    AFix znominal;              // nominal zpos for scaling, 0 = noscale

    void ComputeExtent();       // recompute extent
    void Draw(ACanvas *pcv);    // draw sprite

public:

// Constructor: set scene and x,y,z, sets sprite ptr and scale factor

    AActorSprite(AScene *pscene, ACoord3 &loc, ASprite *psp,
        AFix znominal = 0);

// Set sprite scaling factor, or turn it off
```

```
    void SetScaling(AFix z) {znominal = z;
        scalesInZ = (znominal != AFix(0)); ChangeSprite(psp);}
    void SetScalingOff() {SetScaling(AFix(0));}

// Get/Change sprite ptr

    ASprite *GetSprite() {return psp;}
    void ChangeSprite(ASprite *psp);
};

#endif
```

Constructing AActorSprites

The AActorSprite() constructor takes the same arguments as AActor (scene pointer and *x,y,z* coordinate), plus a sprite pointer and a "nominal" *z*-position. The sprite pointer points to the sprite which should be used when rendering this actor. The 'znominal' argument determines how scaling is to be done. If 0, the sprite is drawn using normal unscaled means via DrawBitmap(). If nonzero, it specifies the *z*-coordinate the sprite should be at in order to draw at a scale of 1.0. When the sprite's *z*-coordinate is less than znominal (closer), the sprite grows in size, and when its *z*-coordinate is greater than znominal (farther), it shrinks in size. Scaled rendering is done via DrawScaledBitmap().

```
AActorSprite::AActorSprite(AScene *pscene_, ACoord3 &loc,
    ASprite *psp_, AFix znominal_) : AActor(pscene_, loc)
{
    psp = psp_;                          // set sprite ptr
    znominal = znominal_;                // set scaling factor
    scalesInZ = (znominal != AFix(0));   // if z-scaling on, notify AActor
    ComputeExtent();                     // compute extent of sprite
    Redraw();                            // and redraw
}
```

Note that the constructor calls ComputeExtent() and Redraw(). All classes derived from AActor should ensure that these methods are called after the object is set up, so that the scene will be updated properly.

It would be nice if the AActor constructor made the calls to ComputeExtent() and Redraw(), so that each derived-class constructor wouldn't have to. The problem is that, at the time the base AActor constructor is called, the information necessary to run ComputeExtent() and Redraw() hasn't been set up yet. After all, the base constructor is called before the derived constructor.

Changing Sprite Pointer and Scaling Factor

AActorSprite::ChangeSprite() can be called at any time to substitute the sprite pointer. As we'll see in the next chapter, classes built off of AActorSprite() can use this to animate the sprite.

```
void AActorSprite::ChangeSprite(ASprite *psp_)
{
   psp = psp_;              // set new sprite ptr
   RedrawNewArea();         // redraw old and new extents
}
```

The scaling factor can be modified or turned off at any time.

```
void SetScaling(AFix z) {znominal = z;
   scalesInZ = (znominal != AFix(0)); ChangeSprite(psp);}
void SetScalingOff() {SetScaling(AFix(0));}
```

Computing the AActorSprite's Extent

When the AActorSprite is initialized, its sprite changed, or its scaling factor altered, ComputeExtent() is called to recalculate the canvas-relative rectangle that the sprite occupies. If scaling is off, this merely involves offsetting the actor's position by the sprite hotspot to get the upper-left corner of the extent, and then adding the sprite's width and height to get the lower-right. Scaling sprites multiply the sprite's width and height by a scaling factor equal to the nominal z-coordinate divided by the real z-coordinate.

```
void AActorSprite::ComputeExtent()
{
// If scaling, scale up size of sprite

   if (znominal != AFix(0))
      {
// Compute fscale scaling factor based on depth (znominal / z)

      AFix fscale = 0;
      if (loc.z > AFix(0))
         fscale = znominal / loc.z;

// Compute new area based on scaling

      area.left = int(loc.x - (fscale * psp->xoff));
      area.top = int(loc.y - (fscale * psp->yoff));
      area.right = area.left + round(fscale * psp->width);
      area.bott = area.top + round(fscale * psp->width);
      }

// Else if not scaling, just find bounding box of sprite
```

```
        else
            {
            area.left = int(loc.x) - psp->xoff; // adjust for hotspot
            area.top = int(loc.y) - psp->yoff;
            area.right = area.left + psp->width;
            area.bott = area.top + psp->height;
            }
    }
```

Drawing AActorSprites

Rendering an AActorSprite, which is done on command from the scene during its Update(), couldn't be much simpler. It uses Draw-Bitmap() or DrawScaledBitmap(), as appropriate.

```
void AActorSprite::Draw(ACanvas *pcv)
{
    if (znominal != AFix(0))
        pcv->DrawScaledBitmap(*psp, area);
    else
        pcv->DrawBitmap(*psp, area.left, area.top);
}
```

Using AActorSprites: An Example

The following code fragment shows how a scene with a single actor can be created, simply by creating the scene and actor, and then using Update() to render the scene. For a static scene, that's all you have to do, period. For animated scenes, stay tuned.

```
// Sample code fragment to create a scene at 320x200 pixels, with a scene
// background color of 3, and one sprite centered on the screen. This
// sample code assumes a sprite array 'sa' is available to get a sprite from.

    ARect sceneArea(0, 0, 320, 200);
    uchar backgroundColor = 3;
    AError err;
    AScene *pscene = new ASceneDos(sceneArea, BMF_LIN8, 320, 200, err,
        0, 0, AScene::UPDATE_FULLAREA, backgroundColor);
    if (err)
        { ... handle error condition ... }
    ACoord3 actorLoc(160, 100, 100);
    AActor *paa = new AActorSprite(pscene, actorLoc, sa[0]);
```

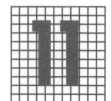

C H A P T E R

Animated Actors and Scrolling Backgrounds

In the last chapter, we developed a scene class to handle screen composition and an actor class to represent graphic objects within the scene. We also subclassed the base actor class with a class which uses a sprite as its graphic representation. In this chapter, we're going to develop three more actor classes, which will give us a lot of power in creating animated scenes. But first, let's look at a concrete example, to see how the scene and actor code developed so far is used.

AQUARIUM: A Scene-Based Demo

The demonstration program we will create is called AQUARIUM, and not surprisingly it consists of an aquarium background with some fish swimming back and forth in it. This doesn't sound too tough, and it isn't. To create this program, we need the following graphic elements:

- Backdrop of water with pebbles and flora at bottom
- Images of some fish, each with a few frames of animation facing left
- Images of the same fish facing right

The Aquarium Actors

The only usable actor class we have right now is AActorSprite (AActor is abstract, and it doesn't have a graphic representation), but that's all we need for this program. The backdrop will be one large sprite which we place at the "back" of the scene. Then, we create some fish sprites at appropriate locations. Now, how do we make the fish swim back and forth?

Each fish is created at a random location in the tank and given a random speed in the left or right direction. Because base class AActor has built-in motion capabilities, our AActorSprite fish will move by themselves. But we need to make them animate, and keep them from swimming right off the screen. So, in our main loop, we'll check each fish's location to see if it has reached the left or right side of the tank. If so, we'll flip its X-speed, so it turns and goes the other way. At the same time, we'll have to change the sprite used by the fish, so that it faces the same direction it's moving. To get animation, as each fish swims we'll periodically rotate its sprite through a few images, so it appears to wiggle its fins as it swims.

That's about all we have to do, other than firing up the graphics mode and handling keypresses to add and remove fish and to end the demo. With actors and scenes, animation is easy!

Aquarium Graphics

Figure 11.1 shows three screen shots. First is the aquarium backdrop, taken from a file called AQUARIUM.PCX. It has a resolution of 640 × 480—the aquarium runs in high resolution. Next to it are AQUAFISL.PCX and AQUAFISR.PCX. These hold all the animation frames for the three fish types, facing left and right. In the actual program, the files AQUAFISL.ASA and AQUAFISR.ASA are used to get the fish animation frames—these files are generated from their PCX counterparts using the GFX2ANM program discussed in Chapter 9.

AQUARIUM: The Code

Figure 11.2 shows the logic flow for the entire AQUARIUM program. The full code listing for the DOS version of AQUARIUM follows. Notice in particular the Rand() and FixRand() functions, which use the C library function rand() to get a random number, but then scale it into a desired range. This is very handy for games and animated demos. Here, it's used for randomizing the type, initial location, direction, and speed of each fish.

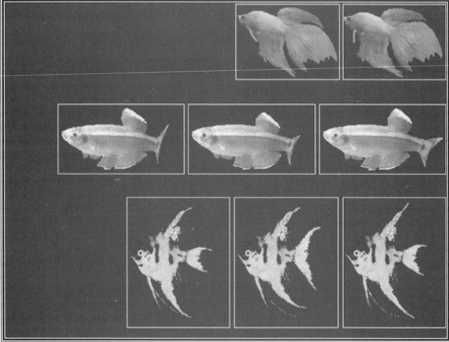

Figure 11.1 Screen shots of AQUARIUM.PCX, the aquarium background and AQUAFISL.PCX.

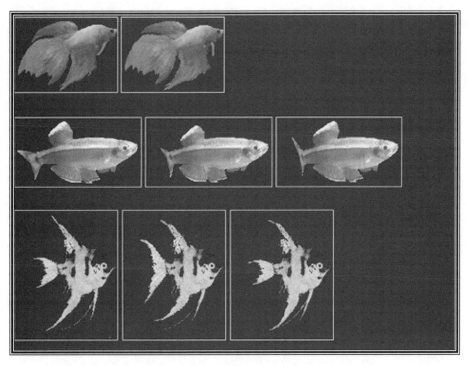

Figure 11.1 (*Continued*) Screen shots of AQUAFISR.PCX, which hold the fish sprites.

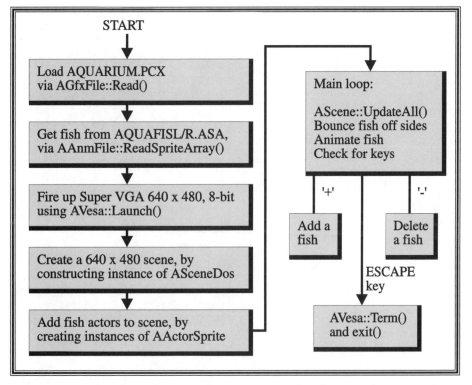

Figure 11.2 Flowchart of AQUARIUM program. Left side is initialization code.

```
//    Aquarium.cpp    Aquarium demo
//    Rex E. Bradford

#include <stdio.h>
#include <conio.h>

#include "agfxfile.h"
#include "aanmfile.h"
#include "ascendos.h"
#include "aactsp.h"
#include "atime.h"
#include "avesa.h"
#include "avga.h"

#define NUM_DEFAULT_FISH 3      // # fish to start in aquarium
#define MAX_FISH 12             // most fish it can hold

typedef struct {
   AActorSprite *pActor;        // ptr to fish actor
   AFix tAnimRate;              // animation rate
   AFix tAnimNext;              // time of next anim
   short type;                  // fish type: 0,1,2
   short index;                 // fish index within type: 0,1,2
   short dir;                   // -1 = left, 1 = right
} Fish;

Fish fish[MAX_FISH];            // array of fishes
int numFish;                    // number of fish in aquarium
AScene *gScene;                 // ptr to scene
ASpriteArray *pFishLeft;        // ptr to spritearray, left-facing fish
ASpriteArray *pFishRight;       // ptr to spritearray, right-facing fish

uchar baseAnim[] = {0,2,5};     // base anim index per fish type
uchar numAnims[] = {2,3,3};     // num anims per fish type

// -----------------------------------------------------------
// ROUTINES TO MAKE, DELETE, AND FEED THE FISH
// -----------------------------------------------------------

int Rand(int low, int high)
{
   long r = rand();
   return (low + ((r * ((high - low) + 1)) / 32768));
}

AFix FixRand(AFix low, AFix high)
{
   float r = float(rand());
   float scale = (float(high) - float(low)) / 32768L;
   r = (r * scale) + float(low);
   return AFix(r);
}
```

```
ASprite *FishSprite(Fish *pFish)
{
    ASpriteArray *psa = pFish->dir < 0 ? pFishLeft : pFishRight;
    return (*psa)[baseAnim[pFish->type] + pFish->index];
}


Fish *MakeFish()
}
// If aquarium full, don't add an unwelcome visitor

    if (numFish >= MAX_FISH)
        return NULL;


// Get new fish slot, randomize type, direction, animation rate

    Fish *pFish = &fish[numFish++];
    pFish->type = Rand(0,2);
    pFish->index = 0;
    pFish->dir = Rand(0,1) ? +1 : -1;
    pFish->tAnimRate = FixRand(.15,.5);
    pFish->tAnimNext = ATime::Read() + pFish->tAnimRate;


// Create new fish actor and give it random location and speed

    ACoord3 loc(Rand(0,400),Rand(50,400),Rand(100,200));
    ASprite *psp = FishSprite(pFish);
    pFish->pActor = new AActorSprite(gScene, loc, psp, 0);
    AFix xspeed = FixRand(30,100);
    if (pFish->dir < 0)
        xspeed = -xspeed;
    pFish->pActor->SetXSpeed(xspeed);

    return pFish;
}


void DelFish()
}
    if (numFish)                            // if there's a fish
        delete fish[--numFish].pActor;      // you must eat it!
}


void FeedFish(Fish *pFish)
{
// Bounce off the walls

    ASprite *psp = pFish->pActor->GetSprite();
    int xleft = int(pFish->pActor->X()) - psp->xoff;
    int xright = xleft + psp->width;
    if (((xleft <= 0) && (pFish->dir < 0)) ||
        ((xright >= 640) && (pFish->dir > 0)))
        {
        pFish->dir = -pFish->dir;
```

```
                    pFish->pActor->ChangeSprite(FishSprite(pFish));
                    pFish->pActor->SetXSpeed(-pFish->pActor->XSpeed());
                    }

        // Animate

            AFix t = ATime::Read();
            if (t >= pFish->tAnimNext)
                {
                pFish->index++;
                if (pFish->index >= numAnims[pFish->type])
                    pFish->index = 0;
                pFish->tAnimNext += pFish->tAnimRate;
                pFish->pActor->ChangeSprite(FishSprite(pFish));
                }
    }


    // -----------------------------------------------------------
    // MAIN PROGRAM
    // -----------------------------------------------------------

    void main(int argc, char **argv)
    {
    // Read aquarium background and fishes

        AError err1,err2,err3;
        ABitmap bmBack;
        err1 = AGfxFile::Read("aquarium.pcx", bmBack);
        pFishLeft = AAnmFile::ReadSpriteArray("aquafisl.asa", err2);
        pFishRight = AAnmFile::ReadSpriteArray("aquafisr.asa", err3);

    // If error, report

        if (err1 || err2 || err3)
            {
            printf("Problem loading aquarium or fishes\n");
            exit(1);
            }

    // Launch graphics mode

        AVesa::Launch(640, 480, 8);
        if (gCanvasScreen == NULL)
            {
            printf("Unable to launch VESA mode\n");
            exit(1);
            }
        if (bmBack.ppalette)
            AVga::SetDAC(bmBack.ppalette->rgb);

    // Make scene with background
```

```
AError err;
ARect sceneArea(0, 0, 640, 480);
gScene = new ASceneDos(sceneArea, BMF_LIN8, 640, 480, err,
    0, 0, AScene::UPDATE_SLOPPY, 0);

ACoord3 loc(0,0,32767);
ASprite spBack(bmBack);
new AActorSprite(gScene, loc, &spBack, 0);

// Throw some fish in the water

for (int i = 0; i < NUM_DEFAULT_FISH; i++)
    MakeFish();

// Infinite loop, handling keys

while (TRUE)
    {
    AScene::UpdateAll();       // move fish, redraw the scene
    for (int i = 0; i < numFish; i++)
        FeedFish(&fish[i]);    // bounce fish off walls & animate

    if (kbhit())
        {
        int c = getch();
        switch (c)
            {
            case '+':          // '+' key, add a new fish
            case '=':
                MakeFish();
                break;

            case '_':          // '_' key, eat a fish
            case '_':
                DelFish();
                break;

            case 0x1B: // ESC key, sell aquarium
                AVesa::Term();
                exit(0);
            }
        }
    }
}
```

Color plate 2 shows a view of AQUARIUM in action.

Animated Actors

In the AQUARIUM program, the fish are animated by changing their sprite representation every so often under program control. This manual animation can get tedious. If we want to create a game with a running person in it, or an educational program with an animated "talking head," we don't want to have to write code to make sure the image changes from each frame to the next at the right time. Clearly, what we need is a new actor class with built-in animation.

Before we go off half-coded, let's think about what kinds of features such a class needs. First, let's discuss a few examples of the kinds of animation we might want to achieve using this new class.

Character Animation

A lot of traditional, old-style games and educational programs feature small sprite characters running around a large backdrop. On video game machines, "side-scrollers" (taken from the fact that the screen scrolls horizontally) are still popular. In these games, little figures jog down hallways, run up and down stairs, climb ladders, leap into the air, and, of course, plummet down into the Pit of Despair. They are pestered by swaggering Evil Henchmen, flying creatures such as bats and dragons, rolling balls and flying spears. For lunch and points, they gobble up energy pellets, floating golden rings, and magic bubbles. And yes, on screen 6387 they finally greet the much sought-after Princess, and together go off happily in search of a sequel.

Recently, many of these titles have begun to incorporate larger characters with more "cartoonlike" animation. See Color plate 3 for an example.

Many of the "props" in these games have very simple animation—usually two to four frames looped over and over again. However, the characters, particularly the player's character, often feature incredibly detailed animation. In *Prince of Persia*, which was a breakthrough game in terms of fluidity of character animation, the player's character has literally hundreds of different frames. How are these frames choreographed together into what appears to be seamless animation?

The trick is to see the animation as a progression of short animated sequences, some of which are "one-shot" and some of which are "looped." A walking or running figure, for instance, is typically created with a loop of 6 to 8 frames of animation. Use less than 6, and the animation appears choppy. Figure 11.3 shows an example walking sequence. Notice how the last frame meshes smoothly with the first, so that the sequence can be played over and over while the figure moves.

Each of the various actions that a running figure takes are similarly represented by a short animation sequence. Some, like a jump or duck, are meant to be played once, at the end of which the figure returns to running or standing. Others, like climbing up a ladder, are

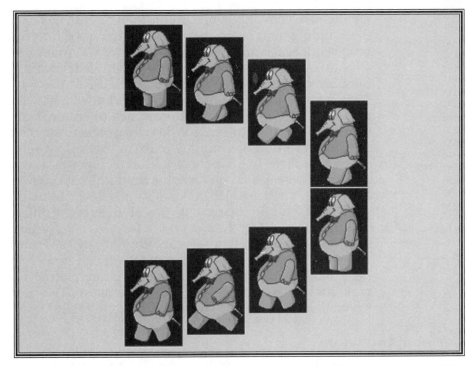

Figure 11.3   Frames of a walking elephant, constructed so that looping is possible.

looped until the program detects that the sequence should stop (and change to some other sequence).

Professional Character Animation

There are a couple more tricks to doing professional-quality character animation, besides developing good artwork, of course. Both involve *synchronization*—tying the animation sequence to something outside itself.

The first of these tricks is synchronization to motion. In many cases, the animation should go faster as the motion of the character or object goes faster. To take a running man as an example, the faster he runs the faster the animation should go, because, after all, in theory the leg motion in the animation is what is making him go. This motion synchonization works only to a point—a walking man is fundamentally a different animation from a running man, not just a slower version.

The second form of synchronization involves the exact mechanics of changing animation sequences. In many cases, it is acceptable for the new sequence to begin on its first frame. For instance, when the standing man begins to run, starting on the first frame of the running sequence is fine. But now take the example of a running man who turns into Big Running Man (BRM) after eating a Mondo Pill. Suppose both the running man and the BRM use 6-frame animated sequences which differ only in size (and maybe hat color). If the running man is on frame 4, and switches to frame 1 of the BRM, the transition will appear jerky. What we want is to switch to the BRM *on the same frame* as the running man, in this case frame 4.

Using these two synchronization techniques, it is possible to create fluid, professional-quality character animation in 2D. But pseudo-3D games, such as DOOM and its ilk, have bitmapped characters which not only animate, but appear to face in different directions. There is no magic to this, just brute force—each frame of animation is created and prestored at several different angles. Typically, 8 different views are used, although software which can render sprites "flipped" horizontally can get by with 4 or 5. Color plate 4 shows a sample graphics file showing various views of a figure. They are all the "same" frame of animation, viewed from different angles.

Cartoon Animation

Cartooning on a computer is mostly a stylistic rather than a technical concept. Cartoon figures are large and have more fluid animation than traditional small "sprite" figures. On the extreme end are full-screen cartoon sequences such as that popularized on computers by the *Dragon's Lair* game. This game features hand-drawn art like the Disney classics (Don Bluth, the creator, was a Disney animator). In this style of animation, a single full-screen "cartoon video" is played to the screen, with periodic transitions to other full-screen sequences based on the player's input.

Doing full-screen anything at a reasonable frame rate is challenging, but in cartooning we can take advantage of the graphic style. In a cartoon, large swaths of the same color are part of the look we want, not an annoying defect which detracts from realism. Our BMF_RLE8 run-length-encoded bitmaps can compress cartoon imagery quite well, and this makes it possible for ARTT to handle cartoon animation.

Other Forms of Animation

Outside the entertainment field, many other forms of animation abound. Digital video playback is one form. Digital video has its own issues, namely compression, compression, and compression. In Chapter 16, we'll discuss digital video in more detail.

In medical and scientific applications, animated windows on data abound. These include real-time display of vital signs such as EKG and EEG, animated "volume visualization" of CAT-SCAN data, and more. In finance, stock price quotation displays show a constant animated stream of raw and summary data (I have a friend in Manhattan who spends all day in her apartment, every day, watching seven such monitors, but now's not the time to get into the personal habits of my friends).

In education, animation is used in a variety of forms. Some of it is the character and cartoon animation we've just discussed, but education applications also feature animations of simulation data, scrolling music scores, scrolling maps with highlight overlays, and a host of other techniques.

In many of these cases, the frames of animation are not pre-stored, like they are for our character and cartoon animation sequences. Rather, each frame is a "snapshot" of some data or simulation results. Animation in this context means computing and rendering successive frames. ARTT is suitable for such styles of animation, as we'll see in the AMUCK sample presented later in this book.

Class AActorAnim: An Animated Actor

Let's design a new actor class to handle sprite-based animation, the most common form we'll need. By deriving it from AActorSprite, our new AActorAnim class will automatically be able to move about the scene and display its current frame. AActorAnim will add the ability to automatically switch frames, taken from a sprite array, based on the passage of time. Additionally, we'll build in these capabilities:

- Loop back to first frame of sequence automatically, if desired.
- Optionally, Kill() sprite after last frame (for explosions, special effects, and other "one-shots").
- Adjust frame rate at any time.
- Optionally, synchronize animation frame rate to horizontal motion speed.
- Switch animation sequence under program control, optionally with synchronized frame index.

What is an animation sequence? Let's define it as a range of frames within a sprite array, which has associated with it its own frame rate. The frame rate is expressed in frames per second, in floating point. The structure AAnimRange, listed below, defines an animation sequence.

```
typedef struct {
   short startIndex; // starting index in array
```

```
        short endIndex;    // last index + 1, or 0 to go to array end
        float frameRate;   // frame rate in frames per second
    } AAnimRange;
```

If we have a sprite array containing a large number of animation frames, ordered in a set of sequences, we can define a set of AAnim-Ranges which describes the sequences in the file. For instance, suppose we have a PCX file named DOG.PCX containing 6 bordered images of a dog running left, 6 bordered images of a dog running right, and 3 frames of facing forward and barking. We could then run GFX2ANM to convert this PCX file into a file-based sprite array, perhaps named DOG.ASA. We can then use AAnmFile::LoadSpriteArray() to load this file into a sprite array.

The sequences of the sprite array can then be described by a set of AnimRanges, as follows:

```
AnimRange dogAnimRunLeft = {0,6,8.0};    // 1st 6 frames, played at 8/second
AnimRange dogAnimRunRight = {6,12,8.0};  // 2nd 6 frames, also 8 frames/sec
AnimRange dogAnimBark = {12,15,5.0};     // last 3 frames, at 5 frames/second
```

To select any given sequence of animation for an animated actor, then, we just supply a pointer to the sprite array from which the frames are taken, and a pointer to the appropriate AAnimRange.

AActorAnim Interface

The header file for class AActorAnim is listed below. AActorAnim is derived from AActorSprite, and so retains all of the capabilities of AActorSprite and its base class, AActor.

```
//   AActAnim.h      Animated sprite Actor class
//   Rex E. Bradford

#ifndef__AACTANIM_H
#define__AACTANIM_H

#include "aactsp.h"
#include "aspritea.h"

typedef struct {
    short startIndex; // starting index in array
    short endIndex;   // last index + 1, or 0 to go to array end
    float frameRate;  // frame rate in frames per second
} AAnimRange;

class AActorAnim : public AActorSprite {

    ASpriteArray *psa;      // ptr to sprite array
    AAnimRange arange;      // animation range/framedur
```

```
    AFix tFrameDur;          // duration of each frame
    AFix tLeft;              // time left for this frame
    AFix tFrameRateBase;     // base frame rate
    AFix framesPerPixel;     // # frames per pixel of motion
    short currIndex;         // current index in sprite array
    ushort autoKill : 1;     // kill when reach last frame
    ushort animSlaved : 1;   // animation slaved to motion

    void SetSlavedFrameRate(); // compute frame rate if slaved to motion

public:

// Constructor: initialize animated sprite actor
    AActorAnim(AScene *pscene, ACoord3 &loc, ASpriteArray *psa,
        AAnimRange *prange, bool autoKill = FALSE);

// Change animation set/range

    void ChangeAnimSet(ASpriteArray *psa, AAnimRange *prange,
        bool autoKill = FALSE);
    void ChangeAnimRange(AAnimRange *prange, bool synchronize = FALSE);

// Set frame rate

    void SetFrameRate(AFix rate) {tFrameDur = AFix(1) / rate;}
    void SetFrameDur(AFix dur) {tFrameDur = dur;}

// Slave animation speed to motion rate, or unslave

    void SlaveAnimToMotion(AFix tFrameRateBase, AFix framesPerPixels);
    void UnslaveAnim() {animSlaved = FALSE;}

// Set motion speed, pause & resume

    void SetSpeed(AFix xspeed, AFix yspeed, AFix zspeed = 0);
    void StopMotion();
    void ResumeMotion();

// Update animation

    void Update(AFix dt);
};

#endif
```

AActorAnim Constructor

The AActorAnim constructor assigns the new animated actor to a scene at a given world coordinate location, like any other actor. It also has arguments to provide an initial sprite array and an AAnim-Range within that array. The last argument tells the animated actor whether to self-annihilate after playing the last frame in the range. This is handy for explosions, temporary special effects, and certain other one-shot animations. This argument defaults to FALSE, which means that the animation will loop over and over until told to do something else.

Notice how AActorAnim initializes the underlying AActorSprite with a sprite pointer taken from the first frame in the supplied range and sprite array. It then hands off most of the initialization to ChangeAnimSet(), which can also be used by the application at any time to change to an entirely new sprite array and animation range at any time.

```
AActorAnim::AActorAnim(AScene *pscene_, ACoord3 &loc,
   ASpriteArray *psa_, AAnimRange *prange, bool autoKill_) :
      AActorSprite(pscene_, loc, (*psa_)[prange->startIndex])
{
   animSlaved = FALSE;              // by default, not slaved to motion
   ChangeAnimSet(psa_, prange, autoKill_);   // "change" anim set
}
```

Changing Animation Sets and Ranges

AActorAnim::ChangeAnimSet(), used by the constructor and available at any time, is listed below. It sets the new sprite pointer and the value of the 'autoKill' flag (by default FALSE, so the animation loops), and then hands off to ChangeAnimRange() to change to a new animation range within that sprite array.

```
void AActorAnim::ChangeAnimSet(ASpriteArray *psa_, AAnimRange *prange,
   bool autoKill_)
{
   psa = psa_;                        // set new sprite array ptr
   autoKill = autoKill_;              // set autoKill flag
   ChangeAnimRange(prange, FALSE);    // change to new anim range
}
```

AActorAnim::ChangeAnimRange() switches to a new animation range. The first argument is a pointer to a new animation range. The second is a "synchronization" flag. If this is TRUE, the new animation sequence is started off at the same *relative* frame index as the current sequence. For instance, if we are at the fourth frame of the dog running left and switch to running right, the new animation will start at the fourth frame of the running right animation. Use this feature with care—if the running right animation has only three frames, odd things can happen! A new frame rate is picked up from the new animation range, unless animation speed has been slaved to motion speed, using the SlaveAnimToMotion() method (to be covered shortly).

```
void AActorAnim::ChangeAnimRange(AAnimRange *prange, bool synchronize)
{
// If synchronized, retain same relative index, else start at beginning

    int relIndex = synchronize ? (currIndex - arange.startIndex) : 0;

// Copy anim range and set current index in it

    arange = *prange;
    currIndex = arange.startIndex + relIndex;

// If animation rate slaved, use it, otherwise use rate in animrange

    if (animSlaved)
        SetSlavedFrameRate();
    else
        SetFrameRate(AFix(arange.frameRate));

// If not synchronized, restart timer countdown

    if (!synchronize)
        tLeft = tFrameDur;
}
```

Controlling Animation Rate, and Slaving Animation Rate to Motion

Animation frame rate is normally controlled by the setting in the current animation range. It may be explicitly set using SetFrameRate() or SetFrameDur(), although these settings last only until the next ChangeAnimRange(), which then picks up the frame rate from the new animation. SetFrameRate() takes a frame rate expressed in frames per second, and computes the duration of each frame (in fixed-point seconds) for internal use. SetFrameDur() is perhaps less intuitive but more efficient in implementation—the frame duration in seconds (for instance, .25 seconds for a 4-frame/second animation) is supplied directly.

```
void SetFrameRate(AFix rate) {tFrameDur = AFix(1) / rate;}
void SetFrameDur(AFix dur) {tFrameDur = dur;}
```

Another method for controlling frame rate is to tie it to the motion rate, using SlaveAnimToMotion(). This method takes a base frame rate to be used when the object is not moving, and a second argument expressed in terms of animation frames per pixel of movement. The formula for calculating the frame rate for a given speed of motion is given by:

```
frameRate = baseFrameRate + (speed * framesPerPixel);
```

Let's take an example. If we assign a base frame rate of two frames per second, and then choose a framesPerPixel setting of .3, what happens to the frame rate at various speeds?

Speed 0 pixels/second → 2.0 + (0 * .3) = 2.0 frames per second
Speed 5 pixels/second → 2.0 + (5 * .3) = 3.5 frames per second
Speed 10 pixels/second → 2.0 + (10 * .3) = 5.0 frames per second

The framesPerPixel setting is very sensitive, and is usually in the range .01 to .5. It literally means the number of frames which should elapse per single pixel of motion, which is why it's usually far below 1.0. By the way, class AActorAnim considers horizontal (*x*-direction) speed only when slaving animation rate to motion. Motion in the vertical direction often has a more complex interpretation than horizontal motion—in 3D views, for instance, motion up the screen often means an object is going "into" the world away from the camera. For more complex animation rate control than slaving to horizontal motion, the animation rate should be reprogrammed directly as needed using SetFrameRate() or SetFrameDur().

AActorAnim::SlaveAnimToMotion() is listed below.

```
void AActorAnim::SlaveAnimToMotion(AFix tFrameRateBase_,
   AFix framesPerPixel_)
{
// Set base frame rate and frames per pixel of motion

   tFrameRateBase = tFrameRateBase_;
   framesPerPixel = framesPerPixel_;

// Mark anim speed as slaved to motion, calculate current frame rate

   animSlaved = TRUE;
   SetSlavedFrameRate();
}
```

To decouple the animation rate from motion, use AActorAnim::UnslaveAnim().

```
void UnslaveAnim() {animSlaved = FALSE;}
```

Overriding the AActor Motion Methods

In order to make animation "rate slaving" work, the AActorAnim object needs to be informed every time the motion speed of the actor is changed, so that the animation rate can be adjusted to match. By default, calls to SetSpeed(), StopMotion(), and ResumeMotion() are handled by class AActor, and our AActorAnim object is never made aware of the new speed settings. We can fix this by overriding these three methods, which are declared virtual in class AActor.

The versions of these methods we define in class AActorAnim call the original methods in AActor, so that the new speed settings are actually processed. Then, additionally, if the animation is in slaved mode, the frame rate is recomputed based on the new speed.

```
void AActorAnim::SetSpeed(AFix xspeed, AFix yspeed, AFix zspeed)
{
    AActor::SetSpeed(xspeed, yspeed, zspeed);    // set x,y,z speed
    if (animSlaved)
        SetSlavedFrameRate();    // if anim slaved, recalc frame rate
}


void AActorAnim::StopMotion()
{
    AActor::StopMotion();                  // set motion flag to FALSE
    if (animSlaved)
        SetFrameRate(tFrameRateBase); // if anim slaved, reset frame rate
}

void AActorAnim::ResumeMotion()
{
    AActor::ResumeMotion();                // set motion flag to TRUE
    if (animSlaved)
        SetSlavedFrameRate();              // if anim slaved, recalc frame rate
}
```

Computing the Slaved Animation Rate

Whenever the animation rate is slaved to motion, and the speed changes, the private method SetSlavedFrameRate() is used to compute the new frame duration.

```
void AActorAnim::SetSlavedFrameRate()
{
// Compute new frame rate and set it

    AFix frameRate = tFrameRateBase;
    if (moving)
        frameRate += abs(speed.x) * framesPerPixel;
    SetFrameRate(frameRate);

// If time left in current frame > frame duration, clamp it down

    if (tLeft > tFrameDur)
        tLeft = tFrameDur;
}
```

Overriding Update() to Animate the Actor

The Update() method, called for each actor from inside AScene::
Update(), is used to give each actor a chance to lean back and reflect
upon the state of the world since last time called (the sole argument is
the amount of time passed since last call), and to take action against
a sea of pixels. The base AActor class does nothing other than move
the actor if it has a current speed. AActorSprite(), having nothing
additional to offer, does not override the AActor::Update() method. In
order for AActorAnim to animate, which is the whole point of this
class after all, Update() must be overridden.

AActorAnim::Update() works as follows. After calling AActor::
Update() to move the actor (if it has a nonzero speed), the amount of
time remaining in the current frame is counted down by the delta-
time argument passed in. If this timer reaches or falls below 0, it is
time to change to a new frame. In this case, the current frame index
is incremented and checked against the end of the animation range.
If the animation has played all its frames as defined in the range, or
if the next frame is outside the range of the sprite array altogether,
the animation is considered to have reached the end of its sequence.
In this case, the 'autoKill' flag is checked. If set, Kill() is used to mark
this actor for deletion. If the 'autoKill' flag is FALSE, the animation
is looped back to the first frame in the range.

In any case, when the frame changes AActorSprite::Change-
Sprite() is called to change the sprite image being presented by this
actor, and the frame timer is reset. Note how this is done. The frame
duration is *added* to the current countdown timer, instead of just
stuffed into it. This keeps our animation from "drifting" off of its true
frame rate.

```
void AActorAnim::Update(AFix dt)
{
// Move actor and count down animation frame timer

    AActor::Update(dt);      // move the actor if moving
    tLeft -= dt;             // count down time left in this frame

// Change frame?

    if (tLeft <= AFix(0))
        {
// Yes, have we reached the end of the animation range?

        if ((++currIndex == arange.endIndex) ||    // check for end index
            ((*psa)[currIndex] == NULL))           // or end of sp array
            {
            if (autoKill)
```

```
              {
              Kill();        // if autoKill set, kill actor
              return;
              }
         currIndex = arange.startIndex; // else restart anim
         }

// In any case (unless killed), change sprite to new frame

    ChangeSprite((*psa)[currIndex]);    // change sprite
    tLeft += tFrameDur;                 // and reset frame timer
    }
}
```

Drawing the Animated Actor

Where's AActorAnim::Draw(), the code to draw the animated actor? We don't need one! The underlying AActorSprite takes care of this, drawing whatever sprite is set into it via ChangeSprite(). AActorAnim is just responsible for animation, and stands on the shoulders of the giants AActor and AActorSprite to handle scene inclusion, motion, and rendering. Vive C++!

Scrolling Backgrounds

When thinking of actors, it's easy to think only of characters and other small objects. But there's nothing to stop an actor from filling an entire screen. A sprite actor of class AActorSprite or AActorAnim can be full-screen in size. The full-screen backdrop in the AQUAR-IUM program is an AActorSprite object. An full-screen animated cartoon could be created using a single AActorAnim (or multiple ones for on-the-fly overlaying!). Can actors get even bigger—bigger than the screen itself?

Sure, why not? Imagine an AActorSprite whose sprite is three screens wide. Presumably, we put this actor behind all the others, so that it doesn't obscure them. Then, moving this sprite is tantamount to *scrolling* the background. Better yet, let's Scroll() the scene itself. All the actors seem to move in the opposite direction of the scene-scrolling, and the effect is that of a camera panning across a scene. Figure 11.4 illustrates.

Scrolling Scenes and Actors

We skipped over scrolling when covering scenes and actors in the previous chapter. Let's return for a look at what we missed. Remember, scenes keep track of their location (defined by the upper-left corner of

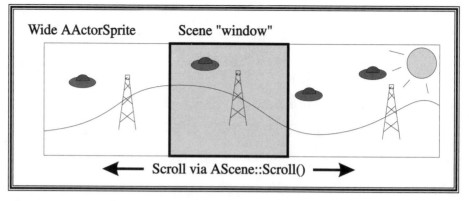

Figure 11.4   Scrolling a scene across a wide AActorSprite.

the scene canvas) in world coordinates. Using world coordinates allows the scene to be thought of as a window into a world which is bigger than the canvas.

AScene::Scroll() is used to move this window in the world coordinate system. The number of pixels to move in *x* and *y* are given as arguments. Scroll() adds these to the current scene world coordinates, gives a scrolling command to each actor to notify them of the change, and then calls Changed() to redraw the entire scene.

```
void AScene::Scroll(AFix dx, AFix dy)
{
// Update world coords

    xWorld += dx;
    yWorld += dy;

// Move all actors to slide with scene, unless they're sticky

    AActor *pActor = pFrontActor; // start at front of list
    while (pActor)
        {
        if (!pActor->sticky)
            pActor->Scroll(dx, dy); // if not sticky, scroll
        pActor = pActor->next;
        }

// Update entire scene

    Changed();
}
```

Now, while scenes keep track of their location in world coordinates, actors keep track of *their* coordinates in off-screen *canvas* coordinates. This is done for efficiency, so that no transformation needs to be done when figuring how to redraw areas of the canvas.

When the world coordinates scroll one way, the actors appear to move in the opposite direction. This is achieved by subtracting the scrolling delta from each actor's canvas location. AActor:: Scroll() follows this by recomputing the actor's extent. Note that AScene::Scroll() only calls AActor::Scroll() on actors which have their 'sticky' flag set to FALSE. If 'sticky' is on, the actor is a "sticky overlay" which keeps its current canvas location while the rest of the scene scrolls.

```
void AActor::Scroll(AFix dx, AFix dy)
{
   loc.x -= dx;        // if scene moves to right, actor loc goes left
   loc.y -= dy;        // similar in y
   ComputeExtent();    // recompute extent of actor
}
```

Multiple Scrolling Planes

Panning across a large background is one use for such scrolling. But we can achieve fancier effects with the same technique. Picture a background sprite behind all the other actors. Now picture a second sprite, much wider than the screen but maybe only 50 pixels tall, with transparency. Let's place this second wide sprite at the bottom of the screen, and in front of all the other actors. By scrolling this sprite at a faster rate than the rest of the scene (calling AActor::Scroll() by hand), we can achieve a *parallax* effect, where this foreground sprite appears to be closer to the camera. See Figure 11.5.

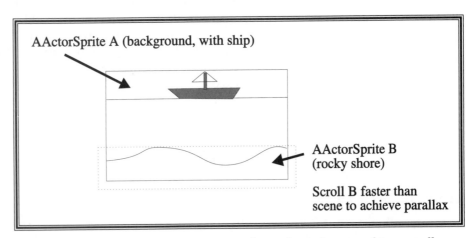

Figure 11.5 Scrolling one sprite at a rate faster than others to achieve parallax.

Clearly, our approach to scrolling has limits. Sprites which are bigger than the screen can take up an awful lot of memory, even in BMF_RLE8 compressed format. And what happens when we've scrolled to the end of the sprite? If we keep going, empty space appears off the sprite's edge. We can write our program to clamp the scrolling of the scene so this doesn't happen, and live with very limited scrolling. There's another approach, though.

Tiled Backgrounds and Tiled Actors

If we want to create a world a hundred screens across, we clearly need a better method than panning across a very large sprite. One hundred 320 × 200 screens would consume 6.4 megabytes in BMF_LIN8 format. On a 640 × 480 screen, the memory requirements are about five times that amount. Yikes.

Two ideas come to mind:

1. Make the background sprite some fixed size, usually larger than the screen but not necessarily, and repeat it as we pan across it. This technique is often called *wraparound*. An infinite world can be created this way, albeit one which gives off a certain sense of déjà vu as it repeats continually.

2. Construct the background out of a set of *tiles*, and define a large world as an array of these tiles, in an interesting and not-too-repetitive pattern. Most side-scrolling video games use this technique. For instance, a world with five unique half-screen tiles, numbered 0 through 4, might present a world which features tiles in this order: 0,1,2,3,4,0,3,0,3,4,2,1,0,3,1,2,etc. See Figure 11.6.

The tiling option still suffers from the fact that the world is limited by the size of the tile index array. However, a lot more tile indexes can be stored in memory than actual bitmapped tile sprites. For instance, a hundred-screen-wide world, composed of half-screen-sized tiles, requires 200 tile indexes to represent it. Even if we use word-sized tile indexes, which gives us an essentially infinite supply of tiles (more than we can fit into memory, certainly), that's only 400 bytes for the tile index array. We still have to store the actual tile sprites, of course—this is the limiting factor in the variety we can put into the world.

There's no reason we can't use wraparound as well, if we want to. When we reach the end of the tile index array, we can always loop back to the beginning of the array.

Tiling in Both Directions

Scrolling doesn't always happen in the horizontal direction, of course. Sometimes we want to scroll vertically—take, for example, a

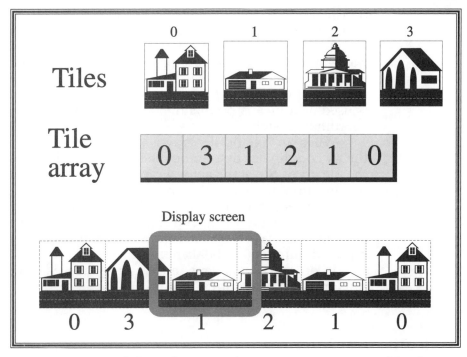

Figure 11.6   A set of tiles, a tile array, and a scene viewing a portion of the tile array.

downhill skiing game or a word processor. (I'll take the skiing game—you take the word processor.) There's no reason we can't support scrolling in both directions. An overhead map of a city, for instance, might be constructed from building and roadway tiles, and permit scrolling in both directions to access different parts of the city.

To support scrolling horizontally and vertically, we just need to turn our notion of an array of tile indexes into a two-dimensional array. The scene can be thought of as a "window" into this two-dimensional array of tiles.

Class AActorTileArray: A Tile Array Actor

Class AActorTileArray is used to create an actor which is a tiled background. It supports scrolling in both the horizontal and vertical directions, by using a two-dimensional array of tile indexes. Each such index is an index into a sprite array, supplied to the AActorTileArray in its constructor. In other words, when AActorTileArray wants to draw a given tile, using its index, it draws the sprite returned by 'sa[index]', where 'sa' is the sprite array. AActorTileArray also supports wraparound in both horizontal and vertical directions.

Actors of this class are a little different from other actors in one way—by definition, an AActorTileArray instance fills the scene in which it is placed. If this is true, what does the actor's x,y location mean? Is it ignored? No, but it has a somewhat different meaning. It is used as a means of anchoring the 2D array of tiles in the world coordinate system.

When an AActorTileArray is supplied its initial x,y,z "location," the x,y coordinates determine the location of the upper-left corner of the tile array. Since the actor wraps, the area above and to the left of this location, if any, is filled by wrapping around. If the x,y coordinates are zero, the tile array is "aligned" with the world coordinate system. Otherwise, the anchoring of the 2D tile array is offset by the amount specified. Figure 11.7 shows how a tile array is itself repeated infinitely in the scene.

In order to avoid gaps in the image, as well as other problems, AActorTileArray requires that all tiles in the sprite array have the same width and height.

AActorTileArray Interface

The header file for class AActorTileArray is listed below. AActorTileArray is derived from class AActor. The constructor is the only public method—everything else in the class is private.

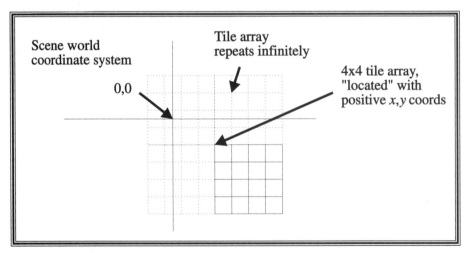

Figure 11.7   A tile array located in scene coordinates, tiling infinitely.

```
//   AActTile.h      TileArray Actor class
//   Rex E. Bradford

#ifndef__AACTTILE_H
#define__AACTTILE_H

#include "aactor.h"
#include "aspritea.h"

class AActorTileArray : public AActor {

   ASpriteArray *psa;         // ptr to sprite array
   ushort *tileMap;           // 2d tilemap array
   short numTilesAcross;      // num tiles across before wrap
   short numTilesDown;        // num tiles down before wrap
   short tileWidth;           // width of a tile
   short tileHeight;          // height of a tile

// Private methods

   int Index(int h, int v) {return((v * numTilesAcross) + h);}
   void ComputeExtent();
   void Draw(ACanvas *pcv);

public:

// Constructor

   AActorTileArray(AScene *pscene, ACoord3 &loc, ASpriteArray *psa,
      ushort *tileMap, short numTilesAcross, short numTilesDown);
};

#endif
```

AActorTileArray Constructor

The AActorTileArray constructor takes several arguments. The scene pointer and initial x,y,z location are passed on to the base AActor constructor. The other arguments include a sprite array pointer and a pointer to a "tilemap," which is the 2D array of tile indexes previously discussed. What are the dimensions of this array? These are supplied in the final two arguments, 'numTilesAcross' and 'numTilesDown'. Think of these as the width and height of the "tiled world," although with wrapping this world will, in fact, repeat indefinitely.

The constructor copies these initializers into member variables, and then computes the extent and redraws.

```
AActorTileArray::AActorTileArray(AScene *pscene_, ACoord3 &loc,
   ASpriteArray *psa_, ushort *tileMap_, short numTilesAcross_,
   short numTilesDown_) : AActor(pscene_, loc)
{
// Set basic info

   psa = psa_;                        // set tile sprite array
   tileMap = tileMap_;                // set ptr to 2D tile mape
   numTilesAcross = numTilesAcross_;  // set # tiles across
   numTilesDown = numTilesDown_;      // and # down

   ASprite *psp = (*psa)[tileMap[0]]; // use tile 0 to set
   tileWidth = psp->width;            // the tile width and height
   tileHeight = psp->height;          // they better be all the same!

// Compute extent and redraw tile array to fill scene canvas

   ComputeExtent();
   Redraw();
}
```

AActorTileArray::ComputeExtent(): Covering the Scene

By definition, the AActorTileArray object covers the scene. Computing its extent is easy, then—it starts at scene-relative location 0,0, and extends to the scene's width and height.

```
void AActorTileArray::ComputeExtent()
{
   area.left = 0;
   area.top = 0;
   area.right = pscene->LogWidth();
   area.bott = pscene->LogHeight();
}
```

Scrolling the AActorTileArray

When a scene is scrolled using AScene::Scroll(), all nonsticky actors receive notification of this using pActor→Scroll(). The implementation in base class AActor just subtracts the scroll amount from its x and y coordinates and calls ComputeExtent() to recompute its extent. This is sufficient for AActorTileArray too. Even though the tile array extends to fill the entire scene coordinate system, its "anchor point" location scrolls just like any other actor.

AActorTileArray::Draw(): Drawing the Tile Map

AActorTileArray::Draw() is a little complicated, primarily because of efficiency considerations. Rather than letting the bitmap clipper do all the work, Draw() figures out which tiles overlap the clip rectangle, and draws only those. The canvas bitmap routine used to draw each tile handles clipping for the ones which lie partially outside the clip area.

After figuring the starting row and column of the array subset which overlaps the clipping rectangle, Draw() gets to work drawing the necessary tiles. At each tile it decides to draw, Draw() uses AActorTileArray::Index() to compute the index into the 2D tile map array at that row and column. This inline method is just a manual version of what a compiler would do with a 2D array, and is implemented as follows:

```
int Index(int h, int v) {return((v * numTilesAcross) + h);}
```

Once an array index is computed for a given row and column this is used to look up a tile index in the tile map array. The tile index is then used as an index into the sprite array associated with the AActorTileArray object. This operation returns a pointer to an ASprite, which can then be rendered using the canvas method DrawBitmap().

```
void AActorTileArray::Draw(ACanvas *pcv)
{
// Assume starting with top row of tile array, at current y

    int startRowIndex = 0;
    int ydraw = loc.y;

// If top row of tiles fully above cliprect, advance to 1st visible row

    if ((ydraw + tileHeight) < pcv->clipRect.top)
        {
        int skipTiles = (pcv->clipRect.top - (ydraw + tileHeight)) /
            tileHeight;
        ydraw += (skipTiles * tileHeight);
        startRowIndex = (startRowIndex + skipTiles) % numTilesDown;
        }

// Else if top row starts below top of cliprect, back up

    else if (ydraw > pcv->clipRect.top)
        {
        int skipTiles = (ydraw - (pcv->clipRect.top - tileHeight)) /
            tileHeight;
        ydraw -= (skipTiles * tileHeight);
        startRowIndex -= skipTiles;
        while (startRowIndex < 0)
            startRowIndex += numTilesDown;
        }

// Assume starting with left column of tile array, at current x
```

```
        int startColIndex = 0;
        int xdraw = loc.x;

// If left column fully to left of cliprect, advance to 1st vis. column

        if ((xdraw + tileWidth) < pcv->clipRect.left)
            {
            int skipTiles = (pcv->clipRect.left - (xdraw + tileWidth)) /
                tileWidth;
            xdraw += (skipTiles * tileWidth);
            startColIndex = (startColIndex + skipTiles) % numTilesAcross;
            }

// Else if left column starts to right of left edge of cliprect, back up

        else if (xdraw > pcv->clipRect.left)
            {
            int skipTiles = (xdraw - (pcv->clipRect.left - tileWidth)) /
                tileWidth;
            xdraw -= (skipTiles * tileWidth);
            startColIndex -= skipTiles;
            while (startColIndex < 0)
                startColIndex += numTilesAcross;
    }

// Loop through visible rows of tile until past bottom of cliprect

        int row = startRowIndex;
        for (int y = ydraw; y < pcv->clipRect.bott; y += tileHeight)
            {

// Within each row, start from leftmost visible tile, go til past right

            int column = startColIndex;
            for (int x = xdraw; x < pcv->clipRect.right; x += tileWidth)
                {

// For each visible tile: get sprite ptr, draw it

                ASprite *psp = (*psa)[tileMap[Index(column,row)]];
                pcv->DrawBitmap(*psp, x, y);

// Advance to next column, wrap around if hit edge of tilemap

                if (++column == numTilesAcross)
                    column = 0;
                }

// Advance to next row, wrap around if hit edge of tilemap

            if (++row == numTilesDown)
                row = 0;
            }
    }
```

Animated Tile Maps

In the game *SimCity*, building rooftops get a flashing electricity symbol on them when they are disconnected from the power grid, which happens when a fire cuts the power lines or Godzilla eats them. *SimCity* is implemented using tiles, and this kind of animation is simply a matter of replacing one tile index with another at the right locations.

You can do the same thing with AActorTileArray The tile map is an array of indexes which is supplied to the AActorTileArray constructor, but lives in memory managed by the application. It could be a static array, it could be in allocated memory (and perhaps read in from a file), or it could even live inside some other object. These tile map indexes can be modified at any time, and the next time that area of the screen is drawn, the new tile index will automatically be used. In order to ensure that the screen is updated when a tile is animated, invoke the AActorTileArray's Redraw() method.

Custom Actor Classes and User-Drawn Actors

Besides the base AActor class, which provides the basic actor interface but can't be instantiated, we've now developed three actor classes. These are AActorSprite, AActorAnim, and AActorTileArray. A lot can be done with just these three classes. In the next chapter we'll introduce another, AActorButton, which can be used to create several varieties of user-interface controls.

The AActor class mechanism is meant to be extended, and it is the primary means by which specialized animation applications can be built without putting undue amounts of work and code into the application itself. If a music application wants to scroll a score across the screen, an AActorScore class should be created. If a scientific application wants to display graphs of various kinds, an AActorGraph class, or better yet, several of them, should be designed and written. A mapping application which provides scrolling through a detailed map might require a special actor class to handle the mechanisms for paging sections of the map into memory from disk. It also might need special actor classes to handle dynamic overlays of information.

The actor classes included in this book and CD are just the basic generic set. Feel free to explore and create new ones. And, if your needs are simple, consider using AActorDraw, the user-drawn actor covered next.

Class AActorDraw: A User-Drawn Actor

All of the actor classes covered so far use sprites as their underlying image representation. Furthermore, they seem to be oriented toward prerendered images, such as those read in from graphics files or sprite array files. This isn't always what we want. The musical-score class hypothesized earlier isn't predrawn; it is formed from a staff and a set of notes.

We don't necessarily need to create new actor classes every time we want an actor with special rendering needs. We already have canvases and a body of code for rendering into them—why don't we just make an actor class which has a user-renderable canvas attached to it? Then, applications can make actors whose graphics can be created on the fly by the application itself. Any time such an application wants to change the actor's visible appearance, it just renders new graphics into the canvas and calls Redraw() to get the results to the screen.

That's exactly what the AActorDraw class does. Derived from AActorSprite, it makes the sprite available for rendering in the form of a canvas. The header file for this class is listed below.

```
//    AActDraw.h      User-draw actor class
//    Rex E. Bradford

#ifndef__AACTDRAW_H
#define__AACTDRAW_H

#include "aactsp.h"

class AActorDraw : public AActorSprite {

    ACanvas *pcvDraw;    // canvas to draw into

// Private method to make sprite

    ASprite *MakeSprite(uchar bmFormat, bool transp, int width,
        int height);

public:

// Constructor: set scene and x,y,z, also bitmap format & width/height

    AActorDraw(AScene *pscene, ACoord3 &loc, uchar bmFormat,
        bool transp, int width, int height, AError &err);

// Destructor: free canvas

    AActorDraw::~AActorDraw();

// Get canvas ptr to draw into (then call Redraw())

    ACanvas *GetCanvas() {return pcvDraw;}
};

#endif
```

AActorDraw Constructor

The constructor for class AActorDraw must pass a pointer to a sprite to initialize the base AActorSprite class. Where does this sprite come from? The constructor uses the static function AActorDraw::Make-Sprite() to build a sprite, with its data bits allocated on the heap. The bitmap format, transparency flag, width, and height are all passed in from the constructor. Because this sprite must be a linear format and renderable, only BMF_LIN8 will work for now. When we add 15-bit and 24-bit support to ARTT in Part 3, however, this class will automatically be capable of creating user sprites in BMF_LIN15 and BMF_LIN24 formats.

The MakeSprite() method used by the constructor is listed below.

```
static ASprite *pspTemp;

ASprite *AActorDraw::MakeSprite(uchar bmFormat, bool transp,
    int width, int height)
{
    ABitmap bmTemp(NULL, bmFormat, transp, width, height);
    pspTemp = new ASprite(bmTemp);
    return pspTemp;
}
```

The constructor is listed below. If MakeSprite() is successful in allocating the data bits for the sprite, a canvas suitable for the bitmap format is created using ACanvas::NewCompatibleCanvas. If the allocation failed, the constructor sets the error return code to AERR_NOMEM.

```
AActorDraw::AActorDraw(AScene *pscene_, ACoord3 &loc, uchar bmFormat,
    bool transp, int width, int height, AError &err) :
        AActorSprite(pscene_, loc,
            MakeSprite(bmFormat, transp, width, height))
{
    if (pspTemp->pbits)
        {
        pcvDraw = ACanvas::NewCompatibleCanvas(*pspTemp, FALSE);
        err = AERR_OK;
        }
    else
        {
        pcvDraw = NULL;   // to protect in case destructor called
        err = AERR_NOMEM;
        }
}
```

AActorDraw Destructor

When an AActorDraw object is destroyed, the canvas allocated in the constructor must be destroyed too. The destructor takes care of this.

```
AActorDraw::~AActorDraw()
{
   if (pcvDraw)
      {
      delete pcvDraw->bm.pbits;   // delete sprite/canvas data bits
      delete pcvDraw;             // delete canvas
      }
}
```

Using AActorDraw Objects

Any time the actor is redrawn, the base class AActorSprite's Draw() method takes care of rendering whatever is currently stored in the AActorDraw's canvas. But we need a mechanism to give us access to this canvas, so we can put new images into the actor. AActor-Draw::GetCanvas() retrieves a pointer to the actor's canvas.

```
ACanvas *GetCanvas() {return pcvDraw;}
```

Now, at any time after the creation of the AActorDraw object, a program can render new contents into the canvas associated with it and invoke the Redraw() method to show the new image. The following sample code shows how this is done:

```
... assume pActorDraw is an object of class AActorDraw ...
ACanvas *pcv = pActorDraw->GetCanvas()
pcv->DrawXxxxx(...);  // draw into canvas with any rendering calls
pActorDraw->Redraw(); // update scene with new image
```

ROMNRACE: A Side-Scroller

This has really been the chapter where the tools for producing animation have switched into high gear, and we now have enough of the toolkit together to produce animation programs of all kinds. Sample program ROMNRACE is a side-scroller which uses class AActor-TileArray to create a long and somewhat varied scrolling backdrop. The game is a one-player timed race set in ancient Rome.

Figure 11.8 is a screen shot from ROMNRACE. See the CD browser or source code for instructions on how to run the game.

Figure 11.8 Screen shot from the ROMNRACE sample program.

Input Devices
and User Interaction

The point of graphics and animation is to communicate with the computer user, whether what is being communicated is a story, a scientific or cultural concept, or an exciting immersive experience. Communication with the user is not one-way. An interactive story follows different branches based on user input, an electronic encyclopedia allows topic selection and searching, and the Simul-Speedway experience is shortlived if there's no steering wheel.

This chapter is an introduction to the tools and techniques of user interaction. It begins with concepts and code for reading "events" from the keyboard and mouse. This is followed by a brief detour into the land of fonts and text rendering. Then, ARTT's facilities for building simple Graphical User Interfaces (GUIs) is presented. While not a full toolbox of user-interface elements such as that presented by Microsoft Windows or the Macintosh OS, this GUI does feature menus, icons, pushbuttons, status bars, and toolbars. Furthermore, ARTT's GUI elements are made from actor classes, and so they may be intermixed in animated scenes with other graphics.

The Keyboard

The keyboard remains a very important input device, even in the realm of mouse-based GUI environments. Until real-time speech recognition in noisy environments is perfected, there is no better way to enter moderate or large amounts of information into a computer. In 3D immersive environments, the keyboard is also a useful adjunct to the mouse—it's hard to select the "Change Carpeting" icon with the mouse while simultaneously using the mouse cursor to steer through a 3D architectural model of a new building.

The operation of a keyboard is pretty simple, at least until you get into the details. On a PC, each time a key is pressed or released, an appropriate *scan code* is sent across the connecting cable to an interface chip in the computer. The term "scan code" is derived from the fact that the keyboard hardware is continually scanning the rows and columns of the keyboard, looking for new presses and releases. Depending on how the keyboard is programmed, scan codes may also be sent repeatedly while a key is held down.

When the interface chip in a PC receives a new scan code, it triggers hardware interrupt 9. Normally, a routine in the BIOS is invoked when this interrupt occurs. The BIOS routine examines the scan code. For normal "key down" events, it places an appropriate key code in the BIOS keyboard queue. Note that the codes placed in the queue are not the same as scan codes—scan codes are numbers which are based on the position of the key on the keyboard, whereas key codes placed in the queue are a superset of ASCII codes. Some keys are handled specially. For instance, presses and releases of the shift key cause a modification of the "shift state," which affects the scan code → key code translation process for subsequent keys, but does not generate a key code itself.

Under DOS, the current program usually checks the keyboard queue periodically using BIOS or DOS calls, and reads key values from the queue. If the program fails to do so, the keyboard buffer may become full (it holds 16 characters by default), and the BIOS routine will ignore subsequent keystrokes and beep. Under Windows, Windows itself takes over the keyboard queue and provides its own event queues for programs to read.

Figure 12.1 illustrates the sequence of events that happens when a key is pressed or released.

Scan Codes and Extended ASCII Key Codes

Under DOS, the keyboard can be "taken over" by a program in order to gain access to scan codes. This is how some games are able to

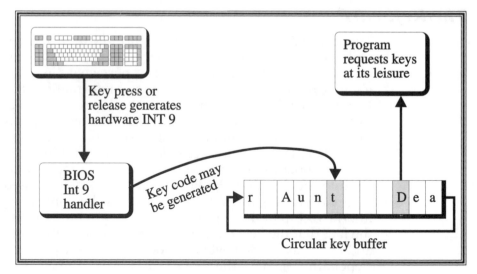

Figure 12.1   Operation of keyboard at hardware and BIOS levels.

respond to the simultaneous depression of multiple keys. The normal BIOS INT 9 handler loses information in its translation of scan codes to key codes. Hold/release information is kept track of for certain shift keys, such as the shift, control, and alt keys. For the bulk of the keyboard, releases are thrown away, and extended ASCII key codes are generated for key presses only. The exact key code depends on the state of the various shift keys—shift-A is not the same as "A", and ctrl-H is not the same as "H". There are also toggle keys to be taken into account, such as the Caps Lock key and the Num Lock key, whose state affects the translation to key codes.

However, taking over interrupt 9 is nontrivial, to say the least. Such a handler must be written in assembly language. Beyond that small hurdle, protected-mode programs must provide separate interrupt handlers for real mode and protected mode, since the hardware interrupt can occur in either mode. Finally, the translation of scan codes to key codes, which even a program using scan codes will still require, takes a fair amount of skill to get right (you must remember to turn on the keyboard's little lights, for instance).

Assuming you don't need the fine control gained by direct keyboard access, life with the keyboard becomes much more straightforward. The stream of key codes which reaches the BIOS can be read via BIOS software interrupt 16h or DOS. C and C++ compilers provide kbhit() and getch(), among other routines, for reading keycodes. Besides normal ASCII codes, many special keycodes (function keys, arrow keys, Page Up and Page Down, etc.) are represented as multibyte sequences, with the first byte the special value 00h. Table 12.1 lists the most important of these special keycodes. See any of several PC programming books for a full listing of scan codes and key codes.

The Keyboard Under Windows

While a keyboard is a keyboard under DOS or Windows, the way in which keystrokes are read by applications differs markedly. Windows programs should not use BIOS or DOS calls to read the keyboard, and they should definitely not try to reprogram the keyboard interrupts. Instead, Windows handles the keyboard on behalf of the application, and sends keystroke event messages to an application's window procedure. As a bonus, Windows programs are informed whenever keys are pressed and released, so that actions can be easily programmed to happen continually while a certain key is held down (for instance, scooting down a hallway while the up arrow is held down). Windows allows access to extended ASCII *translated* key codes, and also provides access to "raw" key presses and releases

Table 12.1 Special Multibyte Key Code Sequences

Key	Codes		
F1	00 3Bh (shift-F1: 00 54h	ctrl-F1: 00 5Eh	alt-F1: 00 68h)
F2	00 3Ch (shift-F2: 00 55h	ctrl-F2: 00 5Fh	alt-F1: 00 69h)
...F3–F10 are 00 3Dh thru 00 44h, shift-Fx, ctrl-Fx, and alt-Fx increment also)			
F11	00 85h (shift-F11: 00 87h	ctrl-F11: 00 89h	alt-F11: 00 8Bh)
F12	00 86h (shift-F12: 00 88h	ctrl-F12: 00 8Ah	alt-F12: 00 8Ch)
Insert	00 52h		
Delete	00 53h		
Home	00 47h		
End	00 4Fh		
Page Up	00 49h		
Page Down	00 51h		
Left arrow	00 4Bh		
Right arrow	00 4Dh		
Up arrow	00 48h		
Down arrow	00 50h		

Table 12.2 Important Keystroke Event Messages	
Message	**Meaning**
WM_KEYDOWN	Raw key just pressed (virtual key code)
WM_KEYUP	Raw key just released (virtual key code)
WM_CHAR	Translated character code (shift and other keys taken into account)

with *virtual key codes.* These have their own coding scheme, and are not the same as scan codes.

There are several different messages which inform an application about keystroke events. The most important are shown in Table 12.2.

Other keystroke events are sent as well, including WM_SYSKEY-DOWN, WM_SYSKEYUP, WM_SYSCHAR, WM_SYSDEADCHAR, and WM_DEADCHAR. A full discussion of Windows key event-handling is beyond the scope of this book—see Chapter 3 of Charles Petzold's *Programming Windows 3.1,* published by Microsoft Press (Appendix E), or any number of other Windows programming texts.

Class AKeybd: ARTT Keyboard Driver

ARTT presents a single interface for dealing with the keyboard under DOS and Windows. It provides support for passing extended ASCII codes to the application. Under DOS, these are gotten from the C library functions kbhit() and getch(). Under Windows, they are taken from WM_CHAR messages. If a Windows ARTT program wants to gain access to virtual key codes, it can simply trap these messages in its window procedure, like any Windows program. Access to scan codes under DOS is a more challenging matter.

Multibyte keycode sequences (00 followed by special keycode) are handled by collecting the two keys into a word-sized quantity, with the second byte in the high half of the word. Thus, the F1 key generates the 16-bit keycode 0x3B00.

Keyboard Driver Design

ARTT maintains its own queue of 16-bit keystroke events, from which an ARTT program must periodically retrieve keys to keep it from becoming full. This queue is filled via calls to kbhit() and getch() in the DOS version of the keyboard class, and from WM_CHAR messages in the Windows version.

The operations supported by the ARTT keyboard driver are basic, and consist of only two public methods:

Read()—Read next key from queue or hardware, return key value or 0 if no keys pending.

InsertKey()—Insert key into keyboard queue.

The second method, InsertKey(), allows a program to place its own "virtual keystrokes" into the keyboard queue and then read them out as if they had been typed. This is handy for supporting scripted control of an application. Also, the GUI system to be developed later in this chapter makes use of this feature to provide notification of menu selections, button presses, and the like.

The header file for class AKeybd, which provides access to the keyboard queue, is listed below.

```
//   AKeybd.h   Keyboard handling
//   Rex E. Bradford

#ifndef__AKEYBD_H
#define__AKEYBD_H

#include "atypes.h"

typedef ushort AKey;              // keycodes are 16-bit values

class AKeybd {

    static AKey keyQueue[];       // queue of pending keycodes
    static short readQ;           // current read position in queue
    static short writeQ;          // current write position in queue

    static AKey ReadKeyboard();   // read direct from keyboard source

public:

    static AKey Read();           // read key from queue/src, 0 if none
    static bool InsertKey(AKey c);     // insert keycode into queue
};

#endif
```

Reading Keycodes

The keyboard queue is defined statically, and is fixed at 64 key events, although this may be changed at will. The queue is circular—keycodes are read from one spot and written to another, and these locations slide around and around the queue, which is implemented as a simple array. Two associated variables, 'readQ' and 'writeQ', keep

---

> *The implementation of class AKeybd is split across three source files, namely AKEYBD.CPP, AKEYDOS.CPP, and AKEYWIN.CPP. Most of the implementation is in AKEYBD.CPP—only the private environment-dependent routine ReadKeyboard() is provided separately for DOS and Windows. Rather than using #ifdefs to separate DOS-specific and Windows-specific code, the linker is used to bring in the appropriate version (from ARTTDOS.LIB or ART-TWIN.LIB). Of course, absolutely no application code changes are needed to switch keyboard operation between DOS and Windows.*

track of where in the queue keys are being read from and inserted into. If they are equal, the queue is empty.

```
#define NUM_KEY_QUEUE 64                  // power of 2 for efficiency
AKey AKeybd::keyQueue[NUM_KEY_QUEUE];     // queue of pending keys
short AKeybd::readQ;                      // where keys read from
short AKeybd::writeQ;                     // where keys inserted to
```

AKeybd::Read() checks the queue and returns the oldest key in it. If the queue is empty, the ReadKeyboard() routine is called to read the "actual" keyboard—under DOS, this is implemented with kbhit() and getch(). If no keys are available at all, ReadKeyboard() will return the special value 0.

There is little need for a method to *wait* until a key becomes available. In an animation program, there is always something to be done between keystrokes, so an AKeybd equivalent of getch() would likely never be called. If a program really has nothing else to do, it can loop waiting for AKeybd::Read() to return a nonzero value.

```
AKey AKeybd::Read()
{
// Check for non-empty queue, if so grab next one from it

    if (readQ != writeQ)
        {
        AKey c = keyQueue[readQ];
        readQ = (readQ + 1) % NUM_KEY_QUEUE;
        return(c);
        }

// If no pending keys, read from key source

    return ReadKeyboard();
}
```

Inserting Keys into the Queue

AKeybd::InsertKey() is used to place a key into the keyboard queue, as if it had just been typed. It returns TRUE if successful, and FALSE if the queue is full.

```
bool AKeybd::InsertKey(AKey c)
{
// Check if room in queue, bail out if not

   if (((writeQ + 1) % NUM_KEY_QUEUE) == readQ)
      return FALSE;

// Add to queue and advance write position

   keyQueue[writeQ] = c;
   writeQ = (writeQ + 1) % NUM_KEY_QUEUE;
   return TRUE;
}
```

Reading the Keyboard Under DOS

The last piece of the keyboard puzzle is environment specific. Under DOS, the keyboard queue is really never used except by keys placed into it using InsertKey(). Normally, AKeybd::Read() checks the queue, finds it empty, and calls AKeybd::ReadKeyboard() to read the BIOS keyboard buffer using kbhit() and getch(). Under Windows, however, the queue is filled as events come in through the windowing system. Providing a queue under ARTT melds these two varied mechanisms into one simple system.

The DOS version of AKeybd::ReadKeyboard is listed below. This is a private method, and is called only by AKeybd::Read().

```
AKey AKeybd::ReadKeyboard()
{
   if (!kbhit())         // check if keypress in BIOS queue
      return 0;          // no, return 0

   AKey c = getch();     // yes, get key code
   if (c == 0)           // if special code 00:
      c = getch() << 8;  // grab 2nd byte, put in high half of word
   return c;             // return 16-bit keycode
}
```

Reading the Keyboard Under Windows

Because we can't read the keyboard directly, the Windows version of AKeybd::ReadKeyboard(), called whenever the key event queue is empty, always returns 0.

```
AKey AKeybd::ReadKeyboard()
{
   return(0);
}
```

How, then, do key events get to our ARTT programs? They are placed into the keyboard queue from the application's window procedure. As a convenience, the AWingWindow::StdHandler() function, which should be called by the window procedures in ARTT programs, does this for us in the case of WM_CHAR messages. The AWingWindow::StdHandler() shown in Chapter 7 left out the following case statement which is present in the real code:

```
case WM_CHAR:
   AKeybd::InsertKey(wParam);
   break;
```

If an ARTT program wishes to handle WM_KEYDOWN and WM_KEYUP messages too, it should put similar code to handle these messages in its window procedure. There is the issue of how to represent key values which are not in the normal ASCII set. In particular, key-up events need to be distinguished from key-down events. Since ARTT keycodes are 16 bits in size, there is plenty of room for devising an encoding scheme which doesn't conflict with the keys generated via WM_CHAR.

Using the Keyboard

In an ARTT program, reading the keyboard and reacting to it is one of the things that is typically done in a main event loop. With the classes developed above, this can work the same in both **DOS** and Windows programs. After initialization and creation of one or more scenes, an ARTT program using scenes and actors might enter a main loop which looks something like this:

```
while (TRUE)
   {
   AScene::UpdateAll();
   ... do other activities, such as checking and manipulating actors, etc.
   int c = Akeybd::Read();
   switch (c)    // return 0 if no key pending
      {
      ... case statements to handle various keys ...
      }
   }
```

The Mouse

In graphics programs, the mouse is often the main input device. The advantage of a mouse over a keyboard is the ability to point at some part of the screen and direct input there. The disadvantage, of course, is that the "input code" is limited by the number of buttons on the mouse. A PC-based mouse typically has two buttons. Table 12.3 lists various types of "mouse gestures" and their common meanings.

Mouse Operation

Most mice in use on PCs are so-called "mechanical" mice. As the mouse is moved across the table, a ball inside the mouse rotates in x- and y-directions. This causes tiny axles attached to gears inside the mouse to rotate. The rotations are detected and fed to a small chip inside the mouse. Changes in the mouse location in *mickeys*, which are related to rotation of the axles and thus absolute mouse movements, are sent to the PC. PC-based mice are typically connected to a serial port, although direct connection to the PC motherboard or a plug-in card ("bus" mouse) is not uncommon.

Mouse position changes, as well as button presses and releases, generate interrupts which are picked up by code in the mouse driver software. For DOS programs, the Microsoft Mouse driver is the standard on PCs; other drivers are compatible with this driver even if they offer special features. The driver, which is loaded into the PC's memory at boot time through the config.sys or autoexec.bat files, is responsible for tracking the mouse position in mickeys and translating it to pixels, under control of the application program. The driver

Table 12.3 Mouse Gestures and Typical meanings	
Gesture	**Typical Meanings**
Move mouse	Point at selection; also "steering" in 3D environments
Click button	Make selection, right click often used for context-sensitive menu popup
Double-click button	Launch program or feature
Press button and drag	Move item to new location
Press both buttons	Rarely used

also keeps track of the current state of the mouse buttons. Figure 12.2 illustrates the overall architecture of the mouse, driver, and application.

Microsoft Mouse Driver

The Microsoft Mouse driver, or its compatible replacement, is accessed by programs through software interrupt 33H. Calls to the driver are made to initialize the mouse, read the current location of the mouse, look for button presses and releases, and change the appearance of the cursor. Other advanced features include the ability to install a routine to be called at interrupt, so that the program may be notified immediately of changes in the mouse state. Table 12.4 lists the most important functions supported by the mouse driver—for a more in-depth treatment, see any book featuring coverage of common device drivers and interrupts.

The Mouse Cursor

Under DOS, the Microsoft Mouse driver can maintain the mouse cursor image, although it can do so only in certain standard graphics modes. In Super VGA modes, and often even in graphics modes supported by the driver, the application program takes over display and movement of the mouse cursor. If possible, the mouse cursor should be updated during interrupts, so that the cursor can smoothly track mouse movements even if the program is busy doing calculations or other activities.

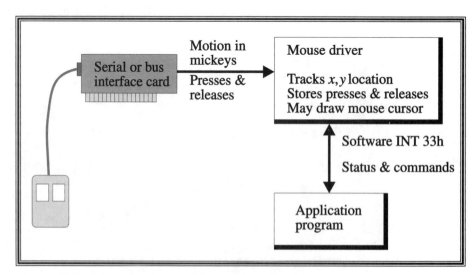

Figure 12.2   Mouse hardware, driver, and application.

Table 12.4 Primary INT 33H Functions in Microsoft Mouse Driver

Function	Purpose
00H	Reset mouse and get status
01H	Show mouse pointer (not supported in all graphics modes)
02H	Hide mouse pointer
03H	Get mouse position and button status
04H	Set mouse pointer position
07H	Set horizontal limits for pointer
08H	Set vertical limits for pointer
09H	Set graphics pointer shape
0BH	Read mouse motion counters
0CH	Set user-defined mouse event handler (real-mode only, unless extender reflects)
0FH	Set mickeys to pixels ratio

In some programs and special modes within programs, the mouse "cursor" may not be as simple as a small arrow or other graphic. For instance, a computer-aided design program may feature screen-sized crosshairs, which are moved continually to be centered around the mouse location. Typically, however, a small sprite graphic is used. This graphic features a "hotspot" around which the graphic is centered—the hotspot represents the true location of the mouse. In ARTT, the ASprite class is perfect for representing mouse cursors.

The Mouse in Windows

Microsoft Windows takes care of the basics of interfacing with the mouse, and presents mouse events to an application through its window procedures. Table 12.5 lists the mouse-related messages.

Windows provides an API for controlling the mouse, including setting the cursor shape from cursor resources stored in the application's EXE file or an external resource file. This means that Windows-based ARTT programs can't set the cursor shape from a sprite—they must use predefined cursor resources like other Windows programs. Another difference is that the DOS-based mouse-handling code included in ARTT doesn't generate double-click events, though it certainly could be modified to do so. Windows, however, detects double-clicks, and these are passed on to the application.

Table 12.5   Windows Mouse-Related Messages

Message	Meaning
WM_MOUSEMOVE	Mouse cursor location changed
WM_LBUTTONDOWN	Left button pressed
WM_LBUTTONUP	Left button released
WM_LBUTTONDBLCLK	Left button clicked shortly after previous click
WM_RBUTTONDOWN	Right button pressed
WM_RBUTTONUP	Right button released
WM_RBUTTONDBLCLK	Right button clicked shortly after previous click

Class AMouse: ARTT Mouse Driver

ARTT provides a mouse "driver" class which makes use of the underlying DOS and Windows drivers. It presents a simple mouse interface which works similarly in both environments. An ARTT program may still access the underlying (environment-specific) driver directly to perform advanced control functions if necessary. The ARTT mouse driver supplies the following functionality:

- Initialization—Detects presence of mouse and initializes underlying driver.
- Location—Returns mouse location at any time.
- Events—Maintains queue of mouse events and reports next event.
- Cursor—Provides graphic sprite cursor, plus methods to hide/show, change sprite, and so on. Cursor shape-changing is not implemented in the Windows version of the driver (use the Windows API instead).

Mouse Events

ARTT maintains a queue of mouse events. These events are:

MOUSE_BUTT1_DOWN	Press of left mouse button
MOUSE_BUTT1_UP	Release of left mouse button
MOUSE_BUTT1_DBLCLK	Second of two successive clicks of left mouse button
MOUSE_BUTT2_DOWN	Press of right mouse button
MOUSE_BUTT2_UP	Release of right mouse button
MOUSE_BUTT2_DBLCLK	Second of two successive clicks of right mouse button

When an ARTT program asks for the next mouse event and no new presses or releases have been placed in the queue, one of the following two mouse events is reported back:

MOUSE_MOVE   Mouse has moved to new location since last event

MOUSE_IDLE   No button event or mouse movement since last event

Each event is wrapped in a structure which includes the mouse event type and the coordinates of the mouse cursor at the time the event was detected. Additionally, the event may be tagged with a window identifier, whose meaning is irrelevant to the mouse code per se. Under Windows, ARTT tags mouse events with the AWing-Window that they were received by. The AMouseEvent structure is defined in AMOUSEVT.H, which is listed below.

```
//    AMousEvt.h   Mouse events
//    Rex E. Bradford

#ifndef __AMOUSEVT_H
#define __AMOUSEVT_H

// Mouse event types

typedef enum {
   MOUSE_NONE,
   MOUSE_MOVE,
   MOUSE_BUTT1_DOWN,
   MOUSE_BUTT1_UP,
   MOUSE_BUTT1_DBLCLK,
   MOUSE_BUTT2_DOWN,
   MOUSE_BUTT2_UP,
   MOUSE_BUTT2_DBLCLK,
} AMouseEventCode;

// Mouse event structure

typedef struct {
   AMouseEventCode code;   // MOUSE_XXX, type of event
   short x;                // mouse xpos at time of event
   short y;                // mouse ypos at time of event
   void *window;           // window event associated with
} AMouseEvent;

#endif
```

A program calls AMouse::NextEvent() to read the next event from the queue. If the queue is empty, NextEvent() still returns a valid mouse event, which is either MOUSE_MOVE or MOUSE_IDLE. The routine returns FALSE when filling in the event structure with a MOUSE_IDLE event, and TRUE for any other event. We'll present the

AMouse class declaration in a moment; for now, here's the prototype for NextEvent():

```
static bool NextEvent(AMouseEvent &evt); // get event if avail
```

How do the mouse events get into the queue? In the DOS version of the ARTT AMouse class, the NextEvent() method itself calls the underlying Microsoft Mouse driver and fills the queue with whatever events have been detected by that driver. In Windows, the application's window procedure must post them to the queue, using AMouse::PostEvent(). The standard window message handler AWingWindow::StdHandler(), which should be called for unhandled messages inside an ARTT program's window procedure, does this automatically. The following exerpt from that method shows how: Note that each event is tagged with 'this', the pointer to the window receiving the message.

```
case WM_MOUSEMOVE:
    AMouse::PostEvent(MOUSE_MOVE, LOWORD(lParam), HIWORD(lParam),
        this);
    break;
case WM_LBUTTONDOWN:
    AMouse::PostEvent(MOUSE_BUTT1_DOWN, LOWORD(lParam),
        HIWORD(lParam), this);
    break;
case WM_LBUTTONUP:
    AMouse::PostEvent(MOUSE_BUTT1_UP, LOWORD(lParam),
        HIWORD(lParam), this);
    break;
case WM_LBUTTONDBLCLK:
    AMouse::PostEvent(MOUSE_BUTT1_DBLCLK, LOWORD(lParam),
        HIWORD(lParam), this);
    break;
case WM_RBUTTONDOWN:
    AMouse::PostEvent(MOUSE_BUTT2_DOWN, LOWORD(lParam),
        HIWORD(lParam), this);
    break;
case WM_RBUTTONUP:
    AMouse::PostEvent(MOUSE_BUTT2_UP, LOWORD(lParam),
        HIWORD(lParam), this);
    break;
case WM_RBUTTONDBLCLK:
    AMouse::PostEvent(MOUSE_BUTT2_DBLCLK, LOWORD(lParam),
        HIWORD(lParam), this);

    break;
```

Drawing the Mouse Cursor

For DOS programs, ARTT provides a mouse cursor in the shape of a sprite, and a method to change its shape by assigning a new sprite pointer. Windows programs must use the Windows function SetCursor() to change the cursor shape. The AMouse class also provides methods to hide and show the mouse cursor—these work in either environment. Under DOS, hiding and showing the mouse cursor is necessary when updating areas of the screen overlapped by the mouse cursor; Windows takes care of this invisibly. It is easy to take for granted that the mouse acts like an "overlay" on top of the screen. In reality, a lot of work goes on behind the scenes to make sure that the cursor can glide over a changing screen surface. Under DOS, the AMouse class has to do this work itself.

First of all, the area under the sprite cursor is captured, using ACanvas::GetBitmap(). This retrieves the image under the rectangular area defined by the cursor, and places these pixels into a bitmap used for this purpose. We haven't seen this method before, so let's look at it now. It is very handy for uses beyond cursor rendering. Any routine which wants to capture part of the screen for later replacement (for instance, before a quicklived menu popup appears) can use GetBitmap().

```
void (ACanvas::*pfGetBitmap[])(ABitmap &bm, int x, int y) = {
   &ACanvas::GetBitmapLin8,
   &ACanvas::GetBitmapLin15,
   &ACanvas::GetBitmapLin24,
   &ACanvas::GetBitmapBadFormat,
   &ACanvas::GetBitmapBadFormat,
   &ACanvas::GetBitmapBadFormat,
   &ACanvas::GetBitmapBadFormat,
};

void ACanvas::GetBitmap(ABitmap &bms, int x, int y)
{
    (this->*pfGetBitmap[bms.format])(bms, x, y);
}
```

GetBitmap(), like DrawBitmap(), uses a table of pointers to methods to get to the proper routine based on the type of bitmap it would like to capture into. The various methods used to capture bitmaps are essentially reverse images of those used to draw bitmaps, and are not reproduced in this book. As always, see the CD.

After the area under the cursor is captured, the sprite cursor is rendered into the screen canvas. When the mouse cursor needs to be moved, the previously captured area is replaced (erasing the cursor), the area under the new location is captured, and the sprite cursor is drawn at the new location. This is the saveunder technique described in Chapter 10, by the way. AMouse::Hide() is used to draw back the captured area, and AMouse::Show() captures a new area and draws the cursor. The process of moving a cursor across an unchanging screen is illustrated in Figure 12.3.

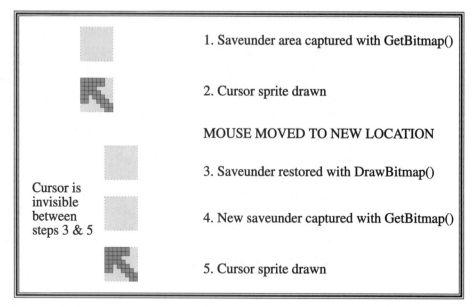

1. Saveunder area captured with GetBitmap()

2. Cursor sprite drawn

MOUSE MOVED TO NEW LOCATION

3. Saveunder restored with DrawBitmap()

Cursor is invisible between steps 3 & 5

4. New saveunder captured with GetBitmap()

5. Cursor sprite drawn

Figure 12.3 Simple method of drawing mouse cursor. Cursor flashes during movement.

This process works fine across a static screen, but what about when new images are rendered to the screen? This must be done without obliterating the mouse cursor, and without making the captured saveunder contents obsolete. The simplest method is to use AMouse::Hide() before rendering any new graphics to the screen canvas, and AMouse::Show() afterwards. The problem with this approach is that the cursor blinks each time this is done. If the screen is being updated continually, the blinking is unacceptable.

The ASceneDOS class provides a solution to the blinking cursor problem. Whenever the scene is blitted to the screen, and the mouse overlaps that area, the mouse cursor is temporarily rendered into the scene's off-screen canvas just before blitting. This way, the image of the cursor is part of what is rendered onto the screen. The rendering is still bracketed by Hide() and Show(), but the image being blitted contains the cursor, so the amount of time that the screen shows no cursor is greatly reduced. This process is illustrated in Figure 12.4— see the full implementation of AScene::RedrawAndBlit() in ASCEN-DOS.CPP on the CD for all the details.

Class AMouse Interface

The full implementation of the mouse interface is contained in AMOUSDOS.CPP (DOS version) and AMOUSWIN.CPP (Windows ver-

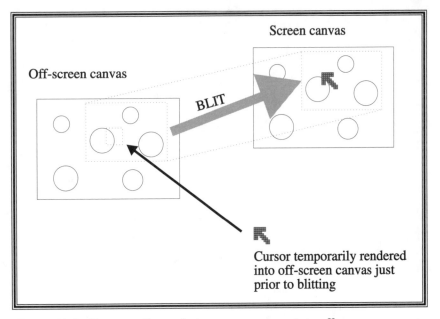

Figure 12.4 Temporarily rendering mouse cursor into off-screen canvas to prevent flashing.

sion). These implementation files are not listed in this chapter—see these files on the CD for the full details. The header file, which defines the interface, is identical across the two versions. It is listed below.

```
//    AMouse.h    Mouse handling
//    Rex E. Bradford

#ifndef__AMOUSE_H
#define__AMOUSE_H

#include "atypes.h"
#include "aerror.h"
#include "amousevt.h"
#include "asprite.h"
#include "acanvas.h"

class AMouse {
    static AMouseEvent eventQueue[];    // event queue
    static short readQ;                 // position where events read from
    static short writeQ;                // position where events posted to

    static bool ReadEvent(AMouseEvent &evt);  // read event from queue

public:
// Initialization and testing
```

```
      static AError Init(ACanvas *pcvScreen);    // init mouse
      static bool IsMouse();                      // is there a mouse?

// Read mouse location & get next event

      static void GetCursorLoc(short &x, short &y);    // get x,y loc
      static bool NextEvent(AMouseEvent &evt);  // get event if avail

// Show, hide, and update cursor

      static void Show();         // decr hide counter & maybe show
      static void Hide();         // incr hide counter, ensure hidden
      static void UpdateCursor(); // update graphic position of cursor
      static bool IsShown();      // is mouse currently shown?

// Set and get cursor sprite

      static void SetCursor(ASprite *sp); // set cursor sprite
      static ASprite *GetCursor();        // get ptr to cursor sprite

// Post event to queue

      static AError PostEvent(AMouseEventCode code, short x, short y,
         void *window);
};

#endif
```

Mouse Handling in Scenes

Unlike keyboard events, mouse events are directed to a particular location on the screen. Rather than just handing such events to a program's main loop, it's preferable to deliver them directly to the entity managing that portion of the screen. The scene and actor classes have facilities for such object-based mouse handling. These were left out of the original discussion in Chapter 10.

Since both scenes and actors have rectangular extents, it's trivial to find both the scene and actor (if any) which is under the mouse cursor. AScene::MouseHandleAll() can be called by an application to pass on the event to the appropriate scene (and eventually actor). It finds the right scene to hand off the event to based on the following algorithm:

1. If some scene has "captured" the mouse, pass event to it.
2. Else test all scenes via virtual method OwnMouseEvent().
3. Else fail by returning FALSE.

```
bool AScene::MouseHandleAll(AMouseEvent &evt)
{
// If some scene has captured mouse, pass event to it.
```

```
    if (pMouseScene)
        return(pMouseScene->MouseHandle(evt));

// Else scan scene list, looking for a scene which "owns" the event.
// In DOS, this is Encloses(). In Windows, it's the event's window
// tag. Anyhow, pass event on to its owner.

    AScene *pscene = pFirst;
    while (pscene)
        {
        if (pscene->OwnMouseEvent(evt))
            return (pscene->MouseHandle(evt));
        pscene = pscene->next;
        }

// No scene owns event, mouse event ignored.

    return FALSE;
}
```

Let's ignore this "mouse capture" business for a second, and focus on OwnMouseEvent(). Which scene gets to own the event, in the absence of an explicit capture? In the base AScene class, Own-MouseEvent() merely tests to see which scene encloses the mouse location.

```
virtual bool OwnMouseEvent(AMouseEvent &evt) { // own mouse event?
    return screenArea.Encloses(evt.x, evt.y);}
```

This works well under DOS, since scenes are not allowed to overlap. Under Windows, however, windows may overlap. A simple screen area test is insufficient. Happily, we previously tagged the mouse events with the pointer to the AWingWindow window they were received by. Now, ASceneWin::OwnMouseEvent() can make use of the fact that each scene also contains a pointer to its window. If the two match, the event is for that scene:

```
virtual bool OwnMouseEvent(AMouseEvent &evt) {
    return (evt.window == pWin);}
```

Well. So far we've found which scene wants the mouse event, and passed the buck to it via MouseHandle(). This method now tries to find the relevant actor. First, the mouse event's screen coordinates are converted to canvas coordinates, offsetting by the scene's upper-left corner and possibly scaling. Then, another mouse-capture check is made. If nobody has captured the mouse, a search for an actor whose extent overlaps the mouse location is made. If such an actor is found, virtual method AActor::MouseHandle() is called to handle the event. This is where the real work of mouse event handling goes down, in the class-specific handler method. If this method returns FALSE, by the way, the search continues. Since actors can overlap, this may turn up another actor who is willing to handle the event. The actors are tested from front to back.

```
bool AScene::MouseHandle(AMouseEvent &evt)
{
// Make copy of mouse event, transform to local screen coords

    AMouseEvent localEvt = evt;
    ConvertScreen2Canvas(localEvt.x, localEvt.y);

// If actor has captured mouse, pass event to it.

    if (pMouseScene == this)
        return(pMouseActor->MouseHandle(localEvt));

// Else start with frontmost actor, look for one which encloses mouse
// loc. Pass event to it. If it returns FALSE, continue with other
// actors behind this one which may overlap mouse loc.

    AActor *pActor = pFrontActor;
    while (pActor)
        {
        if (pActor->area.Encloses(localEvt.x, localEvt.y) &&
            pActor->MouseHandle(localEvt))
                return TRUE;
        pActor = pActor->next;
        }

// Nobody loves us, take zero and go home.

    return FALSE;
}
```

Now, back to this mouse-capture business. Next time you fire up Windows, press on any OK or Cancel button, and don't release the mouse. Now move the mouse around, both inside and outside the button. It pops up and down. The button has "captured" the mouse, and is handling all events until you lift up the button. ARTT supports such mouse capture, and in fact uses it in the AActorButton class developed later in this chapter. AScene::CaptureMouse() captures the mouse on behalf of a particular actor in a scene. CaptureMouse(NULL) releases the capture.

```
AScene *AScene::pMouseScene; // ptr to scene with mouse capture
AActor *AScene::pMouseActor; // ptr to actor with mouse capture
```

```
void AScene::CaptureMouse(AActor *pActor)
{
    pMouseActor = pActor;
    pMouseScene = pMouseActor ? pMouseActor->pscene : NULL;
}
```

These additional inline methods are defined in class AScene:

```
bool IsCapture() {return (this == pMouseScene);}
static bool IsCapture(AActor *pActor) {return (pActor == pMouseActor);}
```

The base actor class AActor defines the interface by which actors handle mouse events. All of these functions are inline, and are presented below. Note that AActor::MouseHandle(), which is virtual, simply returns FALSE. It is up to a derived class to provide a handler which does something useful and returns TRUE.

```
virtual bool MouseHandle(AMouseEvent &evt) {return FALSE;}

void CaptureMouse() {pscene->CaptureMouse(this);}
void UncaptureMouse() {pscene->CaptureMouse(NULL);}
bool IsCapture() {return AScene::IsCapture(this);}
```

Text and Fonts

A picture may be worth just under 1K of words, but text hasn't vanished from the computer screen yet. A somewhat amusing (but highly useful) development in graphical user interfaces is "balloon help," wherein the icon your cursor is dangling uncertainly over becomes tagged with a text overlay which describes what the icon means. This is the icon, remember, that replaced a clunky old text menu item in the first place.

Text is perhaps less important in real-time animation than it is in word processing and other business software. Even so, text is highly important for the following purposes, among others:

- Menus
- Pushbuttons and other user-interface elements
- Status displays and message boxes
- In-view labeling of objects
- Help text

Font Terminology

The shapes of the set of letters making up an alphabet are called a *typeface*. A *type family* is a set of related typefaces, usually with variation in *styles*. A family typically has bold, italic, and other stylistic variations on the basic character shapes. A typeface is often classified as being *serif* or *sans serif* (without serif), serifs being the little ornamental strokes which adorn the endpoints of the major strokes in a character. Common typeface names include Times Roman, Helvetica, Courier, Palatino, and Gothic. An implementation of a particular typeface, realized with a particular style at a particular size, is called a *font*.

The *point size* of a font is the height of the characters in *points*, where a point equals 1/72 of an inch. Thus, a 12-point font has characters which are 12/72, or 1/6, inches in height. In fonts, the term *pitch* refers to character width. Fonts can be characterized as being *fixed-pitch*, wherein all characters have the same width, or *proportional*, where each character carries its own width. Courier is an example of a fixed-pitch font and is used in this book for source listings, in order that characters in the same column line up under one another. Most fonts are proportional, because variable-width characters look better. The *baseline* refers to an imaginary horizontal line at the "base" of the character, below which the *descender* of the character exists and above which is the *ascender*. The *x-height* refers to the distance between the baseline and the top of most lowercase letters. *Leading* is the distance from the bottom of one row of characters to the top of the next. Figure 12.5 illustrates some of these terms.

Another term used in fonts is *kerning*. This describes the process of placing some characters to the left of where they would otherwise be drawn, in order to fit them under the overhang of another character. In Figure 12.5, for instance, the g is kerned to fit better under the overhang of the V. Fonts which support kerning often have a table of *kerning pairs*, which denote particular pairs of characters to be treated specially and how much the right character should be moved left to fit properly.

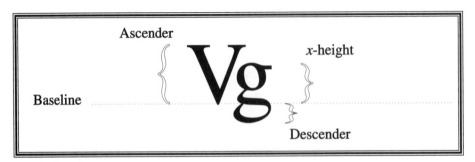

Figure 12.5 Some of the terms associated with a font.

Font Technologies

Three basic technologies have been employed in the representation and rendering of text fonts. These are:

- Bitmapped fonts
- Vector fonts
- Outline fonts

Bitmapped fonts are represented internally, unsurprisingly, as bitmaps. Typically, each character is represented by a monochrome bitmap. Each pixel is represented by a single bit—a value of 1 means that the pixel is *on,* and a 0 means it is *off.* Rendering such monochrome bitmaps onto a color display requires examining each bit and rendering "on" pixels in the desired color. Bitmapped fonts, also called *raster* fonts, are representationally simple, and straightforward to render. Their weaknesses include the fact that changes in style and size require an entirely separate font in order to look good. Simple bitmap scaling works well enough for many kinds of images, but for text characters the blockiness and artifacts introduced are unacceptable.

Vector fonts, where each character is represented by a set of lines (vectors), have some advantages over bitmapped fonts. In a vector font, a character is rendered by drawing each of the lines which make up its definition. Scaling a vector font to a different point size is simply a matter of scaling the endpoint coordinates of the lines before drawing. Styles are also achievable on the fly; for instance, slanting for italics is just a geometric transformation of endpoint coordinates. Vector-based characters drawn with lines which are a single pixel thick tend to look thin when scaled. Even when drawn with thick lines, vector fonts have an angular look.

Outline fonts are based on curve segments, which solves the problem of the angular look of lines. The area between inner and outer outlines is filled, which solves the line thinness problem by allowing the curve thickness to vary as the character definition is scaled up. Even so, at small point sizes outline fonts still have artifacts based on the process of rounding to whole pixels. Scaled outlines by themselves are not enough. Outline fonts now include extra information called *hinting.* This information provides hints to the outline renderer, telling it subtle adjustments to make when scaling to various point sizes. These hints, created by the typeface designer with special visually based software tools, ensure that the font looks good at all important sizes. All this curve-rendering and filling is a heck of a lot of work. In order to speed the process, modern outline font-rendering systems reserve a block of memory for a cache of "realized" font bitmaps, created from the outlines as rendering takes place. The most recently rendered characters at a given size are thus made available in bitmapped form for next time.

Figure 12.6 shows a character represented using each of the three font-rendering technologies. Outline font technology has emerged as the mechanism of choice for high-end text. Both the Macintosh OS and Microsoft Windows use outline fonts, although they both support bitmapped fonts as well. Adobe Postscript "Type 1" fonts and TrueType fonts are both examples of outline fonts.

ARTT Font Technology

Outline fonts are great for high-end text needs, but rendering text from outlines has performance problems which are serious in a real-time environment. ARTT uses bitmapped fonts exclusively. Unlike most standard bitmapped fonts, which are monochrome, ARTT fonts are based on color bitmaps. This allows for colorful text in games and presentations. Also, fonts may have *anti-aliasing* built-in.

One problem with color fonts is that the particular colors are built into the character definition. In Part 3, we'll see how to use color lookup tables to change coloration on the fly, so that a gray font may be rendered in purple, for instance.

The technology for creating and using color fonts is already part of what we have developed so far. In ARTT, a font is a special kind of sprite array—in fact it is class derived from ASpriteArray. The bitmapped characters which make up a font are read from a graphics file, where each character is defined inside a bordered box. Figure 12.7 shows a screen shot of FONT8.PCX, a graphics file which holds a small 8-pixel-tall font.

Class AFont: ARTT Font Class

The header file for class AFont is listed below. It features the following methods:

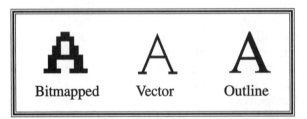

Figure 12.6 A character represented in bitmap, vector, and outline formats.

Figure 12.7 A font defined as bordered characters in a graphics file.

- Two constructors, for building a font from bordered characters
- Several methods to retrieve font information such as character height
- Method Char(), which returns the sprite associated with a given character
- Two methods to determine the size of a string of text

```
//   AFont.h    Font Class
//   Rex E. Bradford

#ifndef__AFONT_H
#define__AFONT_H

#include "aspritea.h"

class AFont : public ASpriteArray {

    short base;                // base character value
    short height;              // font height (copied from 1st char)
    short ascent;              // font ascent (copied from 1st char)
    short maxWidth;        // maximum char width in pixels

// Private method to extract bordered font chars from bitmap

    void ExtractCharsFromBitmap(ABitmap &bm, long borderColor);

public:

// Construct a font from bitmap or file

    AFont(ABitmap &bm, long borderColor, short base);
    AFont(char *filename, long borderColor, short base, AError &err);
```

```
// Character/font info

    int CharWidth(int c) {return((*this)[c - base]->width);}
    int MaxCharWidth() {return maxWidth;}
    int Height() {return height;}
    int Ascent() {return ascent;}
    int Descent() {return(height - ascent);}

// Get character sprite ptr

    ASprite *Char(int c) {return (*this)[c - base];}

// Text sizing

    short TextWidth(char *str, int maxChars = 32767);
    void TextSize(char *str, short &width, short &height,
        int maxChars = 32767);
};

#endif
```

AFont Constructors

The two AFont constructors are used to read the font's characters from a bitmap using the "bitmap finder" code developed in Chapter 8. The first takes a bitmap reference as argument, along with a border color in native format, and a "base character" value. This value defines the lowest value encoded in the font. Character values may range from 0 to 255, but fonts can restrict themselves to a portion of this range. For instance, a font may start with the space character (0x20), which is the first printable character in the ASCII set. All characters in the font should be the same height—the text sizing routines described later assume that all characters are the same height as the first character in the font. Font widths may vary from character to character—such proportional fonts look much better than fixed-pitch fonts.

```
AFont::AFont(ABitmap &bm, long borderColor, short base_)
{
// Set basic fields

    base = base_;
    height = ascent = maxWidth = 0;

// Extract bordered chars from bitmap into font

    ExtractCharsFromBitmap(bm, borderColor);
}
```

The second construct takes a filename as input instead of a bitmap reference, and does the work of opening the file, loading a bitmap from it, and then extracting characters into the font.

```
AFont::AFont(char *filename, long borderColor, short base_, AError &err)
{
// Set basic fields

    base = base_;
    height = ascent = maxWidth = 0;

// Read graphics file into bitmap

    ABitmap bm;
    err = AGfxFile::Read(filename, bm);

// If that worked, extract font chars, clean up bitmap

    if (!err)
        {
        ExtractCharsFromBitmap(bm, borderColor);
        if (bm.ppalette)
            delete bm.ppalette;
        delete bm.pbits;
        }
}
```

Both constructors use AFont::ExtractCharsFromBitmap() to do the bulk of the work. This method is listed below.

```
void AFont::ExtractCharsFromBitmap(ABitmap &bm, long borderColor)
{
// Capture sprites from bitmap into font

    ABitmapFind bmFind(bm, borderColor);
    bmFind.CaptureSprites(*this, TRUE);

// Get ptr to 1st char, fill in font fields from it

    ASprite *psp = (*this)[0];
    if (psp)
        {
        height = psp->height;       // font height is 1st char height
        ascent = psp->yoff;         // look for hotspot ascent marker
        maxWidth = psp->width;      // assume 1st char is widest
        for (int i = 1; ; i++)      // then search all chars for widest
            {
            psp = (*this)[i];
            if (psp == NULL)
                break;
```

```
              if (psp->width > maxWidth) // new widest char, set it
                 maxWidth = psp->width;
          }
       }
    }
```

Font Information Methods

Once a font has been created, several inline methods are available to extract information about the font or a particular character. These are listed below—see the previously listed header file for their definitions.

CharWidth()—Returns width of a given character in pixels

MaxCharWidth()—Returns width of widest character in font

Height()—Returns height of characters in font (should all be same)

Ascent()—Returns number of pixels above baseline

Descent()—Returns number of pixels below baseline

The baseline of the font, like its height, is taken from the first character. The y-coordinate of the sprite's hotspot is used to determine the baseline; the x-coordinate of the hotspot is ignored, as are hotspots for all remaining characters.

Retrieving a Character's Sprite

Since a font is a sprite array, sprite array indexing can be used to retrieve a pointer to the sprite associated with a character. The Char() method takes into account the fact that the font may not start with character 0.

```
ASprite *Char(int c) {return (*this)[c - base];}
```

Rendering Text into Canvases

Drawing a single character in a given font is as simple as retrieving the pointer to the sprite associated with the character using AFont::Char(), and then rendering that character using the Draw-Bitmap() canvas method. ACanvas::DrawCharU() draws a single character from a font at the specified x,y location, unclipped. DrawChar() does the same, restricted to the canvas clip rectangle.

```
void ACanvas::DrawCharU(int c, AFont &font, int x, int y)
{
    ASprite *spChar = font.Char(c);            // get char sprite
    DrawBitmapU(*spChar, x, y - font.Ascent()); // and draw
}
```

```
void ACanvas::DrawChar(int c, AFont &font, int x, int y)
{
    ASprite spChar = *font.Char(c);      // get char sprite
    y -= font.Ascent();                   // offset y by font's ascent
    if (ClipBitmap(spChar, x, y))         // clip the character
      DrawBitmapU(spChar, x, y);          // and draw it
}
```

Drawing a NULL-terminated string of text is done by drawing each character using one of the above methods. The only special character, besides the 0 terminator, is the carriage return character. When encountered, the text position for the next character is moved back to the starting *x*-coordinate, and down by the height of the character.

ACanvas::DrawTextU() draws a string of text using unclipped character-drawing calls.

```
void ACanvas::DrawTextU(char *str, AFont &font, int x, int y)
{
    int xmargin = x;                  // set margin to beginning x
    int c;
    while ((c = *(uchar *)str++) != 0)  // get next char as a uchar
      {
      switch (c)
        {
        case '\n':
          x = xmargin;                // reset x to margin
          y += font.Height();         // and move to next row
          break;

        default:
          DrawCharU(c, font, x, y);   // else: draw char
          x += font.CharWidth(c);     // and advance x
          break;
        }
      }
}
```

Drawing a clipped string of text could be as simple as the above routine, substituting calls to DrawCharU() with calls to DrawChar(). However, DrawText() provides a significant optimization by skipping through all characters which lie above the clip rectangle, and exiting as soon as the text location lies fully below the clip rectangle. Clipping on left and right is left to DrawChar(). With good clipping, an entire "movie credits" listing can be scrolled through a screen. The credits text is represented by a single long string of text, continually redrawn at a *y*-coordinate which scrolls in the negative (upward) direction.

```
void ACanvas::DrawText(char *str, AFont &font, int x, int y)
{
// If top of text is below clip rect, we're outta here
```

```
        if ((y - font.Ascent()) >= clipRect.bott)
           return;


// Start at top of text, scan thru text to skip all rows of text, if
// any, which are completely above the clip rect.

        uchar *p = (uchar *) str;
        while ((y + font.Descent()) < clipRect.top)
           {
           while (*p)   // this row is above cliprect, scan to return
              {
              if (*p == '\n')
                 y += font.Height();
              ++p;
              }
           if (*p == 0)        // if we hit the end of the string, bye
              return;
           }


// Set left margin, now do like DrawTextU() except calling clipped
// version of character draw routine.

        int xmargin = x;
        int c;
        while ((c = *p++) != 0)
           {
           switch (c)
              {
              case '\n':
// When hit returns, check for new row totally below clip rect,
// if so we might as well pack it in now
                 x = xmargin;
                 y += font.Height();
                 if ((y - font.Ascent()) >= clipRect.bott)
                    return;
                 break;


              default:                        // regular char: draw it, advance x
                 DrawChar(c, font, x, y);
                 x += font.CharWidth(c);
                 break;
              }
           }
        }
```

Text Sizing

It's very handy to be able to calculate the width and height of a given string of text. This can only be calculated, of course, in terms of a specific font that the text is to be rendered in. Text sizing is necessary for centering text inside a pushbutton or other screen area, for right-justifying text, and similar uses.

With proportional fonts, the only way to determine the length of a given string of text is to add up the widths of all the characters in it. AFont::TextWidth() determines the width of a string of text in a given font, up to the first carriage return or 0 terminator, or until 'max-Chars' have been encountered. It uses the inline method AFont::Char-Width() to determine the width of each character encountered, and returns the sum of all characters processed.

```
short AFont::TextWidth(char *str, int maxChars)
{
// Setup before scanning through string

   uchar *p = (uchar *) str;      // start at beginning of string
   short width = 0;               // with an accumulated width of 0

// Scan through string, accumulating width

   int c;
   while ((c = *p++) != 0)        // get next char, break out if 0
      {
      if (maxChars-- <= 0)        // if read max # chars, break out
         break;
      if (c == '\n')
         break;                   // if hit end of line, break also
      width += CharWidth(c);      // else add in char's width
      }

   return(width);                 // return accumulated width
}
```

For multilined text, TextSize() computes both the width and height of the text. The width returned is the width of the widest line in the string.

```
void AFont::TextSize(char *str, short &width, short &height,
   int maxChars)
{
// Setup before scanning through string

   uchar *p = (uchar *) str;      // start with beginning of string
   width = 0;                     // with an accumulated width of 0
   height = Height();             // current height is 1 text row
   short currWidth = 0;           // width of this row is 0 so far

// Scan through string, accumulating max line width and height

   int c;
   while ((c = *p++) != 0)        // get next char, break out if 0
```

```
        {
        if (maxChars-- <= 0)        // if read max # chars, break out
            break;
        if (c == '\n')              // if hit carriage return:
            {
            if (currWidth > width)
                width = currWidth;  // if wider than any row, new maxwidth
            currWidth = 0;          // reset current row width
            height += Height();     // bump height by text height
            }
        else
            currWidth += CharWidth(c); // else add in char's width
        }

// After break out of last row, make sure max width accounts for it

    if (currWidth > width)          // stopped accumulating, set width
        width = currWidth;          // if current row is widest
}
```

Graphical User Interfaces

First popularized by the Apple Macintosh, *graphical user interfaces* (GUIs) are all the rage, and will remain so until voice input or other technologies supplement or replace them. Microsoft Windows is by far the dominant such interface for PCs. At its core, a GUI is composed of a set of interface elements. From these elements is built a visual metaphor with user actions and associated effects. Table 12.6 lists some of the common interface elements used in Windows and similar GUIs.

Color plate 6 shows a sample screen from a custom GUI, showing some of the standard GUI elements.

ARTT GUI Elements

ARTT does not include a full graphical user interface, although it includes many of the elements from which one can be built. A scene can be thought of as a window, although it does not have the borders and control gadgets that some windows have in a full user interface—a scene represents only the "client area" of the window. The two classes presented next, AActorButton and AMenu, are capable of looking and behaving like the following elements:

- AActorButton: icon, pushbutton, check box, radio button, status text
- AMenu: menu, menu bar, toolbar

The higher-level constructs, such as bordered windows and dialog boxes, are not included in ARTT, though they can be built using the supplied components.

Table 12.6 Common Interface Elements

Element	*Meaning or Usage*
Window	Screen area for viewing contents of file, program, or system
Icon	Represents file, program, command, or other selectable entity
Menu	List of selectable commands, often applying to current selection
Menu bar	Row of menu selectors
Toolbar	Array of associated icons
Pushbutton	Command initiator
Check box	Option selector
Radio button	Option selector, only one of set selectable at any given time
Scroll bar	Slider for panning view of contents which are too large for window
Slider	Tool for adjusting option in fine increments
Status text	Blank area with status text displayed in it

Class AActorButton: The Button With Many Hats

Most graphical user interfaces impose a "look" as well as a "feel" on their interface elements. Buttons are shaded in gray with a 3D look, for instance, or check boxes have a telltale icon beside the label. ARTT imposes no such visual policy on its user interface elements. It achieves this by requiring that a bitmap be supplied for use as the backdrop for the element. An application can supply any bitmap it chooses (although it must be taken from a sprite array) and may even use different bitmaps for different instances of the same element type. Buttons which require two different visual states, for instance, checked and unchecked versions of a check box, use two adjacent sprites in the array. Text is overlaid on the fly, using a font which again must be supplied.

Class AActorButton can be used, with different initialization parameters, to create icons, pushbuttons, check boxes, radio buttons (with additional logic to uncheck others in the set), and even status text areas. A "button type" is used to determine what happens when the mouse is clicked on the button. Three choices are available:

BUTT_TYPE_NOPUSH	No visual change (icon, status text)
BUTT_TYPE_TWOSTATE	Flip between 2 bitmaps (check box, radio button)
BUTT_TYPE_PUSHDOWN	Use bitmap 2 while mouse down (pushbutton)

A button may have an optional text overlay, and the position and contents of the text are settable. When a button of type NOPUSH or TWOSTATE is pressed, or a PUSHDOWN is released, a desired keystroke may be generated, and inserted into the keyboard system as if it had been typed at the keyboard. This may be a normal ASCII character, or it may be a special-valued character which cannot be typed.

Below is listed the header file for class AActorButton.

```
//    AActButt.h    Button Actor class
//    Rex E. Bradford

#ifndef__AACTBUTT_H
#define__AACTBUTT_H

#include "aactor.h"
#include "aspritea.h"
#include "afont.h"
#include "akeybd.h"

#define BUTT_TEXTPOS_CENTER (-1)

class AActorButton : public AActor {

public:

// Button type: how push interface works

    typedef enum {
        BUTT_TYPE_NOPUSH,     // just 1 icon
        BUTT_TYPE_TWOSTATE,   // switch between icon 1 and 2
        BUTT_TYPE_PUSHDOWN,   // push, uses icon 2 till release
    } ButtonType;

// ButtText: text string, location, and font

    typedef struct {
        char *text;           // text in button
        short xtext;          // xpos of text (or BUTT_TEXTPOS_CENTER)
        short ytext;          // ypos of text (or BUTT_TEXTPOS_CENTER)
        AFont *pfont;         // font to draw text in
    } ButtText;
```

```
private:

    ASpriteArray *psa;      // ptr to sprite array
    short baseIndex;        // base index into sprite array
    ButtText btext;         // button text struct
    ButtonType type;        // BUTT_TYPE_XXX
    AKey keyCode;           // keycode to generate
    short iconNum;          // current icon number (0 or 1)
    short xtext;            // xpos of text (computed)
    short ytext;            // ypos of text (computed)

    void ComputeExtent();   // compute extent of button
    void Draw(ACanvas *pcv); // draw button onto canvas

public:

// Constructor

    AActorButton(AScene *pscene, ACoord3 &loc, ASpriteArray *psa,
        ushort baseIndex, ButtText &btext, ButtonType type, AKey keyCode);

// Change button text (just string, or also location and font)

    void ChangeText(char *str);
    void ChangeText(ButtText &btext);

// Handle mouse events, get/set state

    bool MouseHandle(AMouseEvent &evt);
    int GetState() {return iconNum;}
    void SetState(int state);
};

#endif
```

AActorButton Constructor

The AActorButton constructor takes several arguments. Besides the usual scene and location arguments, these include the sprite array from which bitmaps are taken, the "base index" at which to find the desired sprite (for two-state buttons, the second state is the succeeding sprite), a reference ButtText structure for text contents, font, and placement (see header file), a button type, and a keycode to generate when the button is selected. The constructor mostly copies these into the object, and then draws the button.

```
AActorButton::AActorButton(AScene *pscene_, ACoord3 &loc,
    ASpriteArray *psa_, ushort baseIndex_, ButtText &btext_,
```

```
     ButtonType type_, AKey keyCode_) : AActor(pscene_, loc)
{
   psa = psa_;                // ptr to sprite array holding backdrop
   baseIndex = baseIndex_;    // index of base backdrop sprite
   btext = btext_;            // text string, font, color, position
   type = type_;              // button pushdown type
   keyCode = keyCode_;        // keycode to generate when pushed

   iconNum = 0;               // icon offset index (0 or 1)

   ComputeExtent();           // compute button extent
   Redraw();                  // and redraw button
}
```

Changing Button Text

The text associated with a given button may be changed at any time using AActorButton::ChangeText(). Two versions are supplied, one which takes only a new string pointer, and another which takes an entirely new ButtText structure, for changing font and placement as well.

```
void AActorButton::ChangeText(char *str)

{
   btext.text = str;    // set new string
   ComputeExtent();     // recompute new text offset coords
   Redraw();            // draw button with new text
}

void AActorButton::ChangeText(ButtText &btext_)
{
   btext = btext_;      // copy new text info
   ComputeExtent();     // recompute new text offset coords
   Redraw();            // draw button with new text, font, pos
}
```

Computing Button Extent and Text Placement

Only the bitmap (actually, sprite) backdrop is used in computing extents—the text must fit inside it. The ComputeExtent() method, besides calculating the overall button extent, also precomputes text placement if either the x or y text coordinate is BUTT_TEXTPOS_ CENTER, to avoid having to recalculate this every time the button is rendered. AFont::TextSize() is used to compute the size of the text, and the x,y starting locations necessary to center the text are then derived.

```
void AActorButton::ComputeExtent()
{
// Compute extent area using sprite backdrop
```

```
        ASprite *psp = (*psa)[baseIndex];
        area.left = int(loc.x);
        area.top = int(loc.y);
        area.right = area.left + psp->width;
        area.bott = area.top + psp->height;

// If text on button, calculate its position

        if (btext.text)
          {
          xtext = btext.xtext;     // assume x,y supplied
          ytext = btext.ytext;

// If either x or y text pos is special code, compute specially

          if (xtext == BUTT_TEXTPOS_CENTER) ||
             (ytext == BUTT_TEXTPOS_CENTER))
             {
             short txwidth,txheight;
             btext.pfont->TextSize(btext.text, txwidth, txheight);

             if (xtext == BUTT_TEXTPOS_CENTER)
                xtext = (psp->width - txwidth) / 2;

             if (ytext == BUTT_TEXTPOS_CENTER)
                ytext = btext.pfont->Ascent() +
                    ((psp->height - txheight) / 2);
             }
          }
}
```

Drawing the Button

The backdrop sprite is drawn first when redrawing the button. Then, the button text is drawn. If the button is of type PUSHDOWN, and is in its secondary state, the text is drawn one pixel to the right and down of its normal position. This achieves the 3D pushbutton feel used in most interfaces. If the secondary sprite for the button has appropriate "pushed-in" graphics, the correct effect can be fully achieved. Typically, the primary backdrop has a light border on its upper and left edges and a dark border on its right and lower edges, and the secondary backdrop reverses these. See Figure 12.8.

```
void AActorButton::Draw(ACanvas *pcv)
{
// Draw button backdrop
   ASprite *psp = (*psa)[baseIndex + iconNum];
   pcv->DrawBitmap(*psp, area.left, area.top);

// If text, draw it at its calculated pos (offset by 1,1 if pushdown
// type and pushed down).
```

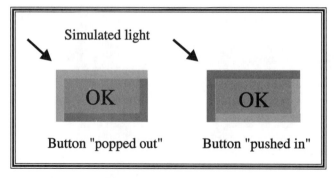

Figure 12.8   Pushbutton featuring "3D look." Left version is unpressed, right version is depressed.

```
if (btext.text)
    {
    int xt = area.left + xtext;
    int yt = area.top + ytext;
    if ((type == BUTT_TYPE_PUSHDOWN) && iconNum)
        {
        ++xt;
        ++yt;
        }
    pcv->DrawText(btext.text, *btext.pfont, xt, yt);
    }
}
```

Handling Mouse Events

Both mouse down and mouse up events associated with the left mouse button are examined by the handler method AActorButton::Mouse-Handle(). For PUSHDOWN buttons, the mouse event stream is captured, so that the mouse-up event which is used to determine keycode generation can be received even if the mouse strays outside the button area (if the up event occurs outside the area, no keycode is generated, however). See the implementation below for full details.

```
// BUTT_TYPE_NOPUSH (simple icon or pushbutton)
//
//    Press: send keycode
//    Release: nothing
//
// BUTT_TYPE_TWOSTATE (toggle)
//
//    Press: flip icon state, send keycode
//    Release: nothing
//
// BUTT_TYPE_PUSHDOWN (animated pushdown icon or pushbutton)
//
//    Press: flip icon state, capture mouse
```

```
//     Release: if mouse inside button, send keycode
//             also flip icon state and release mouse

bool AActorButton::MouseHandle(AMouseEvent &evt)
{
    switch (evt.code)
        {
        case MOUSE_BUTT1_DOWN:

// If two-state or pushdown, flip icon. If pushdown, grab mouse

            if (type != BUTT_TYPE_NOPUSH)
                {
                SetState(!iconNum);
                if (type == BUTT_TYPE_PUSHDOWN)
                    CaptureMouse();
                }

// If not pushdown, send keycode if any

            if (keyCode && (type != BUTT_TYPE_PUSHDOWN))
                AKeybd::InsertKey(keyCode);
            return TRUE;

        case MOUSE_BUTT1_UP:

// If mouse captured (pushdown only), send key if still in button
// Then revert to original state and release mouse

            if (IsCapture())
                {
                if (area.Encloses(evt.x, evt.y))
                    {
                    if (keyCode)
                        AKeybd::InsertKey(keyCode);
                    }
                SetState(0);
                UncaptureMouse();
                }
            return TRUE;
        }

    return FALSE;
}
```

Getting and Setting Button State

Sometimes it's handy to force the button into a particular state, or to retrieve its current state. AActorButton::GetState() and AActorButton::SetState() are available for these purposes.

```
    int GetState() {return iconNum;}

void AActorButton::SetState(int state)
{
    if (state != iconNum)
        {
        iconNum = state;
        Redraw();
        }
}
```

Class AMenu: Menus, Menu Bars, and Toolbars

A *menu* is a list of selectable items, typically vertically arranged. These items are often thought of as strictly text, but they might also be icons. In this case, the menu is called a *toolbar*. The familiar *menu bar* featured at the top of a Microsoft Windows window can be thought of as a menu which happens to be horizontally instead of vertically arranged. Class AMenu creates and groups together an array of AActorButton instances, and can be used to create any of these three types of menus.

All buttons may feature the same bitmap backdrop, or they may each receive their own from sequential entries in a sprite array. A menu may be also composed (entirely) of two-state buttons, each button using two adjacent sprites in the array. All sprites must be the same width and height for alignment purposes. The menu may be arranged vertically, horizontally, or in tabular form with a specified number of columns and rows.

Each button in the menu generates its own unique keycode, taken from an array of keycodes passed in at menu creation time. While all buttons share text, font and positioning, each item receives its own text string.

The header file for class AMenu is listed below.

```
//    AMenu.h      Menu of AActorButts
//    Rex E. Bradford

#ifndef__AMENU_H
#define__AMENU_H

#include "aactbutt.h"

class AMenu {

    AActorButton **pButts;    // array of ptrs to AActButts
    short numButts;           // number of buttons
    short numColumns;         // number of columns

    void DeleteAll();         // delete all buttons in menu
```

```
public:

// Constructor and destructor

   AMenu(AScene *pscene, ACoord3 &loc, ASpriteArray *psa,
      ushort baseIndex, int spIncr, int numButts, int numColumns,
      AActorButton::ButtText &btext, AActorButton::ButtonType type,
      char **text, AKey *pKeyCodes);
   virtual ~AMenu() {DeleteAll();}

// Show/hide all buttons in menu, set all sticky for scrolling

   void Show();
   void Hide();
   void SetSticky(bool onoff);
};


#endif
```

AMenu Constructor

The menu constructor is passed in a large number of arguments. These are:

pscene	pointer to scene in which to place AActorButtons
loc	*xyz* location of upper-left button
psa	pointer to sprite array from which backdrop bitmaps are taken
baseIndex	base index in sprite array at which to find bitmaps
spIncr	sprite increment from button to button (0, 1, or 2)
numButts	number of buttons in menu
numColumns	number of columns to arrange buttons into (1 for vertical)
btext	text font and positioning information
type	type of buttons (must be all the same)
text	pointer to array of pointers to text strings
pKeyCodes	pointer to array of keycodes to assign to buttons

The constructor creates the menu and its associated buttons. If a button creation attempt fails, the buttons created so far are destroyed and the menu fails to materialize.

```
AMenu::AMenu(AScene *pscene, ACoord3 &loc, ASpriteArray *psa,
   ushort baseIndex, int spIncr, int numButts_, int numColumns_,
   AActorButton::ButtText &btext, AActorButton::ButtonType type,
   char **text, AKey *pKeyCodes)
{
// Create array of button pointers and clear it
```

```
        numButts = numButts_;
        numColumns = numColumns_;
        int memAlloc = sizeof(AActorButton *) * numButts;
        pButts = (AActorButton **) new char[memAlloc];
        if (pButts == NULL)
           {
           numButts = 0;
           return;
           }
        memset(pButts, 0, memAlloc);

// Set base x-coord where each row of buttons stats, ptr to 1st sprite,
// initial xyz coord, and other misc setup

        AFix xbase = loc.x;                 // xbase is left margin
        ASprite *psp0 = (*psa)[baseIndex];  // use 1st sprite for sizing
        int column = 0;                     // column counter
        int index = baseIndex;              // sprite array index
        ACoord3 xyz = loc;                  // location of each AActButt

// Create each button in a loop, deleting all upon any failure,
// and resetting x-margin after each column of buttons

        for (int i = 0; i < numButts; i++)
           {
// Create new AActButt at current location in menu

           if (text)
              btext.text = text[i];
           else
              btext.text = NULL;
           pButts[i] = new AActorButton(pscene, xyz, psa, index,
              btext, type, pKeyCodes[i]);

// If failed, clean up by deleting entire menu

           if (pButts[i] == NULL)
              {
              DeleteAll();
              return;
              }

// Advance to next location and sprite index

           if (++column >= numColumns)
              {
              column = 0;
              xyz.x = xbase;
              xyz.y += psp0->height;
              }
           else
              xyz.x += psp0->width;
           index += spIncr; // often 1, but 2 if two-state
           }
}
```

Menu Destruction

When an object of class AMenu is deleted, the DeleteAll() method is invoked.

```
virtual ~AMenu() {DeleteAll();}
```

DeleteAll(), also called when button creation fails during construction, deletes all buttons in the menu.

```
void AMenu::DeleteAll()
{
   for (int i = 0; i < numButts; i++)
      {
      if (pButts[i])
         delete pButts[i];
      }
   delete (char *) pButts;
}
```

Miscellaneous AMenu Methods

It is helpful to work with the entire menu as a unit, rather than each button actor in it. AMenu::Show(), Hide(), and SetSticky() are methods which invoke methods with similar names on each button in the menu.

```
void AMenu::Show()
{
   for (int i = 0; i < numButts; i++)
      pButts[i]->Show();
}

void AMenu::Hide()
{
   for (int i = 0; i < numButts; i++)
      pButts[i]->Hide();
}

void AMenu::SetSticky(bool onoff)
{
   for (int i = 0; i < numButts; i++)
      pButts[i]->SetSticky(onoff);
}
```

Using Buttons and Menus

Assuming a scene has already been created, adding a menu of buttons is easy:

```
// Declare menu initialization data
```

```
static AActorButton::ButtText menuText = {
    NULL, BUTT_TEXTPOS_CENTER, BUTT_TEXTPOS_CENTER, NULL};
static char *menuStrings[] = {"Menu A","Menu B","Menu C"};
static ushort menuKeys[] = {'A','B','C'};
static ACoord3 menuLoc(150,200,1000);

..... create scene ptr 'gScene', font 'gFont', and sprite array 'saMenu'

// Create menu, and make it sticky even if scene scrolls

menuText.pfont = gFont; // since ptr, can't include in static menuText def
AMenu *phMenu = new AMenu(gScene, menuLoc, &saMenu, 4, 0,
    3, 1, menuText, AActorButton::BUTT_TYPE_PUSHDOWN, menuStrings,
    menuKeys);
phMenu->SetSticky(TRUE);
```

AMUCK: A Different Sort of Animation Program

As an example of what can be done with ARTT in a realm outside of animation, I wrote AMUCK, a kind of silly demo program whose components are not so silly after all.

AMUCK features the laboratory instrument panel of a machine built by the mad scientist Ludwig Von Fractalus in 1789. Obviously Ludwig was well ahead of his time. Color plate 5 shows a view from this panel, which in the program is constantly animating. There are waveforms scrolling through display panels, gauges and level meters going wild, and so on. Some of these gadgets are built using class AActorDraw; others feature new actor classes which can be used in your own programs. Versions of AMUCK are provided for both DOS and Microsoft Windows. See the code in AMUCK.CPP and the accompanying art files on the CD. If you are interested in writing "real" animated games, simulations, education titles, scientific visualizations, or other applications featuring animation, looking over the source for this and other sample programs should provide some useful insights for you.

AMUCK allows you to click on various gadgets and drag various sliders, and the view panels change accordingly. The actor classes used are the following:

Background	AActorSprite
Waveform view panels	AActorDraw
Slider controls	AActorSlider
Blinking lights	AActorAnim
VU meters	AActorGaugeNeedle
Clock, tape counter	AActorButton
Thermometer, color bar meters	AActorGaugeBitmap
Pushbuttons	AActorButton

AActorSlider, AActorGaugeNeedle, and AActorGaugeBitmap have not been encountered before. They are fairly simple—see the source code and its comments for details.

With versatile buttons and menus, and the slider and gauge classes featured in program AMUCK, ARTT programs can become truly interactive. The pieces of a full graphics system are falling into place. We have fast static graphics, animation and composition, and now, user interface tools. With these building blocks, we can create snappy and colorful applications. And speaking of color, it's time to add some snazzy real-time color effects, and break through the shackles of 256-color palettes while we're at it. Next stop: the World of Color.

P
A
R
T

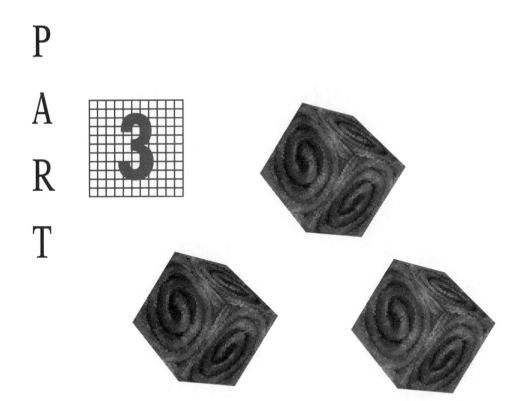

3

Palettes
and Color Effects

C H A P T E R

Color Theory
and Color Palettes

Up to this point, we have assumed that our graphic images are all 8-bit indexed color images. We have further assumed that the 256-entry palette of colors associated with each image is created by magic or by some artist outside our control. In scenes with multiple images, we have assumed that all are drawn from the same palette, or at least from subportions of compatible palettes. Finally, we have assumed that the screen device is operating in an 8-bit indexed-color mode.

In Part 3 of this book, beginning with this chapter, we will blow the doors off of these assumptions. We will learn how to manipulate and control the color palette, and achieve such special effects as screen fading and color cycling. We will work with screen modes featuring 15-bit and 24-bit direct-color bitmaps as their representation, and make use of source images using more than 8 bits of color per pixel. We will explore the mathematics of color manipulation, and use this math to create tables which allow us to achieve a variety of special coloring effects in real time. These real-time effects which are applied to bitmapped images include darkening and lightening (often based on screen "depth"), hazing, translucency, and palette translation.

These three chapters form the gateway to the professional-quality animation of the present and future. Fifteen-bit and 24-bit color displays are the future, and the near one. The color effects developed are by no means a complete tour of the possibilities; they are merely the most important "core effects" subset, and a framework for building upon. Combined with the scene animation and composition mechanisms developed in Part 2, they form a powerful, quality animation programming system.

The Physics of Color

Humans are among a few species of living creatures with color vision. Other animals with eyes similar to ours have retinas featuring receptors composed only of "rods," which respond to *luminosity*. They can distinguish various degrees of lightness and darkness, but no color information. Along with most primates and a few other species, we have "cones" which can distinguish the color of light received as well as its intensity. Presumably, this was an adaptation developed out of some necessity, perhaps the need to distinguish fruits from among the thick forested canopy of trees that was the home of our distant ancestors. While the name Apple was probably chosen for the first color personal computer for mythical reasons (anyone remember the Adam, too?), it kind of fits from the standpoint of evolving visual systems as well.

Color Perception

Before we leave biology and return to the land of curly braces, let's delve a little more deeply into the basics of color perception. At its most basic, color perception is the ability to distinguish various wavelengths of light (wavelength is the reciprocal of frequency). The cones in our retinas are sensitive to wavelengths roughly in the range from 400 nm (nanometers) to 700 nm—light at wavelengths outside this range is colorless or simply unperceived. Pure "tones" of light of different wavelengths, such as might be generated by a laser, are reported by people to represent different sensations of *hue*, such as red, green, yellow, blue, and so on.

Of course, actual light reflected from a surface is composed of a variety of wavelengths at various intensities, depending on the material and other characteristics of the surface, and depending on the makeup of the original light striking it. How do our eyes and our brain make sense of this jumble of information? At the front lines, we have three types of cones in the retina, sensitive to different wavelengths and to the contrast between wavelengths. One type of cone specializes in red-green wavelengths, another type in blue-yellow, and the third in black-white. Even at this receptor stage, information is lost, but the three axes provide enough information for the brain to reconstruct a detailed, if imperfect, range and representation of color. Behind the cones are visual ganglia, which further process the vast amounts of data flooding into the cones and the rods as well, detecting edges and other basic features, and passing this data along to the visual cortex in the brain.

Tri-Chromatic Color Theory

The point of a color generation system, such as a computer monitor, is to provide a simple mechanism which can generate all or nearly all of the color hues, saturation (purity of wavelength), and intensities found in the natural visual world. Computer displays are described by "additive" color systems, in which each color component adds to the overall color result, as opposed to "subtractive" systems such as ink paints, where components absorb color and reduce the overall color when combined. Many additive systems have been presented in theory, and many reduced to practice. The Natural Color System, a descriptive system developed by Hard and Sivik in 1981, closely models the human visual system itself, being based on red-green, blue-yellow, and black-white poles. In far more widespread use are the HLS (Hue/Lightness/Saturation), YUV and YIQ (monochromatic and two poles of chromaticity), and RGB (Red/Green/Blue) systems. Systems based on more than three axes are possible and are capable of covering a greater percentage of the possible "color space." In practice, such systems are more difficult to build and provide little added benefit. Tri-chromatic systems, based on three axes of color, are used in televisions and computer systems exclusively.

Some of the tri-chromatic systems, such as HLS, are useful for color calculations but are difficult to "build" in an actual device. For computer monitors, the RGB system is the standard. As discussed in Chapter 1, the screens of color monitors are covered with tiny triads of phosphor coating, which when struck by electrons produce color in the red, green, and blue wavelengths. By striking the three dots with various intensities of electrons, a wide range of colors and intensities can be reproduced. Figure 13.1 illustrates the RGB "color cube," which shows the colors at the endpoints of the three axes—colors inside the cube have various intermediate hues, various saturations of those hues, and various overall intensities.

This brief tour of color theory barely scratches the surface. For more information, see the excellent discussion in Chapter 13 of Foley et al., *Computer Graphics: Principles and Practice*, and the detailed presentation in *Color and the Computer*, edited by H. John Durrett (see Appendix E).

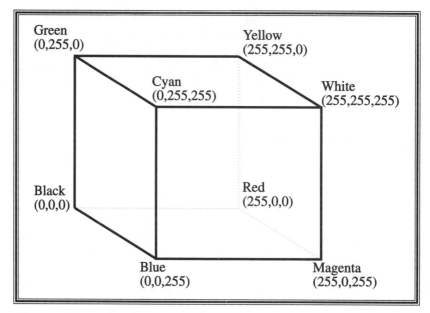

Figure 13.1 RGB color cube. Color components are (Red,Green,Blue), in range 0 to 255.

RGB Color Math

A particular color is represented in RGB color space by its coordinates in the color cube; that is, by its red, green, and blue component values. Often, each component is represented as a continuous floating-point value between 0 and 1.0. For speed of calculation, real-time systems usually use an 8-bit or 16-bit integer value. Eight bits of precision is enough to cover the range of distinguishable colors. The value 200,150,73 (R,G,B) is barely distinguishable from the value 200,150,74, even when they are adjacent. More than 8 bits is wasted except when used to hold intermediate values during calculations, to avoid accumulating roundoff error. Current VGA hardware uses only 6 bits for each component, although many Super VGA cards now feature optional 8-bit DACs. ARTT uses 8 bits per color component, translating down to 6 bits when programming the VGA.

Many mathematical operations can be applied to RGB color values, in order to change the color in some desired manner. Two colors may be added, subtracted, or mixed, for example. Mixing two colors, using either a simple or a weighted average, is done by averaging each of the components separately. Pure green (0,255,0) can be added to pure blue (0,0,255), producing cyan (0,255,255). Pure violet (255,0,255) can be averaged with black (0,0,0) to produce a darker shade

(127,0,127). Or it can be averaged with white (255,255,255) to produce a "hazed," or less saturated, violet (191,127,191). Figure 13.2 shows example addition and mixing calculations.

Other color math operations are possible too. The most common ones are explored in Chapter 15. In general, most such calculations can be done on each of the color components separately.

Palette Fading

What can we do with our new-found color calculation skills? One classic technique, borrowed from the movies and now in widespread use in computer entertainment, is *palette fading*. Here, the entire screen is slowly transformed to or from black or some other color (screens are sometimes faded up to white, for instance). This effect is best achieved by manipulating the color palette, rather than redrawing the entire screen over and over in different colors.

Fading a palette is conceptually simple. Over some number of iterations, a new palette of RGB colors is calculated and used to program the VGA DAC. On each iteration, each RGB color is calculated as a weighted average (mix) of the original RGB color at that index and the "destination" RGB color that is being faded to at that index. The weighting factor used depends on how far through the full fade this iteration is, starting at 0 percent and working to 100 percent.

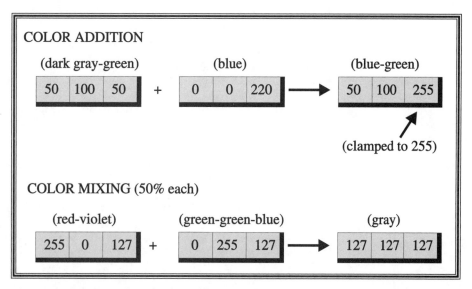

Figure 13.2 Examples of color addition and mixing. Note blue is clamped in addition example.

Calculating each RGB array "from scratch" using weighted averaging is superior to incremental calculations, because it avoids accumulated roundoff error. Fixed-point math is used in calculations because 768 operations must be done each iteration, 3 components times 256 palette entries. In part because of this cost, in general it is not feasible to have animation or other significant processing happening during a fade on current PCs.

Class APalette: Fading

The version of class APalette presented in Chapter 2 was a subset of the actual class definition. Later in this chapter, the full version is presented. Besides the fading methods shown now, color calculation and conversion methods are included in the class.

APalette::Fade To() performs a fade, consuming all processing resources during the fade and only returning when it is complete. Because of its direct VGA DAC access, it works only under DOS. FadeTo() takes a 256-entry RGB array and a number of frames (iterations) as input. Note that there isn't just a single destination fade color for the entire screen. Each color index may fade to a different color—this method may be used to fade from one palette to another, for instance.

```
void APalette::FadeTo(uchar *prgb, short numFrames)
{
    uchar rgbCurr[256 * 3];     // temporary rgb array on stack

    for (int i = 1; i <= numFrames; i++)
        {
        AFix fs1 = AFix(i) / AFix(numFrames);  // factor for supplied rgb
        AFix fs = AFix(1) - fs1;                // factor for starting rgb

        uchar *ps = rgb;          // starting point is current rgb array
        uchar *ps1 = prgb;        // fading toward supplied rgb array
        uchar *pd = rgbCurr;      // with destination buffer on stack

        // for all 256 rgb entries, compute new rgb between start & new

        for (int j = 0; j < (256 * 3); j++)
            *pd++ = round((fs * int(*ps++)) + (fs1 * int(*ps1++)));

        AVga::WaitForVerticalSync();  // wait for vertical sync
        AVga::SetDAC(rgbCurr);        // and then set vga palette
        }

    Set(rgbCurr);     // when all done, update our palette with results
}
```

APalette::FadeTo() calls AVga::WaitForVerticalSync() before each reprogramming of the DAC. This is done to time the fade, but serves the additional purpose of ensuring that the DAC is not updated during midscan. This results in a cleaner fade. AVga::WaitForVerticalSync() uses bit 3 of the VGA's status register to determine whether the device is currently inside the vertical retrace period. Unfortunately, this routine does not work all the time on all SuperVGA devices, as some of them only provide this status bit when running in standard VGA modes.

```
void AVga::WaitForVerticalSync()
{
   while (inp(0x3DA) & 8)      // if in vsync, wait till out
      {}
   while (!(inp(0x3DA) & 8))   // wait while not in vsync
      {}
}
```

Fading to Black or White

For convenience, class APalette includes methods for fading the entire palette to all black or all white. A credit screen, for instance, might fade each name up to the desired palette, hold for a second, and then fade back down to black. The implementations of FadeToBlack() and FadeToWhite() are simple.

```
void APalette::FadeToBlack(short numFrames)
{
   uchar rgb[256 * 3];

   memset(rgb, 0, sizeof(rgb));
   FadeTo(rgb, numFrames);
}

void APalette::FadeToWhite(short numFrames)
{
   uchar rgb[256 * 3];

   memset(rgb, 0xFF, sizeof(rgb));
   FadeTo(rgb, numFrames);
}
```

Palette Animation

Fading is a subset of the general category of *palette animation*. Various forms of palette animation have been in use since the Dawn of Video Games. *Color cycling*, another variant of palette animation, stands for the dynamic updating of the color palette at some particular index, typically from prestored RGB values in an array. The entry in the DAC is continually reprogrammed with a "tape loop" of colors which cycles back to the beginning of the array upon reaching the end.

Color cycling can be used to make water appear to sparkle or flow, to cause fireworks to shimmer, to blink lights with no redrawing, or to call attention to important areas of a scientific rendering, to mention just a few examples. It is important that no other areas of the screen be drawn in a color that is cycling, or they will cycle too. Typically, color slots at one end of the palette, such as indexes 254 or 255, are reserved for this purpose, and not used in any images which don't feature cycling.

Class APalAnim: Color-Cycling Palette Animation

In ARTT, class APalAnim can be used to perform color cycling. For each color index to be animated, an object of this class is created, and two methods are used to time and control the actual palette and DAC updating. Any palette (instance of APalette) may be animated, though typically the palette associated with the screen canvas is the one used. The APalAnim object updates the VGA DAC as well as the palette, and keeps the two in sync.

The APalAnim class consists of three methods:

- Constructor—Create instance of palette animator for one index in a palette

- TimeToAdvance—Detects whether time of next color change has been reached

- Advance—Updates palette with next color in array

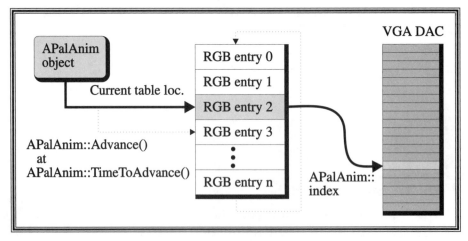

Figure 13.3 An object of class APalAnim, and its connection to an RGB cycle list and the DAC.

The operation of a palette animation object is shown in Figure 13.3. The header file for class APalAnim is listed below.

```
//   APalAnim.h     Palette animation class
//   Rex E. Bradford

#ifndef __APALANIM_H
#define __APALANIM_H

#include "apalette.h"
#include "afix.h"
#include "atime.h"

class APalAnim {
    APalette *palette;     // palette being animated
    uchar *pRgbTable;      // ptr to array of RGB values
    short tabLen;          // table length in bytes
    short tabLoc;          // current table location (byte offset)
    AFix tDelta;           // time between steps
    AFix tNext;            // time of next step
    uchar index;           // index to cycle

public:

// Constructor: set up for palette animation

    APalAnim(APalette *palette, uchar index, uchar *prgb, short numRgb,
        AFix t);

// Return TRUE if time to advance palette entry

    bool TimeToAdvance() {return (ATime::Read() >= tNext);}

// Advance palette entry to next color in cycle

    void Advance();
};

#endif
```

APalAnim Constructor

The constructor for class APalAnim takes five arguments:

palette—palette to be animated (usually palette of screen canvas)

index—index of color to be animated

prgb—pointer to array of red/green/blue values

numRgb—number of RGB triplets in array

t—time between each RGB color advance (in fixed-point seconds)

504

The constructor copies these arguments into internal storage and sets up a couple of internal state variables.

```
APalAnim::APalAnim(APalette *palette_, uchar index_, uchar *prgb,
    short numRgb, AFix t)
{
    palette = palette_;        // palette being animated
    pRgbTable = prgb;          // ptr to table of colors to cycle
    tabLen = numRgb * 3;       // length of table in bytes
    tabLoc = 0;                // current location in table
    tDelta = t;                // time delta between anims
    tNext = ATime::Read();     // time of next anim
    index = index_;            // index of palette entry to animate
}
```

APalAnim Advancing

In order for the palette to actually animate, a program must make periodic calls to do so, invoking methods on any objects of class APalAnim in existence. A sample portion of such code is listed below.

```
// SAMPLE MAIN LOOP WHICH ANIMATES A PALETTE
while (TRUE)
    {
    AScene::UpdateAll();                    // update scenes
    ... do other main loop activities ...
    if (pPalAnim->TimeToAdvance())          // assumes 'pPalAnim' is an APalAnim
        pPalAnim->Advance();
}
```

The TimeToAdvance() method simply checks the current time against the APalAnim's calculated "next advance" time.

```
bool TimeToAdvance() {return (ATime::Read() >= tNext);}
```

APalAnim::Advance() sets the palette entry to the next color in the array, and then advances the current array location, with wrap-around. The time at which the next advancement should occur is calculated too. That's all there is to it—assuming you know what colors to put in the array in the first place! In some cases, like flowing water or blinking lights, lucky guesses at RGB values can work pretty well. In more advanced cases, the color mathematics developed in this and future chapters can be put to work.

```
void APalAnim::Advance()
{
// Set palette and DAC

    palette->Set(pRgbTable + tabLoc, index, 1);
    AVga::SetDAC(pRgbTable + tabLoc, index, 1);
```

```
// Advance table location, with wraparound

    tabLoc += 3;
    if (tabLoc >= tabLen)
        tabLoc = 0;

// Set time of next anim

    tNext = ATime::Read() + tDelta;
}
```

Fifteen-Bit Hi-Color and Twenty-Four-Bit True-Color

The palette fading and animation techniques just covered are intended for the same 8-bit indexed color displays used throughout this book so far. But the days of 8-bit color are numbered, as the price of video memory chips continues to drop (too slowly!), the speed of CPUs continues to increase, and the capabilities of graphics coprocessing hardware continues to escalate. Eight-bit indexed color is a solution to problems which are rapidly disappearing, and its use will begin a serious decline over the next few years.

What is replacing 8-bit indexed color? Direct-color displays, of course, in which each pixel can be programmed with a color value totally independent of all other pixels, chosen from the full spectrum of available colors. Two dominant direct-color formats are emerging, unfortunately with a few side variants. One is 15-bit color, usually called hi-color, and its close variant, 16-bit color. The other is 24-bit color, usually called true-color.

Fifteen-Bit Hi-Color

In a 15-bit color display, each pixel is represented by a two-byte word value. Figure 13.4 shows the layout chosen for this word in virtually all 15-bit displays available on PCs. Happily, this matches Figure 1.11, which is ARTT's 15-bit pixel format. How'd that happen?

Each of the three color components is represented by a 5-bit portion of the word, giving each a range of 32 steps. The sixteenth bit is unused, except in 16-bit color systems, where it is usually used for an extra green bit. Figure 13.5 shows the layout of such 16-bit pixels. Why green, and not red or blue? The eye is more sensitive to green, probably because the natural world holds a lot of green and our distant ancestors needed to navigate through it a lot more than we do, especially those of us living in New York City.

ARTT provides no support for 16-bit color. Fortunately, virtually all Super VGA cards which feature 16-bit color modes also feature 15-bit ones.

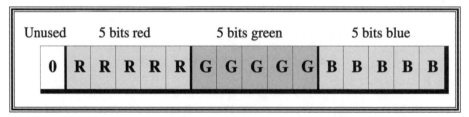

Figure 13.4 Bit-coding of a 15-bit direct-color pixel, with 5 bits of red, green, and blue.

Twenty-Four-Bit True-Color

In a 24-bit color display, each color component is stored in its own byte, and takes on the range 0 to 255. This provides a spectrum of 16.7 million colors, with more color resolution than the eye can distinguish. Unfortunately, not all displays store these three color components in the same order in video memory, but by far the dominant format is the one given in Figure 13.6, where blue is stored first.

Some displays and modes place the components in the opposite order; that is, red, followed by green and then blue. Other displays or modes use 32-bit pixels, with the fourth byte unused, in order to force longword-alignment of each pixel for easier programming. As we shall see, dealing with 3-byte pixels is a royal pain. ARTT supports only blue/green/red ordering, and does not support 32-bit pixel modes featuring the fourth alignment byte. That's not to say that a BMF_LIN32 bitmap format couldn't be invented, it just hasn't been yet. Also, the 24-bit format is a standard format in Windows, while 32-bit layouts are not.

Which Is Better, 15-Bit or 24-Bit?

Fifteen-bit color is a transitional technology, though one which is very useful in the present and for the near future. Within several

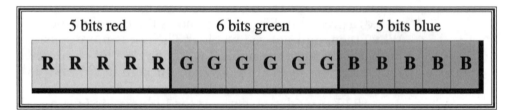

Figure 13.5 Bit-coding of a 16-bit direct-color pixel, with 5 red, 6 green, and 5 blue bits.

Blue byte	Green byte	Red byte
B B B B B B B B	G G G G G G G G	R R R R R R R R

Figure 13.6 Layout of a 24-bit true-color pixel. Blue byte usually appears first.

years, probably 24-bit or perhaps 32-bit pixel layouts will become totally dominant. They simply look better, and the performance penalty, which is their only drawback, will become moot. In the meantime, 15-bit is important, particularly for digital video. The fact that less bytes need to be written (2 per pixel instead of 3), combined with the word-alignment that all pixels feature, gives 15-bit modes substantially better performance.

There are other advantages to 15-bit displays. As we shall see in Chapter 15, many color effects can be achieved in real-time through the use of color lookup tables. In 8-bit modes, such table-driven graphics are commonplace already—each such table requires only 256 bytes of storage. Full-resolution lookup tables for 15-bit graphics require 64K bytes each (32K 2-byte entries), somewhat more daunting but not infeasible. But full-resolution color lookup tables for 24-bit graphics are 48Mb in size, simply impractical in any realistic sense. Other techniques, such as separate lookup tables per component, or on-the-fly color math hardware instead of lookup tables, will eventually be used instead. All the ducks are not quite lined up yet for professional-quality 24-bit graphics with a full suite of real-time effects.

These problems will eventually be overcome, however, and 24-bit is already practical for static image display, image manipulation programs, and other less demanding uses. Fifteen-bit quality is noticeably lesser, though not at all bad. It should be noted that in some ways 8-bit color can be visually superior to 15-bit. This is due to the fact that the resolution of "nearby" shades in the palette, which features 6 or 8 bits per component, is higher than in 15-bit direct color modes, which feature 5 bits per component. An 8-bit scene can show more gradations of a given color, albeit by devoting a portion of its precious palette to such fine-grained color swaths. In general, though, the limited palette available makes 8-bit images look inferior to 15-bit ones. Color plate 7 shows three versions of the same image, in 8-bit, 15-bit, and 24-bit format.

508

Class APalette Revisited

The APalette class definition given in Chapter 2 was incomplete. First of all, each palette instance contains additional data members, beyond the array of 256 three-byte entries shown so far. These are:

- Array of 256 15-bit entries
- Pointer to optional inverse table

The array of 15-bit values, which APalette methods keep in synchrony with the full 24-bit RGB array, is useful in many color calculation routines. The inverse table pointer is optional and often left NULL. If used, an inverse table can be used to dramatically speed up some color calculations. We will visit the topic of inverse tables later in this chapter.

Here is the full listing of the header file for class APalette. Besides the new data members, notice the suite of methods for converting color between 8-bit, 15-bit, and 24-bit formats.

```
//   APalette.h    Palette class
//   Rex E. Bradford

#ifndef __APALETTE_H
#define __APALETTE_H

#include "ainvtab.h"

class APalette {
public:

    uchar rgb[768];     // 256 3-byte RGB entries (blue low, red high)
    ushort rgb15[256];  // 256 15-bit entries (blue in low 5 bits, red high)
    AInverseTable *pInvTab; // ptr to inverse table or NULL

// Palette construction

    APalette() {pInvTab = NULL;}
    APalette(uchar *prgb) {pInvTab = NULL; Set(prgb);}

// Palette set (full or partial palette)

    void Set(uchar *prgb, int index = 0, int num = 256);
    void Set(ushort *pc15, int index = 0, int num = 256);

// Set/get system palette (DAC or window pal)

    static void SetSystemPal(uchar *prgb, int index = 0, int num = 256);
    static void GetSystemPal(uchar *prgb, int index = 0, int num = 256);
```

```
// Conversions

   uchar ConvertTo8(ushort col15) {if (pInvTab) return (*pInvTab)[col15];
      else return FindClosest(col15);}
   uchar ConvertTo8(uchar *prgb) {
      if (pInvTab) return (*pInvTab)[ConvertTo15(prgb)];
      else return FindClosest(prgb);}

   ushort ConvertTo15(uchar col8) {return rgb15[col8];}
   static ushort ConvertTo15(uchar *prgb) {
      return((*prgb >> 3) |
      (ushort(*(prgb+1) & 0xF8) << 2) |
      (ushort(*(prgb+2) & 0xF8) << 7));}

   void ConvertTo24(uchar col8, uchar *prgb) {
      uchar *prgbP = rgb + (int(col8) * 3);
      *prgb = *prgbP; *(prgb+1) = *(prgbP+1); *(prgb+2) = *(prgbP+2);}
   static void ConvertTo24(ushort col15, uchar *prgb) {
      *prgb = (col15 & 0x1F) << 3;
      *(prgb+1) = (col15 >> 2) & 0xF8;
      *(prgb+2) = (col15 >> 10) << 3;}

// Find closest color to rgb or col15, restricted to range

   uchar FindClosest(uchar *prgb, int low = 0, int high = 255);
   uchar FindClosest(ushort col15, int low = 0, int high = 255);

// Palette fade (DOS only)

   void FadeTo(uchar *prgb, short numFrames);
   void FadeToBlack(short numFrames);
   void FadeToWhite(short numFrames);
};

#endif
```

Finding the Closest Palette Color to an RGB Value

In Chapter 9, the FLIC file reader needed a way of replacing color 0 with the closest color to it in the palette. Finding the color closest to a given RGB value is often handy. For instance, you might want to draw red text on an 8-bit display, without knowing ahead of time what color index, if any, holds a red color. APalette::FindClosest() is used to find the color in the full palette, or a subset thereof, which is closest to some desired RGB color.

What does it mean to be "closest"? The best mathematical definition is a *least-squares* difference. For each entry in the palette, the square of the difference between each of its components and the same component of the desired color is calculated, and these three squared differences are added. Mathematically, the "distance" between the colors is the square root of this sum, but there is no need to calculate the square root if all we care to do is find the smallest one. Figure 13.7 illustrates the calculation of the squared distance between two colors.

The implementation of APalette::FindClosest() is given below.

```
uchar APalette::FindClosest(uchar *prgb, int low, int high)
{
// Set up for search

    int imin = 0;
    long diffMin = 256 * 256 * 3;        // current best is real bad
    uchar *pRgbPal = rgb + (low * 3);    // start at rgb[low]

// For each entry, compute squared difference, see if better than
// best so far.

    for (int i = low; i <= high; i++)
        {
// Compute sum of squares of differences in each component

        long bdiff = int(*prgb) - int(*pRgbPal++);
        long gdiff = int(*(prgb+1)) - int(*pRgbPal++);
        long rdiff = int(*(prgb+2)) - int(*pRgbPal++);
        long diff = (bdiff * bdiff) + (gdiff * gdiff) + (rdiff * rdiff);

// If closer than current closest, mark it

        if (diff < diffMin)
            {
            diffMin = diff;
            imin = i;
            }
        }

    return(imin);      // return index of best match
}
```

A variant of the method takes a 15-bit color as input. It merely converts the 15-bit color to 24-bit, using a conversion method, and calls the 24-bit FindClosest().

```
uchar APalette::FindClosest(ushort col15, int low, int high)
{
    uchar rgb[3];

    ConvertTo24(col15, rgb);
    return FindClosest(rgb, low, high);
}
```

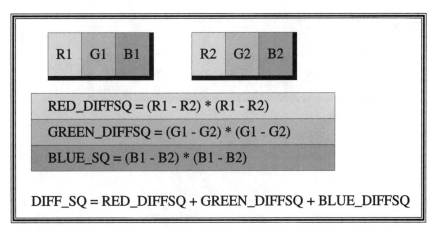

Figure 13.7 Calculating the squared distance between two colors, used in finding closest match.

Color Conversions

With three color formats, 8-bit, 15-bit, and 24-bit, there are six conversions. Four of these require reference to a given palette. The two involving direct-color on both ends, 15-bit → 24-bit and 24-bit → 15-bit, are palette independent. The conversions are all simple, although some have their own idiosyncracies. Additionally, some can be sped up by an inverse table, which we'll look at shortly.

Converting 15-bit and 24-bit representations to 8-bit involves finding the closest match to such a color in the palette at hand. This is where an inverse table, which is a giant table specific to a given palette which takes a 15-bit value as input and produces the closest 8-bit color as output, is used if available. Otherwise, FindClosest() is used.

```
uchar ConvertTo8(ushort col15) {if (pInvTab) return (*pInvTab)[col15];
    else return FindClosest(col15);}

uchar ConvertTo8(uchar *prgb) {
    if (pInvTab) return (*pInvTab)[ConvertTo15(prgb)];
    else return FindClosest(prgb);}
```

Converting 8-bit to 15-bit is simply a matter of looking up the appropriate value in the palette's array of 15-bit values.

```
ushort ConvertTo15(uchar col8) {return rgb15[col8];}
```

Converting 24-bit to 15-bit, which is palette independent, requires packing the 5 most significant bits of each component into the right places of a word value, as Figure 13.8 shows. Truncating

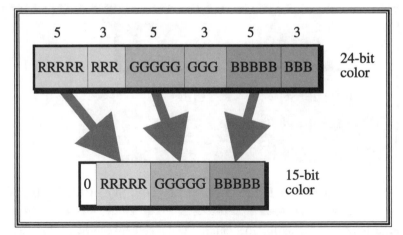

Figure 13.8 Converting a 24-bit color value to 15-bit format.

the least significant bits, rather than rounding them, is done in the interest of speed.

```
static ushort ConvertTo15(uchar *prgb) {
    return((*prgb >> 3) |
    (ushort(*(prgb+1) & 0xF8) << 2) |
    (ushort(*(prgb+2) & 0xF8) << 7));}
```

Converting 8-bit to 24-bit involves looking up the appropriate value in the palette's array of 24-bit values, and copying all three bytes out.

```
void ConvertTo24(uchar col8, uchar *prgb) {
    uchar *prgbP = rgb + (int(col8) * 3);
    *prgb = *prgbP; *(prgb+1) = *(prgbP+1); *(prgb+2) = *(prgbP+2);}
```

Converting 15-bit to 24-bit is independent of any palette, and is a matter of extracting each 5-bit component and expanding it into its own byte, as Figure 13.9 shows. The low three bits of each 8-bit component are set to 0.

```
static void ConvertTo24(ushort col15, uchar *prgb) {
    *prgb = (col15 & 0x1F) << 3;
    *(prgb+1) = (col15 >> 2) & 0xF8;
    *(prgb+2) = (col15 >> 10) << 3;}
```

Palette Setting

Class APalette has two methods for setting the values in a palette. One takes an array of 24-bit colors, the other an array of 15-bit col-

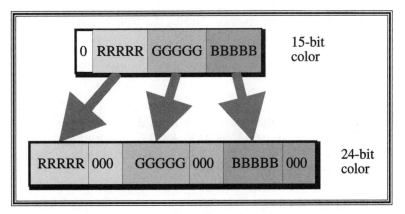

Figure 13.9 Converting a 15-bit color value to 24-bit format.

ors. In each case, both the 24-bit and the 15-bit array in the palette must be updated.

```
void APalette::Set(uchar *prgb, int index, int num)
{
   memcpy(rgb + (index * 3), prgb, num * 3); // set 24-bit entries

   for (int i = 0; i < num; i++, prgb += 3)  // and compute 15-bit
      rgb15[index + 1] = ConvertTo15(prgb);
}

void APalette::Set(ushort *pc15, int index, int num)
{
   memcpy(rgb15 + index, pc15, num * 2);      // set 15-bit entries

   uchar *prgb = &rgb[index * 3];
   for (int i = 0; i < num; i++, prgb += 3)  // and compute 24-bit
      ConvertTo24(rgb15[index + i], prgb);
}
```

Inverse Tables

The methods to convert 15-bit and 24-bit color to 8-bit form make use of some curious entity known as an *inverse table,* if it is present. What is this thing?

Basically, an inverse table is the inverse of the array which looks up a 15-bit or 24-bit RGB color, given an 8-bit index. The table provides a mechanism to do this lookup in reverse, without using the incredibly time-consuming process of finding the closest color using least-squares differencing across the entire palette. The table takes a 15-bit value as input, and produces the closest 8-bit color index as output. With an inverse table, finding a palette's closest match to a given 15-bit color is as simple as:

```
// Conceptually, how an inverse table is used to convert 15->8 bit color
uchar best8BitIndex = inverseTable[some15BitColor]; // NOT ACTUAL SYNTAX!
```

Figure 13.10 shows the operation of an inverse table. While for efficiency the implementation of the inverse table is a simple linear table which uses a 15-bit color as its index, conceptually it can be thought of as a $5 \times 5 \times 5$ three-dimensional table, indexed by 5-bit red, green, and blue values.

Generating Inverse Tables

Where does an inverse table come from? There is no straightforward substitute for using APalette::FindClosest() across all 32,768 table entries to find the closest value to each and every representable 15-bit color and storing that value in the appropriate table slot. This makes inverse table creation extremely time-consuming, the most time-expensive operation presented in this book. Even on a Pentium, it takes several seconds. Thus, inverse tables are often calculated off-line, and loaded in from disk.

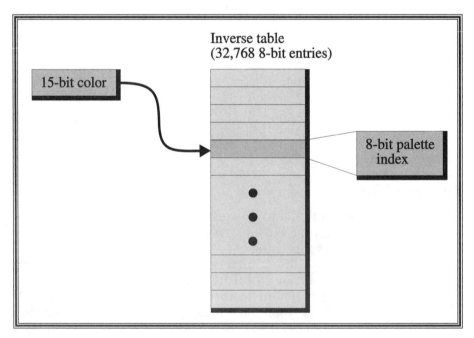

Figure 13.10 Using an inverse table to convert a 15-bit color value to an 8-bit indexed palette entry.

A given inverse table, of course, is only appropriate for a given palette, and becomes out of date if the palette changes. Partial recalculation of the table is difficult, since any changed palette entry might affect any of the inverse table entries. Inverse tables must be used with care. If certain colors are to be animated, for instance, the table should be constructed to avoid using them. The arguments to inverse table creation allow restricting the table to use palette entries in a given range.

Class AInverseTable: An Inverse Table

Class AInverseTable is ARTT's inverse table class. Two constructors are available, one which creates and calculates the entire inverse table, the other of which does nothing. The second form is typically used when the table contents are to be loaded from disk—method TablePtr() is then available to get the pointer of the table for loading into.

The header file for class AInverseTable is listed below.

```
//   AInvTab.h    Inverse Table class
//   Rex E. Bradford

#ifndef __AINVTAB_H
#define __AINVTAB_H

#include "atypes.h"

class APalette;

class AInverseTable {

    uchar tab[32L * 32 * 32]; // 5-bits per r,g,b entry (32K total)

public:

// Constructors (1st empty, 2nd sets itab)

    AInverseTable() {}
    AInverseTable(APalette *palette, int low = 0, int high = 255) {
        Set(palette, low, high);}

// Set inverse table from palette, restrict to range (inclusive)

    void Set(APalette *palette, int low = 0, int high = 255);

// Get raw ptr to table, for loading from file, dumping table, etc.

    uchar *TablePtr() {return tab;}
```

```
    // Look up entry from 15-bit value or 24-bit value

    uchar operator[](ushort c15) {return tab[c15];}
};


#endif
```

AInverseTable Generation

AInverseTable::Set() fills in the entire contents of the inverse table, using a full or partial palette as input. Arguments 'low' and 'high' should be set to 0,255 for an inverse table which can use the full range of the palette. All 32,768 entries of the inverse table are computed in any case—what is restricted is the 8-bit palette indexes which can appear in the table.

This method merely iterates across all 32,768 15-bit values, calling APalette::FindClosest() for each to determine the closest color in the palette. Color components are advanced by 8, which is the proper amount to cover the 256 possibilities in 32 steps (each 5-bit component can take on 32 different values).

```
#define RGB_STEP 8              // range of 256, divided by 32 steps
#define RGB_START (RGB_STEP/2)  // use middle of each range

void AInverseTable::Set(APalette *palette, int low, int high)
{
    uchar rgb[3];

// Go thru 32,768 RGB colors, starting with black (rounded)

    rgb[0] = rgb[1] = rgb[2] = RGB_START;

    for (unsigned int index = 0; index < 32768; index++)
        {
// Find closest match to current RGB color

        tab[index] = palette->FindClosest(rgb, low, high);

// Advance to next color

        rgb[0] += RGB_STEP;        // advance blue fastest
        if (rgb[0] == RGB_START)
           {
           rgb[1] += RGB_STEP;     // then green
           if (rgb[1] == RGB_START)
              rgb[2] += RGB_STEP;  // finally red
           }
        }
}
```

Looking Up Values in an Inverse Table

Once an inverse table is created, it must be "attached" to a palette by setting the palette's 'pInvTab' member to point to it. Then, color conversion routines will automatically make use of it.

As far as using the table for lookup, an inverse table is just an array of 8-bit values, indexed by a 15-bit color value. It is naturally suited to overloading the array indexing operator, and that is, in fact, how values are looked up. Refer back to APalette::ConvertTo8() in this chapter for an example of inverse table usage.

```
uchar operator[](ushort c15) {return tab[c15];}
```

MAKEITAB: A Program for Generating Inverse Tables

As noted earlier, inverse tables are very time consuming to generate. In most cases, it is better to generate them off-line and load them in from disk. MAKEITAB is a program which generates an inverse table from the palette found in a graphics file, and puts the resulting table in an output file. It is suggested that inverse table files be given a distinctive extension, such as INV.

MAKEITAB is run from the command line of the following format:

MAKEITAB gfxfile outfile [low high]

where:

gfxfile	Graphics file holding palette to make table from
outfile	Name of file to create and write inverse table into
low	Low index of palette range to use (defaults to 0)
high	High index of palette range to use (defaults to 255)

An inverse table created with MAKEITAB may be loaded into an AInverseTable and used in a manner such as the following:

```
// Sample code to load in inverse table (assumes 'ppalette' is an APalette)
AInverseTable *pitab = new AInverseTable();   // create empty inverse table
FILE *fp = fopen("someitab.inv");             // open inverse table file
if (fp)
    {
    fread(pitab->TablePtr(), 32768, 1, fp);   // read into inverse table
    ppalette->pInvTab = pitab;                // "attach" to palette
    fclose(fp);                               // close file
    }
// now use color conversion routines with 'ppalette'
```

Color Conversion in Class ACanvas8

The color conversion routines in class APalette, and the inverse tables which can speed up some of these conversions, are of great use to our 8-bit canvases. For instance, sometimes it is handy to specify that a line or rectangle or string of text be displayed in white, or black, or red, without knowing a priori at which palette index such a color is located. Specifying such a color in 15-bit or 24-bit direct format, and letting the canvas convert to 8-bit itself, is what is desired. Conversion to 8-bit makes sense only in the context of some particular palette, of course. Which palette? Read on.

Default Palettes and Private Palettes

Instances of class APalette, remember, are pointed to from within each instance of class ABitmap. Only 8-bit bitmaps (BMF_LIN8, BMF_BANK8, and BMF_RLE8) need palettes; direct-color bitmaps by definition have each pixel specified completely without reference to a palette. Color conversions to or from 8-bit require a palette, as we saw earlier in this chapter. So, we'll need a palette to aid conversion in the following circumstances, among others:

- Set/get current color in 8-bit canvas, when color specified as 15-bit or 24-bit.
- Set/get current color in 15-bit or 24-bit canvas, when color specified as 8-bit.
- Render 8-bit bitmap onto 15-bit or 24-bit canvas.
- Render 15-bit or 24-bit bitmap onto 8-bit canvas.

Note that there is the possibility that more than one palette may be present in the overall "system" of bitmaps and canvases. Several bitmaps may be loaded, each with their own unique palette. This is a problem when using an 8-bit display, because only one of these palettes is set into the actual hardware of the display, and the others are "incorrect." But in 15-bit and 24-bit displays, as we shall see in the next two chapters, it can be very useful to have several 8-bit images, each with their own "private" palette. Figure 13.11 shows the use of private palettes.

Also, even in the case where there is only one palette in use, it can be a nuisance to ensure that each bitmap or canvas we intend to use has its pointer set to that palette. It would be nice if a NULL palette pointer was interpreted correctly in these cases. So, what we need is a "palette finding" policy that is simple and fast to implement but allows us to be sloppy and get good results.

ARTT adopts a "loose" strategy when it comes to associating palettes with 8-bit colors it is handed. For standalone colors, not associated with a bitmapped image, the inline method ACanvas::DefaultPal() implements the following methodology:

1. If the destination canvas has a palette, use it.
2. Else use the "default palette," if any.

```
APalette *DefaultPal() {return (bm.ppalette ? bm.ppalette :
  palDefault);}
```

What is this "default palette?" Well, it's NULL until you set it to something else in your application, using ACanvas::SetDefaultPal(). ACanvas::GetDefaultPal() can be used to retrieve the current setting. In many cases, setting the default palette to the screen canvas's palette (or main window palette, in Windows) is a reasonable default. If the screen or window canvas is not 8-bit, and thus has no palette, a different default can be chosen.

```
static void SetDefaultPal(APalette *pal) {palDefault = pal;}
static APalette *GetDefaultPal(APalette *pal) {return palDefault;}
```

When 8-bit colors are being rendered from a bitmap, that bitmap's palette takes priority. The methodology implemented by ACanvas::BitmapOrDefaultPal() is as follows:

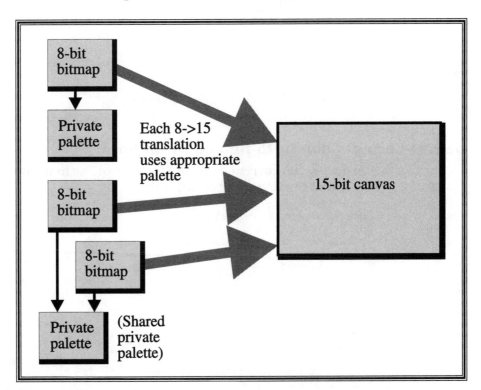

Figure 13.11 Using private palettes to render 8-bit images onto a 15-bit canvas.

1. If bitmap has a palette, use it.
2. Else if destination canvas has a palette, use it.
3. Else use the default palette, if any.

```
APalette *BitmapOrDefaultPal(ABitmap &bms) {
    if (bms.ppalette) return bms.ppalette;
    else return (bm.ppalette ? bm.ppalette : palDefault);}
```

Setting Current Color in 15-Bit and 24-Bit Form

SetColor15() and SetColor24(), defined but unimplemented in ACanvas, can now be implemented in ACanvas8 for all 8-bit canvases. After picking the appropriate palette for conversion, the current color is set from the 8-bit color calculated using an APalette conversion routine. Note that DefaultPal() may return NULL, in which case the color is left unset.

```
void ACanvas8::SetColor15(ushort c15)
{
    APalette *palette = DefaultPal();
    if (palette)
        color8 = palette->ConvertTo8(c15);
}

void ACanvas8::SetColor24(uchar *prgb)
{
    APalette *palette = DefaultPal();
    if (palette)
        color8 = palette->ConvertTo8(prgb);
}
```

Getting Current Color in 15-Bit and 24-Bit Form

Retrieving the current color in 15- or 24-bit format from an 8-bit canvas is just the reverse process.

```
ushort ACanvas8::GetColor15()
{
    APalette *palette = DefaultPal();
    if (palette)
        return palette->ConvertTo15(color8);
    return 0;
}

void ACanvas8::GetColor24(uchar *prgb)
{
    APalette *palette = DefaultPal();
    if (palette)
        palette->ConvertTo24(color8, prgb);
    // IF NO PALETTE, DO NOTHING!
}
```

Drawing Pixels Specified in 15-Bit and 24-Bit Form

Drawing pixels specified in 15-bit and 24-bit form is accomplished with the same conversion, followed by a call to the 8-bit pixel-drawer.

```
void ACanvas8::DrawPixel15U(int x, int y, ushort c15)
{
   APalette *palette = DefaultPal();
   if (palette)
      DrawPixel8U(x, y, palette->ConvertTo8(c15));
}

void ACanvas8::DrawPixel24U(int x, int y, uchar *prgb)
{
   APalette *palette = DefaultPal();
   if (palette)
      DrawPixel8U(x, y, palette->ConvertTo8(prgb));
}
```

Getting Pixel Values in 15-Bit and 24-Bit Form

This is getting boring. Why can't a computer write this code?

```
ushort ACanvas8::GetPixel15U(int x, int y)
{
   APalette *palette = DefaultPal();
   if (palette)
      return palette->ConvertTo15(GetPixel8U(x, y));
   return 0;
}

void ACanvas8::GetPixel24U(int x, int y, uchar *prgb)
{
   APalette *palette = DefaultPal();
   if (palette)
      palette->ConvertTo24(GetPixel15U(x, y), prgb);
   // IF NO PALETTE, DO NOTHING!
}
```

Rendering 15-Bit and 24-Bit Bitmaps

With our newfound ability to render single pixels in 15-bit and 24-bit format on any canvas, we are ready to conquer the world, albeit at the speed of molasses. In class ACanvas, the following methods are able to render bitmaps which are stored in 15-bit and 24-bit format, onto any canvas which implements the DrawPixel15U() and Draw-Pixel24U() methods. We will create improved versions of these in derived canvases, of course.

DrawBitmapLin15U() and DrawBitmapLin15() draw bitmaps stored in BMF_LIN15 format. Note that transparency in 15-bit bitmaps is defined by the pixel value 0. This means that 15-bit bitmaps with transparency may not use 0:0:0, the deepest black color. For foreground black in a transparent 15-bit bitmap, use a color with at least one of the three components set to 1 instead of 0.

```
void ACanvas::DrawBitmapLin15U(ABitmap &bms, int x, int y)
{
// Begin at the beginning, loop through rows

    ushort *p = (ushort *) bms.pbits;
    for (int iy = y; iy < (y + bms.height); iy++)
        {
// Loop through columns

        for (int ix = x; ix < (x + bms.width); ix++, p++)
            {
            if (*p || !bms.transparent)    // if non-zero or non-transp
                DrawPixel15U(ix, iy, *p);  // draw 15-bit pixel
            }

// Advance to next row (tricky because p is a ushort*)

        p += (bms.rowbytes / 2) - bms.width;
        }
}

void ACanvas::DrawBitmapLin15(ABitmap &bms, int x, int y)
{
    ABitmap bmlocal = bms;
    if (ClipBitmap(bmlocal, x, y))
        DrawBitmapLin15U(bmlocal, x, y);
}
```

The methods to draw 24-bit bitmaps are similar. Again, note that the color 0,0,0 is used to signify transparency in transparent bitmaps, and may not be used as a foreground color in such cases.

```
void ACanvas::DrawBitmapLin24U(ABitmap &bms, int x, int y)
{
// Loop through rows

    uchar *p = bms.pbits;
    for (int iy = y; iy < (y + bms.height); iy++)
        {
// Loop through columns

        for (int ix = x; ix < (x + bms.width); ix++, p += 3)
            {
            if (*p || *(p+1) || *(p+2) || !bms.transparent)
                DrawPixel24U(ix, iy, p);   // draw if non-0 or non-transp
            }
```

```
// Advance to next row

     p += bms.rowbytes - (bms.width * 3);
     }
}

void ACanvas::DrawBitmapLin24(ABitmap &bms, int x, int y)
{
   ABitmap bmlocal = bms;
   if (ClipBitmap(bmlocal, x, y))
      DrawBitmapLin24U(bmlocal, x, y);
}
```

Methods to retrieve bitmaps in 15-bit and 24-bit form are also included in class ACanvas, but are not listed here. Their operation is very similar to the above code—see the file ACANVAS.CPP on the CD-ROM for the source listing.

Rendering Scaled 15-Bit and 24-Bit Bitmaps

Rendering scaled versions of bitmaps stored in 15-bit and 24-bit format is very nearly identical to doing so with 8-bit bitmaps (see Chapter 6), except for the pixel-handling code in the inner loop. Methods ACanvas::DrawScaledBitmapLin15() and ACanvas::DrawScaledBitmapLin24() differ from ACanvas::DrawScaledBitmapLin8() in only one line. The line which calls another method to render a given scaled row is changed from:

```
DrawScaledBitmapRowLin8U(sri);      // render row!
```

to

```
DrawScaledBitmapRowLin15U(sri);     // render row!
```

or

```
DrawScaledBitmapRowLin24U(sri);     // render row!
```

The real work goes on in new scaled row-rendering routines, which work with 15-bit and 24-bit bitmap rows. The 15-bit row-scaler built into base class ACanvas is listed below.

```
void ACanvas::DrawScaledBitmapRowLin15U(AScaledRowInfo &sri)
{
// Start at initial source fixed-point x-coord

   AFix fx = sri.srcFx;
```

```
// Traverse from left to right in destination pixel row

    for (int x = sri.destXleft; x < sri.destXright; x++)
      {
      ushort c15 = *((ushort *)sri.srcPbits + int(fx));
      if (c15 || !sri.transparent)         // if non-zero, or not transp
        DrawPixel15U(x, sri.destY, c15);   // draw it at dest
      fx += sri.srcFxStep;                 // step in src w/fraction
      }
}
```

The 24-bit version is very similar.

```
void ACanvas::DrawScaledBitmapRowLin24U(AScaledRowInfo &sri)
{
// Start at initial source fixed-point x-coord

    AFix fx = sri.srcFx;

// Traverse from left to right in destination pixel row

    for (int x = sri.destXleft; x < sri.destXright; x++)
      {
      uchar *p = sri.srcPbits + (int(fx) * 3);
      if (*p || *(p+1) || *(p+2) || !sri.transparent)
        DrawPixel24U(x, sri.destY, p);
      fx += sri.srcFxStep;                 // step in src w/fraction
      }
}
```

Beyond 8-Bit Displays

Rendering 15-bit and 24-bit color onto 8-bit displays is all well and good, and often useful, but the real advances in graphics quality come when the display itself is put into 15-bit and 24-bit modes. The next chapter will do just that. At the same time, we'll create rendering routines in derived canvas classes which cure the speed problems of the generic 15-bit and 24-bit code in this chapter.

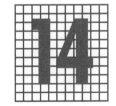

C H A P T E R

Fifteen-Bit and Twenty-Four-Bit Displays

This chapter will be full of code, code, and code. In the previous chapter, we introduced ourselves to the notion that 15-bit and 24-bit displays are the wave of the future, and saw how such direct-color modes represent each pixel using multiple bytes. In this chapter, we will develop the canvas classes necessary for rendering to such display modes. Since there are no standard VGA modes with direct-color capability, this code will be relevant to Super VGA displays only.

Fifteen-Bit Canvases

In 15-bit color display modes, remember, each pixel is represented by a two-byte word. In this word are 5 bits each of red, green, and blue, with the blue bits in the low part of the word. In designing canvas classes to work with 15-bit color, the primary difference from 8-bit canvas classes to keep in mind is the need to write these word-sized direct-color pixels instead of byte-sized indexed-color pixels. In order to do this efficiently, 15-bit canvas classes maintain the "current color" in 15-bit form instead of 8-bit form.

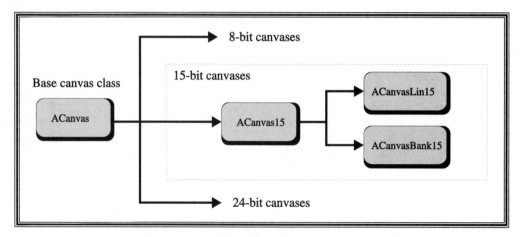

Figure 14.1   Portion of canvas class hierarchy which includes 15-bit direct-color canvases.

Two 15-bit bitmap formats are used in ARTT:

BMF_LIN15   Linear 15-bit canvas
BMF_BANK15   Bank-switched 15-bit canvas

The 15-bit canvas classes include ACanvas15, a base class which maintains the 15-bit current color, ACanvasLin15, the 15-bit linear canvas class, and ACanvasBank15, for 15-bit bank-switched operation. The relevant portion of the canvas class hierarchy is reproduced in Figure 14.1.

Class ACanvas15: Base 15-Bit Canvas Class

Like ACanvas8, class ACanvas15 doesn't have rendering code per se. Its reason for existence is as the resting place for the "current color" in the appropriate format. In this case, that format is a word-sized 15-bit color. ACanvas15, like ACanvas8, is primarily composed of methods to set and get this value from a variety of formats—ACanvas15 provides the appropriate conversions. While ACanvas15 does not include a method to draw a single 15-bit pixel, which is left to derived canvases, it does provide methods to draw pixels in other formats. These do the proper conversion, and then call the unimplemented 15-bit version.

The header file for class ACanvas15 is listed below. Note that "native" color routines use 15-bit color as the native format.

```
//   ACv15.h   Base 15-bit canvas class
//   Rex E. Bradford
```

```
#ifndef __ACANVAS15_H
#define __ACANVAS15_H

#include "acanvas.h"

class ACanvas15 : public ACanvas {
public:

   ushort color15;      // current color is 15-bit

// Constructor: nothing to see here

   ACanvas15(ABitmap *pbm) : ACanvas(pbm) {color15 = 0;}

// Set current color in various flavors

   void SetColor8(uchar c8);
   void SetColor15(ushort c15) {color15 = c15;}
   void SetColor24(uchar *prgb) {color15 = APalette::ConvertTo15(prgb);}
   void SetColorNative(long c) {color15 = c;}

// Retrieve current color in various forms

   uchar GetColor8();
   ushort GetColor15() {return color15;}
   void GetColor24(uchar *prgb) {APalette::ConvertTo24(color15, prgb);}
   long GetColorNative() {return color15;}

// Draw pixel, all convert to 15-bit form, which is not implemented

   void DrawPixel8U(int x, int y, uchar c8);
   void DrawPixel24U(int x, int y, uchar *prgb);
   void DrawPixelNativeU(int x, int y, long c) {DrawPixel15U(x, y, c);}

// Get pixel, all convert from 15-bit form, which is not implemented

   uchar GetPixel8U(int x, int y);
   void GetPixel24U(int x, int y, uchar *prgb);
   long GetPixelNativeU(int x, int y) {return GetPixel15U(x, y);}
};

#endif
```

Let's look at the methods to set the current color. Methods to set the color from most forms are straightforward enough to be inlined:

```
void SetColor15(ushort c15) {color15 = c15;}
void SetColor24(uchar *prgb) {color15 = APalette::ConvertTo15(prgb);}
void SetColorNative(long c) {color15 = c;}
```

Setting the current color in 8-bit format is straightforward, but may be very time-consuming to execute. Conversion from 15-bit to 8-bit format, remember, involves finding the least-squared difference between the desired color and all 256 colors in the palette, and then picking the best. This slow operation is bypassed if an inverse table is attached to the palette (see the implementation of APalette::ConvertTo8() in Chapter 13). Which palette is used? ACanvas::DefaultPal() returns the canvas palette if there is one (since this is a direct-color canvas, any palette attached to it would be solely for the purpose of color conversion such as this), and if not it returns the palette set by ACanvas::SetDefaultPal().

```
void ACanvas15::SetColor8(uchar c8)
{
   APalette *palette = DefaultPal();
   if (palette)
      color15 = palette->ConvertTo15(c8);
}
```

Again, methods to retrieve the current color in most formats are trivial.

```
ushort GetColor15() {return color15;}
void GetColor24(uchar *prgb) {return APalette::ConvertTo24(color15, prgb);}
long GetColorNative() {return color15;}
```

ACanvas15::GetColor8() is a little more involved:

```
uchar ACanvas15::GetColor8()
{
   APalette *palette = DefaultPal();
   if (palette)
      return palette->ConvertTo8(color15);
   return 0;
}
```

Drawing Pixels

While drawing a pixel in 15-bit format is deferred to derived classes, the other format variants can at least do the conversion to 15-bit before passing the buck on to the missing method. Converting an 8-bit pixel for rendering uses a process similar to that used in SetColor8().

```
void ACanvas15::DrawPixel8U(int x, int y, uchar c8)
{
   APalette *palette = DefaultPal();
   if (palette)
      DrawPixel15U(x, y, palette->ConvertTo15(c8));
}
```

Drawing a 24-bit pixel uses the simple conversion ConvertTo15() method in class APalette. ConvertTo15() is a static method, and does not actually use any particular palette. It is located in class APalette because there's no better place to put it.

```
void ACanvas15::DrawPixel24U(int x, int y, uchar *prgb)
{
   DrawPixel15U(x, y, APalette::ConvertTo15(prgb));
}
```

Since "native" form is 15-bit, DrawPixelNativeU() is just a "macro" for DrawPixel15U().

```
void DrawPixelNativeU(int x, int y, long c) {DrawPixel15U(x, y, c);}
```

Getting Pixels

Retrieving the current values of canvas pixels is the reverse of drawing them, and works similarly. The methods are listed below.

```
uchar ACanvas15::GetPixel8U(int x, int y)
{
   APalette *palette = DefaultPal();
   if (palette)
     return palette->ConvertTo8(GetPixel15U(x, y));
   return 0;
}

void ACanvas15::GetPixel24U(int x, int y, uchar *prgb)
{
   APalette::ConvertTo24(GetPixel15U(x, y), prgb);
}

long GetPixelNativeU(int x, int y) {return GetPixel15U(x, y);}
```

Class ACanvasLin15: Linear 15-Bit Canvases

The real 15-bit canvas class we need to implement in this chapter is ACanvasBank15, because 15-bit Super VGAs are bank-switched. However, we still need a linear 15-bit canvas class as well. Our double-buffered scenes use an off-screen canvas, which for most efficient operation should be compatible with the screen canvas class, that is, use the same number of bits per pixel. Class ACanvasLin15 is such a linear 15-bit canvas class for use with off-screen memory.

ACanvasLin15 is similar to ACanvasLin8 in structure. It provides a variety of rendering routines, both geometric (lines, rectangles, and so on) and bitmapped. These routines have a default implementation in ACanvas, and so the rendering routines included here are not strictly necessary. However, the most important ones are reimplemented in this class for efficiency—the ACanvas methods are generic pixel-by-pixel algorithms that are too slow for any but casual use.

The header file for class ACanvasLin15 is listed below.

```
//    ACvLin15.h    15-bit linear canvas class
//    Rex E. Bradford

#ifndef __ACVLIN15_H
#define __ACVLIN15_H

#include "acv15.h"

class ACanvasLin15 : public ACanvas15 {

// Compute pointer from x, y

    ushort *Ptr(int x, int y) {return(ushort *) (bm.pbits +
        (long(y) * long(bm.rowbytes)) + (x * 2));}

public:

// Constructor: once again, pass the buck (bitmap) down the line

    ACanvasLin15(ABitmap *pbm) : ACanvas15(pbm) {}

// Draw pixel: 15-bit version (8/24 conversion supplied by ACanvas15)

    void DrawPixelU(int x, int y);
    void DrawPixel15U(int x, int y, ushort c15);

// Retrieve color of pixel in 15-bit form (8/24 conversion in ACanvas15)

    ushort GetPixel15U(int x, int y);

// Some drawing primitives, replacing slow ones in ACanvas

    void DrawHorzLineU(int y, int xleft, int xright);
    void DrawVertLineU(int x, int ytop, int ybott);
    void DrawRectU(ARect rect);

// Bitmap rendering

    void DrawBitmapLin8U(ABitmap &bm, int x, int y);
    void DrawBitmapLin15U(ABitmap &bm, int x, int y);

// Bitmap row-rendering

    void DrawScaledBitmapRowLin8U(AScaledRowInfo &sri);
};

#endif
```

Drawing and Retrieving Pixels

The inline Ptr() method in class ACanvasLin15 computes a pointer into a linear canvas, given x and y coordinates. This is a matter of starting with the base address of the bitmap, adding the y-coordinate times the "rowbytes", adding the x-coordinate times 2, and finally casting to a ushort pointer. The "times 2" and pointer casting differentiates this method from the Ptr() method in ACanvasLin8. Remember, each pixel is 2 bytes wide.

DrawPixelU() and DrawPixel15U() are about as simple as they can be:

```
void ACanvasLin15::DrawPixelU(int x, int y)
{
    *Ptr(x,y) = color15;
}

void ACanvasLin15::DrawPixel15U(int x, int y, ushort c15)
{
    *Ptr(x,y) = c15;
}
```

GetPixel15U() returns the contents of the word pointer calculated from the x,y coordinate, thus retrieving the 15-bit pixel located there.

```
ushort ACanvasLin15::GetPixel15U(int x, int y)
{
    return *Ptr(x,y);
}
```

Drawing Geometric Primitives

Three geometric primitives are reimplemented in ACanvasLin15 to speed up their default implementation in ACanvas.

ACanvasLin15::DrawHorzLineU() computes the pointer to the leftmost pixel in the horizontal line, and then sets successive pixels. Note that memset() cannot be used to set the pixels, as is done in ACanvasLin8, because memset() does not set wordwide values.

```
void ACanvasLin15::DrawHorzLineU(int y, int xleft, int xright)
{
    ushort *p = Ptr(xleft, y);      // get ptr to leftmost pixel in line
    int w = xright - xleft;         // calculate width
    while (w--)                     // countdown width:
        *p++ = color15;             // draw each pixel and incr ptr
}
```

ACanvasLin15::DrawVertLineU() draws a vertical line by similar means. Note the casting involved in updating the pointer from row to row. The 'rowbytes' field, which is expressed in bytes, must be added to a pointer to char or uchar. Thus, the word pointer is cast to uchar for this addition and then back again to ushort.

```
void ACanvasLin15::DrawVertLineU(int x, int ytop, int ybott)
{
    ushort *p = Ptr(x, ytop);        // get ptr to topmost pixel in line
    int h = ybott - ytop;            // calculate height
    while (h--)                      // countdown height:
        {
        *p = color15;                // set pixel
        p = (ushort *)((uchar *)p + bm.rowbytes); // and advance row
        }
}
```

ACanvasLin15::DrawRectU() draws a filled rectangle. It is similar to DrawHorzLine(), but does successive rows.

```
void ACanvasLin15::DrawRectU(ARect rect)
{
    ushort *p = Ptr(rect.left, rect.top);   // get ptr to upper-left
    int width = rect.Width();               // calc width
    int height = rect.Height();             // and height

    while (height-- > 0)                     // countdown rows:
        {
        int w = width;
        while (w--)                          // countdown columns:
            *p++ = color15;                  // set pixel and incr ptr
        p += (bm.rowbytes / 2) - width;      // end of row, bump to next
        }
}
```

Note that there is no need to provide clipped versions of any of these methods. The clipped versions in class ACanvas perform clipping and then call the unclipped versions. Since these are virtual functions, the derived versions shown here will be invoked.

Drawing Bitmaps

Drawing bitmaps onto a linear 15-bit canvas is similar to doing so onto an 8-bit canvas. The only difference is that 15-bit word-sized pixels must be drawn, including whatever conversion is needed if the source bitmap is not 15-bit.

ACanvasLin15::DrawBitmapLin8U() draws an 8-bit linear bitmap (BMF_LIN8) onto a 15-bit linear canvas. Each pixel must be converted to 15-bit form, which is just a table lookup performed in APalette:: ConvertTo15(). Note that if no suitable palette can be found to perform this conversion, the bitmap is not rendered at all.

```
void ACanvasLin15::DrawBitmapLin8U(ABitmap &bms, int x, int y)
{
// Figure which palette to use, if NULL then cancel

   APalette *palette = BitmapOrDefaultPal(bms);
   if (palette == NULL)
      return;

// Setup

   uchar *ps = bms.pbits;       // get ptr to source bitmap
   ushort *pd = Ptr(x,y);       // get ptr to dest u.1. corner
   int h = bms.height;          // get height for countdown

// Draw all rows

   while (h-- > 0)              // count down rows:
      {
      int w = bms.width;       // get width for countdown
      if (bms.transparent)
         {
         while (w-- > 0)        // transparent: loop thru columns
            {
            if (*ps)           // if non-zero:
               *pd = palette->ConvertTo15(*ps); // then 8->15 and write
            ++ps;              // bump src ptr
            ++pd;              // bump dest ptr
            }
         }
      else                     // else non-transparent:
         {
         while (w-- > 0)        // loop thru columns
            *pd++ = palette->ConvertTo15(*ps++); // 8->15 and write
         }
      ps += bms.rowbytes - bms.width;        // end row: advance src
      pd += (bm.rowbytes / 2) - bms.width;   // and dest ptrs
      }
}
```

Drawing a linear 15-bit bitmap onto a 15-bit linear canvas is even more straightforward, since the source and destination formats are the same. This allows the use of memcpy() in the nontransparent case.

```
void ACanvasLin15::DrawBitmapLin15U(ABitmap &bms, int x, int y)
{
// Setup

   ushort *ps = (ushort *) bms.pbits;  // get ptr to source bitmap
   ushort *pd = Ptr(x,y);              // get ptr to dest u.1.
   int h = bms.height;                 // get height for countdown

// Draw all rows
```

```
      while (h-- > 0)               // count down rows:
        {
      if (bms.transparent)          // if transparent:
          {
          int w = bms.width;        // get width
          while (w-- > 0)           // loop thru columns
            {
            if (*ps)                // if non-zero
               *pd = *ps;           // then write to dest
            ++ps;                   // bump src ptr
            ++pd;                   // bump dest ptr
            }                       // end row: advance src,dest ptrs
          ps = (ushort *)((uchar *)ps + (bms.rowbytes - bms.width));
          pd = (ushort *)((uchar *)pd + (bm.rowbytes - bms.width));
          }
      else                          // else non-transp, memcpy() row
          {                         // and then advance src,dest by rowb
          memcpy(pd, ps, bms.width << 1);
          ps = (ushort *)((uchar *)ps + bms.rowbytes);
          pd = (ushort *)((uchar *)pd + bm.rowbytes);
          }
        }
    }
```

Drawing Scaled Bitmaps

In class ACanvas, methods such as DrawScaledBitmapLin8() and DrawScaledBitmapLin15() provide the overall control flow for drawing scaled bitmaps of any kind. They are aided by "row-rendering" routines, such as DrawScaledBitmapRowLin8U() and DrawScaled-BitmapRowLin15U(). These methods are all implemented in class ACanvas, but the implementations there operate pixel by pixel, calling a virtual function to render each pixel, and so they are fairly slow.

Drawing a scaled 8-bit bitmap onto a 15-bit canvas is particularly slow because DrawPixel8U(), the 8-bit pixel-drawing routine, refigures from scratch each time which palette to use to control the color conversion from 8- to 15-bit. The following override version, ACanvasLin15::DrawScaledBitmapRowLin8U(), uses the palette pointer embedded in the "scaled row info" structure. Each pixel to be drawn needs only to do the 8-bit to 15-bit conversion using this palette, an operation which is a simple table lookup. This version is dramatically faster than the default implementation in ACanvas.

```
void ACanvasLin15::DrawScaledBitmapRowLin8U(AScaledRowInfo &sri)
{
// Can't work without a palette

    if (sri.palette == NULL)
       return;
```

```
// Setup for row

    AFix fx = sri.srcFx;
    ushort *pd = Ptr(sri.destXleft, sri.destY);
    int w = sri.destXright - sri.destXleft;

    while (w-- > 0)                         // loop thru pixels
        {
        uchar c8 = *(sri.srcPbits + int(fx));  // grab source pixel
        if (c8 || !sri.transparent)            // if non-0 or non-transp
            *pd = sri.palette->ConvertTo15(c8); // 8->15 and write
        ++pd;                                  // bump dest ptr
        fx += sri.srcFxStep;                   // advance x by fractional amt
        }
}
```

There is no override implementation of DrawScaledBitmap-RowLin15U(), because the speed savings are not very great. There is no color conversion necessary since both source and destination are 15-bit. Providing a specialized version of this routine in ACanvasLin15 would eliminate the virtual function call to set each pixel, replacing it with a simple pixel copy. While this is certainly worth doing if the routine is to be used a great deal, there is enough overhead in the overall scaling loop that the time savings are not huge.

Class ACanvasBank15: Bank-Switched 15-Bit Canvases

Class ACanvasLin15 is all well and good, but you can't see it on the screen. All 15-bit display modes available on a PC under ARTT are Super VGA modes, programmed by bank-switching. Thus, we also need to develop a bank-switched 15-bit canvas class. Class ACanvas-Bank15 is similar to ACanvasLin15, in that it uses 15-bit pixels, and similar to ACanvasBank8, in that bank-switch crossings must be accounted for during rendering. With this class written, our AVesa class can launch a 15-bit mode with the same ease as an 8-bit one.

The header file for class ACanvasBank15 is listed below. Note the implementation of the inline Vaddr() method, which computes a virtual address from an *x,y* coordinate pair. This is similar to the Vaddr() method in class ACanvasBank8, except that the *x*-coordinate is doubled due to the word-sized pixels.

```
//  ACvBnk15.h   15-bit bank-switched canvas class
//  Rex E. Bradford

#ifndef __ACVBANK15_H
#define __ACVBANK15_H
```

```
#include "acv15.h"
#include "abankmgr.h"

class ACanvasBank15 : public ACanvas15 {

    friend class ACanvas;    // so can access bank manager

    ABankMgr *pBankMgr;      // ptr to bank manager object

// Compute virtual address from x,y

    long Vaddr(int x, int y) {return(bm.vaddr +
        (long(y) * long(bm.rowbytes)) + (x * 2));}

// Hand off to bank manager for easy coding in rendering methods

    ushort *Ptr(long vaddr) {return(ushort*)(pBankMgr->Ptr(vaddr));}
    void EnsureWriteBankAtAddr(long vaddr) {
        pBankMgr->EnsureWriteBankAtAddr(vaddr);}
    void EnsureReadBankAtAddr(long vaddr) {
        pBankMgr->EnsureReadBankAtAddr(vaddr);}
    static bool CrossesBank(long vaddr, int len) {
        return(ABankMgr::CrossesBank(vaddr, len));}
    static int BytesLeftInBank(long vaddr) {
        return(ABankMgr::BytesLeftInBank(vaddr));}

public:

// Constructor: initializes underlying 8-bit canvas

    ACanvasBank15(ABitmap *pbm, ABankMgr *pBankMgr_) : ACanvas15(pbm)
        {pBankMgr = pBankMgr_;}

// Draw 15-bit pixel (8/24-bit conversion supplied in ACanvas15)

    void DrawPixelU(int x, int y);
    void DrawPixel15U(int x, int y, ushort c15);

// Get pixel in 15-bit form (8/24-bit conversion in ACanvas15)

    ushort GetPixel15U(int x, int y);

// Geometric drawing routines

    void DrawHorzLineU(int y, int xleft, int xright);

// Bitmap drawing

    void DrawBitmapLin8U(ABitmap &bm, int x, int y);
    void DrawBitmapLin15U(ABitmap &bm, int x, int y);
```

```
// Bitmap row-rendering

    void DrawScaledBitmapRowLin8U(AScaledRowInfo &sri);
};


#endif
```

Drawing and Retrieving Pixels

Drawing 15-bit pixels is done in a manner very similar to the ACanvasBank8 methods listed in Chapter 5. The virtual address of the pixel is calculated, bank-switching is done if necessary to swap in the bank surrounding this address, and a word-sized pixel is written.

```
void ACanvasBank15::DrawPixelU(int x, int y)
{
    long vaddr = Vaddr(x, y);         // calc virtual addr
    EnsureWriteBankAtAddr(vaddr);     // make sure correct bank is set
    *Ptr(vaddr) = color15;            // calc canvas ptr, set pixel
}

void ACanvasBank15::DrawPixel15U(int x, int y, ushort c15)
{
    long vaddr = Vaddr(x, y);         // calc virtual addr
    EnsureWriteBankAtAddr(vaddr);     // make sure correct bank is set
    *Ptr(vaddr) = c15;                // calc canvas ptr, set pixel
}
```

Retrieving the 15-bit value of a pixel is a similar process.

```
ushort ACanvasBank15::GetPixel15U(int x, int y)
{
    long vaddr = Vaddr(x, y);         // calc virtual addr
    EnsureReadBankAtAddr(vaddr);      // make sure correct bank is set
    return *Ptr(vaddr);               // calc canvas ptr & get
}
```

Drawing Horizontal Lines

The method to draw a horizontal line, ACanvasBank15::DrawHorzLineU(), is almost identical to the implementation in class ACanvasBank8 listed in Chapter 5. Again, the word-sized pixels represent the only real difference in implementation. I know, it seems like a lot of work for a crummy horizontal line; complain to your local SVGA manufacturer.

```
void ACanvasBank15::DrawHorzLineU(int y, int xleft, int xright)
{
// Calc virtual address of 1st pixel, make sure we're in right bank
```

```
      long vaddr = Vaddr(xleft, y);
      EnsureWriteBankAtAddr(vaddr);

// See if horz line lies across a bank boundary, if so split

      int width = xright - xleft;
      if (CrossesBank(vaddr, width * 2))
         {
         int numBytesLeft = 0x10000L - (vaddr & 0xFFFFL);
         int numLeft = numBytesLeft / 2;   // # pixels to left of split
         width -= numLeft;                 // set width for 2nd half later
         ushort *pd = Ptr(vaddr);          // calc canvas ptr
         while (numLeft--)                 // loop thru columns:
            *pd++ = color15;               // set 15-bit pixel
         vaddr += numBytesLeft;            // advance virtual addr to split
         EnsureWriteBankAtAddr(vaddr);     // ensure correct bank now
         }

// Do right case, or entire row if no split

      ushort *pd = Ptr(vaddr);      // calc canvas ptr
      while (width--)               // loop thru columns:
         *pd++ = color15;           // set 15-bit pixel
   }
```

Drawing Bitmaps

Drawing an 8-bit linear bitmap (BMF_LIN8) onto a 15-bit bank-switched canvas involves both color conversion and bank-crossing detection. ACanvasBank15::DrawBitmapLin8U() does both in one fairly large function.

```
void ACanvasBank15::DrawBitmapLin8U(ABitmap &bms, int x, int y)
{
// Pick a palette

   APalette *palette = BitmapOrDefaultPal(bms);
   if (palette == NULL)
      return;

// Setup: get source ptr and compute virtual address

   uchar *ps = bms.pbits;
   long vaddr = Vaddr(x, y);

// Loop through rows

   int h = bms.height;     // count down height of bitmap
   while (h-- > 0)
      {
```

```
// Make sure we're at the right bank for the start of this row

        EnsureWriteBankAtAddr(vaddr); // make sure the bank is right
        ushort *pd = Ptr(vaddr);       // compute ptr to leftmost pixel
        int w = bms.width;

// Does this row lie across a bank boundary?

        if (CrossesBank(vaddr, w * 2))
            {

// Yes, across bank, split into two portions, do left now

            int numLeft = (0x10000L - (vaddr & 0xFFFFL)) / 2;
            long vaddrRight = vaddr + (numLeft * 2);
            w -= numLeft;
            while (numLeft--)
                {
                if (*ps || !bms.transparent)
                    *pd = palette->ConvertTo15(*ps);
                ++ps;
                ++pd;
                }
            EnsureWriteBankAtAddr(vaddrRight);
            pd = Ptr(vaddrRight);
            }

// Second half, or entire row if no split

        while (w-- > 0)
            {
            if (*ps || !bms.transparent)
                *pd = palette->ConvertTo15(*ps);
            ++ps;
            ++pd;
            }

// Update source ptr and virtual address for next row

        ps += bms.rowbytes - bms.width;
        vaddr += bm.rowbytes;
        }
}
```

Drawing a 15-bit linear bitmap (BMF_LIN15) onto the same canvas is similar, but no color conversion is needed.

```
void ACanvasBank15::DrawBitmapLin15U(ABitmap &bms, int x, int y)
{
// Setup: get source ptr and compute virtual address
```

```
        ushort *ps = (ushort *) bms.pbits;
        long vaddr = Vaddr(x, y);

// Loop through rows

        int h = bms.height;      // count down height of bitmap
        while (h-- > 0)
            {
// Make sure we're at the right bank for the start of this row

            EnsureWriteBankAtAddr(vaddr); // make sure the bank is right
            ushort *pd = Ptr(vaddr);      // compute ptr to leftmost pixel
            int w = bms.width;

// Does this row lie across a bank boundary?

            if (CrossesBank(vaddr, w * 2))
                {

// Yes, across bank, split into two portions, do left now

                int numLeft = (0x10000L - (vaddr & 0xFFFFL)) / 2;
                long vaddrRight = vaddr + (numLeft * 2);
                w -= numLeft;
                while (numLeft--)
                    {
                    if (*ps || !bms.transparent)
                        *pd = *ps;
                    ++ps;
                    ++pd;
                    }
                EnsureWriteBankAtAddr(vaddrRight);
                pd = Ptr(vaddrRight);
                }

// Second half, or entire row if no split

            while (w-- > 0)
                {
                if (*ps || !bms.transparent)
                    *pd = *ps;
                ++ps;
                ++pd;
                }

// Update source ptr and virtual address for next row

            ps += (bms.rowbytes / 2) - bms.width;
            vaddr += bm.rowbytes;
            }
        }
```

Drawing Scaled Bitmaps

ACanvasBank15::DrawScaledBitmapRowLin8U() draws a row of a scaled 8-bit bitmap onto the 15-bit bank-switched canvas. The logic to do color conversion as well as bank-crossing, while scaling, makes the routine look a little dense, but it in fact is just an amalgam of by-now familiar techniques. No special row-scaler for 15-bit bitmaps in class ACanvasBank15 is provided, so the default implementation in ACanvas is used in this case. If scaling 15-bit bitmaps onto 15-bit bank-switched canvases is important, a special implementation in this class should be written.

```
void ACanvasBank15::DrawScaledBitmapRowLin8U(AScaledRowInfo &sri)
{
// Can't work without a palette

    if (sri.palette == NULL)
        return;

// Setup for row, make sure correct bank is selected

    AFix fx = sri.srcFx;
    long vaddr = Vaddr(sri.destXleft, sri.destY);
    EnsureWriteBankAtAddr(vaddr);

// Set up ptr into canvas, set width of row

    ushort *pd = Ptr(vaddr);
    int w = sri.destXright - sri.destXleft;

// Check for bank crossing, if so do left half and set up for right

    if (CrossesBank(vaddr, w * 2))
        {
// Split across bank: do left half

        int numBytesLeft = 0x10000L - (vaddr & 0xFFFFL);
        int numLeft = numBytesLeft / 2;    // # pixels on left
        int numRight = w - numLeft;        // the rest on right
        w = numLeft;                       // w = width on left
        while (w-- > 0)                    // count down thru left half
            {
            uchar c8 = *(sri.srcPbits + int(fx));  // get source pixel
            if (c8 || !sri.transparent)            // if non-0 or non-tsp
                *pd = sri.palette->ConvertTo15(c8); // 8->15, write
            ++pd;                                  // bump dest ptr
            fx += sri.srcFxStep;           // advance x by fractional amt
            }
        vaddr += numBytesLeft;             // at end of left, bump vaddr
```

```
            EnsureWriteBankAtAddr(vaddr);   // make sure we're at right bank
            pd = Ptr(vaddr);                // and recalc canvas ptr
            w = numRight;                   // set up width for right half
            }

    // Do entire row, or right half in split case

        while (w-- > 0)                     // loop thru pixels
            {
            uchar c8 = *(sri.srcPbits + int(fx));  // grab source pixel
            if (c8 || !sri.transparent)     // if non-zero or non-transp
               *pd = sri.palette->ConvertTo15(c8);  // 8->15, write
            ++pd;                           // bump dest ptr
            fx += sri.srcFxStep;            // advance x by fractional amt
            }
    }
```

Using 15-Bit VESA Modes

Nope, no code. The implementation of AVesa::Launch() listed in Chapter 5 included calls to create instances of ACanvasBank8, ACanvasBank15, and ACanvasBank24, depending on the depth of the desired mode. Hooked up with an instance of ABankMgrVesa to manage the bank-switching, ACanvasBank15 is ready to roll in 15-bit SVGA modes.

While 15-bit display modes and bitmaps take up twice the memory of 8-bit, and are also slower to render to, the visual results are often worth it. On a sufficiently fast machine, 15-bit graphics is still "realtime," even if perhaps not as peppy as 8-bit. Besides the much wider range of color available on a given display or in a given image, 15-bit solves the enormous headache of matching palettes across a set of images which must be used together. Fifteen-bit displays are becoming standard on the next generation of CD-ROM-based video-game platforms, and are the mode of choice for high-quality digital video playback.

Table 14.1 lists the 15-bit VESA modes.

While Microsoft Windows display drivers support 15-bit color, the current version of WinG does not support 15-bit operation. Windows 95 features CreateDIBSection(), an API call to create a 15-bit drawing surface (bitmap and device context). With a little bit of work, the Windows class AWingWindow could be modified to use CreateDIBSection() instead of WinG, and then 15-bit Windows modes would be at your command.

While the death of 8-bit graphics is easy to exaggerate, 15-bit graphics are already showing up in games, and this trend will continue. Even better-looking, and even less real-time, is 24-bit color, the subject of the next section.

Table 14.1 Fifteen-Bit Vesa Modes

Mode	Resolution	Comments
10DH	320 × 200	Not supported by many video cards
110H	640 × 480	Requires 1 Mb video ram
113H	800 × 600	Requires 1 Mb video ram
116H	1024 × 768	Requires 2 Mb video ram
119H	1280 × 1024	Requires 3 Mb video ram

Twenty-Four-Bit Canvases

In 24-bit color display modes, each pixel is represented by a sequence of three bytes. In most such modes on Super VGA cards, but unfortunately not all, the pixel bytes are in the order blue, green, and then red. ARTT uses this sequence exclusively, and cannot work properly with boards which store the pixels in the reverse order (or any other order).

The three-byte layout is awkward to work with for a variety of reasons. There is no primitive in the C++ language, nor in the underlying hardware for that matter, that can write a three-byte quantity. Other techniques, for instance, three successive byte-sized writes, or a memcpy() call, must be used. Furthermore, bank-switched 24-bit canvases pose another serious problem—if the "rowbytes" is not a power of 2, it is possible for a bank boundary to occur in the middle of a pixel! This complicates the rendering code somewhat.

On current hardware, 24-bit graphics can barely be said to be real time, because of these annoyances and the fact that three times as many bytes need to be written as in 8-bit modes. Still, Pentium chips are getting faster and more common, and further developments are on the way. Twenty-four-bit graphics will be real time soon, if not just now.

Two 24-bit bitmap formats are used in ARTT:

- BMF_LIN24   Linear 24-bit canvas
- BMF_BANK24   Bank-switched 24-bit canvas

The 24-bit canvas classes include ACanvas24, a base class which maintains a 24-bit current color, ACanvasLin24, the 24-bit linear canvas class, and ACanvasBank24, for 24-bit bank-switched displays. The relevant portion of the canvas class hierarchy is reproduced in Figure 14.2.

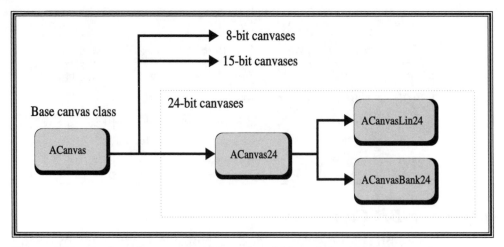

Figure 14.2   Portion of canvas class hierarchy which includes 24-bit direct-color canvases.

Class ACanvas24: Base 24-Bit Canvas Class

Class ACanvas24 is very similar to ACanvas15 or ACanvas8 in structure. The main difference revolves around its representation of the "current color." This value is represented as a union between a small unsigned character array and a longword. Either form can be used in a given operation, whichever is more convenient. The "native" color, for instance, is set by writing the longword portion of the union. In most rendering operations, the first three bytes of the character array are used. The fourth byte, which is the high byte of the longword, is unused.

ACanvas24 provides routines to set and get the current color in each possible format, and to do color conversion when reading and writing pixels. ACanvas24 leaves to derived classes the job of actually reading or writing a 24-bit color pixel.

The header file for class ACanvas24 is listed below.

```
//   ACanvas24.h    Base 24-bit canvas class
//   Rex E. Bradford

#ifndef __ACANVAS24_H
#define __ACANVAS24_H

#include "acanvas.h"

class ACanvas24 : public ACanvas {
public:

    union {
        uchar rgbColor[4];  // color as 3 rgb + pad
```

```
        long rgbColorL;       // color as long
        };

// Constructor: nothing to see here

    ACanvas24(ABitmap *pbm) : ACanvas(pbm) {rgbColorL = 0;}

// Set current color in various flavors

    void SetColor8(uchar c8);
    void SetColor15(ushort c15) {APalette::ConvertTo24(c15, rgbColor);}
    void SetColor24(uchar *prgb) {rgbColor[0] = *prgb;
        rgbColor[1] = *(prgb+1); rgbColor[2] = *(prgb+2);}
    void SetColorNative(long c) {rgbColorL = c;}

// Retrieve current color in various forms

    uchar GetColor8();
    ushort GetColor15() {return APalette::ConvertTo15(rgbColor);}
    void GetColor24(uchar *prgb) {*prgb = rgbColor[0];
        *(prgb+1) = rgbColor[1]; *(prgb+2) = rgbColor[2];}
    long GetColorNative() {return rgbColorL;}

// Draw pixel, all convert to 24-bit form, which is not implemented

    void DrawPixel8U(int x, int y, uchar c8);
    void DrawPixel15U(int x, int y, ushort c15);
    void DrawPixelNativeU(int x, int y, long c) {DrawPixel24U(x, y,
        (uchar *) &c);}

// Get pixel, all convert from 15-bit form, which is not implemented

    uchar GetPixel8U(int x, int y);
    ushort GetPixel15U(int x, int y);
    long GetPixelNativeU(int x, int y) {long temp = 0;
        GetPixel24U(x, y, (uchar *) &temp); return temp;}
};

#endif
```

Setting and Getting Current Color

ACanvas24::SetColor8() uses the DefaultPal() method in class ACanvas to find the palette that it should use to convert 8-bit color to 24-bit form. If the palette to be used is non-NULL, APalette::ConvertTo24(), seen in the last chapter, is used to do the actual conversion (this is a simple table lookup).

```
void ACanvas24::SetColor8(uchar c8)
{
    APalette *palette = DefaultPal();
    if (palette)
```

```
      palette->ConvertTo24(c8, rgbColor);
}
```

Methods to set the color from other forms are straightforward enough to be inlined:

```
void SetColor15(ushort c15) {APalette::ConvertTo24(c15, rgbColor);}
void SetColor24(uchar *prgb) {rgbColor[0] = *prgb;
   rgbColor[1] = *(prgb+1); rgbColor[2] = *(prgb+2);}
void SetColorNative(long c) {rgbColorL = c;}
```

Getting the current color in 8-bit format has problems similar to that encountered in ACanvas15—the palette must be searched for the closest match, unless an inverse table exists. APalette::ConvertTo8() handles the details of this operation.

```
uchar ACanvas24::GetColor8()
{
   APalette *palette = DefaultPal();
   if (palette)
      return palette->ConvertTo8(rgbColor);
   return 0;
}
```

Again, methods to retrieve the current color in other formats are trivial:

```
ushort GetColor15() {return APalette::ConvertTo15(rgbColor);}
void GetColor24(uchar *prgb) {*prgb = rgbColor[0];
   *(prgb+1) = rgbColor[1]; *(prgb+2) = rgbColor[2];}
long GetColorNative() {return rgbColorL;}
```

Drawing Pixels

Like ACanvas15, ACanvas24 implements pixel-draw routines requiring color conversion. It does so by applying the proper conversion, and then calling the 24-bit pixel-drawer, which is left to derived classes to implement.

```
void ACanvas24::DrawPixel8U(int x, int y, uchar c8)
{
   APalette *palette = DefaultPal();
   if (palette)
      {
      uchar rgb[3];
      palette->ConvertTo24(c8, rgb);
      DrawPixel24U(x, y, rgb);
      }
}
```

```
void ACanvas24::DrawPixel15U(int x, int y, ushort c15)
{
    uchar rgb[3];
    APalette::ConvertTo24(c15, rgb);
    DrawPixel24U(x, y, rgb);
}
```

Since "native" form is 24-bit, DrawPixelNativeU() is just a "macro" for DrawPixel24U(), which is itself unimplemented.

```
void DrawPixelNativeU(int x, int y, long c) {DrawPixel24U(x, y,
    (uchar *) &c);}
```

Getting Pixels

Retrieving the current values of canvas pixels is the reverse of drawing them, and works similarly. The methods are listed below. The last, GetPixelNativeU(), ensures that the high byte of the resulting longword is zeroed.

```
uchar ACanvas24::GetPixel8U(int x, int y)
{
    APalette *palette = DefaultPal();
    if (palette)
        {
        uchar rgb[3];
        GetPixel24U(x, y, rgb);
        return palette->ConvertTo8(rgb);
        }
    return 0;
}

ushort ACanvas24::GetPixel15U(int x, int y)
{
    uchar rgb[3];
    GetPixel24U(x, y, rgb);
    return APalette::ConvertTo15(rgb);
}

    long GetPixelNativeU(int x, int y) {long temp = 0;
        GetPixel24U(x, y, (uchar *) &temp); return temp;}
```

Class ACanvasLin24: Linear 24-Bit Canvases

The linear 24-bit canvas class, ACanvasLin24, is very similar to ACanvasLin15 in structure and operation. Only the inner details of the rendering routines are different. The header file for class ACanvasLin24 is not listed here—it is essentially identical to ACanvasLin15. See the file ACVLIN24.H on the CD-ROM for the full listing.

Only one inline method from it is listed below. This is ACanvasLin24::Ptr(), which computes the pointer to a pixel given an *x,y* coordinate pair. Note that the *x*-coordinate is multiplied by 3, because each pixel is 3 bytes wide.

```
uchar *Ptr(int x, int y) {return(bm.pbits +
    (long(y) * long(bm.rowbytes)) + (x * 3));}
```

Drawing and Retrieving Pixels

ACanvasLin24::DrawPixelU() and DrawPixel24U() draw a single pixel in 24-bit format. All this for one pixel? You bet.

```
void ACanvasLin24::DrawPixelU(int x, int y)
{
    uchar *pd = Ptr(x,y);      // calc ptr to pixel at x,y
    *pd++ = rgbColor[0];       // draw blue component
    *pd++ = rgbColor[1];       // green
    *pd = rgbColor[2];         // red
}


void ACanvasLin24::DrawPixel24U(int x, int y, uchar *prgb)
{
    uchar *pd = Ptr(x,y);      // calc ptr to pixel at x,y
    *pd++ = *prgb++;           // draw blue component
    *pd++ = *prgb++;           // green
    *pd = *prgb;               // red
}
```

GetPixel24U() returns the pixel at a given *x,y* coordinate. Read it and weep.

```
void ACanvasLin24::GetPixel24U(int x, int y, uchar *prgb)
{
    uchar *ps = Ptr(x,y);      // calc ptr to pixel at x,y
    *prgb++ = *ps++;           // grab blue component
    *prgb++ = *ps++;           // green
    *prgb = *ps;               // red
}
```

Drawing Geometric Primitives

Like ACanvasLin15, three geometric primitives are reimplemented in ACanvasLin24 to speed up their default implementation in ACanvas. ACanvasLin24::DrawHorzLineU() computes the pointer to the leftmost pixel in the horizontal line, and then sets successive pixels.

```
void ACanvasLin24::DrawHorzLineU(int y, int xleft, int xright)
{
    uchar *p = Ptr(xleft, y);    // get ptr to leftmost pixel
```

```
    int w = xright - xleft;      // calc width
    while (w--)                   // loop thru columns:
       {
       *p++ = rgbColor[0];        // draw blue component
       *p++ = rgbColor[1];        // green
       *p++ = rgbColor[2];        // red
       }
    }
```

ACanvasLin24::DrawVertLineU() works similarly.

```
void ACanvasLin24::DrawVertLineU(int x, int ytop, int ybott)
{
    uchar *p = Ptr(x, ytop);      // get ptr to top pixel
    int h = ybott - ytop;         // calc height
    while (h--)                    // loop thru rows:
       {
       *p = rgbColor[0];          // draw blue component
       *(p+1) = rgbColor[1];      // green
       *(p+2) = rgbColor[2];      // red
       p += bm.rowbytes;          // advance to next row
       }
    }
```

ACanvasLin24::DrawRectU() is fairly simple as well, though barely worth the trouble of implementing at all, instead of relying on ACanvas::DrawRectU() (which would call virtual method ACanvasLin24::DrawHorzLineU() for each row).

```
void ACanvasLin24::DrawRectU(ARect rect)
{
// Setup: get ptr to u.1. pixel, calc width/height, pre-calc amt.
// to advance by from right of one row to left of next.

    uchar *p = Ptr(rect.left, rect.top);
    int width = rect.Width();
    int height = rect.Height();
    int rowAdvance = bm.rowbytes - (width * 3);

// Loop thru rows, drawing each horizontal strip

    while (height-- > 0)
       {
       int w = width;
       while (w--)
          {
          *p++ = rgbColor[0];     // draw blue component
          *p++ = rgbColor[1];     // green
          *p++ = rgbColor[2];     // red
          }
       p += rowAdvance;
       }
    }
```

Drawing Bitmaps and Scaled Bitmaps

DrawBitmapLin8U(), DrawBitmapLin24U(), and DrawScaledBitmap-RowLin8U() are all included in class ACanvasLin24 to speed up the default implementations in ACanvas. If listed here, they would seem like déjà vu all over again. These methods are nearly identical to the ones in ACanvasLin15 listed earlier in this chapter—24-bit pixels are rendered instead of 15-bit ones, but the structure is the same. See the file ACVLIN24.CPP on the CD-ROM for full listings.

Class ACanvasBank24: Bank-Switched 24-Bit Canvases

In order to use an actual 24-bit display mode, we need to develop a 24-bit bank-switched canvas. Class ACanvasBank24 parallels ACanvasBank15. Besides writing 24-bit pixels instead of 15-bit ones, its rendering routines differ somewhat by the need to check for bank-crossings in the middle of a pixel. The header file is not listed below; see ACVBNK24.H on the CD-ROM. One inline method, Vaddr(), is reproduced here. It computes the virtual address of a pixel, given an *x,y* coordinate pair.

```
long Vaddr(int x, int y) {return(bm.vaddr +
    (long(y) * long(bm.rowbytes)) + (x * 3));}
```

Drawing and Retrieving Pixels

The methods to draw a single pixel are distressingly long-winded, a sign that 24-bit bank-switched canvases are good for real-time work only with a very peppy processor. Partly, this complication is due to the fact that a bank-crossing can occur in midpixel. Even the actual execution time for a typical pixel, which does not have such a bank-crossing, is significantly worse than for a 15-bit pixel in a bank-switched canvas.

```
void ACanvasBank24::DrawPixelU(int x, int y)
{
    long vaddr = Vaddr(x, y);          // calc virtual addr
    if (CrossesBank(vaddr, 3))         // check for bank-crossing!!!
        {
        for (int i = 0; i < 3; i++)    // yes (rare), do s-l-o-w-l-y
            {
            EnsureWriteBankAtAddr(vaddr);
            *Ptr(vaddr++) = rgbColor[i];
            }
        }
    else                               // else no bank crossing:
        {
        EnsureWriteBankAtAddr(vaddr); // make sure correct bank is set
        uchar *pd = Ptr(vaddr);       // calc ptr to canvas x,y
        *pd++ = rgbColor[0];          // write blue component of pixel
```

```
        *pd++ = rgbColor[1];            // green component
        *pd = rgbColor[2];              // red component
        }
   }

void ACanvasBank24::DrawPixel24U(int x, int y, uchar *prgb)
{
   long vaddr = Vaddr(x, y);           // calc virtual addr
   if (CrossesBank(vaddr, 3))          // check for bank-cross!!!
      {
      for (int i = 0; i < 3; i++, vaddr++)   // yes (rare):
         {
         EnsureWriteBankAtAddr(vaddr);        // loop thru 3 bytes
         *Ptr(vaddr) = *prgb++;
         }
      }
   else                                // else no bank-crossing:
      {
      EnsureWriteBankAtAddr(vaddr);    // make sure correct bank is set
      uchar *pd = Ptr(vaddr);          // calc ptr to canvas x,y
      *pd++ = *prgb++;                 // write blue component
      *pd++ = *prgb++;                 // green
      *pd = *prgb;                     // red
      }
   }
```

Retrieving the value of a 24-bit pixel is a similarly painful process.

```
void ACanvasBank24::GetPixel24U(int x, int y, uchar *prgb)
{
   long vaddr = Vaddr(x, y);           // calc virtual addr
   if (CrossesBank(vaddr, 3))          // check for bank crossing!!!
      {
      for (int i = 0; i < 3; i++)      // yes (rare), grab 1 at a time
         {
         EnsureReadBankAtAddr(vaddr);
         *prgb++ = *Ptr(vaddr++);
         }
      }
   else                                // else no bank crossing:
      {
      EnsureReadBankAtAddr(vaddr);     // make sure correct bank is set
      uchar *ps = Ptr(vaddr);          // calc ptr to canvas x,y
      *prgb++ = *ps++;                 // grab blue component
      *prgb++ = *ps++;                 // green
      *prgb = *ps;                     // red
      }
   }
```

Drawing Horizontal Lines

The method to draw a horizontal line, ACanvasBank24::DrawHorz-
LineU(), takes the easy way out of bank-crossing detection. If any portion of the line crosses a bank boundary, the entire line is rendered

using pixel-by-pixel function calls. This avoids having to embed more bank-cross checking within each pixel. If the entire line crosses no bank boundary, as is usually the case, a much faster loop is executed.

```
void ACanvasBank24::DrawHorzLineU(int y, int xleft, int xright)
{
    long vaddr = Vaddr(xleft, y);        // calc vaddr of leftmost pixel
    int width = xright - xleft;          // calc width

    if (CrossesBank(vaddr, width * 3))   // check for bank crossing
        {
        for (int x = xleft; x < xright; x++)    // yes:
            DrawPixelU(x, y);            // then do pixel-by-pixel
        }
    else                                 // else no bank-crossing:
        {
        EnsureWriteBankAtAddr(vaddr);    // make sure correct bank
        uchar *pd = Ptr(vaddr);          // calc ptr to leftmost pixel
        while (width--)                  // loop thru columns:
            {
            *pd++ = rgbColor[0];         // for each pixel, blue
            *pd++ = rgbColor[1];         // green
            *pd++ = rgbColor[2];         // red
            }
        }
}
```

Drawing Bitmaps and Scaled Bitmaps

The methods to draw 8-bit and 24-bit bitmaps on a bank-switched 24-bit canvas are very similar to their 15-bit counterparts. See the file ACVBNK24.CPP on the CD-ROM for the listings of ACanvasBank-24::DrawBitmapLin8U() and DrawBitmapLin24U(). Also see the same file for a listing of DrawScaledBitmapRowLin8U(), which draws one row of an 8-bit bitmap scaled onto the 24-bit bank-switched canvas.

Using 24-Bit VESA Modes

As stated previously, 24-bit modes are bulky and slow. The visual quality is worth it when real-time performance is not as important as image representation. As processors speed up, and as hardware-assisted rendering becomes the norm, 24-bit modes will become the standard. Until then, let the viewer beware.

Since rendering routines in 24-bit linear canvases are noticeably faster than those in 24-bit bank-switched canvases, using off-screen buffers can be a help here. Render off-screen into a canvas of class ACanvasLin24, and then blit to the display using ACanvasBank24:: DrawBitmapLin24U(). The scene and actor system uses this method-

Table 14.2   Twenty-Four-Bit Vesa Modes

Mode	*Resolution*	*Comments*
10FH	320 × 200	Not supported by many video cards
112H	640 × 480	Requires 1 Mb video ram
115H	800 × 600	Requires 2 Mb video ram
118H	1024 × 768	Requires 3 Mb video ram
11BH	1280 × 1024	Requires 4 Mb video ram

ology in all screen modes, whether 24-bit or not. This tip applies to 15-bit modes as well as to 24-bit ones.

Table 14.2 lists the 24-bit VESA modes.

While 24-bit graphics can be visually stunning, they are not the last word in color. Of even more importance in many cases are the color effects that can be applied to images to darken, haze, mix, or otherwise alter them to suit the scene. Many of these effects can be applied in real time. The next chapter will show how.

GFXSHOW3: 8/15/24-Bit Image Viewer

GFXSHOW3 is an updated version of GFXSHOW2, the graphics file viewer presented in Chapter 5 (itself updated from GFXSHOW1 in Chapter 3). GFXSHOW3 can display graphics files having 8, 15, or 24 bits of depth, and it can also put the screen into any of these color depths. If the graphics file and screen do not match, color conversion occurs.

GFXSHOW3 is run from the command line using either of these two forms:

```
GFXSHOW3 filename.ext mode              // supply VESA mode number
                                        // (in hex)
```

or

```
GFXSHOW3 filename.ext width height depth    // supply screen resolution
                                            // and depth
```

For instance: GFXSHOW3 somefile.bmp 800 600 15. The source code for GFXSHOW3 can be found on the CD.

C H A P T E R

Color Shading, Hazing, Filtering, and Translucency

By this point, we have the ability to import bitmapped images from outside sources, in a variety of color depths, and display them onto 8-bit, 15-bit, and 24-bit display screens. We can scale their resolution on the fly, not to mention animating an entire overlapping scene of them. This must be it, right? End of story?

Not quite. Any program which uses only the techniques developed so far, whether it be a game, business presentation, kiosk, or home-based educational product, is going to look a little flat. No matter how beautiful the source images displayed, what makes them come alive in a "real scene" is the use of *lighting* and other color effects. Any 3D simulation worth its salt puts great emphasis on local lighting effects, darkening in distant areas, and hazing effects at great distances. Other color effects, such as infrared or other filtered views, and translucency, are very important as well. Color plate 8 shows an outdoor 3D scene featuring such lighting and hazing, as well as an alternate view through an "infrared" filter.

The color theory begun in Chapter 13 is a good base on which to begin our exploration of such color effects. By manipulating RGB colors mathematically, many useful effects can be achieved. Does

(a)

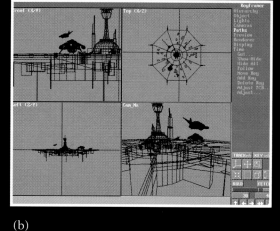

(b)

(c)

Plate 1 Screen captures from Autodesk's 3D Studio. (a) Wireframe view of the scene. Object geometry can be quickly viewed in wireframe for camera placement and overall layout. (b) Wireframe editing windows. Three windows show the scene from along the x, y, and z axes. A fourth window is available for viewing from any camera angle. Object geometry is manipulated in these windows. (c) A scene rendered from the wireframe geometry, with texturing and lighting effects added. Courtesy of LookingGlass Technologies Inc., with permission from Autodesk Inc.

Plate 2 Screen shot of the AQUARIUM sample program. The fish are animate and swim from side to side. The display is 640 x 480 pixels, with a depth of 8 bits per pixel.

Plate 3 Screen shot from *Talk Time with Tucker,* an example of large character, cartoon-like animation. Courtesy of Laureate Learning Systems Inc. and Interactics Inc.

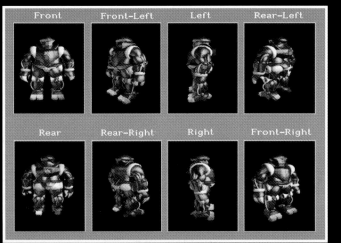

Plate 4 Multiple views of a bitmap taken from different orientations. A pseudo-3D application examines the object's orientation relative to the camera's orientation, and displays the bitmap which most closely approximates the desired result. Courtesy of LookingGlass Technologies Inc.

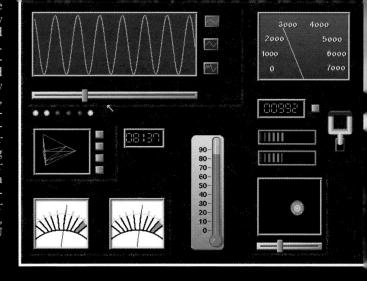

Plate 5 Screen shot of the AMUCK sample program. Many different "actor" classes are used in this animation demo program. These classes include AActorSprite (yellow blinking lights and bouncing ball), AActorDraw (waveform and web displays), AActorButton (waveform selectors, pink web control pushbuttons, time display, frame counter and its pink reset button, and big shutdown switch), AActorSlider (pink sliders under waveform and bouncing ball displays), AActorGaugeBitmap (thermometer and horizontal amplitude bars), and AActorGaugeNeedle (VU meters and RPM gauge).

(a)

(b)

(c)

Plate 7 Three versions of the same image, rendered at different color depths. (a) 24-bit version of image.

(a)

(b)

(c)

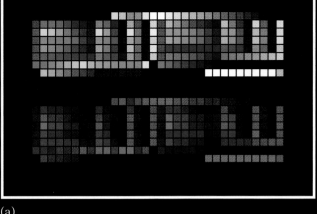

(a)

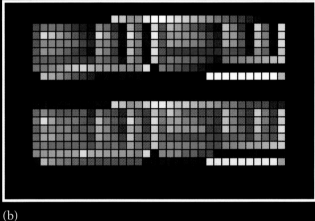

(b)

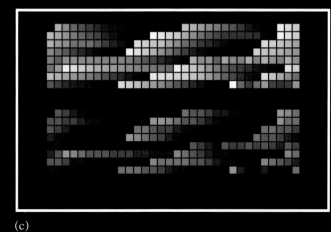

(c)

Plate 9 Sample Color LookUp Tables (CLUTs). (a) Sample shading CLUT. The top half of the screen shows each of the 256 colors in the palette. The bottom half shows darkened versions of each color. All colors come from the same palette, so these are the closest match to the desired (darkened) RGB color. (b) Sample hazing CLUT. In this case, the bottom colors are hazed towards grey. (c) Sample filter CLUT. Each color is the closest match to the original color "seen" through a pinkish-orange filter.

Plate 10 Screen shot from the HELI-FIRE sample program. HELIFIRE is a classic "shoot 'em up" which uses a hazing table for rendering distant helicopters and a blending table to make the crosshair cursor and score background translucent. While it uses bit-maps for all rendering, this program makes use of some of the 3D classes in part 4 of the book.

Plate 11 Adobe's *Premiere* is a very popular desktop video editing tool, and runs on both PCs and Macintoshes. Digital video and audio segments can be captured from analog sources or read from files. Once the video is loaded, Premiere allows easy "cut and paste" of the segments, and also allows overlaying of separate images, a library of transitions such as wipes and fades, and many other features. Courtesy of Adobe Systems Inc.

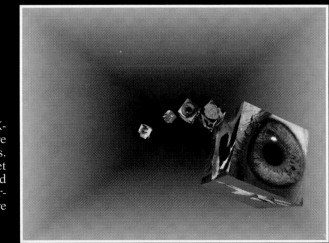

Plate 12 Screen shot from the TEX-CUBES sample program. The cubes are texture mapped with various images. Texture mapping is the fastest way to get realistic-looking objects and terrain, and is now widely used. Video boards incorporating hardware support for texture mapping are becoming available.

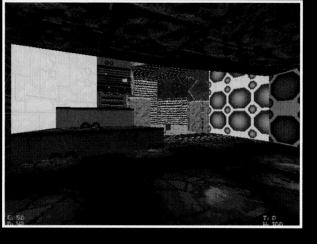

Plate 13 Screen shot from a new ray-casting engine under development. Sophisticated raycasters allow for geometry which is more complex than the basic "square grid of walls" approach. Courtesy of LookingGlass Technologies Inc.

Plate 14 Screen shot of a scene rendered using Criterion's *Renderware,* one of a few commercial 3D engines available for licensing. Renderware uses a sophisticated rendering strategy which features Z buffering "only when necessary" in order to achieve reasonable performance under a variety of uses. Courtesy of Criterion Software Ltd.

Plate 15 Screen shot from *Flight Unlimited,* published by LookingGlass Technologies. This flight simulator features real-time rendering of photo-realistic textured terrain, wrapped over hilly geometry. It uses a custom 3D engine for scene rendering. Courtesy of LookingGlass Technologies Inc.

this mean we are leaving the realm of real-time graphics, and wandering off into image processing? In a word, absolutely not (*okay, two words*). The use of color lookup tables allows these effects to be applied to images in real time, as they are rendered. This chapter, which concludes the 2D core of the ARTT library, launches us into the "big leagues" of real-time animation.

Color Lookup Tables

Any programmer concerned with runtime efficiency will tell you that lookup tables are one of the foremost algorithmic tricks to be employed in the quest for speed. After all, why calculate at runtime what can be precalculated and stored in a table? So how do we apply this tried-and-true technique to color manipulation?

Figure 15.1 shows the conceptual operation of a *color lookup table*, or CLUT. A given color is "looked up" in the CLUT, and the value found there is some modified version of the color. A particular table,. for instance, might darken the color by 50 percent, or mix it with bright green.

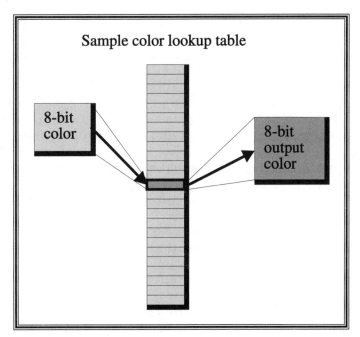

Figure 15.1 Sample color lookup table (CLUT). Eight-bit input color produces 8-bit output color.

Eight-Bit Color Lookup Tables

Let's think about the representation of a CLUT. Figure 15.1 represents a CLUT as taking an 8-bit input and producing an 8-bit result. How was this choice arrived at?

As to how a table is indexed, the obvious choices for indexing are 8-bit, 15-bit, and 24-bit colors. Right away, it's easy to see that using 15-bit or 24-bit colors as table indexes is going to lead to some pretty large tables—32K entries for 15-bit and 16.7M entries for 24-bit! The former is impractical, the latter just about impossible.

Other possibilities exist. For instance, we could have separate lookup tables for each of the red, green, and blue components. For 15-bit graphics, though, this means the "lookup" operation will involve splitting a 15-bit value into three 5-bit indexes, looking up the results for each such component in its corresponding table, and then recombining the 5-bit results into a 15-bit output word. For 24-bit graphics, three tables can be used more directly (each component is already in its own byte), but the three lookups are still time-consuming. Overall, the amount of computation involved in either case makes the multiple-table approach somewhat unsuitable for real-time graphics, at least on current PCs.

So, we are going to limit ourselves to tables indexed by a single 8-bit color index. Therefore, ARTT color effects apply only to 8-bit images. This limitation is not so serious, given that for real-time work, even on 15-bit and 24-bit displays, 8-bit source images are the preferred format. Each 8-bit image may have its own "private" palette, so the overall scene is not limited to 256 colors.

We'll use 8-bit indexes to look up some transformed version of the color in the CLUT. Now, what about the format of the entries found in the table? Should the CLUT hold entries which are 15-bit values, or perhaps 24-bit values? We could have both, in some "supertable." But in a very real sense, an APalette is such a CLUT, having both 15-bit and 24-bit output formats in it, in the rgb15[] and rgb[] arrays. So we already have a "CLUT" that does 8→15 and 8→24 conversions for us—it's our palette! The problem we face is converting back from 15-bit or 24-bit form to 8-bit, which requires an inverse table in order to operate in real time. Inverse tables are themselves big and slow to generate. What if, instead, the CLUT contained 8-bit color values, so that a direct conversion from 8-bit color to 8-bit color was encoded in it? For 8-bit images and displays, this is by far the most direct technique, not to mention the most compact.

In ARTT, our CLUTs will be encoded in such a way. They will convert 8-bit color to 8-bit color directly, without an intervening RGB step. Such tables are still usable with 15-bit and 24-bit displays—they just require an extra palette lookup at the end (to convert the 8-bit result to 15-bit or 24-bit) and are a little inaccurate due to the fact that the CLUT can refer only to colors which exist in the palette, not any possible color.

Uses for CLUTs

There are many possible uses for CLUTs, including:

- Shading—darkening or lightening.
- Hazing—hazing (mixing) toward a specific color, often white or gray.
- Filtering—filtering through a color. Infrared displays are an example.
- Translating—translating colors from one palette to another.

ARTT has CLUT classes for each of these cases, which we will cover in this chapter.

Tables of Tables

By themselves, CLUTs are very useful. But they can be even more useful when grouped into a "table of CLUTs." This is a set of related CLUTs, which can be thought of as a two-dimensional array, indexed by color and table number. Figure 15.2 shows a sample table of CLUTs.

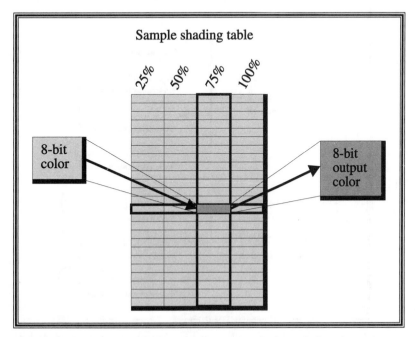

Figure 15.2 Sample shading table, made of a set of CLUTs, each providing a different shading factor.

As an example, let's consider a *shading table*. Each column in the shading table is a CLUT, which serves to darken any 8-bit color by some amount. By what amount? That's where the table comes in. Each column in the table is a CLUT which darkens by a different amount. In a ten-column table, the shading factor might range from 10 percent to 100 percent in steps of 10 percent.

Classes AClut and AClutTable

ARTT features two base classes and several descendent classes relevant to CLUTs. Additionally, many new rendering functions are defined in ACanvas and other canvas classes. Figure 15.3 shows the new classes used to represent CLUTs.

Class AClut

Class AClut is the base class for all CLUTs. It contains a private 256-color uchar lookup array as its only member variable, and a small set of methods for accessing that array. The small set of methods includes:

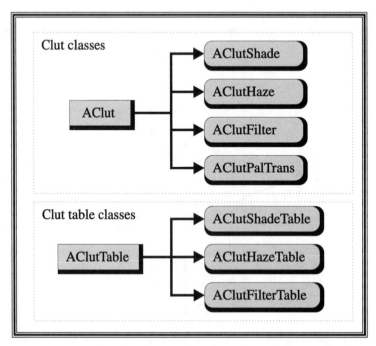

Figure 15.3 The class hierarchies based on AClut and AClut-Table.

- Constructors—One empty constructor and a second which sets the CLUT array values.
- Set()—Sets the CLUT array values by copying from a supplied array.
- TablePtr()—Returns pointer to the internal array.
- Operator[]—The array indexing operator is overloaded for "natural" table lookup.

This last method allows the CLUT to be accessed like a C array.
The header file for class AClut is listed below. All methods are inlined, so no additional code is needed.

```
//   AClut.h      Color Lookup Table class
//   Rex E. Bradford

#ifndef __ACLUT_H
#define __ACLUT_H

#include <string.h>
#include "atypes.h"

class AClut {
    uchar tab[256];           // 256 byte-wide entries

public:
    static AClut identity;   // identity clut: clut[c] == c

// Constructors

    AClut() {}                // empty table, fill in later
    AClut(uchar *pvalues) {Set(pvalues);}  // set table from values

// Other methods

    void Set(uchar *pvalues) {memcpy(tab, pvalues, 256);} // set vals
    uchar *TablePtr() {return tab;}              // get raw ptr to table
    uchar operator[](uchar c8) {return tab[c8];} // look up in table!
};

#endif
```

Class AClutTable

In many cases, what we want is not a single CLUT, but a table of them. In the case of a shading table which darkens colors, we may want 10 CLUTs, each of which darkens the original colors by an additional 10 percent. Then, at runtime the appropriate CLUT can be selected for a given bitmap, based on distance or other lighting conditions, and rendering done through that CLUT.

Class AClutTable implements such a "table of CLUTs." How many CLUTs does a given table need? This should be variable—we may want 4 CLUTs in one case, and 100 in another. We want to make the number of CLUTs variable without imposing any more indirection at runtime than we have to, so a compromise is in order. Rather than allocate a variable-sized array of pointers to the CLUTs, we'll build the pointer array directly into AClutTable. That requires giving the array a size, which we'll fix at 256. Then, any CLUT table can have up to 256 CLUTs in it. This is more than plenty for most purposes, though we'll come up with one use in this chapter where it's just enough.

So an instance of class AClutTable contains an array of 256 pointers to ACluts, plus methods to create and access them. The class declaration for AClutTable, taken from a header file with additional declarations in it, is listed below.

```
class AClutTable {
    AClut *pCluts[256];   // array of 256 ptrs to cluts

protected:
    bool AllocIfIdentity(int i);   // allocate new clut if identity

public:
// Construct empty clut table for later filling.
// Entries initially set to identity clut.

    AClutTable();

// Destroy a table, Free() by reverting to identity clut

    ~AClutTable() {Free();}
    void Free(int low = 0, int num = 256);

// Get ptr or ref to a clut

    AClut *ClutPtr(int index) {return (pCluts[index]);}
    AClut &ClutRef(int index) {return *pCluts[index];}

// Look up entry from 8-bit value

    AClut& operator[](int index) {return *pCluts[index];}
};
```

Must all 256 CLUTs in a given AClutTable be created? No. A cute trick that we're going to pull is to have unused CLUT entries point to an "identity" array. This is a special static CLUT where each entry contains the number of the entry itself. A bitmap rendered by looking up each color in this CLUT remains unaltered! The identity CLUT is in file ACLUT.CPP, and it is defined below.

```
//   AClut.cpp     Color Lookup Table class
//   Rex E. Bradford

#include "aclut.h"

// Identity table: each color maps to itself

static uchar identityArray[256] = {
    0x00,0x01,0x02,0x03,0x04,0x05,0x06,0x07,
    0x08,0x09,0x0A,0x0B,0x0C,0x0D,0x0E,0x0F,
    0x10,0x11,0x12,0x13,0x14,0x15,0x16,0x17,
    0x18,0x19,0x1A,0x1B,0x1C,0x1D,0x1E,0x1F,
    0x20,0x21,0x22,0x23,0x24,0x25,0x26,0x27,
    . . . . .
    0xE8,0xE9,0xEA,0xEB,0xEC,0xED,0xEE,0xEF,
    0xF0,0xF1,0xF2,0xF3,0xF4,0xF5,0xF6,0xF7,
    0xF8,0xF9,0xFA,0xFB,0xFC,0xFD,0xFE,0xFF,
};


AClut AClut::identity(identityArray);
```

AClutTable Methods

The constructor for AClutTable merely sets all CLUT pointers to the identity CLUT. After construction, any pointer may be replaced by constructing a new AClut and pointing at it.

```
AClutTable::AClutTable()
{
    for (int i = 0; i < 256; i++)
        pCluts[i] = &AClut::identity;
}
```

The AClutTable destructor calls method Free(), which frees any tables which have been allocated and pointed to. Note that it skips over any entries which are pointing to the identity CLUT.

```
void AClutTable::Free(int low, int num)
{
    for (int i = low; i < (low + num); i++)
        {
        if (i >= 256)                        // oops - ran off table!
            break;
        if (pCluts[i] != &AClut::identity)   // if non-NULL & non-identity
            {
            delete pCluts[i];                // delete it
            pCluts[i] = &AClut::identity;    // and set back to identity
            }
        }
}
```

Finally, AClutTable::AllocIfIdentity() is used to allocate a new AClut and set an entry to point to it. If the current entry points to the identity CLUT, a new AClut is constructed. If the current entry is an already-constructed AClut, the pointer is left alone and its space reused.

```
bool AClutTable::AllocIfIdentity(int i)
{
    if (pCluts[i] == &AClut::identity)   // only bother if identity now
        {
        AClut *p = new AClut();          // allocate a new clut
        if (p)
            pCluts[i] = p;               // if successful, assign it
        else
            return FALSE;                // else return failure
        }
    return TRUE;                         // success!
}
```

Rendering with CLUTs

Later in this chapter, a variety of rendering routines using CLUTs will be shown. For now, let's just look at a single rendering method, implemented in the base class ACanvas. This method, DrawClut-BitmapLin8U(), renders a bitmap in BMF_LIN8 format onto any canvas. Instead of rendering each 8-bit pixel directly, though, the pixel is run through a CLUT, and the 8-bit value found there is rendered instead.

DrawClutBitmapLin8U() does some setup, filling in an 'ARow-Info' structure. This structure is defined as follows, and is used to aid rendering a row at a time:

```
typedef struct {
    short y;            // row to render
    short xleft;        // left pixel to render in row
    short xright;       // right pixel to render in row
    short transparent;  // is bitmap transparent?
    uchar *pbits;            // ptr to bits to render
    APalette *palette;       // palette to use for conversions
} ARowInfo;
```

After the setup, the rows of the bitmap are rendered using a call to another virtual function, DrawClutBitmapRowLin8U(). This use of a row-rendering function serves a couple of purposes. First, it allows specialized versions to be developed for many canvas classes without them having to rewrite the entire method—they need only supply a canvas-specific row-renderer. Second, bitmaps of format BMF_RLE8 can be rendered using the very same row-renderers, once a different high-level method unpacks each row into linear format.

The high-level method ACanvas::DrawClutBitmapLin8U() is listed below.

```
void ACanvas::DrawClutBitmapLin8U(ABitmap &bms, int x, int y, AClut &clut)
{
// Setup: fill in ARowInfo structure

    ARowInfo ri;
    ri.xleft = x;
    ri.xright = x + bms.width;
    ri.transparent = bms.transparent;
    ri.pbits = bms.pbits;
    ri.palette = BitmapOrDefaultPal(bms);

// Loop through rows, drawing each with clut row-renderer

    for (ri.y = y; ri.y < (y + bms.height); ri.y++)
        {
        DrawClutBitmapRowLin8U(ri, clut);
        ri.pbits += bms.rowbytes;
        }
}
```

The generic row-renderer in class ACanvas is listed below. Note the array indexing syntax used to look up the translated color value in the CLUT.

```
void ACanvas::DrawClutBitmapRowLin8U(ARowInfo &ri, AClut &clut)
{
    uchar *ps = ri.pbits;                    // begin at row start
    for (int x = ri.xleft; x < ri.xright; x++)   // loop thru pixels
        {
        uchar c8 = *ps++;                    // get next pixel
        if (c8 || !ri.transparent)           // if non-0 or non-transp
            DrawPixel8U(x, ri.y, clut[c8]);  // clut and draw
        }
}
```

As an example of how this row-rendering routine can be specialized for a given canvas class, the version of it included in class ACanvasLin8 is listed below. Rather than call DrawPixel8U() to draw each pixel, efficient pointer incrementing is done to move from pixel to pixel. The inner loop of the nontransparent case is extremely simple.

```
void ACanvasLin8::DrawClutBitmapRowLin8U(ARowInfo &ri, AClut &clut)
{
// Setup
```

```
      uchar *ps = ri.pbits;                // get ptr to source pixels
      uchar *pd = Ptr(ri.xleft, ri.y);     // calc ptr to canvas x,y
      int width = ri.xright - ri.xleft;    // calc width

  // Draw row

      if (ri.transparent)          // if transparent:
        {
        while (width-- > 0)        // loop thru columns
          {
          if (*ps)                 // if non-zero
            *pd = clut[*ps];       // look up in clut and write
          ++ps;                    // incr source ptr
          ++pd;                    // incr dest ptr
          }
        }
      else                         // else non-transparent:
        {
        while (width-- > 0)        // loop thru columns
          *pd++ = clut[*ps++];     // clut and write each
        }
  }
```

That's the basics of rendering through a CLUT. Later in this chapter, we'll look at more rendering routines, including those to render a scaled bitmap or one in BMF_RLE8 format. We'll even write a routine to render a BMF_RLE8 encoded bitmap, scaled, through a CLUT! Don't laugh—it's the best way to render your pseudo-3D attack chopper in the distant haze.

Shading Tables: Classes AClutShade and AClutShadeTable

Now that we have the basics of CLUT operation down, let's look at some example CLUT types. In each case but one, we'll develop two classes. The first class will be descended from AClut, and will include at least one constructor and a Set() routine. These are used to initialize or set the AClut with the appropriate values to achieve the desired effect.

The second class will be descended from AClutTable, and will be used to easily generate an entire table of related CLUTs. The desired column of the table can be selected using AClutTable::ClutPtr() or AClutTable::ClutRef(), supplying the index of the desired CLUT.

Darkening and Lightening

Like all 8-bit CLUTs, shading tables make sense only in the context of some palette. In a shading table, each color is replaced by a darkened or lightened version of the same color. Typically, each of the three color components (red, green, and blue) is darkened by the same amount, but this need not be true. Class AClutShade includes constructors and versions of Set() which take one "shading" factor, and versions which take three factors, a different one for each color component.

The color math involved in setting the CLUT values is straightforward. Let's call the shading factor 'f'; for darkening it is less than 1.0, and for lightening greater than 1.0. The red, green, and blue components are computed independently, and each is transformed according to the following formula:

```
cOut = round(int(cIn) * f);   // multiply by shading factor
if (cOut > 255) cOut = 255;   // clamp to maximum of 255
```

The declaration for class AClutShade is listed below.

```
class AClutShade : public AClut {
public:

// Empty constructor: fill later with Set()

    AClutShade() {}

// Construct a shading clut with a shading factor which is
// constant across red, green, and blue.

    AClutShade(APalette *palette, AFix f) {Set(palette, f);}

// Construct a shading clut with independent red, green, and
// blue shading factors.

    AClutShade(APalette *palette, AFix rf, AFix gf, AFix bf) {
        Set(palette, rf, gf, bf);}

// Set an existing shading clut with a shading factor which
// is constant across red, green, and blue.

    void Set(APalette *palette, AFix f) {Set(palette, f, f, f);}

// Set an existing shading clut with independent red, green,
// and blue shading factors.

    void Set(APalette *palette, AFix rf, AFix gf, AFix bf);
};
```

AClutShade::Set() Method

AClutShade::Set() merely traverses all 256 entries in the supplied palette, computing the shaded version of each color and storing it in the CLUT. Note that color computation is done in 24-bit space (8 bits per component), and the final result must be translated back to 8-bit format before storing it in the CLUT. This is inherently lossy—likely there is no entry in the palette which exactly matches the desired color, and the closest one is what is chosen. As can be seen by examining APalette::ConvertTo8(), this process is also sped up dramatically if the palette has an associated inverse table. Otherwise, each of the 256 translations must be tested against each of the 256 palette entries to find the closest match. Often, CLUTs are precomputed, stored on disk, and read in from disk at runtime.

```
void AClutShade::Set(APalette *palette, AFix rf, AFix gf, AFix bf)
{
// Get ptr to beginning of palette, and ptr to clut

    uchar *prgb = palette->rgb;
    uchar *ptab = TablePtr();

// Loop thru all palette colors, shading

    for (int i = 0; i < 256; i++)
        {
        uchar rgb[3];

// Do all 3 components, computing new shade and clamping

        int color = round(AFix(int(*prgb++)) * bf);
        if (color > 255)
            color = 255;
        rgb[0] = color;

        color = round(AFix(int(*prgb++)) * gf);
        if (color > 255)
            color = 255;
        rgb[1] = color;

        color = round(AFix(int(*prgb++)) * rf);
        if (color > 255)
            color = 255;
        rgb[2] = color;

// Convert resulting RGB color to 8-bit and put in table

        *ptab++ = palette->ConvertTo8(rgb);
        }
}
```

Tables of Shading CLUTs

Class AClutShadeTable, derived from AClutTable, contains a table of shading CLUTs. This is very handy when a 3D scene needs each object shaded by a different factor based on its depth, for instance. Typically, 16 shading CLUTs is sufficient for good results. The remaining 240 pointers in the table of CLUT pointers is wasted, but that's okay. Color plate 9 shows a sample shading table.

The class declaration for AClutShadeTable is listed below. Like AClutShade, and like all such classes we will encounter in this chapter, it consists of constructors and Set() methods. The arguments include the starting index at which to put the CLUTs ('low'), the number of CLUTs to generate, and beginning and ending shading factors to use in creating the CLUTs. The intermediate CLUTs are created using interpolated shading factors.

```
class AClutShadeTable : public AClutTable {
public:

// Empty constructor: fill in later with Set()

    AClutShadeTable() {}

// Construct a series of shading CLUTs, each with a different
// interpolated shading factor. Shading factor is constant
// across red, green, and blue in any given CLUT.

    AClutshadeTable(int low, int num, APalette *palette, AFix fBeg,
        AFix fEnd, AError &err) {
            err = Set(low, num, palette, fBeg, fEnd);}

// Construct a series of shading CLUTs, each with a different
// set of interpolated shading factors. Each of red, green, and
// blue shading factors is interpolated independently across the
// supplied ranges.

    AClutShadeTable(int low, int num, APalette *palette, AFix fRedBeg,
        AFix fRedEnd, AFix fGreenBeg, AFix fGreenEnd, AFix fBlueBeg,
        AFix fBlueEnd, AError &err) {
            err = Set(low, num, palette, fRedBeg, fRedEnd, fGreenBeg,
                fGreenEnd, fBlueBeg, fBlueEnd);}

// Set a series of shading cluts into an existing AClutShadeTable,
// each with a different interpolated shading factor. Shading factor
// is constant across red, green, and blue in any given CLUT.

    AError Set(int low, int num, APalette *palette, AFix fBeg,
        AFix fEnd) {return Set(low, num, palette, fBeg, fEnd,
            fBeg, fEnd, fBeg, fEnd);}

// Set a series of shading cluts into an existing AClutShadeTable,
// each with a different set of interpolated shading factors. Each
// of red, green, and blue shading factors is interpolated independently
// across the supplied ranges.
```

```
AError Set(int low, int num, APalette *palette,
    AFix fRedBeg, AFix fRedEnd, AFix fGreenBeg, AFix fGreenEnd,
    AFix fBlueBeg, AFix fBlueEnd);
};
```

AClutShadeTable::Set() is listed below. It interpolates the shading values for each CLUT to be generated, and calls the Set() method of the AClutShade() class to generate a given CLUT, after first allocating it with AllocIfIdentity().

```
AError AClutShadeTable::Set(int low, int num, APalette *palette,
    AFix fRedBeg, AFix fRedEnd, AFix fGreenBeg, AFix fGreenEnd,
    AFix fBlueBeg, AFix fBlueEnd)
{
// Set default RGB to starting values

    AFix fRed = fRedBeg;
    AFix fGreen = fGreenBeg;
    AFix fBlue = fBlueBeg;
    int num1 = num - 1;

// Loop thru all tables to be generated

    for (int i = 0; i < num; i++)
        {

// If can't allocate table, bail out

        if (!AllocIfIdentity(low + i))
            return AERR_NOMEM;

// If more than 1 table, compute intermediate shading factors

        if (num1)
            {
            fRed = fRedBeg + ((fRedEnd - fRedBeg) * i) / num1;
            fGreen = fGreenBeg + ((fGreenEnd - fGreenBeg) * i) / num1;
            fBlue = fBlueBeg + ((fBlueEnd - fBlueBeg) * i) / num1;
            }

// Generate table with these shading factors

        ((AClutShade *) ClutPtr(low + i))->Set(palette, fRed, fGreen,
            fBlue);
        }

    return AERR_OK;
}
```

Uses for Shading Tables

Shading tables have many uses. One use, already mentioned, is to darken objects which are "in the distance" in a 3D scene. Shading tables can also be used to brighten or darken icons on the fly to indicate their selection state, as an alternative to creating and storing separate versions of the icon for that purpose. In this case, only one or a few CLUTs are needed, one for each icon state: normal, selected, disabled. Yet another use is for special effects, lighting up a graphic temporarily when a significant event happens, such as a four-megaton explosion or the correct answer in a math test.

Hazing Tables: Classes AClutHaze and AClutHazeTable

Another effect used often in 3D simulations and games is *hazing,* wherein distant terrain and objects appear more gray or whitish. In reality, this effect is caused by the diffusion of light caused by particles in the atmosphere, which allows more wavelengths to be perceived. The effect can be simulated in a computer by using colors which are "mixed" with a gray or white color.

As in shading, a table of such hazing CLUTs is typically employed, and more highly hazed CLUTs are used for terrain and objects further in the distance. This is easily achieved by using a weighted average of a given color and the hazing color, and weighting the hazing color more heavily in the CLUTs used for distant objects. Color plate 9 shows a sample hazing table.

Hazing Calculations

The weighted averaging is achieved by applying the following formula to each color component of each color in the palette:

```
cOut = round(((1.0 - fHaze) * int(cIn)) + (fHaze * cHaze)));
```

The declaration class AClutHaze is listed below.

```
class AClutHaze : public AClut {
public:

// Empty constructor : fill later with Set()

   AClutHaze() {}

// Construct a hazing clut, hazing toward the supplied RGB
// color by the supplied hazing factor.
```

```
AClutHaze(APalette *palette, uchar *prgb, AFix f) {
    Set(palette, prgb, f);}
```

```
// Set on existing hazing clut, hazing toward the supplied RGB
// color by the supplied hazing factor.
```

```
    void Set(APalette *palette, uchar *prgb, AFix f);
};
```

And here's the class declaration for AClutHazeTable, which produces a table of hazing CLUTs. Two very different methods are available, depending on supplied arguments. In the first, a single color is supplied, along with low and high hazing settings, and a set of CLUTs is generated with interpolated hazing values. This is handy for generating CLUTs to be used for areas of the screen at varying distances from the viewer—the further away, the more hazing is applied (by choosing a higher column of the hazing table). In the second method, a single hazing factor is supplied—each CLUT in the table is created using a different color in the palette as the hazing (mixing) color. With this, a full 256×256 hazing table can be created which has the ability to "mix" any two colors.

```
class AClutHazeTable : public AClutTable {
public:
// Empty constructor : fill in later with Set()
```

```
    AClutHazeTable() {}
```

```
// Construct a series of hazing CLUTs, using a single hazing color,
// and interpolating the hazing factor across the supplied range.
```

```
    AClutHazeTable(int low, int num, APalette *palette, uchar *prgb,
        AFix fBeg, AFix fEnd, AError &err) {
            err = Set(low, num, palette, prgb, fBeg, fEnd);}
```

```
// Construct a series of hazing CLUTs, using hazing colors taken
// from the palette, with a constant hazing factor.
```

```
    AClutHazeTable(int low, int num, APalette *palette, AFix f,
        AError &err) {
            err = Set(low, num, palette, f);}
```

```
// Set a series of hazing CLUTS into an existing AClutHazeTable,
// using a single hazing color, and interpolating the hazing
// factor across the supplied range.
```

```
    AError Set(int low, int num, APalette *palette, uchar *prgb,
        AFix fBeg, AFix fEnd);
```

```
// Set a series of hazing CLUTs into an existing AClutHazeTable,
// using hazing colors taken from the palette, with a constant
// hazing factor.

   AError Set(int low, int num, APalette *palette, AFix f);
};
```

The implementations of the various Set() methods are not included. See the CD-ROM for full listings.

Uses for Hazing Tables

In 3D simulations, hazing tables are often used to mix distant terrain and objects toward some neutral color, usually gray or white. The "hazing color" may be some other color, for instance, light blue—it depends on the scene and what "sky color" is used behind the terrain and objects.

Hazing is really weighted averaging, otherwise known as mixing. Other uses for these "mixing tables" abound. Instead of using shading tables when rendering "disabled" versions of icons, consider mixing the icon with some color like gray. This works well only if the mixing color isn't used in the icon—mixing a color with itself doesn't change it, regardless of the mixing percentages.

Filter Tables: Classes AClutFilter and AClutFilterTable

Another popular color effect is filtering, wherein the displayed colors appear to be seen through a colored filter of some kind. This filter might be blue-tinted glass, for instance, or it might be an infrared vision system which allows only the red component of a color through.

Filter Calculations

In class AClutFilter, a simple algorithm is used to produce such a filter effect. An RGB filter color is supplied as the sole argument besides the palette itself. The value placed in the CLUT for each entry is determined by the intensity (not color) of the palette entry at that index. The intensity is "applied" to the filter color, so that the resulting color matches the hue of the filter with the brightness of the palette entry. This approach for filtering colors isn't particularly grounded in color theory, but it gives pretty good results. Each color component is calculated using the following formula:

```
intensity = (cRed + cGreen + cBlue) / (3 * 256);
cBlueOut = intensity * cBlueIn;
cRedOut = intensity * cRedIn;
cGreenOut = intensity * cGreenIn;
```

The declaration for class AClutFilter is listed below.

```
class AClutFilter : public AClut {
public:

// Empty Constructor : fill later with Set()

   AClutFilter() {}

// Construct a filter clut, using the supplied filter color

   AClutFilter(APalette *palette, uchar *prgb) {Set(palette, prgb);}

// Set an existing filter clut, using the supplied filter color

   void Set(APalette *palette, uchar *prgb);
};
```

The AClutFilterTable class provides a handy means of creating a table which can simulate a form of translucency. Instead of supplying an array of RGB filter colors, the colors are taken from the palette itself. Each CLUT contains an array of color values which are "filtered" values of the entire palette, using a particular palette entry as the filter color. A "full" table of 256 CLUTs can then be used to allow any bitmap to be a multicolor filter to the scene beyond. Later in this chapter, we'll see code which can perform such blended rendering through a CLUT table.

The class declaration AClutFilterTable is listed below.

```
class AClutFilterTable : public AClutTable {
public:

// Empty constructor : fill in later with Set()

   AClutFilterTable() {}

// Construct a series of filter CLUTs, using the colors in the
// palette as filter colors.

   AClutFilterTable(int low, int num, APalette *palette, AError &err) {
      err = Set(low, num, palette);}

// Set a series of filter CLUTs into an existing AClutFilterTable,
// using the colors in the palette as filter colors.

   AError Set(int low, int num, APalette *palette);
};
```

The implementations of the various Set() methods are not included. See the CD for full listings.

Uses for Filter CLUTs and Tables

Filter CLUTs are a handy trick for rendering infrared viewscreens. In this case, a red filter is chosen, and all nonred colors are filtered out. As noted, tables of filter CLUTs are also handy for implementing translucency, a subject we will return to later in this chapter.

Palette Translation: Class AClutPalTrans

When rendering 8-bit images into 8-bit canvases, the implicit assumption all along has been that the image and canvas share the same palette, and so no translation is performed. This certainly is the fastest way to go, copying pixels directly with no lookup or other computation, but it is not always accurate. If the palettes differ, what we want to do is "translate" the colors in the source image/palette into the destination palette.

How can we achieve this? One way is to look up the 15-bit or 24-bit RGB value of each pixel (through the source APalette), and then find the closest match in the destination palette. This match can be done by a search of the entire palette, or through the use of an inverse table. The former approach is far too slow for anything approaching real-time work, but the second is not bad. Basically, each pixel would require two table lookups, as illustrated in Figure 15.4.

This approach has two drawbacks. One, it requires an inverse table, which consumes lots of memory (32K) and is very slow to generate. Second, it requires two lookups at runtime, where it seems one ought to do.

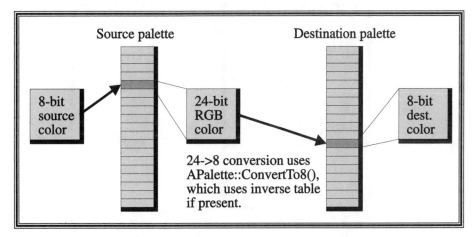

Figure 15.4 Converting an 8-bit color from one palette to another, using only the palettes.

This is where the palette-translation CLUT comes in. By creating a CLUT which "premaps" each 8-bit source palette index into its closest destination match, a single 8-bit to 8-bit lookup can be used to translate each pixel, as Figure 15.5 shows.

The declaration for class AClutPalTrans is listed below.

```
class AClutPalTrans : public AClut {
public:

// Empty constructor : fill later with Set()

   AClutPalTrans() {}

// Construct a palette translation clut, using the supplied
// destination and source palettes.

   AClutPalTrans(APalette *palette, APalette *palsrc) {
      Set(palette, palsrc);}

// Set on existing palette translation clut, using the supplied
// destination and source palettes.

   void Set(APalette *palette, APalette *palsrc);
};
```

The AClutPalTrans::Set() method, which generates the CLUT values, is a very simple routine. Each source color's RGB value is read from the source palette and then simply converted to 8-bit in the

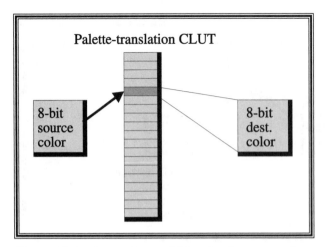

Figure 15.5 Converting an 8-bit color from one palette to another, using a palette-translation CLUT.

context of the destination palette. If the destination palette has an associated inverse table, this process is sped up dramatically, although the table doesn't take too long to generate in either case.

In essence, what we're doing is precomputing for each of the 256 color values what we otherwise would have to do for every pixel at runtime.

```
void AClutPalTrans::Set(APalette *palette, APalette *palsrc)
{
// Set ptr to source palette and table

   uchar *prgb = palsrc->rgb;
   uchar *ptab = TablePtr();

// For each color, compute closest color in dest pal

   for (int i = 0; i < 256; i++, prgb += 3)
      *ptab++ = palette->ConvertTo8(prgb);
}
```

Using Palette Translation CLUTs

The purpose of palette translation CLUTs is pretty obvious and has already been explained. What may not be so obvious is that ARTT doesn't use them without being told to. A more whiz-bang, and less real-time, graphics environment could provide such palette translation as a matter of course whenever rendering bitmaps. But in a high-performance environment, this opens up many questions. If palette translation CLUTs are to be invisibly created as needed, when does this happen, and who cleans up after them? ARTT opts for performance, not even bothering to check if source and destination palettes differ (what would it do if one was NULL?), assuming that unless told otherwise no palette translation is desired. If you need palette translation, use the CLUT-based versions of the bitmap-rendering routines with such CLUTs built at your application's request, or consider building a higher-level interface to ARTT that does this automatically.

Rendering Bitmaps Through CLUTs

Earlier in this chapter, we saw how the DrawClutBitmapLin8U() method was implemented by filling in an 'ARowInfo' struct, which was then passed to a row-rendering routine to draw each row of pixels through the CLUT. We looked at the implementation of the row-renderer, DrawClutBitmapRowLin8U(), in generic class ACanvas. We also saw a specialized version of it in class ACanvasLin8. This

section shows implementations of this row-renderer in other classes, as well as a few other CLUT-related rendering routines.

Drawing BMF_RLE8 Bitmaps Through CLUTs

One of the advantages of the row-based approach is that bitmaps which are encoded in run-length format can be handled using them. DrawClutBitmapRle8U(), implemented in class ACanvas, unpacks each compressed row and then draws it through the same row-rendering routine used by linear bitmaps. A clipped version is available but not reproduced here.

```
void ACanvas::DrawClutBitmapRle8U(ABitmap &bms, int x, int y, AClut &clut)
{
// Setup: fill in ARowInfo structure

    ARowInfo ri;
    ri.xleft = x;
    ri.xright = x + bms.width;
    ri.transparent = bms.transparent;
    ri.palette = BitmapOrDefaultPal(bms);

// Set up reader for RLE8 bitmap

    ARle8Reader rle8rd(bms, FALSE);   // FALSE: don't skip over transp
    ri.pbits = tempBuff;              // use tempBuff[] for decoded row

// Loop through rows, unpacking and drawing each with clut row-renderer

    for (ri.y = y; ri.y < (y + bms.height); y++)
        {
        rle8rd.UnpackRow(tempBuff);
        DrawClutBitmapRowLin8U(ri, clut);
        }
```

Other Implementations of DrawClutBitmapRowLin8U()

The version of the CLUT-based row-renderer in bank-switched 8-bit canvases is somewhat lengthy, mainly because it tries to optimize the transparent and nontransparent cases separately, as well as handle bank-crossings. Here is the implementation of ACanvasBank8::Draw-ClutBitmapRowLin8U().

```
void ACanvasBank8::DrawClutBitmapRowLin8U(ARowInfo &ri, AClut &clut)
{
// Setup a bunch of variables.

    long vaddr = Vaddr(ri.xleft, ri.y); // virtual address of 1st pixel
    EnsureWriteBankAtAddr(vaddr);       // ensure bank set right
```

```
    uchar *pd = Ptr(vaddr);          // and calc ptr to 1st pixel
    uchar *ps = ri.pbits;            // get source ptr
    int width = ri.xright - ri.xleft; // and width of row

// Does this row lie across a bank boundary?

    if (CrossesBank(vaddr, width))
        {
// Split across bank: do left half

        int numLeft = BytesLeftInBank(vaddr);  // # pixels on left
        int numRight = width - numLeft;        // the rest on right
        int w = numLeft;                  // w = width on left half
        while (w-- > 0)                   // count down thru left half pixels
            {
            uchar c8 = *ps++;             // get source pixel
            if (c8 || !ri.transparent)    // if non-zero or non-transp
                *pd = clut[c8];           // lookup in clut and write back
            ++pd;                         // bump dest ptr
            }
        vaddr += numLeft;                 // at end of left, bump virtual addr
        EnsureWriteBankAtAddr(vaddr);     // make sure we're at right bank
        pd = Ptr(vaddr);                  // and recalc dest ptr
        width = numRight;                 // set up width for right half
        }

// Right half or entire row: branch based on transparency

    if (ri.transparent)
        {
        while (width-- > 0)          // transparent: count down pixels
            {
            if (*ps)                 // if non-zero,
                *pd = clut[*ps];     // lookup in clut and write back
            ++ps;                    // bump source ptr
            ++pd;                    // bump dest ptr
            }
        }
    else
        {
        while (width-- > 0)          // non-transparent: count down pixels
            *pd++ = clut[*ps++];     // lookup each in clut and write back
        }
}
```

There is no reason why we can't render an 8-bit image, through a CLUT, onto a 15-bit canvas. The implementation of the row-renderer in class ACanvasLin15 takes each source pixel and looks it up in the CLUT. Then it looks up the 15-bit palette value for the new 8-bit index, and draws that word-sized value into the canvas.

```
void ACanvasLin15::DrawClutBitmapRowLin8U(ARowInfo &ri, AClut &clut)
{
// If no palette, bail out

    if (ri.palette == NULL)
        return;

// Set up source and dest ptrs, calc width

    uchar *ps = ri.pbits;
    ushort *pd = Ptr(ri.xleft, ri.y);
    int width = ri.xright - ri.xleft;

// Loop through columns: if non-zero or non-transp
//
//    1. Look up 8-bit pixel in clut table (clut[*ps])
//    2. Convert to 15-bit and write to dest
//    3. Increment source and dest ptrs

    while (width-- > 0)
        {
        if (*ps || !ri.transparent)
            *pd = ri.palette->ConvertTo15(clut[*ps]);
        ++ps;
        ++pd;
        }
}
```

Versions of DrawClutBitmapRowLin8U() for classes ACanvas-Bank15, ACanvasLin24, and ACanvasBank24 are not included here, but follow very similar approaches to the above code. See the CD for full listings.

Drawing Scaled Bitmaps Through CLUTs

Shading and hazing CLUTs are very important in 3D applications, as they help provide a sense of depth and color realism to a scene. In 3D scenes, of course, scaled bitmaps provide size-adjustment of images, which is also crucial to imparting depth and realism. Therefore, it is highly desirable to provide scaling and CLUT lookup in a single rendering routine. DrawScaledClutBitmapLin8() does just that.

The implementation of this routine, in class ACanvas, uses the same 'AScaledRowInfo' struct used by non-CLUT scaling routines. The main difference between this routine and DrawScaledBitmapLin8() is that the new method uses a different set of scaling row-rendering routines, ones which take an extra CLUT reference argument.

```
void ACanvas::DrawScaledClutBitmapLin8(ABitmap &bms, ARect &area,
    AClut &clut)
```

```
{
// Clip and setup bitmap

    AScaledRowInfo sri;
    if (!ClipAndSetupScaledBitmap(bms, area, sri))
        return;

// Loop thru rows, drawing each (preclipped) strip

    int ysrc = int(sri.srcFy);
    for (sri.destY = sri.destYtop; sri.destY < sri.destYbott; sri.destY++)
        {
        DrawScaledClutBitmapRowLin8U(sri, clut);    // render row!
        sri.srcFy += sri.srcFyStep;                 // advance y fract
        sri.srcPbits += (int(sri.srcFy) - ysrc) * long(bms.rowbytes);
        ysrc = int(sri.srcFy);                      // and src pbits
        }
}
```

The above routine relies on a special scaling CLUT-based row-renderer. The generic scaled CLUT row-renderer defined in class ACanvas is listed below. This method is overridden in some canvases to speed its performance (by eliminating the DrawPixel8U() call in favor of direct canvas bitmap access).

```
void ACanvas::DrawScaledClutBitmapRowLin8U(AScaledRowInfo &sri,
    AClut &clut)
{
// Start at initial source fixed-point x-coord

    AFix fx = sri.srcFx;

// Traverse from left to right in destination pixel row

    for (int x = sri.destXleft; x < sri.destXright; x++)
        {
        uchar c8 = *(sri.srcPbits + int(fx));    // grab source pixel
        if (c8 || !sri.transparent)              // if non-zero, or not transp
            DrawPixel8U(x, sri.destY, clut[c8]); // look up and draw
        fx += sri.srcFxStep;                     // step in src w/fraction
        }
}
```

Another method, ACanvas::DrawScaledClutBitmapRle8(), is called for BMF_RLE8 bitmaps. It is not listed here, but operates in a manner similar to DrawScaledBitmapRle8(), except for the addition of the CLUT reference argument and the fact that a different scaling row-renderer is called.

A derived version of DrawScaledClutBitmapRowLin8U(), the scaled CLUT row-renderer, is defined for class ACanvasLin8. It is

identical to the non-CLUT scaling row-renderer in that class, except for the CLUT lookup applied to each pixel.

```
void ACanvasLin8::DrawScaledClutBitmapRowLin8U(AScaledRowInfo &sri,
    AClut &clut)
{
// Initialize source x-coord, calc ptr into bitmap row, set width

    AFix fx = sri.srcFx;
    uchar *pd = Ptr(sri.destXleft, sri.destY);
    int w = sri.destXright - sri.destXleft;

// Traverse from left to right, writing pixel & stepping x fractionally

    while (w--)
        {
        uchar c8 = *(sri.srcPbits + int(fx));   // grab pixel from source
        if (c8 || !sri.transparent)             // if !0 or non-transp,
            *pd = clut[c8];                     // look up and write
        ++pd;                                   // bump canvas dest ptr
        fx += sri.srcFxStep;                    // advance fractional x
        }
}
```

Specialized versions of DrawScaledClutBitmapRowLin8U() are provided, though not listed here, for classes ACanvasBank8, ACanvasLin15, and ACanvasLin24. No versions are provided for classes ACanvasBank15 and ACanvasBank24—these must rely upon the version in ACanvas. They would not be particularly fast in any case, what with having to handle scaling, CLUT lookup, conversion to 15-bit or 24-bit, and bank-crossing detection. In scene-based rendering, these bitmap operations are usually applied to an off-screen buffer in any case, and such a buffer is linear. Therefore, there is no point in writing huge, complex versions of this routine for bank-switched canvases where it will likely never be called.

Blending Tables

Shading, hazing, filtering, and palette translation are all operations which require only a source image and a CLUT in order to work. The current pixels already lying on the canvas are irrelevant—they are simply overwritten by the new pixels. This is not true of translucency, the last effect to be covered in this chapter. Translucency is one form of a *blending* of the new pixel with whatever color value is already present in the canvas at the time of rendering. If we want the effect of "seeing" through a glass window which is not fully transparent, we are in effect filtering the pixels already present in the scene through the glass color.

For translucency, the filter tables already defined in class AClut-FilterTable will work fine, but the rendering routines won't. We need a new set of methods, ones which make use of both the current canvas pixel color and the color of the "incoming" pixel, and look up the appropriate resulting pixel in a table.

Blended Rectangles

In the simple case, the "image" we are rendering is a solid sheet of color. If this is true, then we can achieve translucency or another blending effect by using a simple CLUT in a novel way. Instead of looking up a source pixel in the CLUT and then rendering it, we take the pixel already present in the canvas and look it up in the CLUT, and then render it back to the canvas. Figure 15.6 illustrates.

Methods DrawClutRectU() and DrawClutRect() perform this operation in a rectangular area. These methods can be used to form the base background for a translucent window or menu atop a scene. Note how each pixel is retrieved with GetPixel8U(), looked up in the supplied CLUT, and then rerendered with DrawPixel8U().

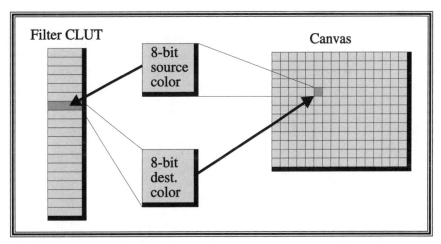

Figure 15.6 Applying a filter by running a canvas pixel through a filter CLUT.

```
void ACanvas::DrawClutRectU(ARect rect, AClut &clut)
{
    for (int y = rect.top; y < rect.bott; y++)
        {
        for (int x = rect.left; x < rect.right; x++)
            {
            uchar cd8 = GetPixel8U(x, y);
            DrawPixel8U(x, y, clut[cd8]);
            }
        }
}

void ACanvas::DrawClutRect(ARect rect, AClut &clut)
{
    if (ClipRect(rect))
        DrawClutRectU(rect, clut);
}
```

DrawClutRectU() is overridden in class ACanvasLin8, replaced with a version which is much more efficient.

```
void ACanvasLin8::DrawClutRectU(ARect rect, AClut &clut)
{
    uchar *p = Ptr(rect.left, rect.top);    // get ptr to u.1. of rect
    int width = rect.right - rect.left;     // precalc rect width

    for (int y = rect.top; y < rect.bott; y++)  // loop through rows
        {
        int w = width;
        while (w-- > 0)                 // for each pixel in row:
            *p++ = clut[*p];            // replace each pixel with clut[pixel]
        p += bm.rowbytes - width;       // advance to next row
        }
}
```

Class ACanvasBank8 supplies an override version as well. Note how both EnsureWriteBankAtAddr() and EnsureReadBankAtAddr() must be used, since each pixel is read as well as written. The read and write bank registers, which may be separate on some Super VGAs, must be kept in sync.

```
void ACanvasBank8::DrawClutRectU(ARect rect, AClut &clut)
{
// Compute virtual address of upper-left, pre-calc rectangle width

    long vaddr = Vaddr(rect.left, rect.top);
    int width = rect.right - rect.left;

// Loop through rectangle from top to bottom

    for (int y = rect.top; y < rect.bott; y++)
        {
// Make sure both read and write banks are located correctly
```

```
EnsureWriteBankAtAddr(vaddr);        // set write bank
EnsureReadBankAtAddr(vaddr);         // we're reading too!
uchar *p = Ptr(vaddr);               // set ptr to 1st pix in row
int w = width;                       // temp copy of width

// Check for this row crossing bank, if so split, do left half

    if (CrossesBank(vaddr, width))
        {
        int numLeft = BytesLeftInBank(vaddr);  // # pixels to left
        w -= numLeft;                          // w = num to right
        long vright = vaddr + numLeft;         // vaddr at bank-switch
        while (numLeft-- > 0)
            {
            *p = clut[*p];                     // clut all pixels
            ++p;
            }
        EnsureWriteBankAtAddr(vright);         // do bank-switch
        EnsureReadBankAtAddr(vright);          // for read bank too
        p = Ptr(vright);                       // set new ptr
        }

// Do right half of split row, or entire unsplit row

    while (w-- > 0)
        {
        *p = clut[*p];
        ++p;
        }

// Advance virtual address to next row

    vaddr += bm.rowbytes;
    }
}
```

Other canvas classes use the base implementation in class ACanvas.

Blended Bitmaps

When a bitmap is to be drawn with translucency or some other color-blending effect, a simple CLUT will no longer do. The source pixel may be any of 256 different values, and it must be blended with any of the 256 colors which may already exist in the destination canvas. Do we need some new 256 × 256 lookup table?

Sort of, but we already have it. The AClutTable class defines a table of 256 CLUTs. This is in effect a 256 × 256 lookup table suitable for blending any source and destination pixels together. But we don't necessarily have to use up 64K for our translucency table. These CLUTs may be all allocated and unique, or some may be directed to point to an "identity" CLUT, which maps each color value to itself. This is handy—we may have translucent images featuring only two or three colors (a smoke cloud, for instance), and it would be a shame to waste 64K on a giant table just to support two or three translucency CLUTs.

Figure 15.7 shows the method by which each pixel in a bitmap is drawn through a *blending table*, implemented as an instance of class AClutTable. The source pixel is used to select which CLUT (column) in the blending table to use. Then, the canvas pixel is used as a lookup index into that CLUT, and replaced with the value found at that entry.

Other than having a new argument of type AClutTable, the ACanvas::DrawBlendBitmapLin8U() method listed below should look pretty familiar, as should the DrawBlendBitmapRowLin8U() row-renderer listed after it.

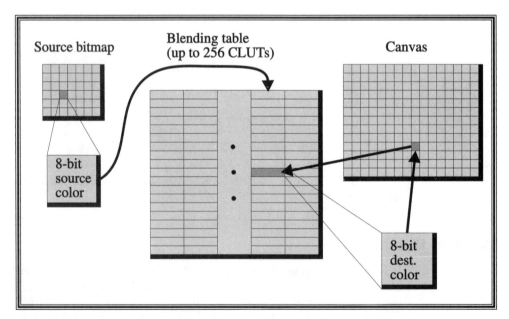

Figure 15.7 Rendering a pixel of a bitmap through a blending table. The source pixel picks the CLUT, and then the canvas pixel is looked up in that CLUT, and replaced with the value found there.

```
void ACanvas::DrawBlendBitmapLin8U(ABitmap &bms, int x, int y,
   AClutTable &clutTab)
{
// Setup: fill in ARowInfo structure

   ARowInfo ri;
   ri.xleft = x;
   ri.xright = x + bms.width;
   ri.transparent = bms.transparent;
   ri.pbits = bms.pbits;
   ri.palette = BitmapOrDefaultPal(bms);

// Loop through rows, drawing with blending row-renderer

   for (ri.y = y; ri.y < (y + bms.height); ri.y++)
      {
      DrawBlendBitmapRowLin8U(ri, clutTab);
      ri.pbits += bms.rowbytes;
      }
}
```

The generic row-renderer for blended bitmaps in class ACanvas is a simple loop. Each pixel is retrieved with GetPixel8U(). The source pixel, meanwhile, is used to choose an appropriate CLUT. Then, the retrieved pixel is looked up in that CLUT, and the result written back to the canvas.

```
void ACanvas::DrawBlendBitmapRowLin8U(ARowInfo &ri, AClutTable &clutTab)
{
   uchar *ps = ri.pbits;                        // begin at row start
   for (int x = ri.xleft; x < ri.xright; x++)   // loop thru pixels
      {
      uchar cs8 = *ps++;              // get next pixel
      if (cs8 || !ri.transparent)     // if non-0 or non-transp
         {
         uchar cd8 = GetPixel8U(x, ri.y);     // read pixel in canvas
         DrawPixel8U(x, ri.y, clutTab[cs8][cd8]); // blend, write
         }
      }
}
```

In the DrawPixel8U() call above, the clutTab[cs8] [cd8] argument looks deceptively like a simple C two-dimensional array lookup. In fact, what is happening is that the first "array indexing" operation is applied to clut-Tab, and the overloaded [] operator produces a reference to the desired AClut. The second array indexing operation is applied to this AClut, which itself overloads operator [] (via a totally different method) to produce the desired pixel value.

A separate high-level routine for BMF_RLE8 bitmaps is provided in class ACanvas but not listed here. Also, more efficient override versions of the row-renderers are supplied in classes ACanvasLin8 and ACanvasBank8. Blended rendering directly onto 15-bit and 24-bit canvases is somewhat problematic, since the retrieved canvas pixels must be converted to 8-bit form before table lookup (and the looked-up value must also be converted back when drawn). This conversion to 8-bit is very slow unless an inverse table is present; even then, blended rendering onto 15-bit and 24-bit canvases is barely a real-time operation.

The blended row-renderer for class ACanvasLin8 is listed below. For the ACanvasBank8 version, see the CD.

```
void ACanvasLin8::DrawBlendBitmapRowLin8U(ARowInfo &ri,
    AClutTable &clutTab)
{
// Setup

    uchar *ps = ri.pbits;              // get ptr to source pixels
    uchar *pd = Ptr(ri.xleft, ri.y);   // calc ptr to canvas x,y
    int width = ri.xright - ri.xleft;  // calc width

// Draw row

    if (ri.transparent)            // if transparent:
        {
        while (width-- > 0)        // loop thru columns
            {
            if (*ps)               // if non-zero
                *pd = clutTab[*ps][*pd];   // look up in blend table, write
            ++ps;                  // incr source ptr
            ++pd;                  // incr dest ptr
            }
        }
    else                           // else non-transparent:
        {
        while (width-- > 0)        // loop thru columns
            {
            *pd = clutTab[*ps++][*pd]; // blend and write each
            ++pd;                  // incr dest ptr
            }
        }
}
```

Scaled Blended Bitmap Rendering

We have scaling, we have blending, we must have scaled blending too, I guess. Hey, I'm just trying to write a complete book here! DrawScaledBlendBitmapLin8U() and, of course, DrawScaledBlend-BitmapRle8U(), are implemented in class ACanvas. They use their own scaled blending row-renderers, implemented in ACanvas and optimized in various derived canvases. See the CD for all the code. If you've been following this chapter all along, you could probably write these routines yourself pretty easily. Just take the scaled CLUT methods and the nonscaled blending methods, and jam them together with your automated code snafuligrator.

Uses for Blending Tables

There are other uses for blending tables besides translucency. If, instead of a filter table, a hazing (mixing) table is used, blending tables can be used for smooth bitmap scaling. Picture a 256 × 256 table, in which two colors can be looked up as row and column, and the value in the table is the mix of the two colors. A table of 256 hazing CLUTs, with the mix factor set to .5, generates just such a table. Then, a special bitmap scaler could be written to interpolate color values using this table. This works easiest when scaling by a power of 2. When scaling up, the new pixel between each pair can be set to the mix of the colors on each side, using the blending table. When scaling down, each pair of pixels can be reduced to a single pixel by looking up their mix in the blending table.

Adding Effects to Actors

Well. We now have a huge library of scaling, blended, CLUT-based rendering routines for linear and run-length-compressed bitmaps, across the full set of canvases. What do we do with it all?

We already have a full screen composition methodology in the system of scenes and actors developed in Chapters 10 and 11. It's time to retrofit the actors, so that instead of just rendering normally, they can take advantage of CLUTs and blending tables. Want an animated scaling shaded sprite? Why not? How about a menu of GUI buttons that are all translucent? Piece of cake.

Retrofitting the AActor Class

The first step in our retrofit is the AActor class, which is where we'll put the methods to allow us to associate CLUTs and blending tables with any actor. The actual rendering routines, of course, are implemented in each derived actor class, but we can still put the AClut and AClutTable specification in AActor.

First, let's add two new member variables to class AActor.

```
AClut *pclut;        // ptr to clut to render with
AClutTable *pBlendTab; // ptr to clut table to blend with
```

Next, let's add some inline methods to set and retrieve these members.

```
void SetClutPtr(AClut *pclut_) {pclut = pclut_;}
AClut *GetClutPtr() {return pclut;}

void SetBlendTablePtr(AClutTable *pBlendTab_)
    {pBlendTab = pBlendTab_;}
AClutTable *GetBlendTablePtr() {return pBlendTab;}
```

The AActor constructor will set these table pointers to NULL by default, but they can later be set to point to the desired tables. If either of these pointers is set, the rendering method in the derived class should use CLUT-based or blending-based rendering. If both are set, by convention 'pclut' overrides. If neither is set, "normal" rendering should occur. Here are the lines we left out in the AActor constructor:

```
AActor::AActor(AScene *pscene_, Coord3 &loc_) : loc(loc_), speed(0,0,0)
{
    pclut = NULL;       // no clut
    pBlendTab = NULL;   // or blend table
    ... other initialization ...
}
```

Rendering in Various Derived Actor Classes

The full Draw() method for class AActorSprite is listed below, replacing the wimpy non-CLUT version we saw a couple of chapters ago. Note that it uses scaling versions of the appropriate rendering method when scaling is enabled. Since classes AActorAnim and AActorDraw are derived from AActorSprite, objects of these classes inherit this rendering functionality as well!

```
void AActorSprite::Draw(ACanvas *pcv)
{
// If scaling enabled, draw scaled to extent area, optionally using
// clut or blend table

    if (znominal != AFix(0))
        {
        if (GetClutPtr())
            pcv->DrawScaledClutBitmap(*psp, area, *GetClutPtr());
        else if (GetBlendTablePtr())
            pcv->DrawScaledBlendBitmap(*psp, area, *GetBlendTablePtr());
        else
            pcv->DrawScaledBitmap(*psp, area);
        }
```

```
// Else not scaled, draw normally or through clut or blend table.

    else
       {
       if (GetClutPtr())
          pcv->DrawClutBitmap(*psp, area.left, area.top, *GetClutPtr());
       else if (GetBlendTablePtr())
          pcv->DrawBlendBitmap(*psp, area.left, area.top,
             *GetBlendTablePtr());
       else
          pcv->DrawBitmap(*psp, area.left, area.top);
       }
}
```

The Draw() method for class AActorTileArray is lengthy; only the relevant portion is reproduced here.

```
void AActorTileArray::Draw(ACanvas *pcv)
{
        ... loop through each tile ...
        ASprite *psp = (*psa)[tileMap[Index(column,row)]];
        if (GetClutPtr())
           pcv->DrawClutBitmap(*psp, x, y, *GetClutPtr());
        else if (GetBlendTablePtr())
           pcv->DrawBlendBitmap(*psp, x, y, *GetBlendTablePtr());
        else
           pcv->DrawBitmap(*psp, x, y);
        ... continue ...
}
```

Finally, the Draw() method for class AActorButton allows the GUI object to be rendered through a CLUT or blending table. The optional text rendered on top of the bitmap is not specially rendered, only the bitmap background receives such treatment. This is generally preferable in order to make the text highly visible anyway.

```
void AActorButton::Draw(ACanvas *pcv)
{
// Draw button backdrop, optionally using clut or blend table

    ASprite *psp = (*psa)[baseIndex + iconNum];
    if (GetClutPtr())
       pcv->DrawClutBitmap(*psp, area.left, area.top, *GetClutPtr());
    else if (GetBlendTablePtr())
       pcv->DrawBlendBitmap(*psp, area.left, area.top,
          *GetBlendTablePtr());
    else
       pcv->DrawBitmap(*psp, area.left, area.top);

// If text, draw it at its calculated pos (offset by 1,1 if pushdown
// type and pushed down).
```

```
if (btext.text)
   {
   int xt = area.left + xtext;
   int yt = area.top + ytext;
   if ((type == BUTT_TYPE_PUSHDOWN) && iconNum)
      {
      ++xt;
      ++yt;
      }
   pcv->DrawText(btext.text, *btext.pfont, xt, yt);
   }
}
```

Classy Actors

If you derive new AActor classes which feature their own Draw() methods, make sure to check the CLUT and blend table pointers and handle rendering appropriately. Then, any actor at all can be rendered with a variety of visual effects, from shading and hazing to palette translation and translucency.

Tips for Making Palettes

In this chapter, we've certainly seen that there's more to color palettes than meets the eye. Here are a few tips to keep in mind when designing 8-bit artwork.

1. It's easier on the programmer, and harder on the artist, to design all artwork using a single palette. Such a palette must be very carefully constructed, by hand, if shading, hazing, and filtering effects are to be employed. If random colors are put in the palette, the closest darkened version of your blue water might be a greenish-gray. If an infrared display is intended, make sure there are plenty of red shades for your filter CLUT to map colors into. If you want to make good use of shading, include several darkened versions of each important color.

2. If you use multiple palettes, keep them confined to separate "screens" in the program. This is akin to using a single palette, but having to change it every so often. Particular artwork which must be used across multiple screen palettes can be translated on the fly, or remapped "in place" once per screen, using palette translation tables.

3. If your destination canvas is 15 or 24 bits deep, consider still using 8-bit source artwork. Each graphic can have its own "private palette." This approach can give you a screen with thousands of colors at once, while reducing memory usage and speeding up rendering. Plus, you get all those neat color effects that 8-bit CLUTs can provide. Blending tables are problematic, however, in 15 or 24 bits.

4. Remember, Windows reserves the first and last ten colors for system use. If you are brave at heart, there are semidocumented ways to steal back 18 of these 20 (leaving black and white untouched, or your soul will be in eternal peril). For maximum compatibility, it's best to live with the middle 236 colors.

MAKECLUT: An Interactive CLUT Builder

Program MAKECLUT allows interactive creation of a CLUT, which can then be saved into a 256-byte binary file for subsequent loading (as an alternative to building CLUTs on the fly within a program). MAKECLUT also generates a view of the resulting CLUT, which allows for experimentation.

Unlike the other ARTT tools, MAKECLUT doesn't take any command line arguments. Instead, it conducts an interactive session, querying the user for the name of an 8-bit graphics file (from which the palette is taken), the type of CLUT desired, and parameters to the CLUT-building function for that type. It then builds the CLUT, prompts for the name of the file to save to, and shows the resulting CLUT on-screen.

HELIFIRE: Sample Program Using CLUTs

HELIFIRE is a helicopter-based "duck shoot." It is set in the future, on some distant mining planet. Hard-pressed colonists are beset by mercenaries trained by MultiMegaCorp for the purposes of sabotaging mining efforts so that the corporation can maintain control of the supplies of . . . [*insert tired, overused plot line here*]. Have fun blasting.

HELIFIRE uses CLUTs in a variety of ways. First, the gunsight is a circular crosshair bitmap, which has a "glassy" translucent look accomplished through a filter blending table (class AClutFilterTable). The backdrop for the score and the restart button use the same filter table to achieve translucency. Also, distant helicopters are hazed through a hazing table (class AClutHazeTable). Color plate 10 shows a screen shot from the HELIFIRE sample program.

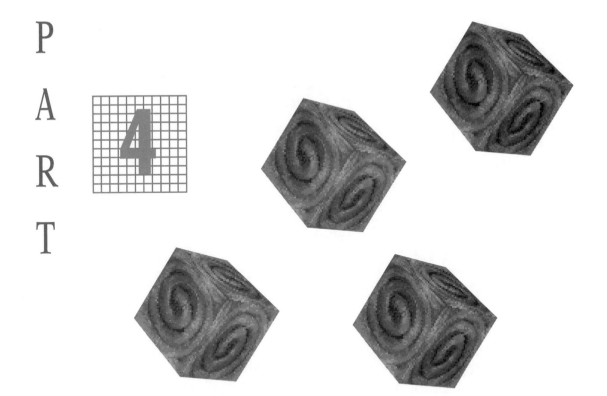

Digital Video, 3D, and Beyond

Digital Video

In the first three parts of this book, we've built a full-featured library for handling 2D bitmapped animation. Part 4 is largely about 3D, which turns the computer screen into a "view portal" into a simulated world. Before we turn our attention to matters of three dimensions, however, there's one 2D topic left which is worth discussion. That topic is *digital video.*

What is digital video? From an end user's standpoint, it means the presentation of TV-like images on the computer screen. Most of the graphics we've seen so far have a distinctly "computery" feel to them. But is that just a choice of artwork? Could we just as easily have been showing digital versions of home movies on the screen, instead of cartoon figures and aquarium fishes? Is digital video just a glorified name for the kind of animation files, such as FLIC files, we've already seen?

In a sense, the answer is yes, but the "glorification" involved is pretty heavy-duty. The animation techniques we've developed so far break down in the face of true digital video, for reasons that will soon be clear. Besides the addition of one or more digital soundtracks, digital video is inherently different from computer animation because it implies natural images, noisy signals, and a moving camera. All these conspire to make digital video data big, really big. How big? *Big.*

Digital Video Basics

To see why digital video data is so big, and therefore why data compression is such an important part of digital video, let's look at some numbers. Let's assume that we want to play a digitized video sequence which measures 320 × 240 pixels, that we want a playback rate of 15 frames per second (just half of television's frame rate), and that we're going to store our image in 15-bit-per-pixel mode in order to get good color quality. Forget the audio track for now. How big are we talking here?

Each frame = 320 × 240 pixels × 2 bytes per pixel = 153,600 bytes per frame (150K)

Each second = 150K × 15 frames per second = 2,250K (2.25 Mb)

There you have it. 2.25 megabytes per second for storing our home movies. At that rate, a vast CD-ROM, holding roughly 650 megabytes, would fill up after less than 5 minutes. Not that you could really use CD-ROM for this movie anyway. A double-speed CD-ROM has a maximum transfer rate of 300K per second, in practice more like 250–270K. So, even if our display code and our display card could keep up, there's no way we could pull this digital video data off CD at anything remotely like the necessary speed. Even current IDE hard disks can't supply sustained data at this rate.

Digital Video Means Compression

To get from 2.25 megabytes per second to 250K per second will take a lot more than converting to 8-bit format or using run-length encoding, the bitmap compression techniques we've used so far. In order to see how bad the situation is, let's express our goal in another way, common to digital video discussions. How many bits can we devote, on average, to each pixel?

320 × 240 = 76,800 pixels per frame (75K)

75K pixels × 15 frames per second = 1,125K pixels per second

250K bytes per second/1,125K pixels per second = .222 bytes per pixel

.222 bytes per pixel × 8 bits per byte ~ 1.75 bits per pixel

Yikes! 1.75 bits per pixel? Data reduction in this range doesn't usually come from an evening spent thinking of a clever hack. And it doesn't come from standard "general" data compression techniques such as LZW, Huffman coding, or PKZIP. What's called for is a specialized technique, one finely attuned to the nature of digital video data. The development of such techniques has been a hotbed of research over the last several years, and great progress has been made. More on these techniques later in this chapter.

Digital Video Means Audio

And what about audio? Is it going to blow up our data storage needs even further? The good news is that audio data is a lot tamer than video, even at high quality. The bad news is that it's still big. CD-quality audio consists of 16-bit samples, digitized at a rate of 44.1 Khz. That's 44,100 samples per second, or 88,200 bytes. Add a second track for stereo, and we're up to 176,400 bytes per second. If we need to pull data off a CD at 250K per second, we can't really afford to use two-thirds of that for audio. In typical game-quality digital video, a single 8-bit 22 Khz audio track is used, requiring 22K of that precious 250K bandwidth. While not of sufficient quality for music buffs, this type of audio is more than adequate for speech and other natural sounds.

How about data compression for audio? This is another area of research, and major breakthroughs have been made in the compression of digital speech. But for general audio, and particularly music, the ear is pretty finicky. Any compression technique which loses quality (and, as we'll see for video, all good compression techniques are *lossy*) is going to sound funny.

Another audio-related issue has to do with how the video and audio streams are mixed in a digital video file. Because CD-ROMs and most other storage devices don't perform well if they have to skip around from track to track, the standard technique is to *interleave* video and audio chunks so that each appears as it's needed during playback. The name of the file format in Microsoft's Video for Windows is AVI, which stands for Audio-Video Interleave. Figure 16.1 shows how interleaving works, and how the two data streams are handled during playback.

Digital Video Recording and Playback

Figure 16.2 provides an overview of the full process of recording and playing back digital video. Recording of video and audio is done with a special video capture card, which can receive standard video signals directly from a camcorder or from another source such as a VCR. Nowadays, capture cards typically have special hardware to compress the video signal on the fly as it is being captured, in order to avoid overtaxing the hard disk onto which the captured data is stored.

After a digital video sequence is stored (in a file) on the hard disk, it can be edited using special software designed for that purpose. So-called *nonlinear editing* software (as opposed to tape-based linear editing) allows image cropping, scaling, and a host of image processing techniques. These include special-effects transitions (fade, wipe,

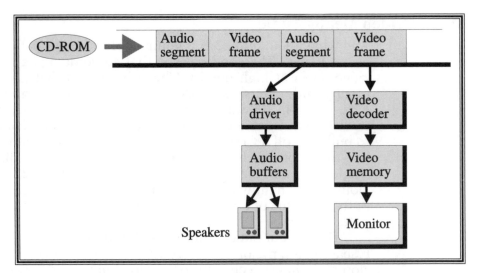

Figure 16.1   Interleaving of video and audio data in an interleaved digital video file.

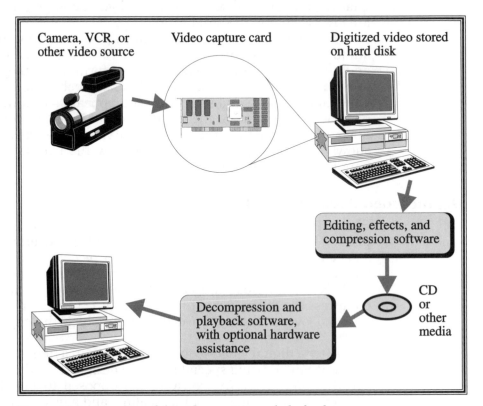

Figure 16.2   Overview of the video capture and playback process.

etc.) and overlaying of titles and other computer-generated images. Manipulation of audio tracks is also possible in these programs. Color plate 11 is a screenshot from *Adobe Premiere,* the most popular personal-use digital video editor, available for both PCs and Macintoshes. In TV stations and among other high-end users, the Macintosh-based Avid Technology system currently reigns supreme.

Digital video editors also allow the file to be *recompressed* into a compression format suitable for final playback. Some compression schemes that work well for playback cannot be used at recording time due to the fact that they are *asymmetrical*—they take far longer to compress than to decompress during playback.

If the digital video file is to be used "in house," it may then be left on a local hard disk, put onto a network file server, and perhaps copied to a CD-ROM for archival purposes. Digital video files which are distributed as part of a product, such as a multimedia or entertainment title, are usually delivered on CD-ROM (it takes a lot of floppies to store even a short movie!).

Finally, playback time arrives. The end user's machine must have the proper software to decode the digital video file and play it back. In particular, it needs the proper decompression software. In the case of proprietary or nonstandard compression techniques, the necessary software is included with the package. But there are digital video standards emerging, as always more than one, and these are often available as part of the operating system. The Macintosh has Apple's QuickTime, and the PC has Microsoft's Video for Windows (VFW), as well as a version of QuickTime called QuickTime for Windows. And then there's MPEG, a true worldwide standard emerging from the Motion Pictures Expert Group. But wait, there's MPEG-1 *and* MPEG-2. Ho ho ho.

Actually, I'm mixing up two distinct concepts here. One is the algorithm by which digital video is compressed. There are a fair number of such techniques, some public and some proprietary, and we'll take a look at a few of them. But QuickTime and Video for Windows are not compression algorithms; they are general file formats and function APIs for digital video storage and playback. They rely on underlying components called codecs (*co*mpressor-*dec*ompressor) to provide interpretation of the bits in a given video frame. QuickTime and VFW manage the overall digital video process, and don't care about the compression technique used in a given file, as long as the appropriate codec is available, as Figure 16.3 illustrates. This is good, because research in compression techniques continues apace, and we don't want to have to invent new file formats and APIs every time there's a breakthrough.

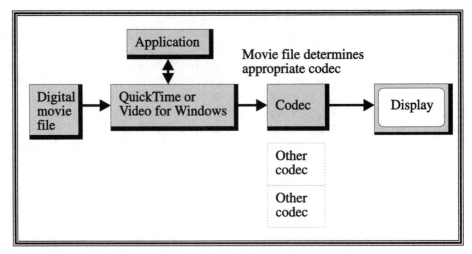

Figure 16.3 Relationship between application, movie file, QuickTime or Video for Windows software, and digital video codecs.

Digital Video Compression Techniques

So what are these mysterious digital video compression techniques, and how do they compress images into the 1.75-bits-per-pixel range? This must be some black art. Or, like everything else once you find out about it, is it really pretty simple?

Compression Techniques that Don't Work

No, Dorothy, digital video compression *is* a black art. Well, maybe dark gray. The bag of tricks we might normally apply to digital video just doesn't cut the mustard. Consider:

- Run-length encoding depends on having runs of adjacent pixels exactly matching in color. This doesn't work for "natural" or noisy images. Furthermore, the exact matches necessary are even less common when we move from 8-bit pixels, where there are only 256 possible values, to 15-bit and 24-bit pixels.

- The FLIC animation file format gets additional compression by encoding only the pixels which have changed in value since the previous frame. Again, for noisy images, or those in which the camera is moving, this technique breaks down. Almost every pixel is changing in digital video, even if only by a slight shade.

- Huffman coding, a standard statistical compression technique, represents data points in terms of "tokens" which vary in length. If we apply this technique to 15-bit pixels, we might find that pixels using frequently occurring colors can be encoded in 5 or 6 bits, while uncommon colors take 20 to 25 bits. This means an average pixel size of over 6 bits, which is not even in the ballpark.

- LZW coding, besides the patent violation issues,[1] is similarly unsuitable. LZW compression encodes commonly occurring strings of data points with a single token. If the image features patterns of recurring pixel sequences, this technique will compress the image somewhat. But again, natural and noisy images simply do not have enough coherence to make this technique appropriate.

Challenging Our Assumptions

So, what to do? Wait for octuple-speed CD-ROM drives holding 10 gigabytes of data? Nope, it's time to sit back and think about the whole issue from a wider perspective. For instance, we've assumed so far that the digital video frames must be preserved with absolute accuracy. But why? Must we preserve every bit of noise introduced by crummy taping equipment? Obviously not. The digital video signal is extremely rich and also imperfect to begin with. If our compression technique distorts the picture a little, maybe that's okay. We can consider *lossy* compression, and, in fact, we must if we're going to get anywhere.

Also, we've assumed that the data we're going to compress is a straightforward image frame, encoded in RGB format with 15 or 24 bits per pixel (or possibly 8 with an associated palette, although this is rarer in digital video than in animation). But the eye is more sensitive to contrasts in lightness than it is to exact color. We could convert the RGB data to a different scheme, one such as YUV, which reorganizes the pixel as a single luminance component and two chrominance (color) components. This color format naturally compresses better, because there is often less change in color from pixel to pixel than there is in luminance, and also the picture is relatively unharmed by encoding the color information with reduced resolution.

The formula for conversion of RGB into YUV is given below. Note that Y, the luminance component, is a weighted sum of the R, G, and B. The total weights add up to 1.0—the values show how much of the total luminance is contributed by each primary (see how important green is). The other YUV components, U and V, are known as color difference values.

```
Y = (R * .299) + (G * .587) + (B * .114)
U = (B * .463) - (R * .147) - (G * .289)
V = (R * .615) - (G * .515) - (B * .100)
```

---

[1] Unisys is the holder of the patent on the LZW compression algorithm, which is used in the GIF file format. At the time of this writing, issues of royalty payments by GIF-handling software developers remain unresolved. Switch to JPEG, I say.

JPEG and the Discrete Cosine Transform

The popular JPEG compression scheme for still images typically starts with an image converted into YUV format, and goes one better. It employs a technique called the Discrete Cosine Transform (DCT), which is a cousin of the Fast Fourier Transform for those of you with a signal-processing background. JPEG stands for Joint Photographic Experts Group, the International Standards Organization body which created the standard. The JPEG algorithm proceeds as follows: After conversion of a bitmap to YUV color space, the algorithm breaks up the bitmap into the three separate component bitmaps, based on Y, U, and V. Each component bitmap is further divided into 8 × 8 pixel blocks, and the following algorithm is applied to each block:

1. A set of 8 by 8 "frequency" coefficients is mathematically derived from the 64 sample points. These encode how much change there is in the component across a range of frequencies. This is a mathematical transformation, and introduces no lossiness.

2. The 64 frequency coefficients are *quantized*. High-frequency components in particular are thrown out or represented by fewer bits than low-frequency coefficients. This is the lossy part of the JPEG algorithm, but it is designed to lose information to which the eye is less sensitive. The U and V chrominance components are subjected to more lossiness than the Y (luminance) component.

3. The quantized frequency values are further compressed (losslessly) using Huffman or arithmetic coding. This represents commonly occurring frequency coefficients in fewer bits than infrequently occurring coefficients, and contributes significantly to the compression ratio.

The decoding of JPEG-compressed images is essentially the reverse of the compression stage. Figure 16.4 diagrams the encoding and decoding process. JPEG compression is complex, and this brief discussion cannot begin to describe it in more than the vaguest terms. The standard also has features not described here, such as a lossless mode and "progressive refinement" features for use across transmission lines. For more information, see the (expensive but excellent) *JPEG: Still Image Data Compression Standard* by Pennebaker and Mitchell, published in 1993 by Van Nostrand Reinhold. This text includes the actual ISO standards documents in its appendices. An excellent introduction to JPEG is contained in the article "The JPEG Still Picture Compression Standard," written by Gregory K. Wallace for the April 1991 issue of *Communications of the ACM*.

Motion JPEG and MPEG

Motion JPEG is the name of a standard whose purpose is to provide a framework for tying together multiple image frames, each of which

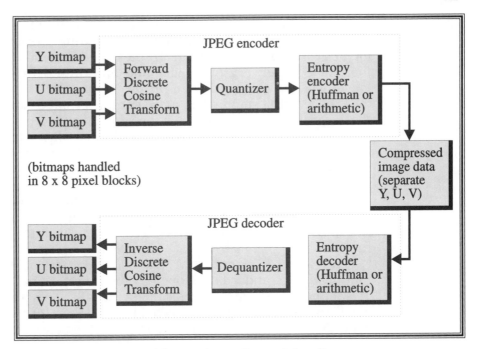

Figure 16.4 Overview of the JPEG encoding and decoding process.

has been independently compressed using JPEG. As such, motion JPEG is a digital video compression technique. MPEG, a standard which has emerged from the Motion Pictures Expert Group, is built upon JPEG but adds a few twists of its own. MPEG looks likely to emerge as the worldwide standard for digital video, one that will be built into the HDTV sets we're going to get any day now, as soon as they figure out how to stuff all the requisite hardware and RAM into a TV set for less than $2,000. All this for *Melrose Place. (Sigh.)*

MPEG takes JPEG as its base, but then goes on to make use of the fact that frames in a digital video sequence are not independent of one another. Rather than try to find exact pixel matches, as the FLIC format does, MPEG recognizes that inexact matches are likely, and further that the camera may be moving, and the best match may not be in quite the same position in the frame. In essence, MPEG works with the same 8×8 pixel blocks as JPEG, but these blocks are not the raw pixel values themselves. Instead, they are the difference between the actual pixels and the predicted values from a motion-derived 8×8 area of the previous frame. The ability to predict what is likely to be in a given 8×8 pixel block, using motion estimation, and to encode only the differences between the actual and the predicted, gives MPEG a big compression boost.

MPEG is an asymmetrical technique. Decoding is not too much more complex than JPEG decoding. Encoding, however, involves a lot of work to search image frames for the "motion" contained therein. For delivery of movies and entertainment CDs, however, long encoding times are not a problem—playback is what is important. The MPEG standard is more complex than described so far, in that not all frames are encoded the same way. For instance, support is included in the encoding for bidirectional play, wherein it is possible to play an MPEG video sequence in reverse order, often with some frame skipping. MPEG is really two standards, also. MPEG-1 is designed for image resolutions of about 360×240 and bit rates of about 1.5 Mbits per second, which is well within double-speed CD-ROM limits. MPEG-2 is designed for higher resolutions and bit rates, and is probably what will find its way into the TV of the future.

A standard related to MPEG is H.261, part of the H.320 full-motion video standard developed by the International Telegraph and Telephone Consultative Committee (CCITT). This standard is oriented toward video teleconferencing, and therefore drops some of MPEG's motion estimation in order to reduce encoding time in line with the needs of two-way video transmission.

As you can probably already tell, Motion JPEG, MPEG, and similar techniques are mathematically intensive, unsuitable for real-time digital video on current desktop PCs, at least without hardware assist. But that hardware is coming fast. There are already chips which can perform the DCT math in hardware. Sigma Designs' Reel-Magic is the first of a wave of low-cost boards which can play back MPEG-encoded movies on a PC. Even by the time you are reading this book, MPEG-equipped video boards may be commonplace.

Vector Quantization

There are several other compression methods which have been applied to image data in a quest for the holy 1.75 bits per pixel. The details of most such techniques remain unknown, since they are considered proprietary by their inventors. Besides DCT-based algorithms, other popular approaches usually fall under the general rubric of *vector quantization.*

Vector quantization is a means whereby the resolution of a set of data is reduced in a controlled way. In the simplest case, we may simply decide that we are going to represent an image with 2 bits per pixel, find the four most common colors, and assign each pixel a 2-bit index into a 4-color palette. This is a form of vector quantization, though not a particularly good-looking one.

Real vector quantization techniques are more involved. A vector-quantization technique I developed for a recent project, which applies only to 8-bit image frames, basically works as follows:

1. Divide each frame into 4 × 4 pixel blocks, which by definition have no more than 16 unique colors in them. Each such block is a delta block, representing pixels which are unchanged from the previous frame with the value 0.

2. Collect the set of unique color values (palette indices) in each block. Look up this set in a table of such sets, which is initially empty. Look for an exact match or a close match. A close match means that each color in the new set has a reasonable RGB match in the set found in the table. If a match is found, remap all color indices into that set. If no match is found, add the new set to the table.

3. Encode the block using 0, 1, 2, 3, or 4 bits per pixel, depending on how many unique colors are in the block. For example, if there are between 5 and 8 unique colors, use 3 bits per pixel. If the entire block is a solid color, use 0 bits per pixel. Add a two-byte "block header" to the block, which signifies which color set is assigned to this block (13 bits) and the number of bits per pixel in the encoding (3 bits).

4. Store the block header words separately from the block data. Collect adjacent runs of the same block header value into run tokens. Then, apply Huffman compression to the entire block header array, representing commonly recurring color set indices in fewer bits. The block data itself remains "uncompressed," other than the fact that the pixels in it are encoded using between 0 and 4 bits, down from the original 8.

Figure 16.5 shows the treatment of each 4 × 4 pixel block, with some simplifications. For instance, runs of fully transparent blocks are encoded as a single token in the Huffman compressor. Also, while each frame is compressed independently, what is encoded is the delta between frames and not the frame itself, in a manner similar to FLIC encoding.

The frame data, counting Huffman-coded block headers and block data, but not counting the color set table itself, which is placed at the head of the movie, averaged just over 2 bits per pixel in our movies. It was somewhat under 2 for sedate, still-camera scenes, and closer to 2.5 or so for full-motion video. Not quite good enough for the big leagues, but then I had never even heard of the term "vector quantization" until the job was done.[2] Maybe the black art is not so black after all if you have a good bag of tricks and the time and willingness to experiment.

Real-world digital video codecs, such as the popular Indeo (Intel) and Cinepak (SuperMac) codecs, are apparently some form of vector quantization, from what I have heard. They are proprietary, so the

---

[2]Not to imply that I slept through math or anything.

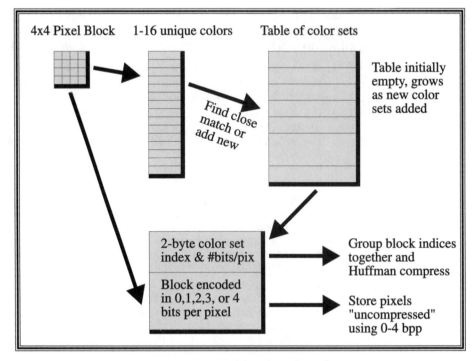

Figure 16.5   Encoding of a 4×4 pixel block in homebrew vector quantization algorithm.

details remain hidden. They work with full-color images and not palettized 8-bit images, so their algorithms are no doubt quite different from the one given above.

For more information on vector quantization and other digital video compression techniques, see Mattison's *Practical Digital Video with Programming Examples in C,* published in 1994 by John Wiley & Sons. This book also features good information on the hardware side of digital video. For us, it's time to leave this enthralling discussion of compression techniques, and explore the higher-level aspects of digital video, such as the file formats, API sets, and environments under which digital video can be played.

QuickTime: Digital Video Arrives

The arrival of Apple's QuickTime 1.0 in late 1991 was not actually the first arrival of low-cost digital video on the desktop. It was predated by several years, in the form of the Amiga, a computer that had built-in video handling from Day 1. But the Amiga got no respect, for reasons both good and bad. Originally, it was too far ahead of its time, featuring preemptive multitasking, a windowing system, and a video graphics system featuring hardware sprites and hardware-assisted blitting. It had video inputs and outputs but no optical drive (or even a hard disk at first) for storing video in digital form, although that didn't stop budding video producers from using the Amiga's genlock feature to turn the machine into a linear tape-based editor with computer-generated overlay graphics. In the end, the Amiga was doomed by poor marketing, a marketplace resistant to nonbusiness computers, and the fact that its giant technology lead was squandered over years of failure to update and improve upon its hardware foundation.

Apple, flush with several years of success in fostering the desktop publishing revolution, has emerged upon a less profitable but still successful attempt to bring "video publishing" to the desktop. The first version of QuickTime featured postage-stamp-sized windows with jerky video and an audio track that dropped out distressingly often, but it was still a marvel to watch. My first exposure to it was a clip of a Todd Rundgren concert, in which the band members danced herky-jerky as my single-speed CD struggled to deliver the data, but I was simply blown away nonetheless. QuickTime 2.0, released in 1994, enhances QuickTime's performance, primarily by improving the codecs available with it. Without hardware support, it still struggles a bit to pump video through a decent-sized window, but the improvement is dramatic nonetheless. Digital video has arrived.

QuickTime Overview

QuickTime, which now also exists on the PC as QuickTime for Windows, has several aspects. First off, there is a QuickTime file format, which is platform-independent. The QuickTime distribution disks also include standalone tools for playing back movies and other tasks, although video enthusiasts will want to buy third-party products such as *Adobe Premiere* for digital video editing and effects processing. QuickTime also consists of software, implemented under Windows as a dynamic-link library (DLL), which provides applications with an API for controlling the playback of movies. Finally, QuickTime includes a set of codecs, one for each type of compression supported—under Windows, these are also implemented as DLLs. Figure 16.6 shows the various components.

QuickTime Applications

Under Windows, QuickTime movies play into a window, of course. In case it's not obvious, QuickTime for Windows does not operate at all

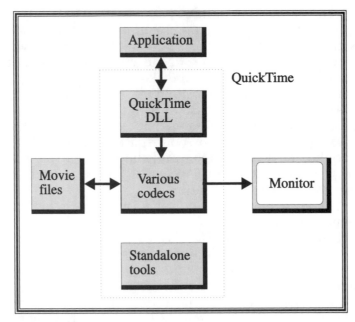

Figure 16.6   QuickTime for Windows components.

under plain DOS. Figure 16.7 shows the overall structure of a simple Windows program which plays a QuickTime movie.

QuickTime File Format

While the interpretation of the data inside a frame is dependent on the codec used to compress the video, all QuickTime files share a common structure. This structure is platform-independent, a fact that causes PC developers who tackle it some grief as they realize they must reverse the byte ordering of each word and longword in the file. The Mac's 68000 processor is big-endian, meaning that multibyte words are stored high byte to low byte, whereas Intel 80×86 processors are little-endian. Hey, at least all computers are still binary, allowing only two states for each bit. It could be worse. In our DNA sequences, each "bit" can take one of four values (adenine, thymine, guanine, or cytosine). Will future biological computers be programmed with quaternary logic, or will we just store two "bits" per DNA node?

Oops. Must . . . stay . . . focused! Okay, QuickTime files are chunk-based files, in that the file is made up of "chunks" of data, each of which has a header which includes its type and length. Chunks are nested—a given chunk may contain more chunks inside of it. Chunk types are four-character names such as 'moov', 'mdat',

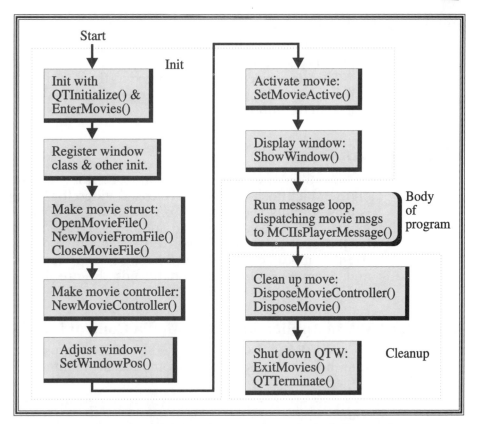

Figure 16.7 Flow of a simple Windows program which plays a QuickTime movie.

'stsc', and so on. Typically, a QuickTime file begins with an 'mdat' chunk, which contains all of the actual video and audio data in an undifferentiated linear mass. This is followed by a 'moov' chunk, which holds all the other chunks within it. These chunks provide all the information needed to interpret the mass of data in the 'mdat' chunk, including compression techniques, offsets to each video and audio frame, playing times for each frame, etc.

The format of individual chunks is beyond the scope of this book, as is a full listing of all chunk types. The best resource for this information is Apple's own *Inside Macintosh* documentation (see Appendix E). Two volumes, *QuickTime* and *QuickTime Components*, together provide all the information necessary to program Quick-Time applications (on the Mac, anyway) and make sense of Quick-Time files. What they don't cover, unfortunately, are the details of compression formats. Not that this information is necessary to work with QuickTime, since the system automatically decompresses video frames for you. But it would still be fun to know.

QuickTime Codecs

Table 16.1 shows the codecs supplied with QuickTime, and other popularly used ones.

The Cinepak codec has emerged as the favorite among users due to its high-quality, good compression ratios, fast decompression, and reasonable compression times.

Video for Windows

In November 1992, about a year after the first release of QuickTime on the Macintosh, Microsoft released Video for Windows 1.0. VFW is conceptually very similar to QuickTime: It consists of a file format for interleaved video and audio (AVI), tools to record and play back digital video files, a software mechanism for applications to use to support digital video, and a set of codecs for compression and decompression of video frames. Figure 16.8 illustrates the main components of VFW.

Accessing VFW in Applications: The Media Control Interface

Video for Windows was preceded by MCI, Microsoft's Media Control Interface. MCI was designed from the start to interface to a wide vari-

Table 16.1 QuickTime Codecs	
Name	*Comments*
Raw	No compression (8, 16, or 24 bits per pixel, linear format)
Anim	Lossy version of run-length compression, useful for computer-generated animation
Graphics	Optimized for 8-bit graphics, not useful for captured video
Video	Apple-developed, fast encoding but mediocre compression ratio
Compact Video	Apple-developed, slow encoding but fast decoding, better compression than Video
JPEG	Great compression ratio, slow encoding and decoding
Cinepak	Developed by SuperMac, very good quality and decoding time, slow encoding

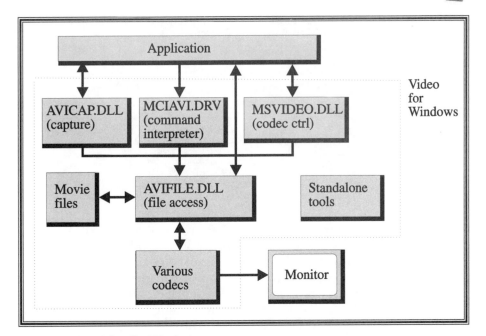

Figure 16.8   Video for Windows components.

ety of audio and video devices, from sound cards to videodisc players. Unlike many other software modules in Windows, MCI is not implemented as a huge API function set. Instead, it is primarily a message-passing interface. Programs communicate using either of two central functions, mciSendCommand() and mciSendString(). The first is a more efficient, command-oriented interface; the second allows English-like text commands to be sent to a device. For advanced uses, message handlers to react to the messages coming back from a device must often be written.

Table 16.2 on page 612 lists the set of MCI commands to which all devices respond.

Table 16.3 lists the optional command messages. Note that they are purposefully "general" in nature, but apply well to many multimedia devices. Specific devices may respond to further messages outside this set.

Sending MCI Commands

The command interface to MCI uses the mciSendCommand() function, which is prototyped as follows:

```
DWORD mciSendCommand(WORD wDeviceID, WORD wMessage, DWORD dwParam1, DWORD
    dwParam2);
```

Table 16.2   Required MCI Commands

Command	Description
MCI_CLOSE	Close an open MCI device
MCI_GETDEVCAPS	Retrieve device capabilities
MCI_INFO	Retrieve device information in text form
MCI_OPEN	Open an MCI device
MCI_STATUS	Retrieve device's current status

Note the similarity to a window procedure, except that a device id appears in place of a window handle (and the first of two message arguments, 'dwParam1', is a DWORD instead of a WORD). The use of the two arguments is message specific. The mciSendCommand() function returns zero if it is successful, or an error code in the low-order word of the return value if not. The function mciGetErrorString() can be used to convert an error code into an error string.

For applications or languages where the C-like format of mciSendCommand() is unsuitable, a text-based interface to MCI devices is provided. The mciSendString() function is prototyped below:

```
WORD mciSendString(char *cmdString, char *returnString, WORD wReturnLength,
    HWND hCallback);
```

Table 16.3   Optional MCI Commands

Command	Description
MCI_LOAD	Load data from a file
MCI_PAUSE	Pause playback or recording
MCI_PLAY	Begin playback
MCI_RECORD	Begin recording
MCI_RESUME	Resume playback or recording after pause
MCI_SAVE	Save data to a file
MCI_SEEK	Seek to location on device
MCI_SET	Set device parameters
MCI_STATUS	Retrieve device's current status
MCI_STOP	Stop playback or recording

The command string is of the form *command device [arguments]*, and might be something such as "play myvideo.avi". The values 'returnString' and 'wReturnLength' are used to provide a known-length buffer to MCI, for it to place response text into. This text can then be shown to the user, for instance. A NULL pointer in 'returnString' signifies that no return text is desired. The 'hCallback' argument is used to provide a window handle for callback messages in certain cases.

An even simpler interface is available through mciExecute():

```
BOOL mciExecute(char *cmdString);
```

Playing Video Using MCI

If Video for Windows is installed on a given system, then MCI commands related to digital video files should, as they say, "just work." The AVI file extension is used to connect the commands to the proper driver, namely MCIAVI.DRV. The MCITEST program included in the Windows 3.1 SDK is a good place to experiment with text-based MCI commands. MCITEST provides a window into which commands can be typed, and in which digital video files can be explored.

Other Interfaces to VFW

In 1994, Microsoft delivered Video for Windows 1.1. Like QuickTime 2.0, this update featured better playback performance, primarily due to inclusion of SuperMac's Cinepak codec, although Intel's Indeo codec is quite good also. A VFW 1.1 Developer's Kit features an extensive API to complement the generic interface to VFW via MCI. Table 16.4 summarizes three new sets of functions included in this developer kit.

These APIs offer tighter control of digital video playback. The best source of information on them is the Video for Windows 1.1 SDK, available as part of the Microsoft Developer Network.

Table 16.4   VFW 1.1 API Sets

Functions	*Description*
MCIWndXxxxx	Window-based video playback API, with VCR control panel and other features
AVICapXxxxx	Window-based interface to audio/video capture
AVIFileXxxxx	Functions to read and write AVI files and streams

The AVI File Format

Just because the VFW 1.1 SDK offers a set of functions for reading and writing AVI files doesn't mean that the AVI format should be a black box. There's nothing magic about it. AVI files are just one of many forms of *RIFF* files. This format is used for more than just video in Windows, and is worth knowing something about.

RIFF Files

RIFF stands for *Resource Interchange File Format,* and it's a chunk-based format designed by Microsoft to hold a variety of data types. WAV sound files are RIFF files, for instance. Each chunk in any RIFF file has an 8-byte header, shown below:

```
typedef unsigned long DWORD; // you probably already knew DWORDs were longs
typedef DWORD FOURCC;        // a long holds four characters

typedef struct {
   FOURCC ckID;              // chunk type (4-char code, much like QuickTime)
   DWORD ckSize;             // size of data to follow, in bytes
} RiffChunkHdr;
```

Some chunk types, notably the 'LIST' chunk, have an extra data field following the chunk header—this is a sort of subtype field:

```
FOURCC ckSubID; // when used with 'LIST', identifies type of LIST chunk
```

RIFF files are a bit less loose than some other chunk-based formats. A given RIFF file must match one of a set of registered "forms." These forms define the layout of a given class of RIFF file, in terms of what chunk types should appear and in what order. Some standard chunk types appear in several different RIFF forms, for instance the 'LIST' chunk, which contains a set of subchunks. Within a given form, custom chunk types relevant to that form may appear. Table 16.5 lists the commonly encountered RIFF forms. A particular form is identified by the chunk ID (type) of the first chunk inside the opening 'RIFF' chunk.

WAV RIFF Files

To make this discussion more concrete, let's look at the format of WAV files, which hold digitized sounds. Each WAV file consists of a 'RIFF' chunk of form type 'WAVE.' The 'RIFF' chunk contains two chunks, a 'fmt' chunk which contains information about the sampling rate and so on of the data, and a 'data' chunk which holds the raw sample data.

Table 16.5   Some RIFF Forms

Chunk ID	Description
'PAL'	Logical Palette
'RDIB'	Device-Independent Bitmap
'RMID'	MIDI Music Sequence
'RMMP'	Multimedia Movie (authored with Macromind Director)
'WAVE'	Digital Audio Waveform
'AVI'	Audio-Video Interleave (digital video movie)

```
RIFF WAVE      Identifies this as a RIFF file, form type: WAVE
     fmt       Number of channels, sample rate, etc.
     data      Contains actual waveform sample data, according to 'fmt'
```

AVI RIFF Files

AVI files are RIFF files too, though they are a little more complex than WAV files. For one thing, AVI files very often hold more than one *stream* of data. A typical AVI has a video stream and an audio stream, though AVI files are not limited to such an arrangement (for instance, an AVI file might have two audio streams, one English and one French, so that language selection could be done at runtime). Below is the chunk layout of a sample AVI file.

```
RIFF AVI       Identifies this as a RIFF file, form type: AVI
  LIST hdrl    List of chunks specifying data format
      avih     Main AVI header (num frames, num streams, width/height, etc.)
    LIST strl  Stream header list (video stream)
        strh   Stream header (playback rate, length, quality, etc.)
        strf   Stream format (BITMAPINFO struct)
    LIST strl  Stream header list (audio stream)
        strh   Stream header
        strf   Stream format (WAVEFORMATEX or PCMWAVEFORMAT struct)
  LIST movi    Actual data chunks (compressed video frames and audio
               segments)
      idx1     Index chunk, gives offset and length of each data chunk
```

AVI Stream Chunks

The first chunk inside the 'RIFF' chunk is a 'LIST' chunk of subtype 'hdrl' (header list). The chunks within this list contain information describing the streams in the file. The first such chunk is an 'avih' chunk, which gives header information about the movie. The data in the 'avih' chunk is in the form of the following structure:

```
typedef struct {
    DWORD dwMicroSecPerFrame;      // period between video frames
    DWORD dwMaxBytesPerSec;        // approximate max data rate for play back
    DWORD dwReserved1;             // unused currently
    DWORD dwFlags;                 // miscellaneous flags
    DWORD dwTotalFrames;           // total number of frames in file
    DWORD dwInitialFrames;         // num frames prior to 1st video frame
    DWORD dwStreams;               // number of streams
    DWORD dwSuggestedBufferSize;   // size of largest record in file
    DWORD dwWidth;                 // width of frame in pixels
    DWORD dwHeight;                // height of frame in pixels
    DWORD dwReserved[4];           // unused currently
} MainAVIHeader;
```

Following the 'avih' header chunk is a 'LIST' chunk for each stream in the file. The subtype for these lists is 'strl' (stream list). Inside each stream list are several chunks. The chunks typically found within a stream list chunk are listed in Table 16.6.

The data in a stream header ('strh') chunk is defined by the following structure:

```
typedef struct {
    FOURCC fccType;              // 'vids' -> video, 'auds' -> audio, 'TXTS' -> text
    FOURCC fccHandler;           // four-character codec name
    DWORD dwFlags;               // miscellaneous flags
    DWORD dwPriority;            // priority of stream
    DWORD dwInitialFrames;       // number of frames before 1st of this stream
    DWORD dwScale;               // time scale (dwRate / dwScale = samples/sec)
    DWORD dwRate;                // data rate (see dwScale comment)
    DWORD dwStart;               // starting time of sequence
    DWORD dwLength;              // length of sequence (in time scale units)
    DWORD dwSuggestedBufferSize; // suggested size of playback buffer
    DWORD dwQuality;             // codec quality setting
    DWORD dwSampleSize;          // sample size, in bytes (0 if varies)
    RECT rcFrame;                // area of output window
}AVIStreamHeader;
```

The data in a 'strf' stream format chunk depends on the type of data in the stream. For video streams, it is a BITMAPINFO structure (see struct BmpInfoHeader in Chapter 3). For audio streams, it is a structure which describes the audio data, including such fields as sampling rate, mono versus stereo, and so on. VFW allows for audio compression as well as video compression.

Other chunks may follow the 'LIST' chunks which define the streams. The Video for Windows Developer's Kit, available as part of

Table 16.6	Chunks Found Within 'strl' Stream List Chunk
Chunk	***Description***
'strh'	Required, contains stream header
'strf'	Required, format depends on type of stream (video, audio, etc.)
'strd'	Optional, additional data for use by codec
'strn'	Optional, text describing stream

the Microsoft Developer Network, is the best source for detailed information on this and other aspects of the AVI format.

AVI Movie Chunks

Following the 'hdrl' list chunk (which contains all the stream chunks discussed so far) is the 'movi' list chunk, which contains the actual video pixels and audio samples. Each is compressed according to the codec defined in its associated stream header. For interleaved video and audio, the audio stream is broken up into segments which are interleaved with the video frames. Video frames are then packaged together with audio segments, each pair inside a 'rec' chunk. Whether grouped inside 'rec' chunks or by themselves, each data chunk inside a 'movi' chunk is one of the types listed in Table 16.7.

In Table 16.7, the chunk names do not actually have the characters '##' in them. These pound signs are place holders for the number of the stream that the data is assigned to, '00' for the first stream, '01' for the second, and so on. So, for instance, a compressed video frame in the first stream would have chunk type of '00dc'.

AVI Index Chunks

Finally, an AVI file may have an optional 'idx1' chunk at its end. This "index" chunk, if present, contains the offsets and lengths of all the video frames and audio segments in the 'movi' chunk, and aids VFW in locating them. The 'idx1' chunk contains an array of index entries, each defined according to the following structure:

```
typedef struct {
    DWORD ckid;          // type of data chunk ('##wb', '##dc', 'rec ', etc.)
    DWORD dwFlags;       // miscellaneous
    DWORD dwChunkOffset; // offset of chunk, relative to 'movi' start
    DWORD dwChunkLength; // length of chunk, excluding 8-byte header
} AVIINDEXENTRY;
```

Table 16.7   Data Chunks Inside 'movi' Chunk

Name	Description
'##wb'	Audio segment, chunk data is audio samples
'##db'	Video frame, chunk data is DIB in format given by 'strf' chunk in video stream header
'##dc'	Video frame, chunk data is compressed according to codec specified in 'strh' chunk
'##pc'	Palette change, chunk data holds new palette entries

Lengthy as this discussion has been, it barely scratches the surface of AVI files. The AVIFileXxxx() functions previously mentioned are documented in the VFW Developer's Kit, and allow access to AVI files at a slightly higher level than the chunk information given here. But it never hurts to know what's going on "under the hood."

VFW Codecs

Like QuickTime, VFW features a set of codecs, and has an extensible architecture which allows for the addition of new ones in the future. Table 16.8 shows the codecs supplied with VFW 1.1.

The Cinepak and Indeo codecs are both in widespread use. With Indeo version 3, Intel has largely caught up with Cinepak in terms of compression ratios and visual quality. Expect further progress by both companies, and other new entrants into the video compression game.

Future Codecs

As MPEG catches on, it seems likely that Video for Windows will supply a standard, built-in MPEG codec, wherein MPEG-encoded frames are embedded within the AVI file format. There are other contestants seeking the "best codec" prize, too. The Duck Corporation has developed a codec named TrueMotion S which has been used by game developers on the 3DO platform and elsewhere. While encoding is currently a time-consuming process, the playback performance of TrueMotion S appears quite amazing. Time will tell whether this codec will find its way into widespread use on personal computers. One factor working against it is the rapid emergence of hardware-assisted digital video playback, which favors standards such as MPEG. If a card maker is going to go to all the trouble to put an algorithm into silicon, they want it to be the right one, and that favors MPEG and perhaps Indeo, which is a product of the semiconductor powerhouse Intel.

Table 16.8   VFW 1.1 Codecs

FOURCC Code	Comments
MRLE	Microsoft run-length encoding, good for computer animation
MSVC	Microsoft Video 1, mediocre quality
JPEG	JPEG encoding
CVID	SuperMac's Cinepak, most popular format
YUV9	Intel 411 YUV format, primarily for capture
RT21	Intel Indeo 2.1, okay but inferior to Cinepak
IV31	Intel Indeo 3.1, competitive with Cinepak

Before we end our detour into the world of digital video, one more development bears examination. It's an add-on to VFW, which builds extra functionality on top of straight digital video playback. It's called WinToon, it's from Microsoft, it's free, and it fits in perfectly with the ARTT rendering system.

WinToon: An AVI-Based Digital Cartooning System

Start with a computer-generated animation. Convert to AVI format. Run through a utility which marks frames with dirty rectangles to speed blitting. Add WinG-based buffering. Mix movie with graphics generated on the fly under program control. Package system as DLL, and give away for free.

Sounds too good to be true, but it's not. It's WinToon, a digital cartooning system available from Microsoft on its JumpStart CD, and downloadable from online services such as CompuServe (see the WinMM forum). WinToon has already been used as the underlying engine in commercial game development, including Disney's *The Lion King*. It's a simple but powerful system, and is definitely worth checking out if you're interested in digital cartooning. In this section, we'll take a tour of what WinToon has to offer.

WinToon Overview

Besides documentation and basic development files such as a C header file and an import library, WinToon is at its heart composed of just two files:

SCANAVI.EXE   Processes AVI file to add dirty-rectangle information

WINTOON.DLL   Run-time DLL necessary for WinToon play-
                   back

The combination of the SCANAVI tool and the WinToon DLL provides two related benefits beyond ordinary AVI playback:

1. Faster playback speed through the use of dirty-rectangle blitting
2. Mixing of AVI digital video frames with program-controlled on-the-fly graphics

This is a powerful combination. The dirty-rectangle optimizations allow WinToon to achieve decent playback rates on full-screen animations. This is assuming that the "video" is actually a computer-generated cartoon and not normal video, where almost every pixel would change at least by a little from frame to frame. In order to get good performance, WinToon relies on the fact that not all of the screen needs updating each frame. WinToon's other major feature, programmable mixing of graphics both behind and in front of the "movie," allows these cartoons to have a degree of interactivity. WinG is used as the buffering mechanism for this mixing, which makes it fast and allows direct access to the buffer by the programmer. For instance, ARTT canvas-based rendering could be used for the programmable graphics. Figure 16.9 shows how the graphics and video are mixed and sent to the screen during the "playback" of a WinToon "movie."

WinToon requires the use of the MRLE codec in AVI files to be used with WinToon. This codec is a variant on the run-length encoding of DIBs and BMP files, which features uncompressed pixel dumps, pixel runs, and "jumps" over transparent pixels. MRLE requires 8-bit graphics. MRLE encodes the delta between frames, so scenes with large unchanging areas have big jumps in them. A frame which features no change from the previous frame can be encoded in 2 bytes! Run-length coding works well with large areas of solid color, and particularly well with scenes in which the camera remains stable, with small sprites flitting about the screen.

How WinToon Works

The steps to making an interactive cartoon are as follows:

1. Create an 8-bit animation using other tools, such as *Autodesk Animator Pro*. Use a digital video editing program to convert to AVI format, using the MRLE codec for video compression.
2. Run SCANAVI on the AVI file. This analyzes the video frames, and adds a third stream of type 'rect'. This stream contains the dirty-rectangle information. Each frame of the animation, which in the original AVI is typically a 'rec' chunk with a video frame and audio segment, has another segment added to it which consists of the dirty-rectangle set for that frame.

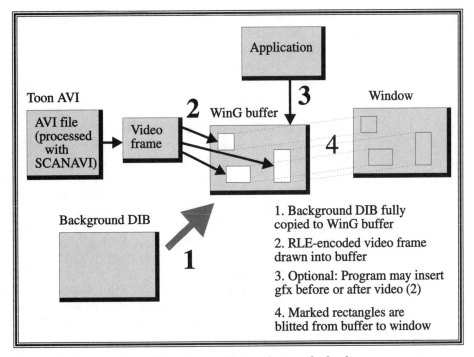

Figure 16.9 Overview of WinToon buffering during playback.

3. Write a program which plays the resulting AVI file, and provides computer-generated overlays and user interaction. This step is nontrivial, but an API provided as part of the WinToon DLL simplifies it considerably.

The SCANAVI Tool

SCANAVI's job is to add the dirty-rectangle information to an AVI file, so that WinToon can use it at runtime to optimize playback. SCANAVI adds a new stream to the file, of type 'rect'. It adds a stream header list for this stream inside the 'hdrl' list, alongside the video and audio stream headers. Then, embedded in the 'movi' chunk along with video frames and audio segments, it adds the dirty-rectangle set for each frame. Figure 16.10 gives an overview of what is added to an AVI file by SCANAVI.

As we've seen in the AScene class, there is no one "right" set of dirty rectangles to describe the difference between two frames. The easy approach would be to find the smallest rectangle which encloses all changed pixels. At the other extreme, a rectangle for each pixel could be specified, although this is clearly silly. SCANAVI adopts an interesting algorithm. It starts with the smallest enclosing rectangle, and then splits it in two, deciding based on some heuristics whether the split was worth it. If the savings to be gained in area are too small to justify the extra overhead of another rectangle and more calls at blit time, the split is discarded. If the split is kept, each of the two resulting rectangles is again split, recursively, until no new splits are acceptable. Some combining of rectangles is done as well.

SCANAVI, which is a Windows program, of course, displays a dialog which lets the animation author control the parameters controlling the split "acceptance" algorithm. Three parameters are under user control. These are listed in Table 16.9.

With all this work, SCANAVI is basically attempting to find the set of rectangles that will minimize blitting time. By the way, WinToon fully recomposes each frame in the off-screen buffer, and uses the rectangles only to minimize window blitting. In this sense it is simpler than AScene, which uses dirty rectangles for both the off-screen buffer and the screen. The optimal set of rectangles is unknowable, since the cartoon may be played back on a machine with different CPU speed and video card performance, and SCANAVI is trying to balance overhead (CPU) and blitting times (video card). But its approach makes sense for a wide range of machines; the user settings allow finer control by an author who knows what the target playback machine is likely to be.

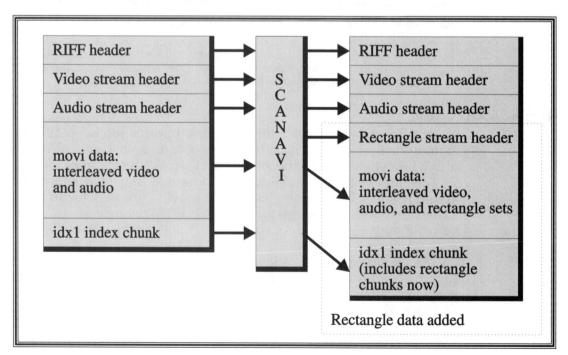

Figure 16.10   Sample AVI file before and after running SCANAVI.

Table 16.9   SCANAVI Rectangle Splitter Parameters

Parameter	*Meaning*
Overhead	Minimum number of pixels saved to justify split
Density	Percentage of active pixels below which split is justified
Fuzziness	Factor affecting combination of nearly intersecting rectangles

Could we use SCANAVI's algorithm in class AScene to speed scene rendering in ARTT? Unfortunately, no. For one thing, SCANAVI is working from a fixed set of frames, whereas AScene is collecting and combining rectangles on the fly as actors are moved around under the unpredictable control of a program. For another thing, SCANAVI can afford to spend a lot of time analyzing the frames, because it is running "off-line." AScene's rectangle manipulation is done as the program is running, and thus its overhead counts as part of what is being optimized.

Toon Playback

Once an AVI file has been processed with SCANAVI, it's ready to be used in a toon-enabled application. If all that's required is to play back the "toon" into a window, the process is no more complex than playing any other AVI file. The WinToon function ToonOpenMovie(), implemented as part of the WinToon API in WINTOON.DLL, is used to open the AVI file and return an MCI device id. Then, normal MCI functions such as mciSendCommand(), mciSendString(), and the MCIWndXxxx() set can be used to play back the toon, pause it, jump to a specified frame, and so on.

Why go to all this trouble just to play back the movie noninteractively? Well, the dirty-rectangle optimizations alone are worth a lot when playing back large animation files. A full-screen animation featuring largely unchanging background might be capable of 15 frames per second on a given machine instead of 5 or 6, and that's worth a lot. WinToon benefits from WinG's speed as well. This does mean, of course, that WinG as well as WinToon must be installed on the playback machine.

A modest amount of interactivity is easily programmed with little special effort. For instance, the window handler could trap WM_LBUTTONDOWN messages, check the mouse coordinates against a set of fixed hotspots, and issue commands which jump the movie to various ranges of frames. In this way, a "hypertext" branching movie could be constructed.

The WinToon API

For full-blown toon control, including overlaying of graphics on the fly, it's necessary to dig into the WinToon API, a set of functions built into WINTOON.DLL. Table 16.10 lists high-level functions used to control overall buffer and window management.

Table 16.11 lists the palette-related portion of the WinToon API. These functions are a thin layer above the basic Windows palette management functions.

The remainder of the WinToon API, listed in Table 16.12, is used to control rendering of the toon. Most of these functions come into play when rendering overlays (or underlays, beneath the active movie frames) along with the toon frames.

A final API function, ToonDefWindowProc(), is a default window procedure built into WINTOON.DLL. If the window procedure for a toon window calls ToonDefWindowProc() for unhandled window messages, much of the "right" behavior happens automatically. For instance:

- WM_CREATE is handled by a call to ToonCreate() to create the WinToon buffer into which frames will be composed.

- WM_DESTROY is handled by a call to ToonDestroy() to destroy the WinToon buffer.

- WM_ERASEBKGND is handled by doing nothing, since the background DIB will be drawn into any window area (DefWindowProc() would fill the area with white, which is unnecessary and causes flashing).

- WM_PAINT is handled by the calls BeginPaint(), ToonPaintDC() to copy from the buffer to the screen, and EndPaint().

- WM_QUERYNEWPALETTE is handled by a call to ToonRealizePalette(), followed by ToonMarkRect() and ToonPaintRects() to repaint the window if the system palette has changed.

- WM_PALETTECHANGED is handled similarly to WM_QUERYNEW-PALETTE, but only if the message has been broadcast from a window other than this one.

- Other messages are passed on to the standard DefWindowProc().

This section is not meant as a complete tutorial on WinToon, so don't worry if things don't seem too clear. WinToon is too big to adequately explain in these few pages; I'm just trying to impart the basics and a flavor for what's available. Before we leave WinToon, though, let's take a peek at how ARTT graphics might be used inside a WinToon interactive cartoon.

Table 16.10   WinToon API—Overall Management

Function	Description
ToonVersion	Return version number of WinToon
ToonOpenMovie	Open AVI file and return MCI device ID
ToonCreate	Create the WinToon buffer
ToonDestroy	Destroy the WinToon buffer
ToonFromWindow	Return WinToon handle, given window handle
ToonWindow	Return window handle, given WinToon handle
ToonDC	Return handle to the WinToon WinG device context
ToonSize	Return the size of the WinToon buffer
ToonResize	Resize the WinToon buffer
ToonIsTopDown	Determine whether WinToon bitmap is top-down
ToonGetDIBPointer	Get pointer to the WinToon buffer's DIB
ToonSetBackground	Set the background bitmap

Table 16.11   WinToon API—Palette control

ToonSetColors	Set the WinToon color table
ToonGetColors	Retrieve portion of WinToon color table
ToonAnimateColors	Call Animate Palette() on behalf of toon
ToonRealizePalette	Realize the WinToon palette

ARTT Graphics in WinToon

A simple WinToon application supplies two sources of imagery: a background DIB, and the AVI file containing the foreground animation. WinToon mixes these two together into the WinG compose buffer, and then blits the changed areas to the screen.

A WinToon program can, however, add its own graphic overlays. Furthermore, it can add them under the animation (between the background and the animation), on top of the animation, or both! This magic is achieved by setting a frame-draw callback using Toon-SetMessage(), passing in the address of the function that WinToon should call every time there is a new AVI frame available. Instead of the default behavior of composing the frame and the background

Table 16.12   WinToon API—Rendering Control

ToonDrawCurrentFrame	Draw current AVI frame into WinToon buffer
ToonSetMessage	Set the WinToon frame-draw callback
ToonMessage	Return the WinToon frame-draw callback
ToonMarkRect	Mark rectangle as dirty
ToonMarkRectList	Mark list of rectangles as dirty
ToonClearRects	Clear the dirty-rectangle list
ToonPaintRects	Paint the screen areas in the dirty-rectangle list
ToonPaintDC	Repaint the screen from the WinToon buffer
ToonRestoreBackground	Restore background for a new frame
ToonSetPaintMethod	Set the WinToon drawing algorithm
ToonPaintMethod	Return the WinToon drawing algorithm
ToonSetPaintList	Set the current paint rectangle list
ToonPaintList	Return the current paint rectangle list
ToonGetRectHeader	Get header of rectangle info

together, the user-defined callback can perform its own composition, including mixing in its own graphics.

Where do these new graphics come from? Anywhere. Any GDI graphics call can be made to render graphics before or after the AVI frame has been drawn. And since the compose buffer is a WinG buffer, whose DIB is accessible, graphics rendered through non-GDI means (ARTT, anyone?) can be used as well. When new graphics are rendered into the compose buffer, care must be taken to inform WinToon that the affected areas must be added to the list of rectangular areas in need of blitting. This is done by calling Toon-MarkRect() or ToonMarkRectList() to add new rectangular areas to the blit list.

Let's get more concrete. Below is a sample callback function, showing the structure that such a function takes and where to add in the rendering code.

```
void SampleToonDrawCallback(HWND hwnd, HTOON htoon, LONG lframe)
{
// By the time we're here, the background has already been placed in the
// compose buffer.
```

```
// If we want to draw below the AVI frame, insert drawing code here:

    HDC hdc = ToonDC(htoon);
    ...render using GDI, or use ToonGetDIBPtr() and render by hand ...
    ToonMarkRect(...); // mark any rectangular areas rendered into

// Now, draw the AVI frame

    ToonDrawCurrentFrame(htoon);

// Now the background and AVI frame are rendered, may add on top

    ... render on top of everything using GDI or hand-rendering ...
    ToonMarkRect(...); // mark areas rendered in this case too
}
```

Imagine a new WinToon scene class, called ASceneWinToon, derived from ASceneWin. Such a class might feature the following methods:

- Constructor: Set up toon, including calls to ToonOpenMovie() and ToonCreate(). Also install a rendering callback, called, for instance, DrawToonArtt(), using ToonSetMessage().
- Destructor: Tear down movie, including call to ToonDestroy().
- RedrawAndBlit: Do nothing! All rendering will be done in the callback installed by ToonSetMessage() in the constructor. This empty override method is needed to avoid having ASceneWin::RedrawAndBlit() do its thing.
- Blit: Unchanged. WinToon takes care of blitting.
- DrawToonArtt: This rendering callback is where the real action takes place. Traverse the scene's actor list, rendering actors and marking their areas with ToonMarkRect(), so that they will be blitted. Those with a z-position greater than some arbitrary or settable "foreground depth" are rendered before the call to ToonDrawCurrentFrame(), and those with closer z-positions are rendered after it. In this way, some of the actors can be behind the video animation, and some in front of it.

Such a scene class would marry WinToon with the full suite of animation features built into ARTT. Well, I've run out of time, not to say pages. But perhaps you might want to pick up the ball and run with this one. One complication you need to address is the possibility of bottom-up WinG DIBs for the WinToon buffer, which will result in upside-down overlays if not taken into account. Using flipped images is the easiest of the possibilities here.

Where's the Code?

This chapter has been long on discussion and very short on code. The design and coding of a digital video system from the ground up could easily fill its own book. Under DOS, there are no standard solutions, and without a massive effort we're simply out of luck. Under Windows, happily, two solid solutions exist, QuickTime for Windows and Video for Windows. Unlike animation, where we can, in fact, write code that performs better than Windows' GDI for our needs, we'd be hard-pressed to outdo Cinepak or Indeo for digital video compression and playback performance. And now that digital video decompression is being built into hardware on-board video cards, there's no point in even trying to roll our own. Enjoy the ride. Learn MCI and even WinToon.

Another aspect of video hardware that is beginning to percolate is in the area of 3D. Boards are emerging that can fill polygons in hardware, and polygons are the basic building blocks of most 3D systems. But it's going to be a while before hardware takes over the world of three dimensions on desktop PCs. For now, 3D programming belongs to the programmers. So let's do it before it's too late! See you in the next chapter.

17

Three-Dimensional Math and Polygon Rendering

Up to this point, the focus in this book has been on two-dimensional graphics. Bitmaps, rectangles, lines, frame animation, dirty-rectangle composing, digital video: These are all concepts that relate to a 2D approach to screen rendering. That's not to say that we haven't already learned some tricks relevant to three-dimensional screens. Scaled bitmaps are at the heart of most "pseudo-3D games," and the shading and hazing tables of Part 3 are used by 3D programmers to help provide the illusion of depth.

In the next three chapters, however, we're going to veer our attention sharply, straight into the land of the third dimension. This chapter will lay the foundations of matrix math and polygon rendering. We'll follow that up with texture mapping, and then discuss a wide range of issues related to 3D scene rendering.

First, the basics.

Three-Dimensional Concepts

If we are interested in the representation and rendering of three-dimensional objects and scenes, we'd better start by figuring out where this third dimension lives. Our two-dimensional world has been based on a coordinate system described by x- and y-axes, as shown in Figure 17.1. Our "scene and actor" system uses two-and-a-half dimensions, adding a z-coordinate for the purpose of depth sorting and even "cheap 3D" scaling of bitmapped objects. Now, we're going to create a real 3D coordinate system.

Three-Dimensional Coordinate System

We can extend our coordinate system by adding a real third z-axis. The 3D coordinate system we'll use for ARTT won't just add a z-axis to ARTT's 2D coordinate system, however. Instead, we're going to go with the more standard coordinate system used in most computer graphics systems. Here, the y axis will point up instead of down (going from negative to positive), and the z-axis points out of the screen. This is mathematically more desirable, as we'll see in a minute. The fact that it doesn't match our 2D coordinate system very well doesn't really matter, as we have to do some pretty heavy math to convert 3D coordinates into 2D screen coordinates anyway, and reversing the direction of the y-axis is the least of our troubles.

This new ARTT 3D coordinate system, depicted in Figure 17.2, is a "right-handed" coordinate system.[1] A right-handed system is one in which, as you hold your right hand so that your fingers curl from the positive x-axis to y-axis, your thumb points in the positive direction

---

[1] Actually, so was our pseudo-3D one.

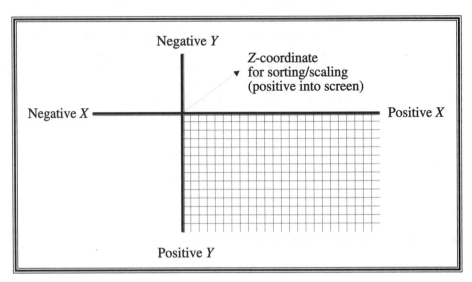

Figure 17.1 ARTT's 2D coordinate system, with third z-coordinate for sorting/scaling.

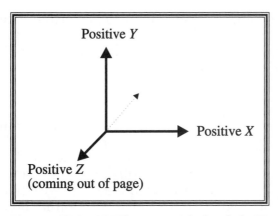

Figure 17.2 ARTT's new right-handed 3D coordinate system.

of the z-axis. Left-handed coordinate systems, in which your thumb would point in the negative direction of the z-axis, are okay and sometimes used too—you just have to be consistent in the math.

Now that we have a coordinate system, we have a way of describing where points and objects are within it. A location in 3D space is defined by three values. Instead of simply an x,y pair, an x,y,z triplet is required. Such a triplet is often called a *vector,* and can be used to describe not only points but also such things as directions and velocities (just as an x,y pair can be used to denote an angle or velocity in two-dimensional space). Shortly we will develop a class, AVector, which can manipulate and perform math on such vectors.

Local, World, View, and Screen Coordinate Systems

Working in three dimensions requires that you get comfortable with more than one *coordinate space.* By this I don't mean other systems in which x goes left instead of right or z goes into the screen. I mean standard, right-handed, 3D coordinate systems, but with different reference points. Even a simple 3D rendering approach usually goes through the following steps when rendering 3D objects onto the screen:

1. Transform object's 3D *local coordinates* into 3D *world coordinates.*
2. Transform 3D world coordinates into camera's 3D *view coordinates.*
3. Project 3D view coordinates onto 2D *screen coordinates.*

Let's get more concrete, and work through these three *transformations* in the context of an example. Let's start with a cube, which is a pretty simple object. How would we define such an object? Let's forget for a moment anything about the coloring of each face, and just concentrate on the shape. Perhaps we intend to draw it in a "wireframe" mode, in which case only the corner points and edge connection information are needed.

Local Coordinates

The eight corners of the cube need to be defined in some coordinate system. Since it may exist at any location in the "world" at any orientation (it may be rotated instead of upright), we don't really want to define our cube in such world coordinates. Let's define the cube in a "local" coordinate system, private to the cube. We'll put the center of its interior at the origin (0,0,0), and align it to the three axes. Figure 17.3 shows how such a cube might be represented.

World Coordinates

Now, suppose we want the cube to exist in some place in the world, perhaps at the location 150,100,–400. Suppose further that the cube has rotated. The cube can be thought of as having a rotation, or orientation, about each of the three axes. Such a cube needs to be *translated* and *rotated* in order to convert its corners from its local coordinate system to world coordinates. See Figure 17.4.

View Coordinates

Now that this cube exists in world coordinates, we'd like to view it on our screen, perhaps in some window. But what does this mean? How

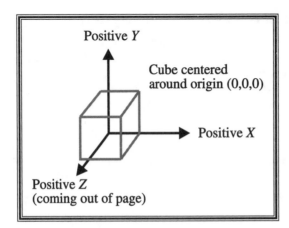

Figure 17.3 Cube defined in local coordinate system, centered around origin.

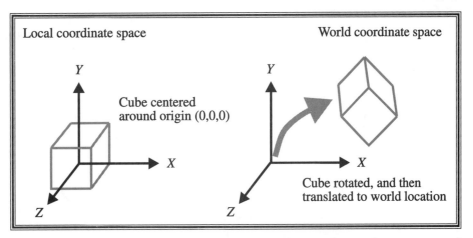

Figure 17.4 Cube converted from local to world coordinates by rotation and translation.

does the screen, which is two-dimensional, relate to our three-dimensional world coordinates? We need a camera, located somewhere in world coordinates and pointing in some direction, with some *field of view* (zoom level). Then, we can figure how to represent the cube on our screen, as seen through this virtual camera.

This is a two-step process as usually implemented. This first step is to map the cube's world coordinates into the reference frame of the camera. This simplifies the second step, which is *projecting* these points onto the screen. I think it was Einstein who said that everything's relative, so we're going to take him at his word and create a *view coordinate system,* with its origin at the location of the camera, its *z*-axis pointing along the line of the camera's direction, and its *x*- and *y*-axes aligned with the camera's tilt. Then we can map the cube's world coordinates into these view coordinates, as Figure 17.5 shows. We're still in a 3D coordinate system now, just one that treats the camera as the center of the universe.

Screen Coordinates

Now that we have a cube in the reference frame of the camera, the process of projecting its corners onto the 2D screen space is relatively trivial, as we'll see later in this chapter. It's essentially a matter of dividing the *x*- and *y*-coordinates of the points by their depth (*z*-coordinate), making sure to treat the signs correctly and flip the *y*-coordinate so that positive faces down. Figure 17.6 illustrates.

There you have it: 3D, or at least basic 3D, in a nutshell. The rest is details, and plenty of them. Starting with some math.

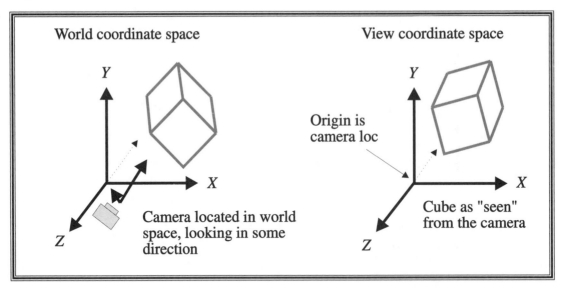

Figure 17.5   Cube converted from world to view coordinates, in the reference frame of the camera.

Vectors

The three-dimensional points, represented by their $x, y,$ and z components, go by another name in traditional 3D graphics. They are called *vectors*. A 3D vector essentially describes some amount of motion along each of three axes—these are the $x, y,$ and z components of the vector. When we use a vector to describe a point in 3D space, we are

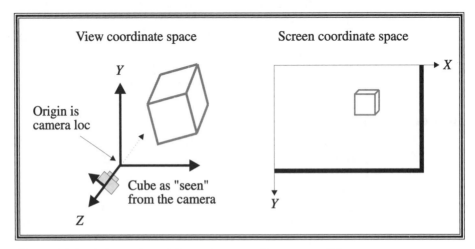

Figure 17.6   Cube projected from view coordinates onto 2D screen.

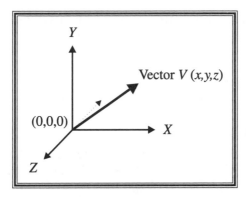

Figure 17.7 A vector can be thought of as a 3D point, or as movement from the origin.

in essence denoting how much motion must occur along each axis to travel from the origin (0,0,0) to that point, as Figure 17.7 shows.

A three-dimensional vector is usually denoted by three components within brackets, for instance:

$$[x\ y\ z]$$

such as:

$$[14\ 20\ -108]$$

Vectors, along with another mathematical construct called a *matrix*, lie at the heart of the mathematical manipulations which are used in transforming 3D points from one coordinate system to another.

Vector Length and Normalized Vectors

Vectors can be used to describe points in 3D space, as we have seen. Vectors can also, not surprisingly, be used to denote the distance between two points (treat one of them as the "origin," and find the vector to the other). One useful bit of information about a given vector is its length, also called its *magnitude*. The magnitude of a 3D vector is an extrapolation of the Pythagorean theorem used to calculate the length of a 2D line:

```
d = sqrt(x*x + y*y + z*z);      // square root of sum of squares
```

A vector which has all of its components divided by this magnitude *d* is called a *normalized vector,* meaning that it has a magnitude of 1.0.

```
Length of [4 -2 4] = sqrt(4*4 + (-2)*(-2) + 4*4) = sqrt(36) = 6
Normalized vector = [4/6 -2/6 4/6] = [.667 -.333 .667]
```

Adding and Subtracting Vectors

Vectors can be added and subtracted. While adding two points may not seem sensible, thinking of vectors as distances along each axis clears things up. To add two vectors, just add the components (distances) along each axis. Thus,

$$[10\ 20\ 30] + [15\ 3\ -20] = [25\ 23\ 10]$$ // just add each component separately

Similarly,

$$[10\ 20\ 30] - [15\ 3\ -20] = [-5\ 17\ 50]$$ // subtract each component in 2nd from 1st

Scaling Vectors

A vector may be scaled in length by multiplying all its components by the same value. This multiplies the length of the vector without changing its "direction," which is the relative ratio of the *x, y,* and *z* components. An example of multiplication by such a *scalar* value is given below.

$$[5\ 10\ -8] * 2 = [10\ 20\ -16]$$ // scale components by 2, length is doubled

Division by a scalar value is equivalent to multiplication by the value's reciprocal.

Angles and Vectors

As stated before, vectors can be thought of as having a "direction" in three-dimensional space. Also, two vectors have an angle between them. Angles are typically measured in radians, where 2π radians equals 360 degrees, a full circle. Angles are measured in a counter-clockwise direction, as shown in Figure 17.8.

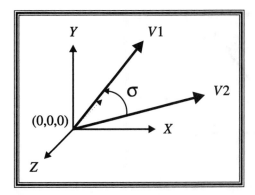

Figure 17.8 Two vectors, and the angle formed between them.

Vector Dot Product

It turns out that there are two useful ways in which to "multiply" two vectors together. The vector *dot product,* also called *inner product,* is the sum of the products of each component. More concretely,

$$A \cdot B = A_xB_x + A_yB_y + A_zB_z$$

The dot product has the interesting property of equaling the product of the magnitude (length) of the two vectors times the cosine of the angle between them. That is,

$$A \cdot B = Mag(A) \;*\; Mag(B) \;*\; cos(\sigma)$$

Vector Cross-Product and Normal Vectors

A different product of two vectors is the *cross-product,* also called *outer product.* The cross-product of two vectors is itself a vector, one whose length is the product of the lengths of the two vectors times the sine of the angle between them. The direction of the result vector is more important than its length, however, as it points perpendicularly to the plane in which the two vectors lie. See Figure 17.9. When normalized to unit length, the vector generated by the cross-product is called a *normal vector.*

The ability to compute a vector which points perpendicularly to a plane can be used to find which surfaces face away from the camera, and thus should not be drawn. As it turns out, we'll bypass the cross-product in favor of a more optimal test, but the cross-product is still a useful part of a 3D system. Its mathematical formula is as follows:

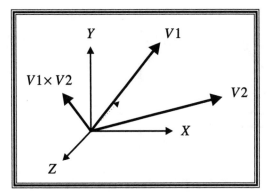

Figure 17.9 The cross-product of two vectors is a third vector, perpendicular to the plane formed by the two vectors.

$$R = A \times B \rightarrow$$
$$R_x = A_y B_z - A_z B_x$$
$$R_x = A_z B_x - A_x B_z$$
$$R_z = A_x B_x - A_x B_x$$

Class AVector

It may still be unclear exactly how we're going to use vectors to manipulate and render 3D objects, but all will become apparent before this chapter is out. In the meantime, let's whip up a simple vector class to implement the concepts listed in the last section. We're going to use floating point numbers for all our 3D math and coordinates. At only 8 bits of fraction, our fixed-point class doesn't really have enough precision to handle some of the calculations we'll be doing without accumulating some serious roundoff error. If you have a Pentium, the good news is that your computer multiplies floating-point numbers faster than fixed-point ones anyway, and multiplication is most of what we'll be doing.

The data members in class AVector will be three floating-point numbers, named 'x', 'y', and 'z'. The operations performed on them will use operator overloading where appropriate. For instance, it's handy to be able to add one vector to another just by typing:

*V*1 += *V*2;   // add vector *V*2 to vector *V*1

The header file for class AVector is listed below. It's definitely worth looking over the method definitions, most of which are inlined for performance.

Since the dot product and cross product operations take the same arguments (two vectors), operator* can't be used for both. Rather than play favorites, both operations are invoked via named methods. Operator* with a single floating-point argument is used for scaling, though.

```cpp
//    AVector.h      3-D vector class
//    Rex E. Bradford

#ifndef __AVECTOR_H
#define __AVECTOR_H

#include <math.h>

class AVector {
public:

    float x,y,z; // 3 floating-point values

// Constructors and assignment

    AVector() {}
    AVector(float x_, float y_, float z_) {x = x_; y = y_; z = z_;}

    AVector &operator=(AVector &v) {x = v.x; y = v.y; z = v.z;
        return *this;}

// Adding vectors together

    AVector &operator+=(AVector &v) {x += v.x; y += v.y; z += v.z;
        return *this;}
    AVector &operator-=(AVector &v) {x -= v.x; y -= v.y; z -= v.z;
        return *this;}

    friend AVector operator+(AVector &a, AVector &b) {
        AVector r;
        r.x = a.x + b.x; r.y = a.y + b.y; r.z = a.z + b.z;
        return r;}

    friend AVector operator-(AVector &a, AVector &b) {
        AVector r;
        r.x = a.x - b.x; r.y = a.y - b.y; r.z = a.z - b.z;
        return r;}

// Scaling vectors
```

```
    AVector &operator*=(float s) {x *= s; y *= s; z *= s;
        return *this;}

    friend AVector operator* (AVector &v, float s) {
        AVector r;
        r.x = v.x * s; r.y = v.y * s; r.z = v.z * s;
        return r;}

// Vector length and normalization

    float Length() {return sqrt((x * x) + (y * y) + (z * z));}
    void Normalize();

// Vector products and normal vector calc

    friend float DotProduct(AVector &a, AVector &b) {
        return((a.x * b.x) + (a.y * b.y) + (a.z * b.z));}
    friend AVector CrossProduct (AVector &a, AVector &b);
    friend AVector Normal(AVector &a, AVector &b, AVector &c);
};

#endif
```

AVector Methods

Three of AVector's methods, Normalize(), CrossProduct(), and Normal(), are too big to be inlined effectively. They are listed below.

```
// Normalize() normalizes a vector to unit length.

void AVector::Normalize()
{
    float recipLength = 1.0 / Length();
    *this *= recipLength;
}


// CrossProduct() computes the cross product of two vectors, and
// returns the resulting vector.

AVector CrossProduct (AVector &a, AVector &b)
{
    AVector r;
    r.x = (a.y * b.z) - (a.z * b.y);
    r.y = (a.z * b.x) - (a.x * b.z);
    r.z = (a.x * b.y) - (a.y * b.x);
    return r;
}


// Normal() computes a vector perpendicular to a plane, where that
// plane is defined by three points. The direction of the normal
// vector is outwards from the convex angle defined by a->b->c, where
```

```
// the connection moves in a counter-clockwise direction. The
// resulting normal vector is normalized before being returned.

AVector Normal(AVector &a, AVector &b, AVector &c)
{
   AVector norm = CrossProduct(b - a, b - c);
   norm.Normalize();
   return norm;
}
```

Polygons and Polyhedra

Ok, what do we have so far? We have vectors, which can be used to represent locations in a 3D coordinate system. Not only that, they can also be used to represent directions in three-dimensional space. We've got a class, AVector, that implements some basic operations on vectors.

Now, how do we go about using these vectors to describe and render three-dimensional graphic objects? This begs the question of what our 3D objects even look like. Previously, we've seen how we can scale bitmaps to any appropriate size based on "depth," and we can imagine selecting from predrawn bitmaps which show an object at some particular angle. In this chapter, however, we're going to drop bitmaps in favor of the standard representation in "real" computer graphics: *polyhedral* objects—that is, objects built from *polygons*.

Polygons

A polygon is a bounded planar (flat) surface. Its boundaries are defined by its vertices, which are the "corners" of the polygon. A triangle is the simplest polygon, containing three vertices and thus three sides. Polygons may have three, four, five, or more sides.

Polygons can be classified according to their "complexity." A *convex* polygon is one whose interior angles are all less than 180 degrees. Any line drawn through the polygon intersects its edges at most twice. A *concave* polygon has one or more angles greater than 180 degrees, and doesn't fulfill the two-intersection limit. Convex polygons can be rendered with simpler and faster methods than concave polygons. More complex still are *self-intersecting* polygons, where it isn't necessarily clear what areas lie inside the polygon and what areas lie outside. Figure 17.10 shows some polygons of various types.

Each vertex of a polygon which exists in three-dimensional space can be represented by a vector. The full polygon can be represented by an ordered list of such vectors, arranged in either clockwise or coun-

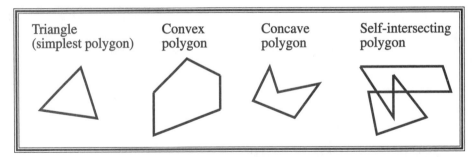

Figure 17.10   Various types of polygons.

terclockwise order. In ARTT, we will work with only convex polygons, and will arrange their vertices in counterclockwise order.

Polyhedral Objects

A set of polygons in 3D space can be put together to build a full three-dimensional object called a *polyhedron* (plural: *polyhedra*). A *convex polyhedron* is one whose interior angles are all less than 180 degrees. An interesting property of a convex polyhedron is that, no matter what angle it is viewed from, no visible face obscures another face that would otherwise be visible (only those that are facing away are obscured). Figure 17.11 shows a convex polyhedron, and one that is nonconvex.

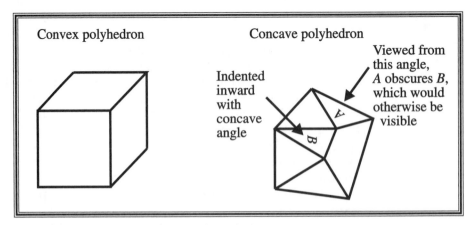

Figure 17.11   Convex and concave polyhedra. In the concave case, polygon *A* can obscure polygon *B,* which would otherwise be visible from the camera.

The faces of polyhedra are polygons. Polygons may be rendered with a solid color, with various smooth shading techniques, or with bitmaps in a process known as texture mapping. For now, let's not worry about how the polygons are rendered and drawn. Even if we're going to color each face with a solid color, we still need to figure out how the shape of a 3D polyhedron gets converted into some form which can be viewed on a two-dimensional screen. We need to transform its representation, and for that we're going to use a mathematical construct called a matrix.

Matrices and Transformations

Earlier in this chapter, we talked about the process of transforming coordinates from local space to world space to view space, and finally to screen space. Now we know that the coordinates we're interested in transforming are vectors, and they represent the vertices of polygons in our polyhedral object. The job at hand, then, is to transform a vector from one coordinate system to another. The types of transformations we want to achieve are the following:

Scaling	Scale magnitude of a vector
Rotation	Rotate vector about some point or axis
Translation	Move a vector some direction in x, y, z

All the transformations we are interested in, except the final perspective transformation which maps 3D view coordinates onto 2D screen coordinates, involve some combination of these three types of transformations.

Matrix Basics

A matrix is a two-dimensional array of numbers. In ARTT, we will be working with 3×3 matrices, having 3 rows and 3 columns. An example of a matrix is

$$M = \begin{bmatrix} 1 & 2 & 3 \\ 4 & 5 & 6 \\ 7 & 8 & 9 \end{bmatrix}$$

What do the numbers in the matrices really mean? That's a big question, and one which is outside the scope of this book. Matrices are well-defined in mathematics with rules governing their manipulation; what we're interested in here is what matrices can do for us.

Multiplying a Vector by a Matrix

One important thing we can do is multiply a vector by a matrix. When we do so, we get a new vector as the result. This operation will be the primary means by which we can transform vectors from one coordinate space to another. All we need is the right matrix. The multiplication of a vector by a matrix is shown below:

$$[V_x \ V_y \ V_z] \times \begin{bmatrix} M_0 & M_1 & M_2 \\ M_3 & M_4 & M_5 \\ M_6 & M_7 & M_8 \end{bmatrix} = [(V_xM_0 + V_yM_3 + V_zM_6) \ (V_xM_1 + V_yM_4 + V_zM_7) \ (V_xM_2 + V_yM_5 + V_zM_8)]$$

Each of the three components of the resulting vector is the sum of the products of the three original vector components times a different column of the matrix.

Multiplying Two Matrices

Another useful computation is the multiplication of a matrix by another matrix, which produces a matrix result. In the case of two 3 × 3 matrices, the formula for the multiplication is given below:

$$\begin{bmatrix} A0 & A1 & A2 \\ A3 & A4 & A5 \\ A6 & A7 & A8 \end{bmatrix} \times \begin{bmatrix} B0 & B1 & B2 \\ B3 & B4 & B5 \\ B6 & B7 & B8 \end{bmatrix} =$$

$$\begin{bmatrix} (A0B0 + A1B3 + A2B6) & (A0B1 + A1B4 + A2B7) & (A0B2 + A1B5 + A2B8) \\ (A3B0 + A4B3 + A5B6) & (A3B1 + A4B4 + A5B7) & (A3B2 + A4B5 + A5B8) \\ (A6B0 + A7B3 + A8B6) & (A6B1 + A7B4 + A8B7) & (A6B2 + A7B5 + A8B8) \end{bmatrix}$$

Matrix multiplication is associative but not commutative. That is, *AB* is not the same as *BA*, but (*AB*)*C* is the same as *A*(*BC*). This property is very useful in computer graphics, particularly high-end 3D systems which feature complex objects built of subparts which have their own local coordinate systems. If each of the transformations needed to scale, rotate, or translate a vector into a new coordinate system is described by a matrix, then these matrices can be *concatenated* together, and the full set of transformations applied all at once.

Scaling Transformations

Now that we have seen the basic matrix math, let's see how we construct matrices capable of performing typical transformations. The first case we'll examine is the scaling transformation, which multiplies each component of a vector by a scaling factor. The scaling factors need not be the same for the three components.

The matrix which performs scaling is given below:

$$S = \begin{bmatrix} Sx & 0 & 0 \\ 0 & Sy & 0 \\ 0 & 0 & Sz \end{bmatrix}$$

Let's work out the math to see for ourselves:

$$[Vx \ Vy \ Vz] \times \begin{bmatrix} Sx & 0 & 0 \\ 0 & Sy & 0 \\ 0 & 0 & Sz \end{bmatrix} = [(VxSx + 0 + 0) \ (0 + VySy + 0) \ (0 + 0 + VzSz)]$$

It works! Each component of the vector is scaled by the appropriate scaling factor in the scaling matrix.

Take a look at the following matrix:

$$\begin{bmatrix} 1 & 0 & 0 \\ 0 & 1 & 0 \\ 0 & 0 & 1 \end{bmatrix}$$

When a vector is multiplied by this special matrix, it scales each component by 1. The result is same as the original vector. This special matrix, with 1 along the diagonal and 0 elsewhere, has a name. It is called the *identity matrix*. Its special property applies for multiplication by another matrix too—multiplying a matrix by the identity matrix yields the original matrix.

Rotation Matrices

Rotating a vector implies an axis of rotation, about which the rotation can occur. Rather than covering the general case of rotation about any axis, we're going to restrict our discussion to rotations about one of the three coordinate axes. Rotation about the *x*, *y*, and *z* axes is depicted in Figure 17.12.

The elements in a rotation matrix are the sines and cosines of the angle of rotation. In our right-handed coordinate system, positive angles move in a counterclockwise direction, when looking down an axis from positive to negative.

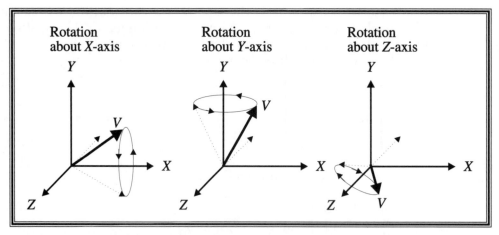

Figure 17.12   Rotation of a vector about the *x*, *y*, and *z* axes.

The matrices for rotation about the three axes are given below:

$$Rx = \begin{bmatrix} 1 & 0 & 0 \\ 0 & \cos(\sigma) & \sin(\sigma) \\ 0 & -\sin(\sigma) & \cos(\sigma) \end{bmatrix}$$

$$Ry = \begin{bmatrix} \cos(\sigma) & 0 & -\sin(\sigma) \\ 0 & 1 & 0 \\ \sin(\sigma) & 0 & \cos(\sigma) \end{bmatrix}$$

$$Rz = \begin{bmatrix} \cos(\sigma) & \sin(\sigma) & 0 \\ -\sin(\sigma) & \cos(\sigma) & 0 \\ 0 & 0 & 1 \end{bmatrix}$$

Translation and Homogeneous Coordinates

Now we come to translation, arguably the simplest transformation of all. Translation is accomplished by adding some amount to each of the *x*, *y*, and *z* components of the vector. So what's a translation matrix look like?

Good question, bad answer. There isn't any 3 × 3 matrix which can be multiplied by a vector to accomplish translation. Sorry. Guess we should pack up our bags and head back to Flatland! Actually, we have two choices besides giving up. One is to simply use math other than matrix multiplication for translation. In fact, simple vector addition clearly works:

$$[Vx\ Vy\ Vz] + [Tx\ Ty\ Tz] = [(Vx + Tx)\ (Vy + Ty)\ (Vz + Tz)]$$

There is one hitch in this little scheme. Earlier, we noted that we could concatenate the matrices for all our transformations together into one "master" matrix, and then multiply our vectors by it to accomplish all the transformations at once. If we're only converting one vector, doing this isn't worth the trouble, but the picture changes if we have a set of transformations we want to apply to a large number of vectors. By concatenating the matrices together into one master matrix, we can save time, because then each vector need only be multiplied by the single matrix. But if translation can't be done with matrix multiplication, we can't build such a master matrix, because we have to insert translation at various steps along the way.

The way out of this dilemma, for most 3D systems, is to use *homogeneous coordinates*, and 4×4 matrices instead of 3×3. Homogeneous coordinates are outside the scope of this book, and we won't use them in ARTT. Instead, we'll perform our transformations in a few stages, interspersed with translation by vector addition when needed. For our simple uses, this approach can actually be more efficient, since multiplying with 3×3 matrices involves far less calculations than with 4×4 matrices. Homogeneous coordinates really become handy when sub-object nesting is used such that each vector needs conversion through several coordinate systems, or when matrix multiplication hardware is available. For us, with simpler needs and no hardware, it's a toss-up.

For more information on homogeneous coordinates and how 4×4 matrices solve the matrix concatenation problem, consult any book on 3D geometry, such as *Computer Graphics: Principles and Practice*. Appendix E lists several good sources.

Class AMatrix

Before we start using matrices to transform our polygon vertices from local to world to view space, let's look at class AMatrix, which implements a 3×3 matrix. As in the AVector class, we'll use floats for our elements, to avoid precision problems. Class AMatrix includes two constructors and an assignment operator; the members are public too, so that elements may be assigned by hand. It also features two methods:

SetIdentity()	Set the matrix elements to the values of the identity matrix
ScaleXYZ()	Scale each column by the appropriate component of the specified vector

and two friend functions:

operator*()	Multiply a matrix by a vector, yielding a vector
operator*()	Multiply a matrix by a matrix, yielding a matrix (operator* is overloaded)

The header file for class AMatrix is listed below:

```
//    AMatrix.h     3x3 matrix class
//    Rex E. Bradford

#ifndef __AMATRIX_H
#define __AMATRIX_H

#include <string.h>
#include "avector.h"

//    Matrix layout:
//
//    m[0] m[1] m[2]
//    m[3] m[4] m[5]
//    m[6] m[7] m[8]

class AMatrix {
public:
    float m[9]; // array of [9] is quicker to access than [3][3]

// Constructors and assignment

AMatrix() {}
AMatrix(float m00, float m01, float m02, float m10, float m11,
    float m12, float m20, float m21, float m22) {
    m[0] = m00; m[1] = m01; m[2] = m02;
    m[3] = m10; m[4] = m11; m[5] = m12;
    m[6] = m20; m[7] = m21; m[8] = m22;
    }
AMatrix &operator=(AMatrix &a) {
    memcpy(m, a.m, sizeof(m)); return *this;}
void SetIdentity() {memset(m, 0, sizeof(m));
    m[0] = 1; m[4] = 1; m[8] = 1;}

// Matrix computations

    void ScaleXYZ(AVector &v);
    friend AVector operator*(AVector &v, AMatrix &m);
    friend AMatrix operator*(AMatrix &a, AMatrix &b);
};

#endif
```

AMatrix Methods and Friend Functions

The ScaleXYZ() method scales each column of the matrix by a different scaling factor, as given by a three-element vector. ARTT's virtual camera uses this function when constructing the world-to-view transformation matrix, to control for the field of view of the camera in horizontal and vertical directions.

```
void AMatrix::ScaleXYZ(AVector &v)
{
    m[0] *= v.x;    // scale first column by vector's x
    m[3] *= v.x;
    m[6] *= v.x;

    m[1] *= v.y;    // scale second column by vector's y
    m[4] *= v.y;
    m[7] *= v.y;

    m[2] *= v.z;    // scale third column by vector's z
    m[5] *= v.z;
    m[8] *= v.z;
}
```

The first operator* takes a vector and matrix as arguments, and returns a vector result. This multiplication of a vector by a matrix is the fundamental operation used in transforming polygon vertices from one coordinate system to another. Overloading the multiplication operator allows us to use convenient syntax, such as:

```
// Example of multiplying a vector times a matrix
AVector v(0,0,50);
AMatrix m(10,20,30,100,200,300,9,5,3);
AVector vresult = v * m;
```

Here's the implementation, for which we've already seen the formula:

```
AVector operator*(AVector &v, AMatrix &m)
{
    return AVector(
        (v.x * m.m[0]) + (v.y * m.m[3]) + (v.z * m.m[6]),
        (v.x * m.m[1]) + (v.y * m.m[4]) + (v.z * m.m[7]),
        (v.x * m.m[2]) + (v.y * m.m[5]) + (v.z * m.m[8]));
}
```

The second operator* takes two matrices, and returns a matrix as its result. Multiplying matrices is the way in which transformations can be concatenated together. Even though we won't be building a "master matrix" in ARTT, we still want to be able to concatenate together the three rotation matrices for a given coordinate system transformation, so this method will still be quite handy.

650

```
AMatrix operator*(AMatrix &a, AMatrix &b)
{
    AMatrix r;

    r.m[0] = (a.m[0] * b.m[0]) + (a.m[1] * b.m[3]) + (a.m[2] * b.m[6]);
    r.m[1] = (a.m[0] * b.m[1]) + (a.m[1] * b.m[4]) + (a.m[2] * b.m[7]);
    r.m[2] = (a.m[0] * b.m[2]) + (a.m[1] * b.m[5]) + (a.m[2] * b.m[8]);
    r.m[3] = (a.m[3] * b.m[0]) + (a.m[4] * b.m[3]) + (a.m[5] * b.m[6]);
    r.m[4] = (a.m[3] * b.m[1]) + (a.m[4] * b.m[4]) + (a.m[5] * b.m[7]);
    r.m[5] = (a.m[3] * b.m[2]) + (a.m[4] * b.m[5]) + (a.m[5] * b.m[8]);
    r.m[6] = (a.m[6] * b.m[0]) + (a.m[7] * b.m[3]) + (a.m[8] * b.m[6]);
    r.m[7] = (a.m[6] * b.m[1]) + (a.m[7] * b.m[4]) + (a.m[8] * b.m[7]);
    r.m[8] = (a.m[6] * b.m[2]) + (a.m[7] * b.m[5]) + (a.m[8] * b.m[8]);

    return r;
}
```

The Perspective-Viewing Pipeline

Let's review our goal for this chapter. We're interested in taking a polyhedron, or at least one polygon (face) of such an object, and representing it on the screen. This will involve transforming its vertices from a local coordinate system to a world coordinate system, then to a view coordinate system, and finally to the screen coordinate system.

Let's talk more concretely about what the steps might be for a single polygon:

1. Rotate polygon to its desired orientation in world coordinates.
2. Translate polygon from local coordinates to world coordinates.
3. Translate polygon from world coordinates to view coordinates.
4. Rotate polygon about camera's orientation.
5. Scale polygon based on viewport aspect ratio and field-of-view.
6. Project polygon's view coordinates onto screen coordinates.
7. Draw the projected polygon!

Steps 1 and 2 comprise the transformation from local coordinates to world coordinates, and we can implement them using the vector and matrix math encountered so far. To rotate a polygon in any of x, y, and z, we construct a matrix which is the concatenation of three rotation matrices, one for each axis of rotation. Then we multiply each polygon vertex by this matrix. To translate the rotated polygon to world coordinates (step 2), we just use vector addition to offset each vertex by the distance from the implied local coordinate origin of 0,0,0 to the new world coordinate location.

Steps 3 through 6, which transform world coordinates into view coordinates, require a reference frame for the view coordinates to be based on. Where are we viewing from, exactly? For that, we need to specify the location and orientation of a virtual camera, and some other information about it as well.

The Virtual Camera

There are several ways in which we might go about specifying a virtual camera. The camera certainly needs a location in 3D world coordinate space, so that it has some location relative to the other objects in world space. This location is not "where the computer screen is," by the way. It is a spot "back away from" the screen, behind the camera lens as it were, ideally about where you are really sitting back a bit from your real computer screen, although it's obviously hard to control the user's head position from inside a program.[2]

The camera also needs an orientation. We'll define our camera's orientation in terms of pitch, heading, and bank. Pitch is rotation about the *x*-axis, heading is rotation about the *y*-axis, and bank is rotation about the *z*-axis. Equivalent terms often used instead of heading and bank are yaw and roll. Figure 17.13 shows our virtual camera.

We're not quite done specifying our camera yet. Two real cameras may have the same location in the world (well, not at the same time I guess) and the same orientation, but one may have a telephoto lens and the other not. They won't take the same picture. What's dif-

---

[2]Though it won't be long now, I'm sure.

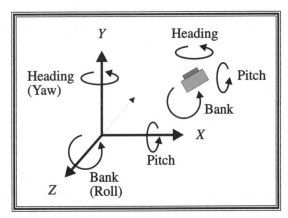

Figure 17.13 Camera located in world coordinate space with pitch, heading, and bank.

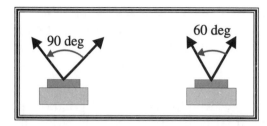

Figure 17.14 Two cameras with different fields of view.

ferent is the camera's *field of view,* which represents the spread of the angle of space taken in by the camera. See Figure 17.14. Also, if the size of the viewport on which we are viewing the camera's results is not square, then the field of view in the horizontal direction is different from the field of view in the vertical direction.

View Coordinate Transform

Now that we have a virtual camera, we can describe how to convert world coordinates into camera-relative view coordinates. Looking back at our seven-step list, step 3 is to translate the polygon from world coordinates to view coordinates. This is accomplished by subtracting the camera's location from the polygon coordinates, in order to represent the polygon in coordinates relative to the camera. Step 4 is to rotate the polygon in *x, y,* and *z,* in the opposite amounts that the camera is rotated about these axes. The three rotation matrices are concatenated so that this operation is performed by a single matrix multiplication. In fact, this concatenated matrix can include the transformation in step 5 as well. Step 5 scales the polygon based on the camera's viewport *aspect ratio* and field of view. This gives our virtual camera a "zoom" capability. If the field of view is narrow, the objects we do see will appear larger. The viewport aspect ratio is used to control for viewports which are not square, so that we don't get elongation in the horizontal or vertical direction. In essence, it provides for the vertical field of view to vary from the horizontal field of view, based on the viewport height and width.

Perspective Transform

The final step before rendering, step 6, is to transform the view coordinates into screen coordinates, or more correctly viewport coordinates. In ARTT, we will project onto a viewport which is defined by a canvas. This is the easiest step mathematically. Essentially, we simply divide each of the *x* and *y* components by the *z*-component, which serves to "project" these coordinates onto the screen and cause more distant objects to appear smaller. The formula is slightly more complicated because it makes an adjustment to make view coordinate 0,0 to project to the center of the viewport. Also complicating the formula is the fact that the sign of z must be reversed (it is negative in front of the camera, remember), and the y-coordinate must be flipped upside down to match our top-down 2D coordinate system. Here's the real formula:

```
Xscreen = ((Xview / -Zview) * ViewportWidth) + (ViewportWidth / 2) + 0.5
Yscreen = ViewportHeight - (((Yview / -Zview) * ViewportHeight) + (ViewportHeight
          / 2) + 0.5)
```

Figure 17.15 shows the perspective transform in action.

Projection is not quite that simple, unfortunately. If the z-coordinate in view space is positive, which means it is behind the camera, its projection to screen space is undefined. We simply must avoid projecting a vertex with a positive z. The right solution is to clip a polygon containing such vertices in 3D space. In essence, we clip the polygon against the pyramidal section of space viewable from the camera, which does not include anything behind the camera. Then we project the clipped polygon and render it. In ARTT, we're going to punt on polygon clipping (except in 2D screen space, where we clip to the canvas, which is straightforward). Instead, we'll simply avoid drawing polygons which are partially behind the camera. This will work for simple needs, but a "real" 3D system must include 3D clipping.

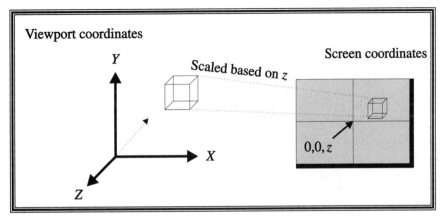

Figure 17.15 Projecting from 3D view coordinates to 2D screen coordinates.

Rendering the Polygon

With the polygon's vertices transformed to screen coordinates, all that's left is to draw it. We're going to come back to that in a minute. First, let's create a virtual camera class to add to our 3D system.

Class ACamera: The Virtual Camera

Class ACamera implements a virtual camera for our growing 3D system. It keeps track of the camera's location and orientation in world coordinate space, its field of view, and the width and height of the viewport through which the world is viewed. It provides methods to retrieve and modify these parameters. Every time they change, it recomputes a transformation matrix, one which can be used to transform vectors from world coordinate space to view coordinate space.

The camera's field of view is specified in radians, the unit used for all 3D angles in ARTT. A full 360-degree circle equals 2π radians. The constant FOV_90 is supplied in the ACamera header file and represents a 90-degree field of view ($.5\pi$ radians). Other angles can be computed from this if needed.

The methods of class ACamera, besides those used to maintain the camera itself, include the following:

World2View	Transforms a vector from world space to view space, using the matrix
Project	Projects a vector from view space to 2D screen space
IsFacing	Determines whether a polygon is facing the camera

The header file for class ACamera is listed below. Note that the private method CalcViewMatrix() is called every time the camera's parameters change.

```
//   ACamera.h    3-D camera class
//   Rex E. Bradford

#ifndef __ACAMERA_H
#define __ACAMERA_H

#include "atypes.h"
#include "afix.h"
#include "amatrix.h"
#include "apolygon.h"

#define FOV_90 1.5708      // 90-degree field of view
```

```
class ACamera {
    AVector loc;              // camera location
    AVector dir;              // camera pitch, heading, bank
    float fov;                // field of view, in radians
    int viewportW;            // viewport width
    int viewportH;            // viewport height
    float viewportAspect;     // viewport aspect ratio (height / width)
    AMatrix m;                // matrix to xform world->view coords

    void CalcViewMatrix();    // recompute world->view matrix

public:

// Constructors

    ACamera() {}
    ACamera(AVector &loc_, AVector &dir_, int vpw, int vph,
        float fov_ = FOV_90) {
            SetViewport (vpw, vph, fov_, FALSE);
            SetLocAndDir(loc_, dir_);}

// Read current state of camera

    AVector GetLoc() {return loc;}
    AVector GetDir() {return dir;}
    float GetFOV() {return fov;}
    int GetViewportWidth() {return viewportW;}
    int GetViewportHeight() {return viewportH;}
    float GetViewportAspect() {return viewportAspect;}

// Set camera params

    void SetLoc(AVector &loc_) {loc = loc_; CalcViewMatrix();}
    void SetDir(AVector &dir_) {dir = dir_; CalcViewMatrix();}
    void SetLocAndDir(AVector &loc_, AVector &dir_) {
        loc = loc_; dir = dir_; CalcViewMatrix();}

    void SetViewport(int w, int h, float fov_, bool recalc = TRUE) {
        viewportW = w; viewportH = h; fov = fov_;
        viewportAspect = float(h) / float(w);
        if (recalc) CalcViewMatrix();}
    void SetFOV(float fov_) {fov = fov_; CalcViewMatrix();}

// Transform and project points

    void World2View(AVector &ptsrc, AVector &ptdest);
    bool Project(AVector &ptsrc, APolyVertex &pvdest);

// Check if xformed poly (screen coords) is facing forward

    static bool IsFacing(APolyVertex &v1, APolyVertex &v2,
        APolyVertex &v3);
};

#endif
```

Calculating and Using the View Matrix

The private method CalcViewMatrix() is called whenever the camera's location, orientation, field of view, or viewport changes. It computes a matrix which is capable of performing the rotations and scaling needed to transform a vector from world coordinates to view coordinates. Conceptually, it performs the following steps:

1. Set the matrix to the identity matrix.
2. Multiply the matrix by the reverse of the camera's rotation about the x-axis (pitch).
3. Multiply the matrix by the reverse of the camera's rotation about the y-axis (heading).
4. Multiply the matrix by the reverse of the camera's rotation about the z-axis (bank).
5. Scale the x-column of the matrix by the viewport aspect ratio (ratio of viewport height to viewport width—field of view actually represents the vertical field of view).
6. Scale the y-column of the matrix by 1.0 (no operation).
7. Scale the z-column of the matrix by the field of view divided by FOV_90.

The code for ACamera::CalcViewMatrix() doesn't look as involved as the above. The first four steps have been collapsed into some custom code which sets each of the nine elements of the matrix directly from what the results of these steps would have been. The enterprising reader may work out the matrix multiplications by hand to verify these. The last three steps are accomplished by a single call to AMatrix::ScaleXYZ(), which has been previously seen.

```
void ACamera::CalcViewMatrix()
{
// Combine (reverse) rotation about x, y, and z in one fell swoop

    AVector rdir(-dir.x, -dir.y, -dir.z);

    m.m[0] = cos(rdir.y) * cos(rdir.z);
    m.m[1] = cos(rdir.y) * sin(rdir.z);
    m.m[2] = -sin(rdir.y);
    m.m[3] = (sin(rdir.x) * sin(rdir.y) * cos(rdir.z)) -
        (cos(rdir.x) * sin(rdir.z));
    m.m[4] = (sin(rdir.x) * sin(rdir.y) * sin(rdir.z)) +
        (cos(rdir.x) * cos(rdir.z));
    m.m[5] = sin(rdir.x) * cos(rdir.y);
    m.m[6] = (cos(rdir.x) * sin(rdir.y) * cos(rdir.z)) +
        (sin(rdir.x) * sin(rdir.z));
    m.m[7] = (cos(rdir.x) * sin(rdir.y) * sin(rdir.z)) -
        (sin(rdir.x) * cos(rdir.z));
    m.m[8] = cos(rdir.x) * cos(rdir.y);

// Scale by viewport aspect ratio and field-of-view
```

```
    AVector vscale(1.0 * viewportAspect, 1.0, fov / FOV_90);
    m.ScaleXYZ(vscale);
}
```

Once we have the proper matrix, using it to convert vectors from world space to view space is trivial. ACamera::World2View() first translates the vector relative to the camera location, then multiplies this new vector by the matrix. The resulting vector is in view coordinate space.

```
void ACamera::World2View(AVector &ptsrc, AVector &ptdest)
{
    ptdest = (ptsrc - loc) * m; // translate, then rotate/scale
}
```

Projecting onto Screen Space

The projection from view space to screen space must take care to avoid projecting points which lie behind the camera. These have a positive z-component in our right-handed coordinate system. Furthermore, we must not project points with z equal to 0, as this will cause a divide-by-zero exception. ACamera::Project() checks the z-component and avoids projection, returning FALSE to alert the caller. It is the responsibility of the calling code not to try to render a polygon for which *any* of its points (vectors) have failed to be projected. As stated earlier, a more robust 3D system would clip the polygons to the *viewing volume* in front of the camera to avoid this problem.

If the z-test passes, the x- and y-components are divided by the z-component, and other math is done to shift the center of view to the center of the screen, and to flip the y-coordinate from our 3D system (y goes up) to our 2D system (y goes down). The 2D points produced by this method are fixed-point numbers, not floating point. Once in screen space, our heavy-duty transformation days are over, and we want the lightweight efficiency of fixed-point coordinates for our rendering routines.

The x,y fixed-point numbers produced by ACamera::Project() are bundled into a structure called APolyVertex, which is defined in APOLYGON.H and looks like this:

```
typedef struct {
    AFix x;        // x-coord of vertex
    AFix y;        // y-coord of vertex
} APolyVertex;
```

Here's ACamera::Project():

```
bool ACamera::Project(AVector &ptsrc, APolyVertex &pvdest)
{
// If behind camera, whoo boy!
```

```
    if (ptsrc.z >= 0)
        return FALSE;


// Project! Screen x is view x divided by distance (z), scaled
// by viewport width, and centered. Screen y is view y divided
// by distance (z), scaled by viewport height, and centered. Also,
// y is flipped from bottom-up in view coords to top-down in screen.

    pvdest.x = ((ptsrc.x / -ptsrc.z) * viewportW) +
        (viewportW / 2) + 0.5;
    pvdest.y = viewportH - (((ptsrc.y / -ptsrc.z) * viewportH) +
        (viewportH / 2) + 0.5);
    return TRUE;
}
```

Backface Culling

The final method in class ACamera, IsFacing(), requires some discussion. It's important to point out that a polygon has two sides to it, a front and a back. In order to know which is which, we have to define our polygons as a list of vertices in some defined order. Let's say the front face, the one that we want to draw, has vertices defined in counterclockwise order. On the other side of the polygon, the back face has the same vertices in clockwise order. See Figure 17.16.

When we view an arbitrary polygon from some camera angle, we might be looking at either the front face or the back face. If we are looking at the back face, we don't want to draw the polygon. The front face is facing away from the camera in this case.

Another way of thinking about this is that we don't want to draw the interior of polyhedral objects. Think of a cube. The six faces which point outward are all front faces. The other side of each face looks toward the inside of the cube, and can never be seen (unless the camera gets inside the polyhedron, and we shouldn't let that happen).

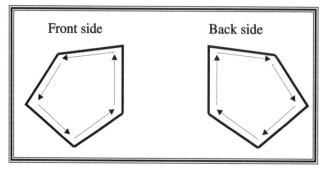

Figure 17.16   Front face of polygon has vertices in counterclockwise order, back face is clockwise.

The process of identifying polygons which face away from the viewer is called *backface removal*, or alternatively *backface culling*. In a typical polyhedron, half of the faces will be facing away. In a convex polyhedron, backface culling is all that need be done to ensure that all the visible faces of the object are drawn in proper sorting order—no visible face can obscure another in such objects, so they needn't be drawn in any special order. More complex polyhedrons require advanced algorithms to make sure the polygons are drawn in the proper sorted order. We will return to this topic in Chapter 19.

How do we determine whether a polygon is facing away from us? We could try to examine its vertices and see if they are still geometrically in counterclockwise order, or if they have flipped to clockwise order. There are easier ways, however. We can compute the cross-product of any three adjacent vectors in the polygon. This produces a vector perpendicular to the polygon, remember, and in the case of a convex polygon this resulting vector points out in the direction that the polygon is facing. If we do this operation in screen coordinates, all we need to do is check the *z*-component of this vector. If it is positive, the polygon is facing away from the camera and need not be drawn. If it is negative, it is facing toward the camera and should be drawn. (This may seem backwards—the reason is that we are working in screen space now, where *y* is pointing down and therefore positive *z* points into the screen to preserve right-handedness.)

If all we're interested in is backface culling, though, it's wasteful to compute the complete cross-product, which has *x* and *y* components which we don't care about as well. ACamera::IsFacing() just does the minimum necessary to compute the *z*-component of the cross-product, and returns TRUE if the polygon is facing.

```
bool ACamera::IsFacing(APolyVertex &v1, APolyVertex &v2, APolyVertex &v3)
{
// Compute z-component of cross product, if < 0 then polygon is facing

    float x1 = v3.x - v2.x;
    float x2 = v1.x - v2.x;
    float y1 = v3.y - v2.y;
    float y2 = v1.y - v2.y;
    return ((x1*y2 - y1*x2) < 0);
}
```

Rendering Polygons

Finally, the math is done, and we can return briefly to the comfortable world of 2D rendering. Now that we've done the hard part of transforming our polygon to screen coordinates, drawing it will seem simple indeed. For now, we're just going to fill the polygon with a solid color—this is called *flat shading*. In the next chapter, we'll delve into a very cool technique called *texture mapping*, whereby we can stretch a bitmapped image across the polygon's face.

The header file APOLYGON.H, as we saw earlier, contains the definition for the APolyVertex structure, which defines a polygon's vertex. In ARTT, an entire polygon is described by a structure of type APolygon. It contains the following fields:

colorNative	The polygon's face color, in "native" format
tmap	The bitmap to use when texture mapping (unioned with colorNative)
type	type of rendering (flat shaded or texture mapped—selects from above union)
numVerts	Number of vertices in the polygon
pVerts	Ptr to array of vertices (type APolyVertex)
vertIndex[]	Array of vertex indices
pTmapCoords	Ptr to array of texture map coordinates

Ignore the texture mapping fields for now (tmap, type, and pTmapCoords). What's left is the polygon's color, the number of vertices, and a pointer to the vertices themselves. But wait. There's an extra field, an array of vertex indices. What's this all about?

If all we were going to ever do is draw solitary polygons, there would be no need for the 'vertIndex[]' array. The 'pVerts' field would point to a (counterclockwise) list of polygon vertices, and that would be that. But in polygon-based objects, each vertex is shared by more than one face. In fact, by definition, each vertex is shared by at least three faces. See Figure 17.17.

It would be wasteful to spend time transforming the same point three times, each time in the context of a different polygon face of the

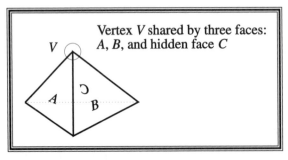

Figure 17.17   In a closed polyhedron, each vertex is connected to at least three faces.

same object. Ideally, each vertex would be transformed just once, and the transformed vertex used by all polygons which share it. That's just what we're going to do, when we get to polygon-based objects in the next chapter.

In the meantime, we're going to set up our APolygon structure to anticipate this. Each polygon points to a list of vertices, which will be a "master list" of all vertices in the polyhedron. Then, each polygon is defined by a pointer to this shared list, and by the indices of the particular vertices that this polygon is made of. Figure 17.18 shows this structure.

Below is the full definition of the APolygon structure, including the fields related to texture mapping:

```
#define MAX_POLY_VERTICES 8    // maximum vertices in a polygon
#define POLY_TYPE_FLAT 0       // filltype: flat-shaded polygon
#define POLY_TYPE_TMAP 1       // filltype: texture-mapped polygon

typedef struct {
   union {
      long colorNative;        // native-format color
      ABitmap *tmap;           // texture map ptr
      };
   ushort type;               // POLY_TYPE_XXX
   short numVerts;            // number of vertices
   APolyVertex *pVerts;       // ptr to array of vertices
   uchar vertIndex[MAX_POLY_VERTICES]; // indices into vertex array
   ATmapCoord *pTmapCoords;   // ptr to array of tmap coords, or NULL
} APolygon;
```

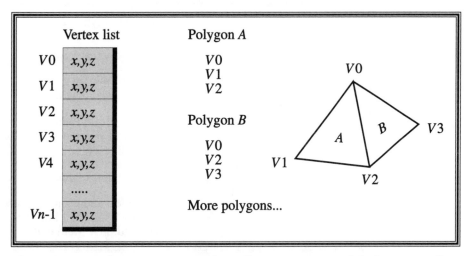

Figure 17.18 Polygons represented by indices into master polyhedron vertex list.

Drawing Flat-Shaded Convex Polygons

Earlier we noted that a convex polygon has the property that any line passing through it intersects the polygon at most twice and thus creates a single span of filled area along that line. We're going to make use of that property in our polygon-rendering routine. In essence, we're going to pass horizontal lines through the polygon, and draw the span inside the polygon for each such row. We can thus use DrawHorz-Line() to do the actual pixel-drawing, which is good because we have an optimized version of this routine in each canvas class. The overall polygon-drawing routine will be in class ACanvas, and need not be customized for each class.

ACanvas::DrawFlatConvexPolygon() will first find the top vertex in the polygon, and then work downwards, filling in a horizontal row of pixels between the left and right sides of the polygon on each row. An incremental process, similar to our line-drawer, is used to move the left and right sides by fractional pixel amounts as we scan down the polygon. On the left and right edges of the "current" sides of the polygon at any given time, fixed-point steppers are used to adjust the left and right *x*-coordinates, while vertically one pixel is stepped each iteration. The only hard part is setting up these "digital differential analyzers" which control the fractional stepping, and starting up new ones whenever a vertex is reached and a new side of the polygon must be started. Figure 17.19 illustrates the overall process of convex polygon filling.

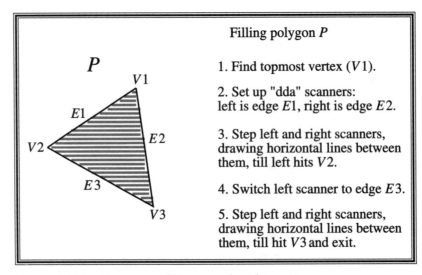

Figure 17.19   The steps in filling sample polygon *P.*

Let's look at ACanvas::DrawFlatConvexPolygon(), and then at the two "helper" routines which it uses. Much of the work is done in ACanvas::SetupPolyDda(), which sets up the digital differential analyzer structure which controls the fractional stepping along the left and right sides. Vertical stepping is done a whole pixel at a time, and this structure determines how far in the horizontal direction the current polygon side needs to step at each iteration. Much of the rest of the logic goes into determining when to stop, including detecting the special case when the bottom side of the polygon is flat.

```
void ACanvas::DrawFlatConvexPolygon(APolygon &poly)
{
// Find topmost vertex of the polygon, set index in vmin

    int vmin = FindTopmostPolyVertex(poly);

// Set starting line

    APolyDda ldda,rdda;
    int y = int(poly.pVerts[poly.vertIndex[vmin]].y);
    ldda.yend = rdda.yend = y;

// Set up a polygon scanner for left side, starting from top vertex

    SetupPolyDda(poly, ldda, vmin, +1);

// Set up a polygon scanner for right side, starting from top also

    SetupPolyDda(poly, rdda, vmin, -1);

// Set color for all subsequent drawing

    SetColorNative(poly.colorNative);

// Scan till one line-drawer finishes

    while (TRUE)
       {

// Check for left dda hitting end of polygon side

        if (y >= ldda.yend)         // check for end of left drawer
           {
           if (y >= rdda.yend)      // yes, also hit end of right?
              {
              if (ldda.vertNext == rdda.vertNext) // if same vertex, done
                 break;
              // Check for flat bottom
              int vnext = rdda.vertNext - 1;
```

```
            if (vnext < 0)
                vnext = poly.numVerts - 1;
            if (vnext == ldda.vertNext)
                break;
            }
        SetupPolyDda(poly, ldda, ldda.vertNext, +1); // reset left sc.
        }

// Check for right dda hitting end of polygon side, if so reset scanner

        if (y >= rdda.yend)
            SetupPolyDda(poly, rdda, rdda.vertNext, -1);

// Fill span between two line-drawers, advance drawers when hit vertices

        if (y >= clipRect.top)
            DrawHorzLine(y, round(ldda.x), round(rdda.x));

// Advance left and right x-coords by fractional amounts

        ldda.x += ldda.dx;
        rdda.x += rdda.dx;

// Advance ypos, exit if run off its bottom

        if (++y >= clipRect.bott)
            break;
        }
}
```

ACanvas::FindTopmostPolyVertex(), called at the start of Draw-FlatConvexPolygon(), scans all the vertices and returns the index of the topmost one (minimum *y*-coordinate).

```
int ACanvas::FindTopmostPolyVertex(APolygon &poly)
{
    AFix ymin(32767);              // assume impossible minimum
    int vmin;
    for (int i = 0; i < poly.numVerts; i++)
        {
        if (poly.pVerts[poly.vertIndex[i]].y < ymin) // smaller y?
            {
            ymin = poly.pVerts[poly.vertIndex[i]].y;  // yes, mark y
            vmin = i;                                 // mark index, too
            }
        }
    return vmin; // return minimum vertex index
}
```

ACanvas::SetupPolyDda(), the other helper routine, fills in a structure of type APolyDda for a given side of the polygon. It is passed in the index of the topmost vertex and the "direction" to go in to find the other (+1 for counterclockwise, −1 for clockwise). The APolyDda structure is defined in APOLYGON.H and is reproduced below. Ignore the two texture-mapping fields at the bottom of the structure for now.

```
typedef struct {          // polygon line-stepper dda
   short vertIndex;       // index of vertice scanning from
   short vertNext;        // index of next vertex
   AFix x;                // current x value
   AFix dx;               // stepping factor in x
   short ybeg;            // beg y-coord of span
   short yend;            // end y-coord of span
// Only if texture-mapping:
   ATmapCoord tc;         // texture-map coord
   ATmapCoord tcDelta;    // x,y delta to texture-map coord
} APolyDda;
```

The SetupPolyDda() method is listed below:

```
void ACanvas::SetupPolyDda(APolygon &poly, APolyDda &dda,
   short ivert, int dir)
{
// Set current and next vertex (next = current +- 1, with wraparound)

   dda.vertIndex = ivert;                  // set current vertex
   dda.vertNext = ivert + dir;             // move to left or right
   if (dda.vertNext < 0)                   // if left to vert -1,
      dda.vertNext = poly.numVerts - 1;    // wraparound to last one
   else if (dda.vertNext == poly.numVerts) // or if right past last,
      dda.vertNext = 0;                    // wraparound to vert 0


// Set starting/ending ypos (dda.ybeg,yend) and current xpos (dda.x)

   dda.ybeg = dda.yend;    // start where last left off
   dda.yend = round(poly.pVerts[poly.vertIndex[dda.vertNext]].y);
   dda.x = poly.pVerts[poly.vertIndex[dda.vertIndex]].x;


// Calculate fractional number of pixels to step in x (dda.dx)

   AFix xdelta = poly.pVerts[poly.vertIndex[dda.vertNext]].x -
      poly.pVerts[poly.vertIndex[dda.vertIndex]].x;
   int ydelta = dda.yend - dda.ybeg;
   if (ydelta > 0)
      dda.dx = xdelta / ydelta;
   else
      dda.dx = 0;
}
```

Polygon Clipping

The DrawFlatConvexPolygon() routine relies on the DrawHorzLine() routine to do all left/right clipping. For clipping entire rows above the clip rectangle, DrawFlatConvexPolygon() runs the dda's without call-

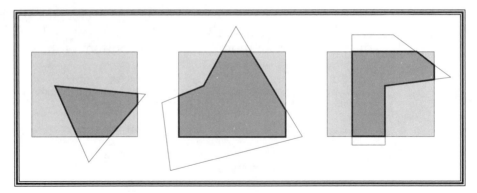

Figure 17.20   Examples of clipped convex polygons.

ing DrawHorzLine(). And as soon as the bottom of the clip rectangle is reached, the routine exits. A better implementation would preclip the polygon to the clipping rectangle, and render only what lies inside. A convex polygon, when clipped to a rectangle, produces another convex polygon (or nothing at all). Figure 17.20 shows some examples of clipped convex polygons.

As we noted before, however, polygon clipping really needs to happen in 3D space, before projection to 2D screen space. We won't be doing such 3D clipping in this book, but there are many good sources for implementing such a clipper; see Appendix E. For immersive games featuring entire worlds composed of polygons, 3D polygon clipping is a fine art, some would say a lost art after watching the bugs and glitches that appear on many a computer gaming screen.

POLYSPIN: A 3D Example

This chapter has been pretty heavy-duty. The reward is the program POLYSPIN, which shows just how straightforward it is to use the code we've developed so far. POLYSPIN doesn't actually spin a polygon. Instead, it spins the camera about the z-axis. This is, literally according to the theory of relativity, the same as spinning the polygon in the opposite direction. The camera is also pitched downward slightly, and this accounts for the fact that the polygon does not stay centered, but instead moves around the screen in a circle. At the same time, the camera is moved toward the polygon, so the polygon grows larger as it gets closer to the camera. When the camera passes by the polygon, one or more points will fail to project. At this point, the program exits. A more polite program would simply skip the polygon rendering at this time, but in our case we'd just have to stare at a black screen forever after that anyway.

It's a humble example, to be sure—we'll be dropping single polygons in favor of full polyhedra in the next chapter, and texture mapping them too. The code for the **POLYSPIN** program is listed below:

```
//   POLYSPIN    Polygon-spinning example
//   Rex E. Bradford

#include <stdio.h>
#include <stdlib.h>
#include <conio.h>

#include "amode13.h"
#include "acvlin8.h"
#include "acamera.h"
#include "apolygon.h"

// Spinning square data

#define COLOR_BLUE 1            // standard VGA palette says so
#define COLOR_GRAY 7            // ditto
APolyVertex squareScreen[4];    // space for projected vertices
AVector squareView[4];          // space for view-space vertices
APolygon square = {             // the square polygon definition
    COLOR_BLUE,POLY_TYPE_FLAT,4,squareScreen,0,1,2,3,0,0,0,0,NULL};
float squareWorld[] = {         // polygon vertices in world coords
    50,-50,-400,
    50,50,-400,
    -50,50,-400,
    -50,-50,-400,
};

void main()
{
// Bring up screen

    AMode13::Launch();

// Define camera location and orientation, tilted down slightly

    AVector camLoc(0,0,0);
    AVector camDir(-.2,0,0);
    float fov = FOV_90;
    ACamera cam(camLoc, camDir, gCanvasScreen->bm.width,
        gCanvasScreen->bm.height, fov);

// Create off-screen canvas to compose into

    ABitmap bmOff(NULL, BMF_LIN8, FALSE, gCanvasScreen->bm.width,
        gCanvasScreen->bm.height);
    ACanvas *pcvOff = new ACanvasLin8(&bmOff);
```

```
// Forever:
//    1. Blank offscreen buffer
//    2. Rotate camera about z-axis and move towards polygon
//    3. Transform & project polygon to screen coords, exit if past camera
//    4. Draw polygon into offscreen buffer
//    5. Blit offscreen buffer to screen

    while (TRUE)
       {
// 1. Blank offscreen buffer

       pcvOff->SetColor8(COLOR_GRAY);
       pcvOff->DrawRect(0, 0, pcvOff->bm.width, pcvOff->bm.height);

// 2. Rotate camera about z-axis

       AVector camDir = cam.GetDir();
       camDir.z += .05;
       cam.SetDir(camDir);
       AVector camLoc = cam.GetLoc();
       camLoc.z -= 1;
       cam.SetLoc(camLoc);

// 3. Transform & project polygon to screen coords, exit is past camera

       for (int i = 0; i < 4; i++)
          {
          cam.World2View(*(AVector *)&squareWorld[i*3], squareView[i]);
          if (!cam.Project(squareView[i], squareScreen[i]))
             {
             AMode13::Term();
             exit(0);
             }
          }

// 4. Draw polygon in offscreen buffer

       pcvOff->DrawFlatConvexPolygon(square);

// 5. Blit offscreen buffer to screen

       gCanvasScreen->DrawBitmapLin8U(pcvOff->bm, 0, 0);
       }
    }
```

Figure 17.21 captures the spinning polygon in action.

Figure 17.21 Screen shot from sample program POLYSPIN.

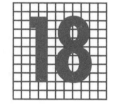

C H A P T E R

Polyhedral Objects and Texture Mapping

This chapter is really a continuation of the last one. When we left our hero, it was a mere lone polygon spinning about the screen. In fact, it wasn't even spinning, the camera was. In this chapter, we'll build upon the same mathematical base, creating a class to represent polyhedral objects. Furthermore, we'll use the bitmapping skills we've developed throughout this book to spruce up the look of the polygons which make up such an object. We'll use texture mapping, wherein a bitmap is stretched across the surface of a polygon. Finally, we'll develop an actor class for these polyhedral objects, so that they can be included in ARTT scenes.

Polyhedral Objects

It's time to take our lone polygon, and join it with its friends into a full polyhedron, an object built from polygons. This object might be as simple as a cube, or it might be a giant battle robot. While the world of "high-end" 3D employs other modeling techniques such as bicubic surface patches, polygon-based objects are the way to go for real-time 3D on our "low-end" PCs. Even bicubic surface patches are typically reduced to lots of tiny polygons for rendering purposes, so learning about polygons is useful even at the high end.

On one level, a polyhedron is just an array of polygons. Each polygon has enough information to be rendered through some camera, so a well-chosen array of them can represent a 3D object. But we're going to add a little more information to our polygon array when we turn it into a polyhedral object. If you look back to the POLYSPIN example of the last chapter, you'll notice that the polygon was defined in world coordinate space. What about the local coordinates that were supposed to be the first step in the list of transformations? That stage was skipped, and that's why we couldn't rotate the polygon itself, and had to instead spin the camera.

Local Coordinates for Object Definition

In our polygon object class, we're going to give the entire object a location in world coordinates, and an orientation vector which shows where it's facing in the world in terms of rotation about the x, y, and z axes. The polygons which make up the object should then be defined in a local coordinate space, and the object itself is assumed to be centered around the origin $(0,0,0)$ of that coordinate space and oriented upright and facing down the z-axis toward the negative direction.

Then, the first step of our transformation series will rotate all the polygons toward their true orientation in world space, and translate the polygons to world space based on the object's world location, as shown in Figure 17.4 in Chapter 17.

Other Benefits of an Object Class

Besides having a place to store the overall object's world location and orientation, having a polyhedral object class provides other benefits. We noted in the last chapter that each vertex in a closed polyhedron (one which fully encloses some space, as does a cube) is shared by at least three polygon faces. It would be a waste to transform these vertices from local to world to view to screen space three times each. Our polygon object will have just one array of vertices, in local coordinates, and we'll transform each one once.

The polygon object will maintain separate arrays for the vertices in local, world, and screen space. View space coordinates are temporary and need not be stored, as we'll see. The advantage of keeping world coordinates hanging around is that, if the object doesn't move or rotate from one view to the next (perhaps only the camera does), the local-to-world transformation doesn't need to be recomputed. The object also has a pointer to its array of polygons, each of which denotes which vertices are used by that face and also includes other rendering information. In order for the object-handling code to communicate properly with the rendering code, the pointer to the fixed-point screen-space vertex array built into each polygon must match the array pointer built into the overall object itself. Figure 18.1 illustrates the relationship between polyhedral objects and the polygons themselves.

Class APolyObj

Class APolyObj is fairly simple. The member variables consist of:

pVertLocal	Ptr to array of vertices defining the object, in local coordinates
pVertWorld	Ptr to space in which to store the world-coordinate vertices
pVertScrn	Ptr to space in which to store the fixed-point screen vertices
loc	Object's location in world coordinates (center of object)

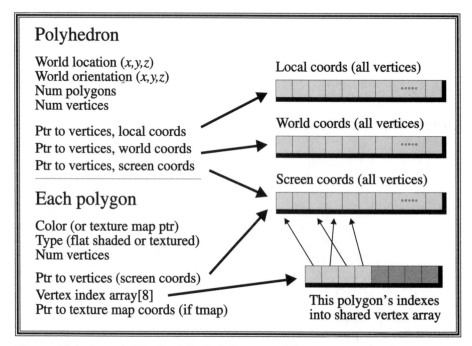

Figure 18.1   Data fields of polyhedral objects and their associated polygons.

orient	Object's orientation (x,y,z rotation) in world space
polys	Ptr to array of polygons
numPolygons	Number of polygons in 'polys' array
numVertices	Number of vertices in 'pVertLocal', 'pVertWorld', 'pVertScrn'

Two constructors are provided—an empty one which allows subsequent setting of the members by hand, and one which takes a long series of arguments, and stuffs each member variable. All members are public, so this class has the benefit of being easy to play with, and the cost of being unsafe to play with.

Other than constructors, only four methods are defined:

TransformLocal2World	Transforms all vertices from local to world coordinates
TransformWorld2Screen	Transforms all vertices from world to view to screen coordinates
Draw	Draws all visible polygons
BoundingBox	Computes smallest screen rectangle enclosing all polygons

The header file for class APolyObj is listed below:

```
//   APolyObj.h      Polygon object class (polyhedron)
//   Rex E. Bradford

#ifndef __APOLYOBJ_H
#define __APOLYOBJ_H

#include "apolygon.h"
#include "avector.h"
#include "arect.h"

class ACamera;
class ACanvas;

class APolyObj {
public:

    AVector *pVertLocal;     // ptr to array of vertices in local coords
    AVector *pVertWorld;     // ptr to array of vertices in world coords
    APolyVertex *pVertScrn;  // ptr to array of vertices in screen coords
    AVector loc;             // location in world coords
    AVector orient;          // orientation in world coords
    APolygon *polys;         // ptr to array of polygons
    short numPolygons;       // number of polygons
    short numVertices;       // number of vertices

// Constructors
```

```
APolyObj() {}
APolyObj(AVector *pvl, AVector *pvw, APolyVertex *pvs, AVector loc_,
    AVector orient_, APolygon *polys_, short numPolys, short numVerts)
        {pVertLocal = pvl; pVertWorld = pvw; pVertScrn = pvs;
        loc = loc_; orient = orient_; polys = polys_;
        numPolygons = numPolys; numVertices = numVerts;}

// Transform from local->world, and world->screen (includes project)

    void TransformLocal2World();
    bool TransformWorld2Screen(ACamera &cam);

// Draw projected polyhedron

    void Draw(ACanvas *pcv);

// Return 2D bounding box of projected polyhedron

    void BoundingBox(ARect &rect);
};


#endif
```

APolyObj::TransformLocal2World

This method does the transformation from local to world coordinates, using the object's current world location and orientation. The world coordinates do not overwrite the local coordinates—the object has a separate array in which to put them. This means that this method need not be invoked unless the object has moved or rotated.

The same trick which ACamera::CalcViewMatrix() used, preconcatenating all three rotation matrices into one, is employed here. Then each vertex is run through this matrix, and the world location is added.

```
void APolyObj::TransformLocal2World()
{
// Create local->world rotation matrix

    AMatrix m;

    m.m[0] = cos(orient.y) * cos(orient.z);
    m.m[1] = cos(orient.y) * sin(orient.z);
    m.m[2] = -sin(orient.y);
    m.m[3] = (sin(orient.x) * sin(orient.y) * cos(orient.z)) -
        (cos(orient.x) * sin(orient.z));
    m.m[4] = (sin(orient.x) * sin(orient.y) * sin(orient.z)) +
        (cos(orient.x) * cos(orient.z));
    m.m[5] = sin(orient.x) * cos(orient.y);
    m.m[6] = (cos(orient.x) * sin(orient.y) * cos(orient.z)) +
        (sin(orient.x) * sin(orient.z));
```

```
m.m[7] = (cos(orient.x) * sin(orient.y) * sin(orient.z)) -
    (sin(orient.x) * cos(orient.z));
m.m[8] = cos(orient.x) * cos(orient.y);

// For each vertex, multiply by matrix and move to world loc

    for (int i = 0; i < numVertices; i++)
        pVertWorld[i] = (pVertLocal[i] * m) + loc;
}
```

APolyObj::TransformWorld2Screen

APolyObj::TransformWorld2Screen() really performs two transformations. For each vertex, it transforms from world coordinates to view coordinates, using the supplied camera. Then it projects this vertex to screen coordinates. If any projection fails (z-component of view coordinate is $>= 0$, behind the camera), the method exits immediately, returning FALSE. The caller must not attempt to draw the object in this case. Not only has a vertex failed to project, but the remaining vertices have not even been transformed at all. A more robust system would use 3D polygon clipping, or at least keep track of which polygons have projected and which ones have not, so that at least some of the polygons could be drawn. APolyObj uses an all-or-nothing approach to rendering the object.

```
bool APolyObj::TransformWorld2Screen(ACamera &cam)
{
    AVector v;

    for (int i = 0; i < numVertices; i++)  // loop thru all vertices
        {
        cam.World2View(pVertWorld[i], v);   // convert world->view
        if (!cam.Project(v, pVertScrn[i]))  // project
            return FALSE;                   // if project failed, bail
        }
    return TRUE;
}
```

APolyObj::Draw

APolyObj::Draw() draws all the polygons in an object which are facing the camera, using the method ACamera::IsFacing() on each polygon to make this decision. Note that each polygon can be drawn either in solid color or via texture mapping, which will be covered later in this chapter.

```
void APolyObj::Draw(ACanvas *pcv)
{
    for (int i = 0; i < numPolygons; i++)    // for all polys in obj:
```

```
    {
    APolygon &poly = polys[i];                  // get poly, check facing
    if (ACamera::IsFacing(pVertScrn[poly.vertIndex[0]],
       pVertScrn[poly.vertIndex[1]], pVertScrn[poly.vertIndex[2]]))
       {
       if (poly.type == POLY_TYPE_FLAT)
          pcv->DrawFlatConvexPolygon(poly);     // flat shaded
       else
          pcv->DrawTmappedConvexPolygon(poly);  // texture mapped
       }
    }
}
```

APolyObj::BoundingBox

It's often handy to know the extent of the screen area covered by a polygon object. This can aid the recomposing process—we saw in our scene and actor classes how screen redraw could be sped up through the use of dirty rectangles. The actor classes have a method which returns the bounding area of the object to allow the scene system to compute the screen areas in need of redraw. Figure 18.2 shows a typical polyhedral object and its bounding box.

An aid to such recomposing code, APolyObj::BoundingBox(), computes the minimum rectangle which encompasses all the polygons in the object. Like APolyObj::Draw(), it should not be called if TransformWorld2Screen() returns FALSE. Note that BoundingBox() does not bother to check for which polygons are backfacing—in a convex polyhedron, the bounding box is identical whether these are included or not, and it is actually faster to compute using them than to spend the time figuring which are backfacing.

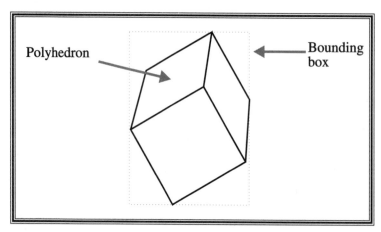

Figure 18.2   Sample polyhedron and its bounding box.

```
void APolyObj::BoundingBox(ARect &rect)
{
// Set initial impossible coords for box

    rect.left = 32767;
    rect.right = -32767;
    rect.top = 32767;
    rect.bott = -32767;


// Loop thru all vertices. If any outside box, extend box.

    int i;
    APolyVertex *pv;
    for (i = 0, pv = pVertScrn; i < numVertices; i++, pv++)
        {
        if (int(pv->x) < rect.left) rect.left = int(pv->x);
        if (round(pv->x) >= rect.right) rect.right = round(pv->x) + 1;
        if (int(pv->y) < rect.top) rect.top = int(pv->y);
        if (round(pv->y) >= rect.bott) rect.bott = round(pv->y) + 1;
        }
}
```

Sprucing Up Polygon Objects

That's all there is to our polygon object class. Rather than employ it immediately, we're going to spruce up its current flat-shaded appearance. Then, we'll bundle the polygon object into an actor class, so we can use it in scenes with minimal effort on our part.

Visual Realism and Polygon Shading

Not to scoff at the 3D skills we've developed so far, but drawing polygon objects in solid colors, even if each face can have its own unique color, is kind of old-fashioned. The quest for visual realism has blazed a trail far beyond such capabilities, and we're going to explore a bit of that path. The ultimate goal of high-end 3D computer graphics is to reproduce the natural world in all its intricate glory on the computer screen, and maybe create a few not-so-natural worlds as well. Real-time computer graphics has this goal as an ideal, tempered by the need to create such images on the fly under severe processing constraints.

One realm of visual realism is the set of effects produced by light on a surface. After all, without light we wouldn't see anything at all, so modeling light at some level is a good place to start. Some methods of rendering 3D objects and scenes, for instance, *raytracing*, literally attempt to model light at the level of millions of individual rays bouncing off surfaces and eventually finding their way into the viewer's eyes. Others, such as *radiosity,* attempt to model overall light-

ing behavior through sophisticated mathematical analysis. Neither raytracing nor radiosity are real-time processes, however.

Ambient Illumination

Let's start by assuming that each face of a polygon has some inherent color, perhaps expressed as an RGB triplet. In reality, this color is created by the fact that the surface's material absorbs some frequencies in the visible spectrum and reflects others into the viewer's eye, but we can ignore these aspects—the polygon simply has a color associated with it.

But if there is no light in the scene, all the polygons appear black. We need to add some *ambient light* to the picture. This causes the scene in which the object appears to be globally illuminated by some level of light. The light is assumed to be colorless, in that it does not affect the color associated with a polygon, only that color's intensity. In more mathematical terms:

$$I^1 = I * k_a$$

where I is the original intensity of the color, k_a is the level of ambient light, and I^1 is the new intensity. The relative levels of red, green, and blue making up the original intensity should be preserved in the new intensity. Each color component is scaled by the ambient light level:

$$R^1 = R * k_a$$
$$G^1 = G * k_a$$
$$B^1 = B * k_a$$

This doesn't get us very far yet. If all the sides of a cube have the same color, ambient light will just give them all the same new intensity of that color. In the real world, some parts of an object are brightly lit, and others are darker or even in shadow, based on *light sources*.

Diffuse Illumination

For simplicity's sake, we will assume a single point source of light, infinitely far away from the object, or at least far enough away to avoid worrying about differences in the angle at which the light enters each portion of the object and scene.[1] Surfaces which exhibit

---

[1]If the light were really infinitely far away, it would need an infinite amount of energy (or is it infinity squared?) to reach us with any intensity. This is impractical unless you rewire the phase charge coupling inverter, which can take twenty minutes unless the Cardassians are really bearing down on you, in which case, maybe five.

diffuse reflection, also known as *Lambertian reflection,* appear equally bright from all viewing angles when reflecting such light, but the amount reflected is dependent on the relative angle at which the light strikes the surface. If the light is traveling perpendicular to the surface, the most light is emitted. This amount is reduced as the light strikes the surface at more oblique angles, because less surface area is hit by a given "volume" of light. The exact amount is a function of the cosine of the angle between the direction to the light source and the surface's normal vector (perpendicular to surface). Figure 18.3 illustrates diffuse reflection.

The formula for diffuse illumination of a surface is given below:

```
I¹ = I * k_d * cos(σ)
```

The angle between the light vector and the surface normal is nontrivial to calculate, especially since both are typically represented as vectors, not angles in 3D space. However, we can take advantage of the vector math covered in Chapter 17. There, we noted that the dot product of two vectors was equal to the magnitude of the vectors times the cosine of the angle between them. This formula is repeated below:

```
A · B = Mag(A) * Mag(B) * cos(σ)
```

If we make sure that our two vectors are normalized, that is to say scaled to length 1, then the above formula can be reduced. With $Mag(A) == Mag(B) == 1$, then the cosine of the angle is simply equal to the dot product. Therefore, our diffuse illumination equation becomes:

```
I¹ = I * k_d * N · L
```

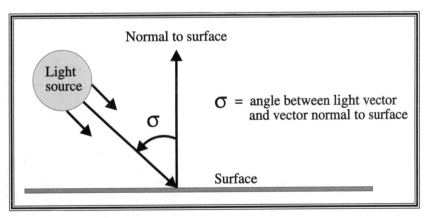

Figure 18.3 Diffuse illumination by a light source.

where N is the vector normal to the polygon's surface, and L is the vector directed toward the light source, both normalized. We can put our ambient and diffuse illumination models together into one formula:

```
I¹ = I * k_a + I * k_d * N · L
```

or, split into the red, green, and blue components:

```
R¹ = R * k_a + R * k_d * N · L
G¹ = G * k_a + G * k_d * N · L
B¹ = B * k_a + B * k_d * N · L
```

With both ambient and diffuse illumination, each polygon in an object is lit according to the angle of light striking it from some light source, plus an overall ambient component. This is a definite step up from our fixed-color polygon model, and adds a certain amount of realism. Multiple light sources can even be employed, and their results added together.

Objects of class APolyObj can use this illumination technique with no extra coding, other than the lighting calculations themselves. With diffuse lighting, each face of a polyhedron is "lit" based on its angle relative to the light. Since each polygon face is still rendered with a single solid color in this lighting model, no change need be made to the polygon rendering code in the canvas classes. All that's needed is that, before rendering, each visible face's color be computed according to the formulas given above, and stored into the polygon's color field. The ambient and diffuse illumination constants (k_a and k_d) are fixed for a given scene. The direction vector to the light source, L, is fixed. The only changing factor is N, the vector normal to the polygon. This is a world-coordinate vector, and needs to be recomputed using AVector::Normal() every time the polygon changes orientation in world space. The normal can be recomputed after transformation to world space. A more efficient approach, but one that would require changes to class APolyObj, would be to store a precomputed local-coordinate normal vector along with each polygon, and then transform this vector along with all the others into world coordinates. This would then *be* the normal vector in world coordinates, and the call to AVector::Normal() could be skipped.

ARTT provides the tools to do ambient and diffuse lighting, but does not provide any classes for light sources or methods for these calculations. This is left as an exercise for the motivated reader.

Gouraud Shading

Unless an object is composed of many tiny polygons, the flat shading of each polygon leaves something to be desired. Also, an effect called *Mach banding* highlights the intensity difference at the edges where polygons meet. In many cases, the polygons which make up an object are really only themselves approximations of what is supposed to be a curved surface, so perhaps there is a way to change color intensity across a single polygon to mimic what would really happen across that curvature. This is essentially what *Gouraud shading* does.

The concept behind Gouraud shading is to calculate a normal vector at each *vertex* instead of each polygon. Then, color intensities associated with each vertex are computed, using the formulas derived above for lighting polygons. Finally, a rendering routine interpolates these colors smoothly across the face of the polygon, using iterative fractional math just like that used to track the polygon edges. What is being interpolated here, however, is not 2D coordinates but instead "coordinates in color space," or more simply, RGB colors. Figure 18.4 contrasts interpolation of surface normals with interpolation of color values. Gouraud shading, which is an inaccurate but speedy approximation, interpolates colors rather than normals.

It's not necessarily obvious what is meant by the normal vector of a vertex. A vertex is a point, not a surface, so which direction is perpendicular to it? In cases where the polygon object itself is being created as an approximation of some shape, the program or process creating the polygons may "know" what the vector normal to each vertex is. Barring that, a decent approximation is simply to average the normals of all the surfaces which meet at a given vertex, as depicted in Figure 18.5.

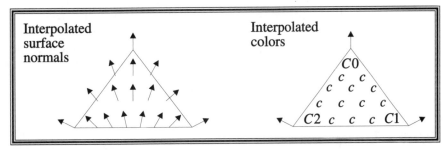

Figure 18.4 Interpolation of surface normals, compared with direct interpolation of color values.

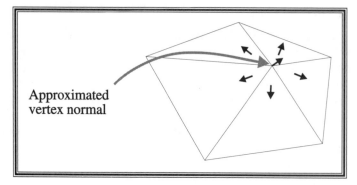

Figure 18.5 Approximating a vertex normal by averaging adjacent surface normals.

Implementing Gouraud Shading in ARTT

ARTT does not implement Gouraud shading. To do so would require:

- Storage of a surface normal at each vertex, created ad hoc or by adjacent surface averaging.

- Light sources and methods to perform the lighting equations, and store a computed color value at each vertex.

- A new polygon rendering routine in class ACanvas, one which vertically interpolated color values during the edge-scanning process, and then called a special row-rendering routine capable of horizontally interpolating color values.

- A row-rendering routine for class ACanvas, and optimized versions for other canvas classes. This would interpolate color values in RGB space from left to right, with fractional resolution (possibly using AFix for each color component). Availability of an inverse table for converting back to 8-bit color would be extremely desirable.

The effort would be well worth the results. Smoothly shaded surfaces look much nicer than flat-shaded ones. Even better would be to add specular reflection, which shows the highlights where light strikes a shiny surface. In *Phong shading,* specular intensity is related to the cosine of the angle of light striking the surface, but in a nonlinear way. A typical implementation involves interpolating the surface normal across a polygon, and then computing the color intensity at each pixel from this value. Phong shading, unlike Gouraud shading, cannot be done in real time without hardware support.

Texture-Mapping Concepts

Surfaces in the real world have far more complexity than can be modeled with the simple illumination models given above. Wood, fabric, dirt, and other materials have complex coloring patterns. These patterns could be simulated by breaking the surface down into huge numbers of polygons, but the vertex transformation time expands exponentially as we subdivide surfaces into smaller areas.

Real-world computer graphics, especially for games and other PC multimedia products, doesn't have to be so scientific. An old adage in program optimization, that of precomputing as much information as possible, can be applied in the visual realm as well. What if we prerendered the graphic look of a given surface, and stored that look as a bitmap? And what if we then "wrapped" that bitmap onto the surface of a polygon, taking 3D orientation into account? We'd have reduced our problem to that of copying pixels from our source bitmap onto our destination polygon, albeit in a nontrivial manner. We'd have the hottest technique in modern PC graphics, called *texture mapping*.

Texture-Mapping Basics

The astute reader may be wondering how a bitmap, which is inherently rectangular, can be mapped onto an arbitrary polygon, which might be a triangle or a hexagon. What we really need is some portion of the bitmap, one which matches the shape or at least the number of vertices of the polygon to be mapped onto. In texture mapping, this extra information is supplied as a list of *texture coordinates*. Each vertex in the polygon is assigned some corresponding coordinate in the bitmap, which in this context is called a *texture map*. The texture map coordinates, which are fractional x,y offsets into the texture map, typically go by the letters u,v instead of x,y. Figure 18.6 illustrates.

How are these texture map coordinates assigned? They can be specified by hand, if the programmer knows what portion of a tex-

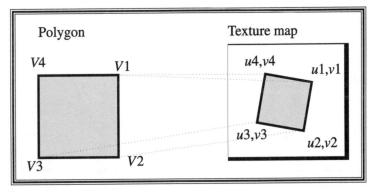

Figure 18.6 A polygon and its vertices' corresponding coordinates in a texture map.

ture map should be used to texture a given polygon. They are often generated by tools which can wrap a large texture map across a set of connected polygons, or even around an entire object. The geometry and algorithms for such wrapping are beyond the scope of this book; suffice it to say that modeling programs such as Autodesk's *3-D Studio* provide them as a standard feature.

The process of rendering a polygon using texture mapping shares some similarities with the bitmap scaling techniques developed earlier in this book. An overall polygon rendering routine steps through the polygon vertically, just like the flat-shaded polygon renderer of the previous chapter, except that u,v texture map coordinates are interpolated along with horizontal edge x-coordinates. Then, within each row, a special method is called to scan out a strip of the texture onto that row of the polygon. The hard part is that this strip, which is horizontal across the polygon, is not horizontal across the source texture map. Figure 18.7 shows a typical case.

Also, since the number of pixels in a row of the destination polygon is unlikely to match the number of pixels in the corresponding "row" of the texture map, the pixel copying must also feature scaling. In ARTT, we will use simple scaling algorithms like those used for bitmap scaling, wherein source pixels are simply skipped or replicated to fill the destination's requirements. Fancier (and slower) algorithms use pixel-averaging to provide smoother results.

Figure 18.8 shows a texture map on the left, and a polygon mapped with that texture on the right.

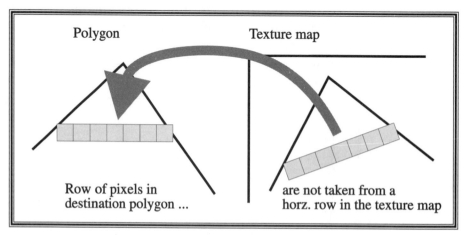

Figure 18.7   A row of polygon pixels is drawn from a "row" of texture pixels which need not be horizontal.

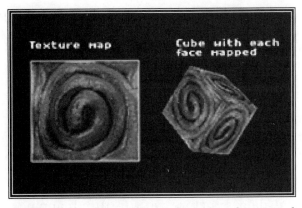

Figure 18.8   A texture map (left), and a cube mapped
with that texture (right).

Texture-Mapping Data Structures in ARTT

The structures related to polygon objects and polygon rendering presented in the last chapter contained fields relevant to texture mapping. We ignored these fields at that time, but return to them now. The first is the APolygon structure, which describes a polygon's coordinates and how it is filled. This structure is reproduced below, with texture-mapping fields highlighted:

```
#define MAX_POLY_VERTICES 8    // maximum vertices in a polygon
#define POLY_TYPE_FLAT 0       // filltype: flat-shaded polygon
#define POLY_TYPE_TMAP 1       // filltype: texture-mapped polygon


typedef struct {
   union {
      long colorNative;        // native-format color
      ABitmap *tmap;           // texture map ptr
      };
   ushort type;                // POLY_TYPE_XXX
   short numVerts;             // number of vertices
   APolyVertex *pVerts;        // ptr to array of vertices
   uchar vertIndex[MAX_POLY_VERTICES]; // indices into vertex array
   ATmapCoord *pTmapCoords;    // ptr to array of tmap coords, or NULL
} APolygon;
```

The 'tmap' field points to the bitmap which should be used for texturing. This field is unioned with, and thus replaces, the 'color-Native' field. The 'type' field specifies what technique should be used when drawing, and is set to POLY_TYPE_TMAP in order to indicate texture mapping instead of flat shading. The last field, 'pTmapCoords', points to an array of texture coordinates, whose dimension should match the number of vertices specified in 'numVerts'. These coordinates are of class ATmapCoord, which holds a *u,v* pair and is defined below:

```
class ATmapCoord {
public:
    AFix u;                      // u-coord of texture map
    AFix v;                      // v-coord of texture map
    ATmapCoord() {}
    ATmapCoord(AFix u_, AFix v_) {u = u_; v = v_;}
};
```

The final data structure with texture-mapping information is the APolyDda structure, which is internally used by the polygon-drawing routine. APolyDda, remember, is used to control the fractional stepping down one side of the polygon. Two such structures are active at any time, one on the left side and one on the right, and each is reinitialized any time a vertex is encountered on that side.

```
typedef struct {             // polygon line-stepper dda
    short vertIndex;         // index of vertice scanning from
    short vertNext;          // index of next vertex
    AFix x;                  // current x value
    AFix dx;                 // stepping factor in x
    short ybeg;              // beg y-coord of span
    short yend;              // end y-coord of span
// Only if texture-mapping:
    ATmapCoord tc;           // texture-map coord
    ATmapCoord tcDelta;      // x,y delta to texture-map coord
} APolyDda;
```

The last two fields in struct APolyDda are relevant here. The 'tc' field holds the "current" value of the *u,v* texture map coordinate. This indicates the exact location in the texture map which the row-rendering routine should use for this edge of the row. The 'tcDelta' field is used to fractionally step the 'tc' field from one row to the next, as the scanning of the polygon moves downward toward the next vertex.

Texture-Mapping Methods

Class ACanvas has a method called DrawTmappedConvexPolygon(), which is called to render a polygon of type **POLY_TYPE_TMAP**. This method is very similar to DrawFlatConvexPolygon(), listed in the previous chapter. The texture-mapping version varies in the following ways:

1. SetupTmapPolyDda() is called instead of SetupPolyDda() at each vertex. This method calls SetupPolyDda() for basic setup of the APolyDda struct, and then adds its own initialization of the 'tc' and 'tcDelta' fields.

2. No call to SetColorNative() is made, since the row-rendering routine does all pixel setting.

3. Instead of DrawHorzLine(), a special row-rendering method called DrawTmapRow8U() is called to render the row. Note that only 8-bit linear bitmaps (BMF_LIN8) may be used for the texture map in this version. Also, since DrawTmapRow8U() does no clipping, the main driver routine must clip the left and right edges, and also adjust the texture coordinate of the left edge if it is clipped.

4. After each row is rendered, incremental update of the texture map coordinates is done in addition to the update of the left and right edge coordinates.

Otherwise, the methods are identical. ACanvas::DrawTmapped-ConvexPolygon() is listed below:

```
void ACanvas::DrawTmappedConvexPolygon(APolygon &poly)
{
// Find topmost vertex of the polygon, set index in vmin

    int vmin = FindTopmostPolyVertex(poly);

// Set starting line

    APolyDda ldda,rdda;
    int y = int(poly.pVerts[poly.vertIndex[vmin]].y);
    ldda.yend = rdda.yend = y;

// Set up a polygon scanner for left side, starting from top vertex

    SetupTmapPolyDda(poly, ldda, vmin, +1, *poly.tmap);

// Set up a polygon scanner for right side, starting from top also

    SetupTmapPolyDda(poly, rdda, vmin, -1, *poly.tmap);

// Scan till one line-drawer finishes

    while (TRUE)
        {
// Check for left dda hitting end of polygon side

        if (y >= ldda.yend)         // check for end of left drawer
            {
            if (y >= rdda.yend)     // yes, also hit end of right?
                {
                if (ldda.vertNext == rdda.vertNext) // if same vertex, done
                    break;
```

```
                    // Check for flat bottom
                    int vnext = rdda.vertNext - 1;
                    if (vnext < 0)
                        vnext = poly.numVerts - 1;
                    if (vnext == ldda.vertNext)
                        break;
                    }
                SetupTmapPolyDda(poly, ldda, ldda.vertNext, +1, *poly.tmap);
                }

// Check for right dda hitting end of polygon side, if so reset scanner

            if (y >= rdda.yend)
                SetupTmapPolyDda(poly, rdda, rdda.vertNext, -1, *poly.tmap);

// Fill span between two line-drawers, advance drawers when hit vertices

            if (y >= clipRect.top)
                {
                int xleft = round(ldda.x);        // get width of span
                int xright = round(rdda.x);
                int width = xright - xleft;
                if (width > 0)                    // if width > 0, draw
                    {
// Set up and draw texture mapped row of polygon

                    ATmapCoord tc = ldda.tc;
                    ATmapCoord tcStep((rdda.tc.u - tc.u) / width,
                        (rdda.tc.v - tc.v) / width);
                    if (xleft < clipRect.left)
                        {
                        tc.u += (tcStep.u * (clipRect.left - xleft));
                        tc.v += (tcStep.v * (clipRect.left - xleft));
                        xleft = clipRect.left;
                        }
                    if (xright > clipRect.right)
                        xright = clipRect.right;
                    DrawTmapRow8U(y, xleft, xright, *poly.tmap, tc, tcStep);
                    }
                }

// Advance left and right x-coords by fractional amounts

            ldda.x += ldda.dx;
            rdda.x += rdda.dx;

// Advance left and right tmap coords by fractional amounts

            ldda.tc.u += ldda.tcDelta.u;
            ldda.tc.v += ldda.tcDelta.v;
            rdda.tc.u += rdda.tcDelta.u;
            rdda.tc.v += rdda.tcDelta.v;

// Advance ypos, exit if run off its bottom
```

```
        if (++y >= clipRect.bott)
            break;
        }
    }
```

The FindTopmostPolyVertex() method used to find the top vertex in the polygon is the same one used by the flat-shading renderer. SetupTmapPolyDda() is new, however, and is listed below. After calling SetupPolyDda() to set up all the basic fields in the APolyDda structure, it computes 'tc' and 'tcDelta'.

Computing 'tc' is easy—there is already an entry in the texture map coordinate array for this vertex. Rather than just copying the coordinate, however, it is scaled up by the texture map's width and height. This step is necessary because the polygon's texture coordinates are specified in the range 0 to 1.0, to make them independent of any particular bitmap width and height. The 'tc' field used in the texture map row-renderer, however, expects fractional *pixel* coordinates.

The other field, 'tcDelta', is a little more complicated. It is computed by taking the texture map coordinate of the next vertex, subtracting the current texture map coordinate, and dividing by the number of rows between them. This gives the amount to adjust the 'tc' field after each row, so that by the time the next vertex is reached, the 'tc' field will match the value associated with that vertex.

```
void ACanvas::SetupTmapPolyDda(APolygon &poly, APolyDda &dda,
    short ivert, int dir, ABitmap &tmap)
{
// Do normal poly scanner setup

    SetupPolyDda(poly, dda, ivert, dir);

// Compute initial u,v tmap coords: scale up to w,h of bitmap

    ATmapCoord &tc = poly.pTmapCoords[dda.vertIndex];
    dda.tc.u = tc.u * tmap.width;
    dda.tc.v = tc.v * tmap.height;

// Compute texture-map delta "stepping factors"

    ATmapCoord &tcn = poly.pTmapCoords[dda.vertNext];
    ATmapCoord tcNext (tcn.u * tmap.width, tcn.v * tmap.height);
    int ydelta = dda.yend - dda.ybeg;
    if (ydelta > 0)
        {
        dda.tcDelta.u = (tcNext.u - dda.tc.u) / ydelta;
        dda.tcDelta.v = (tcNext.v - dda.tc.v) / ydelta;
        }
    }
```

Texture Map Row Rendering

After all the setup, the actual row rendering is a little bit of a letdown. It's very similar to a bitmap scaling row-renderer, except that fractional stepping is done in both *x* and *y*, since the source "row" may travel at any angle through the texture map. Here's the generic implementation of DrawTmapRow8U() in class ACanvas, which is short enough to explain itself.

```
void ACanvas::DrawTmapRow8U(int y, int xleft, int xright,
    ABitmap &tmap, ATmapCoord &tc, ATmapCoord &tcStep)
{
    for (int x = xleft; x < xright; x++)     // loop thru dest pixels
        {
        uchar c = *(tmap.pbits + (int(tc.v) * tmap.rowbytes) +
            int(tc.u));             // look up pixel in texture map
        DrawPixel8U(x, y, c);       // draw it
        tc.u += tcStep.u;           // step texture u coord
        tc.v += tcStep.v;           // step texture v coord
        }
}
```

Calling DrawPixel8U() to set each pixel in the polygon is not ideal, of course. That's why DrawTmapRow8U() is declared virtual, to encourage us to write faster versions in various canvas classes. The version for ACanvasLin8, our linear 8-bit canvas class, is listed below. Note how it precomputes the address of the first destination pixel in the row, and then just steps incrementally from there. Otherwise, it's essentially the same as the version in class ACanvas.

```
void ACanvasLin8::DrawTmapRow8U(int y, int xleft, int xright,
    ABitmap &tmap, ATmapCoord &tc, ATmapCoord &tcStep)
{
    int width = xright - xleft;     // calc width
    uchar *pd = Ptr(xleft, y);      // calc ptr to canvas x,y

    while (width-- > 0)                    // loop thru dest columns
        {
        *pd++ = *(tmap.pbits + (int(tc.v) * tmap.rowbytes) +
            int(tc.u));                    // look up tmap pixel and write
        tc.u += tcStep.u;                  // step texture u coord
        tc.v += tcStep.v;                  // step texture v coord
        }
}
```

The version of DrawTmapRow8U() in class ACanvasLin15 differs only in its need to set a 15-bit destination pixel, which requires finding a palette relevant for the source bitmap. BitmapOrDefault-Pal() takes this palette from the bitmap, or if there isn't one there, from a default source. Then, each 8-bit pixel is "converted" using APalette::ConvertTo15(), which amounts to nothing more than an inline table lookup. The 24-bit version in ACanvasLin24 differs from this one only in its need to convert to 24-bit form instead of 15-bit form, and isn't listed.

```
void ACanvasLin15::DrawTmapRow8U(int y, int xleft, int xright,
    ABitmap &tmap, ATmapCoord &tc, ATmapCoord &tcStep)
{
// See if palette in texture map, canvas, or default, else cancel.

    APalette *palette = BitmapOrDefaultPal(tmap);
    if (palette == NULL)
        return;

// Setup: calculate dest ptr and width

    ushort *pd = Ptr(xleft, y);
    int width = xright - xleft;

// Draw row

    while (width-- > 0)                      // loop thru dest columns
        {
        uchar c = *(tmap.pbits + (int(tc.v) * tmap.rowbytes) +
            int(tc.u));                      // get texture pixel
        *pd++ = palette->ConvertTo15(c);     // 8->15, write pixel
        tc.u += tcStep.u;                    // step texture u coord
        tc.v += tcStep.v;                    // step texture v coord
        }
}
```

Class ACanvasBank8 also has an implementation, which is conceptually similar to the one in ACanvasLin8 but is practically complicated by the nuisances of bank-crossing detection and bank-switching. This version is not listed—see the accompanying CD. Override versions for ACanvasBank15 and ACanvasBank24 are not implemented—these classes rely instead on the generic implementation in class ACanvas.

Advanced Texture Mapping

The texture mapping code shown above is just the entry point into the wide world of texture mapping. This section is a brief introduction to other destinations in that world.

Perspective Mapping

The technique of applying a source texture map onto a polygon through linear interpolation is called *linear texture mapping,* and though fast, it is not mathematically correct. Texture pixels should appear bigger at the closer edge of the polygon than those at a more distant edge,[2] but they don't with our linear mapper. This doesn't really matter for polygons whose distance from the camera far outweighs the relative distance between edges. But if the polygon is a stretch of wall, and we're close to one end of that wall and looking down it, the inaccuracy is quite dramatic indeed. *Perspective texture mapping* cures this problem, by doing a portion of the perspective transformation at each pixel along the way. In essence, a "reverse projection" is performed, whereby a pixel in the destination canvas is projected back to the texture map, and the pixel found there is drawn. Perspective mapping requires a divide operation per pixel, and is thus slower than linear mapping. It can be done in real time, however, and good 3D systems use it when it makes a difference, and drop back to linear mapping where the user won't notice.

Lit Texture Mapping

When discussing illumination earlier in this chapter, we saw how surface normals and light sources could be used to calculate new color intensities. In the simple case of ambient lighting only, each polygon is "lit" with a constant intensity. Our current texture mapping code simply copies pixels from the texture map to the canvas with no modification, but an alternate version could use each texture pixel as a lookup value into a lookup table (a CLUT). The techniques and classes developed in Chapter 15 could be used to build a set of shading tables, and the appropriate one selected for use with each polygon based on its illumination.

We can do even better than this simple "per polygon" lighting. Remember Gouraud shading, which does linear interpolation of color values across a polygon. An extension of this technique can do smooth lighting changes across a textured polygon. By interpolating overall intensity between the vertices, and using the intensity of a given pixel to determine which lighting CLUT to use for that particular pixel from a table of such CLUTs, the texture may be smoothly lit across its surface. This alleviates the "jump" in intensity from polygon to polygon, and is important in making 3D scenes look natural.

Translucent and Transparent Textures

Speaking of lookup tables for color effects, we also saw in Chapter 15 how blending tables could be used to simulate translucency. The

---

[2]Actually, the pixels don't really change size. Near the closer edge, we should be stepping through pixels with a smaller step value, which causes us to copy the same source pixel more often, and skip source pixels less often.

same technique can be applied to texture mapping, in order to put a see-through window in a scene, for instance. Transparent texture maps, where pixels of value 0 are simply not drawn, are possible as well. Neither of these cases is appropriate for closed polyhedra, where the interior of the object (and the backside of other faces) would become visible. However, their use in 3D textured scenes is abundant. Transparent textures can be used for gates and grates, oddly shaped doorways, and opened (or opening) windows.

Animated Textures

There is no reason, of course, why the texture assigned to a polygon must stay fixed forever. Just like 2D sprites, textures may animate. The texture map pointer might be rotated among several possibilities in a canned loop, or the texture map itself might be rendered into on the fly. It is just a bitmap, after all, and a canvas can be easily attached to make it renderable.

Tiled Texture Mapping

Texture maps, like any bitmap, can get pretty large. What if you want to cover the side of a brick building with a brick pattern? It's pretty annoying to have to make a large bitmap with a thousand repeating bricks in it—why not just have the texture mapper routine do the repeating? A *tiled texture mapper* can accept coordinates outside the 0 to 1.0 range, and use them to determine how to repeat the texture across the polygon. For instance, if a given span had to range from .5 to 6.5, the texture would be repeated six times across that row.

Bump Mapping

Rough surfaces such as fabric or brick can be simulated using well-drawn texture maps, but a more direct modeling approach is possible. In *bump mapping*, perturbations to the surface normal of the polygon are added in at each pixel, and an illumination value appropriate to that normal calculated. Lookup tables can be used to drive the process. The resulting pixels can have a quite "natural" feel if the perturbation values are carefully chosen. The illumination values can be used to create a color value without any texture map at all, or can be used to modify the color of a texture map pixel.

Procedural Mapping

Procedural mapping abandons the notion of a source texture altogether. At each pixel, a procedure is called, passing in relevant information about the location in the polygon to be drawn. The procedure, using any algorithms, texture maps, or data tables at its disposal, colors the pixel. The *RenderMan* rendering system, developed by Pixar, includes a procedural shading language customized for this purpose. Needless to say, procedural mapping is not an especially real-time process. Looks great in the movies, though.

Class AActorPolyObj: Scene-Based Polyhedron

If we can manipulate and render a polyhedral object, we ought to be able to put it into a scene. Full 3D scene rendering is a large and difficult topic unto itself, as will become clear in the next chapter. Short of a full 3D scene, we can put 3D objects into our current 2-and-a-half-D scene and actor system. To do so, we'll need to create a camera in addition to the polygon objects. Then, we'll need to add the appropriate actors to the scene. Let's create an actor class derived from AActor, one which has an associated polygon object. This actor class will be responsible for rendering the object, determining its 2D extent, and assigning it an *x,y,z* coordinate in the scene's coordinate system, which differs from the 3D object's coordinate system.

AActorPolyObj Data Members

Class AActorPolyObj, an instance of which is responsible for a single polygon object in a scene, is derived from class AActor. It provides the following member variables in addition to those of its base class:

pobj	Ptr to polygon object of class APolyObj
cam	Reference to camera of class ACamera
speed3d	Speed of object in 3D world coordinates
rotate3d	Rotational speed of object
clipped	Flag for whether object is currently clipped (projection failure)

Note that in addition to providing an actor-based wrapper around an APolyObj, class AActorPolyObj adds fields to support automatic movement and rotation along three axes. In the header file listing for class AActorPolyObj given below, note the inline methods for getting and setting these speeds, which default to 0. There are also inline methods for changing the polygon object associated with this actor, so that animation across a series of predefined polyhedron definitions can be achieved.

```
//    AActPoly.h    PolyObj Actor class
//    Rex E. Bradford

#ifndef __AACTPOLY_H
#define __AACTPOLY_H
```

```
#include "aactor.h"
#include "apolyobj.h"

class AActorPolyObj : public AActor {

    APolyObj *pobj;              // ptr to polygon object
    ACamera &cam;                // reference to camera
    AVector speed3d;             // 3d speed
    AVector rotate3d;            // 3d rotational speed
    bool clipped;                // if TRUE, don't render

    void ComputeSceneLoc();      // recompute scene loc
    void ComputeExtent();        // recompute extent
    void Draw(ACanvas *pcv);     // draw polyobj

public:

// Constructor: set scene & object stuff

    AActorPolyObj(AScene *pscene, APolyObj *pobj, ACamera &cam);

// Get/Set at underlying polyobj

    APolyObj *GetPolyObj() {return pobj;}
    void SetPolyObj(APolyObj *pobj_) {pobj = pobj_;}

// Adjust 3d motion speed and rotational speed

    void Get3DSpeed(AVector &speed3d_) {speed3d_ = speed3d;}
    void Set3DSpeed(AVector &speed3d_) {speed3d = speed3d_;}
    void Get3DRotationSpeed(AVector &rotate3d_) {rotate3d_ = rotate3d;}
    void Set3DRotationSpeed(AVector &rotate3d_) {rotate3d = rotate3d_;}

// Update

    void Update(AFix dt);
};

#endif
```

AActorPolyObj Constructor

The constructor for class AActorPolyObj takes three arguments: a
scene pointer, a pointer to an APolyObj, and a reference to a camera.
It initializes the base AActor, and then calls the following methods:

ComputeSceneLoc()	Transforms and projects the 0,0,0 center of the object (in local coordinates), and uses the result to assign a location in the scene coordinate system

ComputeExtent()	Transforms and projects the entire polygon object, and computes its bounding extent in scene coordinates
Redraw()	Marks the object's scene extent for redrawing

```
static ACoord3 dummyLoc(0,0,0);

AActorPolyObj::AActorPolyObj(AScene *pscene_, APolyObj *pobj_,
    ACamera &cam_) : AActor(pscene_, dummyLoc), cam(cam_)
{
    pobj = pobj_;                                   // set obj ptr
    speed3d.x = speed3d.y = speed3d.z = 0;          // zero speed
    ComputeSceneLoc();                              // xform to 2D
    ComputeExtent();                                // the usual
    Redraw();
}
```

AActorPolyObj::Update()

This method is called by the scene every time AScene::Update() is called. It gives the actor a "timeslice" in which to perform periodic update. In this case, that means moving and rotating the object, and causing it to be redrawn. This redrawing is done every time through, because the camera may have moved or altered its orientation.

```
void AActorPolyObj::Update(AFix dt)
{
// Convert time delta to floating point

    float fdt = float(dt);

// Move object in 3D world space (if moving)

    if (speed3d.x || speed3d.y || speed3d.z)
        {
        pobj->loc.x += speed3d.x * fdt;
        pobj->loc.y += speed3d.y * fdt;
        pobj->loc.z += speed3d.z * fdt;
        }

// Rotate object in 3D world space (if rotating)

    if (rotate3d.x || rotate3d.y || rotate3d.z)
        {
        pobj->orient.x += rotate3d.x * fdt;
        pobj->orient.y += rotate3d.y * fdt;
        pobj->orient.z += rotate3d.z * fdt;
        }

// Compute scene loc and redraw old and new area
```

```
        ComputeSceneLoc();
        RedrawNewArea();
    }
```

AActorPolyObj::ComputeSceneLoc()

AActorPolyObj::ComputeSceneLoc() transforms the polygon object from world coordinates to view coordinates, and then projects those onto screen coordinates. If the projection is successful, the projected screen coordinates are converted to scene coordinates. How is this done? The x and y coordinates are fine as is, but the projected screen coordinates have no z! For lack of a better approach, z is taken from the object's view coordinates. The z-coordinate is negated, in order to match the scene's coordinate system, where positive z goes into the screen.

```
void AActorPolyObj::ComputeSceneLoc()
{
    AVector zeroWorld(pobj->loc);       // obj center in world coords
    AVector zeroView;                   // store view coords here
    APolyVertex zeroScreen;             // store screen coords here

    cam.World2View(zeroWorld, zeroView);   // convert world->view
    if (cam.Project(zeroView, zeroScreen)) // project to screen
        {
        ACoord3 newloc(zeroScreen.x, zeroScreen.y, -zeroView.z);
        MoveTo(newloc);                 // move to scene x,y,z loc
        }
}
```

AActorPolyObj::ComputeExtent()

AActorPolyObj::ComputeExtent() computes the extent of the actor, as an aid to screen recomposing. This implementation transforms and projects the entire polygon object, and notes in the 'clipped' field whether projection succeeded. If projection failed, the object is not visible, and the new bounding box is set to the empty rectangle. If projection succeeded, APolyObj::BoundingBox() is called to compute the new extent of the object in screen coordinates.

```
void AActorPolyObj::ComputeExtent()
{
// Transform and project object, set bounding box unless clipped

    pobj->TransformLocal2World();               // local->world
    clipped = !pobj->TransformWorld2Screen(cam); // world->view->screen
    if (clipped)
        area.left = area.top = area.right = area.bott = 0; // clipped
    else
        pobj->BoundingBox(area);                // not clipped
}
```

AActorPolyObj::Draw()

This is the easy part. As long as all the polygons have successfully projected, as marked in the saved flag named 'clipped', drawing can occur. This is done by passing the buck to APolyObj::Draw().

```
void AActorPolyObj::Draw(ACanvas *pcv)
{
   if (!clipped)
      pobj->Draw(pcv); // only draw if not clipped away
}
```

TEXCUBES: *Putting it All Together*

The TEXCUBES sample program creates an infinite stream of spinning texture-mapped cubes in a full-screen scene, and flies them at the viewer. Press a key when you can't stand it any longer. The source for the Windows version of this program is listed below. A sample screen shot from TEXCUBES is shown in color plate 12.

```
//    TEXCUBES   Texture-mapped cube-spinning sample
//    Rex E. Bradford

#include <windows.h>
#include <stdio.h>
#include <stdlib.h>

#include "wing.h"
#include "awingwin.h"

#include "acamera.h"
#include "agfxfile.h"
#include "abmfind.h"
#include "ascenwin.h"
#include "aactpoly.h"
#include "aactsp.h"
#include "akeybd.h"
#include "atime.h"


// Application info

static char *szAppName = "TEXCUBES";  // app name (window class name)

AWingWindow *pMainWin;  // ptr to window obj

AScene *gScene;

#define WIN_WIDTH 512
#define WIN_HEIGHT 384
```

```
int PASCAL WinMain(HANDLE, HANDLE, LPSTR, int);
LRESULT CALLBACK WndProc(HWND, UINT, WPARAM, LPARAM);


// Cube polygon data

ABitmap bmTmap[6];          // 6 texture maps

ATmapCoord tc[4] = {        // bitmap covers face of cube
    ATmapCoord(0,0),
    ATmapCoord(0,.999),
    ATmapCoord(.999,.999),
    ATmapCoord(.999,0)};

APolygon cubeFaces[] = {    // polyvertex ptr NULL, must fill in!
    (long)&bmTmap[0],POLY_TYPE_TMAP,4,NULL,0,3,2,1,0,0,0,0,tc,
    (long)&bmTmap[1],POLY_TYPE_TMAP,4,NULL,0,4,7,3,0,0,0,0,tc,
    (long)&bmTmap[2],POLY_TYPE_TMAP,4,NULL,0,1,5,4,0,0,0,0,tc,
    (long)&bmTmap[3],POLY_TYPE_TMAP,4,NULL,1,2,6,5,0,0,0,0,tc,
    (long)&bmTmap[4],POLY_TYPE_TMAP,4,NULL,3,7,6,2,0,0,0,0,tc,
    (long)&bmTmap[5],POLY_TYPE_TMAP,4,NULL,4,5,6,7,0,0,0,0,tc,
};

float cubeLocal[] = {    // cube vertices in local coordinates
    -50,-50,50,
    50,-50,50,
    50,-50,-50,
    -50,-50,-50,
    -50,50,50,
    50,50,50,
    50,50,-50,
    -50,50,-50,
};

#define NUM_CUBE_FACES 6          // num faces on a cube
#define NUM_CUBE_VERTICES 8       // num vertices on a cube

#define MAX_CUBES 5
AActorPolyObj *pCube[MAX_CUBES];   // ptrs to cube objects

AFix tNextCube;          // time at which to create next cube;

//#define HARD_PATH      // uncomment to look for art in current dir

// -----------------------------------------------------------
//
// Rand() computes a floating-point random number within a given range.

float Rand(float low, float high)
{
    float rand0to1 = float(rand()) / 32768;
    return(low + (rand0to1 * (high - low)));
}
```

```
// ------------------------------------------------------------
//
// MakeCube() makes a new cube, and sets it spinning toward the camera.

AActorPolyObj *MakeCube(AScene *pscene, ACamera &cam)
{
// Allocate space for screen vertices

   APolyVertex *pverts = new APolyVertex[NUM_CUBE_VERTICES];

// Allocate polygon defs, copy from basic def, fill in vertex ptrs

   APolygon *faces = new APolygon[NUM_CUBE_FACES];
   memcpy(faces, cubeFaces, sizeof(APolygon) * NUM_CUBE_FACES);
   for (int i = 0; i < NUM_CUBE_FACES; i++)
      faces[i].pVerts = pverts;

// Create polygon object

   AVector loc(Rand(-50,+50), Rand(-50,+50), -3000);
   APolyObj *pPolyObj = new APolyObj(
      (AVector *) cubeLocal,  // local vertices
      new AVector[NUM_CUBE_VERTICES], // world vertices
      pverts,                 // screen vertices
      loc,                    // world loc
      AVector(0,0,0),         // world orientation
      faces,                  // polygon defs
      NUM_CUBE_FACES,         // num polygons
      NUM_CUBE_VERTICES);     // num vertices

// Create polygon actor, assign motion and spin

   AActorPolyObj *pActorPoly = new AActorPolyObj(pscene, pPolyObj, cam);
   AVector speed(Rand(-40,+40), Rand(-40,+40), Rand(100,200));
   pActorPoly->Set3DSpeed(speed);
   AVector rotate(Rand(-1.5,+1.5),Rand(-1.5,+1.5),Rand(-1.5,+1.5));
   pActorPoly->Set3DRotationSpeed(rotate);

// Return actor

   return pActorPoly;
}


// ------------------------------------------------------------
//
// DelCube() deletes a cube, cleaning up its memory use.

void DelCube(AActorPolyObj *pcube)
{
   APolyObj *pPolyObj = pcube->GetPolyObj();
   delete[] pPolyObj->pVertWorld;
   delete[] pPolyObj->pVertScrn;
```

```
      delete[] pPolyObj->polys;
      delete pPolyObj;
      pcube->Kill();      // don't delete - let scene do that!
}


// -----------------------------------------------------------
//
// CubePastCamera() returns TRUE if cube has flown by us.

bool CubePastCamera(AActorPolyObj *pcube)
{
    APolyObj *pPolyObj = pcube->GetPolyObj();
    return (pPolyObj->loc.z >= 0);
}


// -----------------------------------------------------------
//
// WinMain() is the program's entry point.

int PASCAL WinMain(HANDLE hInstance, HANDLE hPrevInstance, LPSTR
lpszCmdLine, int nCmdShow)
{
// Register window class

    if (!hPrevInstance)
        {
        WNDCLASS wndclass;
        wndclass.style = CS_BYTEALIGNCLIENT | CS_VREDRAW |
            CS_HREDRAW | CS_DBLCLKS;
        wndclass.lpfnWndProc = WndProc;
        wndclass.cbClsExtra = 0;
        wndclass.cbWndExtra = 0;
        wndclass.hInstance = hInstance;
        wndclass.hIcon = NULL;
        wndclass.hCursor = LoadCursor(NULL, IDC_ARROW);
        wndclass.hbrBackground = (HBRUSH) NULL;
        wndclass.lpszMenuName = NULL;
        wndclass.lpszClassName = szAppName;
        if (!RegisterClass(&wndclass))
            {
            MessageBox(NULL, "Can't register class\n", NULL, MB_OK);
            return FALSE;
            }
        }

// Read texture maps

    ABitmap bmTmapFile;
#ifdef HARD_PATH
    if (AGfxFile::Read("\\artt\\samples\\texwin\\tmaps.pcx", bmTmapFile))
#else
    if (AGfxFile::Read("tmaps.pcx", bmTmapFile))
#endif
```

```
            {
            MessageBox(NULL, "Can't load texture maps!\n", NULL, MB_OK);
            return 1;
            }

        ABitmapFind bmfind(bmTmapFile, 255);
        for (int i = 0; i < 6; i++)
            {
            if (!bmfind.NextBitmap(bmTmap[i], FALSE))
                {
                MessageBox(NULL, "Can't extract textures from tmaps.pcx!",
                    NULL, MB_OK);
                return 1;
                }
            }

    // Clear system palette and create palette

        AWingPal::ClearSystemPal();
        APalette *gPalette = new APalette();
        gPalette->Set(bmTmapFile.ppalette->rgb, 0, 256);

    // Create window

        DWORD windowStyle = WS_OVERLAPPED | WS_CAPTION | WS_SYSMENU |
            WS_MINIMIZEBOX | WS_MAXIMIZEBOX | WS_THICKFRAME;
        AError err;
        pMainWin = new AWingWindow(err, WIN_WIDTH, WIN_HEIGHT,
            gPalette,
            szAppName,
            "Textured Cubes",
            windowStyle,
            CW_USEDEFAULT, CW_USEDEFAULT,
            WIN_WIDTH, WIN_HEIGHT,
            NULL,
            NULL,
            hInstance,
            NULL);
        HWND hWndApp = pMainWin->hwnd;

    // If can't create, bail out

        if (err)
            {
            delete pMainWin;
            UnregisterClass(szAppName, hInstance);
            MessageBox(NULL, "Can't create window\n", NULL, MB_OK);
            return 1;
            }

    // Define camera location and orientation

        AVector camLoc(0,0,0);
        AVector camDir(0,0,0);
```

```
    float fov = FOV_90;
    ACamera cam(camLoc, camDir, WIN_WIDTH, WIN_HEIGHT, fov);

// Create scene

    ARect sceneArea(0, 0, WIN_WIDTH, WIN_HEIGHT);
    gScene = new ASceneWin(pMainWin, AFix(0), AFix(0),
      AScene::UPDATE_SLOPPY, 0);

// Add background

    ABitmap bmBack;
#ifdef HARD_PATH
    if (AGfxFile::Read("\\artt\\samples\\texwin\\texback.pcx", bmBack))
#else
    if (AGfxFile::Read("texback.pcx", bmBack))
#endif
        {
        MessageBox(NULL, "Can't load texback.pcx!\n", NULL, MB_OK);
        return 1;
        }
    ACoord3 loc((WIN_WIDTH - bmBack.width) / 2,
        (WIN_HEIGHT - bmBack.height) / 2, 32767);
    ASprite spBack(bmBack);
    new AActorSprite(gScene, loc, &spBack);

// Show window

    AScene::UpdateAll();
    ShowWindow(hWndApp, nCmdShow);

// Poll messages from event queue, update

    MSG msg;
    while (TRUE)
        {
        if (PeekMessage(&msg, 0, 0, 0, PM_REMOVE))
            {
            if (msg.message == WM_QUIT)
                break;
            TranslateMessage(&msg);
            DispatchMessage(&msg);
            }
        else
            {
            AScene::UpdateAll();
            for (int i = 0; i < MAX_CUBES; i++)
                {
                if (pCube[i] && CubePastCamera(pCube[i]))
                    {
                    DelCube(pCube[i]);
                    pCube[i] = NULL;
                    }
```

```
            }
        if (ATime::Read() > tNextCube)
            {
            for (int i = 0; i < MAX_CUBES; i++)
                {
                if (pCube[i] == NULL)
                    {
                    pCube[i] = MakeCube(gScene, cam);
                    tNextCube = ATime::Read() + AFix(Rand(2,8));
                    break;
                    }
                }
            }
        int c = AKeybd::Read();
        if (c == 0x1B)
            PostQuitMessage(0);
        }
    }

// Delete window, unregister class, and exit

    delete pMainWin;
    UnregisterClass(szAppName, hInstance);
    return msg.wParam;
}


// ------------------------------------------------------------
//
// WndProc() is the window message handler.

LRESULT CALLBACK WndProc(HWND hwnd, UINT message,
    WPARAM wParam, LPARAM lParam)
{
// Handle messages not handled by StdHandler() or DefWindowProc().

    switch (message)
        {
        case WM_DESTROY:
            PostQuitMessage(0);   // when window destroyed, close up shop
            return(0);
        }

// Pass the rest on to StdHandler(), some go on to DefWindowProc

    return pMainWin->StdHandler(hwnd, message, wParam, lParam);
}
```

19

Three-Dimensional Scene Rendering

In the last two chapters, we built up a body of classes capable of rendering texture-mapped convex polyhedral objects in a scene. This is great, but it's hardly the end of the line in 3D rendering. Most objects we might want to represent are nonconvex, so that visible faces in the same object can obscure each other, and need to be somehow sorted properly. Furthermore, there is the issue of 3D landscapes and terrain. Are the floor and walls of a maze "objects" in any sense, or do we want to render them using some other 3D technique? And what about complex objects in which part of object A is in front of object B, and part of it is behind? No matter which object we render first, it doesn't work! Welcome to 3D scene rendering, the most challenging aspect of real-time 3D graphics.

Hidden Surface Removal

Look at the object in Figure 19.1. It is nonconvex, meaning that it features angles between some polygon edges which are greater than 180 degrees. Of more importance, this means that the polygons which make up the object cannot be drawn in any random order, because visible polygons can obscure one another when viewed from various

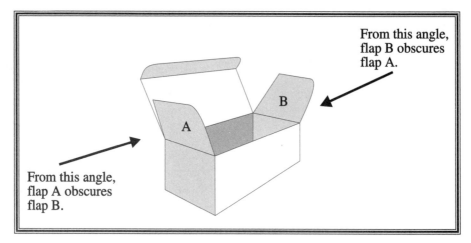

From this angle, flap B obscures flap A.

B

A

From this angle, flap A obscures flap B.

Figure 19.1   A nonconvex polyhedron. No polygon drawing order sorts correctly from all view angles.

angles. If we draw the front one first and then the back one, the back one will incorrectly "show through."

If off-screen composition is the art of 2D graphics, then *hidden surface removal* is the black art of 3D graphics. The proper rendering of nonconvex polygons can be viewed as a three-dimensional sorting problem. If we can order the polygons in a particular way, perhaps one that is view dependent, then we can simply draw them all back to front using this ordering, and thereby allow polygons in front to overlay those which are behind. The trick is to find such an ordering. Or maybe not—it turns out that there are other ways of creating the correct resultant image which don't require sorting at all. Let's have a brief look at some of the range of techniques that have been invented.

Z Buffering

The simplest approach to hidden surface removal was proposed by Catmull in 1974. An area of memory called a Z buffer is used alongside the viewport's frame buffer (canvas bitmap, in ARTT). Each x,y location in the viewport has a corresponding x,y location in the Z buffer. Instead of holding pixel colors, however, the Z buffer holds the depth (z-coordinate) of the pixel drawn at that location. See Figure 19.2.

The Z buffer requires rendering routines to write not only into the pixel buffer, but also into the Z buffer, recording the depth of the pixel rendered into the corresponding location in the pixel buffer. Furthermore, such rendering routines must not write into either the

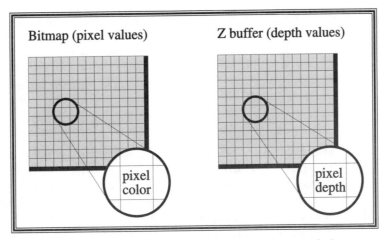

Figure 19.2 A Z buffer accompanying a bitmap of the same dimensions.

pixel buffer or the Z buffer any pixel which is more distant than the one already recorded in the Z buffer. Sample code for a hypothetical DrawPixelZ() is given below.

```
// SAMPLE CODE FOR HYPOTHETICAL ROUTINE WHICH DRAWS Z-BUFFERED PIXEL
// (assumes canvas has zbuffer which can be accessed like a 2D array)
void ACanvas::DrawPixelZ(int x, int y, int z)
{
    if (z < zbuffer[x][y])    // assumes smaller z is closer
        {
        DrawPixel(x,y);       // if so, draw pixel
        zbuffer[x][y] = z;    // and record its depth in z buffer
        }
}
```

In one fell swoop, all sorting issues are resolved. Polygons or other primitives may be rendered in any order, as long as the rendering routines update and respect the Z buffer. Problem solved.

Solved, that is, for the well-off among us. In the long run, Z buffering will probably win out as the ultimate sorting algorithm due to its simplicity and ease of implementation in hardware. And hardware implementations already exist. The Intel i860 processor, not available in your PC of course, actually has a single instruction which checks the value in a Z buffer, and writes to both a pixel buffer and the Z buffer if the current value is closer. Until such hardware becomes commonplace, however, Z buffering is too costly for real-time use on PCs. The technique is tough to implement efficiently in software for the following reasons:

- The Z buffer must use at least 16 bits per pixel for reasonable accuracy, so memory costs are high (a 640×480 16-bit Z buffer uses over 600 K).

- The Z buffer must be reset by filling its contents with a "very distant" value at the beginning of each frame, which is time consuming.

- Rendering algorithms must all be written to check and modify the Z buffer, adding to their complexity and slowing their performance.

- Good rendering algorithms must interpolate Z values across the surface of the polygon or other surface, further slowing performance.

The Z buffer size issue can be solved by rendering the scene in multiple passes, each time clipped to a different horizontal "strip," which may be as short as a single scan line. This saves memory, but at the cost of the time spent reprocessing the scene multiple times. For such a scan-line algorithm to work well, all polygons should be collected into a giant list, sorted vertically, and then processed by a special algorithm which keeps track of "active" polygons which intersect the current row being processed. Even so, the overhead of collecting and sorting all the polygons can be large.

Z buffering is at the foundation of some 3D software systems, such as OpenGL. But you won't find it used in your favorite moving-camera PC simulation for another few years at least.

Depth-Sorting

So much for Z buffering. Maybe sorting polygons into depth order isn't so bad an idea after all. We have their z-coordinates in view space, which is exactly what we need to sort by. We'll just collect our polygons into a list, sorted by each polygon's z-coordinate, and render back to front.

Not so fast. First of all, a polygon doesn't have a z-coordinate, a vertex does. Each polygon has three or more such vertices. Which one is the real depth of the polygon? None of them, of course. The polygon has a different depth at each point on its surface, at least if its vertices have different depths. But we can easily find the minimum and maximum z-coordinate of the polygon by checking all the vertices. If the furthest z-coordinate of polygon A is closer than the closest z-coordinate of polygon B, then polygon A is fully closer than polygon B and should be drawn after it in sorting order.

This helps, but by no means solves the full sorting problem. There will be a great many cases in which polygons overlap in the z-dimension. In fact, polygons which share an edge in a polyhedron, and therefore share two vertices, will almost always overlap in the z-dimension. We need to do more work to sort these cases properly. We can check x,y bounding boxes. In cases where the bounding boxes of two polygons don't overlap, we can sort the two polygons arbitrarily—if they don't overlap on the screen, who cares what order they are drawn in? But there are more complex cases too. The following steps, not all of which are trivial to implement, can be used to properly depth-sort two polygons:

1. If there is no overlap in the polygons' *x*-extents or *y*-extents (view coordinates), they can be drawn in either order.
2. If one polygon is entirely on one side of the plane of the other polygon, this determines drawing order.
3. If there is no overlap in the pixels covered by the two polygons (compare edges), they can be drawn in either order.
4. If sorting cannot be determined in the first three steps, split one polygon using the plane of the other, and repeat.

Depth sorting is a reasonable approach, but still requires collecting polygons together into a big list and applying sorting steps which are complex and time consuming in the tough cases. This amount of overhead isn't terrible, but isn't small either.

By the way, there is a special name for a simplified case of depth-sorting, when each polygon to be rendered has a constant *z*-component. In the *Painter's Algorithm*, *z* extents can't overlap, so sorting is simply a matter of ordering by *z*. The scene and actor system developed in Part 2 uses the Painter's Algorithm, albeit with bitmaps instead of polygons as the graphic elements to be sorted and rendered.

Area Subdivision

Another class of sorting techniques, the *area subdivision* algorithms, look at things from an entirely different angle, as it were. Instead of focusing on the polygons themselves, these algorithms focus on the screen. *Warnock's Algorithm,* one of the most popular area subdivision methods, recursively divides the screen into smaller and smaller rectangles, in an attempt to find screen areas which are completely encompassed by a single polygon. Any given polygon intersects a rectangular screen area in one of the four ways depicted in Figure 19.3.

When a rectangle is completely surrounded by a single polygon, or by more than one polygon with a simply determined ordering relationship, the rectangle need be subdivided no further. Otherwise, the rectangle is split into quadrants, and the algorithm rerun on these quadrants. Figure 19.4 shows the screen division necessary to render a very simple scene. This recursion can proceed right down to the level of a single pixel, in which case multipolygon conflicts which still exist can be resolved by computing the *z*-coordinate of each polygon at that particular pixel, and choosing the closest. This algorithm is well-suited to anti-aliasing the edges of polygons by subdividing past

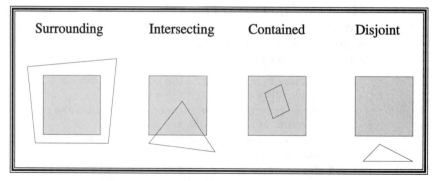

Figure 19.3 A polygon may have four relations to a rectangular area, as shown.

the resolution of a single pixel, and then averaging the results of the subpixel quadrants.

This method is conceptually simple, and the ease with which anti-aliasing can be built in is attractive, but the technique has severe performance problems for real-time work. For one thing, a full list of the polygons in the entire scene must be created and maintained, just

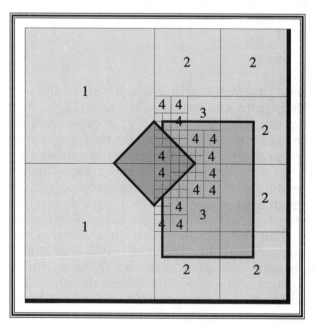

Figure 19.4 Simple scene, consisting of two polygons, divided using Warnock's algorithm. Each square is marked with its level of subdivision.

as in depth-sorting. The traversing of this polygon list to determine the outcome for a given rectangular area is time consuming, although well-coded versions of the algorithm will make use of the fact that polygons which don't intersect a given rectangle cannot intersect its "children," and thus should not be considered at all.

Finally, rendering the rectangles, which may be as small as a single pixel (or smaller, in the subpixel anti-aliasing version) is simple for flat-shaded polygons, but requires extra calculations for Gouraud shaded or texture-mapped polygons. The unit of rendering is no longer a polygon but some (small) rectangular area of a polygon, which requires computation of the corner colors of the rectangle in the case of Gouraud shading, and of the u,v texture map coordinates in the case of texture mapping. This adds to rendering overhead, although it is somewhat offset by the fact that the rendering primitive is always a rectangle, which allows optimization of the rendering routine. The overall verdict: not ready for real time.

Binary Space Partitioning

We seem to be running out of options for sorting in real time. Fortunately, the final sorting technique we'll look at *is* suitable for real-time use, subject to various caveats and onerous restrictions. Nobody said 3D was easy!

Binary space partitioning (BSP) relies on a straightforward observation. If a plane can be found which divides a set of polygons into two "clusters," then the polygons on the same side of the plane as the camera can obscure, but not be obscured by, any polygons on the other side of the plane. With suitable *separation planes*, which can't always be found without sometimes splitting polygons into two pieces, this process can be recursively repeated. The end result is called a *BSP tree*, whose branch nodes are separation planes and whose leaves are polygons. Such a BSP tree can be used to drive a sorting process based on an arbitrary view location. Figure 19.5 shows a simple set of polygons, depicted in two dimensions for ease of visualization, and the separation planes which might be used to build a BSP tree from them.

In order to render a set of polygons described by such a BSP tree, a "tree-walking" algorithm is used. This algorithm starts at the root of the tree, and computes which side of the root's separation plane the camera is on. It proceeds to the subtree on the side of the plane opposite to the camera, in order to render those polygons first, and then renders the polygons on the side of the tree shared with the camera. Either "half" can be a polygon or list of polygons (there can be more than one in the same leaf), or it can be a subtree, in which

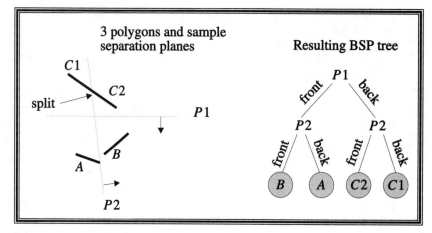

Figure 19.5 Polygons divided into clusters by separation planes, and the resulting BSP tree.

case the same process is recursively run. When it comes time to render an individual polygon, backface-culling is applied to avoid rendering those facing away from the camera. Happily, the algorithm detects these as part of its tree-walk, so a separate facing computation is unnecessary. Sample C++ code for such a tree-walking renderer is given below.

```cpp
// Sample code to render a BSP tree

class BSPTree {
    BSPTree *backChild;       // child tree on back side of plane
    BSPTree *frontChild;      // child tree on front side of plane
    Plane *separationPlane;   // separation plane
    Polygon *polys;           // list of polygons at this node
    ... methods ...
};

void BSPTree::Render()           // called for root tree, recurses
{
    if (PlaneFacingCamera())     // if this sep. plane is facing the camera
        {
        if (backChild != NULL)   // then render sub-tree on back side first
            backChild->Render();
        DisplayPolygons(polys);  // followed by polygons in this node
        if frontChild != NULL)
            frontChild->Render(); // followed by sub-tree on front side
        }
    else                         // else sep. plane is facing away from camera
        {
        if (frontChild != NULL)  // then render sub-tree on front side
            frontChild->Render();
```

```
      // camera behind this plane, don't render (backface culling)
      if (backChild != NULL)
         backChild->Render();  // followed by polygons on back side
      }
}
```

Pay attention now, because here comes the good part. A BSP tree which describes a set of polygons and their separation planes is valid *regardless of the camera view direction!* No matter which direction the camera is facing in, the tree-walker will render the polygons in correct sorting order. The tree can thus be created in world-coordinate space or even local space. As long as the polygons don't move relative to each other, the tree remains valid. The computation of whether a given separation plane is facing the camera depends on the view location and direction, of course. The normal vector pointing out of the separation plane can be computed in view space, or it can be pre-stored in the tree in local or world space and transformed. Then, the plane-facing test reduces to the sign of the z-component of the (transformed) normal vector.

Note that there are multiple valid BSP trees for a given set of polygons. The possible trees are not all equally efficient—the best BSP representation for a given set of polygons will have as few nodes as possible, and as many leaves containing multiple polygons as possible. Also, it is desirable to split as few polygons as possible. Creating leaves with multiple polygons in them essentially means finding "good" separation planes that divide polygons into clusters which have unambiguous sorting between them.

The BSP algorithm exemplifies the time-honored tradition of pushing computation back to the time before a program is even run. A BSP tree for a given set of polygons can be computed ahead of time, and stored as data along with the polygons themselves. Then, the only runtime computation is that done during tree-walking.

So, have we found the ideal solution to sorting polygons in real time? Yes and no. For a set of polygons which doesn't animate, BSP representation is pretty ideal. An architectural walkthrough of a proposed building, for example, could make use of a BSP tree describing the entire building. Representing an entire complex building as a single BSP tree might be a little much, actually, since traversing the parts of the tree for the third floor is wasted time when you're on the first. In a real application, some connected set of multiple BSP trees would probably be used.

The problem with BSP trees is that they represent a static set of polygons, which isn't adequate for most 3D work. Polygon cars should turn their wheels as they roll down the polygon highway; polygon robots should flex their arms and legs. BSP sorting by itself doesn't work in the face of such relative motion and animation, and recomputing BSP trees is too slow to do on the fly. So while binary space partitioning can be used for static entities, it can't sort an entire animated scene. It can play a role in scene rendering, but can't handle the whole job.

This coverage of various sorting algorithms has necessarily been brief. For more information, consult Foley et al., *Computer Graphics: Principles and Practice,* or other 3D references listed in Appendix E. Until we all hang up our software hats and employ hardware Z buffers, sorting is probably the most challenging aspect of real-time 3D rendering.

Terrain Rendering

In high-end "pure" computer graphics systems, 3D scenes are allowed to be arbitrarily complex, and a robust sorting algorithm (typically Z buffering) is employed to render the scene properly. If the scene includes room interiors or an exterior landscape, these are simply more polygons thrown into the overall soup as far as sorting and rendering is concerned.

On current PC systems, this purist approach doesn't cut the mustard. There is no general sorting algorithm which can render 3D scenes in real time, with the exception of BSP sorting, which can't sort an entire scene in which relative motion or animation is occurring. What's needed is a new approach. If the kind of scenes which can be rendered properly is restricted, perhaps it is possible to invent a new sorting approach which works for those scenes, even if it can't handle all possible scenes.

Scene = Terrain and Objects

The real world in which we live does not feature arbitrary collections of shapes. Suppose we are indoors, in some house or building. The geometry of walls, floors, and ceilings is fairly constrained, and most objects in the room are placed on the floor or hanging from a wall or ceiling, but not floating in space. If we are outdoors, there is a landscape with elevation changes, but there aren't chunks of terrain hanging in the air. In both the indoor and outdoor case, we can describe a typical scene in terms of terrain and objects. This is the simple but key observation which can point us toward rendering strategies which render the visible terrain before us, while also rendering the visible objects correctly sorted among each other and the terrain.

Indoor Terrain

The geometry of indoor terrain can be very simple, as in the case of a square room with four walls, a floor, and a ceiling. Given a camera viewpoint inside such a room, these six polygons can be rendered in any order, since non occlude any other. Furthermore, all objects inside the room can be rendered after all terrain elements. Figure 19.6 shows a top-down view of a very simple room with a couple of objects.

Sorting the objects correctly between themselves still needs to be done somehow. If they don't move or animate, BSP sorting can be used. Otherwise, a new approach is needed for them.

Figure 19.7 shows a more complex indoor terrain layout, one in which sorting is not so straightforward. A BSP tree can handle this terrain, of course, but the fact that the terrain itself can obscure objects means that we can't adopt a rendering model which says "terrain first, sorted objects after." The rendering of terrain and objects must be interleaved, and this is where the complexity arises. Later in this chapter, we'll look at some of the issues which are encountered when trying to support such interleaved sorting.

Outdoor Terrain

Another common environment for 3D simulations is outdoors, where the terrain is a landscape instead of room interiors. Real landscape has continuously varying elevation, which can be simulated with a reasonable amount of accuracy via a mesh of texture-mapped triangles. Various textures can be devised for various terrain "types" such as grass, sand, water, rocks, snow, roads, and so on. Such textures

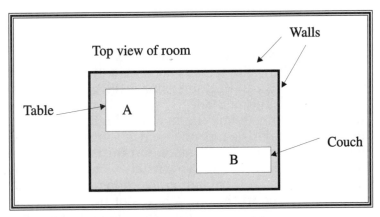

Figure 19.6 Top view of a room with a few objects in it.

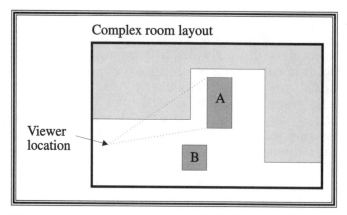

Figure 19.7   In this room layout, object A cannot be drawn in front of all walls or behind all walls. It must be sorted in with terrain polygons.

should "tile" well; that is, the edges of each texture should blend well into other copies of itself or other textures it might appear adjacent to.

Outdoor terrain rendering shares with indoor rendering the issue of correctly interleaving objects with terrain. If a figure is coming over a hill and is partially obscured by it, this means that the polygons which make up the hill must be rendered after the object (assuming a back-to-front rendering strategy is used, instead of Z buffering or some other approach in which polygon drawing is order independent). However, if the same figure is standing on a flat plain in front of the viewer, it is drawn after the terrain squares under its feet. Figure 19.8 illustrates the two cases.

Sorting Terrain Polygons

The first step in 3D scene rendering is to design a rendering strategy which can draw the terrain itself in correct sorted order from any viewpoint. This can be done using a BSP tree for the terrain, assuming it doesn't animate and is not subject to deformation, either of which would invalidate the tree. For highest throughput, it is better to write a "rendering pipeline" which is optimized toward the kind of terrain being rendered. Indoor terrain is geometrically simple and indoor renderers are often written using raycasting, a technique described later in this chapter. Outdoor terrain renderers are more challenging due to the smoothness of the terrain elevation fluctuations (that's the goal, anyway) and the fact that much more distant terrain and objects must be included in the view.

This moonman is in front of terrain

This moonman is behind hilly terrain

Figure 19.8   Moonmen must be properly interleaved with terrain polygons.

Suppose a terrain map is broken down into triangles (two per square), with a side length of 4 meters. The floor of a huge room 16 meters by 16 meters has only:

```
16/4 x 16/4 = 16 squares, x 2 = 32 triangles
```

An outdoor view with the same size terrain triangles will have to draw many more triangles. Suppose we wish to see terrain just 200 meters distant (50 squares), which is not that far. With a 90-degree field of view (one quadrant of a circle), we need to render in excess of 1,250 squares, or more than 2,500 triangles. This is a lot of rendering, and it's also a lot of vertices to transform and project. Good outdoor renderers, like those found in games such as the upcoming *Terra Nova*, use hybrid techniques which draw distant areas using non-polygon techniques.

Sorting the triangles in an outdoor view is fundamentally a matter of traversing them in the correct order. The typical approach is to render horizontal or vertical strips of terrain squares, split by the view direction into left and right halves. Each strip is rendered from outside to inside, and then the next closer strips are rendered. See Figure 19.9. Within a square, the rendering order for the two triangles is based on which terrain corners are on the near and far sides.

Sorting Objects With Terrain

In many simulations such as airplane flying, car racing, and robot zapping, the terrain is populated with objects, both fixed and moving.

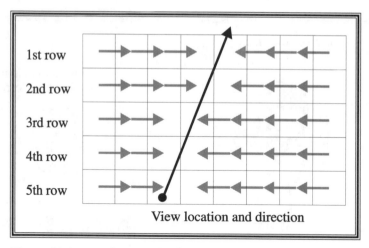

Figure 19.9 Rendering order for terrain squares, given a particular view location and direction.

These objects are often rendered using polygons which are texture mapped, Gouraud shaded, flat shaded, or some combination of these. Often, objects are rendered using bitmaps. Natural objects such as trees, bushes, humans, and other creatures don't look very good when rendered using polygons. This is due to the sharp angles and overall jagged nature of polygons, which can only be overcome by using large numbers of small polygons. This cure, of course, is worse than the disease, since objects with huge numbers of polygons can't be rendered very quickly due to the vertex transformation and projection overhead.

Whether rendered using polygons, bitmaps, or some other technique entirely, objects must be drawn in the proper sorting relation to the terrain on which they stand or above which they hover. In the general case, this may involve splitting the object into parts, since part of an object may be in front of a given terrain polygon and another part behind it. Figure 19.10 illustrates this situation via a depiction of a multilegged creature coming over a hill.

In most computer games today, such situations are dealt with using a very simple strategy. They are punted. That is to say, the rendering strategy simply does not deal with them correctly, and the objects in the game are designed with an eye toward minimizing the likelihood of noticeable sorting anomalies. After all, there is no federal law saying that every frame of the scene *must* be rendered with no errors. As long as the overall effect works and such inaccuracies are rare enough that the viewer isn't constantly distracted by them, who cares if a few small polygons are out of order sometimes? The game player would rather have that than an equivalent game

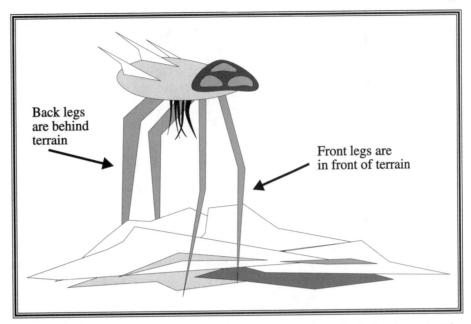

Figure 19.10   Object which can't be drawn wholly in front of or behind terrain. The object's polygons must be individually sorted into the terrain.

which uses a Z buffer for total accuracy and runs at one-third the frame rate.

One strategy for dealing with objects is to make their "footprint" smaller than the size of the terrain polygons on which they are placed. This minimizes the likelihood of the sort of "straddling" problem illustrated by the multilegged creature. But no matter how small an object is, if it moves it will come close enough to an edge to straddle more than one polygon. The best strategy in this case is usually to render it immediately after rendering the terrain polygon it straddles which is closest to the viewer. See Figure 19.11.

The data structures required to support interleaved rendering of terrain and objects are not trivial. They must provide a link between terrain polygons and the objects residing "on" them, and these links change in real time as objects move and are created and destroyed. Furthermore, there must be a straightforward way to determine which of the terrain polygons that an object straddles is closest to the viewer. The design of these data structures, and the rendering pipeline which renders a scene from them, is one of the real black arts in real-time 3D simulations. The requirements of different simulations, whether they be indoor or outdoor, high-flying or low to the ground, demand unique methods if maximum performance is desired. And it always is.

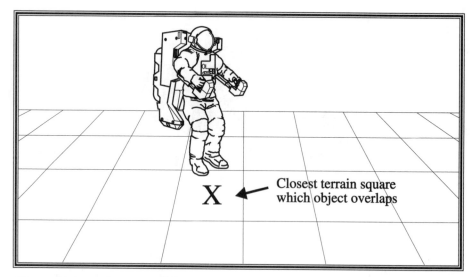

X ← Closest terrain square
which object overlaps

Figure 19.11 Object straddling terrain polygons, rendered after closest terrain square it straddles.

Raycasting Engines

When a programming task seems intractable, it's often a good idea to sit back, stare at a corner of the ceiling,[1] and let go of your assumptions. Just as the Z buffer is a radically different way of looking at polygon sorting, so are there radically different ways to approach terrain and object rendering. One clever approach to the rendering of indoor scenes made its debut with the shareware game *Castle Wolfenstein*. This game features texture-mapped floors, walls, and ceilings, arranged in a fairly rigid gridlike formation. It sure looks like a bunch of polygons being rendered, with bitmapped objects in each room. But in fact no polygons are ever drawn, not as such anyway. The rendering algorithm, which has since been adopted and enhanced by large numbers of game developers, comes at the screen from a whole different angle, so to speak. It renders the scene in vertical strips, each one pixel wide. This technique is called *raycasting*.

Raycasting Terrain Layout

Let's start with the most basic raycasting engine, and then talk about the bells and whistles. In the simplest case, the indoor environment consists of a floor, vertical walls which occur only at right angles, and a ceiling. Any or all of these may be textured. Figure 19.12 shows a possible layout of walls.

---

[1]and paint the ceiling blue, eh Mike?

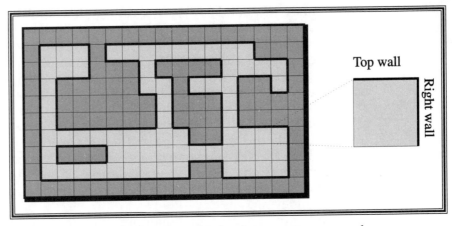

Figure 19.12 A "maze" grid suitable for the raycasting approach.

It's possible to represent such an environment by a grid. Each element might contain a pointer to the texture of the floor square at that grid location, the presence or absence of walls at each side and their texture, and the texture of the ceiling. Such a two-dimensional array of grid elements completely describes this simple indoor layout. While there are many ways of representing an element in this grid, the structure shown below would do the trick:

```
typedef struct {
    ABitmap *floorTmap;      // texture map for floor
    ABitmap *ceilTmap;       // texture map for ceiling
    ABitmap *rightWallTmap;  // texture map for wall at right, or NULL
    ABitmap *bottWallTmap;   // texture map for wall at bottom, or NULL
} AGridRaycast;

AGridRaycast theGridWorld[32][32]; // a world composed of such grid squares
```

In the above data layout, only the walls at the right and bottom sides of a grid square (when looking from above) are assigned a texture. The left wall is obtained by looking at the right wall of the square to the left, and the top wall is obtained by looking at the bottom wall of the square above.

Basic Raycasting Algorithm

The raycasting approach is related to ray tracing, wherein light rays are cast "backwards" from the eye through each pixel on the screen, and into the scene beyond, in a kind of reverse replay of what actually happens in the real world. In raycasting, the simplified geometry of the environment makes it possible to cast one ray for each vertical strip on the screen, instead of one for each pixel. In a low-resolution screen mode like mode 13H, this reduces the number of rays cast from $320 \times 200 = 64,000$ to just 320.

Each of the 320 rays in this case are cast out at different angles from the eye into the scene. Each ray "snakes" out from the eye through the bottommost pixel of a given vertical strip, where it typically hits some area of floor. Then, the ray slithers along the floor at the appropriate angle. Each time the ray hits the boundary of a grid square, two things happen. First, the one-pixel-wide strip of texture which the ray has just slithered through is rendered by copying it to the vertical strip of screen pixels, scaled based on distance according to perspective calculations. Then, a check is made to see if a wall has been encountered. If so, the algorithm switches to wall-rendering.

Walls are rendered in a manner similar to floors, taking into account that the walls are vertical and not horizontal. In the simple case we are describing, all walls are the same height, so only a single pixel-strip transfer operation occurs. Unless the person is close to the wall, the top of the wall will be below the top of the screen, and so then the algorithm switches to ceiling rendering, which is like floor rendering in the reverse direction, without the need to check for walls.

The above algorithm operates for each vertical pixel strip, each at an angle determined by the camera field-of-view and the horizontal resolution of the screen or viewport being rendered into. Figure 19.13 shows a sample grid and an associated view, using solid colors instead of textures for the floors, walls, and ceilings.

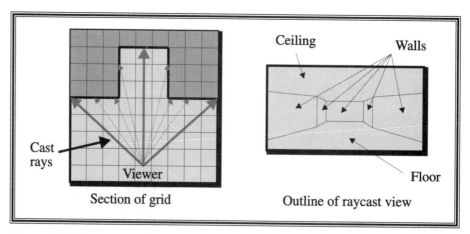

Figure 19.13   An area of a grid-based indoor world, and an outline of a raycast view generated from it.

Raycasting Enhancements

The basic raycasting engine has been enhanced in a number of ways by many developers. Some of these improvements are highlighted below.

Height Mapping

Having a flat floor and walls of all the same height can get pretty boring. To alleviate this, each grid square can be assigned a different height, creating sunken floor areas and raised platforms. Instead of each square having "wall" or "no wall" on its sides, each square has a wall whose height may range from 0 to "full height," along with an accompanying wall texture. A raycasting renderer for such a layout must be able to switch back and forth multiple times between floors and walls, instead of assuming that the first such wall will encounter the ceiling. Some height-mapping variations have two levels of grid resolution, a coarse one for determining textures and major height changes, and a fine level used only for certain grid squares which have detailed height variations.

Lighting

A large part of visual realism is derived from effective lighting. Raycasting engines may, instead of just copying strips of pixels, run them through a CLUT to change their shade. In this way, more distant floors, walls, and ceilings can appear darker. Additionally, local lighting can be applied to each grid square. The amount of light associated with a square, combined with a distance factor, is used to determine the particular shading CLUT that is used. In order to avoid lighting discontinuities at grid boundaries, the pixel strip copier can be modified to interpolate lighting levels, and switch lighting tables (CLUTs) smoothly at appropriate pixels.

Transparency and Translucency

Real interiors have doorways, archways, windows, and so forth. If a texture has some amount of transparency in it, there needs to be some way to continue the raycasting beyond the wall to fill in the transparent pixels, while not having that further raycasting overwrite the pixels which are present in the current texture. The easiest way to handle a wall with transparency is to draw nothing at the point it is encountered, instead putting the necessary information "on a stack" for later processing, and continuing the raycasting as if the wall didn't exist. When the raycaster finishes the entire strip, the transparent slivers on the stack can be rendered, in reverse order from back to front, overdrawing any pixels covered by nontransparent pixels in the sliver. Translucency can be handled by the same mechanism, except that the translucent pixels, when finally rendered, are done via an appropriate blending table.

Objects

It wouldn't be much of a world without objects, of course. Bitmapped objects are reasonably straightforward to handle in a raycasting engine. Given the knowledge of an object's location in the grid and its size, it's not hard to determine the set of angles it encompasses, and therefore the set of strips which encounter it. When a given square of floor is encountered, the appropriate sliver of any objects in that vertical strip can be "stacked" in a manner similar to transparent wall handling. The reverse pass through the stack then renders these slivers. Note that objects hidden by walls are never even processed, since the floor section they stand on isn't encountered.

Polygon-based objects are tougher, because rendering such objects in vertical strips is difficult and requires a lot of overhead. A possible approach, one which has its own overhead, is to render the entire object into a separate off-screen bitmap, and then treat it like any other bitmapped object. A minor optimization of this approach would be to do the above but clipped to the strips which are known to be visible.

Animating Textures

There is no reason why the texture assigned to a given floor, wall, or ceiling square need remain constant. These bitmaps may be changed on the fly in real time as each frame of the scene is rendered. Floors may represent animating water or lava, or even simulated grates and trapdoors. Walls may animate to represent opening doors, video wallscreens featuring a speech by Our Exalted Leader, or simulated views into the animated world outdoors. Another form of animation, animation of lightsources, can be a very effective way to affect the mood of a game.

More Complex Layouts

The grid layout gives a mazelike feel which is getting a bit tired. While raycasting relies on a simple geometry to work properly and speedily, alternate geometries which feature diagonal walls and height-mapped areas with complex shapes can be rendered using a modified raycasting engine.

If you're interested in writing a raycaster, definitely pick up a copy of *Gardens of Imagination*, written by Christopher Lampton and published in 1994 by The Waite Group. This book develops code for a raycaster which features height mapping, lightsourcing, and bitmapped objects, and provides in-depth treatment of the theory behind the engine.

Beyond Raycasting

Raycasting is in widespread use for indoor maze games as I write this book. It is appealing because it is simple to code, at least compared to the alternatives, and well-written raycasters render at very high speeds. The restrictions on terrain geometry make it unsuitable for really complex indoor environments, like those featured in games such as *System Shock,* developed by LookingGlass Technologies and published by Origin. However, advanced raycasters can create some pretty interesting environments. Color plate 13 shows a screen shot from a new raycasting engine under development.

Raycasting is not particularly suitable for outdoor environments, due to the continuous variation in elevation which does not map well onto the concept of "floors and walls." Other techniques are used in the best outdoor simulations, some of which feature raycast-like strip processing in the distant portions of the view.

The development of these rendering pipelines is a hotbed of research and activity. Some of the techniques developed are suitable only to a very restricted environment. Others are more widely applicable, usually at some performance cost due to their generality. Many companies in the software business regard these rendering methods as the "family jewels," and work incessantly on them to maintain a competitive edge. There are now 3D rendering engines commercially available on the market, however, and this trend toward open standards (and lots of them, no doubt) will increase. The next sections of this chapter look briefly at a few of them.

OpenGL: Landing on the Desktop

Probably the most well-known 3D rendering engine is OpenGL. OpenGL is a standard being promulgated by the OpenGL Architecture Review Board. It is based on a graphics engine developed at Silicon Graphics for its line of 3D workstations. Microsoft has made OpenGL available for Windows NT, and it seems likely to migrate to Windows 95 at some point. OpenGL's hardware and memory requirements are not insignificant, which may keep it off the average desktop for a little while.

OpenGL Overview

OpenGL is a polygon-based rendering engine, although it supports rendering of bitmaps as well. Polygons may be flat shaded, Gouraud shaded, or texture mapped. Support for animating polygon objects is included via "nested instancing," whereby a cluster of polygons may be attached to its "parent" cluster with a relative location and relative orientation. For instance, a car may have four wheels, each of which uses the same local polygon model but is independently located and oriented. Texture maps may be rendered using a basic algorithm such as that shown in the previous chapter, or more sophisticated filtering options may be selected, to blend together the texture pixels which would otherwise be entirely skipped over.

Besides the basics, which obviously include a controllable camera, OpenGL adds support for many advanced features. These include multiple light sources, anti-aliasing, translucency, fog, environment mapping (texture mapping other parts of the scene onto a "reflective" polygon), curved surfaces, shadows, and motion blur. Not all of these features are particularly amenable to real-time implementation, but they may be individually enabled and disabled.

OpenGL and Z Buffering

OpenGL implements sorting via a Z buffer. While very simple scenes can be rendered in real time without specialized hardware, OpenGL is not particularly suited to real-time use without such support. That's not to say that OpenGL isn't an important standard. The relentless push of video board hardware development is rapidly making high-resolution, full-color 2D accelerators a commodity item. The next challenge for hardware manufacturers is 3D rendering support, and products are already appearing on the market. OpenGL is already popular on high-end graphics workstations. Within a very few years, hardware capable of providing for OpenGL's needs will be widely available on the PC, and it may very well become the standard for 3D rendering. By that point, OpenGL will be criticized more for features it lacks than for its performance-hungry nature. Its support for texture mapping could be improved in a number of ways, for instance, bump mapping and procedural texture mapping. OpenGL has no notion of terrain, other than as a large set of polygons.

OpenGL API and Extensions

OpenGL is an API and associated data structures, implemented in a library which is (dynamically) linked with an application. OpenGL procedures are available for camera placement, polygon object specification, coloring and texturing selection, lighting placement, and so on. Each procedure is named beginning with the letters *gl*—examples include glLight, glMaterial, glTexCoord, and so forth. OpenGL provides *display lists* for polygon storage, so that calls need not be made to respecify the polygons each time a frame is to be rendered.

Several libraries related to OpenGL are available:

OpenGL Utility Library

As part of the OpenGL system, the GLU routines provide some higher-level services. In particular, there is support for curved surfaces and methods to *tesselate* them, that is, to approximate them with a set of polygons. The names of routines in this library all begin with *glu*—examples include gluSphere, gluNurbsSurface, and gluTessVertex.

OpenGL Extension to the X Window System

This provides mechanisms to connect OpenGL buffers to visible windows in the X-Window system. X Windows is the graphics and windowing system available on most UNIX implementations. Routines in this library have names beginning with *glX*.

Open Inventor

This is an object-oriented toolkit based on OpenGL, written in C++.

For more information, see the *OpenGL Programming Guide* and the *OpenGL Reference Manual*, written by the OpenGL Architecture Review Board and published in 1993 by Addison-Wesley. There are also books available on Open Inventor.

Other 3D Rendering Engines

OpenGL is not the only option for those seeking to use a commercially available rendering engine. The intense focus on 3D games and simulations, and the amount of money to be made in the business, has begun to spawn an industry to provide a variety of tools to game and simulation developers. Among these tools are rendering engines. These typically feature a linkable library with an API accompaniment, and often also include various tools for converting data formats of polygon models from 3D Studio to a "native" format of some kind. The good ones are not cheap by any means, but that too will change with time. Brief highlights of a few of these engines are included below.

Real-Time Engines

I'm writing this chapter a week after Microsoft's acquisition of RenderMorphics. This purchase leads one to believe that Microsoft is not going to wait for the hardware to catch up to OpenGL, and intends to make a 3D gaming engine of some kind available. RenderMorphics' Reality Lab is one of several competing engines suitable for real-time work. Others include Argonaut's BRender and Criterion's RenderWare. These engines, which must handle a wide variety of 3D scenes, feature sophisticated "hybrid" rendering strategies which use Z buffers or other slow algorithms only in the portions of the scene which require them. They also will be featuring support for 3D hardware as it becomes available. Color plate 14 shows a screen shot produced by RenderWare, and Color plate 15 shows a screen shot of a product using a custom 3D engine.

RenderMan

If you think OpenGL has hefty processing requirements, think again. Invented by the folks who brought you the computer imagery in *Star Wars* and then went on to found Pixar, RenderMan is a rendering engine based on *procedural shading,* of which procedural texture mapping is just a part. At its heart is the RenderMan Shading Language, which is a C-like language specialized to the purpose of writing procedural shaders. Shading in RenderMan is not restricted to polygons or even curved surfaces—the passage of light through smoky air, for example, can be represented via a shader. In RenderMan, shading is a general organizing mechanism, by which light is colored as it travels from light sources to or through objects, through intervening materials including air and water, and finally into the eye.

The RenderMan engine features built-in anti-aliasing, depth of field (focus) effects, motion blur, bump mapping, environment mapping, shadows, and more. It works well with curved surfaces, and doesn't require that they be broken down into polygon approximations. With the right scene model, RenderMan generates highly realistic pictures.

All this functionality has a price. When RenderMan is able to generate a scene in real time, we will all be plugging virtual video-music chips into a socket behind our ears for entertainment, and making dinner in our recombinant DNA ovens. Maybe twenty years from now.

The Future of 3D Scene Rendering

If you aren't currently engaged in writing texture mappers and vertex projectors and polygon-sorting algorithms, you may never have to. That's not to discourage you—in fact such work is enormously enjoyable as well as challenging. Plus, it's never a bad idea to learn, by doing, how things work under the hood, even if you never make direct use of the code you write.

The reason that these 3D techniques are soon to be rendered obsolete is because they will be implemented at the hardware level. This won't happen overnight, but before the end of the millenium 3D rendering hardware will be commonplace. Repent now! That's not to say that all 3D skills will become obsolete overnight—actually there's a lot more to 3D than Gouraud shading and texture mapping, most importantly the modeling and realistic animation of objects and terrain.

After all, the hardware takeover is already well under way in the 2D realm, what with $100 video boards featuring hardware support for bitmap blitting and scaling, text rendering, and line-drawing. More expensive boards feature hardware-assisted video decompression and other advanced 2D features. This fact hasn't stopped me from writing this book, which is largely devoted to 2D animation topics. Why? Because 2D rendering is a much broader topic than just pixel-copying. Video boards may have 2D acceleration, but they don't currently handle moving sprites, overlay composition, and CLUT-based coloring effects, to name just a few topics we've covered. Until video boards make another quantum leap in capability, 2D rendering software skills will remain important.

The same is true in the 3D realm. The initial crop of 3D accelerator boards will feature flat shading, Gouraud shading, and simple texture mapping of polygons. Some will provide a Z buffer; the cheaper ones won't even do this, relying on software to perform sorting. For a while, vertex transformation and polygon clipping will remain a function of software, as will the bulk of the rendering pipeline. These aspects of 3D rendering will be handled more and more by standardized packages such as OpenGL and the others noted in the previous section. Because 3D rendering is inherently more complex than 2D, most developers will rely on these packages and treat them as black boxes.

Hopefully, this chapter has given you some glimpse of what's going on inside those black boxes. Maybe you will be the creator of one of them. And the rest of us will stand on your shoulders, working on the physics of jointed motion or modeling the backspin of a golf ball in flight through the misty air being rendered by your 3D engine. And wondering whether that purple triangle just beyond the sand-trap is a bug in your rendering code, or just bad data in that new fractal terrain model.

Optimizing, Porting, and Enhancing ARTT

I hope this book has been half as much fun to read as it has been to write. In this final chapter, I'd like to present my thoughts on what interested readers might be able to do with the information in this book. In particular, I'm going to give my ideas on how the ARTT toolkit can be improved and built upon. I'm not afraid to point out ARTT's shortcomings, and give you pointers on what to do about them if you have the motivation. The ARTT toolkit presented in this book was developed under several constraints, not the least of which is a total lack of assembly language, and this chapter will guide you should you wish to relieve some of those limitations.

Optimizing ARTT via assembly language is one direction to take the toolkit in. In the other direction lies the opportunity to port it to other platforms, since C++ is pretty much a lingua franca these days. In fact, one of my motivations for avoiding assembly language, which I know quite intimately thank you and no I'm not being defensive am I, was to aid those interested in porting ARTT to other platforms or processors.

Finally, ARTT is hardly the last word in 2D rendering and animation in terms of overall functionality. From adding support to new file formats, to writing new rendering primitives, to adding a full graphical user interface, there are many ways to extend and enhance ARTT. In this chapter, we'll talk about a few and how to fit these enhancements into the existing toolkit.

So without further ado, here come some insider's tips on taking ARTT to the next level.

Optimizing ARTT via Assembly Language

If you're a competent assembly language programmer, there are several portions of ARTT which can be sped up fairly dramatically. Rewriting the whole toolkit in assembly is a waste of time and effort. An old adage says that 90 percent of the execution time is spent running 10 percent of the code. Get a profiler and find that 10 percent, or use this section as your guide to the methods that need an "assembly fix" the most. If you don't know assembly language, go read up on it first, and then read Michael Abrash's *Zen of Code Optimization* (full reference in Appendix E).

Fixing Class AFix

Assembly language sometimes offers more than just pure speed. There are some cases where a language like C++ simply doesn't let you get at hardware features that are important. Class AFix is a case in point. Remember, our fixed-point numbers are internally represented in AFix by a 32-bit long value, of which 8 bits are used for fraction, 16 are used for the whole part, and 8 are used only during intermediate calculations. If class AFix were written in assembly language, we could devote 16 bits to fraction and 16 bits to whole part, gaining precision and eliminating overflow problems (multiply AFix(500) by AFix(500) and see what you get—you won't be amused).

What magic does assembly have to offer? Look at Figure 20.1. When a 32-bit number is multiplied by another 32-bit number on a

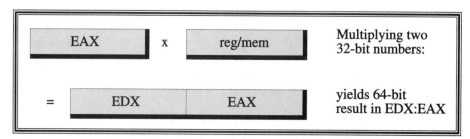

Figure 20.1 Multiplying two 32-bit numbers yields a 64-bit result on an Intel 32-bit CPU.

386/486/Pentium CPU, the result goes into a 64-bit result register (actually, half in EAX, half in EDX).

In C or C++, the high 32 bits of this result are simply thrown away, because there is no mechanism in the language for dealing with an integer larger than a long, which is 32 bits in our case. In assembly, however, we can multiply two 32-bit numbers into a 64-bit result, then shift that result down by 16 bits to slide the fixed point back down to the proper position. Such an assembler sequence might look something like this:

```
IMUL EAX,EDX     ; multiply 32-bit fixed-point EAX by 32-bit fixed-point EDX
SHRD EAX,EDX,16  ; shift 64-bit result (EDX:EAX) down 16 bits
```

One of the best ways to optimize ARTT and enhance its precision is to recode much of the AFix class in assembly language, using 16 bits for fractional resolution instead of 8. Division as well as multiplication has to be changed to shift by 16 instead of 8. Table 20.1 lists the methods most in need of conversion to assembler.

The definition of the constant AFix::max would need changing as well if fractional resolution changed from 8 to 16 bits.

Since the AFix methods are all defined inline, it would be counterproductive to convert these to assembly language *functions*. Instead, inline assembly language should be used. The Watcom compiler provides excellent capabilities for specifying register arguments to such inline functions; other compilers' abilities to handle this job vary.

Speeding up ACanvas Methods

The biggest performance gains in ARTT can be obtained by rewriting rendering methods in assembly language. This should not be done indiscriminately. Some methods are rarely called, depending on the type of graphics and animation you are doing. Others work

Table 20.1	Most Important AFix Methods to Recode Using Inline Assembler
operator*=(AFix a)	member function: multiplication by another AFix
operator/=(AFix a)	member function: division by another AFix
operator*(AFix a, AFix b)	friend function: multiply two AFix's
operator/(AFix a, AFix b)	friend function: divide one AFix by another

pretty well in C++—most compilers will optimize memset() and memcpy() into inline assembler, for instance, so any method which uses these functions for its inner loop may already be operating at peak efficiency.

It may be better to rewrite a given method in assembly in its entirety, or it may be better to use inline assembler only for the inner loop. If a method is small, perhaps 10 lines or less, it is probably better to go all-assembler, and pay attention to register usage across the entire routine. For large methods, recoding the inner loop using inline assembler is more cost-effective and less error-prone. Use your judgment, or try it both ways in a few cases and time the results.

The choice of which methods to optimize depends on which ones you make heaviest use of. Table 20.2 should be taken only as

Table 20.2 Canvas Methods Worth Considering for Assembly Optimization (optimize in any canvas class in which the method is used heavily)

DrawPixelU	Draw pixel in current color
DrawPixel8U	Draw pixel in supplied color
GetPixel8U	Get pixel
DrawBitmapLin8U	Draw BMF_LIN8 bitmap
DrawTmapRow8U	Row of texture mapper (any canvas)
DrawClutBitmapRowLin8U	Row of linear 8-bit CLUT bitmap renderer
DrawBlendBitmapRowLin8U	Row of linear 8-bit blended bitmap renderer
DrawScaledBitmapRowLin8U	Row of linear 8-bit scaled bitmap renderer
DrawScaledBitmapRowLin15U	Row of linear 15-bit scaled bitmap renderer
DrawScaledBitmapRowLin24U	Row of linear 24-bit scaled bitmap renderer
DrawScaledClutBitmapRowLin8U	Row of linear 8-bit CLUT scaled bitmap renderer
DrawScaledBlendBitmapRowLin8U	Row of linear 8-bit blended scaled bitmap renderer

general advice, to be tempered with knowledge of your own usage. The row-rendering routines used by bitmap scalers and texture mappers are obvious candidates; others are my best guess.

Other Assembly Candidates

Besides the canvas-based rendering classes, there are a smattering of other places where assembly language could be used to achieve noticeable performance improvements. The best places I can think of to look at include:

ARle8Reader::SkipRow—Used a lot when clipping BMF_RLE8 bitmaps.

ARle8Reader::UnpackRow—Used constantly when rendering BMF_RLE8 bitmaps. This one is a clear win if you use run-length encoding.

APalette::FindClosest—Used to convert from 15/24-bit to 8-bit, on the fly or when building an inverse table.

ARect methods—Many methods of class ARect are used a lot, especially in dirty-rectangle composition. Depending on the compiler, they may be okay. Disassemble and conquer.

AMatrix and AVector methods—Used heavily in 3D transformations, disassemble and decide.

If you invested in a huge assembly language effort, and rewrote most of the above routines, I would expect a performance boost of well over 50 percent in overall frame rate, depending on the mix of rendering routines and other computational overhead. It's certainly worth the effort if you're psyched.

Optimization Without Assembly

Rendering routines in ARTT are first developed in class ACanvas, using generic pixel-by-pixel algorithms or relying on other previously written methods to do the actual pixel manipulation. This is because class ACanvas is so generic that it doesn't know the format of a pixel in its canvas. In most cases, more efficient versions of each routine have been developed for each canvas class. This isn't true in all cases, however—I made decisions as to which methods were important enough to provide an efficient version of, and which should just rely on the version provided in ACanvas. If you really need an optimal version of the routine which renders 8-bit run-length-encoded bitmaps through a CLUT, scaled, onto a 24-bit bank-switched canvas, you may have to write it yourself, because I probably didn't think it was useful enough to hand-code. Profile your applications, and determine where the bottlenecks are. Then, make sure the C++ is right before you reach for assembler.

Porting ARTT to Other Platforms

One of ARTT's primary design goals was to be portable to environments beyond DOS and Windows, and machines beyond IBM compatibles. Possible platforms/environments to port to include OS/2, X Windows, and the Macintosh. Before discussing issues specific to each of these platforms, some general comments are in order.

General Porting Issues

In one sense, writing portable code is not so hard. Don't depend on byte ordering and integer size, and don't interface with any input or output devices, and you're pretty much all set. However, in a graphics library which also features keyboard, mouse, and timer input, this is clearly an impossible goal. ARTT has been written to be portable to a variety of computers and operating systems, subject to the following general constraints:

- C++ compiler or cross-compiler must be available.
- Screen must use 8, 15, or 24 bits per pixel in an ARTT-approved linear or bank-switched format, or must provide a blitting mechanism which takes one of these as input.
- Integer size must be at least 16 bits (preferably 32 for better performance).
- Keyboard, mouse, and timer services must be available.

Systems with the following features require a little extra porting effort, particularly in the file-reading classes:

- 64-bit integer size (modify AWORD16 and AWORD32 definitions in ATYPES.H)
- Big-endian byte ordering (Intel CPUs are little-endian, meaning least-significant bytes in a word appear first)

Most ARTT C++ classes are 100 percent portable, or at least they are supposed to be. Table 20.3 lists the classes which may need to be modified or replaced in porting to another environment.

More general issues are worth considering too. On systems which feature native graphics and file formats other than BMP, PCX, and FLC, new derived classes to handle these formats are a good idea. Systems with extensive hardware capabilities, such as sprite overlays and fast blitters, may demand even more of a good port. Reworking the classes listed above is sufficient to get ARTT up and running well on a new system, however.

OS/2, X Windows, and the Macintosh

OS/2 on IBM compatibles shares a heritage with Windows. Presentation Manager, the windowing interface to OS/2, was originally

Table 20.3 ARTT Classes Which May Need Modification or Replacement When Porting

Class name	Issues
ABmpFile	Current implementation is little-endian
AFlcFile	Current implementation is little-endian
AKeybd	Must implement ReadKeyboard() method
AMem	Provides access to physical video memory if necessary
AMouse	Mouse location, button press, and cursor services
APcxFile	Current implementation is little-endian
ASceneDos/Win	Need derived scene class for window attach & redraw/blit
ATime	Must implement Read() method
AWingWindow/AWingPal/AVga	Must provide access to screen windows and system palette

planned as the successor to Windows. Then it faltered and Windows 3.0 took off in popularity, and Microsoft switched lanes and made a beeline to the bank. The upside-down nature of DIBs has its genesis in OS/2. By the time you read this, OS/2 may also be running on PowerPC machines. The architecture of these machines, which includes a different CPU, may cause additional incompatibilities.

X Windows is the graphics and windowing system in most widespread use on workstations, which feature a wide range of CPUs, word sizes, and other differences. Some X Windows machines feature monochrome screens, which ARTT does not support (ARTT can work on 8-bit gray-scale screens, with the caveat that colors keep their luminance but lose their color). Workstations running X Windows may be big-endian or little-endian, may have 64-bit CPUs, and in general encompass more variety (read: *more porting problems*) than the other environments.

The Macintosh has a graphics toolkit built into ROM. Named Quickdraw, this toolkit has a reasonable set of features, is well implemented given its general nature, and provides direct support for accelerator cards. Quickdraw lies at the base of the Mac's famed GUI, and it provides some pretty advanced features such as support for multiple monitors on the same "virtual desktop." Even so, Quick-draw has no animation, no composition, no CLUT-based rendering, nor other features that ARTT supplies. Porting to the Mac nowadays means porting to the PowerMac, which features the PowerPC CPU chip instead of a member of the 680x0 line.

The following porting issues are common to all of the above environments:

- File-reading code may need to be rewritten to be big-endian, or even worse, to work either way based on a runtime decision. Abandoning structures in favor of byte-at-a-time collating of words is the best way to go, even though it makes the code less readable.
- Machines with 64-bit integers could pose a tough problem, if there is no native 16-bit word size (e.g., long is 64 bits, short is 32 bits). Again, abandoning structures is the best way to make file-reading code portable.
- BMP file headers are somewhat different under OS/2, so the ABmpFile class would have to be modified accordingly.
- The keyboard, mouse, and timer classes need to be modified. OS/2 Presentation Manager is very like Windows in that its windows are message-based, so the Windows version is a good guide. On the Mac and under X Windows, code can poll for keyboard and mouse events, and a system timer is generally available, so these would actually resemble their DOS counterparts more.
- Each of these three environments features system-maintained windows. Some class like AWingWindow is needed to handle the tying of canvases to windows, and to provide palette access and blitting.
- A new scene class, similar to ASceneWin, is needed to connect window-based scenes to the new window class described above.

Enhancing the Canvas Classes

There are several ways in which the canvas classes could be built upon. Some general areas for enhancement include:

- New bitmap formats
- New geometric rendering primitives
- Color effects for 15-bit and 24-bit sources
- Support for accelerator cards

New Bitmap Formats

ARTT supports seven bitmap formats. There are linear and bank-switched versions of 8-bit, 15-bit, and 24-bit pixel layouts, plus a run-length-encoded 8-bit format. This last one, BMF_RLE8, is the only compressed bitmap format that ARTT handles, if you don't count the fact that the file-reading classes decode images compressed by other means into ARTT formats. Possibilities for new bitmap formats are discussed on the following page:

BMF_MONO

Monochrome displays are getting rarer but are not unknown. Most printers are still monochrome, so extending ARTT to support printers certainly means creating a new monochrome format. An uncompressed, one-bit-per-pixel format is simple in concept, but several practical decisions loom. What happens when applications set colors? Does a monochrome canvas attempt to dither patterns of black and white, or does it just require that applications be "monochrome aware" and use only black and white colors? And what about sprite transparency? Does a transparent monochrome sprite just have "on" and "off" pixels, or does transparency require having a separate "mask" bitmap to denote which pixels are active?

BMF_LIN16

Many SVGA cards support a format which has 5 bits of red, 6 bits green, and 5 bits blue. The sixth green bit gives more color resolution in the component to which the eye is most sensitive. For that gardening simulation, you may want the extra shades of green. Besides a new canvas class and new rendering routines, a 16-bit format requires rethinking the palette and inverse table classes, which currently are hard-coded for 15-bit operation.

BMF_LIN32

Many SVGA cards also offer a 32-bit format, which has the same 8 bits each of red, green, and blue, plus an extra byte per pixel. In the card's video memory, this byte is unused; it serves to align pixels on longword boundaries for faster access. Much of the complexity of the 24-bit canvas classes arises from working with 3-byte pixels, which are awkward. With 4-byte pixels, for instance, bank-crossings can't occur within a pixel. For use in source bitmaps, many high-end systems treat the fourth byte as an *alpha channel*, which means it determines the level of transparency of the pixel. This is a very powerful concept which can be employed in methods that render 32-bit bitmaps.

BMF_BANK16 and BMF_BANK32

In order to support 16-bit and 32-bit SVGA modes in bank-switched operation, these two new formats need to be implemented, along with associated canvas classes. If the 16-bit and 32-bit modes are only to be accessed via Windows or through VESA 2.0's linear screen memory option, the bank-switched formats can be punted.

Before you get a bee in your bonnet and start firing off these new formats, beware. Fully supporting a new format requires not only writing a new canvas class, but also modifying all existing canvas classes to handle rendering source bitmaps in the new format. The combination of canvas classes and bitmap formats turns adding a format into an n-squared increase in effort. The row-based nature of many methods is an attempt to avoid the explosion of methods that N canvases $\times M$ bitmap formats implies. Furthermore, some canvas classes require even more design work related to colors, palettes, and color lookup tables. Of the above, I would say that BMF_LIN32 holds the most future promise, because of the effects possible with an alpha channel.

Regarding compressed bitmap formats, which is another direction to go in, this is a lot harder than it sounds. Writing a method to render some image compressed using JPEG or Huffman coding or whatever is easy enough. Now, write methods to render such compressed images scaled, or through CLUTs, or both. ARTT has myriad such combinations built in, many of which work a row at a time, which is problematic if the compression technique is not row-based. Better to decompress these images in their entirety into a common ARTT format, and then render using the decompressed bitmap.

New Geometric Rendering Primitives

ARTT is strong on bitmap manipulation and weak on geometric primitives. It currently supports rendering of lines, rectangles, and polygons. New primitives which could be added include:

- Circles, ellipses, and arcs
- Curves, such as Bezier curves and B-splines
- Lines with varying thickness or styles

These can all be implemented in class ACanvas, and performance would probably be satisfactory across all canvases. If the overhead of calling DrawPixel() slows them down too much, there is an alternative to writing optimized versions in the canvas classes. Circles, ellipses, arcs, and curves can all be approximated using short line segments. Consider writing these rendering routines to decompose the curved primitive into lines, to a degree of fineness determined by an argument passed in, and then use ARTT's underlying line-drawer to do the rendering of these short segments. Then write super-fast versions of the line-drawer in all classes, and get *all* the line and curve types humming.

Color Effects for 15-bit and 24-bit Sources

Many of the color effects in ARTT are handled via lookup tables, and therefore require 8-bit source images. Shading, hazing, and translucency filtering effects are all achieved via tables which take 8-bit input pixels and produce 8-bit output pixels. This design was chosen because table lookup is far faster than performing such shading, hazing, and filtering effects in RGB color space, and after all this is a book about real-time graphics.

However, as 15-bit and 24-bit graphics become more and more prevalent, the 8-bit techniques will begin to fall by the wayside. Eventually, the horsepower will become available to assign a pixel-processing procedure to a graphics primitive, and have that routine merrily manipulate red, green, and blue components according to some algorithm, eventually arriving at an output RGB value that creates the desired effect. Is there, however, an intermediate step between the present troubled earth and that eventual procedural bliss?

First, let's consider extending our lookup tables to cover these new formats. A CLUT taking 15-bit values as input and producing 15-bit values on output would be:

```
2^15 = 32,768 entries of one word each = 64 Kbytes
```

Kind of big, but not necessarily out of the question. A blending table would consist of up to 32,768 such tables, and is clearly not in our budget.

What about 24-bit images? The simple calculation for a CLUT is:

```
2^24 = 16 million entries of 3 bytes each = 48 Mbytes
```

Now, 48 megabytes will someday dance on the head of a pin, but by then there will also be an individual CPU operating behind each pixel on the screen doing its own raytracing, so let's stop right here. No, don't even think about the 16-million-entry blending table, with each entry containing 48 Mbytes.

There's an alternative, though, and a pretty good one. The shading, hazing, and filtering tables created in Part 3 of this book all treated red, green, and blue independently when computing the values that go into these tables. We can do the same at runtime. A 24-bit lookup table can be composed of three 8-bit tables, one for each component. This is only $3 \times 256 = 768$ bytes, a much more familiar and happy number. An operation to look up a value in such a table might look something like the following:

```
// Sample 24-bit table lookup
uchar redNew = tableRed24[redOld];
uchar greenNew = tableGreen24[greenOld];
uchar blueNew = tableBlue24[blueOld];
```

Not as fast as an 8-bit lookup table, but not bad at all. For fifteen-bit table lookup, there's no real need to break the word into its three color components. Instead, carefully-built tables allow the following:

```
// Sample 15-bit table lookup (using two bytewide tables)
uchar tableHigh[256] = {...};    // look up high half of word here
uchar tableLow[256] = {...};     // look up low half of word here
ushort cNew = (((ushort) tableHigh[cOld >> 8]) << 8) |
        tableLow[cOld & 0xFF];
```

Support for Accelerator Cards

Super VGA graphics cards featuring hardware acceleration of rendering functions abound. It's hard to find one without these features nowadays. Manufacturers of such boards include ATI, Diamond, Paradise, Matrox, Number 9, and others. At the heart of each of these boards is one or two large chips which do all the hard work. Some board manufacturers such as ATI use chips of their own design. Others buy them from S3, Weitek, and other companies which specialize in the design and manufacture of such chips.

ARTT treats all video boards equally, using them as "dumb" linear or bank-switched frame buffers, and performing its own pixel computations for all rendering. Doing so is unavoidable in most routines—accelerator boards (currently, anyway) provide very fast versions of only the basics, such as 8-bit bitmap blitting and line-drawing, and often bitmap scaling. There are no accelerators with routines for CLUT-based bitmap rendering, blending table usage, run-length-encoded bitmaps, and so on.

Still, using the hardware for the basics is appealing. Most 2D programs use off-screen buffers anyway, which by the way these cards can't support unless the off-screen buffer is in unused video memory, so the main thing we'd like to use is simply blitting of our off-screen buffer to the screen. Scaled blitting would be nice too, especially the interpolated smooth-scaling available in some cards.

Putting support for such accelerator hardware into ARTT is not impossible, although it has its perils. Windows users get it for free, as WinG uses these features of the boards for blitting the off-screen buffer to the window. For DOS development, it's simply a matter of following a few simple steps:

1. Obtain from the board or chip manufacturer a programmer's guide to the board you want to support. The array of boards and underlying chips is the biggest Tower of Babel we've come across in this book, and even variations of the same line of boards feature different programming techniques.

2. Write a new canvas class for a particular combination of board and color depth, deriving it from the appropriate linear or bank-switched class. Write a Launch() method which uses VESA or direct programming to launch the mode, and write a Term() method to return to text mode. If you're bypassing VESA and using bank-switching, create a bank manager class with the appropriate code for bank-switching this board.

At this point, you should have a working "driver" canvas, albeit one which doesn't yet make use of hardware acceleration. Now:

3. Rewrite any relevant methods, such as DrawBitmapLin8U() or DrawLineU(), to use the i/o ports or other mechanisms of the board to achieve the same effect. This will require careful study of the board's interface, and probably a few three-finger salutes in the process.

That's it in a nutshell. Now repeat for 300 different board designs. After all your hair is gone, switch to Windows.

Supporting More Graphics and Animation File Formats

The version of ARTT developed in this book includes support for reading and writing PCX and BMP graphics files. It also reads FLIC animation files, and reads and writes animations in a private ASA format. Both the graphics file and animation file code are designed to be extended. Class AGfxFile is the base graphics file class from which any new format can be derived, and class AAnmFile is the base class for animation files. Studying the existing derived classes should give you a clear idea of what to do to support a new format.

Graphics Files

Graphics file formats which are common and you might wish to write classes for include:

GIF   Used by CompuServe, encodes 8-bit images very compactly

TIFF   Most common format for 24-bit images

See Chapter 3 for a list of other formats worth considering adding support for. Look over the graphics file format books in your local bookstore, and find one which describes in detail the formats you're interested in. Magazines like *Dr. Dobbs* (see Appendix E) often have good articles on file formats, too.

Animation Files

Thankfully, there are fewer commonly used animation file formats than there are graphics file formats. The Autodesk FLIC format is by far the most prevalent, although it handles only 8-bit animations.

Adding the ability to write FLIC files as well as read them is not hard and is worth the effort—imagine pressing a hotkey to begin recording all the action as you run your animation program!

Two digital video formats, which add audio but are otherwise conceptually similar to animation files, were briefly discussed in Chapter 16. These are AVI, Microsoft's file format for its Video for Windows, and MOV, Apple's QuickTime file format. Reading (and writing) these files should be done using the relevant toolkits, since the compression formats are proprietary and you won't have much luck reading the video frames unless you are Mr. or Ms. Reverse Engineer par excellence.

Microsoft provides a toolkit for reading and writing AVI files as part of its VFW Software Development Kit, available as part of the Microsoft Developer Network. Apple provides a QuickTime for Windows developer's kit as well. Maybe ARTT can play a part in the movie-making studio you create in your basement! No royalties please, just invite me to the Oscars ceremony.

Keeping Up With VESA and Windows

The VESA-related code in ARTT (Classes AVesa and ABankMgrVesa) is written to version 1.2 of the VESA VBE specification. Version 2.0 arrived in early spring of 1995, and offers some new features of interest. Support in video cards' ROM for the 2.0 spec, of course, will arrive slowly over time. If you have a 2.0-compatible card and would like to play with the new features, only minor adjustments to ARTT are needed.

See Chapter 5 for information on some of the new capabilities. One of the most important new features is the support for "linear" SVGA modes. In a linear SVGA mode, the entire screen bitmap is located in extended memory, and can be addressed as a single linear block. Such a bitmap is accessible with a linear-format canvas, such as ACanvasLin8, ACanvasLin15, or ACanvasLin24. The AVesa:: Launch() routine could be modified to create such a canvas instead of a bank-switched one. Note that only 32-bit protected-mode programs can access linear buffers, since they appear above the 1 Mb boundary.

Windows 95 and CreateDIBSection

Windows 95 supports WinG, so ARTT-based windows programs should work fine. However, the off-screen buffer in such programs must have a depth of 8 bits (BMF_LIN8 format). Win95 offers an alternative mechanism for allocating off-screen buffers in the CreateDIBSection call. With CreateDIBSection, 15-bit and 24-bit off-screen buffers may be created. Consult the relevant Win95 programmer documentation for more information on this capability. Minor rework of the AWing-Window class would be required to replace WinG with CreateDIBSection and the related blitting functions.

Enhancing ARTT's Graphical User Interface

The GUI classes presented in Chapter 12, AActorButton and AMenu, do a lot for such weeny little things. They can behave as clickable icons, pushbuttons, check boxes, menu bars and menus, and even static text fields. With a little help from the surrounding application, they can function as radio buttons (somebody has to deselect the other buttons when a new one is selected).

Needless to say, these classes don't implement a full graphical user interface, nor were they intended to. They're adequate for the basics of user interaction and option selection, but they don't compete with the huge array of fancy controls available to Windows developers. Windows developers are probably better off sticking with these, although ARTT's buttons and menus can still be handy for "in-scene" hotspots.

Dialog Boxes

For DOS developers, enhancing ARTT's humble GUI might be useful. The most prominent missing feature is the dialog box, which wraps up a bunch of controls into a window. Since ARTT's scene system doesn't handle overlapping windows, such dialogs would have to either be modal (all scenes freeze while the dialog is on top of them), or appear in a nonoverlapping screen area. In either case, the place to start would be by writing a dialog class. Such a class would be responsible for creating its collection of controls and handling interaction with them.

Determining a format for a dialog template, which would define the controls and their layout, is probably the most challenging aspect, and wouldn't it be nice to have a graphical tool for dialog layout as well? Assuming that such a template can be handed to a dialog's constructor, the following methods in the dialog class would be most important:

Constructor—Create new scene and all actor controls in the scene.

Destructor—Delete dialog's scene.

HandleKey—ARTT's controls generate "virtual keystrokes" when clicked. The dialog, rather than the application, wants to handle these events. The main loop of an application with dialog boxes would presumably call

ADialog::HandleKey() to give dialogs a chance to handle key events before the application gets a crack at them. The dialog box class could automatically handle some (OK and Cancel, for instance), and pass others on to a user-installed dialog handling procedure. This procedure would be responsible for monitoring all key events and updating the state of the dialog box in some memory structure available to the application.

There are many ways to structure the data flow between applications and dialog boxes, and the thoughts above are not meant as the only possible scenario. For instance, an easier approach to dialog layout would be to require a dialog creation procedure, which creates the actors in code instead of from some dialog template. This puts more work on the creator of individual dialogs, but less on the dialog box system itself.

Overlapping Scenes

As stated before, ARTT does not handle overlapping scenes. That's not strictly true—scenes may overlap under Windows, as the clipping and overlap mechanisms are handled by the operating system itself. Under DOS, however, scenes may not overlap. Changing the scene class to handle overlap is not really that difficult, however.

First off, the no-overlap rule really applies only to scenes which are active. A scene may overlap others, as long as no attempt is made to Update() any overlapped scenes. If an application is careful to use AScene::Update() only on scenes which are not obscured, avoiding AScene::UpdateAll(), everything works fine. When a scene which has been obscured is uncovered, usually because an overlapping scene has been deleted, a call to AScene::Changed() should be made to ensure redrawing of the exposed area.

Support for full overlapping of active windows is possible, too. Since each scene has its own off-screen buffer, regardless of overlap, the trick is making sure that scenes which are obscured don't blit to the screen over their obscuring windows. The ARectList class can come in handy here. Each scene can maintain a visible region which consists of a set of rectangles. These rectangles describe the visible area of the scene. Figure 20.2 shows a sample obscured scene and its visible region.

Whenever a scene is created, destroyed, resized, or moved, the visible regions for all scenes need to be recomputed. The stacking order of scenes can be handled with a scene-depth coordinate (which is unrelated to the z-coordinates of actors within a scene), or via a tree structure of links. With all this in place, the RedrawAndBlit() mechanism needs to be modified to clip any areas to the scene's visible region. The methods in class ARect and ARectList can come in handy here too.

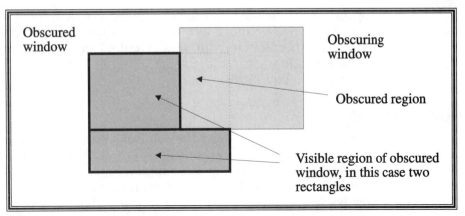

Figure 20.2 The visible region of an obscured window can be described by a list of rectangles.

Finally, a full user interface could provide mechanisms for moving, resizing, and closing these scene windows. A full-fledged scene frame might consist of a title bar for dragging, a menu bar for menu selection, clickable icons for zooming and iconization, and a thick frame for resizing. Oh, and scroll bars, drag and drop, and all your other favorite Windows features. Yes, my own personal user interface, with 3D spinning icons and translucent dialog boxes, animated cursors, help balloons with a video of my dog in them, and pie-shaped graphic menus appearing under the cursor! Master of my realm, after I just fix these last few bugs!

Don't do it. That way leads to the Dark Side.

Extending 3D and Virtual Reality Support

ARTT provides some starter classes for working in 3D. The basics of vector and matrix math, including vertex transformation and projection, are included. There is a camera class for viewing 3D scenes, along with a class for representing polyhedral objects. These objects may be flat shaded or texture mapped, but must have a convex shape in order to be rendered correctly.

This is just the beginning of a 3D system, a full implementation of which could easily fill another book of this size. There are both major and minor ways in which ARTT's 3D capabilities can be enhanced and extended. This section discusses a few of them.

Light Sourcing

ARTT provides flat shading of polygons, but the colors must be specified directly in the polygon structure, or at least placed there by the program. A class ALightSource might provide the mechanism for specifying one or more light sources. Class APolyObj could then be modified to calculate the shade (color) of each face based on its default shade and the current set of light sources. See Chapter 18 for the relevant equations.

Gouraud Shading

Gouraud shading, wherein the color of a polygon face blends smoothly between vertices of different colors, is a useful adjunct to the flat shading and texture mapping already developed. Gouraud shading is discussed in Chapter 18. Basically, each vertex needs its own RGB color, probably specified in full 24-bit format. RGB vertex colors, like polygon face colors, can be subject to lightsourcing calculations. Then, a new polygon rendering routine named DrawGouraudConvexPolygon() could be written which does the proper RGB interpolation down the left and right edges. The rendering of a row of such a polygon also requires a new method, one which performs interpolation in RGB space across the row, pixel by pixel. In 24-bit canvases, this color can be set directly into the destination bitmap. In 15-bit canvases, APalette::ConvertTo15() can be used to map down to 15 bits. In 8-bit canvases, APalette::ConvertTo8() can be used.

Advanced Texture Mapping

Chapter 18 also contains some discussion of advanced texture mapping concepts. The only type of texture mapping ARTT includes code for is linear texture mapping, so named because the fractional pixel interpolation is done linearly. No attempt is made to account for true perspective, wherein texture pixels closer to the camera should be somewhat larger. Such perspective texture mapping is one enhancement which can be added to ARTT. Others include lit texture mapping, wherein each vertex gets a predetermined or computed lighting value, and CLUT-based methods are used to shade the texture pixel as they are laid down. Bump mapping is another technique, where the effect of light on simulated surface normal perturbations can add realism to a surface. Procedural texturing is a powerful approach, though not particularly well-suited to real-time use.

Terrain Rendering

The class AActorPolyObj, which allows convex polyhedra to be included in what is really a 2-and-one-half-D scene, is a stopgap measure which allows use of 3D objects but doesn't begin to qualify as a true 3D rendering system. The discussions in the previous chapter should alert you to the complexity of such a system. If you're interested in developing the 3D system further, the first place to start is by developing an engine for rendering terrain. Indoor terrain is easier than outdoor terrain, because of the constrained geometry and the fact that the view does not extend very far into the distance. Several books describe the techniques of raycasting in detail, so this is probably the best place to start. Raycast scenes work well with bitmapped objects, so the bitmap rendering and animation techniques covered in this book will prove very useful in such a venture. The discussion in Chapter 19 should help you should you decide to add darkened corridors with spot lighting, translucent windows, and mist effects to your raycaster.

Virtual Reality

Well, I couldn't finish an entire book of this size without including this overused buzzword. *Virtual reality* is really just what we've always called 3D simulation, but coupled with some cool new hardware gizmos. The most important of these is the VR headset, a helmet with goggles that puts the computer screen right in front of your eyes. By the time this book is published, there should be several reasonably priced VR headsets on the market. Figure 20.3 is a photo of one such product, the VFX1 Headgear from FORTE Technologies, Inc.

Since these headsets are driven by the VGA card, nothing special needs to be done to put an image onto the tiny LCD screens inside them. Some headsets, however, allow independent programming of the left and right screens, which can be employed to provide a true 3D stereo vision effect. This is not that difficult to support—each eye just gets the same scene rendered from a slightly different camera position and angle. The frame rate gets cut about in half because of the extra work of rendering two screens, but the effect is pretty stunning.

VR headsets also feature sensors which can report the pitch, heading, and bank of the helmet (pitch, yaw, and roll in VR parlance). Feeding this information back into the program, and using it to control the corresponding parameters of the virtual camera, creates an experience in which you can "look around" a virtual scene. Coupled with stereo vision and stereo audio using the built-in headphones, the entire effect is very "immersive." Don't forget to eat dinner.

Miscellaneous Ideas

Software, that virtual sandbox, can be pulled like taffy in a million directions. Sometimes, if you're not careful in your planning and design, the result can be just as gooey. Below are a few oddball directions in which to pull the ARTT taffy.

Figure 20.3 The VFX1 Headgear from FORTE Technologies, Inc. Photo courtesy FORTE Technologies, Inc.

File-Based Canvases

The division of labor between the bank-switched canvas classes and the bank-manager class (ABankMgr) opens the door to an interesting possibility. Bank-switched memory needn't refer to video memory, and it needn't even refer to memory per se. A disk-based file is a form of "address space," and a bank-manager class can be designed to allow access to the 64K banks which make up such a file.

What could be done with such a scheme? Imagine a very large bitmap, perhaps 8000 × 8000 24-bit pixels, that you'd like to render into. Such a bitmap is 192 megabytes in size! Clearly, new() is going to have a tough time fulfilling your bitmap allocation request. But now suppose that the bitmap is kept in a large disk file, and only 64K is kept in memory at any one time. But who does the "paging" of the file, and when?

With the right bank-manager class attached to existing bank-switched canvases, everything "just works." Such a bank-manager class, let's call it ABankMgrFile, is derived from ABankMgr. It implements SetReadBank() and SetWriteBank(), plus a constructor to set things up and a destructor to shut things down. See the sample interface below.

```
// HYPOTHETICAL FILE-BASED BANK MANAGER
class ABankMgrFile : public ABankMgr {
    int page;                          // current bank # in memory
    uchar *pageBits;                   // ptr to 64K allocated page

    void SwitchWriteBank(int bank);    // write out curr page, read in new
    void SwitchReadBank(int bank);     // write out curr page, read in new
public:
    ABankMgrFile(FILE *fp);            // open file, alloc page, init self &
                                       // base ABankMgr

    ~ABankMgr();                       // close file and free page bits
};
```

SetReadBank() and SetWriteBank(), rather than calling VESA or fiddling bits in some register, would actually use file i/o operations to ensure that the proper "bank" of the file is kept in a single memory buffer. Figure 20.4 illustrates how such a file-based canvas might operate.

The simple scheme of keeping one 64K bank in memory can be enhanced by including a cache of such 64K sections. The contents of the cache, and determining which bank to jettison when an unavailable one is needed, can be handled by a least-recently-used (LRU) algorithm. When a new bank is read in, the current one must first be written back to the file. With modification to EnsureWriteBank() to

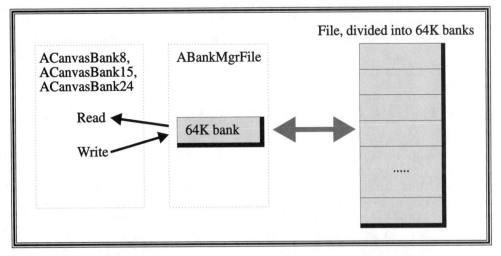

Figure 20.4 Interaction between a bank-switched canvas, the file-based bank manager, and a file.

maintain a dirty bit, the bank manager could tell whether an application has modified the bank, and avoid writing it back if not.

What good are file-based canvases? They certainly aren't very real time, but they are a mechanism for creating very detailed renderings, including those that might be saved to a large TIFF file and later printed on a color printer. Such printers can typically handle 300 or 600 dots per inch, so the 8000-pixel example is hardly extravagant.

Overlaid Scenes

In ARTT's scene and actor system, the scene is essentially a composition buffer, and the actors are graphic elements which render into that buffer. Minor modifications to this design could allow the stacking of transparent scenes, one on top of the other. The output to the screen would be the composition of all of these scenes, overlaid using transparency or even translucency. In a sense, each scene would be a sort of actor in a "super scene" which would handle the final screen blitting, after all the scenes had been composed into the super-scene buffer.

Uses for this kind of system abound. A mapping program might feature a base scene for the overall map, plus overlaid scenes for roadways, tourist attraction markers, custom route pathways, and so on. A "map" of the human anatomy might feature skeletal overlays, muscular overlays, organ overlays, and so forth.

Another way of implementing such an overlay system would be to give a single scene multiple lists of actors, with individual control over the visibility of entire lists. A still simpler scheme would make use of the 'hidden' flag already present in class AActor, and traverse the scene's actor list to hide or show actors which are part of a given "overlay set." Perhaps an 'overlay set' field could be added to class AActor to automate determination of which actors are in which set.

Morphing, Fractals, Particle Systems, and More

The number of interesting special effects which are being used every day in computer graphics is astounding. Books are available which describe the mathematics and algorithms behind such techniques as morphing, fractal terrain generation, particle systems, grammar-based modeling, and volume rendering, to mention just a few. This book has not featured coverage of these primarily because they are not, in general, real-time processes, although clever optimizations bring some of them into the ballpark of real time.

Last Thoughts

I tell ya, computer graphics keeps moving on ahead of ya. When I was your age, laddie, we had sprites that were 8 pixels by 8 pixels, just one solid color, and we were glad to have it! The kids today, I'll tell ya. They got their scaling-interpolated YUV blitters, and they got their Gouraud triangle shaders. They got lazy, that's what they got! We used to read each pixel by hand every morning, shade its color in the afternoon, and put it onto the screen that evening. And then we got up the next morning and did the same thing, by gum, seven days a week! We worked hard; none of this "where's the blitter function?" or "which DLL implements the control?" We started at one end of a line, and we inched across all the way to the other end, that's what we did.

The kids today. You'll get yours, though. You'll be in the Old Programmers' Home, and the new hotshots will come in, looking to hear stories of the old days when there were such things as flat computer screens. Before the immersive holographic web and its "paw-and-scrape" interface. Before the 65,536-processor P12 array took over all imaging functions, assigning CPUs on the fly to different octants of the virtual display space. Yeah, you'll get yours. Maybe they won't even want to hear your old stories. Maybe they'll just shake their heads, turn their gaze upwards a little, and flick on the Microsoft Media MindMeld Magazine. There's an interesting virtual forum on group-enabled sub-vocal interfaces happening.

Yeah, you'll get yours. Me, I'm still having fun inventing new things to do with these little pixels. Always something new to do in the sandbox. What's up today? An interpretive scripting language for animated scenes, that's it! Hey, gotta go. See you on the computer screen, while they still have them.

 **ARTT Class Hierarchy**

 Tools and Sample Programs

 Installing ARTT from the CD-Rom

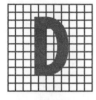 **Compiling ARTT**

 Recommended Reading

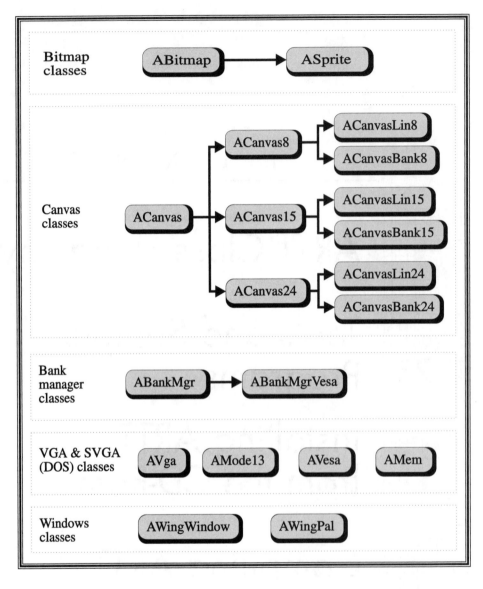

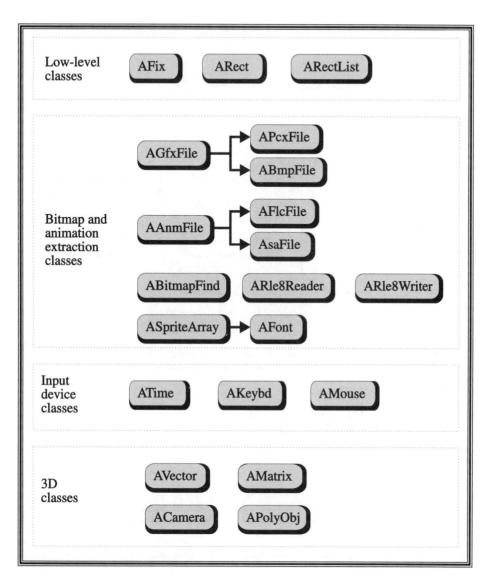

Low-level classes

AFix   ARect   ARectList

Bitmap and animation extraction classes

AGfxFile → APcxFile
AGfxFile → ABmpFile

AAnmFile → AFlcFile
AAnmFile → AsaFile

ABitmapFind   ARle8Reader   ARle8Writer

ASpriteArray → AFont

Input device classes

ATime   AKeybd   AMouse

3D classes

AVector   AMatrix
ACamera   APolyObj

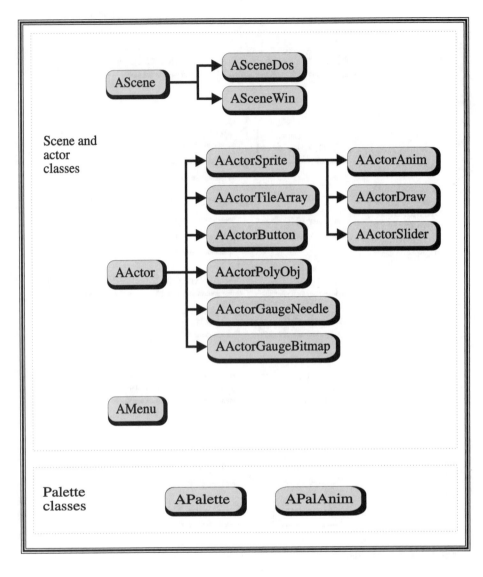

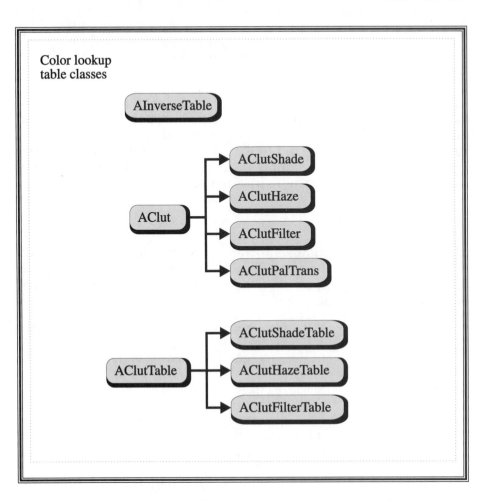

Color lookup
table classes

Tools and Sample Programs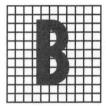

The ARTT toolkit contains a number of executable "tools" which provide useful functions in an animation environment. Also contained on the CD-ROM are several sample programs, which illustrate features of the class library and toolkit. This appendix provides a brief synopsis of each tool or sample program—see the interactive documentation on the CD for more information.

Tools

The sources and executables for all tools are found in the **TOOLS** directory under the main **ARTT** directory. Each tool is briefly described below. The chapter of the book in which the tool is introduced is included for reference.

GFXSHOW1	Views a low-resolution 8-bit graphics file in VGA mode 13H (Chapter 3)
GFX2GFX	Converts a graphics file from one format to another (Chapter 3)
PIXBLITZ	Rendering speed test program (Chapter 4)
VESALIST	Lists available VESA SVGA modes (Chapter 5)
GFXSHOW2	Views any 8-bit graphics file in VGA or SVGA mode (Chapter 5)
GFXPLAY	Plays bordered images in a graphics file as an animation sequence (Chapter 8)
ANIMPLAY	Plays an animation file (Chapter 9)
ANIMVIEW	Single-steps through an animation file (Chapter 9)
ANM2ANM	Converts an animation file from one format to another (Chapter 9)
GFX2ANM	Converts a series of bordered images into an animation file (Chapter 9)
ASALIST	Lists information about each sprite in an ASA-format animation file (Chapter 9)
MAKEITAB	Makes an inverse table and stores it in a file (Chapter 13)
GFXSHOW3	Views any 8/15/24-bit graphics file in any 8/15/24-bit SVGA mode (Chapter 14)
MAKECLUT	Makes a color lookup table and stores it in a file, allows viewing too (Chapter 15)

Sample Programs

Sample programs are found in the SAMPLES directory under the main ARTT directory. Some samples are DOS-only, some are Windows-only, and some appear in two versions. The program in each directory is briefly described below, along with chapter reference.

BBALL	Bouncing ball demo, **DOS** (Chapter 2)
SCALSHOW	Sample scaling bitmap, **DOS** (Chapter 6)
WEB	Sample WinG program, features gyrating web, **WINDOWS** (Chapter 7)
AQUADOS	Fishtank plus fish swimming back and forth, scene based, **DOS** (Chapter 11)
AQUAWIN	**WINDOWS** version of above (Chapter 11)
ROMNRACE	Scrolling-background cartoon race game, **DOS** (Chapter 11)
AMUCKDOS	Wacky laboratory panel with waveforms and gadgets, scene based, **DOS** (Chapter 12)
AMUCKWIN	**WINDOWS** version of above (Chapter 12)
HELIDOS	Helicopter shoot-'em-up, featuring color lookup tables, **DOS** (Chapter 14)
HELIWIN	**WINDOWS** version of above (Chapter 14)
POLYSPIN	Simple spinning polygon, **DOS** (Chapter 17)
TEXDOS	Texture-mapped cubes coming out of nowhere, whizzing by, **DOS** (Chapter 18)
TEXWIN	**WINDOWS** version of above (Chapter 18)
WGFXVIEW	**WINDOWS**-based file viewer (not referenced in book—See CD browser).

Installing ARTT from the CD-ROM

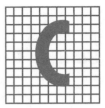

Installation

The accompanying CD contains ARTT, which holds all code and artwork for the C++ class library, tools, and sample programs. It also contains ARTT.HLP, an interactive browser. Besides ARTT, the CD contains two system components from Microsoft, Win32s and WinG. These are necessary to run Windows-based ARTT programs, but may already be on your system.

Installation instructions:

1. Install the Win32s extensions, unless:
   a) You already have Win32s installed (most compilers do this for you).
   b) You are running Windows 95 (only Windows 3.1 requires this extension).

To install Win32s from Windows, use the Program Manager, select RUN from the FILE menu, and type d:WIN32INS\SETUP, where d: is your CD drive letter.

2. Install the WinG extension, unless you already have WinG installed.

To install WinG from Windows, use the Program Manager, select RUN from the FILE menu, and type d:WINGINST\SETUP, where d: is your CD drive letter.

3. Install ARTT. From the Windows Program Manager, select RUN from the FILE menu, and type d:SETUP, where d: is your CD drive letter. A full install requires somewhat under 15 megabytes of hard disk space.

If you locate the toolkit in some directory other than the default directory \ARTT, some features of the interactive browser will not work (launching of sample programs and viewing of some graphics and animation files).

Using the Browser

The ARTT interactive browser is a WinHelp file named ARTT.HLP, located in the directory \ARTT\DOC. Double-click on the ARTT HELP icon to launch WinHelp. You will be placed at the contents page of the ARTT interactive browser.

Further instructions on compiling the ARTT library, tools, and sample programs can be found in Appendix D, and more detailed information is contained in the browser.

Compiling ARTT

Directory Structure

The ARTT toolkit is comprised of the following components:

- DOS-based library
- Windows-based library
- Tools
- Sample programs

The ARTT directory structure looks like this:

```
ARTT
   BIN        Executable versions of tools
   DOC        Help file (ARTT.HLP) and associated data
   H          Header files for all ARTT classes, both DOS & Windows
   ICONS      Windows icons for sample programs
   LIBDOS     C++ source files and makefiles for DOS classes
   LIBWIN     C++ source files and makefiles for Windows classes
   TOOLS      C++ source files and makefiles for tools
   SAMPLES
      ....    Various sample programs, each in its own directory
   WING       WinG library files
```

Libraries

Any source file with the same name in both the **LIBDOS** and **LIBWIN** directories is a generic class source file, and has an identical implementation in the two places. Files which are specific to **DOS** or Windows appear in only one of these directories. The limitations of the various compiler MAKE utilities made it impossible to have just one copy of these duplicated files in a separate directory.

The makefile in the **LIBDOS** directory builds **ARTTDOS.LIB**, and the makefile in the **LIBWIN** directory builds **ARTTWIN.LIB**. DOS tools and samples link with **ARTTDOS.LIB**; Windows samples link with **ARTTWIN.LIB** and the appropriate WinG library.

The ARTT class library can be compiled under various compilers, into either 16-bit or 32-bit format. Most source files have no compiler-dependent code in them. Some of the **DOS** library source files do have compiler dependencies, particularly when it comes to accessing physical memory or BIOS functions from 32-bit protected mode. See **AMEM.CPP**, **AMOUSDOS.CPP**, **AVESA.CPP**, and **AVGA.CPP**. Also, **APALETTE.CPP** in both libraries uses one of two variants for method APalette::FindClosest(), depending on whether the word size is 16 or 32 bits.

Tools

The source for all tools is found in \ARTT\TOOLS. All tools are DOS-based, and are built from a single makefile.

Sample Programs

Each sample program appears in its own directory. Many sample programs have both a DOS and a WinG implementation in separate directories. All necessary artwork files for each sample program are present in its directory.

Compilers

Three compilers have been tested and makefiles developed for them. These are:

- Borland C++ 4.5
- Symantec C++ 6.11 and 7.0
- Watcom C++ 10.0

There are some limitations with some of these compilers. In particular, Symantec C++ 6.11 does not link properly with the 32-bit version of WinG. Therefore, Symantec 6.11 users must compile ART-TWIN.LIB in 16-bit mode (32-bit DOS compilation works fine). For 6.11 users, this means that some of the sample WinG programs, which require 32-bit operation, cannot be compiled. This limitation does not apply to Symantec C++ 7.0. Also, Borland C++ does not support 32-bit DOS development. However, ARTT supports the Borland PowerPack add-on. If you own this add-on, you can compile DOS programs in 32-bits (Borland 32-bit Windows operation works fine without the PowerPack). Due to the manner in which memory below 1 Mb (including the screen) is accessed in 32-bit DOS with Borland C++, DOS programs compiled in this way may not run properly under all windowing environments. The Watcom compiler has no particular restrictions to note.

Each library, tool, and sample directory has multiple makefiles in it. The appropriate makefile must be copied to the file MAKE-FILE, and then MAKE run from the command line.

For More Information

For more information on how to build the libraries, tools, and sample programs, refer to the ARTT interactive browser. See Appendix C for information on how to access the browser.

Recommended Reading

The Classics

Foley, James, Andnes van Dam, Steven Feiner, and John Hughes, *Computer Graphics: Principles and Practice,* 2nd edition, Addison-Wesley, 1987. Used widely as a textbook for undergraduate and graduate-level computer science courses, this book is a "must have." It covers in detail the theory behind 2D and 3D graphics, with an emphasis on high-end realism.

Newman, William M. and Robert F. Sproull, *Fundamentals of Interactive Computer Graphics,* 2nd edition, McGraw-Hill, 1973. This ancient book shows how much theoretical work was done even before there was reasonable hardware available for practical use. It is still a solid introduction to line, curve, and polygon rendering, and 3D projection and rendering mathematics.

VGA and SuperVGA Programming

Abrash, Michael, *Zen of Graphics Programming,* Coriolis Group Books, 1995. This tour de force of optimized assembly-language graphics programming is big and full of good stuff. Its usefulness is somewhat marred by its focus on obscure graphics modes such as 16-color modes and the undocumented "Mode X"—essentially no code can be used directly by Super VGA or Windows programmers. Still, it's a joy to watch the master at work. A fun activity is to photocopy the family stories which begin each chapter, show them to a friend, and ask him or her to guess what graphics topic might be even remotely related to such a story.

Ferraro, Richard, *Programmer's Guide to the EGA, VGA, and Super VGA Cards,* 3rd edition, Addison-Wesley, 1994. Weighing in at over 1,600 pages, this paperback tome has a wealth of information on VGA and Super VGA cards and programming. My enthusiasm is somewhat dampened by the equally vast wealth of typos and other errors.

Wilton, Richard, *Programmer's Guide to PC Video Systems,* Microsoft Press, 1994. As an introduction to VGA and Super VGA programming, this book is better organized and less daunting than Ferraro's.

Video Electronics Standards Organization, *VESA BIOS Extension (VBE).* Go to the source for the full story on the VESA VBE specification. A copy of the specification can be obtained from VESA, whose address is given below.

> Video Electronics Standards Association
> 2150 North First Street, Suite 440
> San Jose, CA 95131-2029
> Phone: 408-435-0333
> Fax: 408-435-8225

Graphics and Animation File Formats

Kay, David C. and John R. Levine, *Graphics File Formats,* **2nd edition, Windcrest/McGraw-Hill, 1995.** One of many fine books on graphics file formats, this short book covers the basics.

Kent, Jim, "The Flic File Format," *Dr. Dobbs Journal,* **March 1993.** Written by the author of Autodesk Animator Pro, where the flic file format made its debut, this article is short but helpful.

Swan, Tom, *Inside Windows File Formats,* **Sams Publishing, 1993.** Not just a graphics file formats book, this one sheds light on many Windows-related file formats, including BMP, ICO, CUR, FNT, and even GRP, PIF, and EXE. On an accompanying disk is a help file containing the TrueType font specification.

Bitmapped Animation

Thompson, Nigel, *Animation Techniques in Win32,* **Microsoft Press, 1995.** How can you resist a book with a foreword by Dave Barry? This book implements a Windows-based C++ class library for sprite-based animation. While fairly short, it does include good discussions of DIBs and the Windows Palette Manager.

Microsoft Windows

King, Adrian, *Inside Windows 95,* **Microsoft Press, 1994.** Is this book, published roughly a year before Windows 95's release, a vaporbook? While not a programmer's book per se, it features detailed information on the internals of Windows 95 relevant to any Windows programmer.

Petzold, Charles, *Programming Windows 3.1,* **3rd edition, Microsoft Press, 1992.** *The* reference on Windows programming. This book is another "must have." Can't wait for *Programming Windows 95.*

General PC Programming

Duncan, Ray, *Advanced MS-DOS Programming,* **2nd edition, Microsoft Press, 1988.** A good overview of DOS from a programmer's perspective, although probably hard to find nowadays. Also covers the ROM BIOS and the Microsoft Mouse driver. Old but still applicable, although 32-bit extended DOS programming requires many new skills.

Kyle, Jim and Ralf Brown, *PC Interrupts,* **2nd edition, Addison-Wesley, 1994.** This book is a detailed listing of the vast set of PC-related APIs. A CD-ROM version of this book and its companion *Network Interrupts* is entitled *Uninterrupted Interrupts,* and is also published by Addison-Wesley. This CD version puts all this information at your fingertips, which may be reaching for it often. And you thought the days of disk-shuffling ended when software stopped running directly from floppies.

Norton, Peter, Peter Aitken, and Richard Wilton, *PC Programmer's Bible,* **3rd edition, Microsoft Press, 1993.** Another good introduction to both DOS and the BIOS. This book has a good amount of low-level information, such as keyboard scan codes and timer hardware operation.

Game Programming

LaMothe, André, John Ratcliff, Mark Seminatore, and Denise Tyler, *Tricks of the Game Programming Gurus,* **Sams Publishing, 1994.** While not as good as *Gardens of Imagination* as a raycasting 3D tutorial, this book has other goodies to offer the budding game developer. Such topics include sound and music, artificial intelligence, and networking, among others. This book is a good general introduction to the techniques used by modern computer game designers.

Lampton, Christopher, *Gardens of Imagination,* **The Waite Group, 1994.** The best of the "3D texture-mapped maze game" programming books. It builds, chapter by chapter, a raycasting engine that includes variable-height floors, local lighting effects, and bitmapped objects. A great place to start for any budding DOOM cloner.

Digital Video

Mattison, Philip, *Practical Digital Video with Programming Examples in C,* **Wiley, 1994.** Written by an Intel engineer, this book provides detailed coverage of digital video hardware and software. Video fundamentals and color space representation and conversion topics are followed by in-depth discussion of digital video compression. Covers QuickTime, Video for Windows, JPEG, MPEG, and more.

Apple Computer, *Inside Macintosh: QuickTime,* **Addison-Wesley, 1993.** This volume and its companion, *Inside Macintosh: QuickTime Components,* are vast references on the programming and internals of QuickTime. The only missing topic is specifications on the (proprietary) digital video compression algorithms.

Graphics Data Compression

Nelson, Mark, *The Data Compression Book,* **M&T Books, 1992.** Oriented more toward generic compression techniques than graphics, this book is still a good introduction and worth having. It covers Huffman coding, arithmetic coding, dictionary-based techniques such as LZW, and lossy compression of speech and graphics.

Pennebaker, William B. and Joan L. Mitchell, *JPEG: Still Image Data Compression Standard,* **Van Nostrand Reinhold, 1993.** If you want to immerse yourself in the JPEG algorithm, reach deep into your wallet and buy this book. Appendices include the actual text of the ISO standards.

Wallace, Gregory, "The JPEG Still Picture Compression Standard," *Communications of the ACM,* **April 1991.** This article is an excellent discussion of the algorithms used in the JPEG compression standard.

Three-Dimensional Graphics and Animation

Artwick, Bruce, *Applied Concepts in Microcomputer Graphics,* **Prentice-Hall, 1984.** Though dated, this book describes techniques which are still useful in making 3D practical on a desktop computer. Artwick is the author of the original Flight Simulator, and has much to say about algorithmic optimization. I can't believe the publisher made him add a final chapter about business graphics.

Harrington, Steve, *Computer Graphics: A Programming Approach*, 2nd edition, McGraw-Hill, 1987. The coverage of 3D fundamentals, particularly matrix computations and perspective viewing transformations, is the clearest I've seen in any book. This book builds a 3D code library as it goes, although I don't care for the Pascal-like pseudolanguage and reliance on global variables.

Watt, Alan, *Fundamentals of Three-Dimensional Computer Graphics*, Addison-Wesley, 1989. Although its contents overlap *Computer Graphics: Principles and Practice*, this book's unwavering focus on 3D shading and rendering makes it a favorite of mine.

Edited by Durrett, John, *Color and the Computer*, Academic Press, 1987. This collection of articles provides in-depth discussions of the physics, perception, specification, and ergonomics of computer-generated color.

Edited by Glassner, Andrew, *Graphics Gems*, Academic Press, 1990. This is the first of four numbered volumes (so far) in this series. Graphics Gems is a hefty collection of short articles aimed at graphics programmers, each highlighting a technique, tidbit, or optimization. Articles are organized into topic categories which include 2D geometry, 2D rendering, image processing, frame buffer techniques, 3D geometry, 3D rendering, matrix techniques, and more. C code is available for many articles, and volumes I through III are now available on CD-ROM. The articles may, however, be on the brief side for those who don't already know a given topic pretty well.

Advanced (Non Real-Time) 3D

Ashdown, Ian, *Radiosity: A Programmer's Perspective*, Wiley, 1994. This book provides in-depth discussion and code on the topic of radiosity. Radiosity is a non-real-time, photo-realistic rendering approach which bears some similarity to raytracing, but overcomes some of raytracing's limitations.

Watt, Alan and Mark Watt, *Advanced Animation and Rendering Techniques*, Addison-Wesley, 1992. The successor to *Fundaments of Three-Dimensional Computer Graphics*, this one is a heavy-hitter for those who have gotten the basics of 3D under their belts. Topics include parametric surfaces, shadow generation, texture-mapping, raytracing, radiosity, animation of three-dimensional models, and more.

Edited by Glassner, Andrew, *An Introduction to Ray Tracing*, Academic Press, 1989. This book is a collection of articles which together provide a solid introduction to raytracing.

Three-Dimensional Toolkits

Upstill, Steve, *The RenderMan Companion*, Addison-Wesley, 1990. A good introduction to the RenderMan 3D rendering engine and shading language.

OpenGL Architecture Review Board, *OpenGL Programming Guide*, Addison-Wesley, 1993. The standard introduction to the OpenGL system. Its companion is the *OpenGL Reference Manual,* which is a detailed rundown of API functions and data structures.

C++

Meyers, Scott, *Effective C++*, Addison-Wesley, 1992. This collection of 50 C++ "tips" is very thought-provoking and useful to seasoned programmers. I would love to mud-wrestle Meyers over the necessity of using the *const* keyword.

Stroustrup, Bjarne and Margaret A. Ellis, *The Annotated C++ Reference Manual*, Addison-Wesley, 1990. While this text, co-authored by the inventor of the C++ language, may be thick going for novices, there is no better source for in-depth understanding of C++. This text serves as the Base Document for the ANSI standardization of the language.

Stroustrup, Bjarne, *The Design and Evolution of C++*, Addison-Wesley, 1994. If the *Annotated C++ Reference Manual* is the "what" of C++, this book is the "why." Highly recommended for those who already know C++ reasonably well.

Assembly Language and Optimization

Abrash, Michael, *Zen of Code Optimization*, Coriolis Group Books, 1994. "The best optimizer is between your ears" is the title to Chapter 1 of this book. This book covers algorithmic optimization relevant to C++ programmers as well as tight, cycle-counting assembly-language. Here the book really shines, providing detailed information on instruction pipelining and why the "official" timings given in the 486 and Pentium manuals are only the starting point for true code speed.

Subscription Sources

Microsoft Developer Network CD. If you can't afford the $495 entrance fee to Level 2 of the *Microsoft Developer Network* (or can't find room to store the 20 CDs that appear at your door every three months), at least pony up the $195 for Level 1. Every three months, you will receive a CD-ROM packed with technical articles, sample code, working tools, and more. The full text of Petzold's *Programming Windows 3.1* can be found buried several directories deep on the CD!

Dr. Dobb's Journal. My favorite of the programmer's magazines, Dr. Dobb's is a treasure trove of algorithms and code. Each July features an issue devoted to graphics.

Microsoft Systems Journal. If you want in-depth technical information about Windows and can't afford to join the Microsoft Developer Network, subscribe to this magazine. The first detailed discussions of WinG and WinToon appeared here.

CompuServe Information Service. Online services such as CompuServe host several forums relevant to graphics programmers. CompuServe has the GRAPHICS, WINMM (Windows Multimedia), and GAMDEV (Game Developers) conferences, among others. Download graphics and code, post questions to the experts, and watch your phone bill spiral heavenward.

Index

t indicates an entry in a table.